DATE DUE

MAR 3 1993	
16	
JUL 1 8 1996	
NOV 1 9 1996	

The
Military
in
America

The
MILITARY
in
AMERICA

*From the Colonial Era
to the Present*

New, Revised Edition

Edited by
PETER KARSTEN

THE FREE PRESS
A Division of Macmillan, Inc.
NEW YORK

The Free Press
A Division of Macmillan, Inc.
866 Third Avenue, New York, N.Y. 10022

Printed in the United States of America

printing number
1 2 3 4 5 6 7 8 9 10

Library of Congress Cataloging-in-Publication Data

The military in America.

1. United States—Armed Forces—History.
2. Sociology, Military—United States. I. Karsten,
Peter.
UA23.M5626 1986   355′.00973   86–7605
ISBN 0–02–919190–4

Contents

THE EARLY REPUBLIC

THE CIVIL WAR ERA

FROM CIVIL WAR TO WORLD WAR I

Contents

CONTENTS

THE COLD WAR YEARS

THE VIETNAM ERA AND BEYOND

An Introduction

Armies "fight and die"; they also "live and breathe." Recruits are "ordered"; they also "self-select." Branches of the armed services "cooperate and complement"; they also "contend and compete." Officers may be "capable"; they may also be "careerists." Military units have "missions"; they also have "interests." Commanders "obey" civilian leaders; they also "interact" with them. People "admire" warriors; they also "regard" them. Military systems "serve" nations; they may also "reflect" them. The former of these expressions are the stock in trade of an older, more "traditional" military history; the latter are the hallmarks of a newer one. Both describe accurately the same phenomena. The former do so within the framework of the military sciences; the latter, within the framework of the social and behavioral sciences. This volume offers students of American society and of its military some of the more interesting recent work of those who regard the military with the eyes of social and behavioral scientists, and it provides as well several primary sources that illustrate these insights.

For many years American military historians were primarily concerned with past efforts at organizing and managing combat armies and navies. Most studies dealt with battles, tactics, strategy, logistics, and command, and many of those who wrote them were themselves active or former military personnel. Necessarily, most of these studies were only peripherally concerned with the relationship between the military and the greater society. Few concerned themselves for long with such issues as the social origins of military personnel, the process of socialization and value inculcation in the military environment, public attitudes toward military systems, military attitudes toward the public, the relation of military to economic and political elites, the development of interservice rivalries, or the effect of military service on the individual. Students of tactics, logistics, or command were preoccupied (for understandable enough reasons) with the reasons that battles were lost or won.

A few scholars, like Bell Irwin Wiley and Dixon Wecter, began to give special attention to the broader social questions as early as the 1930s. Although some of what was produced a generation or more ago is still of considerable value to students of the military in society, much of the analytically rich research on one or another of the relationships of the military to society is of fairly recent vintage. Beginning, I believe, in the 1960s, a number of scholars have published studies that treat the military as a system interactive with the rest of the society. Military history of this sort is often really social history, and some of it is exceptionally good.

This is not to say that the earlier "drum and trumpets" type of military history is without merit. No one would deny the quality of many of the products of this persistently inventive school. A case in point is Allan Millett and Peter Maslowski's *For the Common Defense*. But the new work on "the military in society" deserves its own place in the literature, in a volume that both complements its "battlefields" counterpart and may serve as a supplement to general surveys of American social history. In this volume I have sought to assemble as many of the better examples of recent work as possible, adding from time to time an original document that may illuminate a conclusion of one or another author. Complementary to this volume is another book of mine, *Soldiers and Society* (Greenwood Press, 1978), an edited collection of primary sources designed to explore the related question of the extent to which the military may be said to have affected the lives of Americans in the past two centuries.

Why the new fascination with the military as process, as institution, and as system interactive with society? One answer is certainly the increased contact with the social and behavioral sciences (and especially those studies of military systems produced in those fields) that American history graduate students experienced in the past two decades. A graduate student minoring in sociology, who had in mind a dissertation on a military subject, would have learned of Morris Janowitz's *The Professional Soldier: A Social and Political Portrait*, Stanislav Andreski's *Military Organization and Society*, and Kurt Lang's annotated bibliography, *Military Institutions and the Sociology of War*. One minoring in political science with a military-related dissertation in the back of her mind would have been told of Samuel P. Huntington's *The Soldier and the State: The Theory and Politics of Civil-Military Relations* and perhaps Harold Stein's collection of essays *American Civil-Military Decisions: A Book of Case Studies*. One minoring in social psychology would surely have learned of the four-volume *Studies in Social Psychology in World War II: The American Soldier* and possibly of Peter Bourne, *Men, Stress and Vietnam*; Roy Grinker and J.W. Spiegel, *Men Under Stress*; or D. G. Mandelbaum, *Soldier Groups and Negro Soldiers*. (As for myself, I chose to minor in law, but shortly before completing my dissertation I happened upon Lang's magnificent volume. Thereupon, without any training beyond what I read, I began careening off, from model, to empirical data base, to generalizations.) For those whose basic diet had been the standard "meat and potatoes" history (a look at what others had said of the early army or the *fin de siècle* navy, followed by a lonely search for a "topic," a year or so in the archives, and another constructing a revisionist view of "the topic"), this social science literature was heady stuff. It raised questions rarely addressed in the historical literature, and it suggested scientific methods of addressing them.

But interest in the social and behavioral sciences is only part of the story. Another is a function of a basic change in the character of the military itself beginning in 1940 or perhaps 1948, the years that peacetime Selective Service Acts were passed. Until then American historians, if they knew the American military at all, knew it as a wartime phenomenon, "for the duration." Scholars maturing since World War II have seen a vast and pervasive *peacetime* establishment, and some of them have served in it. As such, these scholars may have less fascination with the questions of strategy, tactics, leadership, and logistics that captivated many of those who lived through World War II, and more interest in the process of recruitment and socialization, and inter- and intraservice rivalries, the questions of value transformation, and the relation of the military to society, issues that caught their attention in the last forty-odd years when the peacetime U.S. military usually numbered well over two million men and women.

It is also possible that the war in Vietnam may have led some to study the American military who would not otherwise have been so inclined. To the extent that this occurred, it meant that scholars with the perspectives of social, demographic, intellectual, or cultural history, who had not previously studied the military, now brought those perspectives to military history.

Several of the better studies utilized by "new" military historians have been written by sociologists, social psychologists, and political scientists who did not think they were writing history, but who from our perspective could fairly be said to have done so. Moreover, some studies quite explicitly sociological, containing little or no "time-series" analyses, are still of great value, for they provide us with valuable information about the recent past that can serve as "benchmarks" and should, in every sense, be the stock in trade of the "new" military historian.[1]

Two examples of what I mean may be in order. Frederic Bergerson, a political scientist, recently published a fine study of the development by army "insurgents" of modern combat helicopter aviation, a process in which army aviators struggled to survive Air Force (and some Army) efforts to quash the movement. But Bergerson described his book as "a case study" in "analytic deduction," because he was after bigger game than a mere history of the phenomenon: "I think it is necessary to study diffuse longitudinal phenomena if we are not to be stuck with . . . a single-decision bias, or a bias towards survey methodology [and if we are to achieve] a model that may explain bureaucratic politics generally."[2] Fortunately for us, Bergerson provided us with a marvelous historical study of recent interservice rivalry and innovation while building his model of bureaucratic politics.

Second example: During World War II, Samuel Stouffer and his associates questioned tens of thousands of American GIs about their training, morale, combat experiences, and attitudes with the objective of providing the U.S. Army with useful information and advice. In the process, they also generated theories of social process and socialization and played significant roles in the history of sociology and social psychology. But their efforts also provided a wealth of information to historians, and a few examples of "new" military history have used the Stouffer data as "benchmark" information in comparative analysis of Americans at war before and after World War II.[3] The Stouffer study is now a rich slice of history itself and should be employed widely by those teaching about America's military past (as well as by students of American society who are *not* concerned with the military *per se*, but with race relations, class consciousness, and American values more generally in the 1940s).

RECRUITMENT

Many recent studies have focused on the two central questions regarding the process whereby youth "join up": the whys and wherefores of government intentions and policies, and the motives of those who join or who resist joining. As to the first of these, the early terrain was described in John Shy's "New Look at the Colonial Militia" (Selection 1 in this volume), an article that points to the regional diversity of colonial militia recruitment policies and practices, a diversity reflecting the needs and resources of tightly knit, relatively compact New England townships and parishes, on the one hand, and the more diffusely settled and socially stratified Chesapeake area, on the other. In the earliest stages of settlement every man was a warrior. As threats from Indian tribes receded and settlements became more economically specialized and complex, militia acts began to resemble the modern selective service system, with deferments for ferryboatmen, millers, attorneys, and others vital to economic life. An example is the North Carolina Militia Act of 1774 (Selection 3).

Among the detailed accounts of the ways colonial and Revolutionary War–era militia were organized and maintained, the most interesting may be Richard Buel's study of Connecticut, *Dear Liberty* (1980). Buel focuses on the state's mobilization of its economic and human resources. State leaders devised a variety of ingenious schemes to raise forces for state and continental regiments. The increasingly complex offers that Buel reports regarding provisions, pay, time of service, tax moratoria, and accoutrements (all devised to spur lagging enlistments) suggest that the conclusion of another recent study of eighteenth-century American enlistments, on "contractual principles and military conduct during the Seven Years War," by F. W. Anderson (Selection 2) applies to Connecticut in 1778–1781 as well. Eighteenth-century Americans, Anderson argues, viewed military service as a free and voluntary act, a contract between equal parties, *not* as a political or social obligation of a deferential tenant to his socially "better" landlord, as was the case in some European communities at the time.[4]

Recent studies of United States government policies during the Civil War and the *fin de siècle* make the same point: After the first surge of voluntary enlistments prompted by pure enthusiasm, social pressures, and ideological commitments, the government did not expect to find men willing to serve out of a sense of political obligation. A draft designed to generate fees and the hiring of substitutes during the Civil War was the logical product of a market economy view of military service as a relatively unappealing and dangerous *job*, and can be equated with eighteenth-century offers. Similarly, the efforts to attract better naval personnel in the late nineteenth and early twentieth centuries, recently described by Frederic Harrod, did not consist of an appeal to patriotic sentiments but reflected rather an understanding of the sailor's creature comforts (food and living quarters), his treatment within the disciplinary system, his pay and promotion opportunities, his sense of adventure, and his retirement and other benefits.[5]

It is not until the era of World War I, over 250 years since the draft militia units of the earliest settlements, that we again see a concerted (and successful) effort by political and social leaders to compel men to serve. This effort and its anticonscription counterpart, analyzed recently by John Chambers (Selection 26), represents a clash between those localistic, antistatist traditional foes of compulsory service and more cosmopolitan statists, who argued that the social consciousness of the modern progressive state warranted a corresponding measure of political-military obligation on the part of its citizens.

Terminated after World War I, the draft was revived in 1940 and again in 1948. A memorandum prepared by the Selective Service System in 1965 (Selection 37) described the "indirect manner" in which the system worked.

The second question before us concerns the motives of those who joined up and those who resisted recruitment efforts. Here two sorts of studies have appeared: those that stress the ideological and patriotic motives for enlistment, and those that find economic, and less lofty motives. Recently I assembled evidence regarding the various reasons that men enlisted in the distant as well as the recent past in an effort to generalize about those reasons and their implications,[6] but herein we will review studies of particular times and settings. John Ferling claims that religious impulses were powerful recruitment motives in the early colonial era but gave way to more ideological and political ones by 1775. However, his evidence, while accounting for some recruits, is not, in my view, as substantial as that of F. W. Anderson, whose colonial New England soldiers were disproportionately the younger sons of yeomen farmers who had yet to inherit any land of their own. They viewed military service as a means of acquiring an income, a modest nest-egg, and a modicum of personal independence (from home), and saw themselves primarily as contracting employees. Charles Royster insists that economic motives alone are inadequate in understanding the enlistment and reenlistment of Continental Line Soldiers: "The distinguishing feature of the recruits was their willingness." He is responding (with only partial success) to the evidence that Mark Lender (Selection 6) and several others have offered to the contrary. Marcus Cunliffe discovered a fascinating world of mid-nineteenth-century volunteer military companies and drill squads where economic incentives played no role whatever (Selection 13). However, these were not regulars; they were private citizens, subject to no government but their own by-laws, and each with his own livelihood aside from the Sunday strut on the parade-grounds.[7]

In the early stages of the Civil War some evidence indicates that ideological or political commitment inspired men to join the ranks of Union or Confederate forces. My comparison of Union Army volunteer and draft figures by civilian occupation suggests substantial voluntary, elite support for the cause, support that stemmed variously from a general appreciation for the North's war aims, from a general sense of how the secession might adversely affect one's personal opportunities and ambitions, from pietistic religious concerns with "the sin of slavery," and from the more cosmopolitan and politically informed citizen's sense of duty (see also Selection 14). Peter Levine and Robert E. Sterling have identified resistance to the 1863 draft among Democrats, Catholics, and foreign-born, which suggests that decisions to submit or to resist were culture-driven, a point similar to one the "new" political historians have made regarding voter behavior in the second half of the nineteenth century. Some early volunteers, however, had their personal welfare in mind. Don. R. Bowen carefully analyzed those from Jackson County, Missouri, who "rode with Quantrill," the Confederate guerrilla of western Missouri and Kansas, and concluded that the Union Army's extralegal liberation of slaves in 1861 and 1862 explained much. The eldest sons of substantial slave-holding families joined in disproportionate numbers, apparently to defend their long-term interests.[8]

As time passed, casualties mounted, enthusiasm waned, voluntary enlistment fell, and draft resistance spread throughout the North. When in 1864 the North's three-hundred-dollar commutation fee was abolished, and the only alternatives remaining to service when drafted were active resistance or the purchase of a substitute (costing about fifteen hundred dollars in Ohio), the men drafted tended to be those lower on the socioeconomic scale, a pattern consistent with the evidence from the Revolutionary War army.[9]

The motives of officer candidates appear to have been different from those of enlisted men. My study of Naval Academy candidates from the

1840s to the 1920s found some (especially from the Reconstruction South) who saw Annapolis essentially as a free college education, but most candidates who left a record of the decision were motivated by a spirit of adventure, militarism, patriotism, or an amalgam of the three. The same may be said of both the officer and enlisted volunteers for the brief war with Spain in 1898, as Gerald Linderman's analysis of those from Galesburg, Illinois, and Clyde, Ohio, would suggest (Selection 25). Yet when more than a relative handful of men were sought, as in World War I, enlistment was supplanted by compulsion, and the results show that the less developed, localistic South was underrepresented among enlistees. This was in large part due to the lack of interest shown by Southern blacks, as noted in Arthur Barbeau's *The Unknown Soldiers* (1974), but the enlistment rates of Southern whites were also below the norm. Thus, during the early stages of World War II, before voluntary enlistment gave way to conscription, whites as well as blacks from the less industrialized counties in South Carolina were less likely to enlist than those from the more industrially developed counties (Selection 30). Once again, this seems consistent with similar evidence from the Civil War era.[10]

Economic conditions and job security counted heavily in peacetime. During the 1920s and 1930s, as Fredric Harrod and Robert K. Griffith have shown, a clear correlation existed between adverse economic conditions and good quality enlistees, high reenlistment rates, and low desertion rates in both the army and the navy (see Selections 29 and 48). A Congressional study in 1963 indicated that long-term regional income levels were more significant than current unemployment levels in predicting voluntary enlistment rates.[11] It would be useful to know whether or not this was the case in other times.

Many blacks who could gain access to the army felt like Richard Johnson, who served from 1899 to 1922. "Having discovered the security of the army," Johnson wrote, "I had shed that forlorn and hopeless feeling that once possessed me." Studies of the Cold War era in particular show that blacks have found the military a place of opportunity, relative to civilian employment, and that their reenlistment rates persistently exceeded those of whites.[12]

TRAINING AND SOCIALIZATION

The process of familiarizing recruits with the military's mores and preparing them to perform their duties, like the process of recruitment, has two dimensions: the goals and policies of the military trainers, and the effects that the process has on the trainees. With regard to the former, my study of Naval Academy socialization of midshipmen from the 1840s to the 1920s includes an attempt to uncover those objectives. It can be compared with similar studies of the other service academies in the twentieth century. W.

Bruce White has described the purposes and processes of Army socialization of ethnic and racial enlisted minorities in the years from the Civil War to the 1920s (Selection 28), and John Faris has described basic training in more recent years, but neither Faris nor anyone else demonstrates the purposes that the military itself sees in "boot camp" with the kind of detail that White provides for the earlier "Americanizing" enterprise.[13]

The military reinforces training with disciplinary codes and leadership methods to ensure that missions are accomplished. These codes and methods sometimes change, reflecting changes in the larger society's value system or new demands within the military itself. Morris Janowitz has suggested certain trends in the "patterns of organizational authority" within the American military since World War II. As the military became more technologically sophisticated, employing more "military specialists," its need to reenlist such specialists grew, but these specialists were like "free professionals"—averse to arbitrary authority. Indeed, many former specialists have indicated that they had left the military because of its coercive ways. Hence, out of need, military elites slowly devised and provided less coercive (more "persuasive") forms of leadership than had prevailed before. Gary Wamsley provides us with a look at what may have been one such specific change in Air Force aviation training, which resulted in higher rates of pilot completion of the program.[14]

Military socialization is not limited to basic training or the service academies, of course. It is an ongoing, sometimes conscious, more generally unprogrammatic process inherent in the routine of barracks or shipboard life. My study of naval officers before 1925 and Morris Janowitz's study of officers of all services in the twentieth century explore the effects of this ongoing socialization process on the officers involved.[15] One modest measure of the socializing importance of the postacademy years can be detected in James L. Morrison's account of the resignation of West Point officers and candidates during the secession crisis of 1860–61. Nearly all of the Southern-born *cadets* went over to the Confederacy by April, 1861, whereas about 15 percent of those Southern-born *graduates* of West Point (including all those graduates who had left the service shortly after graduation) fought on the Union side during the war.[16] Day-in, day-out service under the flag had clearly prompted many to think of themselves as servants of the nation rather than of their state of birth.

The Stouffer study of GIs during World War II thoroughly investigated changes in attitudes and behavior that could be attributed to military service, but Stouffer and other more recent studies clearly demonstrate the importance of personality traits and values acquired prior to entering the military. For example, my study of the careers of the cadets of 1946 and midshipmen of 1920 found that their fathers' occupation and their own religious affiliation were modest but statistically significant predictors of their eventual successful attainment of high rank. Peter Peterson, similarly, found that the values expressed in answers to questionnaires put to army officer candidates in 1969, before they began their training, were important predictors both of their completion of OCS training and of their decision to remain in the army after the first tour of duty. William Cockerham and David Mark Mantell have argued that the process of self-selection into airborne training and "Green Beret" service, due to values these men already possessed, was as important as the training or duty assignments thereafter in explaining their posttraining or postservice attitudes and values. Johnnie Daniel and Arthur Korotkin found several preservice experiences to be good predictors of successful adjustment and advancement for naval enlistees in 1978. In short, the impact of training and efforts to transform attitudes can be overstated. "Militarization" can be confused with the reinforcement of established values.[17]

MORALE

The Stouffer team study of *The American Soldier* in World War II reported that few combatants were primarily motivated by patriotic or idealistic impulses; rather, they saw themselves as fighting to defend their immediate comrades-in-arms ("the primary group") and for their own survival. Peter Maslowski analyzed the content of some fifty diaries and collections of letters of Civil War common soldiers with the Stouffer study's questions by his side, in an effort to compare their morale to those of World War II GI's (Selection 16). He found their orientation similar to those of their counterparts eighty years later. Where the Stouffer team saw the primary group (the rifle team or squad) as the central unit of morale, and Roger Little saw "the two-man buddy system" as the comparable unit in the Korean War, Charles Moskos maintained that by the time of the Vietnam War the infantryman's motivation tended to be based largely on his own survival ("not getting zapped, and dry socks tomorrow") (see Selection 39). In like fashion, Richard Gabriel and Paul Savage claimed that the officer corps of the 1960s had become afflicted with "careerism" (an increased concern with one's own career and promotion opportunities), which led to "ticket punching" (the cycling of promotion-minded officers through command billets during the Vietnam War). Less concerned for their men and the cause than for themselves, and unable to acquire command skills in their too-brief tours of duty, these officers and the system that sent them there were responsible for some of the army's morale problems in Vietnam, as well as the deaths of some of their men.[18]

These linear historical trends should not be overstated, however. Martin Van Crevald's comparison of American and German fighting units in World War II has demonstrated that the "managerial leadership" Gabriel and Savage associated with the 1960s was present in the early 1940s. Van Crevald has explained how and why the American military's leadership, doctrine, training, and replacement policies produced a fighting force with lower morale than its German counterpart.[19] Tamotsu Shibutani has described the progressive demoralization and disintegration of a Nisei military unit in World War II, and Eli Ginzberg and his colleagues have documented the existence of hundreds of thousands of badly utilized, "ineffective soldiers" in World War II. Moreover, morale problems similar to those observed in Vietnam can also be found, to one degree or another, in F. W. Anderson's study of contentious colonial troops during the French and Indian war, John Alexander and Steven Rosswurm's rebellious and radicalized Revolutionary War Pennsylvania militiamen, Richard Kohn's Newburgh conspirators, Christopher McKee and Harold Langley's mistreated sailors of the early nineteenth-century navy, or any of several accounts of deserters from the Revolutionary War through World War II (see Selection 17). Morale may well have been lower in Vietnam, especially during the more static, post-Tet period, than in other wars, but we must examine more evidence to establish both the fact and the causes of lessened morale. Even if there is less use of coercion and more use of persuasion now than in the past, there were many officers in the progressive era quite alert to the notion that less arbitrary and coercive measures would boost morale and cut the desertion rate.[20]

When social psychologists and sociologists in World War II examined the Army's segregated units, and brief integration of some units during the Battle of the Bulge, they concluded that the racial integration of units would result in the improved morale and more effective use of blacks, and correctly predicted that white troops would quickly come to accept blacks as comrades-in-arms. David Mandelbaum and Leo Bogart have made the evidence and the reasoning of these and later Korean War studies available to use (Selection 36), and others have described the use of blacks in World War II and their effective integration thereafter.[21] Once again, one feels a bit of *déjà vu*. Historians have demonstrated that a similar process ensued during the Civil War. Many whites in the Union Army also acquired respect for the black soldiers and teamsters they observed.[22]

COMBAT: ITS NATURE AND ITS EFFECTS

"New" and "old" military history are more difficult to distinguish when it comes to studies of combat; nonetheless, one distinction exists: The "better" analyses of combat have explored its nature from the perspective of the individual soldier as well as from that of the commander. Few such studies have appeared, and we still know very little of combat "from the bottom up" as a process.[23] Greg Denning recently asked what "the face of battle" meant to men of the USS *Essex* during the naval Battle of Valparaiso in 1814. Such naval combat was intense and extremely lethal; it also prompted brave gestures and heroic conduct. The participants on the *Essex* (with only one exception) had steeled themselves for the fight, each reinforcing the other's nerve and verve, and that adrenalin-fueled resolve prompted dying exclamations of the noblest sort. Yet several historians (most notably, John Ellis) have reported the existence in various wars of other kinds of combatants, some uncertain, others shocked by the killing, many confused by the fog of battle, frightened, unable to relate what they had been told about combat with what was happening.[24] Perhaps intense, close-range combat requiring group cooperation (as with crew-fed weapons) overcomes some of the individual soldier's sense of terror.

During World War II, General S. L. A. Marshall and his teams of observers from the Army's Human Resources Research Office discovered that only about one in every five GIs in some four hundred combat infantry units "actually fired at the enemy . . . during the course of an entire engagement" (Selection 31). Marshall attributed this, in part, to a Judeo-Christian "fear of killing."[25] Marshall's study first appeared in 1947; to date no one has attempted a systematic analysis of the "fear of killing" in any other war or battle in which American (or, to my knowledge, any other nation's) armies have participated.

What are the consequences of one's having experienced extensive combat? During the Vietnam War some psychologists and psychiatrists claimed that the consequences of such combat to the individual's psyche were severe. Survivor guilt and post-traumatic stress disorder (PTSD) could be the result (see Selection 45 for a critical review of such contentions). Others argued that much of the distress that noncombat veterans or veterans of moderate combat suffered could be attributed to personality traits that existed before military service.[26] The Grinker and Spiegel and the Stouffer studies did establish that the "shell-shock" seen in the trenches of World War I was clearly evident in World War II as well ("combat fatigue" it was called then). After prolonged periods of combat, the din of battle, the sight of dying comrades, and the fear of death produced "the shakes" and other symptoms of mental collapse in many GIs[27] (see, for example, Selection 33). Psychiatrists observed similar disorders in Vietnam, but relatively fewer, because the rotation system in Vietnam exposed men to fewer months of combat than the average combatant, for example, in the Italian theater during World War II. Nonetheless, two separate comparisons of groups of Vietnam combat veterans, noncombat Vietnam-era Veterans, and a peer cohort who saw no service have demonstrated that, ten years after the war, veterans of heavy combat are about twice as likely to experience PTSD as any of their peers.[28] We might find similar evidence of PTSD in the histories of combat veterans of Cowpens, Gettysburg, or Belleau Wood, though the search for evidence, combatants, and a control group of nonvets would be quite difficult.

Finally, there have been a number of recent studies of another combat-related subject—the ethical conduct of Americans at war. Some have studied specific atrocities: Phillip Paludan's *Victims* (1981) is a carefully crafted, sensitive study of the massacre of Southern Appalachian Unionists by

Confederate militia during the Civil War. John Brinsfield offers a shrewd, historically sound defense of the legal and ethical facets of General William Sherman's march through the South. Stan Hoig's *The Sand Creek Massacre* (1961) thoroughly explores that act of butchery in Southeastern Colorado and its aftermath. Ronald Schaffer meticulously unveiled the efforts of Army Air Force leaders, devoid of ethical concerns, to mask and depict deceptively their terror-bombing of German targets in the winter and spring of 1945[29] (Selection 32; see also 34).

Others have explored the ethics of American military leaders independent of a specific incident. William Skelton and Thomas Leonard (Selection 23) have shown that many army officers, both before and after the Civil War, were distressed by their Indian-fighting role. Often filled with respect for their Native American opponents, sometimes troubled by the injustice of their government's demands, they nevertheless carried out their orders; none resigned. Douglas Kinnard similarly found that many generals who had served in Vietnam had been deeply upset by their government's policies; yet none publicly protested or resigned (but see Selections 13 and 44). My own study of the origins of the laws of war and of violations thereof asked why some violated and others scrupulously adhered to these laws, and identified certain personality traits, ethnocentricity, combat conditions, the nature of the weapons employed and, especially, poor leadership as the factors producing war crimes.[30]

Others have asked about how the American public has reacted to questions about the ethics of Americans at war. W. Darell Gertch has described "the mutation of American values" regarding strategic bombing between 1937 (when Americans criticized Spanish Fascist and Japanese aerial attacks against urban populations) and 1945 (when, in general, the public displayed little concern for the incendiary bombing of German and Japanese cities). Herbert Kelman and Lee Lawrence have sagely analyzed the public's divided reaction to the My Lai massacre and the court-martial of Lieutenant William Calley[31] (Selection 43).

OTHER CONSEQUENCES OF MILITARY SERVICE

Quite independent of the trauma of combat, soldiers in American history were sometimes affected in other ways by their service for a substantial period of time in a "total institution" very different from their preservice environment.

Political perspectives might alter. Certain Revolutionary War soldiers, the subjects of studies by William Benton (Selection 8), Edwin Burrows, and E. Wayne Carp, seem to have experienced a change in political perspective. Officers from Pennsylvania and New York who served outside their own states tended to adopt more cosmopolitan political positions after the war, as did some enlisted men. Others who had not left their state but were similar in age, nativity, religion, social class, and country affiliation to those who had also exhibited an outlook altered by their army experiences; one group had seen more of the Confederation and its plight, and had seen the need of stronger bonds, in the form of a new Constitution. Some artisans and laborers, deferential in 1774, became politically independent beings by 1783 as a consequence of their treatment at military hands. Arthur Barbeau found a similar development in many black soldiers serving in World War I.[32]

Nancy Phillips, in a sophisticated study of World War II veterans and a control group of nonveterans, has demonstrated that those who served became more "hawkish," regardless of whether they had volunteered or been drafted. John Helmer reported that some working-class veterans of the Vietnam War in the Boston area, the subjects of his study *Bringing the War Home* (1974), were radicalized by their experiences, but he gave inadequate attention to the *pre*service values of his subjects; other studies indicate that radical Vietnam veterans were generally men who had opposed the war before entering the service (see Selection 44). Indeed, those testing the hypotheses that military service in the 1960s or 1970s has "militarized" those who served, made them more authoritarian, or led them to acquire guns have found little or no evidence to support these hypotheses.[33]

Nonetheless, military service has altered the lives of certain GIs in significant ways. Evon Vogt and John Adair described those changes for certain Navajo and Zuni young men who had served in World War II; the ability to communicate in English was the key there. Robert Havighurst described the "cosmopolitanizing" effects of service on Euro-American veterans of World War II. Harvey Browning, Sally Lopreato, and Dudley Poston demonstrated that, when one controlled for level of education, race, and occupation and then examined the differences in income of men aged twenty-five to fifty who had served and those who had not, the Chicano and (to a lesser extent) black veterans were doing better in 1971 than their nonveteran counterparts. The military regimen and insistence on the use of the majority culture's language, symbols, and habits may have acculturated the youth from the *barrio* in ways that improved their ability to move into and function within the job market, but Browning and his colleagues do not speculate in any depth on explanations of the differences they detected. In any event, Josphina Card's survey in 1981 of Vietnam-era veterans and nonveterans (who had first been surveyed in 1960 while in the ninth grade) confirmed what other studies in the 1940s, 1960s, and 1970s had indicated: The majority of veterans described their military experience positively.[34]

Opinion polls conducted by Robert Havighurst in 1951 and the Gallup and Harris organizations in 1969, 1971, and 1979 provide an opportunity to compare the views of a random sample of veterans of World War II, Korea, and Vietnam, and the public as a whole. Veterans of all three wars tend to hold similar views, and the opinions of Vietnam veterans about various aspects of that war are not notably different from those of the general public.

INTER- AND INTRASERVICE TENSIONS

Beneath the deceptively placid surface rhetoric of the military services, one often detects a tug-of-war between units within a particular service, or between services. My study of the regular army in the *fin de siècle*, for example, revealed a fear among some officers that the National Guard might displace the regulars as the central defense force of the nation and the chief recipient of Congressional largesse (Selection 24). Both Monte Calvert and I have described severe tensions within the late-nineteenth-century Navy between line and engineering officers. Several scholars have noted the persistent fears (some of them legitimate) that Marines have had since the early twentieth century that the Navy or the Army or both were about to succeed in extinguishing the Corps. Robert O'Connell's dissertation highlighted the struggle in the 1910s and 1920s between naval "young Turks," impressed by the submarine and the aircraft carrier, and older, more conservative battleship-oriented admirals. Fred Greene identified the fight in the mid-1930s between the Army General Staff, bent on redefining national interests in the Far East to the advantage of Army appropriations, and naval leadership, determined to prevent a change so devastating to them. Yet Greene merely describes the fight; he does not explore its interservice implications. Louis Morton analyzed a more specific rivalry between the army and the Marine Corps, both of whom had battalions in north China in the late 1930s when the Japanese drove south. Neither wanted to be the first to leave, as that would "leave the field clear" for the other service, to the detriment in a future crisis of the one that had "bugged out" first.[35]

Interservice rivalries and tensions between Army field commanders and the Army Air Force continued during World War II, and after the war these tensions culminated in the creation of a separate Air Force within a "unified" Department of Defense. Perry Smith, Vincent Davis, and Paul Hammond have illuminated some of the struggles between Air Force and navy leaders in the late 1940s. Frederic Bergerson's study of how "The Army (got) an Air Force" (the helicopter assault groups of the Vietnam era) offers another example of interservice rivalries and "institutional insurgency"; his young Turks are army helicopter aviators who built a case for themselves by demonstrating both their own ability to perform the mission and the Air Force's unwillingness to provide adequate close air support of assault troops.[36]

Another source of intraservice tensions lay in the rate of promotion. Junior officers in the mid- and late nineteenth century found that advancing in rank was extremely slow, due to a surplus of senior and middle-level officers. This situation irked ambitious young achievers, who contrasted their stagnation to the rapid rise of their nonservice peers in law and business. It led to lobbying efforts in the 1850s and the late nineteenth century, efforts that ultimately led to promotion reform in 1899 and 1916, to the system of "selection up or out" (see Selection 24). (This is the system that Gabriel and Savage faulted recently for producing the "careerist" officers of the 1960s.)[37]

Interservice rivalries can result in mindless duplication of services, but these rivalries *can* be of some use to those in the Congress or administration who want to put a lid on military spending or second-guess the strategic vision of a service Chief of Staff. Lewis Dexter found that the members of the House Armed Services Committee in the 1950s were consciously using interservice rivalry as an instrument to "find out from the Air Force or from Strategic Air Command about Air Defense." As a key committee figure put it: "You'll learn only what they in the service want you to learn, *unless there is interservice rivalry.*"[38]

QUESTIONS OF CIVILIAN CONTROL

One aspect of the military's relation to the greater society is that of civilian control. In the seventeenth and eighteenth centuries this subject was taken very seriously. Timothy Breen has shown the symbiotic relationship between Puritan Massachusetts society and its "covenanted militia." He points to the collective memory these former East Anglicans had of Charles I's Irish soldiers and relates this to the localistic insistence of the Massachusetts towns that they control such matters as the militia's election of officers rather than permitting the crown's officials in Boston to name the officers. When the British naval and military presence was felt, it frequently prompted colonial alarm and distress, and was central to the movement of colonists "toward Lexington" and revolution (see Selections 4 and 5). Yet John Phillip Reid reminds us that the British military under General Gage in the decade before Lexington was *not* acting outrageously or, by British standards, unconstitutionally; indeed, it was unwilling to intervene unless a civil magistrate first read the Riot Act. By the 1770s few such magistrates could be found in New England.[39]

Lawrence Cress, Richard Buel, and Richard Kohn have explored the tension in the 1790s between those with a localistic distrust of a centralized armed force and the cosmopolitan "realism" of those who favored a federally organized, professional military. Both Kohn and Cress document the political monopolizing of the new standing army's officer corps in the late 1790s by Federalists, to the distress of I-told-you-so Jeffersonians. In addition, Theodore J. Crackel has demonstrated that the Jefferson Administration first identified Federalist foes and Republican friends within the officer corps and then reorganized the armed services in order to purge some of those Federalists, to control the Army's officer training process at the source, and to "hasten the day when Jefferson's appointees would constitute a majority in the army."[40]

Questions of civilian control of the military surfaced during the Civil War and Reconstruction. In the past fifteen years several scholars have offered detailed accounts, at both the local and the national level, of the tension between the Army and its radical republican allies in the Congress on the one hand, and President Andrew Johnson and his moderate allies on the other (see Selections 18 and 19).[41]

POLITICAL LOBBYING

If the military in America was satisfactorily "controlled" by Congress and the President, if the officers did not devote their evenings to planning Cromwellian coups, that does not exhaust the ways they might, and sometimes did, conspire politically. Professional soldiers have, from Newburgh to the present, sought to secure benefits for their branch of the service, their corps, their peer group, or themselves. Examples of this appear in studies by Richard Kohn on the Newburgh Conspiracy (Selection 7), William Skelton on the lobbying of antebellum army officers (Selection 11), Harold Hyman on the army's concern for its status in the South in 1866 and 1867 (Selection 18), Martha Derthick on the National Guard's politicking, my work on naval "young Turk" lobbying in the late nineteenth century (Selection 24), and Vincent Davis on "the Admiral's lobby" of the twentieth century.[42]

Soldiers need not have personal or corporate interests at stake to become politically active, of course. During the American Revolution some militia units had two missions—defense and political indoctrination—as John Shy suggests.[43] The wavering or indifferent had to be taught that there was "no remaining neuters"; Tories had to be identified, taxed, and made to toe the line. More recently, during the Cold War many officers offered their men highly political courses in "Militant Liberty" (as one military-generated anticommunist program was called), and showed films created by the Defense Department depicting the "Red Menace." A few commanders offered specific advice on which candidates for public office merited support, and which did not. Thomas Palmer has provided us with a good account of these activities (Selection 38).

INTERACTIONS WITH SOCIETY

Quite independent of its formal relations with President and Congress, the American military has long interacted with society in a variety of ways that have been the subject of the "new" military history. Two may be summarized briefly: First, the military has, on occasion, been used as a protector of property and restorer of "law and order." Such missions tended to be accomplished more speedily and with less bloodshed when regulars were employed, rather than militia or National Guard units drawn from the immediate area of the confrontation and which sometimes represented a particular ethnic or social group (see, for example, Selection 22).[44]

Second, army, navy, or militia units have, quite naturally, served as the interim government of occupied territory, or more recently, as military advisers in "client" countries, providing legal forms, order, advice, training, and basic services (as in the Reconstruction South, the Western territories, the Philippines, Samoa, Cuba, Haiti, China, Germany, Japan, and modern Latin America). Often these occupation forces sought to "uplift" the habits, values, or political ways of the occupied state.

The precise ways that the military and society interact often depend on context. For example, Frank Schubert has found that black soldiers on the late-nineteenth-century frontier were treated with much civilian fear and loathing, except for those black units located between white settlements and potentially dangerous Indian communities. Indians appear to have served as a negative reference group in those cases. In a different time and place, American GIs in Britain during World War II generally enjoyed good relations with their hosts. Norman Longmate has imaginatively assessed the nature of that interaction. Yet when GIs were stationed in a less familiar culture, as were Cold War airmen at a base in Turkey in the 1950s and 60s, the interaction was far more strained, and the actual contacts were reduced to a minimum, as Charlotte Wolf has shown.[45]

Samuel Huntington argued in 1957 that the army officer corps of the late nineteenth century was isolated from American society, and that this isolation helped the officers become more professional and innovative, but John Gates, in a fine reexamination of the evidence, recently demonstrated that Huntington was wrong: The officer corps was *not* isolated; rather it was fully immersed in the progressive mainstream of *fin de siècle* life.[46] Resting on such precarious evidence, Huntington's conclusion, regarding the desirability of the self-isolation of the military, becomes highly suspect.

Another commonly believed hunch about the military and society has also been challenged. Many have assumed that the typical voter prefers a veteran for public office to a nonveteran, all other things being equal. Albert Somit and Joseph Tannenhaus have, indeed, established that those political leaders who selected House candidates in the 1950s for the primaries disproportionately put forward veterans. Yet when they compared *election* day veteran–nonveteran races, they found that the public did not express a similar preference.[47] The party strategists had assumed a preference that was not there.

Any theory of how "the military" is perceived by "the society" founders on the fact that almost as many different societal images of "the military"

as there are units in society. Whenever we probe the relation of the military to society, we tend to uncover new links and overlays, new indications that, for all its unique structures and missions, the American military is still both the product and the property of the greater society; that to one extent or another it reflects that greater society's failings of sexism, racism, drug abuse, and self-centeredness; that it reflects its traditionalism and modernity, its interest group behavior in the nation's capital, its concerns for equity, efficiency, and personal achievement. To say that the military and society enjoy a symbiotic relationship is not to deny that tensions or differences exist; it is only to acknowledge what most Americans tend to forget: that our military has always been, far more so than is the case in most other states, the creature of our culture, not its mentor.

NOTES

1. For a review of this literature see Peter Karsten, "The New American Military History: A Map of the Territory, Explored and Unexplored," *American Quarterly*, Fall 1984, pp. 389–418. This introduction is a revised version of that essay.
2. Frederic Bergerson, *The Army Gets an Air Force: Tactics of Insurgent Bureaucratic Politics* (Baltimore: Johns Hopkins Press, 1980), pp. 18, 82.
3. Samuel Stouffer *et al.*, *Studies in Social Psychology During World War II: The American Soldier*, 4 vols. (Princeton, N.J.: Princeton University Press, 1948–52). One imaginative "benchmark" use of Stouffer is by Peter Maslowski, "A Study of Morale in Civil War Soldiers", *Military Affairs*, 34 (1970): 122–125, reprinted herein.
4. Richard Buel, Jr., *Dear Liberty* (Middletown, 1980), pp. 250, 80, 179, 212, *passim*; F. W. Anderson, "Why Did Colonial New Englanders Make Bad Soldiers? Contractual Principles and Military Conduct during the Seven Years War," *William and Mary Quarterly*, 38 (1981): 395–417.
5. See Eugene C. Murdock, *One Million Men: The Civil War Draft in the North* (Madison: University of Wisconsin Press, 1971), pp. 3–177; Hugh G. Earnhart, "Commutation: Democratic or Undemocratic?" *Civil War History*, 12 (1966): 132–42; James W. Geary, "A Lesson in Trial and Error: The U.S. Congress and the Civil War Draft, 1862–1865," dissertation, Kent State University, 1976. Regarding naval recruitment, see Fredric Harrod, *Manning the New Navy: The Development of a Modern Naval Enlisted Force, 1899–1940* (Westport, Conn.: Greenwood Press, 1978).
6. Peter Karsten, "Consent and the American Soldier: Theory Versus Reality," *Parameters*, 12 (1982): 42–49.
7. Anderson, "A People's Army: Provincial Military Service in Massachusetts during The Seven Years War, *William and Mary Quarterly*, 40 (1983): 499–520; John Ferling, "The New England Soldier: A Study in Changing Perceptions," *American Quarterly*, 33 (1981): 26–45; Charles Royster, *A Revolutionary People at War: The Continental Army and American Character, 1775–1783* (Chapel Hill:

University of North Carolina Press, 1979), pp. 65, 268, 373–78; Robert Gross, *The Minutemen and Their World* (New York: Hill & Wang, 1976), pp. 146–53; Mark Lender and James Kirby Martin, *A Respectable Army: The Military Origins of the Republic, 1763–1789* (Arlington Heights., Ill.: Harlan Davidson, 1982), pp. 218–19; Edward C. Papenfuse and Gregory A. Stiverson, "General Smallwood's Recruits: The Peacetime Career of the Revolutionary War Private," *William and Mary Quarterly*, 30 (1973): 117–32; John R. Sellers, "The Common Soldier in the American Revolution," in S. J. Underdal, ed., *Military History of the American Revolution* (Washington, D.C.: GPO., 1976), 151–66; Buel, *Dear Liberty*, 179. Marcus Cunliffe, *Soldiers and Civilians: The Martial Spirit in America, 1775–1865* (New York: Free Press, 1976), pp. 200–247.

8. Peter Karsten, *Soldiers and Society: The Effects of Military Service and War on American Life* (Westport, Conn.: Greenwood Press, 1978), pp. 66; Peter Levine, "Draft Evasion in the North during the Civil War, 1863–1865," *Journal of American History*, 67 (1981): 816–34; Robert E. Sterling, "Civil War Draft Resistance in the Middle West," dissertation, Northern Illinois University, 1974. Cf. Judith L. Hallock, "The Role of the Community in Civil War Desertion," *Civil War History*, vol. 29, 1983; and Grace Palladino, "The Poor Man's Fight: Draft Resistance and Labor Organization in Schuylkill County, Pennsylvania, 1860–1865," dissertation, University of Pittsburgh 1983, ch. 6. Regarding late-nineteenth-century voter behavior, see Paul Kleppner, *The Third Electoral System, 1853–1892* (Chapel Hill: University of North Carolina Press, 1980). Don R. Bowen, "Guerrilla War in Western Missouri, 1862–1865: Historical Extensions of the Relative Deprivation Hypothesis," *Comparative Studies in Society and History*, 19 (1977): 30–51.

9. Levine, "Draft Evasion"; Earnhart, "Commutation."

10. Peter Karsten, *The Naval Aristocracy* (New York: Free Press, 1972), pp. 5–19; Gerald Linderman, "The War and the Small-Town Community," ch. 3 of *The Mirror of War: American Society and the Spanish-American War* (Ann Arbor: University of Michigan Press, 1974); Fred Baldwin, "The American Enlisted Man in World War I," dissertation, Princeton Univ. 1964, pp. 61–62; Arthur Barbeau, with F. Henry, *The Unknown Soldiers: Black American Troops in World War I* (Philadelphia: Temple Univ. Press, 1974); Karsten, *Soldiers and Society*, pp. 69–71.

11. Harrod, *Manning the New Navy*, 185, 198; Robert K. Griffith, Jr., *Men Wanted for the U.S. Army: America's Experience with an All-Volunteer Army Between the World Wars* (Westport, Conn.: Greenwood Press, 1982); U.S. Congress, Joint Economic Committee, *Economic Effects of Vietnam Spending*, 90th Cong., 1st Sess. (Washington, D.C.: GPO, 1967), I: 317.

12. Marvin Fletcher, *The Black Soldier and Officer in the U.S. Army, 1891–1917* (Columbia: University of Missouri Press, 1974), p. 77; H. Wool, *The Military Specialist*, p. 144; Charles Moskos, "Racial Integration in the Armed Forces," *American Journal of Sociology*, 72 (1966): 140.

13. Karsten, *Naval Aristocracy*, ch. 2; John Lovell, *Neither Athens nor Sparta: The American Service Academics in Transition* (Bloomington: Indiana University Press, 1979); Joseph Ellis and Robert Moore, *School for Soldiers: West Point and the Profession of Arms* (New York: Oxford University Press, 1974); and Judith H. Stiehm, *Bring Me Men, and Women: Mandated Change at the U.S. Air Force*

Academy (Berkeley: University of California Press, 1981). W. Bruce White, "The Military and the Melting Pot: The American Army and Minority Groups, 1865–1924," dissertation, University of Wisconsin, 1968; John Faris, "The Impact of Basic Combat Training: The Role of the Drill Sergeant in the All-Volunteer Army," *Armed Forces and Society*, 2 (1975): 116–27; On ROTC, see Peter Karsten, "Anti-ROTC: Response to Vietnam or 'Consciousness III?'" in John Lovell and Philip Kronenberg, eds., *New Civil-Military Relations* (New Brunswick: Transaction Books, 1974), pp. 111–28.

14. Morris Janowitz, "Changing Patterns of Organizational Authority: The Military Establishment," *Administrative Science Quarterly*, 3 (1959): 473–93; Gary Wamsley, "Contrasting Institutions of Air Force Socialization: Happenstance or Bellwether?" *American Journal of Sociology*, 1972, pp. 399–417.

15. Karsten, *Naval Aristocracy*, chs. 3 and 5: Janowitz, *Professional Soldier*, chs. 7–13.

16. James L. Morrison, "The Struggle Between Sectionalism and Nationalism at Ante-Bellum West Point, 1830–1861," *Civil War History*, 19 (1973): 138–48, esp. 147. It remains for someone else to sort out the Southern-born graduates who remained loyal, by graduating class, and to separate those who remained on active duty from those who resigned early in their careers. Cf. William S. Dudley, *Going South: U.S. Navy Officer Resignations and Dismissals on the Eve of the Civil War* (Washington: Naval Historical Foundation, 1981).

17. Peter Karsten, "Ritual and Rank: Religious Affiliation, Father's Calling, and Successful Advancement in the U.S. Officer Corps of the Twentieth Century," *Armed Forces and Society*, 9 (1983): 427–40; Peter Peterson, *Against the Tide* (New Rochelle, N.Y.: Arlington House, 1974), pp. 148, 182; William Cockerham, "Selective Socialization: Airborne Training as Status Passage," *Journal of Political and Military Sociology*, (1973): 215–29; David Mark Mantell, *True Americanism: Green Berets and War Resisters* (New York: Teachers College Press, 1975); J. Daniel and A. Korotkin, "The Effect of Premilitary Experiences on Military Success," *Journal of Political and Military Sociology* 9 (1981): 255–61.

18. Samuel Stouffer et al., *Studies in Social Psychology during World War II: The American Soldier*, 4 vols. (Princeton, Princeton University Press, 1948–1952), I: 484–89; Peter Maslowski, "A Study of Morale in Civil War Soldiers," *Military Affairs*, 34 (1970): 122–25; Roger Little, "Buddy Relations and Combat Performance," in *The New Military*, ed. Morris Janowitz (New York: Russell Sage Foundation, 1964), pp. 195–225; Charles Moskos, *The American Enlisted Man: The Rank and File in Today's Military* (New York: Russell Sage Foundation, 1970), pp. 144–46.

19. Martin Van Crevald, *Fighting Power: German and U.S. Army Performance, 1939–1945* (Westport, Conn.: Greenwood Press, 1982).

20. Tamotsu Shibutani, *The Derelicts of Company K: A Social Study of Demoralization* (Berkeley: University of California Press, 1978); Eli Ginzberg et al., *The Ineffective Soldier: Lessons for Management and the Nation*, 3 vols. (New York: Columbia University Press, 1959); Anderson, "Contractual Principles and Military Conduct"; Steven Rosswurm, "Arms, Culture and Class: The Philadelphia Militia and 'Lower Orders' in the American Revolution, 1765–1783,"

dissertation, Northern Illinois University, 1979; John K. Alexander, "The Fort Wilson Incident of 1779: A Case Study of the Revolutionary Crowd," *William and Mary Quarterly*, 31 (1974): 589–612; Lender and Martin, *A Respectable Army*, pp. 131–32; Richard Kohn, *Eagle and Sword: The Beginnings of the Military Establishment in America* (New York: Free Press, 1975), ch. 2; Christopher McKee, "Fantasies of Mutiny and Murder: A Suggested Psycho-History of the Seaman in the U.S. Navy, 1798–1815," *Armed Forces and Society*, 4 (1978): 293–304; Harold O. Langley, *Social Reform in the U.S. Navy, 1798–1862* (Urbana: University of Illinois Press, 1967); Richard Bardolph, "Inconstant Rebels: Desertion of North Carolina Troops in the Civil War," *North Carolina Historical Review*, 41 (1964): 163–89; Ella Lonn, *Desertion*; Escott, *After Secession*, 131–32; Hallock, "Role of the Community," pp. 29–43; Harrod, *Manning the New Navy*; Jack Foner, *The U.S. Soldier Between Two Wars* (New York: Humanities Press, 1970); Arnold Rose, "The Social Psychology of Desertion," *American Sociological Review*, 26 (1951): 618–24.

21. David Mandlebaum, *Soldier Groups and Negro Troops* (Berkeley: University of California Press, 1952); Leo Bogart et al., *Social Research and Desegregation of the Armed Services* (Chicago: University of Chicago Press, 1969); Ulysses Lee, *The U.S. Army in World War II: The Employment of Negro Troops* (Washington: Office of Chief of Military History, U.S. Army, 1966); Morris MacGregor, Jr., *The Integration of the Armed Forces, 1940–45* (Washington: Center for Military History, U.S. Army, 1981); Richard Dalfiume, *Desegregation of the U.S. Armed Forces: Fighting on Two Fronts, 1939–1953* (Columbia: University of Missouri Press, 1969); Moskos, "Racial Integration," pp. 132–48. Cf. Alan M. Osur, *Blacks in the Army Air Forces During World War II* (Washington Office of Air Force History, 1977); Bradley Biggs, *The Triple Nickels* (Hamden: Archon, 1984).

22. Clarence Mohr, "Southern Blacks in the Civil War: A Century of Historiography," *Journal of Negro History*, 59 (1974): 177–95; Mavin R. Cain, "A 'Face of Battle' Needed: An Assessment of Motives and Men in Civil War Historiography," *Civil War History*, 29 (1982): 5–27; James M. McPherson, *Marching Toward Freedom* (New York: Knopf, 1967), pp. 30–35, 52–67.

23. See Bell Irvin Wiley's studies of Civil War soldiers; John Ellis, *The Sharp End: The Fighting Man in World War II* (New York: Scribner's, 1980); or John Keegan, *The Face of Battle* (London: Routledge & Keegan Paul, 1976), for good examples.

24. Greg Denning, "The Face of Battle: Valpariso, 1814," *War and Society*, 1 (May 1983): 25–42; Bell Irvin Wiley, *The Life of Johnny Reb* (Indianapolis: Bobbs-Merrill, 1944), 32–35, 215; Linderman, "War and the Small-Town Community," pp. 104–05; Stanley Cooperman, *World War I and The American Novel* (Baltimore: Johns Hopkins Press, 1967); Ellis, *The Sharp End*, esp. chs. 2–4, 6.

25. S. L. A. Marshall, *Men Against Fire* (New York: Harper & Row, 1947), pp. 5–10, 50–60, 70–80.

26. Edgar Nace et al., "Adjustment Among Vietnam Drug Users Two Years Post Service," in Charles Figley, ed., *Stress Disorders Among Vietnam Veterans* (New York: Brunner/Mazel, 1978), pp. 71–128; E. R. Worthington, "Demographic and Pre-service Variables as Predictors of Post-Military Service Adjustment," *ibid.*, pp. 173–87; Jonathan Borus, "The Reentry Transition of the Vietnam

Veteran," *Armed Forces and Society*, 2 (Fall 1975); G. A. Braatz *et al.*, "The Young Veteran as a Psychiatric Patient in Three Eras of Conflict," *Military Medicine*, 136 (1971): 455–57.

27. Karsten, *Soldiers and Society*, 26–45; Roy Grinker and J. Spiegel, *Men Under Stress* (Philadelphia: Lippincott, 1945), p. 350; Stouffer, *American Soldier*, II: 81, 204, 374–81.

28. 97th Cong., 1st Sess., House Committee on Veterans Affairs, Arthur Egendorff *et al.*, *Legacies of Vietnam: Comparative Adjustment of Veterans and Their Peers* (Washington: GPO, 9 March 1981); Josephina Card, *Lives After Vietnam: The Personal Impact of Military Service* (Lexington, Mass.: Lexington Books, 1983).

29. Phillips S. Paludan, *Victims: A True Story of the Civil War* (Knoxville: University of Tennessee Press, 1981); John Brinsfield, "The Military Ethics of General William T. Sherman: A Reassessment," *Parameters: Journal of the U.S. Army War College*, 12 (June 1982): 36–48; Stan Hoig, *The Sand Creek Massacre* (Norman: University of Oklahoma Press, 1961); Ronald Schaffer, "American Military Ethics in World War II: The Bombing of German Civilians," *Journal of American History*, 67 (1980): 337–74.

30. William Skelton, "Army Officer Attitudes Toward Indians, 1830–1860," *Pacific Northwest Quarterly*, 67 (July 1976): 113–124; Richard N. Ellis, "The Humanitarian Generals," *Western Historical Quarterly*, 3 (1972); 170–78; Douglas Kinnard, "The Vietnam War in Retrospect: The Army Generals' Views," *Journal of Political and Military Sociology*, 4 (1975), 17–28; Peter Karsten, *Law, Soldiers, and Combat* (Westport, Conn.: Greenwood Press, 1978).

31. W. D. Gertch, "The Strategic Air Offensive and the Mutation of American Values, 1937–1945," *Rocky Mountain Social Science Journal*, 11 (Oct. 1974): 37–50.

32. Edwin G. Burrows, "Military Experience and the Origins of Federalism and Antifederalism," in *Aspects of Early New York Society and Politics*, ed. Jacob Judd and Irwin Polishook (Tarrytown, N.Y.: Sleepy Hollow Restorations, 1974), pp. 83–92; E. Wayne Carp, "Supplying the Revolution; Continental Army Administration and American Political Culture, 1775–1783," dissertation, University of California, Berkeley, 1981; Barbeau, *The Unknown Soldiers*, last two chapters.

33. Nancy Phillips, "Militarism and Grass Roots Involvement in the Military-Industrial Complex," *Journal of Conflict Resolution*, 17 (1973): 625–55; John Helmer, *Bringing the War Home* (New York: Free Press, 1974); James Fendrich and Michael Pearson, "Black Veterans Return," in Martin Oppenheimer, ed., *The American Military* (Chicago: Aldine, 1971), pp. 163–78; M. K. Jennings and G. B. Markus, "Political Participation and Vietnam-Era War Veterans: A Longitudinal Study," in Nancy Goldman and David Segal, eds., *The Social Psychology of Military Service* (Beverly Hills: Sage, 1976), pp. 175–200; Mary Senter, "Civil–Military Relations in the Mass Public: An Analysis of Interpersonal Civil–Military Ties in Metropolitan Detroit," dissertation, University of Michigan 1982; Norma J. Wikler, "Vietnam and the Veteran's Consciousness: Pre-political Thinking Among American Soldiers," dissertation, University of California, Berkeley, 1973; Alan Lizotte and David Bordua,

"Military Socialization, Childhood Socialization, and Vet's Firearms Ownership," *Journal of Political and Military Sociology*, 1980, pp. 243–56.

34. Evon Vogt, *Navajo Veterans: Changing Values* (Cambridge: Peabody Museum, Harvard University Press, 1951); Evon Vogt and John Adair, "Navajo and Zuni Veterans," *American Anthropologist*, 51 (1949): 547–61; Robert Havighurst *et al.*, *The American Veteran Back Home* (New York: Longmans-Green, 1951); Browning, Lopreato and Poston, "Income and Veteran Status," *American Sociological Review*, 1973, pp. 74–85; Card, *Lives After Vietnam*.

35. Peter Karsten, "Armed Progressives: The Military Reorganizes for the American Century," in Jerry Israel, ed., *Building the Organizational Society* (New York: Free Press, 1973), 196–232; Monte Calvert, *The Mechanical Engineer in America, 1839–1910: Professional Cultures in Conflict* (Baltimore: Johns Hopkins Press, 1965); Karsten, *Naval Aristocracy*, pp. 65–69, 355–57. Cf. Edward W. Sloan III, *Benjamin Franklin Isherwood: Naval Engineer* (Annapolis: U.S. Naval Institute, 1965); Robert O'Connell, "Dreadnought? The Battleship, The U.S. Navy, and the World Naval Community," dissertation, University of Virginia 1974; Fred Greene, "The Military View of American National Policy, 1904–1940," *American Historical Review*, 66 (1961): 354–77; Louis Morton, "Army and Marines on the China Station: A Study in Political and Military Rivalry," *Pacific Historical Review*, 29 (1960): 51–74.

36. Perry Smith, *The Air Force Plans for Peace, 1943–1945* (Baltimore: Johns Hopkins Press, 1970); Vincent Davis, *Postwar Defense Policy and the U.S. Navy, 1943–1946* (Chapel Hill: University of North Carolina Press, 1966); Paul Hammond, *Super-carriers and B-36 Bombers: Appropriations, Strategy, and Politics* (Indianapolis: Bobbs-Merrill, 1963). Frederic Bergerson, *The Army Gets an Air Force: Tactics of Insurgent Bureaucratic Politics* (Baltimore: Johns Hopkins Press, 1980).

37. James E. Valle, *Rocks and Shoals: Order and Discipline in the Old Navy, 1800–1861* (Annapolis: U.S. Naval Institute Press, 1980); Karsten, *Naval Aristocracy* pp. 279–93, 356–60. Cf. James L. Abrahamson, *America Arms for a New Century* (New York: Free Press, 1981), who correctly stresses the legitimate security objectives of the "Young Turks," but incorrectly discounts the significance of their career anxieties.

38. Lewis Dexter, "Congress and the Making of Military Policy," in *New Perspective on the House of Representatives*, ed. Nelson Polsby and Robert Peabody (Chicago: Rand McNally, 1963), pp. 175–94, 310–24.

39. John Shy, *Toward Lexington: The Role of the British Army in the Coming of the American Revolution* (Chapel Hill: University of North Carolina Press, 1981); Timothy Breen, "English Origins and New World Development: The Case of The Covenanted Militia in Seventeenth-Century Massachusetts," *Past and Present*, 1972, pp. 75–96; John Phillip Reid, *In Defiance of the Law* (Chapel Hill: University of North Carolina Press, 1981).

40. Cress, *Citizens in Arms*, chs. 7 and 8; Buel, *Dear Liberty*, 100; Kohn, *Eagle and Sword*, chs. 12 and 13; Theodore J. Crackel, "Jefferson, Politics, and the Army," *Journal of the Early Republic*, 2 (Spring 1982): 21–38; Crackel, "The Founding of West Point: Jefferson and the Politics of Security," *Armed Forces and Society*, 7 (1981): 528–44.

41. Hans Trefousse, "The Joint Committee on the Conduct of the War: A Reassessment," *Civil War History*, 10 (1964): 5–17; James Sefton, *The United States Army and Reconstruction, 1865–1877* (Baton Rouge: Louisiana State University Press, 1967).

42. Kohn, *Eagle and Sword*, ch. 2; Harold Hyman, *Era of the Oath: Northern Loyalty Test During the Civil War and Reconstruction* (Philadelphia: University of Pennsylvania Press, 1954); Martha Derthick, *The National Guard in Politics* (Cambridge: Harvard University Press, 1965); Karsten, *Naval Aristocracy* ch. 6; Vincent Davis, *The Admirals Lobby* (Chapel Hill: University of North Carolina Press, 1967).

43. John Shy, "The American Revolution: The Military Conflict Considered as a Revolutionary War," in Stephen Kurtz and James Hutson, eds., *Essays on the American Revolution* (Chapel Hill: University of North Carolina Press, 1973), pp. 121–56.

44. Barton Hacker, "The U.S. Army as a National Police Force: The Federal Policing of Labor Disputes, 1877–1898," *Military Affairs*, 32 (1969): 255–64; Jerry M. Cooper, *The Army and Civil Disorder: Federal Military Intervention in Labor Disputes, 1872–1900* (Westport, Conn.: Greenwood Press, 1980).

45. Frank Schubert, "Black Soldiers on the White Frontier: Some Factors Influencing Race Relations," *Phylon*, 32 (1971): 410–17. Cf. Marvin Fletcher, *The Black Soldier and Officer in the U.S. Army 1891–1917* (Columbia: University of Missouri Press, 1974), chs. 3, 8 and 9; Ann J. Lane, *The Brownsville Affair* (Port Washington, N.Y.: Kennikat Press, 1971), ch. 1; Norman Longmate, *The G.I.s: The Americans in Britain, 1942–45* (London: Hutchinson, 1975); Charlotte Wolf, *Garrison Community: A Study of an Overseas American Military Colony* (Westport, Conn.: Greenwood Press, 1969).

46. Samuel P. Huntington, *The Soldier and the State* (Cambridge: Harvard University Press, 1957), ch. 9, esp. p. 229; John M. Gates, "The Alleged Isolation of U.S. Army Officers in the Late 19th Century," *Parameters*, 10 (1982): 32–45.

47. Albert Somit and Joseph Tannenhaus, "The Veteran in the Electoral Process," *Journal of Politics*, 19 (1957): 184–202.

The Colonial Era

1

A New Look at Colonial Militia

JOHN W. SHY

Some have argued that military systems are major forces, shaping the political and social order; others see them as essentially reflective of the societies they serve. The history of the several compulsory and voluntary militia and expeditionary military organizations of the colonial era provide evidence relevant to these questions.* John Shy's "new look at colonial militia," a comparison of the military systems of different colonies throughout the seventeenth and eighteenth centuries, certainly suggests a diversity of experience, reflecting differing colonial social and economic settings and political purposes.

*See Timothy Breen, "English Origins and New World Development: The Case of the Covenanted Militia in Seventeenth Century Massachusetts," *Past and Present*, 1972, pp. 75–96.

THE SUBJECT OF THE MILITIA has produced some passionate writing by American publicists, soldiers, and historians. Defenders of the militia—those who believe that a universal military obligation is the proper way to defend a society—are fond of stressing that only when free men must themselves fight to protect their liberty are they likely to remain free. The colonial militia, in particular, represents the happy uniqueness of America, where Englishmen in the seventeenth century revived this military relic of the middle ages just as in Europe it was sinking beneath the superiority of the politically dangerous mercenary army on the battlefield. Critics of the militia—many of them professional soldiers—point a different moral, one that rests on the apparent inefficiency of militia in combat, and on

SOURCE: John W. Shy. "A New Look at Colonial Militia," *William and Mary Quarterly*, 20 (April 1963): 175–185. Copyright 1963 by John W. Shy. Reprinted by permission.
EDITOR'S NOTE: Most of the citations to the sources consulted by the author in this essay have been omitted from this volume for brevity and economy. The reader should consult the original source of the essay for the complete scholarly documentation.

the way that the myth of defense by militia led again and again to tragic unpreparedness for war.

There is one point, however, where critics and defenders appear to agree: it is on the assumption that the militia, especially the colonial militia, is a fairly static institution; once its simple theory of organization has been described, there seems little need to watch it as closely for signs of deviation and change as one would watch, say, political institutions. Historians have tended to go along with this assumption, as they have generally accepted the major tenets of both defenders and critics; in short, the militia is usually regarded as both politically healthy and militarily inefficient, but in any case relatively uncomplicated.

My aim is simply to raise a question about this conventional view; and to suggest that the early American militia was a more complicated—and more interesting—institution, that it varied from province to province, that it changed through time as the military demands placed upon it changed, and that these variations and changes are of some historical importance. My motive is not to bolster either the Pentagon or the House Armed Services Committee in their latest disagreement over the concept of the citizen army, or even to provide a new key to the reinterpretation of the American Revolution, but only to offer ways of thinking about our early military history, and of more satisfactorily relating that history to the general history of colonial America.

It is not difficult to understand why the militia has been treated in terms of an unvarying sameness; one has only to read the laws to know the answer. In 1632 the Virginia Assembly told every man fit to carry a gun to bring it to church, that he might exercise with it after the service. One hundred forty-four years later, the legislature of Revolutionary Massachusetts ordered men between the ages of sixteen and fifty to be enrolled in the militia, to provide their own weapons and equipment, and to be mustered and trained periodically by their duly commissioned officers; that is, the same thing Virginia had said if in less sophisticated language. In other ways, the laws are much alike. Certain minor groups of men are exempted from duty. In time of emergency, individuals may be impressed or levied or drafted—the word varies—from their militia companies for active service. In most cases, the law provides that anyone so drafted can be excused by paying a fine, sometimes also by finding an able-bodied substitute. The one case of a clear legal difference—that company officers are elected by their men in New England while they are appointed by governors elsewhere—turns out on inspection to have made little difference in practice. As in the case of colonial politics, men of the "better sort" usually appear in office whatever the process of selection; military organization and social structure seem as yet undifferentiated.

In the beginning, of course, this is true quite literally; social and military organization were the same thing. When John Smith wrote of "soldiers," he meant only those inhabitants who at that moment had guns in their hands and who had been ordered to help Smith look out for danger. But military change in Virginia began very early. To make everyone a soldier when men were still concerned about starving was to ensure that no one would be much of a soldier, as Virginia learned several times. First, a few forts and garrisons were established, either by appropriated funds or, more often, by land grants. Then Negroes, and later most indentured servants, were excused from militia duty. Indian policy had a direct bearing on military organization. For a time, Virginia attempted to treat all Indians as hostile, *ipso facto*. But the military requirements of such a policy were too great, demanding large forces to make almost continuous raids into Indian country. The policy was changed, and the system of defense changed with it; henceforth, Virginia relied on a buffer of friendly Indians, on several forts along the frontier, and—after Bacon's Rebellion—on a few dozen paid, mounted soldiers who "ranged" between the forts—the first rangers of American history.

The year of Bacon's Rebellion, when both Chesapeake and New England colonies waged war against the Indian, affords a convenient opportunity for comparison. Though there are many similarities in the way Virginia and Massachusetts responded to this danger, differences are equally evident and may be more important. Virginia had fewer enemies to contend with, and yet suffered political breakdown in the process of fighting the war, while Massachusetts did not. Governor William Berkeley's strategy of defense, which called for five hundred soldiers in the pay of the colony, required a level of taxation that most Virginia planters believed they could not bear. When Nathaniel Bacon and his followers later reshaped strategy, they called for a thousand soldiers, but planned to use them in raiding and plundering the Indian settlements; thus, Virginians would get not only the satisfaction of hitting back at their tormentors, but also the chance to make a burdensome war profitable. The change from Berkeley to Bacon is more than a little reminiscent of European mercenary armies of the sixteenth and early seventeenth centuries, when a government often lost control of a war while trying to wage it more effectively. Massachusetts and Plymouth lost many more lives than did Virginia in 1675–76, but their governments never lost control of the war. Crucial to New England's success was its ability to draft large numbers of men when and where they were needed. Of course there were grumbling and evasion as war-weariness set in, but the point is that Boston could do it and apparently Jamestown could not.

The reasons for this difference are not altogether clear. There is always danger of neglecting the effect of the particular economic and political situation in each colony while making a military comparison. There is also the possibility that if danger to Virginia had been greater, it might have unified and invigorated that colony. But it would seem that the principal factor is the different pattern of settlement. New England towns were more scattered than Chesapeake farms, but each town had a capacity for armed resistance that was lacking in an individual plantation. A town could bear the burden of a military draft and still hope to maintain itself against attack, while the loss of a man or two from a single, remote household often meant choosing between abandonment and destruction. Despite shortages and complaints, a New England town could usually house and feed a company of soldiers besides its own, thus acting as an advanced military base. Even the meetinghouse, large and centrally located, often doubled as the "garrison house," strong point and refuge in case of attack. New England promised its soldiers plunder in the form of scalp bounties, profits from the sale of Indian slaves, and postwar land grants, but such promises were contributory, and not essential as they were in Virginia, to the procurement of troops. The contrast between New England and the Chesapeake can be exaggerated, because many New England towns were destroyed or abandoned during King Philip's War. But there remains an important difference: the clustering of manpower and the cohesive atmosphere in the town community gave New England greater military strength.

This point about the importance of atmosphere can be sharpened by adding the case of New York to the comparison. The Dutch West India Company made the initial error of promising protection to settlers of New Netherland, and it never thereafter could correct its mistake, although it tried. Organized solely as a commercial enterprise, the colony acquired a social heterogeneity and an attitude toward war that subverted militia organization. The English conquest in 1664 brought the stereotype militia law, but it also brought a small garrison of regulars that tended to perpetuate the Dutch atmosphere of military dependency. Moreover, an accident of geography gave New York not the twohundred-mile frontier of Massachusetts or Virginia, but a single center of danger—the Anglo-Dutch city of Albany, a city constantly torn by internal disputes. More straggling in its pattern of settlement than Virginia, and with much less of the sense of community that makes men fight for one another, New York depended for protection on its diplomatic and commercial connection with the Iroquois Confederation rather than on an effective militia; in time of trouble, it had to call for help.

By the end of the seventeenth century, the principal threat to the British colonies was changing. Europeans—French and Spanish—became the main danger. Virginia found itself so little troubled by the new threat, and her Indian enemies so weak, that militia virtually ceased to exist there for about a half century, a time when a handful of semi-professional rangers could watch the frontier. When the Tuscarora momentarily menaced Virginia in 1713, Governor Alexander Spotswood had little success in ordering out the militia. He then tried to recruit two hundred volunteers from the counties along the frontier ("for those that are far enough from it are little inclined to adventure themselves"), but soon learned that frontiersmen were understandably reluctant to leave their homes in time of danger. Spotswood, finally convinced that he could not make war, made peace.[1]

During the same period, the frontiers of Massachusetts were under sporadic attack by French-supported Indians. After the loss of Deerfield in 1704, the colony developed a net of what have been called, in another time and place, "strategic villages," from Hadley to Wells in Maine, each protected by its own militia, and augmented by provincial troops who used horses in the summer, snowshoes in the winter, to connect the towns by patrols and to conduct raids into Indian country. Clearly the New England militia was retaining much of its vitality.

But it was not just the prevalence or absence of an external threat that determined military change. As New England bore the brunt of war with France, South Carolina occupied the post of danger against Spain. The Carolina militia came in from the country to repulse a Spanish attack on Charleston in 1706, and it rallied—with some help from North Carolina and Virginia—to save the colony during the Yamassee War in 1715, though not before most of the outlying settlements had been abandoned. But South Carolina came to have a more scattered population than either Virginia or New York. In 1720, the Council and Assembly complained to the British Board of Trade that it was difficult to react to any sudden danger because the colony's 2,000 militiamen were spread over 150 miles. In 1738, Lieutenant Governor William Bull reported to the Board that, brave as the Carolinians might be, an effective defense was, as he phrased it, "Inconsistent with a Domestick or Country Life."

Bull neglected to mention South Carolina's other major difficulty in defending itself—slavery. Under the earliest militia law, officers were to "muster and train all sorts of men, of what condition or wheresoever born." In the Yamassee War, four hundred Negroes helped six hundred white men defeat the Indians. But as the ratio of slaves to whites grew rapidly, and especially after a serious slave insurrection in 1739, Carolinians no longer dared arm Negroes; in fact, they hardly dared leave their plantations in time of emergency. The British government tried to fill the gap, first by organizing Georgia as an all-white military buffer, then by sending a regiment of regulars with Oglethorpe in 1740. But increasingly the South Carolina militia became an agency to control slaves, and less an effective means of defense.[2]

Elsewhere the new, European threat of the eighteenth century called forth responses that went far beyond the original conception of militia. War against France and Spain required larger forces, serving for a longer time and traveling greater distances. These were volunteer forces, paid and supplied, often armed and clothed, by the government. The power of the governor to raise and command the militia accordingly came to mean less and less, while the military role of the legislature grew larger. The shift in power from royal governor to colonial Assembly had many causes, but the change in the character of warfare was not the least of them.

Less important perhaps, but also less obvious, was the changing character of recruitment in the eighteenth century. So long as military service was nearly universal, one might imagine that volunteers for active duty necessarily must have been militiamen who received a reminder of their military obligation along with a little tactical drill at the militia muster, three or four times a year. This, it would appear, is not wholly true. There were several classes of men, whose total number was growing after 1700, who fell outside the militia structure. These classes were: friendly and domesticated Indians, free Negroes and mulattoes, white servants and apprentices, and free white men on the move. These were precisely the men who, if given the chance, were most willing to go to war. As the militia companies tended in the eighteenth century to become more social than military organizations, they became the hallmarks of respectability or at least of full citizenship in the community. Evidence gathered so far is not full nor does it admit of any quantitative conclusions, but it does indicate that a growing number of those who did the actual fighting were not the men who bore a military obligation as part of their freedom.[3]

It is difficult to believe that the colonial volunteers of the eighteenth century had more in common with the pitiable recruits of the contemporary European armies than with the militia levies of an earlier period; nevertheless, changes in the social composition of American forces between about 1650 and 1750 were in that direction. By impressing vagabonds in 1740, the Virginia Assembly filled its quota of men for the expedition against Cartagena. Six years later, when Governor William Gooch sought to recruit volunteers for another expedition, he found few men willing to enlist, the usual sources apparently depleted by the previous draft.

Perhaps the vital change was in the tone of active service: with more social pariahs filling the ranks and military objectives less clearly connected to parochial interests, respectable men felt not so impelled by a sense of duty or guilt to take up arms. Only when a war approached totality (as in the Puritan crusade to Louisbourg in 1745, when an impressive percentage of Massachusetts manpower served in the land and sea forces) might the older attitude appear. Otherwise fighting had ceased to be a function of the community as such. It seems never to have crossed the introspective mind of young John Adams that he was exactly the right age to serve in the Seven Years' War, and he was shocked when a friend expressed envy in 1759 of the heroic warriors who had begun to win victories in North America.

In fact, volunteer units so constituted could perform well under certain circumstances, but generally suffered from low morale and slack discipline. At least one British general in the Seven Years' War understood that there were two kinds of provincial troops: those levied from among the militia on the basis of a legal military obligation, and those who were recruited for all the wrong reasons—money, escape, and the assurance of easy discipline.[4] It is instructive to note that before Pitt's promise of reimbursement permitted the colonial governments to pre-empt the recruiting market with high pay and enlistment bounties, British regiments, despite their notoriously low pay and harsh discipline, enlisted about 7,500 Americans after Braddock's arrival. Again in 1762, when the colonies themselves used supplementary bounties to recruit regulars for General Jeffery Amherst, almost 800 enlisted. There are hints that some of these recruits—for the provincial as well as the regular regiments—were Indians and Negroes, and better evidence that many of the white men were second-class citizens of one sort or another.

The generally low opinion acquired by most British officers of the American fighting man, an opinion that later would have disastrous consequences for them, originated with the kind of provincial units they saw during the Seven Years' War. Even when Massachusetts and Virginia resorted to the draft to fill their quotas, they now provided first for the impressment of "strollers," and "idle, vagrant, or dissolute persons." Once the British had seen the American encampment at the head of Lake George in 1756—"nastier than anything I could conceive," reported one officer—most provincial regiments were relegated by the British command to an auxiliary function, becoming toward the end of the war "hewers of wood and drawers of water," as James Otis put it. This was ignoble and backbreaking work, often on short rations, so that low morale and poor discipline declined still further. Add to this the frequency of epidemics among the Americans, whose officers probably had never heard of the elementary rules of field sanitation set down by Dr. John Pringle in 1752 and could not have enforced them even if they had. Contributory to certain kinds of disease was the absence—not the presence—of women among the provincial troops. These poor creatures—ridiculed in the drawings of Hogarth and maligned by the Puritan clergy—at least kept some semblance of cleanliness about the camp, hospitals, and person of the British regular.

Because the Seven Years' War in America was primarily an attack on Canada with New England supplying most of the provincial troops, it was the Yankee in particular who came to be regarded as a poor species of fighting man. This helps explain the notion of the British government that Massachusetts might be coerced without too much trouble in 1774. The government and most British officers failed to understand that those provincials who had mutinied, deserted, and died like flies during the Seven Years' War were not militia units; those who did understand the difference apparently failed to see that the New England militia had not decayed to the extent that it had elsewhere. Even after Bunker Hill, General Thomas Gage seems still to have been somewhat confused: "In all their Wars against the French," he wrote to the Secretary of State, "they never Shewed so much Conduct Attention and Perseverance as they do now."[5]

It would be wrong, I am sure, to push either of the arguments advanced herein beyond certain limits. A good deal of research remains to be done before these comparisons are fully established, or perhaps modified. But the main points seem to me clearly borne out by the evidence turned up so far. The approach to early American warfare that promises new insight into the nonmilitary facets of colonial history—into political behavior, social structure, economic activity, even religious belief—is the approach that emphasizes regional diversity and continual change.

NOTES

1. In a long report to the Board of Trade in 1716, Spotswood proposed the abandonment of the militia system in Virginia in favor of a force that would comprise only one-third of the available military manpower, but would be paid by a tax on the other two-thirds who would be excused from service. Spotswood's proposal has a certain similarity to the modern American Reserve and National Guard. He was certain that most Virginians would be happy to pay a small tax to avoid traveling 20 or 30 miles to muster, but foresaw opposition from "Persons of Estates," who "would not come off so easily as they do now." As Spotswood saw it, under the militia system, in practice "no Man of an Estate is under any Obligation to Muster, and even the Servants or Overseers of the Rich are likewise exempted; the whole Burthen lyes upon the poorest sort of people."

2. In a memorial to the King, April 9, 1734, the Governor, Council, and Assembly argued that the presence of three Negroes for every white man made provincial self-defense impossible. *Cal. State Papers, Col., Amer. and W. Indies, 1734–1735* (London, 1953), pp. 173–175.

3. There is scattered evidence for the existence of migratory free white men not enrolled in the militia: Nathanial B. Shurtleff, ed., *Records of the Governor and Company of the Massachusetts Bay in New England* (Boston, 1853–1954), V: 242; *Colonial Laws of New York from the year 1664 to the Revolution* (Albany, 1894–96), I: 454; Governor Dudley to the Council of Trade and Plantations, Nov. 15, 1710, in Headlam, ed., *Cal. State Papers, Col., Amer. and W. Indies, 1710–June, 1711* (London, 1924), p. 268, where Governor Dudley reported that all his "loose people" had gone in the expedition to Nova Scotia; Abbot E. Smith, *Colonists in Bondage: White Servitude and Convict Labor in America* (Chapel Hill, 1947), pp. 281–282, which discusses the impressment of vagrants; Colonel George Washington to Governor Dinwiddie, Mar. 9, 1754, in R. A. Brock, ed., *The Official Records of Governor Robert Dinwiddie . . .* (Richmond, 1883–84), I: 92, where George Washington complains that his soldiers in 1754 are "loose, Idle Persons that are quite destitute of House and Home." For Indians, either as allies or as individual recruits, examples abound. Perhaps the over-all tendency was exemplified by the New York Assembly in 1711; when asked to provide 600 men for the expedition against Canada, it voted 350 "Christian" volunteers, 150 Long Island Indians, and 100 Palatine Germans, who were not only outside the militia system but recently had been disarmed for their unruly behavior. In addition, 100 more Palatines were sent by the Assembly as recruits to the four British regular companies stationed in the province.

4. In a private letter to the Earl of Loudoun, Feb. 25, 1758, Major General James Abercromby urged that the provincial troops be improved "by drafting them out of the militia, in place of whom they send out at an extravagant premium

the rif-raf of the continent." Loudoun Papers, No. 5668, Henry E. Huntington Library, San Marino, Calif.

5. Though the hypotheses advanced in this article are meant to apply only to the colonial period, the author being willing to admit that the Revolution brought rapid and extensive changes, there remains at least a trace of persistent difference between Virginia and Massachusetts after 1775. In 1777, Jefferson opposed a draft from the Virginia militia: "It ever was the most unpopular and impracticable thing that could be attempted. Our people even under the monarchial government had learnt to consider it as the last of all oppressions." Adams, in reply, agreed that it was "only to be adopted in great Extremities." But he added: "Draughts in the Massachusetts, as they have been there managed, have not been very unpopular, for the Persons draughted are commonly the wealthiest, who become obliged to give large Premiums, to their poorer Neighbours, to take their Places." Jefferson to Adams, May 6, 1777, and Adams to Jefferson, May 26, 1777, in Lester J. Cappon, ed., *The Adams–Jefferson Letters: The Complete Correspondence Between Thomas Jefferson and Abigail and John Adams* (Chapel Hill, 1959), I: 4–5.

2

Why Did Colonial New Englanders Make Bad Soldiers?

Contractual Principles and Military Conduct During the Seven Years' War

F. W. ANDERSON

As John Shy points out, British officers had a low opinion of colonial American soldiers during the Seven Years' War (1756–63). Fred Anderson has recently studied New England's soldiers in that war and their relations with their officers, and has shed new light on the character of the colonial soldiery, British misperceptions, and Anglo-American cultural divergence on the eve of the Stamp Act Crisis.* What was the nature of this misperception?

*For his most complete treatment of these questions see Fred Anderson, A People's Army: Massachusetts Soldiers and Society in the Seven Year's War (Chapel Hill, 1984), also available in paper from W. W. Norton.

BRITISH ARMY OFFICERS who served in North America during the Seven Years' War never tired of reminding one another that the American colonists made the world's worst soldiers. As they saw matters, provincial troops were overpaid and underdisciplined, a sickly, slack, faint-hearted rabble incapable of enduring even the mildest privations, officered by men unwilling to exercise authority for fear of losing favor with the mob. The

SOURCE: F. W. Anderson, "Why Did Colonial New Englanders Make Bad Soldiers: Contractual Principles and Military Conduct During the Seven Years' War," William and Mary Quarterly, 38 (1981): 395–417.
EDITOR'S NOTE: Most of the citations to the sources consulted by the author in this essay have been omitted from this volume for brevity and economy. The reader should consult the original source of the essay for the complete scholarly documentation.

populace as a whole seemed as bad as its soldiery: a greedy, small-minded people incapable of disinterested action in defense of the Empire. Contacts between regulars and New England provincials largely fostered this image of Americans, and the image in turn created the dominant British impression of colonial military abilities at the outset of the War for Independence.

Although this was a profoundly mistaken impression, it was in no sense a groundless one: provincials in the Seven Years' War often behaved unprofessionally or in ways detrimental to the war effort. Yet their behavior was not unreasoned, nor was it merely self-interested, as the British too readily assumed. Instead, the unmilitary deportment of New Englanders, in every rank from general officer to private soldier, reflected an almost unfailing tendency to base arguments and actions upon contractual principles whenever they confronted what they regarded as the unwarranted pretension of superiors.

These principles were explicitly articulated in the course of a seemingly minor dispute between the provincial officers of Massachusetts, headed by Major General John Winslow, and the supreme commander of the British forces, John Campbell, fourth earl of Loudoun, in the summer of 1756. Contractual principles, like the ones Winslow and his officers invoked, were applied throughout the war by enlisted men to justify much of the unmilitary behavior—the mutinousness and desertion—that so appalled regular officers. Far from being merely bad soldiers, as the British assumed and subsequent historians have agreed,[1] colonial New Englanders were bad soldiers in a special way, and for reasons that help illuminate late colonial attitudes toward authority—especially the sovereign authority of the crown.

Seventeen fifty-six brought a French victory—the capture of Fort Oswego, Great Britain's main fur-trading post on Lake Ontario—and a change in the British command. In July, the earl of Loudoun, "a rough Scotch lord, hot and irascible," succeeded Major General William Shirley, governor of Massachusetts and an amateur soldier who had been commander in chief since the death of Edward Braddock. The change produced an intermission in offensive military activity that left plenty of time for quarrels between regular and provincial officers. The most significant dispute concerned the rank of colonial officers and the extent of the supreme commander's authority over provincial troops; and the course of this argument showed that Loudoun and the provincial officers of Massachusetts espoused fundamentally antagonistic conceptions of military service.

Lord Loudoun took command only after the campaign of 1756, as planned by Shirley, was well under way. The centerpiece of the effort was an action against the French forts at Crown Point and Ticonderoga on Lake Champlain; the expeditionary force was composed wholly of New England and New York provincial troops under the leadership of Major General John Winslow, one of Massachusetts's most able and distinguished commanders. In order to induce the New England assemblies to contribute men and money, Shirley had given assurances that the command would be independent, that the officers would be New England men, and that the troops would serve only within a strictly bounded area in New York. By these undertakings, Shirley in effect promised that he would not try to turn the provincial troops into regulars—the sine qua non for suspicious assemblymen who feared the consequences of unlimited military service (that is, service during the pleasure of the crown), and who regarded protection from such oppression as a part of their charter privileges.

If Shirley did not in fact exceed his authority in making such commitments, he was at least offering guarantees that only he was prepared to honor. For example, by promising an independent command to Winslow, he effectively bound himself not to combine the provincial army with any regular force during the campaign, since to do so would make the provincials explicitly and unpleasantly subordinate to regular officers. The Rules and Articles of War stipulated that in cases of joint service between redcoats and provincials, colonial field officers—those holding the ranks of major and above—were to rank as "eldest captains" of the regular establishment. In practice, this meant that the admixture of so much as a battalion of regulars would reduce the whole command structure of the provincial army to a subordinate role; Winslow himself would be subject to orders from the most junior redcoat major in the field. Beyond this, the Mutiny Act of 1754 required that colonial troops serving jointly with regulars be subject to British military justice, not to the milder provisions of the colonies' mutiny acts. Applied together, the Rules and Articles of War and the Mutiny Act would virtually have achieved what the assemblies had sought guarantees against: the transformation of provincial troops into regulars.

Lord Loudoun, of course, in no way felt bound to honor Shirley's highly irregular promises. Indeed, as Loudoun saw it, he had been sent to America to straighten out the horrible mess Shirley had made of the war. One of the new commander's first acts, therefore, was to summon Winslow with his chief subordinates to headquarters in Albany in order to inform them that he considered a junction between regulars and provincials both desirable and well within his authority. The provincial major general and his officers maintained in response what they had announced even before Loudoun's arrival: that the conditions under which the provincials had been raised could not be altered without extreme prejudice to the colonial war effort. To Loudoun, who had engineered the confrontation to force the balky colonials to submit to his authority, their refusal to be overawed amounted to insubordination, almost mutiny. He tried to raise the stakes by requiring Winslow to make a formal response to a heavily loaded query: "I desire to be informed by you, in writing, whether the Troops now raised by the several Provinces & Colonies of New England, and Armed with His Majesty's Arms, will in Obedience with His Majesty's Commands,

. . . Act in Conjunction with His Majesty's Troops and under the Command of His Commander in Chief, in whose hands he has been pleased to place the Execution of all those Matters."

Winslow's reply was carefully weighed, respectful, and completely obdurate. He had consulted with his principal subordinates, he wrote, and they all agreed that the provincials would indeed consent to being joined with His Majesty's regular troops, provided, however, "that the Terms & Conditions Agreed upon & Established, by the Several Governments to whome they Belong and upon which they were rais'd be not altered." He directed one of his colonels to write another letter to Loudoun "with the Termes, and Conditions, on which the Provincial Troops, now on their March towards Crown Point were raised." The specifications were that the commander of the expeditionary force should be an officer from Massachusetts; that the pay, bounties, and provisions of the men should be as set by the provincial assemblies; that the service would not extend south of Albany or west of Schenectady, and that its term should not exceed twelve months from the date of enlistment. The provincials, in other words, gave no ground at all.

Loudoun, who was keenly aware that he could not defend the New York frontier without the aid of his stubborn auxiliaries, now realized that he could not bully them into acquiescence. Reluctantly, he compromised. On August 12 he extracted a declaration of the provincial officers' allegiance to the king; in return he promised to refrain from bringing about a junction of forces for the time being and to allow the expedition against Crown Point to proceed under Winslow's command.

The supreme commander, of course, was hardly pleased with this modus vivendi. Once Winslow left Albany to return to his army at Lake George, Loudoun sent to Whitehall a long complaint about military affairs in America. The stubborn opposition of the provincials, he believed, came from the meddling of his predecessor, Shirley, who had raised a faction among the Massachusetts officers in the army and who even now was conspiring to thwart the whole war effort. Shirley and his accomplices had been profiting handsomely from the war, Loudoun wrote, and, fearful of being exposed, were doing their utmost to undermine the honest and efficient administration he was trying to establish.

Just as Loudoun was finishing his report—on August 19—the post brought a long letter from Shirley, enclosing among other items a letter from John Winslow that explained provincial opposition to joint service. Aware that Loudoun intended to blame him for the sorry state of the American war, Shirley had busily been gathering information, from Winslow and others, with which to defend himself. Now he was writing to Loudoun in defense of his conduct, and attempting to explain the Massachusetts officers' behavior as well. Shirley's letter and the one from Winslow that Shirley had enclosed vexed Loudoun mightily; furious, he annotated both to show the "fallacious Assertions" they contained and sent them off to Whitehall with his report. In Winslow's letter he underlined the phrases that he found especially repugnant.

> The grand Debate with the Officers in regard to the Junction arises from the General and Field Officers losing their Rank and Command which they were Universally of Opinion they could not give up as the Army was a proper Organiz'd Body and that they by the Several Governments from whom these Troops were rais'd were Executors in Trust which was not in their power to resign, and, even should they do it, it would End in a DISSOLUTION OF THE ARMY as the Privates Universally hold it as one part of the Terms on which they Enlisted that they were to be Commanded by their own Officers and this is a Principle so strongly Imbib'd that it is not in the Power of Man to remove it.

As Loudoun angrily perceived, Winslow saw the provincial army as the creature, not of the crown, but of the provincial governments. The army as Winslow portrayed it was organized on the basis of contractual understandings. Officers understood when they received their commissions that they would hold specific ranks and exercise the authority granted by law; privates understood when they enlisted that they would serve under the men who enlisted them. Such understandings made the army "proper"; if the conditions of the contract were violated, the army would cease to exist. Appropriately, Winslow used an everyday legal metaphor to describe his officers' position: they regarded themselves as "Executors in Trust," like the executors of an estate, men named in a will or court proceeding to settle an estate's just debts and distribute legacies. Once made, the contract could not be altered by any human agency, although it *could* be destroyed. Officers had it "not in their power to resign" their "Trust"; even the privates had "so strongly Imbib'd" the principle of service under "their own Officers . . . that it [was] not in the Power of Man to remove it" without dissolving the army along with the agreement. This was a homely argument, rooted in the officers' social experience; they were, after all, the sort of men who would be named the executors of estates, and all of them had surely seen such trustees at work. In vocabulary and conception, it suggests that Winslow and his comrades understood military relationships to be founded in principle upon contracts. Theirs was an argument especially resonant in New England, a society fairly stepped in convenants: marriage covenants binding husbands and wives, church convenants among members of congregations, the great covenant of salvation between God and his chosen people. It did not, however, particularly resonate for Lord Loudoun.

Loudoun fixed upon this passage in Winslow's letter because to him its reasoning seemed wholly, self-evidently specious. The order concerning the rank of provincial officers was the *king's* order; the provincial troops were royal subjects; the king or his representative might command them as he saw fit in defense of the realm. That they could characterize themselves as the "executors" of some "trust" other than the prompt execution of their superiors' commands was virtually seditious. When Loudoun thought of proper command relationships and soldierly qualities, he thought first of obedience, loyalty, and subordination. He unhesitatingly obeyed his own direct superiors, the duke of Cumberland and George II; it was quite incomprehensible to him that the bumpkins of New England could fail to understand so basic a relationship. The only reasonable conclusion, and the one Loudoun drew, was that the provincials were self-interested, perverse, and actively opposed to his (hence, the king's) authority.

What the irascible Scot failed to understand was that the provincial field officers had had no firsthand experience with the two institutions that had fostered his ideas of proper social and military relationships: a professional army and a highly stratified social system. English society, with its elaborate clientage networks and its vast distances between the great and the humble, operated on far different assumptions and followed different rules from the much smaller-scale societies of colonial North America.

At about the time Loudoun was composing his report to Whitehall, he received a letter from Governor Thomas Fitch of Connecticut that made explicit some of the curious assumptions of the colonial world. Fitch had learned of the possibility of a junction between regular and provincial troops and was writing to register his concern. Loudoun doubtless found the letter meddlesome and offensive, full of the same egregious sophistry that Winslow and his officers had employed to justify their resistance to his authority. Fitch, the elected governor of a highly insular colony, was very much a product of the same small world as the provincial officers, and the principles he articulated were their principles, too. "Your Lordship will see," he wrote,

> that these [provincial] Troops were not raised to act in conjunction with the Kings Troops, as we were then [when the provincials were raised] altogether unacquainted with his Majesty's Intentions respecting the Operations that would be Directed for annoying the Enemy: Yet are nevertheless raised for the same Service and Sent forth under the command of Officers appointed and commissioned for that purpose; it therefore seems necessary that these Troops be continued under the same Command and Employed agreeable to the Design of their Enlistments, otherwise the Contract between them and their Constituents made for promoting his Majesty's service in this particular may be broken and their Rights violated; the Consequence of which may be greatly prejudicial not only to the King's Interest and the Safety of the Country at this Time but may prove a great Discouragement on future Occasions.

None of the key ideas Fitch employed—the "Rights" of the soldiers, the "Contract between them and their Constituents"—had any compelling meaning for Loudoun; yet New Englanders thought in precisely these terms. The governor was explaining that the operative relationship, so far as the provincial soldier was concerned, was between himself and the province that he understood to be his employer. Although he surely assumed that he was fighting on the king's behalf, the soldier did not regard himself as an employee of the king; it was, after all, the colony that paid his wages and supplied him with food, according to the contract ("made for promoting his Majesty's service") to which he subscribed at enlistment. The idea of the king's intervening, by virtue of his sovereign authority, to alter the terms of an agreement to which he was not a party made no sense: no contract could be changed without the mutual consent of the parties involved. An enlistment contract was no exception: any unilateral attempt to change the agreement simply nullified it and voided the soldier's contractual responsibilities. Such thinking produced an army that was wholly alien to Loudoun's experience: an army made up of men who assumed that soldiers' rights and the conditions of their enlistment had a real bearing on day-to-day operations—men who behaved as if they were in fact the equals of their leaders.

To Lord Loudoun, the talk of contractual commitments and obligations was a smokescreen generated by a few provincial officers who were intent on keeping their rank and command; who were, moreover, intent on thwarting him and the war effort to promote their own fortunes and those of the master conspirator, William Shirley. Loudoun sincerely thought that the provincial privates were amenable to joint service with the regulars, and that whatever fears had grown up among them had been "industriously raised" by Shirley's henchmen. Evidence exists, however, to suggest that this was not the case. Numerous soldiers' diaries that survive from the war demonstrate that the men in fact agreed with their officers about the centrality of contract, although they frequently disagreed over the application of the principle. A survey of thirty journals, mostly those of junior officers and enlisted men, reveals instances of soldiers' actions that reflected motivating ideas of contract, from the beginning to the end of the American phase of the war.

Virtually every private's diary begins with a formalized entry. For example: "April 5 1758 I Lemuel Lyon of Woodstock Inlisted under Captain David holms of Woodstock in newingLand For this present Cannody Expordition—I Received of Captain Holms £2.0s.,od." Or this one, by Jonathan French of Andover: "there Being Orders By the great and Generall Court or Assembly to raise 1800 Men Under the Command of His Excelency ye Right Honle the Earl of Loudoun; for the Defence of His Majestys Colonies and for the anoyance of His Majties Enemies in North:America and upon Consideration of Six dollars Bounty and Some other articles I inlisted in Sd Service William Arbuthnot of Boston being apointed Capt of a Company in the Rigmt Comanded by Coll Joseph Fry." Such entries record the undertaking of an agreement (enlistment), its parties (the soldier and the enlisting officer), and the receipt of a consideration by which the contract was confirmed. The province, of course, kept muster lists and payrolls—official records of service that conveyed the same information—so the diarists did not in fact need to record the data they habitually placed in their initial entries. That they did so with great consistency suggests that the soldiers were consciously keeping track of the bargain between themselves and their province, as well as its fulfillment—a written record to which they could refer in case their employer reneged on any part of its obligation. Hence the frequent notations concerning the issue and quality of provisions take on additional significance, since the province agreed to supply the men with stated quantities of food and rum each week, as well as specified articles of bedding and clothing.

The province sometimes failed to keep its soldiers supplied with the articles it had promised; conveying huge volumes of provisions and other necessaries across vast stretches of wilderness was always difficult and frequently impossible.[2] When the logistical system broke down, the diaries reveal that the troops often took concerted action in the form of mutiny or mass desertion to register their discontent with what from their perspective looked like an employer that was failing to live up to its end of the bargain. The fourteen instances of troop disorder mentioned in the diaries indicate that Winslow and his fellow officers were not in the least exaggerating their warnings to Loudoun.[3] Once they became convinced that the province had broken faith with them, provincial soldiers did not hesitate to show their dissatisfaction by refusing to work or by marching off. Furthermore, these instances of willful disobedience demonstrate remarkable consistencies in causation and in the actions undertaken by the protesting troops.

The causes the diarists ascribed to each of the mutinies and desertions (and they invariably gave each incident a cause) fall into three broad categories. In about a third of the cases, the soldiers were convinced that the army had failed to fulfill its obligations to provide food and rum; half of the instances reflect the soldiers' conviction that they were being forced to serve longer than they had agreed at the time of enlistment; in the remainder, the troops sought assurances that they would be additionally compensated for work not covered in their initial understanding.[4] In every case, the grievance was essentially a matter of contract, and each collective action bespoke the soldiers' concern for their compensation. This in turn suggests that provincial troops were motivated at least in part by the expectation of monetary gain.[5]

The intermingling of contractual and pecuniary concerns in the common soldiers' reactions to deficiencies in supply comes through clearly in Private Obadiah Harris's description of a near-mutiny among Massachusetts troops in Colonel Timothy Ruggle's regiment a few miles north of Albany in August 1758:

> the 20th Day The Saborth Nothing Remarcable but full of fatgue and our Provision Grows Short—
> the 21 Day—We Eate up all Clean that was in our Tents and whare to get the Next Mouth full we Know not but hope that Providence will provide for us Now men are so Cross and tachey that they Cant Speak to one and other

what Shall we do for Sumthing to Eate is the Crye The old Saing is a days Life is hunger and Ease and used to Compare it to a Solders Life but hunger and toyl is our Present State.

Such grousing is common enough in the soldiers' diaries; but Harris, uniquely, continued his complaint in fourteeners, New England's traditional ballad meter:

> And Now when times are Grown so bad
> and our Provision Dun
> Let Every one take up his Pack
> and Make a March for home
> for if we stay within the Camp
> and on our Wages Spend
> We Shall have Nothing for to take
> When our Campane will Eand

The next day, supplies arrived, grumbling ceased, and Harris commemorated the event with twelve more couplets. That he had taken the time and effort necessary to turn his complaint into verse, however, and that he had not obviously been uneasy about seditiously advocating that "Everyone take up his Pack/ and Make a March for home," imply that he thought little of subordination and service to the cause once the provisions ran out. Similarly, the candor of diarists in recording their participation in mutinies and desertions, and the very frequency and openness of such rebellions, indicate that ideas of duty and loyalty mattered less to provincial soldiers than equity, once they concluded that they were being abused. Such considerations justified resistance and protest of a sort that was, by military definition, irresponsible.

Beyond their consistency in cause, the mass desertions and mutinies show a striking consistent pattern of action—what might be characterized as a protocol of protest governing the behavior of the rebels and the responses of their commanders. Two cases from the diaries, one an account of a mutiny, the other of a desertion, exemplify provincial patterns of resistance.

Gibson Clough was a private soldier who served at Louisbourg in 1759 and 1760. A native of Salem and a mason by trade, Clough had lived at home until he had enlisted at age twenty-one in Colonel Jonathan Bagley's regiment, one of the units that garrisoned the fortress. He and his fellows joined in April for what they thought would be the standard eight-month tour. A month before their enlistments expired, they began to worry that they would not be allowed to go home as promised.

[30 September 1759] Cold weather—hear a great talk of things uncertain and thus time spends a way and so we spend our days. . . . [C]old weather is coming on apace which will make us look round about us and put [on] our Winter Clothing and we shall stand in need of good Liquors for to keep our Spirits on cold Winter's days, and we being here within Stone walls are not likely to get Liquors or Clothes at this time of the year and although we be Englishmen Born we are debarred Englishmens Liberty therefore we now see what it is to be under Martial Law and to be with the regulars who are but little better than slaves to their Officers; and when I get out of their [power] I shall take care how I get in again.

At the end of October, the provincials' worries were realized.

31[October] And so now our time has come to an end according to enlistment, but we are not yet got home nor are like to.
    NOVEMBER
    1 The Regiment was ordered out for to hear what the Coll. had to say to them as our time was out and we all swore that we would do no more duty here so it was a day of much Confusion with the regiment.

In effect, what happened on November 1 was that the soldiers of Bagley's regiment determined to go on strike. Since their term of service had expired, they felt no particular responsibility to perform their duties. They may indeed have reasoned that to serve without a new agreement might obligate them to service over which they could exercise no control at all. At any rate, the regiment stuck as a unit, and as a unit accepted the consequences.

2nd [November] The Regiment was turned out for duty and we all stood to it that we would not do any duty at all, for which we was all sent to the Guard house prisoners, but myself and three men were released because we belonged to the Kings works [Clough had recently been detailed to the engineers who were at work refurbishing the fortifications], and there was a letter read to the regiment which came from the governor and Council [of Massachusetts] which informed us that we were to Stay here till the first of December or till we have news from Genl Amherst which I hope will be very soon for our Redemption from this Garrison.

There were obvious problems with imprisoning a whole regiment, amounting to a quarter of the complement of the fortress, and the command soon decided to compromise by releasing some of the men to return to Massachusetts. This, in combination with a carefully orchestrated show of force, was enough to break the strike:

3rd [November] The Regiment was turned out for to hear their doom for denying their duty and for sending a round robin [petition] to the Coll desiring him to get us sent home according to enlistment, which they say was mutiny but it was all forgave by the Genll [Brigadier General Edward Whitemore, military governor of Louisbourg] and a detachment of 140 embarked on board of the Ship Oliver, a transport bound to Boston and the three Regular regiments was drawn up on the grand parade, so was our regiment all but the prisoners and they were brought up by four files of men and place in the centre and the General made a speech to them ye articles of war was read to us and the letter that come from Boston, and then the Coll. made a speech to us and told us that we was to stay one month more at least and more if wanted.

On December 5, a brig and two schooners arrived from Boston, with word that the regiment would be required to remain all winter. Bagley thereupon promised the remaining troops that he would carry their cause to the General Court; three weeks later, he and another officer left for Boston. This plunged Clough into gloom: "and now the Major [Ezekiel Goldthwait] takes command of the Reg't here according to orders and we are all like to be here all winter and God Help us."[6]

Clough's experiences in many ways typify mutinous resistance among provincial troops. A similar response was desertion, an option not readily available to the members of a garrison on the isolated northeastern tip of Cape Breton Island. The constraints of isolation, however, did not apply in the case of John Woods, a private from Worcester who in 1759 was serving in Colonel Abijah Willard's regiment at Fort Ticonderoga. Like Clough, he had enlisted at the beginning of April for an eight-month tour of duty. On October 27, Woods mentioned "a great Stir a Bout going home," but noted no further unrest until

> Nov. 1 This morning a Pertition Carried in to the Coll Willard for a Discharge the Coll agreed to send to the General [Amherst] for one—So then went back to work & to our duty
>
> 2 Last night the Sargent Came back from the Gene'l with orders we should no go of. . . .
>
> 2 This morning Draw'd up to hear what the Gen. orders was when heard all agreed to go of all got there packs went on to the perade Leut French march't us off march't one mile made a halt, Came three officers and Said they were coming after us to bring us back But not minding Kept on our march a Bout Twelve miles Then Came Three more officers and would have us come back & that the Coll had sent to Coll Lyman & that he had sent 3 hundred men & one hundred highlanders Down the South Bay to Stop us But Refused to go back A good Day. . . .
>
> 3 This morning Cloudy but march't off Soon began to Rain & held all Day met with nothing worse than the mountains went about twelve then Campt
>
> 4 About three oClock Cle'd of Cold & look like A fair day about Sun Rise set out & made a fine march this day met with Nothing to scare us at all.

Several characteristics of the troops' activity in these cases were apparent in virtually every rebellion. In the first place, there was nothing secretive about the actions of the discontented soldiers, and they made no attempt to conceal their identities. Unlike the classic desertion—an individual soldier slipping away from an encampment under the cover of darkness or ducking out of the line of march—the provincial desertions occurred in broad daylight, and usually after some notice had been given, either informally or by a petition to the commanding officer. Furthermore, they were always corporate, involving from a score or two of men to several hundred. Provincial mutinies did not resemble the classic mutiny in regard to the participants' disposition toward authority; rather than seeking to overthrow or kill their commanders, the rebellious troops apparently either behaved with respect toward them or treated them with simple indifference. In this it would seem that the mutineers were in effect informing their commanding officer that they no longer acknowledged his authority, and that they would not do so until he had made a proposal that they as a group found acceptable. Their actions also bespoke a sharp limitation in their goals: rather than permanently rejecting the leadership of their officers, they did so only until the grievance had been rectified or until they were forced by superior strength to submit. In line with these characteristics, it is noteworthy that the mutinies were nonviolent in every case; although the soldiers retained their arms, there is no mention of any use or threatened use of them.

Mutinies seem sometimes to have been led by junior officers, and the band of deserters to which John Woods belonged marched under the leadership of one "Leut French." This suggests, at the very least, a degree of identification between company officers and enlisted men that would simply have been incomprehensible in the British or any other European army. In a larger sense, the actions of mutineers and deserters seem to reflect an achieved consensus not dissimilar to that of a small town meeting. Clough and his fellow mutineers "all swore" that they "would do no more duty," and "all stood to it that [they] would not do any duty at all" when threatened with the stockade; Woods's deserters "all agreed to go of[f]" together. Another diarist, Private Enoch Poor of Newbury, noted in June 1760 that everyone in the three provincial companies that garrisoned Fort Frederick, in Nova Scotia, "was of One Mind [and] That was Not To work with thout Pay" for extra duties not comprehended in the enlistment understanding. Evidence that whole units, like Clough's regiment, submitted to imprisonment after being given the opportunity to reconsider their conduct suggests that the solidarity of the mutineers could be sustained under considerable stress.[7]

The discontented soldiers often acted in richly symbolic, even theatrical ways. Several diarists note that participants in mass desertions marched off with "clubbed arms": they carried the muskets over their shoulders, grasping the weapons at the muzzles, not by the buttstocks—a posture that, in contemporary drilling conventions, signalled the completion of duty.[8] Furthermore, the fact that the men marched off carrying arms that were for the most part crown property indicates an additional measure of defiance, a signal that the rebels intended to appropriate their own compensation.

The sequence of events in the mutiny and the desertion described above, and indeed in most of the other rebellions for which a good record of events exists, closely paralleled the sequence described by Nathaniel Knap of Newbury in his account of a refusal to work at Louisbourg in 1759. Significantly, Knap was not a soldier but a civilian artificer employed as a ship carpenter at the fortress. Although he worked directly for the military and was, to a degree, subject to military discipline, he was explicitly a contract worker, employed under a twelve-month agreement. The striking similarity between the dispute he described and the mutinies and desertions discussed above suggests the great extent to which New Englanders' military behavior derived from civilian patterns of response that were clearly governed by reasoning from contractual principles. When soldiers and civilian workers were confronted with the expiration of their contracts, their reactions were not merely parallel: they were identical, and reflected identical assumptions. Knap's account of the event begins:

Monday the 19th [of March 1759] this Day fair Weather & it being Our Freedom Day we all kept a holiday & Gave the Day to the King the Govenor [Edward Whitemore] would not let but three men go home & we Draw'd Lots & I got a Blank

teusday the 20th this Day fair Weather went to work on Mr Laslys Scooner Capt herriman Sail'd to Day & Isaac Ridgway & frances Holiday & Rd Lowell went home with him they got the Lot to go home & the Govenor Said that we Should all be Discharg'd in three Months if we would stay

Three months later, Knap and his fellow carpenters found that Whitemore still required their services.

Sunday June the 17th 1759—this Day fair Weather . . . we went to the Govenor to Day for our Discharge but we Could not Get a Direct Answer he wanted us to tarry till we had Relief sent us from Boston. . . .

Monday 18th this Day fair Weather We all Concluded not to Do any work and was still trying for a Discharge Coln Bagley is our Agent and he Came and told us that if we would stay one fortnight Longer that the Govenor would pay us our wages and pay our Passage home and allows us 14 Day Pay and 14 Day Provisions all this on the Govenors word and honour.

Once again, they returned to work. Two weeks later, Whitemore again proved unwilling to dismiss the homesick artisans. As before, they refused to work without an agreement.

Monday July the 2 1759 this Day fair Weather none of us Did any work the Govenor said that there should be but 12 men Go home and that the Married Men Should go which is 8 that Desir'd to go and 4 young men then there was 4 of them that Came from Snt Johns allow'd to go

teusday the 3 this Day foul Weather I am one that's to go home and I am a getting Ready

Teusday the 3 this Day foul Weather the Govenor Rather than Come under a Bond he said that all the Compe mite go home & we ware a Geting Ready to go home.

No soldier, of course, could ever threaten to make his commander execute a bond for the fulfillment of an agreement, as the carpenters evidently threatened to make Whitemore do—the tactic by which they secured their release. Because the governor was compelled to deal with the carpenters as civilians, not soldiers, he was unable to coerce them by applying force, as a military commander might apply it to stubborn soldiers. The carpenters' repeated strikes and Whitemore's hapless attempts to renegotiate their work contract thus offer exceptionally clear examples of the process at work in the mutinies and desertions of provincial troops. In military cases, the commander's duty and legal right to suppress the rebellion by force of arms (if not his actual ability to do so), complicated the pattern; but the important fact is that the rebellious troops' behavior reflected assumptions identical to those of the carpenters. In case after case, the aggrieved soldiers notified their commander that they intended to take independent action if the commander did not remedy the grievance. Sometimes an officer responded as Governor Whitemore did, agreeing to the demands of the rebels or offering a compromise. More often, the leader responded by reminding the soldiers of his authority and threatening them with severe punishment should they carry through their threats. Despite such warnings, troops persisted: like the carpenters, they waited until the agreed deadline and then refused to work, or they proceeded to muster themselves without orders and march out of camp in a body. Here the soldiers acted out their defiance symbolically—openly disregarding orders, clubbing muskets, and so on—a dramatized version of the carpenters' repeated refusal to go to work. Commanders reacted to these challenges in several ways: by trying to reason with the mutinous men; by offering to represent their case to the next higher commander; by giving in; or by trying to suppress the disorder by force. This was the point at which the command generally performed its own symbolic counter-theater, to give point to its power—perhaps by surrounding the rebellious troops with regulars, bayonets fixed, and beating the prisoners' march; perhaps by seizing and summarily punishing a ringleader, if one could be identified and caught. Finally, the mutinous soldiers determined whether to accept the conditions offered or to continue to resist. The most frequent solution was to accept the commander's offer; the most frequent outcome was some form of accommodation. In only one instance was a troop rebellion crushed by force (and that without bloodshed); every other incident either ended peacefully, with some degree of success for the rebels, or circumstances changed in such a way as to eliminate the grievance.

New England provincial officers and enlisted men conceived of military service in terms that were worlds apart from those familiar to British professional officers. The New Englanders for the most part lacked a military ethos recognizable to officers like the earl of Loudoun, who identified loyalty, subordination, discipline, and regularity as the primary martial virtues. When defining their relationship to military and civil authority, provincials seemed instead to regard themselves as employees of their provinces, contracted workers whose work consisted of bearing arms against the French and Indians.[9] Accordingly, they conducted themselves exactly as civilians would when confronted with the expiration of a work contract or when faced with an unacceptable alteration in the terms of their employment.

To Loudoun and those like him, the provincials looked like incredibly bad soldiers and, given their professional perspective on the matter, the New Englanders *were* bad. On the other hand, the provincials believed they were adequate (if not perfect) soldiers, whose actions were above all consistent, sensible, and necessary. From their point of view, anyone who tried singlehandedly to alter previously agreed arrangements was behaving in a dangerously unacceptable way. The truth, of course, is that the regulars and provincials were operating from contradictory premises about society, warfare, and military service. Colonials and regulars, without realizing it or even having a name for it, were culturally different from each other; and because they did not recognize that the premises from which they reasoned differed so profoundly, each believed the worst about the other.

The behavior of the provincial officers in opposing Loudoun in 1756, and of provincial troops in their various mass desertions and mutinies throughout the war, demonstrates that contractual ideals were not only deeply held but broadly shared among men of all the social standings represented in the colonial forces. Contractual relations had been much more central to their social experience than either royal authority or highly deferential social relationships. The cultural context of a convenanted society and the demands of the provincial economy made contracts a part of everyday life and talk, while notions of royal sovereignty and of a naturally superior, titled elite remained for the vast majority of the colonists rather distant and abstract. The long-standing practice of fighting wars against the French without direct aid from the mother country had generated at all levels of New England society assumptions of autonomy that complemented this home-grown contractualism. New Englanders, accustomed to having their own governments raise, direct, supply, and pay the provincials, automatically identified the colonial assemblies as the agencies responsible for defense. For the soldier, the locus of authority was the annually negotiated contract of enlistment that tied him to his government, specifying the service he would render and the care and compensation he would receive in return.

The Seven Years' War transformed the scale of colonial military conflict and introduced the immediate participation and command of professional British soldiers. It also brought a sharp and unexpected confrontation with New England's tradition of a contract-based soldiery. No matter how hard they tried, however, British officers found that they could not prevent provincial soldiers from acting on ingrained notions about the contractual nature of military service. The result was twofold. On one hand, regular officers concluded that New Englanders (and by extension, all Americans) lacked the character to make good soldiers. Ultimately, their belittling of Americans' martial virtue would lead to one officer's famous boast in 1774 that he could take a thousand grenadiers to America "and geld all the Males, partly by force and partly by a little Coaxing." On the other hand, the war eventually put under arms a third or more of all men in New England who were eligible to serve, and directly exposed them to imperial authority, even as it graphically illustrated the divergences between British and American thinking. Just as the regulars drew conclusions from the war about Americans, so New Englanders drew their own conclusions about the British. The war was an education for both sides, and the lessons each learned would inform the crucial decisions made in the years that followed the Peace of Paris [1763].

NOTES

1. Such discussions have usually taken place in the context of a venerable debate over the relative merits of regular troops versus militia, deriving from the post–Civil War writings of Emory Upton and John A. Logan. The emphasis has been on describing (or excusing) provincial misconduct, not on explaining it. A notable exception to this partisan tendency is John W. Shy's brief and influential essay, "A New Look at Colonial Militia," *William and Mary Quarterly*, 3d Ser., XX (1963), 175ff [Selection 1]. Shy contended that 18th-century provincials were drawn increasingly from socially marginal groups and consequently fought with less commitment than men who believed that they were fighting for their homes and families. For reasons I hope are clear from this article, I disagree. Nonetheless, Shy's work marks an advance in the interpretation of colonial and Revolutionary military affairs without which this article would not have been possible; my debt is, I trust, evident in the very formulation of the question addressed here.

2. As John Shy has pointed out, the problem of supply was paramount in the Seven Years' War, in which even the small forces deployed in the wilderness were "huge in terms of logistical effort" (*Toward Lexington* [Princeton, N.J., 1965], 88).

3. These 14 "disorders" were not, of course, all of the mutinies and desertions among provincials during the war but only the ones that happened to be recorded in the diaries.

4. In 4 of the 14 cases, the cause ascribed was a deficiency in supply. . . . In 7 cases, troops rebelled as a consequence of the expiration of their term of enlistment or the fear that they would be retained beyond the end of their term. . . . In the remaining 3 cases, troops protested by refusing to work unless paid additionally for extra duty. . . .

5. For wage rates see *The Acts and Resolves, Public and Private, of the Province of the Massachusetts Bay*, XV (Boston, 1908), 442, 454–455. These represented a rate about double that at which regulars were paid, even if the provincials' bounties were not included. See Pargellis, *Loudoun*, 281–285. A private's wages

were almost the same as those a civilian agricultural laborer would receive, according to wages quoted in William B. Weeden, *Economic and Social History of New England, 1620–1789*, II (Boston, 1891), 896–898.

6. Gibson Clough, Dec. 22, 1759. Col. Bagley succeeded in obtaining an additional bounty for the men detained over the winter but did not himself manage to return until June 13, 1760, two weeks ahead of the replacement troops for his regiment. In the meantime, on Apr. 1, Clough and his remaining comrades had all, more or less unwillingly, reënlisted for the 1760 campaign. Clough finally returned to Salem on Jan. 1, 1761, overjoyed at the end of what he had come to regard as his captivity.

7. See also Samuel Morris, Nov. 1, 1759. These collective actions by soldiers show obvious affinities to those of civilian crowds in the late colonial and Revolutionary periods, as described in a now-voluminous secondary literature. The deserters and mutineers do not seem, however, to have been acting to extend the authority of the community by extra-legal means, nor were they expressing explicit class (or proto-class) antagonisms. In their motivation by principle, they were behaving in much the same way as English crowds that sought to enforce their conceptions of "moral economy," but differed from the English case in that they appealed to a principle on which colonial New Englanders of every social station agreed.

8. Seth Pomeroy, Sept. 1, 1755; Samuel Chandler, Nov. 22, 1755; Caleb Rea, July 22, 1758. Rea: "[July] 22nd . . . This Day the Regt of Royal Hunters [the nickname of Col. Oliver Partridge's regiment] Clubbed Muskets and were marching out of the Camp by reason the allowance of Provision (which at this time was very mean thro' the whole Camp) had been detain'd one Day or more, but Col. Preble [Jedediah Preble of Massachusetts] persuaded'm to stop (after they had march'd near a mile) and he wou'd see they had the allowance imediately, which they had and returned."

9. I wish to reiterate that they regarded themselves as such in legal or formal terms. There is also abundant evidence that New Englanders were motivated by a sense of millennial mission in opposing the French and Indians, whom they identified with Antichrist. See Nathan O. Hatch, *The Sacred Cause of Liberty; Republican Thought and the Millennium in Revolutionary New England* (New Haven, Conn., 1977), 21–55. Here I have meant to address the question of how they in practice defined their position with regard to military and civil authority, not the larger question of their motives in joining the army. [Ed. This "larger question" clearly warrants more attention, Nathan Hatch's evidence notwithstanding.]

3

North Carolina Militia Act of 1774

As colonial societies and economies developed, their military systems tended to change as well, reflecting increases in economic and political sophistication. A kind of early "selective service system" emerged as trades and professions critical to the colonies were made exempt. The original militia law for the Carolinas, for example (drafted by John Locke in 1669), read: "All inhabitants and freemen of Carolina, above 17 years of age and under 60, shall be bound to bear arms, and serve as soldiers whenever the grand council shall find it necessary." Passages from the more discriminating Militia Act of 1774 are reprinted here.

WHEREAS A MILITIA may be necessary for the defence and safety of this province.

I. Be it Enacted by the Governor, Council and Assembly and by the Authority of the same That all Freemen and Servants within this province between the Age of Sixteen and Sixty shall compose the Militia thereof and that the several Captains of the same shall Enroll the names of all such Freemen and Servants of which their several Companies consist and shall at their respective General Musters return a Copy thereof to the Colonel of their respective Regiments under the Penalty of Five Pounds Proclamation money to be levied by a Warrant of Distress from the Colonel of their Regiment directed to the Sheriff of the County to which the said Regiment belongs which Sheriff shall be paid out of the said Penalty the sum of ten Shillings: and in case any Sheriff shall neglect or refuse to serve such Warrant he shall forfeit and pay the sum of five pounds to be recovered by action of Debt in any court of Record and be applied as hereinafter directed which Copy so returned shall by every Colonel be returned to the Governor or Commander in Chief for the time being under the like Penalty and that all persons after being so Enrolled who shall at any time (Unless rendered incapable by sickness or other accident) neglect or refuse when called upon to appear at such times and places where Ordered by the Colonel or Commanding Officer, there to be mustered,

SOURCE: Walter Clark, ed., *State Records of North Carolina*, 26 vols. (Winston-Salem, N.C., 1895–1914), 23: 940–941.

Trained and exercised in Arms and be provided with a well fixed Gun shall forfeit and pay if at a private Muster five Shillings, if at a General Muster Ten Shillings and shall also be provided with a Cartouch Box, Sword, Cutlass, or Hanger, and have at least Nine Charges of powder made into Cartridges and sizeable Bullets or Swann Shot and three Spare Flints a Worm and a picker under the Penalty if at a private Muster the Sum of two Shillings and Six pence if at a General Muster Five Shillings to be levied by a Warrant of distress from the Captain of the Company directed to the Serjeant of the same who is hereby impowered to Execute the said Warrant and distrain for the said Fines and Penalties in the same manner as Sheriffs are impowered to distrain for public Taxes and shall make return thereof to the Captain which Serjeant shall deduct one Shilling and four pence out of every Fine so levied and in Case such Serjeant or Serjeants shall neglect or refuse to serve any Warrant or Warrants to him or them so directed he or they for such Neglect or refusal shall be fined Twenty Shillings to be recovered by a Warrant from the Captain directed to any other Serjeant under the same Penalty to be accounted for and applied as other fines in this Act directed. . . .

III. Provided also, That no member of his Majesty's Council, no member of Assembly, no Minister of the Church of England, no Protestant Dissenting Minister regularly called to any Congregation in this Province, no Justice of the Superior Courts, Secretary, Practising Attorney, no man who has borne a Military Commission as high as that of a Captain or Commissioned Officer who has served in the army, no Justice of the Peace, nor any Person who hath acted under a Commission of the Peace, no Clerk of the Court of Justice, Practicing Physician, Surgeon, Schoolmaster having the Tuition of ten Scholars, Ferryman, Overseer having the care of six Taxable Slaves, Inspectors, Public Millers, Coroners, Constables, Overseers and Commissioners of Public Roads, Searchers, or Branch Pilots so long as they continue in office shall be obliged to enlist themselves or appear at such musters.

IV. Provided nevertheless, That in case any such Overseer having the Care of six Taxable Slaves shall be seen in the muster Field on the days of General or Private musters they shall be liable to a Fine of forty shillings to be levied by a Warrant from the Colonel or Commanding Officer and applied as other Fines in this Act directed.

V. And be it further Enacted, by the Authority aforesaid, That if the Captain, Lieutenant, or Ensign, or any Two of them shall adjudge any Person or Persons enrolled as aforesaid, to be incapable of providing and furnishing him or themselves with the Arms, Ammunition, and Accoutrements, required by this Act, every such Person shall be exempt from the Fines and Forfeitures imposed by Virtue of this Act until such Arms, Ammunition, and Accoutrements, shall be provided for and delivered him by the Court Martial; to be paid for out of the Fines already collected, and that may hereafter be collected. . . .

4

The Boston Press Gang Riot of 1747

Britain's eighteenth-century imperial wars created seasonal demands for additional naval personnel. English conscription techniques of the day were simple and direct: the vessel in need sent a "press gang" ashore to draft (impress) unwary subjects in the area who had no skill or trade exempting them. The colonists were as opposed in the practice as their counterparts in the homeland, as this selection* from Governor Thomas Hutchinson's history of Massachusetts indicates.

*See also William Pencak and John Lax, "The Knowles Riot . . .," *Perspectives in American History* 10 (1976): 163–214.

IN 1747 (NOV. 17th) HAPPENED a tumult in the town of Boston equal to any which had preceded it, although far short of some that have happened since. Mr. Knowles was commodore of a number of men of war then in the harbour of Nantasket. Some of the sailors had deserted. The commodore . . . thought it reasonable that Boston should supply him with as many men as he had lost and, sent his boats up to town early in the morning, and surprized not only as many seamen as could be found on board any of the ships, outward bound as well as others, but swept the wharfs also, taking some ship carpenters apprentices and labouring land men. However tolerable such a surprize might have been in London it could not be borne here. The people had not been used to it and men of all orders resented it, but the lower class were beyond measure enraged and soon assembled with sticks, clubs, pitchmops, etc. They first seized an innocent lieutenant who happened to be ashore upon other business. They had then formed no scheme, and the speaker of the house passing by and assuring them that he knew that the lieutenant had no hand in the press they suffered him to be led off to a place of safety. The mob increasing and having received intelligence that several of the commanders were at

SOURCE: Thomas Hutchinson, *The History of the Colony of Massachusetts-Bay* . . . , 2d ed., 3 vols. (London, 1765–1828), vol. 2, pp. 489–492.

the governor's house, it was agreed to go and demand satisfaction. The house was soon surrounded and the court, or yard before the house, filled, but many persons of discretion inserted themselves and prevailed so far as to prevent the mob from entering. Several of the officers had planted themselves at the head of the stair way with loaded carbines and seemed determined to preserve their liberty or lose their lives. A deputy sheriff attempting to exercise his authority, was seized by the mob and carried away in triumph and set in the stocks, which afforded them diversion and tended to abate their rage and disposed them to separate and go to dinner.

As soon as it was dusk, several thousand people assembled in king-street, below the town house where the general court was sitting. Stones and brickbatts were thrown through the glass into the council chamber. The governor, however, with several gentlemen of the council and house ventured into the balcony and, after silence was obtained, the governor in a well judged speech expressed his great disapprobation of the impress and promised his utmost endeavours to obtain the discharge of every one of the inhabitants, and at the same time gently reproved the irregular proceedings both of the forenoon and evening. Other gentlemen also attempted to persuade the people to disperse and wait to see what steps the general court would take. All was to no purpose. The seizure and restraint of the commanders and other officers who were in town was insisted upon as the only effectual method to procure the release of the inhabitants aboard the ships.

It was thought advisable for the governor to withdraw to his house, many of the officers of the militia and other gentlemen attending him. A report was raised that a barge from one of the ships was come to a wharf in the town. The mob flew to seize it, but by mistake took a boat belonging to a Scotch ship and dragged it, with as much seeming ease through the streets as if it had been in the water, to the governor's house and prepared to burn it before the house, but from a consideration of the danger of setting the town on fire were diverted and the boat was burnt in a place of less hazard. The next day the governor ordered that the military officers of Boston should cause their companies to be mustered and to appear in arms, and that a military watch should be kept the succeeding night, but the drummers were interrupted and the militia refused to appear. The governor did not think it for his honour to remain in town another night and privately withdrew to the castle. A number of gentlemen who had some intimation of his design, sent a message to him by Col. Hutchinson, assuring him they would stand by him in maintaining the authority of government and restoring peace and order, but he did not think this sufficient.

The governor wrote to Mr. Knowles representing the confusions occasioned by this extravagant act of his officers, but he refused all terms of accommodation until the commanders and other officers on shore were suffered to go on board their ships, and he threatened to bring up his ships and bombard the town, and some of them coming to sail, caused different conjectures of his real intention. Capt. Erskine of the Canterbury had been seized at the house of Col. Brinley in Roxbury and given his parole not to go aboard, and divers inferior officers had been secured.

The 17th, 18th and part of the 19th, the council and house of representatives, sitting in the town, went on with their ordinary business, not willing to interpose lest they should encourage other commanders of the navy to future acts of the like nature, but towards noon of the 19th some of the principal members of the house began to think more seriously of the dangerous consequence of leaving the governor without support when there was not the least ground of exception to his conduct. Some high spirits in the town began to question whether his retiring should be deemed a desertion or abdication. It was moved to appoint a committee of the two houses to consider what was proper to be done. This would take time and was excepted to, and the speaker was desired to draw up such resolves as it was thought necessary the house should immediately agree to, and they were passed by a considerable majority and made public.

In the house of representatives, Nov. 19th, 1747.

Resolved, that there has been and still continues, a tumultuous riotous assembling of armed seamen, servants, negroes and others in the town of Boston, tending to the destruction of all government and order.

Resolved, that it is incumbent on the civil and military officers in the province to exert themselves to the utmost, to discourage and suppress all such tumultuous riotous proceedings whensoever they may happen.

Resolved, that this house will stand by and support with their lives and estates his excellency the governor and the executive part of the government in all endeavors for this purpose.

Resolved, that this house will exert themselves by all ways and means possible in redressing such grievances as his majesty's subjects are and have been under, which may have been the cause of the aforesaid tumultuous disorderly assembling together.

T. Hutchinson, Speaker.

The council passed a vote ordering that Captain Erskine and all other officers belonging to his majesty's ships should be forthwith set at liberty and protected by the government, which was concurred by the house. As soon as these votes were known, the tumultuous spirit began to subside. The inhabitants of the town of Boston assembled in town meeting in the afternoon, having been notified to consider, in general, what was proper for them to do upon this occasion, and notwithstanding it was urged by many that all measures to suppress the present spirit in the people would tend to encourage the like oppressive acts for the future, yet the contrary party prevailed and the town, although they expressed their sense of the great insult and injury by the impress, condemned the tumultuous riotous acts of such as had insulted the governor and the other branches of the legislature and committed many other heinous offences.

The governor, not expecting so favorable a turn, had wrote to the secretary to prepare orders for the colonels of the regiments of Cambridge, Roxbury and Milton and the regiment of horse to have their officers and men ready to march at an hour's warning to such place of rendezvous as he should direct; . . . Commodore [Knowles] dismissed most, if not all, of the inhabitants who had been impressed, and the squadron sailed to the great joy of the rest of the town.

5

A Letter from Samuel Adams

The founders of the Massachusetts Bay Colony had dour memories of the newly created standing army of Charles I. Colonists of the late seventeenth century had the "new model" Army of the Lord Protector Oliver Cromwell to consider, for good or ill, as well. Educated colonists knew of the private armies of Marius, Caesar, and their imitators, the Praetorian Guard of the Roman Empire, the mamelukes and janissaries of the Middle East, the condotierri *of Italy, and the constant threat that these mercenaries posed to civil liberties, personal property, and political power. Colonists in the 1760s, then, had ample historical cause to fear the presence of a "foreign" body of soldiers.* But the crown's deployment and use of large numbers of British land forces both during the French and Indian Wars and after, in the days of colonial resistance to the Sugar, Stamp, and Townsend Acts (quite independent of naval press gangs), gave immediacy and reality to the opinions of radicals like Samuel Adams, one of whose letters on the subject to the editor of the* Boston Gazette *in 1768 is reprinted here.*

*See John W. Shy, *Towards Lexington: The Role of the British Army in the Coming of the American Revolution* (Princeton, 1965) and Lawrence Cress, *Citizens in Arms* (Chapel Hill, 1982). See also Jesse Lemich, "The American Revolution Seen from the Bottom Up," in *Towards a New Past*, ed. Barton Bernstein, (New York, 1968), pp. 3–45, for evidence of American working-class conflict with these regulars in the decade prior to the Revolution.

IT IS A VERY IMPROBABLE SUPPOSITION, that any people can long remain free, with a strong military power in the very heart of their country:— Unless that military power is under the direction of the people, and even then it is dangerous.—History, both ancient and modern, affords many instances of the overthrow of states and kingdoms by the power of soldiers, who were rais'd and maintain'd at first, under the plausible pretence of defending those very liberties which they afterwards destroyed. Even where there is a necessity of the military power, within the land, which by the

SOURCE: Article signed "Vindex," *Boston Gazette*, December 12, 1768, as given in *The Writings of Samuel Adams*, ed. H. A. Cushing (Boston, 1904–1908), 1: 264–268.

way but rarely happens, a wise and prudent people will always have a watchful & a jealous eye over it; for the maxims and rules of the army, are essentially different from the genius of a free people, and the laws of a free government. Soldiers are used to obey the absolute commands of their superiors: It is death for them, in the field, to dispute their authority, or the rectitude of their orders; and sometimes they may be shot upon the spot without ceremony. The necessity of things makes it highly proper that they should be under the absolute controul of the officer who commands them; who saith unto one come, and he cometh, and to another go, and he goeth. Thus being inured to that sort of government in the field and in the time of war, they are too apt to retain the same idea, when they happen to be in civil communities and in a time of peace: And even their officers, being used to a sort of sovereignty over them, may sometimes forget, that when quartered in cities, they are to consider themselves & their soldiers, in no other light than as a family in the community; numerous indeed, but like all other families and individuals, under the direction of the civil magistrate, and the controul of the common law—Like them, they are to confine their own rules and maxims within their own circle; nor can they be suppos'd to have a right or authority to oblige the rest of the community or any individuals, to submit to or pay any regard to their rules and maxims, any more than one family has to obtrude its private method of oeconomy upon another.

It is of great importance, and I humbly conceive it ought to be the first care of the community, when soldiers are quartered among them, by all means to convince them, that they are not to give law, but to receive it: It is dangerous to civil society, when the military conceives of it self as an independent body, detach'd from the rest of the society, and subject to no controul: And the danger is greatly increased and becomes alarming, when the society itself yields to such an ill grounded supposition: If this should be the case, how easy would it be for the soldiers, if they alone should have the sword in their hands, to use it wantonly, and even to the great annoyance and terror of the citizens, if not to their destruction. What should hinder them, if once it is a given point, that the society has no law to restrain them, and they are dispos'd to do it? And how long can we imagine it would be, upon such a supposition, before the tragical scene would begin; especially if we consider further, how difficult it is to keep a power, in its nature much less formidable, and confessedly limited, within its just bounds!—That constitution which admits of a power without a check, admits of a tyranny: And that people, who are not always on their guard, to make use of the remedy of the constitution, when there is one, to restrain all kinds of power, and especially the military, from growing exorbitant, must blame themselves for the mischief that may befall them in consequence of their inattention: Or if they do not reflect on their own folly, their posterity will surely curse them, for entailing upon them chains and slavery.

I am led to these reflections from the appearance of the present times; when one wou'd be apt to think, there was like to be a speedy change of the civil, for a military government in this province. No one I believe can be at a loss to know, by whose influence, or with what intentions, the troops destin'd for the defence of the colonies, have been drawn off, so many of them, from their important stations, and posted in this town. Whether they are to be consider'd as marching troops, or a standing army, will be better determined, when the minister who has thus dispos'd of them, or G. B———d,* or the Commissioners of the customs, if he or they sent for them, shall explain the matter; as they who did send for them, assuredly will, to Britain and America. I dare challenge them, or any others to prove that there was the least necessity for them here, for the profess'd purpose of their coming, namely to prevent or subdue rebels and traitors: I will further venture to affirm, that he must be either a knave or a fool, if he has any tolerable acquaintance with the people of this town and province, nay, that he must be a traitor himself who asserts it. I know very well, that the whole continent of America is charg'd by some designing men with treason and rebellion, for vindicating their constitutional and natural rights: But I must tell these men on both sides the atlantic, that no other force but that of reason & sound argument on their part, of which we have hitherto seen but precious little, will prevail upon us, to relinquish our righteous claim:—Military power is by no means calculated to convince the understandings of men: It may in another part of the world, affright women and children, and perhaps some weak men out of their senses, but will never awe a sensible American tamely to surrender his liberty.—Among the brutal herd the strongest horns are the strongest laws; and slaves, who are always to be rank'd among the servile brutes, may cringe, under a tyrant's brow: But to a reasonable being, one I mean who acts up to his reason, there is nothing in military atchievement, any more than in knight errantry, so terrifying as to induce him to part with the choicest gift that Heaven bestows on man.

But whatever may be the design of this military appearance; whatever use some persons may intend and expect to make of it: This we all know, and every child in the street is taught to know it; that while a people retain a just sense of Liberty, as blessed be God, this people yet do, the insolence of power will for ever be despised; and that in a city, in the midst of civil society, especially in a time of peace, soldiers of all ranks, like all other men, are to be protected, govern'd, restrain'd, rewarded or punish'd by the Law of the Land.

[EDITOR'S NOTE: "G. B———d" refers to the Massachusetts Bay Colony's Governor, Francis Bernard; direct reference to Bernard might have invited a charge against the *Boston Gazette* of seditious libel.]

The Revolutionary Era

6

The Social Structure of the New Jersey Brigade

The Continental Line as an American Standing Army

MARK EDWARD LENDER

Two military systems served the patriot cause during the War of Independence: the reorganized militias and the Continental Congress's own brigades. For brief periods the militia appears to have included large percentages of the eligible population. It served in a number of different capacities: as a support force for the Continental regulars when they were in the region, as saboteurs and guerrillas in other instances, and, on occasion, as a kind of political thought-police, keeping the pressure on listless or unsupportive citizens.* The Continentals, on the other hand, were soldiers "for the duration" and were, in a very real sense, akin to the very mercenaries they had been hired to fight. Mark Lender's study of the Continentals from New Jersey identifies their origins and the fears they engendered.

*See John W. Shy, "The American Revolution: The Military Conflict as a Revolutionary Conflict," in *Essays on the American Revolution*, ed. Stephen Kurtz and James Huston (Chapel Hill, 1974), pp. 121–156.

EDITOR'S NOTE: A number of notes reporting the sources of the author's evidence, present in the first edition of this volume, have been omitted from this edition. The reader should consult the first edition or Lender, *The Regular Line: The Continental Soldiers of New Jersey, 1775–1783* (forthcoming), chapter 5, for full scholarly citations.

EIGHTEENTH-CENTURY AMERICANS lived in particular dread of standing armies. As the colonists matured politically in the years before the Revolution, they adopted as their own the dictum of over a century of British whig thought: standing armies threatened the social stability and political order of any nation maintaining them in peacetime. The rank and file came from the lowest reaches of society, with no bonds of property or sentiment to the civilian world and, therefore, with no stake in the maintenance of its liberties and institutions. Lacking such attachments, they could too easily become the agents of designing generals or other would-be tyrants. Indeed, whigs pointed to examples as distant as ancient Rome and as close as seventeenth-century Denmark to illustrate how such armies might destroy the liberties of the peoples they were supposed to defend.[1] Moreover, they alleged that standing armies fought poorly, for the soldiers were not fighting for their own rights and property. Their sole incentives, argued a British whig, were their wages "for slaughter and bloodshed." By the opening shots of the Revolution, then, whigs on both sides of the Atlantic could agree with the warning of Samuel Adams: standing armies, even in war, were "dangerous to the Liberties of the People." The troops were "distinct from the rest of the Citizens," he said, and loyal only to their officers. "Such a Power," he noted solemnly in 1776, "should be watched with a jealous Eye."

Central to the question over standing armies was the social composition of a nation's military. Whigs clearly saw that, if the defense of a country was not to be entrusted to standing regiments, men with an interest in society's preservation had to assume a military obligation. In his *Argument* against standing armies John Trenchard insisted that a national army should consist of "the same persons as have the property." If this were the case, Adams's fear of a soldiery "distinct" from the citizenry evaporated. The troops became no more than "bodies of armed citizens," noted Richard Price, and would have no reason to overthrow the state. Adams himself conceded that, because a militia was "composed of free Citizens," there was "therefore no Danger of their making use of their Power to the destruction of their own Rights." Society, then, had nothing to fear as long as its citizenry had "virtue" enough to defend itself. The peril came, as Edward Montagu warned, when military duties passed to "the dregs of the people."

America's tradition of a Revolutionary army of "embattled farmers" emerged from these whig preferences for citizen-soldiers. During the War for Independence, many patriots claimed (at least in public) to have fashioned their army after their ideology. Their soldiers, they said, were sturdy farmers and mechanics, classic whig battalions of armed freemen who had left their homes to defend liberty. And since the Revolution most historians have accepted this image of the patriot forces largely at face value, concluding that the rebel army was basically "republican." Scholars arrived at these conclusions, however, not through analyses of military personnel but, rather, by focusing on the ideological rhetoric of patriot leadership (particularly the military leadership). Thus the question of who actually served in the Revolutionary military, and what meaning their service gave to the nature of the Revolution, has gone largely unexamined.

Recently, however, a few historians have addressed the issue by probing the social composition of the Continental troops (although without including their officers). Investigations of the enlisted men of Massachusetts, Virginia, and Maryland revealed an army recruited mostly from the young and the poor. The troops were generally the sons of poor farmers, laborers, and drifters; many were recent immigrants without roots in American society. Socially, they were something less than the yeomen of Fourth of July oratory. But, as excellent as these studies are, they are only the first steps in uncovering the social origins of the Continental Line.

This essay examines the personnel of the New Jersey Continental regiments, or the New Jersey Brigade, as these units were known collectively. Moreover, it suggests that the social status and origins of the patriot regulars exerted an important influence on popular attitudes toward regular armies in general. For, if the Jerseymen, like the troops of Maryland, Massachusetts, and Virginia, prove not to have been the yeomanry of legend, perhaps the Continental regiments were in many respects similar to their European opponents. And, if the American regulars were comparable to the rank and file of the Old World standing armies, did patriots recognize the fact and form their views on their own military accordingly? If so, Whig pronouncements against standing forces were not mere ideological cant; rather, it suggests that many Americans genuinely feared that a war fought in the name of "liberty" and "virtue" had produced an institution that they considered the very antithesis of these noble goals—a classic standing army, with all its potential for political and social disruption.

I

This analysis is based on social and economic data on 88 New Jersey officers and 710 enlisted men. Jersey Brigade muster rolls completed between late 1776 and mid-1780 (later enlistment records were insufficiently detailed for analytical purposes) supplied the names of the troops under consideration. Besides names, these records also listed the physical descriptions, townships of enlistment, and usually the ages of each recruit. Some of them had additional data on residency, on occupation, and on whether a soldier had enlisted as a substitute. By collating these muster roll data with information from the state township ratables lists, it was possible to reasonably ascertain the soldiers' social and economic status. The tax statements recorded the real and personal property of all free adult males and the head taxes paid by men who owned no taxable property. Sufficiently distinctive surnames on the muster rolls were matched with their counterparts on the ratables lists (many men were eliminated from the analysis when their names could not be matched with certainty), a task facilitated by the use of New Jersey genealogical sources and local histories. If a soldier did not appear on the tax records because he was too young to own any taxable property himself (ages of enlistment are in Table 1), or if he paid only a head tax as a propertyless son of a more prosperous family, family data were located whenever possible. These family data were then used as representative of the soldier's condition.

Using this matching technique, the muster rolls and ratables list provided either family or personal data on 289 (41 percent) of the 710 enlisted men. These ratable soldiers were, because their names appeared on the tax rolls, assumed to be residents of the towns from which they enlisted. Of the men not appearing on the ratables list, the muster rolls specifically identified 146 (21 percent of the total 710, but about 35 percent of all the nonratable troops) as nonresidents; they came from a variety of other areas and will be discussed separately later. No direct residency or economic data were available for the remaining 275 untaxed soldiers, but nonquantitative sources made it possible to draw conclusions on their social status as well. This analysis reveals that the men as a group, both taxed and untaxed alike, constituted a force quite dissimilar from the propertied freemen envisioned by most whigs. Instead, the Jersey troops came largely from the poorest levels of society and were generally not engaged in the defense of families or farms. In fact, many of them were propertyless with no settled place in the civilian world.

A look at the 289 men with available tax data clearly illustrates the poverty of many of the troops. The Jersey Brigade came from a state with large disparities in the distribution of wealth. In this regard, New Jersey was typical of other northern states: the richest 10 percent of the taxpayers held about 45 percent of all ratable wealth, whereas the upper third of the taxable residents owned fully 85 percent. In contrast to this favored group were the Jerseymen in the two lower wealthholding thirds of the ratable population, which together shared only some 15 percent of the state's total

TABLE 1
Age at Enlistment of New Jersey Troops

AGE	NUMBER	%	CUMULATIVE %
–18	57	10.5%	10.5%
18–22	238	44.1	54.6
23–27	101	18.7	73.3
28–32	48	8.9	82.2
33–36	38	7.0	89.2
37–41	33	6.1	95.3
41–	25	4.6	99.9

Note: Based on 540 cases with reported ages.

assessed wealth. In fact, about 21 percent of the taxpayers owned no ratable property at all. Land distribution, like the distribution of total wealth, also demonstrated the commanding economic position of the wealthiest citizens. Only some 30 percent of the assessed populace owned farms of over 100 acres. (See Table 2). The largest and most productive farms were concentrated in the hands of the privileged few. Thus the distribution of wealth in Revolutionary New Jersey was skewed in favor of the well-to-do.

The army reflected the disparities of the civilian world; a man's rank in the New Jersey Brigade paralleled his position in New Jersey society. The officers, as we shall see later, came chiefly from the wealthiest third of society, while the rank and file originated largely in the lowest classes. (See Table 3.) Of the rank and file on whom we have tax data, fully 90 percent of the privates and noncommissioned officers came from the poorest two-thirds of the ratable population (61 percent from the poorest third, 29 percent from the middle third). Indeed, 46 percent of them owned no taxable property at all (more than twice the proportion of propertyless in the general ratable populace); and well over half of the ratable soldiers were either landless or had too little acreage to farm for a livelihood (or came from families in such a situation). While some 30 percent of the general taxpayers owned farms of a hundred acres or more, only 9 percent of the soldiery had similar holdings. (See Table 2.) The families of only three soldiers owned any slaves, and none of the troops (or their families) held a taxable interest in any commercial, fishing, iron-working, or any other nonagricultural sector of the state economy. If the lower limits of a New Jersey "middle class" were set at a farm of twenty-five to thirty acres, with livestock and other taxable wealth, the soldier's economic problems become even more apparent. Only 20 percent of the assessed troops held that much property, while in contrast slightly over 45 percent of the state's general taxpayers owned that much or more.

Although there were a few enlisted men from "respectable" circumstances, only 9 percent of all the ratable soldiers owned enough to be in-

TABLE 2
Distribution of Farms by Percentage of Ratable Population

ACRES	ALL NEW JERSEY	SOLDIERS	OFFICERS
Landless	37.0%	56.7%	2.3%
1–24	12.8	12.5	6.8
25–99	20.5	21.8	20.4
100–199	18.7	7.6	38.6
200–299	6.7	1.4	18.2
300–399	2.1	0.0	4.5
400–	2.2	0.0	9.1

Note: Based on data in Lender, "Enlisted Line," chap. 4.

TABLE 3
Distribution of Enlisted Men and Officers over Wealthholding Thirds
of Total Ratable State Population[1]

Percentage of Enlisted Men from:		
Lower Third[2]	Middle Third	Upper Third[3]
61%	29%	10%
Percentage of Officers from:		
Lower Third	Middle Third	Upper Third[4]
0	16	84

[1]Based on data in Lender, "Enlisted Line," chap. 4.
[2]Includes 46 percent propertyless soldiers.
[3]Includes 1 percent of the soldiers in the wealthiest tenth.
[4]Includes 31.8 percent of the officers in the wealthiest tenth.

cluded in the wealthiest third of Jersey society, while only 1 percent came from families in the richest upper tenth. Of these men, all were either draftees who chose to serve rather than hire a substitute or were members of leading patriot families with strong commitments to the cause. Caleb Kimble, for example, owned 240 acres in Sussex County, with over twenty head of stock, when he was drafted in 1778. Young Amos Cresse, who owned little himself, enlisted from an active and wealthy Cape May family that sent a number of officers and men into the militia and regular forces. The prominent Hand and Ogden families also had sons fighting throughout the war in commissioned and enlisted grades. These troops, however, were but a minority of the men, a small middle- and upper-class group in a largely poor soldiery.

The social status of the 146 nonresident soldiers was apparently similar to their ratable comrades in arms. These men were largely from out of state or foreign-born poor with no visible roots in New Jersey society. Their origins were as follows: other towns, 7; other counties, 45; other states, 62 (New York, 40; Pennsylvania, 16; Maryland, 3; Virginia, 2; North Carolina, 1); foreigners, 32 (Ireland, 16; Britain, including Scotland, 10; Germany, 3; Canada, 1; France, 1; Holland, 1). Typical of these recruits was Job Polk, who came from Buck's County, Pennsylvania, to enlist in South Jersey, or a group of seventeen New Yorkers who enlisted in early 1777 when part of the Jersey Brigade was posted in their state. Among these men, many of whom were probably drifters, were several cited as bounty jumpers from the regiments of other states. Other soldiers, like Cornelius Van Reid and Vincent LeFord, joined the brigade after immigrating, respectively, from Holland and France.

Although the enlistment records singled out only 4–5 percent of the 710 soldiers as foreigners, other sources indicate that in fact they composed a much larger—if not precisely quantifiable—part of the Jersey Line. John Adams, for instance, thought that the middle states' regiments included a large proportion of immigrants. They held too few Americans, he felt, and too many Irish and German redemptioners and transported convicts. A Jersey militia colonel, who witnessed the organization of the new regular battalions in 1777, reported that the Continentals were "mostly" foreigners. Most of these foreign soldiers were probably deserters from the British forces and prisoners held by the Americans: New Jersey patriot leaders did not want to use such men, arguing that they had no attachment to the cause and that once in ranks they could not be exchanged for captured Americans. Yet the need for troops was so great that recruiters accepted whatever manpower they could find. Throughout the war, Hessian prisoners and deserters (to whom Congress had directed special appeals not to fight for the English) worked for patriot civilians and bore arms in the New Jersey Brigade. The colonel of the Second New Jersey Regiment even arranged special protection for one Hessian, knowing that he risked execution if recaptured by the British. English soldiers also enlisted with the Continentals. Sergeant George Grant, for example, who played an important part in the 1781 mutiny of the Jersey Line, was probably a British deserter; it is likely that some of the Irish in the Jersey ranks were also deserters. And, in allowing enemy personnel to serve in their regiments, the Jersey whigs were evidently little different from others. Even Washington allowed a condemned Englishman to enlist rather than hang, and Nathanael Greene claimed that he relied heavily on British deserters to fill the battalions of his Southern Army. The foreign-born soldier, then, frequently of enemy origin, was an important part of the Continental Line.

The 275 men who lack available residency or tax data also appear to have been quite poor, and many of them were probably similar to the nonresident troops already discussed. Others, if they in fact lived in the townships listed on the muster rolls, escaped the attention of the local tax assessors and thus did not appear on the ratables books. Privates James Sarge and William Gallaspe, for example, supposedly resided, respectively, in Kingwood and Bethlehem townships in Hunterdon County. Yet a search of area tax and genealogical sources produced no record of either man or of their families. They either did not live in these towns or were too poor to be included on the tax lists. In some cases these troops were not even freemen, which would also account for their absence from the ratables books. John Evans, a black who cited Reading Township as his home, and William Holmes, an Indian who said he came from Cumberland County, were probably in this situation; neither of them was assessed. Samuel Sutphin, however, was a nonrated soldier who did live in his town of record; he was a Somerset County slave, sent into the army as a substitute by an owner who declined to serve in person. (About 2 percent of the Jersey regulars were nonwhites, and it is likely that some of them served in circumstances similar to those of Sutphin, Evans, and Holmes.)

The state gave many of these untaxed men plenty of opportunities to enlist as substitutes. In 1778 and 1780, for instance, New Jersey drafted militiamen into the Continental Line; and hundreds of these draftees, unwilling to serve, hired men to take their places. Some areas sent no one but substitutes. In 1778 a Middlesex County muster roll carried twenty-eight men raised under the draft laws—all of them hirelings. Others were enlisted to take the place of men already in ranks. Private Thomas Ireland of the Second New Jersey, deciding that there was more profit in privateering than in soldiering, hired a substitute to take his place and went to sea. Still other substitutes were indentured servants and slaves sent by wealthier residents. Indeed, the state encouraged the enlistment of such substitutes during a manpower crisis in 1777.[1] It granted militia exemptions to any two citizens who sent a Continental substitute in their stead, and to masters who sent their servants or slaves. In addition, some servants broke their contracts by running away and enlisting on their own, while, as noted earlier, an occasional freeman purchased a slave specifically to serve military tours for him.

The precise number of substitutes will never be known because not all muster rolls identified them. But among all the nonresident or otherwise untaxed troops just over 28 percent carried substitute labels, while 10 percent of those with confirmed residency served under similar circumstances. This means that enlistment records specifically identified a minimum of 21 percent of the Jersey Continentals as substitutes, and we can safely assume that the actual total was much greater, perhaps as high as 40 percent. The fact that there were almost three times as many nonresident as resident substitutes suggests that many of the nonresidents deliberately looked for areas where their services were in demand, enlisting there for the extra substitute pay. For whatever reasons they enlisted, however, the fact is that at least one-fifth of the Jersey Brigade was in the ranks because an equal number of civilians did not want to be and purchased the services of others instead of serving themselves.

Other Continentals entered the ranks involuntarily or volunteered under duress. New Jersey's large tory population contributed its share of these recruits, although neither patriots nor loyalists were happy about the situation. The loyalists naturally did not want to bear arms against the king, and the whigs knew that coerced, politically hostile men seldom made reliable soldiers. Yet manpower needs were so great that even Governor William Livingston, a firm Jersey whig, agreed to force the enemies of the Revolution into its service. Consequently, patriot courts often forced tories arrested for treason to choose between joining the Continentals or risking a trial for their lives. Beginning in 1777, men brought before the New Jersey Council of Safety, over which Livingston presided, for "suspicious Circumstances surrounding their Conduct" often enlisted rather than submit to further investigation. After that, persons suspected of any sort of loyalism faced the possibility of coerced enlistment.[2] In 1777, for example, a civilian court in Morristown sentenced thirty-five tories to hang. Two were duly executed, while the others, reprieved "if you will enlist in the

American army for the remainder of the war," were sent to Continental recruiters. On another occasion, the Morristown court hanged two of seventy-five tories and sent the rest into the army. In 1779, patriots in Gloucester County sentenced seventeen men to the noose for high treason and then pardoned all but one of them. Two of the lucky ones were exiled, while six are known to have enlisted as a condition of their pardons and the rest probably did likewise.

Another source of manpower apart from the formal recruiting structure was the criminal court. Although Congress ruled recruiting from prisons illegal in 1776, New Jersey still used some felons as soldiers. For example, John Sanders, a horse thief, was sentenced to two floggings in 1777. After the first, he "signified his willingness to enlist in the Continental Service" and the court remitted his second lashing. Livingston pardoned one Benjamin Bartholomew of Gloucester County, sentenced to death as a burglar, on condition of his enlisting, while other Jerseymen also escaped jail terms in the same fashion.

We cannot know exactly how many felons and tories entered New Jersey regiments. Too few court records survive, and muster rolls only infrequently recorded the legal history of a particular soldier. But there must have been plenty of them; available records can account for almost a third of a battalion of these reluctant recruits. Furthermore, the policy of enlisting criminals or tories did not necessarily produce bad soldiers. Of the thirty-five tories reprieved at Morristown in 1777, eleven of twenty-one with traceable war records deserted; but four of these returned and the rest apparently served satisfactorily. One, Barnett Banghart, who remained in the ranks until 1783 and was even wounded in action, received a warrant for a veteran's land grant—one of the same grants due to men who enlisted under the most patriotic circumstances.

Thus the New Jersey enlisted men—both taxed and untaxed—were a mixed lot. But most of them shared an important common denominator: that of lower-class origins. If they were taxable residents they usually came from the poorest families. If they were untaxed residents, they were probably servants, slaves, or others with no ratable property. And, if they were nonresidents, they had no stake in local social or economic affairs. It is little wonder, then, that so many found the payments offered to substitutes, together with army pay and bounties, attractive. Such men had filled the provincial regiments during the colonial wars, and the Continental Army provided a similar chance for poor men to reach for a better life than civilian society could offer.

II

A dramatic difference existed between the enlisted men and their officers. One French officer noted that his American counterparts, regardless of state, were of the best families, sophisticated, generally well educated, and usually "farmers and farmers' sons of independent or easy fortunes. Many of them," he said, "have been bred to the learned professions." Some were tradesmen, he wrote, while pointing out that "a tradesman in America is quite a different creature from a tradesman in Europe." They were all zealous for liberty, and many "would not pass unnoticed in the politest court in Europe."

In New Jersey the tax data clearly support this general view of the officer corps. In stark contrast to the rank and file, fully 84 percent of the officers came from the wealthiest third of society and almost 32 percent from the richest tenth (none came from the poorest third, and only 16 percent from the middle third). (See Table 3.) While there were a few poorer officers, none ever advanced farther than captain in rank, and the highest field ranks were held by men of considerable prominence in the state. Together, such officers as Generals William Alexander (Lord Stirling), William Maxwell, Elias Dayton, Matthias Ogden and David Forman, and Colonel Israel Shreve and Ephraim Martin and their relatives owned tens of thousands of acres. The officer corps also owned proportionately more of the largest farms than either the enlisted men or civilians (see Table 2), and the farms of just over 31 percent of the officers used slave labor. The Jersey officer corps, then, represented the state's social and economic elite.

These figures are hardly surprising, as Americans fully expected their officers to come from the leading social circles. Jerseymen assumed the social superiority of commissioned rank; and the state's procedures for granting Continental commissions almost guaranteed that only the socially influential would become officers. When men petitioned the legislature for commissions, they forwarded endorsements in their favor from prominent neighbors, military figures, or anyone else considered to have influence. These supporting letters took care to point out that the would-be officers were "gentlemen," "of good family," or "Men of Property and Character." Applicants without sufficient social status were less likely to know anyone with enough influence in the legislature to assure action on their behalf. The way was thus clear for those from the highest social levels, where well-placed friends and relatives could lend support.

A large number of cases illustrate this pattern, as hopeful candidates sought help from such men as "Lord Stirling," Governor Livingston, and other officers and civilian officials. When Richard Cox, for example, applied for a lieutenancy in 1776, he not only assured the legislature of his zeal for the cause but also sent the endorsements of the New Brunswick Committee and Militia General Philemon Dickinson. Anthony Walton White, one of the richest men in Middlesex County, sent no less than three endorsements: one from the mayor and aldermen of New Brunswick, another from "sundry" freeholders, and one from the Middlesex Committee. The sons of prominent officers sometimes won commissions on the favor of their fathers. John Shreve, son of Colonel Israel Shreve of the Second New Jersey, served as an ensign in his father's unit at the age of thirteen; and Jonathan Ford Morris of Morris County received an ensign's commission at sixteen through the influence of his father, the company commander. Holding a commission was thus a prerogative of the best connected Jerseymen.

Only occasionally were officers commissioned from the ranks. After years of campaigning with a fine service record, Sergeant Moses Sproule rose to ensign; John Brewer received a company commission in 1776 after distinguishing himself as a sergeant. Others gained their rank by guaranteeing that they could bring a body of recruits with them. In January 1776, Lord Stirling requested ensign's rank for a Jerseyman who had already assembled most of an infantry company. One William Bostwick sent two commission requests to the legislature in late 1776. His previous experience was only that of militia private, however, and these notes did him little good. Then, on November 27, he sent a third petition for a lieutenancy, this time stressing that he had thirty-two men willing to serve under him. Bostwick was commissioned within two days. But the Bostwicks, Sproules, and Brewers were the exceptions, for less than 2 percent of the officers rose from the ranks. The leadership of the New Jersey Brigade, then, was firmly in the hands of those who led New Jersey society.

III

The New Jersey Brigade thus generally reflected the structure of the society for which it fought. It was officered by the "best" men of society while the rank and file came from those who composed much of the populace at large—the poor, the least influential, and the nonresident drifting lower class. The brigade therefore contained a preponderance of men to whom army pay and bounties represented more than their meager stake in civilian life.

The gulf between the ideal and the reality of Continental personnel was such that informed contemporaries could hardly ignore it. A genuine "yeoman" in New York, for example, recognized the low social origins of the soldiery. "My situation in life was that of a farmer in respectable circumstances," he said, "and rather above that which furnished the usual recruits for the regular army." Washington referred with evident condescension to "common soldiers" or "such People as compose the bulk of an army." Patriot governments also admitted the condition of their rank and file: in 1775 a dismayed Congress found that the Continentals were being jailed because they could not pay small civilian debts. New Jersey had to prohibit such arrests by statute on two occasions (1776 and 1777) to stop a damaging drain on its battalions. Patriots generally made these observations only when they were forced to by circumstances—they were obviously at variance with official rhetoric on an ideal army—but it is clear that they recognized the real nature of the Continental forces.

Contemporary accounts of the army strengthened this view. The French, who had no commitments to a whig military ideal, were under no illusions regarding the Continentals. One Bourbon officer asserted that the American "regular soldiers had a bad reputation with the general public." The Continental regiments, he said, "were composed entirely of vagabonds and paupers; no enticements or tricks could force solid citizens to enlist, inasmuch as they had to serve in the militia anyway." Another Frenchman, writing under the name "DeLisle," took an equally hard look at the regulars in the *New Jersey Gazette*. He argued that most American farmers and familymen were unwilling to "forego the sweets of domestic life for three, four, or seven years service," and therefore fought only in the militia; the men who had enlisted as Continentals were of the same "class of men who compose the common soldiers of Europe"—the propertyless and single. There were a few landed and familymen in the regulars, he admitted, but he noted that they enlisted in the early days of the war "in a fit of enthusiasm, when the salvation of America was thought to rest entirely upon her success in filling up the Continental regiments."

And, even if the French—who were used to dealing with the lower-class regulars of Europe—were unfavorably biased in their estimates of the Continentals (although there is no evidence of this), the same cannot be said of an even harsher New Jersey view. This was the opinion of John Taylor, a man whose judgment commands respect. Taylor was a dedicated whig and a devoted faculty member of fledgling Queen's College (now Rutgers) in New Brunswick; he was also a colonel of the Middlesex County militia. While on active duty near Princeton in 1777, Taylor saw firsthand the nature of the American army then being organized. The situation appalled him: the militia "yeomanry"—the country's "original safeguard"—were extremely backward in the cause (too many, he said, were ill-disciplined or tories), and the nation's regulars hardly inspired confidence. The Continentals were "mostly foreigners," he lamented, and were "really mercenaries . . . [with] no attachment to the country, except what accrues from the emoluments of the service." The army, and therefore the cause, was in trouble, he concluded. His advice was to "Hope for the best, but at the same time fear the worst."

Other whigs, realizing what kind of an army they had raised, were indeed "fearing the worst." Before the war was two years old, Charles Lee was deeply concerned for the army's future: some means had to be found to rally the yeomanry, he said (in the form of militia), or else the patriot army would pose a threat to the country. He maintained that "when the soldiers of a community are volunteers [that is, regulars], war becomes quite a distinct profession. The arms of a Republic get into the hands of its worst members." Over the course of the war Lee's judgment proved questionable on occasion, but events bore him out in this instance. John Adams was referring to "standing" forces by 1777 when talking of the Continentals, and after the war he recalled a prediction he had made in 1776: raising a regular army would attract only the "meanest, idlest, most intemperate and worthless, but no more." It was useless, said Adams, to appeal to the sons of the yeomanry and the mechanics—the marrow of a republican army—for they had better things to do. "Was it creditable," he asked, "that men who could get at home a better living, more comfortable lodgings, more than double the wages, in safety . . . would bind themselves for the war [for the duration]? I knew it to be impossible." George Washington also knew his own army. In 1783 he noted that, once his veterans had "frolicked a while among their friends, and find they must have recourse to hard labor for a livelyhood," they would reenlist on "almost any Terms" in any future "regular or standing force." Patriots thus found themselves with a classic standing army—and knew it.

Worse, the Continentals gave reason enough to fear that they might act like an Old World standing force. An alarming number of incidents suggested that the army was not fully satisfied with its subordination to civilian authority. Continental units had, after all, mutinied, or threatened to, in the face of deplorable service conditions; and it was no secret that they blamed their problems on Congress and on their states. Nor were the officers happy: they shared the problems of inadequate pay and supplies with their men, and they had been embroiled with Congress over the issue of half-pay pensions since 1778. On occasion, the officers went to extremes in articulating their complaints. In 1779 part of the New Jersey officer corps provoked a confrontation with their state when it threatened to resign *en masse* in a pay dispute; and in April 1783 congressional opposition to half pay provided the tinder for the Newburgh conspiracy. Clearly, not all the officers were willing to accept civilian decisions on the army without question. Moreover, as patriots watched these events, they were also aware of the social composition of the army; the disgruntled officers commanded a rank and file that was, as Sam Adams had feared, "distinct from the rest of the Citizens." America in 1783 faced the age-old combination for army mischief—angry, upper-class officers and poor, restless troops. Thus, while the army never attempted a coup, Americans could hardly be blamed for fearing the worst from the Continental units stationed at Newburgh.

The social composition of the Continental Line was therefore deeply disturbing to patriots and could not help influencing their views on the military. They had watched as "public virtue" proved too weak to draw "solid citizens" into the regulars, and they had seen the army filled by men they considered a world apart from those who should have rallied to liberty's cause. It is little wonder, then, that whigs were apprehensive about maintaining the army a day longer than necessary. At one point, the Connecticut delegates in Congress urged a statute forbidding postwar regulars under any circumstances; and the New Jersey legislature opposed "any . . . military Establishment whatever" after the war. In Congress, the Jerseymen disagreed with the decision to furlough the army in 1783; they wanted to disband it completely, thus forgoing the possibility of recalling them even if the peace failed and hostilities resumed. And, when Congress sent the men home, it did so with final warning on the dangers of standing armies. Patriots, in short, had seen nothing in the Continental Line to assuage their fears of standing regiments, and they dreaded them as much after the war as before it.

NOTES

1. The crisis stemmed from a congressional request that New Jersey raise a fourth regiment, despite the fact that the 1776 defeats had drastically curtailed recruiting and the desertion rate in the 1777 battalions was over 40 percent.
2. If whig authorities feared the desertion of these coerced recruits, they sent them into the Continental Navy instead of to the army. See William Maxwell to Washington, May 27, 1780, *Washington Papers*, 4th ser., Library of Congress, Washington, D.C.

7

The Inside History
of the Newburgh Conspiracy

America and the Coup d'Etat

RICHARD H. KOHN

A number of American military units vigorously appealed to their civilian lead-
ers, generally for a more prompt redress of their financial arrears, at one time
or another during the Revolution. Some actually marched on their elected leg-
islators. Perhaps the most significant of these incidents was the last—the New-
burgh conspiracy. As Richard Kohn says of this moment, "America did stand at
the crossroads in March, 1783." Theoretically, George Washington could have
become the first American monarch (or "Protector"); the newly formed Society
of the Cincinnati (a hereditary organization of Revolutionary War officers) could
have become our aristocracy; and the Newburgh conspiracy could have set a
dangerous precedent of military interference with civilian control. Professor Kohn
points out another important characteristic of this incident, a characteristic that
does recur: the use of military disquiet by one faction of the civilian leadership
to secure a political objective.

AT THE CLOSE of the American Revolution, after the preliminary articles
of peace had been signed, but before knowledge of them had reached
America, there occurred at the Continental Army's Newburgh cantonment one of the most bizarre and little understood events in the history
of the United States. At the very moment of victory, the officer corps

SOURCE: Richard H. Kohn, "The Coup d'Etat That Failed," *Society* (May-June 1975), pp.
30–36. Adapted from "The Newburgh Conspiracy: Nationalism and Militarism, 1783,"
chapter 2 of Richard H. Kohn, *Eagle and Sword: The Beginnings of the Military Establishment
in America* (New York: Free Press, 1975), pp. 17–39. Reprinted by permission of the author.

responded to an anonymous appeal from one of its members and met to consider mutiny against constituted civilian authority. The Newburgh conspiracy was the closest an American army has ever come to revolt or coup d'etat, and it exposed the fragility of civil-military relations at the beginning of the republic. Had the army cast off civilian control at the critical moment of the nation's birth, a national military establishment might have been impossible for generations afterward.

Behind the events at Newburgh in March, 1783, lay a complex plot which involved not only certain leaders of the army, but of Congress as well, most importantly the very same men who would be responsible in the following years for founding an American military establishment. The willingness of these men to risk shattering the delicate bond of trust between the army and the American people, in violation of the deep-rooted tradition against direct military interference in politics and the long-standing warnings about the dangers of an army, revealed a flaw which would dog the Federalist party throughout its existence.

* * *

Although the roots of the crisis went back several years, the first stage in the conspiracy began in late 1782. In the last week in December, Major General Alexander McDougall and Colonels John Brooks and Matthias Ogden rode into Philadelphia with a petition to Congress from the army encamped at Newburgh. The major grievance was pay. Officers and men had not received their salaries in months. More important, the officers were concerned about receiving the half-pay pensions promised by Congress in 1780. To the officers, half-pay was "an honorable and just recompense for several years hard service" during which their "health and fortunes" had been "worn down and exhausted." But they feared, and with good reason, that its general unpopularity might induce Congress to repudiate the promise. Therefore, they were willing to accept a commutation of half-pay to some equivalent lump sum payment. For all its moderation and plea for sympathy, however, the petition spoke in thinly veiled threats: "any further experiments on their [the army's] patience may have fatal effects."

The petition capped almost six months of continual turmoil in the northern encampment, and within the officer corps, agitation which had surfaced over compensation five years earlier. Earlier efforts to settle the pay problem with state governments had failed, and when Congress considered the question of half-pay in the summer of 1782, the resurgence of all the old arguments in opposition only heightened the officers' desperation. Pay and half-pay, however, were only symptoms of a deeper malaise in Newburgh. Most officers were apprehensive about returning to civilian life. Many had been impoverished by the war while friends at home had grown fat on the opportunities provided by the war. For all, the end of hostilities meant reentering a society that had adjusted to their absence, and in traditionally antimilitary New England, a society that would accord none of the advantages or plaudits that returning veterans expect to receive. During those long, boring months of 1782, a growing feeling of martyrdom, an uncertainty and a realization that long years of service might go unrewarded—or perhaps even hamper their future careers—made the situation increasingly explosive.

In mid-November, their patience exhausted, the officers decided to petition Congress once more. Major General Henry Knox drafted the address and, in correspondence with Secretary at War Benjamin Lincoln, carefully laid the groundwork for its reception in Philadelphia. On his part, Lincoln took the utmost pains to press the seriousness of the situation on delegates in Congress. From Philadelphia General Arthur St. Clair explained the political situation to McDougall's committee, and advised the officers to tell Congress "in the most express and positive terms" that unless action was immediate, it could expect "a convulsion of the most dreadful nature and fatal consequences." Events were rapidly approaching a crisis.

Although few in the army knew it, the petition's timing was perfect. The same week that McDougall journeyed from Newburgh to Philadelphia, political conditions shifted abruptly in Congress. On December 24, Congress was shocked to learn that Virginia had repealed her ratification of the Impost of 1781. Since Rhode Island had refused earlier to ratify, the measure was now dead. Most shocked of all were Superintendent of Finance Robert Morris and the clique of nationalists under his leadership in Congress. Based chiefly in the Middle states, but with pockets of strength in the South and New England, merchants and lawyers and planters and elements of the old colonial aristocracy, conservative on questions of finance and fearful of the excesses of popular rule, the nationalists had come to power in 1780 at the low point in the war. Immediately they embarked on reforms to rejuvenate the war effort, strengthen congressional authority and administer public affairs more efficiently. Throughout the war, then as the guiding force behind the Constitution in 1787 and as the nucleus of the Federalist party, the nationalists drove persistently to add to the power and authority of the central government. In the early 1780s, the impost was the heart of their program, and its significance followed naturally from the design of centralization. "Without certain revenues," Hamilton had declared in 1780, "a government can have no power; that power, which holds the purse strings absolutely, must rule."

The nationalists were overjoyed by McDougall's petition. To pay any of the army's claims, Congress would have to find new sources of money. Paper money would no longer circulate, and nationalists could argue that new foreign loans could not be floated without some visible means to meet interest payments. The only alternative was a new funding system; to the nationalists, this meant a new impost amendment giving Congress the power to tax imports. The air of crisis and possible mutiny would bludgeon

Congress into another impost. When Congress then presented it as a measure to repay its victorious army, the states and the public could not possibly refuse.

Within 24 hours of their arrival, McDougall and his officers conferred with Robert Morris. Within another week, the nationalist leadership had convinced McDougall and his colleagues that the army's only hope for payment lay in a new funding system. But unless McDougall and the army cooperated fully, the nationalists threatened, "they would oppose" referring army claims to the states "till all prospect of obtaining Continental funds was at an end." McDougall's first task was to gain the support of the whole officer corps. His second duty was to buttonhole individual congressmen, spreading rumors of the army's uneasiness and the dire prospects if Congress refused satisfaction.

The nationalist leaders would take care of the rest. Certainly not all of the nationalists were involved—only Hamilton, Financier Robert Morris and assistant financier (but no relation) Gouverneur Morris for certain. Others participated with varying degrees of enthusiasm. Some were uninformed of the machinations; others ignored them, willing to work for nationalist ends regardless of the means employed. Madison probably knew nothing directly of the manipulations behind the scenes, but he felt that without an increase in national authority, the union would collapse and the states would degenerate into small units warring with each other constantly. In the weeks ahead, Madison's skill in debate and his incisive political understanding would perfectly complement the stratagems of the nationalist floor leaders, Hamilton and James Wilson. After the army had set the stage and spread the threats, the nationalists would forge an acceptable funding system and maneuver it through Congress.

On January 6, Congress received the army memorial and referred it to a grand committee of one delegate from each state. The next day this committee talked with Robert Morris. At a meeting marked by "loose conversation" on the "critical state of things," the financier stated "explicitly" that his office could not advance the army any pay, and could not even promise any "until certain funds should be previously established." On January 13, McDougall and the army committee intensified the pressure. At a meeting with the grand committee, the officers depicted the resentment in camp in unmistakable terms. When a congressman asked them what, specifically, the army might do if not satisfied, one colonel replied that Congress could expect "at least a mutiny." By the end of the conversation, the grand committee was convinced that a powder keg would explode in Newburgh unless Congress acted quickly. Therefore it appointed Hamilton, Madison and John Rutledge of South Carolina to draft a report on the army's claims, after consulting with Robert Morris to determine the monetary resources at the Confederation's disposal. Pressure tactics were working. Soon the tense and solemn mood of the meeting with McDougall pervaded the halls of Congress.

For the next ten days, while Hamilton and the committee prepared a report on the army's claims, Robert Morris and his associates maneuvered to bring consideration of a new revenue system before Congress. Using the full weight of his personal prestige and the authority of his office as arbiter of national finance, Morris delayed congressional efforts to refurbish the old Confederation taxing system and turned aside initiatives to seek new foreign loans. On January 22, the grand committee submitted its report. In the midst of debate the financier suddenly tendered his resignation. In a bitter letter he declared that his own integrity and position as financier were "utterly unsupportable" because of the Confederation's financial distress. If "permanent provision for the public debts of every kind" was not established by the end of May, he threatened, Congress would have to find a new superintendent.

In the wake of Morris's action, the strain of McDougall's scare campaign, and the urgency of the army's unquestioned discontent, the nationalists gained their first victory. On January 25, after three days of debate on Hamilton's report, Congress agreed to leave the first two claims of the army—present pay and the settlement of unpaid salaries—to Morris's discretion. To support his efforts, it promised to "make every effort in [its] power to obtain—from the respective states substantial funds, adequate to the object of funding the whole debt of the United States."

But the nationalist victory was incomplete. The heart of the report was a provision for commuting half-pay into an outright grant, the one point which would solidly wed the army's interests to those of other public creditors. Twice on January 25, the nationalists tried to shove the measure through, but both times a coalition of New England and New Jersey delegates voted no. Rhode Island and Connecticut were bound by instructions from their legislatures to oppose half-pay in any form, and other eastern congressmen well knew the popular aversion to anything resembling pensions. The nationalists dropped the matter for the moment, Congress referred it to a committee of five, including Hamilton and Wilson, and then turned its attention to a new impost proposal.

Despite this setback, the nationalist program seemed on the surface to be faring well. But in reality, the Morrises and Hamilton were stymied at several points. Knox's silence—it had been three weeks since McDougall had written to him—was ominous. Unless the officer corps cooperated, by keeping up or increasing the pressure from Newburgh and agreeing not to seek half-pay from the states, the whole nationalist design could collapse.

The greatest obstacle of all, however, was Congress's reluctance to adopt commutation of the pensions. Hamilton's committee of five, appointed in January to reshape the measure, recommended it again on February 4, but New England's opposition remained adamant and subsequent debate led nowhere. Commutation was critically important. The fear of a mutinous army might prod Congress into resolving national revenues, but the state legislatures, scattered over the continent far from the army's potential grasp, would not necessarily ratify such an amendment. The Confederation must be committed to paying the huge sums commutation entailed; then like it or not, the states would have to agree to the revenue system or abandon a long-standing promise to the new nation's army. For this reason, the Morrises and Hamilton were willing to use any tactic that could ram commutation down congressional throats.

Overshadowing all these obstacles was the likelihood that news of a peace treaty would arrive at any moment. Peace was the one contingency that could not be manipulated by the nationalist leadership. Should definite word arrive, the crisis would be over, the need to buttress national authority lost and the nightmares of mutiny dispelled in the euphoria of victory. Peace would also destroy the army's political leverage. No longer needed, it would be quickly demobilized to save money and allow the rank and file to return home. Nationalist leaders understood these possibilities all too well. When commutation lost for the second time on February 4, they began the preparations to use force.

The second stage in the plot began on February 8, when Colonel Brooks left Philadelphia to corner Knox and commit the army to the nationalist program. In his dispatch pouch, Brooks carried two letters for Knox. One, from McDougall and Ogden, reported to the entire army in detail on the political situation and emphasized the dim prospects for commutation. The other was a personal message from Knox's "dear friend" Gouverneur Morris, lamenting the state of the nation and pleading for a union of the officers with other public creditors to enact permanent taxes. Four days later a secret letter, more explicit, more conspiratorial and more pressing, left Philadelphia for Knox. Under a prearranged pseudonym, McDougall wrote that the army might well have to mutiny in order to gain its just due— declare publicly that it would not disband until it could be paid and assured of commutation. Such a move would be very dangerous, he admitted; Knox should wait for definite instructions. Meanwhile their friends would decide whether to introduce a motion to this effect on the floor of Congress.

What the nationalists wished when they sent Brooks back to Newburgh was the active cooperation of Knox and the other leaders of the army's effort for redress. Should all the rumors and parliamentary maneuvers in Philadelphia fail, a declaration by the army that it would not disband might frighten Congress into passing commutation, then passing another funding system to raise the money. Such a declaration, while constituting only a passive mutiny, would definitely convey overtones of more positive action in the future, perhaps even a military takeover. Congress would have no choice: accept commutation or risk the consequences.

The dangers in the scheme were considerable. In the first place, a statement by the army that it would not lay down its arms would disgrace the national government. It would proclaim to the world that in its first breath of independence, the United States was unwilling to treat its victorious soldiery with justice. Secondly, it might lead to a wholly unpredictable chain of events. No one could possibly foresee the consequences of the military's declaring its independence from the civil power. Yet in the first week of February, anticipating the worst, the Morrises and Hamilton were willing to take the chance. Knox and the other leaders in Newburgh were responsible men, and could be depended upon to keep the situation in hand.

The nationalists did have another alternative, one they eventually used, and one that historians of the conspiracy have never fully understood. If an incident had to be staged in Newburgh, they could foment a real mutiny among the officers. But it was even more risky since it would involve not only a confrontation with Congress, but also with the military's legitimate leadership. For some time Robert Morris and the others had known of a dissident element in camp which could be persuaded to force an explosion, though the manipulations required would be far more delicate than the rather direct approaches they were making to Knox.

There was a group of young officers, a small extremist wing of the corps, which was angrier, more dogmatic and hotheaded, and which fumed at Washington's moderate leadership. Unlike many older officers, these men had grown up in the army and had less to look forward to on returning to civilian life. They sensed more deeply the impending loss of their military status and privilege. These Young Turks naturally gravitated to Horatio Gates, the "hero of Saratoga," an overbearing and sensitive general whose bad blood with Washington was long-standing. For Gates the discontent in Newburgh could be used to recoup his reputation and, incidentally, to snatch the army away from his rival. Fed by disillusionment, frustration and personal dreams of glory, Gates and his young zealots evidently lost all sense of reality and began planning a full-fledged coup d'etat. The exact nature of the group and its plans will probably never be known. But there are strong hints that they talked of replacing Congress and ruling themselves, either as individuals under a new form of government or through a military dictatorship.

Apparently they approached Robert Morris in January. The financier, recognizing in them another tool should an uprising in Newburgh prove necessary, cynically encouraged their hope for a coup. It was far safer for the nationalists to rely on Knox. Under regular leadership, a declaration by the officers that they would not disband would represent the united voice of the whole army. The Gates group could never speak for all the officers, most of whom revered Washington. Yet Gates and his men, if handled with cunning, could be used to kindle an insurrection in camp that might very well scare Congress more, especially if the mutiny were partially directed against Washington's authority. The scheme, however, involved a desperate gamble. If Gates successfully snatched the army from Washington, the military takeover and civil war the nationalists were determined to avoid might become reality. Furthermore, the nationalists mistrusted Gates, but if they could not push their program through Congress, and if Knox would not cooperate, then Hamilton and the Morrises would have no choice but to use Gates.

In the first week of February, Gates was only a last resort. Then on February 12, news arrived in Philadelphia that George III, in a speech to Parliament, had mentioned preliminary articles of peace signed between Great Britain and the United States. While the report was only hearsay, the nationalists thought peace was certain. Haste was now imperative. Though Knox was yet to be heard from, the nationalists now felt that they must prepare to use Gates just as a safeguard. Through him, they would incite a mutiny in the army—spark the explosion—then make certain it was immediately snuffed out. It was a treacherous double game, fraught with uncertainty. But to the nationalists the whole future of the country was at stake.

The other side in the double game, the means by which the confusion would be harnessed, was George Washington, the patient, persevering commander whom the nationalists knew would never brook direct military interference in politics. The day after the king's speech arrived, the nationalists readied Washington for the coming storm. Hamilton began his letter by pointing out the injustice the army felt and the possibility that the oncoming peace would justify its fears. In a political sense, however, the army might assure itself justice while at the same time easing the country's financial dilemma. The problem would "be to keep a *complaining and suffering army* within the bounds of moderation." This would be Washington's duty, *"to take the direction"* of the army's anger, preserving its confidence in him without losing that of the nation. But Washington should prepare for the worst; there was a real danger of the army rejecting his leadership.

Brooks was already in Newburgh when Hamilton's letter arrived, trying to establish direct channels between the nationalists and Knox. Knox was the pivot in the nationalist scheme. As the leader in all the agitation at Newburgh since mid-1782, as a friend of the most important officers and as a respected member of Washington's military family, Knox could best influence the corps to cooperate. But Knox was also extremely cautious. While he sympathized deeply with nationalist goals, he was first and foremost a soldier, with his career tied to Washington's and to the reputation of the army. Not only were these plans risky, potentially damaging to the army's image, but they would throw him into direct conflict with his patron. The Massachusetts General would not risk a show of force. He undoubtedly said as much to Brooks, and on February 21, he wrote McDougall and Gouverneur Morris to the same effect.

The final stage of the conspiracy began when Knox's rebuffs reached Philadelphia near the end of February. The nationalists acted without hesitation. For the last three weeks their efforts in Congress had been losing momentum. The impost proposal was mired in violent arguments over detail. The nationalists could not muster enough votes without conceding both the appointment of collectors by the states and a limitation on the number of years the measure would be in effect. Even worse than the debates and interminable delays was the appearance of antinationalist counterattacks on the very foundations of the impost. On February 18, Rutledge and John Francis Mercer proposed that all the revenue from any impost be appropriated for the exclusive use of the army—for salaries and half-pay—rather than to provide generally for the restoration of public credit. The restriction cleverly reversed the chief nationalist argument— that permanent funds were needed to satisfy the army's claims—and thus attacked the whole concept of an impost as adding to the strength of the central government.

Although nationalist leaders easily blocked these attacks, it was obvious that the impost would not pass strictly on its own merits. Immediately they shifted attention to commutation. Again, however, Congress deadlocked. New Englanders, still mindful of the unpopularity of pensions in their region, continued to vote in opposition. At one point the nationalists had to choke off an attempt to recommend half-pay back to the states. Faced with such obstacles, the nationalists amplified their campaign of rumor. Washington, they hinted, was losing control of the officers; the army would not lay down its arms, would declare so soon and had even made plans to support itself in the field. By the end of the month, the Massachusetts delegation and Oliver Wolcott, Sr., of Connecticut had swung over to commutation. But threats were not enough. The air of crisis and the shaky coalition supporting commutation could evaporate at a moment's notice. Now, with Knox's refusal to help, it was the last possible moment for action.

On February 26, the nationalists opened their final offensive. To incite the army, McDougall penned one last frenzied letter to Knox, suggesting that there was no hope left for the officers' claims and that the army might soon be split into separate detachments to prevent rebellion. In a similar move, Robert Morris requested permission to make his resignation public, in order not to mislead those who had "contracted engagements" with him. The explanation sufficed, and "without dissent or observation" Congress agreed. News of his resignation, as he well realized, would rock the army and call into question the whole fabric of Confederation finance. After a short while to let these maneuvers take effect, the nationalists alerted Gates.

The emissary was Walter Stewart, a Pennsylvania colonel, former aide of Gates and now inspector of the Northern Army. Stewart reached the cantonment on Saturday, March 8. Although there is no record of the meeting, Stewart undoubtedly pledged Morris's support for any action the officers might take and assured Gates and his followers that the public creditors were fully behind them. Apparently nothing passed that hinted of the nationalists' planned treachery; Stewart probably knew as little of their true intentions as Armstrong and Gates. The officers and their ambitious leader still thought that the first initiatives had been theirs, and that Morris was the unwitting tool.

Within hours rumor flew around camp that "it was universally expected the Army would not disband until they had obtained justice," that the public creditors would join the officers in the field, if necessary, to redress their grievances, and many in Congress looked favorably on the venture. Then on Monday morning, the conspirators published anonymously a call for a meeting of all field officers and company representatives on Tuesday at 11 A.M. to consider McDougall's report of February 8 and to plan a new course of redress. Simultaneously, William Barber, Stewart's assistant in the inspector's department, took several copies of an unsigned address to the adjutant's office where officers from various lines gathered each morning to receive general orders. When the officers saw it, and later, as copies circulated around the encampment, bedlam ensued.

Written by Armstrong and copied by Christopher Richmond, another of Gates's aides, the first of the famous Newburgh addresses urged the officers to forget "the meek language of entreating memorials" and "change the milk-and-water style" of their last petition to Congress. In the most inflammatory rhetoric, Armstrong recalled the army's suffering and glory, comparing them with "the coldness and severity of government," and the country's ingratitude to the men who had placed it "in the chair of independency." Whom would peace benefit? Not the officers, who could look forward only to growing "old in poverty, wretchedness and contempt." Could they, he asked, "consent to wade through the vile mire of dependency, and owe the miserable remnant of that life to charity, which has hitherto been spent in honor?" If so, they would be pitied, ridiculed, for suffering this last indignity. They had bled too much, but they still had their swords.

In a menacing reference to Washington, Armstrong demanded that they "suspect the man who would advise to more moderation and longer forbearance." Draw up one last strong remonstrance, Armstrong argued, and send it to Congress as an ultimatum. If the terms of the December petition were met, the army would keep its faith. If not, the army would have its alternatives.

In response, Washington threw the conspirators on the defensive. On Tuesday morning, March 11, he issued general orders which objected to the address and invitation to a meeting as "disorderly" and "irregular." An assembly with his personal approval would take place at noon on Saturday to discuss McDougall's letter from Philadelphia. The senior officer present—undoubtedly Gates—would preside, and, implying his own absence, Washington requested a full report of its deliberation afterwards. The ploy had possibilities. Five days' hiatus might cool down passions. In any event, Washington planned to attend the meeting and confront the officers in person, with Gates in the chair, strictly circumscribed by procedure and unable to speak out or manipulate the proceedings.

On Saturday morning tension was high. Officers from every unit stationed near Newburgh filed up the low hill to the public meeting house. As Gates opened the proceedings, the Commander-in-Chief entered and asked permission to address the gathering. Gates could hardly refuse, and Washington mounted the stage. Instead of pleading for delay, he took the offensive, denouncing the anonymity of the first summons to a meeting as "unmilitary" and "subversive of all order and discipline." Then he attacked Armstrong's address directly. Would the officers leave wives and children and all their property to desert the country "in the extremest hour of her distress," to "perish in a wilderness with hunger, cold and nakedness?" Or worse, could the army actually contemplate "something so shocking" as turning its swords against Congress, "plotting the ruin of both, by sowing seeds of discord and separation" between military and civil?

Washington reminded the officers of their duty and the disgrace that would follow any step that might sully the army's glory or tarnish its deserved reputation for courage and patriotism. Congress, like any large body "where there is a variety of different interests to reconcile," moved slowly. But ultimately it would justify the army's faith, and Washington pledged himself "in the most unequivocal manner" to press its case.

He then produced a letter from his friend, Joseph Jones, as proof of Congress's good intentions. After reading the first paragraph, Washington paused to put on his spectacles. Unaffectedly, the tall general murmured that he had grown gray in the service of his country and now found himself going blind. The assemblage was stunned. In his speech, Washington had forced them to face the implications of rash action—civil war, treason and the undoing of eight years' effort. The contrast with this simple dramatic gesture, an act that blended Washington's charismatic influence with the deepest symbolic patriotism, was overpowering. The tension, the imposing physical presence of the Commander-in-Chief, the speech and finally an act that emotionally embodied the army's whole experience, combined all at once and shattered the officers' equanimity. Spontaneously they recoiled. Some openly wept.

In a moment Washington was gone, the meeting now firmly in the grasp of his lieutenants. After a brief interval, Knox introduced motions that reaffirmed the army's "attachment to the rights and liberties of human nature" and its "unshaken confidence" in Congress and asked the Commander-in-Chief to write Congress again on the army's behalf. The officers accepted these unanimously, declaring their "abhorrence" and "disdain" of the "infamous propositions" advanced in the addresses, and their "indignation [at] the secret attempts of some unknown persons to collect officers together, in a manner totally subversive of all discipline and good order."

Even as the officers left the hall, news of the incident was on the way to Philadelphia. Tuesday afternoon Washington had posted copies of the addresses and his general orders. Coming on the heels of other serious problems, the "alarming intelligence" according to Madison induced "peculiar awe and solemnity . . . and oppressed the minds of Cong[res]s with an anxiety and distress which had been scarcely felt in any period of the revolution." Immediately the nationalists seized the initiative. As an embarrassment to the men involved, the committee appointed to consider Washington's dispatches consisted exclusively of opponents of commutation and the impost. Both measures had languished for days. The explosion in Newburgh, properly represented, would add new urgency.

The one obstacle left to commutation was Eliphalet Dyer, a Connecticut delegate who reflected his constituents' dislike of pensions and felt bound by his instructions to oppose half-pay in any form. Badgered by the nationalists and McDougall, told that only he prevented the measure, that he had become the focus of resentment from everyone in the army, that commutation was more publicly acceptable than half-pay, that it alone "would quiet and pacify the Army," Dyer finally caved in. Two days later, a committee of Hamilton, Dyer and one other delegate submitted a report recommending five years' full pay to all officers entitled to half-pay. With Connecticut now in agreement, commutation passed.

Superficially, the nationalist intrigue had worked well, and within another month Congress approved a new impost amendment. But it was not a clearcut victory for the nationalists. The impost contained such a jumble of compromises, so many concessions to sectional jealousy and state sovereignty, that even Hamilton could not bring himself to vote for it. It was limited to twenty-five years, the revenues restricted to paying debts, and its enforcement uncertain since the states would appoint collectors. Yet it was all the nationalists could muster. News of peace had arrived on March 12, the army was disintegrating and Robert Morris's resignation was public.

The same day that Congress voted its approval of commutation, it received Washington's speech and the proceedings of the March 15 meeting. Even though apprehension lingered over the army's mood, the news dissipated "the cloud" of fear and "afforded great pleasure" to the delegates. Instead of arousing suspicion and distrust by its flirtation with mutiny, the army emerged from the Newburgh affair with enhanced prestige and honor. Few knew how close to calamity the officers had really come. The public record belied any conspiracy, showing only a loyal officer corps rejecting the seductions of despair despite deep and abiding grievances.

The Newburgh affair was significant for what did not happen. No tradition was broken and no experience with direct military intervention occurred to haunt future American political and military life. The only precedent set, in fact, positively reaffirmed Anglo-American tradition: the first national army in American history explicitly rejected military interference and military independence from civilian control. The disbanding of the Continental Army without a damaging incident assured that civilian control of the military for the foreseeable future would be more an administrative than a political problem. America did stand at the crossroads in March, 1783. Today, as one weighs an impossible number of variables and attempts to judge the alternatives without the certainty that hindsight normally offers, the significance of the event is vague and indistinct. Perhaps contemporaries understood the question more clearly. To them the shape of the country's political institutions, even whether or not the disparate sections could live together in union, was uncertain. Thomas Jefferson was describing a general feeling when he claimed "that the moderation and virtue of a single character has probably prevented this revolution from being closed as most others have been by a subversion of that liberty it was intended to establish."

8

Pennsylvania Revolutionary Officers and the Federal Constitution

WILLIAM A. BENTON

The effect that military service has on servicemen has often been exaggerated; the typical G.I. returns to civilian life with his values and attitudes pretty much intact, largely unaffected by his service experience. Habits and traits acquired in childhood are not easily altered, even by the discipline of the regiment or the hardship and trauma of the campaign.* But some servicemen do experience certain changes as a result of their military experiences. William Benton demonstrates this for Revolutionary War officers from Pennsylvania and relates these changes to the political controversy that divided the nation within five years of the war's end.†

*See Peter Karsten, *Soldiers and Society* (Westport, Conn., 1978).

†Compare Benton's findings with those of Edwin Burrows, "Military and the Origins of Federalism and Antifederalism," in Jacob Judd and Irwin Polishook, eds., *Aspects of Early New York Society and Politics* (Tarrytown, N.Y., 1974), pp. 83–92.

THOUGH MUCH HAS BEEN WRITTEN about the forces which contributed to the adoption of the federal Constitution of 1787, the possible influence of the military experiences of the Revolutionary War has been relatively neglected. One of the purposes of the writers of the Constitution was "to provide for the common defence." *The Federalist* treats military issues at some length. If provision for military defense of the United States was an

SOURCE: William A. Benton, "Pennsylvania Revolutionary Officers and the Federal Constitution," *Pennsylvania History* 31, 4 (October 1964): 419–435. Copyright © 1964 by the Pennsylvania Historical Association. All rights reserved. Reprinted by permission.
EDITOR'S NOTE: Most of the citations to the sources consulted by the author in this essay have been omitted from this volume for brevity and economy. The reader should consult the original source of the essay for the complete scholarly documentation.

important matter to the writers of the Constitution, it should also have seemed important to the former officers of the Revolutionary army, who remembered the severe trials of the war.

Certain assumptions about the probable attitudes of the Revolutionary officers towards the Constitution immediately suggest themselves. It would not be surprising to discover that the Revolutionary officers, remembering how the weakness of the central government had contributed to their trials, were among the advocates of a stronger central government through the Constitution. It seems likely, too, that officers who had witnessed the numerous failures of the militia so often deplored by George Washington might have favored the Constitution as a means of substituting a stronger standing army for reliance on the militia. This article will attempt to test such assumptions with respect to the Pennsylvania veterans of the Revolutionary officer corps. It will examine the part they took in the ratification struggle in Pennsylvania, the possibility that the issue of a standing army versus the militia system affected their judgments, and the possibility that other factors, such as economics, religion, and geography, influenced the ex-officers.

In attempting to approach these issues I have limited myself to studying men who held the rank of major or above. This method offers a manageable number of subjects and concentrates on the more prominent Pennsylvania officers. In analyzing these men I have divided them into three general classifications: Continental Army officers, militia officers who became Federalists, and militia officers who became Antifederalists.[1]

One of the most serious questions to be answered in the establishment of a new federal government was whether a standing army should be formed or the militia of the various states should continue to be virtually the only protection which the country had against foreign invasion or Indian attack. This issue was one upon which the ex-military officer was likely to focus his war experiences, to enable him to reach a decision.

Article One, Section Eight of the United States Constitution states:

> The Congress shall have Power To . . . declare War . . . , raise and support Armies . . . , make rules for the Government and Regulation of the land and naval Forces; To provide for calling forth the Militia to execute the Laws of the Union, suppress Insurrections and repel Invasions:
>
> To provide for organizing, arming, and disciplining the Militia, and for governing such part of them as may be employed in the Service of the United States, reserving to the States respectively, the Appointment of the Officers, and the Authority of training the Militia according to the discipline prescribed by Congress.

Article Two, Section Two says:

> The President shall be Commander in Chief of the Army and Navy of the United States, and of the Militia of the several States, when called into the actual service of the United States.

These two sections of the Constitution provide for a national standing army with the President of the United States as Commander in Chief. As it was likely that George Washington would be the first President, the officers who had served under him during the Revolution would seem likely to have given strong support to these sections of the proposed Constitution. Under the Articles of Confederation it was virtually impossible to raise a standing army or even to appoint a commander in chief, since unless nine states agreed, Congress was powerless. When Arthur St. Clair was president of Congress he wrote to the governor of Connecticut bemoaning this fact:

> We have appointed an assembly, and invested it with the sole and exclusive power of Peace and War, and the management of all national concerns. And during the course of, almost, a whole year, it has not been capable, except for a few days, for want of a sufficient number of Members to attend to these matters. Since the first monday in November last to this time there has been a Representation of nine States, only Thirty Days—and ten States, only three days.

The issue of a standing army raised a question in Pennsylvania, and in the rest of the United States, upon which Federalists and Antifederalists could not agree. To the Federalists a standing army was a necessary part of the powers of the government-to-be. And the ratification struggle proved, as we might expect, that this issue found the ex-Continental Army officers among the Federalists. During the Revolution these officers had seen militia troops refuse to serve outside the borders of their own states, panic due to inadequate training, or leave when their enlistments were over—even if they left the remainder of the army in an untenable position.

Soon after the battle of Long Island, General George Washington wrote to the Continental Congress saying that the defeat had

> dispirited to [sic] great a proportion of our troops and filled their minds with apprehension and dispair. The militia . . . are dismayed, intractable and impatient. . . . Great numbers of them have gone off; in some instances, almost by whole regiments. . . . I am obliged to confess my want of confidence in the generality of the troops.

Washington had declared that American liberty might be lost

> if their defence is left to any but a permanent standing army.

The Federalists believed that a standing, permanent army was necessary. They held that the United States needed one for purposes of internal and external defense. James Wilson, although not an officer during the Revolution, expressed the issue very clearly when he said in the Pennsylvania Constitutional ratifying convention:

> Ought Congress be deprived of power to prepare for the defense and safety of our country? Ought they to be restrained from arming until they divulge

the motive which induced them to arm? I believe the power of raising and keeping up an army in time of peace is essential to every government. No government can secure its citizens against dangers, internal and external, without possessing it. . . .

When we consider the situation of the United States, we must be satisfied that it will be necessary to keep up some troops for the protection of the western frontiers and to secure our interest in the internal navigation of that country.

In what is probably the greatest and most important work in political science written in the United States, *The Federalist Papers*, Alexander Hamilton, James Madison, and John Jay devoted eight essays to the issue of a standing army and the inadequacy of the militia system. Their most succinct argument was presented by John Jay when he wrote:

[The United States government] can apply the resources and power of the whole to the defense of any particular part, and that more easily and expeditiously than State governments or separate confederacies can possibly do, for want of concert and unity of system. It can place the militia under one plan of discipline, and, by putting their officers in a proper line of subordination to the Chief Magistrate, will, in a manner, consolidate them into one corps, and thereby render them more efficient than if divided into thirteen . . . independent bodies.

In contrast, the military sections of the Constitution were abhorrent to the Antifederalists and were vigorously repudiated by them. They believed that a standing army was inimical to the freedom and liberty of the people of the United States. The militia system was capable of dealing with any emergency which could possibly arise to threaten the freedom of the country, while securing the country from tyranny by affording a civilian army. An impassioned plea to this effect was published on September 23, 1787, shortly after the Constitution was first published in Pennsylvania:

Had we a standing army when the British invaded our peaceful shores? Was it a standing army that gained the battles of Lexington and Bunker Hill, and took the ill-fated Burgoyne? Is not a well regulated militia sufficient for every purpose of internal defense? And which of you, my fellow citizens, is afraid of any invasion from foreign powers that our brave militia would not be able immediately to repel?

On December 13, 1787, the Constitution was ratified by the Commonwealth of Pennsylvania. The vote in the ratifying convention was 46 for ratification, 23 opposed. The Constitution was adopted, but the Antifederalists still did not give up in their fight to oppose a standing army. On December 18, they published their "Address and Reasons of Dissent of the Minority of the Convention of the State of Pennsylvania to their Constituents." In this address they gave a prominent place to four objections to Article One, Section Eight, and Article Two, Section Two of the recently adopted Federal Constitution:

Standing armies in the time of peace are dangerous to liberty. They ought not to be kept up. . . ,

Congress shall not have authority to call or march any of the militia out of their own State, without the consent of such State. . . .

A standing army in the hands of a government placed so independent of the people, may be made a fatal instrument to overturn the public liberties. . . . An ambitious man who may have the army at his devotion, may step into the throne, and seize upon absolute power.

The absolute, unqualified command that Congress have over the militia may be made instrumental to the destruction of all liberty, both public and private; whether of a personal, civil, or religious nature.

Although they had lost the fight over ratification, the Pennsylvania Antifederalists did not give up their fight to retain an independent militia system and ban a standing army. In September 1788 a large group of them met in Harrisburg to decide upon a slate of candidates for the coming state and congressional elections. They also proposed amendments to the Constitution. Among these amendments were:

That no standing army of regular troops shall be raised or kept up in time of peace, without the consent of two-thirds of both Houses in Congress. That each state respectively shall have power to provide for organizing, arming, and disciplining the militia thereof. . . . That the militia shall not be subject to martial law, but when in actual service in time of war . . . nor shall the militia of any state be continued in actual service longer than two months under any call of Congress, without the consent of the legislature of such state.[2]

Thus one of the prime issues of contention between the Federalists and Antifederalists was the issue of a standing army, to be controlled by the national government, as opposed to the state-controlled militia system which was then current. The Antifederalists did not give up their opposition to a standing army even after the Constitution had been adopted.

The ex-officers of Pennsylvania played their part in this controversy. As it developed, the ex-militia officers generally favored the militia system, unless they had served nationally during the Revolution. On the other hand, service outside the state seemingly demonstrated the inadequacies of the militia system through travel with the Continental Army and contact with the militia of other states; those militia officers who had served outside Pennsylvania proved more likely to be Federalists than those who had not. The ex-Continental Army officers generally became firm supporters of a standing, national army.

The ex-Continental Army officers were well organized through their membership in the Society of the Cincinnati. This organization was founded in 1783, ostensibly to continue and strengthen the ties of friendship which had been developed during the Revolution among the Continental Army officers. But one of the main purposes of the organization in the eyes of many of its founders was to create an hereditary officer corps. Many of the officers had a desire to continue in the military establishment and wanted to create an army on the European model; on the European pattern they wanted, and demanded, one-half pay for life and the establishment of a military caste system based upon an hereditary officer corps. The Confederation offered none of these things for them. The officers who had founded the Society of the Cincinnati, therefore wanted to see the Articles of Confederation changed, and welcomed the Constitution with its standing army.

Pennsylvanians were prominent among the ex-Revolutionary officers who took advantage of the opportunities presented when the Constitution opened the way to a new standing army. Brigadier General Richard Butler became a major general in the United States Army in 1789 and was second in command to a fellow Pennsylvanian, Arthur St. Clair, in the Northwest Territory. Lieutenant Colonel Josiah Harmar became General in Chief of the army until 1792, when he retired and was succeeded by Major General Anthony Wayne. All of these men were Pennsylvanians, members of the Society of the Cincinnati, and wished to maintain the military connection.

Some of the ex-Continental officers, notably two Pennsylvanians, Lewis Nicola and Anthony Wayne, wanted a more authoritarian central government than was established by the Constitution. As early as May, 1782, Nicola was advocating the creation of a monarchy with George Washington as king. Anthony Wayne seems to have had a similar idea soon after the Constitution was adopted. He wrote: "Our illustrious friend General Washington will be her first 'president' (or by whatever name the world may please to call him). I wish he had a *Son.*" Yet short of a more authoritarian government, they accepted the Constitution and were ardent Federalists.

The ex-army officers were well represented in the Pennsylvania ratifying convention. Of the 69 members, 17 had been high-ranking officers in the Continental Army or the militia during the Revolution. Three of these were Antifederalists, the remainder were Federalists. Nicholas Lutz, Antifederalist leader of Berks County, had been a lieutenant colonel in the state militia. The Federalist delegation was led by such men as Colonel Thomas McKean of Philadelphia, Major General Anthony Wayne of Chester County, Colonel Stephen Chambers of Lancaster County, and Colonel Timothy Pickering of Luzerne County. These men were among the leaders of their respective parties. Their importance, along with the importance of such men as the following, was very great in Pennsylvania politics: Major General Edward Hand, Federalist of Lancaster County and presidential elector in 1789; Major General Thomas Mifflin, first governor of Pennsylvania and a Federalist; Major General Arthur St. Clair, Westmoreland County Federalist and president of Congress in 1787; Brigadier General Samuel Meredith, Federalist and first Treasurer of the United States; Lieutenant Colonel Samuel Maclay, Antifederalist of Northumberland County and member of the United States House of Representatives; Major General James Potter, Northumberland County Antifederalist; and Colonel Timothy Matlack, Philadelphia Antifederalist. The ex-officers from Pennsylvania who were Federalists were generally a more influential and prominent group than were their Antifederalist counterparts. The Antifederalist officers seem to have had influence only within their respective counties, while many of the Federalists had statewide, if not national, prominence.

In attempting to discover whether other factors, besides military service, influenced these officers, I have compiled and analyzed data concerning the branches of service, positions on the Constitution, ages, occupations, membership in the Society of the Cincinnati, religions, and counties of residence of as many of the 590 officers of Pennsylvania who held rank of major or above, as possible. Sixty of these officers either died or moved from Pennsylvania before the United States Constitution was written. I was able to discover the political views of only 99 of the remaining men. Of the original 590 officers, 131 served in the Continental Army during the Revolution and 459 in the militia. There were $3\frac{1}{2}$ times as many militia officers because the militia usually served for only short periods of time. Their enlistments were never of more than six months' duration, and the same officers rarely served more than one enlistment. Continental Army officers were commissioned for the duration of the war and there was a much smaller turnover in personnel.

Of the 99 officers whose political opinions are known to me, 44 served in the Continental Army and 55 in the state militia. Of the 60 officers who had died by 1787, 24 were Continentals and 36 militia officers. My results are therefore based upon a knowledge of 41 per cent of all the Continental Army officers and 13 per cent of the militia officers. Therefore, while it is possible to reach a fairly definite conclusion about the Continentals, only tentative conclusions can be reached concerning the militia officers.

The results of a branch of service-politics survey are extremely revealing. Of the 44 Continentals whose political opinions are recorded, all were Federalists. The militia officers were divided; 23 of them were Federalists, 32 were Antifederalists. It appears that this division was based at least in part upon the type of service seen by these militia officers. Of the 23 Federalist militia officers, 13 are known to have served outside the state of Pennsylvania, either in Canada, New York, or in the southern campaigns. Only four of them are known not to have served outside the state.

An examination of the Antifederalist militia officers tells us a different story. Only one of them is known to have served outside Pennsylvania's borders, while 24 are known not to have served outside the state. These facts lead us to the tentative conclusion that the militia officer who served outside the state became a Federalist more readily than one who served only within the state. This may well have been true because, having served outside Pennsylvania, a militia officer, like the Continental Army officers, saw the meaning of national unity and national defense, and re-alized the need for these things in the United States.

The society of the Cincinnati plays an interesting role in this analysis. Of the 44 Pennsylvania Continental Army officers who were Federalists, 32 were members of the society. There were 16 militia officers who were eligible for membership in the society, having had three years of service during the Revolution. yet only three of them chose to join. All three were Federalists. Eight Antifederalists were eligible for membership, but not one of them chose to join the society. It would seem, therefore, that member-ship in the Society of the Cincinnati is one way of obtaining an indication as to whether or not an ex-officer became a Federalist or an Antifederalist. This is not surprising, as the society's major goal was the preservation of the officer class. The Constitution, with the standing army which it au-thorized, seemed to re-establish an officer class. The members of the So-ciety of the Cincinnati would, therefore, support the adoption of the Con-stitution.

Several historians, notably Charles Warren, have made an age distinc-tion between Federalists and Antifederalists. Using a select group of ten Antifederalists and nine Federalists, Warren found that Antifederalists were much older than Federalists. Jackson Turner Main rejects this view and makes the statement that the Federalists were younger than their oppo-nents by an average of about two years, which is not a significant age difference. My own investigation shows that the Pennsylvania Antifeder-alist officers average seven years older than the Federalist opponents.[3] My sampling might or might not be representative of the age of the Antifed-eralists, as the ages of only 15 out of 32 are known. In any case, I do not believe that this age difference is a particularly notable distinction. The four oldest officers were Colonel Jacob Morgan (71 in 1787), Lieutenant Colonel James Read (71), Major General John Armstrong (70), and Colo-nel Lewis Nicola (70). Two of these men were Antifederalists, two Feder-alists. It is, therefore, not likely that age was much of a factor in deter-mining whether or not one of the ex-officers became a Federalist.

Whether a man was native or foreign born did not make any difference when he took a position on the adoption of the Constitution, at least not in Pennsylvania. Thirteen Federalists and four Antifederalists were not born in America, about 15 per cent of each group. There is no significance in these figures, although it is interesting to note that 11 of the 17 were born in Ireland, and 14 of the 17 in the British Isles.

An analysis of the religions of the 99 officers reveals that this factor seems to have played a very small role in determining a man's politics. The religions of 29 of the Federalists and 9 of the Antifederalists are known. These results are somewhat fragmentary but are instructive because they reveal no difference between Federalists and Antifederalists. There were fewer Quakers in the Antifederalist ranks, and more Calvinists and Catholics in the Federalist ranks. The Quakers in this survey were "Free Quakers." They were barred from the regular Quaker meetings because of their military service and organized their own churches, or meetings. These results do not reveal anything significant to us, since the Antifederalist results are so scanty. A wider sampling of both would probably reveal little difference between the two sides.

Several historians, notably Charles Beard and Jackson Turner Main, have attributed economic motives to the writers and supporters of the Constitution. I have therefore investigated the civilian occupations of the 99 officers in order to determine whether or not there was any division along occupational lines in this group. This is not a survey of the wealth of these individuals, but of their occupations.

Jackson Turner Main analyzed the occupations of the 69 members of the Pennsylvania ratifying convention and came to the conclusion that 54 per cent of the Federalists but only 22 per cent of the Antifederalists were in the wealthy or educated classes. Thirteen per cent of the Federalists were farmers, compared with 48 per cent of the Antifederalists. This data would seem to be significant, except for the fact that my results, on the same type of survey and using Main's criteria, for the officer group reveal an entirely different picture. I found that some 84 percent of the Federalists and 83 per cent of the Antifederalists belonged to the wealthy or educated classes, while 11 per cent of the Federalists and 11 per cent of the Antifederalists were farmers. There is no significant difference of any kind.

One significant occupational difference does come to light, however. Twelve per cent of the Federalists were professional military officers, while none of the Antifederalists were.[4] It is also noteworthy that six of the seven professional officers were members of the Society of the Cincinnati and ex-Continental Army officers. This is a striking contrast and one which seems to emphasize the importance of the role played by the military in the adoption of the Constitution.

So far we have seen that, except for the professional soldiers, there was little difference in the social status or ages of the Federalist and Antifederalist officers from the state of Pennsylvania. The only difference between them seems to have been in their branches of military service, but this conclusion has not yet been conclusively proven. The next group of figures is extremely revealing, as this table reveals that military service was an important criterion in determining the political position of these men in 1787.

John Bach McMaster and Frederick Stone, and Orin G. Libby have made case studies of the geographical distribution of the vote on the Constitution in Pennsylvania. The people of the late 1780's did the same, and saw a definite correlation between residence and politics. Philadelphia, Bucks, Chester, Lancaster, York, Northampton, Northumberland, Montgomery, Luzerne, and Huntingdon counties were overwhelmingly Federalist in sentiment; while Berks, Bedford, Cumberland, Westmoreland, Fayette, and Dauphin were Antifederalist. Washington and Franklin counties were split in their voting. If the officers do not follow this pattern, then it must be assumed that other factors influenced their opinions about the adoption of the Constitution.

Analysis of the residences of the officers, by county, reveals some striking results. Two per cent of the Federalists and six per cent of the Antifederalists came from counties which were split on the issue of the Constitution, and can therefore be discounted. What cannot be discounted is that 27 per cent of the Federalists came from Antifederalist counties, and 56 per cent of the Antifederalists came from Federalist counties. These results are very significant. Philadelphia and Cumberland counties, the former strongly Federalist and the latter strongly Antifederalist, account for 42 per cent of the total number of officers. Forty-four per cent of the Federalists came from these two counties, 30 per cent from Philadelphia, and 14 per cent from Antifederalist Cumberland. The residences of the Antifederalists are even more significant. Fifteen per cent of them came from Cumberland County, while 25 per cent came from Philadelphia. It is very clear that we must look beyond local issues to find why these people stood as they did upon the adoption of the Constitution.

The officers with whom I am dealing do not conform to any pattern or theory which has been evolved to explain why people stood as they did upon the issue of the adoption of the Constitution in the years 1787 and 1788. To be sure, this small percentage of the population was specialized, but they do represent a cross-section of Pennsylvania life in the period following the American Revolution. Anthony Wayne, Arthur St. Clair, James Potter, Edward Hand, and John Armstrong were respected as the state's leading military officers. Samuel Meredith and Jacob Morgan were among the wealthiest men of the state; others were average industrious citizens. They were representative of the Pennsylvania of their day.

Many of these officers gained national prominence after the Revolution, if this had not already been accomplished. Josiah Harmar, Arthur St. Clair, and Anthony Wayne became generals in chief of the army. John Armstrong, Jr., an ardent Federalist who later became a Jeffersonian Republican, was United States Minister to France from 1804 to 1810, and was Secretary of War during the War of 1812. Samuel Meredith was made first Treasurer of the United States by President Washington in 1789 in recognition of his financial ability. He served in that capacity until 1801. Arthur St. Clair was president of Congress in 1787 and served as the first governor of the Northwest Territory from 1787 to 1802. Ten other officers served in Congress, representing the Commonwealth of Pennsylvania. Other officers were prominent on the state level. Thomas McKean was chief justice of Pennsylvania, and later, governor of the state. Joseph Hiester also served a term as governor, as did Thomas Mifflin.

It is fair to assume that the ex-Revolutionary officers had a greater influence upon public affairs than their numbers can account for. It would therefore be instructive to attempt to discover why they became Federalists or Antifederalists. The statistical evidence for this question has already been presented, although much of it is of a negative nature. But the negative factors are important, for if it can be shown that the generally accepted theories do not apply to this group of officers, then a new approach to the reasons for the adoption of the Constitution must be found, at least for the officer class. Occupational, religious, and residential factors have all been shown to have little or no influence upon the group with which we are dealing, while the difference in ages has been discounted.

What then were the differences between the Federalist and Antifederalist officers? There were three major factors separating the two groups, none of which is a complete answer in itself. The first was the officer's branch of service. No officer from Pennsylvania who had served in the Continental Army became a known Antifederalist. This factor is not difficult to account for. As has been related above, I believe that the Continental Army officer, due to his nationwide service, developed a nationalistic outlook and saw the necessity of a strong central government. Josiah Harmar, soon to be general in chief of the army, wrote just before the Constitutional Convention:

> I sincerely hope that the proposed convention will be able to revise and amend the Confederation, or frame an entire new government, as without a federal head, and proper powers rested in Congress, the country must soon become a scene of Anarchy and Confusion.

William Irvine was worried about the external threat to the United States, especially from British North America, due to the weakness of the national government under the Confederation:

> We are entering in a critical situation, and should the Convention break up and leave us in the unsettled state we now are, I am really afraid of the Consequences. By the last accounts from Canada it appears that Lord Dorchester is using every exertion to [place (?)] the Militia of his province on a respectable footing. . . . If something is not done to cure or at least alleviate the disorders in the federal government, our situation may invite the attack of nations who have fewer resentments to gratify than Great Britain.

A second way of distinguishing between the two parties is by the extent of officer service in each group. In this manner it is possible to distinguish between the militia officers who became Federalists and those who became Antifederalists. The Continental Army officers all served outside the state, as did at least 13 of the Federalist militia officers. The Antifederalists were distinguished mostly by short lengths of service, limited to within the state of Pennsylvania. Only one Antifederalist, Nicholas Lutz, is known to have served outside the state. Many of the others served for short lengths of time; Frederick Antes, Christian Lower, Timothy Matlack, William Montgomery, and Jonathan B. Smith served only for a short time in 1775, while Samuel Maclay served for three months in 1776. Many of the militia Federalists served for longer periods of time; Stephen Balliet, John Nixon, Thomas Smith, Henry Slagle, and many others served for over a year. Some, notably Nixon and Slagle, served for more than two years. It would seem, therefore, that the more time an officer served on active duty, the more likely he was to have become a Federalist.

The third distinction between the two groups is membership in the Society of the Cincinnati. Much has already been said about this organization, but it must be reiterated that over 50 per cent of the Federalists were members, while no Antifederalists were, although at least eight were eligible for membership.

The only distinctions between the two groups are those mentioned above. All deal with the military service of these officers during the Revolution. These factors seem to have had a decisive influence upon the political opinions of the officer class. Perhaps this influence was subconscious in many cases. The men themselves probably did not recognize it at the time, yet their military service did influence them in 1787.

Military service during the Revolution helps to explain why these officers either supported or rejected the Constitution in Pennsylvania in 1787. If this theory can be extended to the high ranking officers of the other states, then it helps to explain why the Constitution was written and adopted. I do not believe that I am superseding, or even disputing, the generally accepted theories which have been offered concerning the adoption of the Constitution. My conclusions are valid solely for those who served in a military capacity during the Revolution. The writings of Charles Beard, Forrest McDonald, Orin Libby, Merrill Jensen, George Bancroft, and Jackson Main are ample proof of the fact that my approach to this problem, although valid, is a narrow one.

NOTES

1. Those officers who served in both the Continental Army and in militia units will be considered as Continental Army officers for the purposes of this discussion. In all cases they spent more time in the national service than in active militia service.

2. *Independent Gazetteer*, September 15, 1788. These amendments were signed by 33 Antifederalists, of whom 9 were ex-high ranking officers of the militia.

3. The 15 Antifederalists whose ages are known averaged 53 years of age in 1787, while 55 Federalists averaged 46 years; 24 Continentals averaged 43 years of age; 18 militia Federalists, 48 years of age.

4. By professional military officers I mean those men who devoted their lives to military service after the Revolution.

The Early Republic

9

Excerpt from Governor Samuel Adams's Farewell Address, 1797

Governor Samuel Adams's "farewell address" to the legislature of Massachusetts on January 27, 1797, presented the case for the localistic antifederalists, friends of the state militia, in the debate that raged throughout the first century of the new republic. Keep in mind that "the danger of standing armies in times of peace" that he refers to was not theoretical. Adams's nemeses, the nationalistic Federalists in the new Federal Congress, had created a 5,000-man regular army and were on the verge of creating a regular navy and marine corps. They had deployed the army in 1794 against western Pennsylvanians and would deploy it in 1799 against northeastern Pennsylvanians. They would carefully select Federalists for the officer corps. For those and other actions they would lose control of the Federal government in 1800 to men more sympathetic to Samuel Adams's point of view.*

*See Kohn, *Eagle and Sword*, chapters 8–13; and Theodore Crackel, "Jefferson, Politics, and the Army," *Journal of the Early Republic*, II (Spring 1982): 21–38.

. . . PERMIT ME TO CALL your attention to the subject of the Militia of the Commonwealth.—A well regulated militia "held in an exact subordination to the civil authority and governed by it," is the most safe defence of a Republic.—In our Declaration of Rights, which expresses the sentiments of the people, the people have a right to keep and bear arms for the common defence. The more generally therefore they are called out to be disciplined, the stronger is our security. No man I should think, who possesses a true republican spirit, would decline to rank with his fellow-citizens, on the fancied idea of a superiority in circumstances: This might tend to introduce fatal distinctions in our country. We can all remember the time when our militia, far from being disciplined, as they are at present, kept

SOURCE: Harry Alonzo Cushing, ed., *The Writings of Samuel Adams* (New York, 1907), 4: 402–3.

a well appointed hostile army for a considerable time confined to the capital; and when they ventured out, indeed they took possession of the ground they aimed at, yet they ventured to their cost, and never forgot the battle of Bunker Hill. The same undisciplined militia under the command and good conduct of General Washington, continued that army confined in or near the capital, until they thought proper to change their position and retreated with haste to Halifax.—If the Militia of the Commonwealth can be made still more effective, I am confident that you will not delay a measure of so great magnitude. I beg leave to refer you to the seventeenth article in our Declaration of Rights, which respects the danger of standing armies in time of peace. I hope we shall ever have virtue enough to guard against their introduction.—But may we not hazard the safety of our Republic should we ever constitute, under the name of a select militia, a small body to be disciplined in a camp with all the pomp & splendor of a regular army? Would such an institution be likely to be much less dangerous to our free government and to the morals of our youth, than if they were actually enlisted for permanent service? And would they not as usual in standing armies feel a distinct interest from that of our fellow-citizens at large? The great principles of our present militia system are undoubtedly good, constituting one simple body, and embracing so great a proportion of the citizens as will prevent a separate interest among them, inconsistent with the welfare of the whole.—Those principles, however, I conceive should equally apply to all the active citizens, within the age prescribed by law.—All are deeply interested in the general security; and where there are no invidious exemptions, partial distinctions or privileged bands, every Man, it is presumed, would pride himself in the right of bearing arms, and affording his personal appearance in common with his fellow-citizens. If upon examination you shall find, that the duties incident to our present system bear harder on one class of citizens, than on another, you will undoubtedly endeavour, as far as possible, to equalize its burthens.

10

Father's Occupation of West Point Cadets and Annapolis Midshipmen

The career officer corps of the nineteenth century were like their eighteenth-century (British) counterparts. They were disproportionately of the more hierarchic, ritualistic faiths (especially the Episcopal faith) and (as these tables indicate) from more well-to-do families than the typical eligible male. An interesting difference exists between father's occupations of West Point cadets and Annapolis midshipmen, suggesting a relationship between certain types of "navy-minded" occupations in society and Annapolis and certain "army-oriented" occupations and West Point.

Father's occupation of cadets entering West Point, 1845–1867

	CADETS ENTERING WEST POINT		
FATHER'S OCCUPATION	1845–1860 N = 993	1861–1867 N = 416	1845–1867 N = 1409
None	47 (5%)	29 (7%)	76 (5.4%)
Business			
Merchant	96 (10%)	68 (16%)	164 (11.8%)
Manufacturer, miller	28 (2.7%)	13 (2.5%)	41 (3%)
Broker, agent, spec.	21 (2%)	6 (1.5%)	27 (2%)
Grocer, hotelkeeper, self-employed	12 (1.1%)	6 (1.5%)	18 (1.2%)
Banker, insurance	15 (1.4%)	11 (2.5%)	26 (1.9%)
Clerk	20 (1.9%)	5 (1%)	25 (1.8%)
Professional			
Contractor, engineer	23 (2.2%)	3 (.8%)	26 (1.9%)
Physician	58 (5.5%)	31 (7%)	89 (6.5%)
Clergyman, educator	28 (2.5%)	27 (6%)	55 (4.5%)
Editor, publisher	11 (1%)	5 (1%)	16 (1.1%)
Lawyer, judge	117 (11%)	57 (14%)	174 (12.2%)
Govt. official (high)	11 (1%)	3 (.8%)	14 (1%)
Govt. official (low)	16 (1.5%)	8 (2%)	24 (1.8%)
Worker			
Machinist, mechanic	26 (2.5%)	26 (6%)	52 (4%)
Other skilled worker	26 (2.5%)	5 (1%)	31 (2.2%)
Laborer, enlisted man	5 (.5%)	6 (1.5%)	11 (.8%)
Farmer, planter	345 (34%)	69 (16.4%)	414 (30%)
Officer	88 (8.7%)	48 (12%)	136 (9.5%)

SOURCE: Compiled from archival records at the U.S. Military Academy at West Point, N.Y., by Peter Karsten, summer 1977.

Naval Academy officer candidates, 1847–1900, segregated
by father's occupation, compared to cross-section of mature[a] male
national work force, drawn from the 1870 census[b]

FATHER'S OCCUPATION TOTAL SAMPLE: 1,560 (WIDOWS EXCLUDED)	PERCENTAGE OF CANDIDATES APPOINTED	PERCENTAGE OF MATURE MALE WORK FORCE, 1870	RATIO OF COLUMNS 2 & 3
Officer (161)	10.3%	.03%	343.3
Banker (86)	5.5	.15	36.6
Attorney, judge (194)[c]	12.4	.5	24.8
Manufacturer (114)	7.3	.5	14.6
Government official (123)[c]	7.9	.6	13.1
Physician, druggist, civil engineer (150)	9.6	1.1	8.7
Merchant (282)	18.1	2.5	7.2
Clergyman, educator, artist (80)	5.1	1.1	4.6
Shopkeeper, agent, hotelkeeper (111)[c]	7.1	2.0	3.6
Artisan, clerk (104)[c]	6.5	skilled—10 unemp. & unskilled—30.2 total—40.2	.65 .16
Planter, farmer, rancher (157)[c]	10.0	prop. farmers—30 agri laborers—21 total—51	.30 .19

[a]Extrapolated from census figures for males 16 years of age and older, and adjusted for occupations such as physician, judge, or manufacturer with a greater proportion of older members, and for occupations such as artisan, clerk, or agricultural laborer, which contained a disproportionate number of younger persons.

[b]U.S. Bureau of Census, *Ninth Census* Vol. III, *The Statistics of the Wealth and Industries of the United States* (Wash., 1872), 797–843.

[c]Analysis of the 483 officer candidates appointed in 1915 and 1925 reveals a slight decrease in the percentage of those whose fathers were farmers (corresponding to the general decrease in the national percentage of farmers), attorneys, and government officials, and a virtual doubling of the percentage (from 14.2 to 25.4) of those whose fathers were artisans, clerks, or shopkeepers. Perhaps the tripling of the size of the Academy between 1900 and 1920 resulted in a saturation of the upper and upper-middle class sources of officer candidates; perhaps the increased use of competitive exams explains the increases in middle and working class origins. I don't know which is more likely.

SOURCE: Peter Karsten, *The Naval Aristocracy: The Golden Age of Annapolis and the Emergence of Modern American Navalism* (Free Press, 1972), table 1–2, p. 9.

11

Officers and Politicians

The Origins of Army Politics in the United States before the Civil War

WILLIAM B. SKELTON

Civilian control of the military in America has been a persistent phenomenon, but military interaction with politicians to secure personal or service objectives has been just as persistent. Officers do not directly challenge civilian leadership, but they do seek to influence it, in much the same way as other lobbyists do. In this essay William Skelton describes this interaction of officers and politicians in the years before the Civil War.

ONE OF THE MOST CHERISHED of America's political ideals is civilian control of the military establishment. At least until the involvement of the armed forces in national policy-making during the Cold War era, army and navy officers overwhelmingly accepted the supremacy of their civilian superiors. The only major exception to this pattern was the so-called Newburgh Conspiracy at the end of the Revolution, but that was a brief and ambiguous affair, manipulated by civilian leaders and eventually contained within the army itself. Its failure left the fabric of civil supremacy intact. Perhaps the most important characteristic separating the American pattern of political "modernization" from those of developing nations in the twentieth century was the peripheral role of the professional officer corps in that process.

SOURCE: William B. Skelton, "Officers and Politicians: The Origins of Army Politics in the United States before the Civil War," *Armed Forces and Society,* vol. 6, no. 1 (Fall, 1979). Printed by permission of the publisher and the author.
EDITOR'S NOTE: Most of the citations to the sources consulted by the author in this essay have been omitted from this volume for brevity and economy. The reader should consult the original source of the essay for the complete scholarly documentation.

Given the significance of civil supremacy in United States history, it is surprising that historians have devoted so little attention to its origins and development. However, a variety of influences seems to have contributed to civil control. One was the long-standing distrust of standing armies in Anglo-American political culture, deriving from the bitter controversies surrounding the army in seventeenth-century England and reinforced in America by the militia tradition and the experience of British occupation before and during the Revolution. The founding fathers only reluctantly accepted the government's power to maintain permanent armed forces and wrote into the Constitution elaborate checks on military authority. Antimilitarism became a staple of American political ideology, periodically renewed in the democratic reform movements of the nineteenth century and only temporarily submerged after World War II.

A second influence was the general stability of American political life: the absence of the bitter class and tribal conflicts which plague many developing nations; the long experience with the electoral process; the density and perceived legitimacy of civilian institutions. In contrast to events in Third World societies, the United States armed forces have neither seen the necessity nor been offered the opportunity for political intervention to restore order in time of upheaval or to arbitrate irreconcilable political controversies. Even the extraordinary conditions of the Civil War did not deprive the rival governments of broad popular support or create power vacuums for the exploitation of a "man on horseback." Finally, civil supremacy arose in part from the internal character of the military establishment. American officers have always derived from a relatively broad spectrum of society; thus the armed forces have not been the preserve of a single social class or geographical region which might use military power to acquire or defend a privileged position. At any rate, the permanent armed forces were small and geographically isolated until the mid-twentieth century, lacking the power to dominate civilian institutions even if they had been so inclined.

However, the interplay of these factors merely defined the outer boundaries of civil-military relations in the United States, precluding direct and open intervention in the civilian political process. Within this framework, much latitude existed for less direct and less threatening types of political involvement. Concentrating on the twentieth century, social scientists have analyzed a complex variety of political activities by military men: lobbying for weapons systems and for strategic and foreign policy doctrines; pushing service interests; aligning with local and private groups for mutually beneficial spending programs; propagandizing a strong military posture generally. As Samuel P. Huntington has shown, the constitutional separation of power actually encourages such behavior, as it blurs the civilian chain of command and permits officers to play one branch of the government against others. American officers have usually been nonpartisan, but they have been anything but apolitical.

Although most visible and controversial in recent years, the basic patterns of military politics emerged in the first half of the nineteenth century. During that period, professional army officers began to work out for the first time their collective role in relationship to politics. While professional ideology rejected partisanship and discouraged taking sides on purely civilian issues, officers eagerly embraced political means to pursue goals defined as *professional*: individual advancement within the military hierarchy; the interests of particular branches of the service; the welfare of the army as a whole. Frequently, they rationalized personal or group interest on the basis of national security. Military politics have grown more complex in the twentieth century, but their basic outlines have not significantly changed. Thus, the development of officers' political attitudes and activities before the Civil War had a major impact on the conduct of civil-military relations in the United States.

From the formation of the regular army in 1784 to the end of the War of 1812, no clear pattern marked officers' political relations. The dominant characteristic of the army during this period was instability. No consensus existed in Congress or the nation as a whole as to the size or specific functions of the military establishment. Reductions, expansions, and reorganizations of the army were frequent and kept the officer corps in a continual state of flux. Military careers were short: only 17 percent of the men on the 1789 army list and 12 percent of those on the 1797 army list served twenty years or longer. The army lacked uniform regulations, systematic administrative procedures, and effective institutions to educate aspiring officers and instill group values. Except for a small minority of careerists, the officer corps consisted of a mass of individuals, still closely linked to civilian life, whose brief military experiences did not produce uniform, professionally defined patterns of thought or behavior.

Political conditions in the early Republic blurred the distinction between civil and military affairs. During the Revolution, state and regional jealousies and the ill-defined powers of the Continental Congress created a tangle of command problems which, at times, threatened to disrupt the Continental Army. Military appointments, promotions, and assignments became highly charged political issues, as commanders maintained local bases of support and freely maneuvered for advancement. Under the Articles of Confederation, initiative in military matters rested mainly with the states. Congress lacked the power to raise revenue, and the constitutionality of a permanent army remained in doubt. Officers found it necessary to lobby continually both in Congress and in the states for pay, benefits, and even decisions on relative rank. While the Constitution gave the federal government the clear authority to raise an army, the development of political parties during the 1790's added another complication. Political leaders viewed the army as a source of patronage and, at least in the case of certain Federalists, as a potential tool to quell internal opposition. Because of the lateral appointment policy—the practice of appointing citizens directly to high rank—political considerations continued to influence the chain of command. During the Quasi-War with France, the size and character of the military establishment became central issues in national politics. The struggle between John Adams and Alexander Hamilton over the "New Army" of 1798—in the opinion of one historian, the "only completely political army in American history"—divided the Federalist party and contributed to its defeat in 1800.

Although the Jefferson administration inherited a predominantly Federalist officer corps, it made no concerted attempt to purge its opponents.[1] However, the Democratic Republicans continued to use military appointments for patronage purposes and hoped to make the army a bastion of the administration. When Congress expanded the army in 1808, the War Department consulted prominent Republicans on appointments. "As we have quite a sufficient number of our opponents political now in the Army," the Secretary of War wrote a Connecticut Republican, "it may be advisable to pay some attention to the political feelings of the Candidates." The army's role in enforcing the controversial Embargo Act increased administration interest in the political orthodoxy of the officer corps. By the War of 1812, lateral appointments had given the high ranks of the army the appearance of a Democratic Republican political caucus: of the thirty-five men who served as general officers between 1808 and 1815, eight had supported the administration in Congress, four had been Republican state or territorial governors, and at least five others had been Republican state legislators. The middle rungs of the officer corps included scores of former officeholders and journalists, overwhelmingly Jeffersonian in their politics.

Under these circumstances, military and political life interpenetrated at all levels. Not all officers engaged in politics, of course; much depended on the individual's family and social standing. The Articles of War, the basic code of military justice, prohibited officers from openly criticizing the president or Congress. However, officers demonstrated little awareness of military life as a separate realm of endeavor, distinct from the political forum and guided by its own code of values. Military men appealed to their political friends for redress on professional matters, publicized personal quarrels in the press, cultivated ties in the regions where they were stationed, and took open stands on general political issues. During the 1790's, for example, General James Wilkinson carried on a complex intrigue in both Congress and the army to replace Anthony Wayne as commander of the army. Officers in the Trans-Appalachian West participated in that region's web of expansionist and secessionist schemes; perhaps more than twenty regulars, General Wilkinson among them, were involved in the Burr Conspiracy. At St. Louis, New Orleans, Mackinac, and other army stations, military men exercised civil as well as military authority, serving as judges, postmasters, customs collectors, and even territorial governors. Inevitably, civil-military intimacy prevailed, and officers plunged into local political affairs. Before and during the War of 1812, the appointment of Republican politicians and editors intensified the overlap between politics and the army. In one of the most flagrant cases, William Duane of Philadelphia continued to publish his Republican newspaper and advise the administration on political matters while holding a regular army commission.

The years following the Peace of Ghent marked no abrupt change in the traditionally confused patterns of army politics. The euphoric nationalism of the postwar period briefly submerged popular antimilitarism; scores of returning veterans received heroes' welcomes and mingled in prestigious political circles. Most high-ranking officers had entered the army as recently as 1808 or 1812 and few were in the strict sense careerists. The senior generals, Andrew Jackson and Jacob Brown, established their headquarters at their personal residences, where they mixed military administration with farming and political interests. The complex political infighting of the Era of Good Feelings absorbed the attention of many regulars. The candidacy of Secretary of War John C. Calhoun was particularly popular in the army: several officers supported him in the press, and General Brown served as intermediary when Calhoun agreed to run for vice president under John Quincy Adams in 1824.

Beneath the surface, however, the changing circumstances of army life led officers to view their relationship with politics in a somewhat different light. Most basically, the period after 1815 brought a new stability to the military profession. In 1821 the last major peacetime reduction and reorganization of the army in the nineteenth century occurred. From that point forward, the trend was toward a gradual, though uneven, expansion of the officer corps—from 532 in 1823 to 1,108 in 1860. With the sporadic encouragement of the executive branch of the government, officers worked out a common conception of their professional role, emphasizing the development of expertise and organizational efficiency in preparation for a future conflict with a major European power. The introduction of tactical manuals, standardized regulations, and uniform administrative procedures brought regularity to all phases of the military establishment. Under the supervision of Sylvanus Thayer, the United States Military Academy emerged as the most important entry point into the officer corps and an effective means of socializing young men into military life.

Perhaps the most significant change of the post-War of 1812 period was the stabilization of military careers. No longer were officers faced with imminent disbandment. The decreasing use of lateral appointments, except in wartime, assured young men entering the army as second lieutenants of gradual upward mobility within the military hierarchy. Although officers continued to complain about low pay, slow promotion rates, and the lack of public esteem for their profession, more and more of them found military life sufficiently attractive to make a long-term career commitment. The median career length for officers on the 1797 army register, for example, was ten years; for those on the 1830 list, it was twenty-two years.

The percentage of officers who would serve twenty or more years rose from 12 percent of the 1797 total to 59 percent of the 1830 total.

The interaction of these trends—the regularization of military procedure, the emergence of West Point as a socializing institution, the lengthening of military careers—gave the profession of arms a cohesion and a permanence which it had previously lacked. Increasingly, military men manifested common patterns of thought and behavior, determined more by their experiences as cadets and officers than by their social backgrounds or their contacts with the civilian world. Political attitudes reflected this transition. By the 1820's and 1830's, officers had begun to distinguish between military and political life. As military professionals, their principal responsibility was to the nation as a whole rather than to a particular section, faction, or party. Their involvement in a centralized, restrictive bureaucratic institution led them to emphasize hierarchical values—order, obedience, discipline—which set them apart from the rough-and-tumble egalitarian flavor of contemporary political life. West Point administrators stressed the Academy's national image and tried to isolate cadets from civilian politics.

Officers' perception of the political environment reinforced their tendency to separate the military from the civilian sphere. The regular army enjoyed considerable prestige immediately after the War of 1812. By the early 1820's, however, antimilitary sentiment was resurfacing in Congress. The initial stimulus was rivalry between Secretary of War Calhoun and Secretary of the Treasury William H. Crawford, both candidates for the presidency in 1824. To embarrass Calhoun and cut back government expenditures, Crawford's congressional supporters sponsored a series of investigations into the War Department and led the struggle to reduce the army in 1821. Congressional hostility, or at least indifference, continued through the Adams administration. While specific military programs fared better under the Jacksonians, the regular army was continually a target for congressmen, state legislators, and editors, who found its authoritarian structure and reliance on specialized expertise incompatible with egalitarian values. Antimilitary rhetoric peaked during the depression years of the early 1840's, as economy-minded congressmen considered reductions of the army and the abolition of West Point. The danger was more apparent than real: the expanding frontier and threats of foreign war brought periodic increases in military strength. Officers exaggerated the extent of public hostility, however, and came to see politicians as adversaries. Immersion in the world of civilian politics might provoke the wrath of Congress, threatening both the army as an institution and their personal careers with it.

Though seldom expressed in theoretical form, officers developed a conception of the army as an apolitical instrument of public policy. As servants of the nation, they should stand aloof from party and sectional strife and avoid taking sides on civilian political issues. Colonel Henry Atkinson favored Andrew Jackson for the presidency in 1824 but felt himself "too delicately situated (being an officer in the army) to take an active part." Colonel Duncan L. Clinch stated in 1829 that he had "always deprecated the practice of officers of the Army interfering in elections, either of a general or local character, except so far as respects an honest and moderate expression of their opinions—and have never approached the polls, or given a vote, since I have been in the Army." Brigadier General Edmund P. Gaines opposed partisan allegiances by officers: "In war we must serve our country with all our hearts, and with all our soul, and with all our strength; we are thus rendered incapable of serving a political party." According to a correspondent to a military periodical, officers' political attachments might turn the army into "an armed mob, dangerous in its nature to the vital interests of the government, and subversive of the honor belonging to the profession of arms." By accepting a commission, an officer voluntarily surrendered his rights of political action.

A corollary of officers' distinction between political and military life was a negative view of politicians. In contrast to the discipline and devotion to duty which allegedly typified the military profession, politicians appeared shifty, divisive, self-serving, and too willing to compromise principles. They were "loafers" and "demagogues" who courted the "mob" and failed to appreciate the sacrifices of the army. They placed sectional and party welfare above the national interest. Individual officers privately questioned the desirability of democratic government. "I am no longer a democrat," wrote Lieutenant John Sedgwick on learning of disorders among volunteer troops in the Mexican War. "I go for an empire, governed by a strong hand, reserving the right of revolutionizing—when opposition becomes too hard." Captain Thomas Williams blamed the secession crisis on universal manhood suffrage and favored "an hereditary Executive, an hereditary Senate, property qualifications for voters; property qualifications for Representatives. . . . "

It would be misleading to take at face value officers' professions of political neutrality. After both the War of 1812 and the Mexican War, senior commanders harbored political ambitions; General Winfield Scott desperately pursued the presidency through his long career. As earlier, civil-military intimacy often prevailed at frontier posts. However, the dissociation of the military profession from politics was not entirely rhetorical. By the 1830's, most career officers were demonstrating little interest in political issues not directly relevant to the army. When they expressed a preference for a particular candidate or party, they usually did so on the basis of *professional* considerations—the potential impact on military programs or their personal careers. Officers' private correspondence rarely mentioned such staple issues of the Jacksonian Era as the tariff, the National Bank, or even sectional controversies. National elections frequently passed unnoticed or were dismissed with comments similar to that of Colonel Abraham Eustis in 1840, who thought life "not long enough to devote any portion of it to reading long speeches, pro & con, on Log-cabins & Hard Cider." This tendency is especially striking when compared to the overwhelming popular interest in politics which marked the 1830's and 1840's.

Officers' political energies were not lacking but were channeled into the pursuit of professional goals. These goals were of three general types: personal career advancement; the interests of particular branches of the service (often reflecting intraservice rivalries); the army interest as a whole. In seeking these goals, officers institutionalized patterns of political behavior which would survive into the twentieth century.

The most widespread variety of political activity by military men was advancement of their personal careers. Matters of rank and promotion took on special significance in the United States Army. First, American culture generally emphasized competition and individual advancement, never more strongly than in the mid-nineteenth century. Second, the officer corps was recruited from a relatively broad social base. In contrast to contemporary European armies, officers did not derive from an aristocratic ethos which could afford them secure status independent of the army; instead, they tended to come from middle class farming and professional families, often in declining economic circumstances. Most of them identified with military rank as the principal determinant of both their status and their financial well-being, an inclination reinforced by lengthening career commitments. In the opinion of one correspondent to a military journal, rank constituted "the substance of all [the military man] can hope of advancement in the scale of social being . . ." Captain Orlando B. Willcox stated the same sentiment more dramatically in his novel based on military life: "Promotion! promotion! give men promotion or they die!"

The regularization of military administration after the War of 1812 somewhat restricted the scope of political patronage. Lateral appointments to high rank became rare in peacetime; seniority strictly governed regular promotions through the grade of colonel. However, the army's personnel system included important areas where political sponsorship could further an officer's career. Congressmen determined most appointments to West Point, by far the most common entry point to the officer corps, and political considerations influenced the granting of direct citizens' commissions, especially when new regiments were raised.[2] More important to the internal functioning of the army was the use of political influence in such matters as assignments to detached service, leaves of absence, transfers from line regiments to desirable staff positions, and the issuance of brevet rank—honorary rank above an officer's regular grade, awarded for gallant or meritorious conduct or for ten years service in one grade. In addition, promotions to the rank of general lay outside the seniority system, as did the periodic bonanzas of irregular promotions caused by expansions of the army.

To obtain these advantages, officers suppressed their generalized disdain for politicians and cultivated influential supporters. The nature of the political system facilitated their efforts. The army was a national bureaucracy existing in a decentralized, community-oriented social order. Officers retained ties in their former localities and often knew their congressmen personally; many extended their contacts through marriage or through prolonged service in a particular region. Although the War Department denied that political pressure affected its personnel decisions, each reorganization or expansion of the army and each death of a general officer brought a rush of officers' claims which the government could ignore at its own risk. Under this pressure, army administrators usually tried to strike a rough geographical balance in distributing favors, with political patronage playing a significant role. A veteran of War Department bureaucracy explained the facts of military life to a candidate for a staff appointment in 1857:

> You have enough of army recommendations, you want some political ones. Do not let this word deter you, from using in your own defence lawful weapons, which have been already turned against yourself. . . . Virginia influence is now in the ascendancy, and that, through your wife's relatives you can command. By all means, use it. . . . Request your friends, to watch for a vacancy, and, on the occurrence of one, to *lose no time*, in pressing your claim, in person, if they can, if not by letter.

Examples of such activity abound. The reduction and reorganization of the army in 1821 created a tangle of politically charged claims which disrupted military administration for years. Officers and their sponsors aired their cases in the press; controversy over appointments kept the Adjutant General's Office without a permanent chief until 1825 and the Second Artillery Regiment without a colonel until 1832. When the Commanding General of the army died in 1828, a bitter struggle ensued over succession to his office. The political implications of choosing among rival candidates led John Quincy Adams to favor abolishing the office altogether. When Adams did make a decision, one of the disappointed candidates openly defied the administration and appealed for redress to Congress. Similar controversy surrounded the appointment of officers to the newly formed Ordnance Department in 1832 and First Dragoons in 1833; the selection of a brigadier general to replace Winfield Scott after his promotion to commanding general in 1841; the granting of brevet promotions for Mexican War service; and the nomination of officers to the four new regiments added in 1855. Of course, political intervention for leaves, transfers, and favorable assignments was continual. In 1833, the beleaguered Secretary of War prohibited officers from visiting the capital except on official business. This order was soon rescinded, however, probably because officers charged that it interfered with their rights. Captain Samuel P. Heintzelman expressed a common opinion in 1855: "I must get to Washington & try to get promotion. . . . There is nothing like being on the spot."

The use of political support for individual career advancement mainly continued and confirmed practices common before the War of 1812. The second category of officers' political action—pushing the interests of particular branches of the army—marked a significant new development. The principal source of this trend was the period of military reform after the War of 1812, which brought a greater degree of specialization within the officer corps. In place of the previously fluctuating organization, a stable regimental structure emerged in the line or "combat" portion of the army, consisting of four artillery and seven (by 1860 ten) infantry regiments. The reintroduction of mounted regiments in the 1830's added a third combat arm. Most importantly, staff and support functions earlier performed by civilians or by officers scattered through the geographical commands were concentrated in separate General Staff departments, or bureaus, headquartered at Washington. These bureaus—quartermaster, ordnance, medical, pay, engineers, and others—were largely autonomous within the army, responsible in most matters directly to the secretary of war. They were headed by high ranking chiefs and staffed by relatively permanent cadres of officers who identified strongly with department interests.

The result of this internal segmentation was a great deal of intraservice rivalry—perhaps the most distinguishing characteristic of nineteenth-century military administration. The line branches and staff bureaus frequently fought among themselves: infantry officers, for example, envied the desirable seaboard posts of the artillery, while the Corps of Engineers quarreled sporadically with the Corps of Topographical Engineers over politically popular internal improvements projects. However, the principal divisions were between staff and line. Staff officers wished to perpetuate and expand their departmental jurisdictions; line officers resented the size and independence of the bureaus and tried to curb the alleged privileges in pay, promotion, and stations enjoyed by their staff colleagues. Of course, personal ambition interacted with group interest—virtually any change in military organization would affect individual careers. Much intraservice friction was contained within the army, taking the form of angry exchanges of official correspondence and appeals to the War Department for redress. However, all sides frequently resorted to political channels. The staff departments had obvious advantages: their headquarters were in Washington and their chiefs had easy access to the president, secretary of war, and congressional committees. Line officers, scattered at small posts along the frontier and coastline, looked to the commanding general as their spokesman and made use of local political connections.

Political activity in pursuit of branch objectives took several forms. Most common were appeals by individual officers to their congressmen or their influential friends and relatives. Another important channel was the press. For example, two of the principal adversaries of intraservice feuding, the artillery regiments and the Ordnance Department, carried on an acrimonious pamphlet war during the 1840's and 1850's, the artillery pushing for a merger of the two branches, the ordnance seeking to preserve its independence. Other intraservice quarrels were aired in newspapers, military periodicals, and even literary magazines. Officers used circular letters and memorials to win congressional support and actively lobbied in Washington. When possible, they established ties with regional and local interests in a civil-military version of log-rolling. Most successful in this respect was the Corps of Topographical Engineers, the department in charge of army exploration and many internal improvements projects. Beginning in the 1820's, topographical officers worked on a wide variety of canals, railroads, harbor and river improvements, and other civil works which brought them into contact with businessmen and politicians. They aligned with powerful southern and western leaders in support of territorial expansion and a southern route for the transcontinental railroad. While sometimes a center of controversy, the corps profited from these relationships. Between 1830 and 1860, it achieved independent bureau status, improved promotion opportunities, and nearly a four hundred percent increase in personnel. Individual topographical officers, as well as many from other branches, used contacts made through civil projects to obtain lucrative positions on leaving the service.

Perhaps the most politically oriented branch of the army was the Corps of Engineers. Since its formation in 1802, this corps had enjoyed an elite status within the military establishment. Its duties were defined as "the most elevated branch of military science" and each year it drew the top graduates of West Point. As with the topographical engineers, the engineers supervised various civil works and thus benefited from local political alliances. However, the engineers had responsibility for two programs on which there was no public consensus. One was the Military Academy itself, frequently under attack during the Age of the Common Man as a seedbed of elitism and authoritarianism. The second was the construction of seacoast fortifications. The government had begun a systematic program of coastal fortification after the disastrous experiences of the War of 1812. In the absence of a strong foreign threat, however, congressional skeptics constantly criticized its expense and sometimes reduced or delayed appropriations. Moreover, developments in military technology—rifled artillery, explosive shells, steam-powered naval vessels, railroads which could concentrate large forces at threatened spots—raised questions as to the military effectiveness of the entire system. In defending its vulnerable programs, the engineers could not expect united support from the army as a whole. While the artillery and the Ordnance Department had a vested interest in the fortification program, all branches resented the corps' elite position, especially its exclusive control of West Point, and frequently lobbied against it.

The Corps of Engineers countered these threats by developing an array of political weapons. Senior officers in Washington kept in close contact with the executive branch and Congress, promoting and even drafting bills which might benefit the corps. Lower ranking engineers looked after the corps' interests in the areas where they were stationed. When the Connecticut legislature passed resolutions in 1842, calling for the abolition of West Point, Captain George W. Cullum rushed to repair the damage: "I spent a day or two spouting to the loafers and trust I have put some right ideas in their heads." The chief engineer attempted to stifle internal dissent potentially harmful to engineer programs and encouraged his subordinates to write articles for the civilian press, designed to convince the public of the vital importance of coastal fortifications and formal military education.

The most elaborate political campaign waged by the Corps of Engineers before the Civil War occurred during the early 1850's. In 1851, the House of Representatives tabled the annual appropriation bill for fortifications, in part because of the unsettled state of military technology, in part because of western suspicions that the program was a useless pork barrel scheme to benefit the coastal states. At the same time, junior officers in several staff departments favored legislation to speed promotion in their branches. An ambitious young engineer officer stationed at the Coast Survey Office in Washington, Lieutenant Isaac I. Stevens, coordinated a lobbying campaign to push the two programs. Stevens and other officers at the capital personally solicited the support of scores of congressmen. They raised funds from the corps to print memorials and reports bolstering their case which they distributed to prominent men in the federal government and the states. On Stevens' advice, engineer officers lobbied in the districts where they were stationed, published articles in local newspapers, and mobilized their influential friends and relatives. The campaign succeeded; the army appropriation bill for 1853 restored the funds for fortifications and, much to the resentment of the line, provided engineer, topographical, and ordinance lieutenants with automatic promotion to captain after fourteen years service. Stevens hoped that "our officers hereafter will realize their responsibilities as American Citizens, and will discharge, what I consider their bounden duty to enlighten the public mind."

A variation on the theme of intraservice friction was the occasional attempt by an individual officer who differed with his branch or with the administration on policy questions to take his case directly to Congress or the public. Through the 1830's and 1840's, for example, Brigadier General Edmund P. Gaines urged the War Department to adopt a military program based on mobile "floating batteries" for harbor defense and a federally constructed railway system, radiating from the interior states to the seacoast and capable of concentrating masses of militia to repel an invasion. When the administration showed little interest, Gaines doggedly pushed his ideas through his influential friends, the press, public lectures, and even memorials to Congress. Another military gadfly, Major Wiliam H. Chase of the Corps of Engineers, clashed with the leadership of his branch on a variety of issues and did not hesitate to appeal to higher authority. In his opinion, unquestioning obedience to the chief engineer would make every officer "but a paid hireling, bound to do all or any work required of him no matter how injurious it may be to the commonwealth." Among other things, Chase publicly attacked pay differentials favoring staff over line officers, lobbied against a bill to form a company of engineer troops, and criticized the orthodox fortification program during the 1850's.

In common with such twentieth-century mavericks as General William Mitchell and Admiral Hyman Rickover, service critics irritated their superiors. However, there were few disciplinary means at their disposal, short of potentially embarrassing courts-martial. The seniority rule protected critics from the subtle pressures of "merit" evaluations; prolonged service in particular areas allowed them to develop local ties and enjoy a considerable degree of autonomy.

The third area of officers' political activity—the pursuit of general army interests—was of only limited importance before the Civil War. Military men were certainly aware that they constituted a group distinct from the rest of society; they frequently portrayed themselves as a devoted band of brothers, serving an ungrateful and rather degenerate public. However, this identity only sporadically found expression through political channels. In contrast to the immediate, tangible nature of individual and branch interests, the army interest was poorly defined. Antimilitary rhetoric notwithstanding, a general consensus usually existed in the government that the regular army should be retained and even increased occasionally to meet the demands of westward expansion. Army-navy rivalry was not yet a significant incentive to internal service solidarity. The two services had relatively clear, mutually exclusive functions; service appropriations were determined by separate congressional committees and had little bearing on one another. The navy occasionally crossed swords with the Corps of Engineers on the perennial issue of coastal fortifications, but many line officers were indifferent to that program and viewed it as a branch rather than a service matter. In other words, few political issues compelled army officers as a group to close ranks. Moreover, regulars were wary of actions which might appear to challenge civil control and thus provoke congressional retaliation.

Nevertheless, officers occasionally did evoke general service interests. The desire of high commanders to enhance the army's public image subtly influenced decisions on troop distributions, the opening and closing of military posts, and army participation in transportation projects. In 1820, for example, Major General Jacob Brown suggested stationing additional troops in Maine in order to make that state's congressional delegation more favorable to the army. He also hoped that regulars would, through military road building, "achieve a victory over some of the prejudices of the country by their useful labours in peace if they could not by their deeds of arms in War." Officers lobbied almost continually for higher pay and other economic benefits. They pushed for a retirement and pension system, intended both to increase military efficiency and speed promotion for junior officers. Military humanitarians supported bills to improve the condition of enlisted men, especially the establishment of "military asylums" for old soldiers. The congressional economy drive following the Depression of 1837 caused some activity in defense of general service interests, though intraservice squabbling was a more typical reaction. The officer corps as a whole favored the addition of new regiments in 1855.

The Mexican War briefly intensified service solidarity. That conflict followed a period of demoralization within the officer corps, caused by the frustrating, controversial Second Seminole War and the pressures of the congressional retrenchment campaign. Even officers with misgivings about Manifest Destiny greeted the outbreak of fighting with an enthusiasm bordering on euphoria. Dreams of glory and rapid promotion infatuated subaltern and gray-haired veteran alike. Moreover, the war provided an opportunity to prove the professional skills of the regular army and permanently silence its civilian critics.

Battlefield experience confirmed the army's hopes, both individual and institutional. However, the seemingly partisan direction of the war effort by the administration of James K. Polk soon produced dissatisfaction. Officers resented the large-scale callup of volunteers, the appointment of citizens to the temporary "regular" regiments created for the emergency, and the commissioning of prominent Democrats as generals. No opinion was as pervasive within the officers corps as contempt for citizen soldiers, and the administration's reliance on "mushroom generals" and its promotion of "partisans lawyers and quacks" over regulars and West Point graduates seemed a conscious plan to degrade the army. Captain William H. T. Walker predicted that every regular officer "with one spark of chivalry" who could make a living outside the army would resign after the war. "I would rather serve as a private in a foreign army than to be a captain in an army which is trodden upon as ours is by its government." The ultimate insult was Polk's suspension of General Winfield Scott from command of the forces in Mexico City early in 1848, after his spectacular conquest of the enemy capital. Although the outgrowth of factional conflict which involved regular as well as volunteer officers, the "martyrdom" of Scott appeared to many regulars the epitome of the army's suffering. The simmering resentment of politicians came to the surface. Lieutenant Francis Collins, who "was not ignorant of the foul workings of a contemptible scheme of political partyism," found Polk's action beyond belief. Lieutenant Colonel Ethan Allen Hitchcock considered the army in Mexico, aside from a small clique of dissidents, universally opposed to Scott's suspension. "We all see the enormity of the conduct of the President—deplore and abhor it."

However, this upsurge of army solidarity was short-lived. Temporarily isolated in Mexico, officers could take little immediate action beyond writing indignant letters home. The briefness and the overwhelming success of their campaign rapidly defused resentment. The budding militance of the officer corps dissipated as veterans returned to heroes' welcomes, saw their most popular commander elected president, and scrambled for individual rewards, especially brevet promotions. The Mexican War left an important legacy for the regular army in the form of professional pride. It did not create an alienated praetorian class, prepared to use united political action on behalf of group interests.

Another characteristic of officers' political behavior working against a unified army interest was the relatively bipartisan—or perhaps nonpartisan—nature of the officer corps. In contrast to the pre-War of 1812 army, regulars appear to have favored neither politial party consistently. Although it is risky to generalize from the limited evidence available, a sampling of officers' preferences during the period of the second party system (approximately 1828 to 1852) reveals a nearly even division: thirty Democrats; thirty-two National Republicans or Whigs (or at least anti-Jacksonians). In addition, officers' party identifications were remarkably "soft" when compared to the intense partisanship in the larger society. Even in private correspondence, they usually expressed their allegiances obliquely, even apologetically, and tended to view their party as the lesser of two evils. Presidential candidates with military backgrounds inspired surprisingly little enthusiasm. During the 1820's, a number of influential officers supported John C. Calhoun, Monroe's popular secretary of war, but Andrew Jackson and William Henry Harrison drew only mixed responses from the army. While many regulars favored Zachary Taylor in 1848, partly as a rejection of the Polk administration, the similar Whig candidacy of Winfield Scott four years later aroused little noticeable support within the officer corps and even some active opposition.[3]

Several factors help explain the absence of a strong partisan bias in the antebellum army. The first is ideological. As Richard Hofstadter has demonstrated, Americans by the 1830's were moving toward a conception of parties and party conflict as legitimate and even beneficial institutions—necessary to check the concentration of power, to publicize important issues, and generally to structure political conflict in a sprawling, heterogeneous society. On the other hand, the emerging professional ideology of the officer corps, with its emphasis on service to a unified nation, perpetuated the older view of partisanship as divisive and potentially disruptive. Officers might use party connections to pursue professional goals, but they saw such ties as a necessary evil—a compromise with an imperfect world—rather than as a virtue.

Second, the military appointment process tended to divide and weaken the officer corps' party allegiances. Before the War of 1812, the executive branch controlled all appointments and inevitably favored its supporters. Thus the political coloration of the officer corps reflected the party in power: largely Federalist through the early 1800's; overwhelmingly Republican after 1808. By the 1820's, however, the War Department had adopted the practice of appointing most West Point cadets on the recommendation of congressmen, a procedure confirmed by law in 1843. Military commissions continued to be a form of patronage, of course, but mainly congressional rather than executive patronage. Thus, the political allegiances which officers brought to the army—blurred in most cases by four years at West Point—resembled the party composition of Congress, and presumably of the nation as a whole. Beginning in 1832, the use of professional examining boards to determine medical appointments weakened political patronage in the Medical Department.

A final factor softening officers' partisanship was the relative insignificance of military policy as an issue in party conflict. From the 1790's to the reduction of the army in 1821, military affairs had frequently inspired intense political debates. After 1821, however, the size and organization of the army aroused only occasional interest in Congress. Although there has been no detailed analysis of congressional voting on military questions, neither Democrats nor Whigs seem to have consistently supported or opposed army interests. On six House of Representatives roll calls involving relatively well-defined army interests, for example, Whigs voted in favor of the army position by a 56.9% majority while Democrats did so by a 52.6% majority. The expansionist foreign policy of national Democratic leaders, especially in the 1840's, appealed to officers' hopes for action and promotion; the usual Democratic control of the federal government eased the passage of certain military bills. On the other hand, many regulars disliked the egalitarian flavor of Democratic political rhetoric, which they associated with opposition to West Point and the regular army, and felt more comfortable with the seemingly conservative Whigs. Divisions on some military issues tended to follow regional rather than party lines: the eastern seaboard usually supported coastal fortifications while western states were more likely to favor expansions of the infantry and mounted regiments and the appointment of citizens directly to the army. At any rate, military policy remained a secondary issue through the antebellum period, subordinated to debates over foreign policy, government expenditures, and other more controversial matters. Thus, officers principally interested in professional objectives saw little consistent basis for choice between the major parties.

By the 1850's, regular army officers had come to manifest consistent patterns of thought and behavior in their relationship with the political world. The most important influence had been the emergence of a distinct military profession after the War of 1812. Regulars developed a professional ideology which distinguished clearly between military and political life. While the army was dedicated to politically neutral national service, politicians and especially parties seemed divisive and self-serving. Although officers continued to engage in political activity, both ideology and the quest for career security channeled their energies almost exclusively toward professional goals: individual career advancement; branch objectives; and, to a limited extent, the general interest of the army. In the process, the more politically oriented regulars grew familiar with such common strategies of the second party system—and of interest group politics generally—as congressional lobbying, the manipulation of patronage, and the use of the press to gain public support.

The sectional crisis of the late 1850's and 1860's temporarily disrupted these patterns. As politics polarized North against South, military men found it increasingly difficult to concentrate on professional matters to the exclusion of the general political environment. Although the army contained both abolitionists and ardent secessionists, most officers were moderate in their views and genuinely alarmed by the sectional split. Not only did the crisis threaten the national unity so central to their professional ideology, but also the army itself and their personal careers within it. Predictably, they tended to blame the nation's troubles on political leaders, whom they accused alternately of self-serving opportunism and blind fanaticism. "Most [congressmen] are more interested in making sensation speeches for their immediate constituents than in working for the good of the country," wrote a Virginia-born officer late in 1860. "I have heretofore thought them to be harmless; but they have finally succeeded in bringing the country to the verge of dissolution. . . , "A Pennsylvanian attributed the crisis to "fanatics who regard the principles (?) of a political party as paramount to the interests of their country and the welfare of a few miserable negroes of more importance than the perpetuity of the American Union." With the emergence of the Republican party in the late 1850's, the bipartisanship of the officer corps temporarily declined, as regulars looked to the Democrats, whatever their flaws, as the best hope for national unity.[4]

Secession split the officer corps. Forced to choose between their budding professional identities and older sectional, state, and especially family loyalties, most southern-born officers and a few northerners with ties in the South resigned and joined the Confederacy. The Civil War and Reconstruction confronted military men with unprecedented problems—organizing and commanding mass armies of volunteers, "nation building" in the South—which further eroded the line separating the army from the civilian world. As the sectional crisis receded, however, prewar patterns of political behavior reemerged and continued into the twentieth century. With the rise of efficiency reports and other methods of evaluating "merit," outside political support for career advancement became less conspicuous, though it did not disappear. The growth of interservice rivalry added a strong incentive to internal service solidarity. By the mid-twentieth century, the vast size of the armed forces and their symbiotic relationship with the industrial economy made military politics more complicated than they had been in the days of the old army. Nevertheless, nonpartisan pressure group action in pursuit of professionally defined objectives continues to characterize the officer corps' relationship to the political world.

The nature of officers' political behavior suggests an additional explanation for the strength of the American tradition of civil control. On one hand, the conditions mentioned at the start of this essay—the historical suspicion of standing armies, the general stability of the political system, the small size and relatively broad recruitment base of the professional officer corps—placed constraints on regular army officers, discouraging them from forming an exclusive praetorian elite. On the other hand, military men enjoy rather free access to political channels. Rather than standing haughtily aloof or attempting as a group to dominate the political process, regulars entered politics at a number of levels and for a variety of often competing objectives. Thus, the "military interest" did not constitute a united front but an array of interests—individual, intraservice, service—which tended to diffuse the impact of officers' political action. In their political behavior, regulars were both military professionals and American citizens. Professional concerns shaped the goals they sought, but the methods which they adopted lay very much in the mainstream of political life. In other words, American political culture in the nineteenth century both coerced and co-opted army officers into accepting the principle of civil control.

NOTES

1. An anonymous person, very probably General James Wilkinson, listed the political affiliations of regular army officers on the Army Register of 1801, presumably for the use of the new Democratic Republican administration. He found 12 officers to be Republicans and 51 to be opposed in varying degrees to the administration. In addition, 70 were listed as politically apathetic or of undetermined affiliation. Only 12 were described as "professionally the soldier without any political creed." War Office Register, July 24, 1801, Thomas Jefferson Papers, Library of Congress. Noble E. Cunningham, Jr., has found little correlation between party affiliation and dismissal of officers when the army was reduced in 1802. Cunningham, *The Jeffersonian Republicans in Power: Party Operations, 1801–1809* (Chapel Hill, 1963), 66–68. On the Federalist leanings of officers in the early nineteenth century, see Joseph G. Swift, *The Memoirs of Gen. Joseph Gardner Swift, L.D.D., U.S.A., First Grad. of the U.S.M.A., West Point* (Worcester, Mass., 1890), 23, 42–43.

2. In 1846, for example, President James K. Polk decided to officer the newly created Regiment of Mounted Riflemen almost exclusively through citizens' appointments. He reported that the rush of candidates and their political sponsors was "beyond anything of this kind which I have witnessed since I have been President." While favoring western Democrats, Polk allowed Whig senators to choose the regimental major and "three or four" lieutenants. James K. Polk, *The Diary of James K. Polk During His Presidency, 1845–1849*, ed. Milo M. Quaife (4 vols., Chicago, 1910), I, 412–417.

3. Lt. Isaac I. Stevens, organizer of the engineers' lobby of the early 1850's, and several other officers supported Franklin Pierce in 1852, partly because they

had known him as a temporary general in the Mexican War. Stevens was rewarded with the governorship of Washington Territory.

4. Of 35 regular army officers whose party identifications I have positively determined for the period 1856–1860, 25 were Democrats, 7 were Republicans, and 3 supported the Constitutional Union ticket in 1860. The Democratic edge was almost certainly much greater. Undoubtedly, southern officers were virtually unanimous in opposition to the Republicans. While many northern-born officers did not openly express their party allegiances in their correspondence, their emphasis on moderation and compromise and their conservative views on slavery strongly imply "doughface" Democratic leanings. After the *fait accompli* of secession, of course, officers who remained with the Union generally rallied in support of the Lincoln administration and favored the use of force to suppress the rebellion.

12

A Crisis of Conscience

ETHAN ALLEN HITCHCOCK

The citizen who does not approve of a particular decision for war need not volunteer, and (if he is not conscripted) he may decide to speak out against the policy (as did Henry David Thoreau, Theodore Parker, and others during the Mexican War). The regular soldier has fewer options. As one pledged to carry out the orders of his government, he is in a real dilemma if he deems those orders to be unconscionable. Many professional soldiers have experienced a "crisis of conscience" at one time or another in their careers.* The longer one's tenure, the more difficult the resignation (unless one is about to retire). In the years prior to the Civil War, some career officers were upset by the federal government's treatment of Indian tribes and Mexico.†

Ethan Allen Hitchcock was the grandson of Ethan Allen, of Revolutionary War fame, and the son of a prominent judge. He attended West Point during the War of 1812 and continued to read widely throughout a successful military career. During the Civil War he helped Francis Lieber draft General Order No. 100, rules governing the conduct of Union troops in the field. He was a Unitarian, and a man with a conscience. His diary entries and correspondence, some of which are reprinted here, display his midcareer "crisis of conscience" and show how he resolved his dilemma.

* See Peter Karsten, Law, Soldiers, and Combat (Westport, Conn., 1978).
† See William B. Skelton, "Army Officer Attitudes toward Indians, 1830–1860," Pacific Northwest Quarterly 67 (July 1976): 113–124.

SOURCE: W. A. Croffut, ed., Fifty Years in Camp and Field (New York: Putnam, 1909), pp. 111, 120, 122, 123, 198, 202, 212, 214, 225, 228, 229, 237, 411–412.

JULY 8, 1836. "I hardly know what it is proper to do. When I left General Gaines all was quiet on the Sabine. I was temporarily attached to his staff and had his orders to return to him from Washington, but I thought the order was for my accommodation, and, believing active service in that quarter at an end, I did not hesitate to avail myself of Major Smith's offer to relieve him at New York. Now I hear that General Gaines has actually crossed the Sabine and gone with his army to Nacogdoches in Texas. I am puzzled what to do. I regard the whole of the proceedings in the Southwest as being wicked as far as the United States are concerned. Our people have provoked the war with Mexico and are prosecuting it not for 'liberty' but for land, and I feel averse to being an instrument for these purposes."

"June 22 [1840]. We are ordered to St. Louis (Jefferson Barracks) and then, after the sickly season, to Florida. I saw the beginning of the Florida campaigns in 1836, and may see the end of them unless they see the end of me. The government is in the wrong, and this is the chief cause of the persevering opposition of the Indians, who have nobly defended their country against our attempt to enforce a fraudulent treaty. The natives used every means to avoid a war, but were forced into it by the tyranny of our government."

"Nov. 1 [1840]. . . . The treaty of Payne's Landing was a fraud on the Indians: They never approved of it or signed it. They are right in defending their homes and we ought to let them alone. The country southward is poor for our purposes, but magnificent for the Indians—a fishing and hunting country without agricultural inducements. The climate is against us and is a paradise for them. The army has done all that it could. It has marched all over the upper part of Florida. It has burned all the towns and destroyed all the planted fields. Yet, though the Indians are broken up and scattered, they exist in large numbers, separated, but worse than ever. . . . The chief, Coocoochee, is in the vicinity. It is said that he hates the whites so bitterly that 'he never hears them mentioned without gnashing his teeth.'"

"Nov. 14 . . . General Armistead is entirely subdued and broken-spirited. His confidence in his success has been boundless and his letters to Washington have doubtless been written in that temper. I cannot help thinking it is partly his own fault. If he had freely offered the Indians an ample reward to emigrate, or the undisturbed possession of the country south of Tampa Bay, he might have secured peace. I have suggested his making the overture now, but he declines. Not only did he refuse to make the offer he was authorized to make, but at the very time when Halec [Tustenugga] was here in amicable talk he secretly sent a force into his rear, threatening his people at home!. . . . I confess to a very considerable disgust in this service. I remember the cause of the war, and that annoys me. I think of the folly and stupidity with which it has been conducted, particularly of the puerile character of the present commanding general, and I am quite out of patience."

"C[orpus] C[hristi], 28th Aug. [1845]. . . . Colonel Kinney's position here is an extraordinary one. While an object of suspicion to both Texans and Mexicans, he seems to be regarded as a man of power by both sides and capable of serving both sides. He seems to have no concealments, but frankly declares that the Texans have no right to go (or claim) to the Rio Grande."

"29th Aug. Received last evening . . . a letter from Captain Casey and a map of Texas from the Quarter-master-General's office, the latter being the one prepared by Lieutenant Emory; but it has *added to it* a distinct boundary mark to the Rio Grande. Our people ought to be damned for their impudent arrogance and domineering presumption! It is enough to make atheists of us all to see such wickedness in the world, whether punished or unpunished."

"1st Oct. . . . [T]his morning . . . as frequently of late, [General Zachary Taylor] introduced the subject of moving upon the Rio Grande. I discovered this time more clearly than ever that the General is instigated by ambition—or so it appears to me. He seems quite to have lost all respect for Mexican rights and willing to be an instrument of Mr. Polk for pushing our boundary as far west as possible. When I told him that, if he suggested a movement (which he told me he intended), Mr. Polk would seize upon it and throw the responsibility on him, he at once said he would take it, and added that if the President instructed him to use his discretion, he would ask no orders, but would go upon the Rio Grande as soon as he could get transportation. I think the General wants an additional brevet, and would strain a point to get it."

"2d Nov. Newspapers all seem to indicate that Mexico will make no movement, and the government is magnanimously bent on taking advantage of it to insist upon 'our claim' as far as the Rio Grande. I hold this to be monstrous and abominable. But now, I see, the United States of America, as a people, are undergoing changes in character, and the real status and principles for which our forefathers fought are fast being lost sight of. If I could by any decent means get a living in retirement, I would abandon a government which I think corrupted by both ambition and avarice to the last degree."

"25th March [1846]. . . . As to the right of this movement, I have said from the first that the United States are the aggressors. We have outraged the Mexican government and people by an arrogance and presumption that deserve to be punished. For ten years we have been encroaching on Mexico and insulting her. The Mexicans have in the whole of this time done but two wrong things: one was the destruction of the Constitution of 1824, which would have converted Texas into a mere department of Mexico; this gave Texas the right of revolution, and she established her independence as far west as the Nueces,—no further; the other was the cold-blooded and savage murder of Fannin's men at Goliad—an individual piece of barbarity which has deprived the Mexican army of all respect among civilized people. Beyond these, I know of nothing Mexico has done to deserve censure. Her people I consider a simple, well disposed, pastoral race, no way inclined to savage usages."

"26th March. . . . My heart is not in this business; I am against it from the bottom of my soul as a most unholy and unrighteous proceeding; but, as a military man, I am bound to execute orders."

"P.M. We are waiting the return, hourly expected, of General Taylor from Point Isabel. It is impossible to note the multitude of camp stories in circulation. One represents that Colonel Carabahal told Lieutenant Smith of my regiment (both Masons, 't is said) that General Canales has been following up our rear with several hundred men, ostensibly to annoy us but really to co-operate with us against Paredes's forces: that the moment the army of Paredes shall be defeated by us (an event which he anticipates) 7000 men will rise against the Paredes government and declare the independence of the northern provinces, and that these provinces are willing to concede the Rio Grande as the boundary between them and the United States. Another story is that General Ampudia, with 2500 men, was to arrive at Matamoras to-day, and it is supposed that he will cross the river and be ready to give us battle to-morrow, with such additional force as can be collected in and about Matamoras—in all about 4000 men. Colonel C. told Smith, also, by the way, that General Mehia, commandant of Matamoras, who issued the other day a furious proclamation, was actually in the interest of the contemplated revolt and issued the proclamation to deceive his government. Affairs seem to be very much involved, and we shall have either tolerably smooth sailing or a very boisterous time, for if Canales and Carabahal are playing a deep game against us, we shall have this whole country on us—several thousand men."

Sunday, May 24. . . . "I am necessarily losing, from a military point of view, all the honors of the field. I was hoping that no collision would take place. . . . My absence from my regiment at such a time as this is a species of death; yet the doctor says I must not think of going south in the hot weather, as he has another surgical operation to perform. . . . "

"10th Nov. I am very much disgusted with this war in all of its features. I am in the position of the preacher who read Strauss's criticism of the *Gospel History of Christ*. Shall he preach his new convictions? Shall he preach what his audience believe? Shall he temporize? Shall he resign? Here the preacher has an advantage over the soldier, for, while the latter may be ordered into an unjust and unnecessary war, he cannot at that time abandon his profession—at all events, not without making himself a martyr. In the present case, I not only think this Mexican war unnecessary and unjust are regards Mexico, but I also think it not only hostile to the principles of our own government—a government of the people, securing to them liberty—but I think it a step and a great step towards a dissolution of our Union. And I doubt not that a dissolution of the Union will bring on wars between the separated parts."

"New Orleans, Dec. 15, 1846. High time to use my notebook. Left St. Louis on 21st, and got here the 31st. With other officers have since waited for a steamer to take us to the Brazos at St. Iago in western Texas. Report is fully confirmed that General Scott will take the conduct of the war, and it is considered settled that the castle of San Juan at Vera Cruz is to be assailed. My regiment is with Taylor at Monterey."

"My feeling towards the war is no better than at first. I still feel that it was unnecessarily brought on by President Polk, and, notwithstanding his disclaimers, I believe he expressly aimed to get possession of California and New Mexico, which I see, by his message received here to-day, he considers accomplished. Now, however, as the war is going on, it must, as almost everybody supposes, be carried on by us aggressively, and in this I must be an instrument. I certainly do not feel properly for such a duty, particularly as I see that my health is almost sure to fail me—not only from the nature of the disease with which I left the country in April last, but because I know the remains of that disease are still with me. I feel very much like making a sacrifice of myself and drawing the curtain between me and this life. I am convinced that no contingency connected with this war can affect that in me which, by its nature, is immortal, and the end must be the same be my passage to it what it may. As a matter of taste and choice, I should prefer a more quiet career, and one in which I could pursue my favorite studies, of philosophy. But this is not to be."

February 27, 1847. Colonel Hitchcock to Theodore Parker: "I coincide with you in your views of this abominable war. Humble as I am, I wish not to fall a victim to this war without entering my protest against it as unjust on our part and needlessly and wickedly brought about. I am here, not from choice, but because, being in this army, it is my duty to obey the constituted authorities. As an individual I condemn, I abominate this war: as a member of the government I must go with it until our authorities are brought back to a sense of justice."

May 1854. . . . "[We] make a quarrel with Spain, really for the purpose of seizing the island of Cuba. I have not the smallest sympathy with the movement. I think that republican principles would be injured by the annexation of Cuba to the United States."

"I have been seriously thinking of resigning from the army. . . . I consider the slavery in our country an element guided by passion, rather than by reason, and its existence among us is shaking the whole fabric of our government. Abolitionists would abolish the institution of slavery as the real evil, whereas the real evil is the want of intelligence from which slavery itself took its rise. Men in a passion, as Plato says, are already slaves."

"As to leaving the army: I may do so if I choose at this time and no one notice me, for I am unknown except to a few friends. If I wait and a war with Spain be forced on us by the headlong ambition or false policy of the Cabinet at Washington it might be hazardous to retire, even though in principle opposed to the war, not only as unjustifiable towards Spain but as impolitic and injurious as respects ourselves. I do verily believe that such a war would be a downward instead of an onward step for our republican institutions, and might easily justify my own conscience in refusing to be an instrument in the unjust campaign."

"I might draw a line between my duty to remain in the army to repulse any attempt made from abroad upon us, and the questionable duty of going beyond our borders to inflict a direct wrong upon another people, with probable injury to us in the end. I had this point in consideration on entering into the Mexican War, the grievous wrong of which was perfectly apparent to me, but I did not resign. My principles were not then so clear to me as they have since become, and it would have been more difficult to act freely then than now—in case, I mean, of a war with Spain manifestly for the acquisition of Cuba. . . . "

"New York, May 31. I am in doubt as to leaving the army, wishing to do so, but uncertain as to the result. I do not wish to be moved by the slightest disposition to avoid service and responsibility. One point of weight with me is my personal opinions, after reading Plato, as I have, and finding myself more than ever a cosmopolite. The truth is, I am not sufficiently devoted to my profession, or even to my government, to make *service* a pleasure. I consider war an evil, whether necessary or not. It indicates a state of comparative barbarism in the nation engaged in it. I am also doubtful as to governments, and feel disposed to think that with my views I ought to live under what Plato, in the *Statesman*, speaks of as the 7th government. The question remains whether I can pass from a practical to a theoretical life, and whether, being a member of society, I am not bound to act with it. If I resign I wish to do so in such a frame of mind as to have no after regrets. This, in fact, is the principle which I wish to have guide me in whatever I do, for my eternity is here and now."

13

Elmer Ellsworth

Marcus Cunliffe

The formal, state-run militia systems were largely moribund by the 1820s, but the regulars were not left alone on the field by the amateurs. While compulsory militia forces had failed, voluntary organizations flourished. Throughout the land volunteer companies sprang up, imitative of British and European forces. Inspired by anomie, ancestor worship, or a purely militaristic impulse, these lovers of helmet, plume, epaulette, and lance gave to the new communities of antebellum America an air of Napoleonic militarism. In the following selection, Marcus Cunliffe, the preeminent student of this phenomenon, describes the career of one of the more interesting of these "volunteers."

BUT ANOTHER CASE is worth looking at: that of Elmer E. Ellsworth, "the first martyr of the Civil War," who is so perfect an epitome of the volunteer psychology as to be almost a caricature. Ellsworth was born in New York State in 1837, of poor and unschooled parents. Typically, he wished to enter West Point; but he was unable to prepare to the proper educational standard. He had to be satisfied with amateur soldiering, and in Stillwater, New York, organized a company with the extravagant yet typical enough name of the Black Plumed Riflemen. When his family moved out to Chicago, Ellsworth sought a suitable company, but being still wretchedly poor could not afford to join the ones he admired. Then he met a Frenchman who had served with a Zouave regiment in the Crimea, and who taught him the peculiar Zouave drill. Having made a few friends among the militia he was able to find part-time work as a drillmaster in Illinois and Wisconsin. He was a small man, but wiry and quick, and so much in earnest that

SOURCE: Marcus Cunliffe, *Soldiers and Civilians: The Martial Spirit in America, 1775–1865* (New York: Free Press, 1976), pp. 241–247.

he soon knew far more about soldiering than his acquaintances. He also fell in love and became engaged to Miss Carrie Spafford.

His prospective father-in-law, a banker, was understandably not impressed by Ellsworth's career thus far. The young man was penniless and obviously could not make a living by teaching drill to sundry volunteer companies. Mr. Spafford made Ellsworth promise to study law. For some while he rubbed along on the margin of starvation, picking up a few dollars as a law copyist, with only one suit to wear and no bed to sleep on. The contrast between his meager, obscure existence and that of Mr. Spafford or of his prosperous young contemporaries was nearly unbearable. He was sustained by a comprehensive fantasy of martial excellence. The lawbooks on his table would enable him to draft a complete system for a reformed militia. His wretched diet and his bare room, rightly understood, were signs not of civilian failure but of soldierly austerity. The easygoing young clubmen with whom he consorted were to be the instruments of his ambition.

His chance came in 1859 when these companions elected him captain of a moribund company, the National Guard Cadets of Chicago. No doubt Mr. Spafford disapproved, but Ellsworth saw the situation as a challenge. He reorganized the company as the United States Zouave Cadets: a grander name and one embodying a novel idea, since this was the first Zouave unit in the whole country. They adopted the picturesque Zouave costume—red cap, sash and loose trousers—and those who were hairy enough grew moustaches and goatee beards. He devised a strict code of conduct—no drinking while in uniform, or gambling or billiards or swearing. Unconsciously they anticipated the penitential national mood of two years later.

Ellsworth taught his men the complicated Zouave drill, a kind of rapid gymnastics, and thanks to his fanatical zeal they began to attract attention. A Zouave, said a Chicago newspaper, is a fellow "who can climb a greased pole feet first, carrying a barrel of pork in his teeth—that is a Zouave. A fellow who . . . can take a five-shooting revolver in each hand and knock the spots out of the ten of diamonds at 80 paces, turning somersaults all the time and firing every shot in the air—that is a Zouave." Someone else said that whenever Ellsworth's "dazzling company" appeared in Chicago, the street at once filled with spectators: "At double-quick and at the call of the bugle, these sixty or more young athletes would form figures of crosses, double crosses, squares, triangles, like the dissolving figures of the kaleidoscope." The bugle notes replaced shouted words of command, and as they perfected their drill Ellsworth was able even to dispense with the bugle. They adopted too a special Zouave yell, in which may perhaps be recognized the old ritual of the Boston Light Infantry, and the genesis of subsequent cheerleading techniques: "Each man doffed his cap, and jerked it up and down in front of him with a pumphandle movement, shouting in chorus at the same time, 'One! two! three! four! five! six!' and winding up with an Indian-like shout of 'Zouave! tig-e-r-r!'"

Two events now transformed Ellsworth's existence. First, he met Abraham Lincoln in Springfield, became a nominal student in the law firm of Lincoln & Herndon, and watched the friendly lawyer blossom in 1860 into a presidential candidate. Here was luck at last, after a run of family misfortunes. The candidate might well be elected, as Ellsworth was no doubt assured by a new friend, John G. Nicolay of the Springfield Grays, who was to become one of Lincoln's private secretaries. Then at last Ellsworth would have some backing, a bed to sleep in, a more sustaining menu than dry biscuits, and something tangible to present to the hardheaded Mr. Spafford, not to mention father-dominated Miss Carrie. He began to urge on Lincoln the idea of a Bureau of Militia, to be established within the Department of War. He submitted an elaborate draft of a militia bill to the Illinois legislature.

The second event was for the moment more astounding. In the summer of 1860 Colonel Ellsworth—he had by now acquired this militia title—took his company on a drill tour of twenty American cities. The tour did not cost very much; the railroads offered excursion rates and hospitality was provided by volunteer companies along the way.

The tour was a sensation. The Zouaves traveled from Adrian, Michigan, to Detroit, to Cleveland, to Niagara Falls, to Rochester, to Syracuse, to Utica, Troy, Albany. At each point they challenged the local companies to compete in drill. Their own display, which lasted from three to four hours, was so scintillating that the newspapers, and tens of thousands of spectators as well as more official judges, agreed that the Chicago Zouaves were unrivaled. At Albany the elegant Burgesses Corps was most impressed. Huge, excited crowds applauded them in New York City. Lincoln's other private secretary, John Hay, said that Ellsworth's portrait "sold like wildfire in every city of the land. Schoolgirls dreamed over the graceful wave of his curls, and shop-boys tried to reproduce the *Grand Seigneur* air of his attitude. Zouave corps, brilliant in crimson and gold, sprang up, phosphorescently, in his wake, making bright the track of his journey." A Zouave company, for example, immediately appeared in Albany, and others in places North and South that Ellsworth never visited. The Irish-born poet Fitz-James O'Brien (who died of a Civil War wound in 1862) wrote a poem on the Zouaves in seven stanzas, apparently after watching the Chicago company perform in New York. The poem pictures French Zouaves in an encounter with a "sallow Arab troop" whom they vanquish. The first stanza reads:

> To bugle-note and beat of drum
> They come—the gallant Zouaves come!
> With gleams of blue and glints of red;

With airy, light elastic tread;
With dashing, wild, insouciant air;
With figures sinewy, lithe, and spare;
With gait replete with fiery grace;
With cloudless eye and boyish face,
And agile play of feet and hands,
Swift as a Bedouin of the sands,
They come—they gay Zouaves!

The final stanza declares:

Your Zouave corps, O haughty France!
We looked on as a wild romance,
And many a voice was heard to scoff
At Algiers and at Malakoff;
Nor did we Yankees credit quite
Their evolutions in the fight.
But now we're very sure what they
Have done can here be done to-day,
When thus before our sight deploys
The gallant corps from Illinois,—
American Zouaves!

Ellsworth's team moved on to acclaim in Boston and Salem (where the Light Infantry was quickly transmuted into the Salem Zouaves). Their severest test came at West Point, where they showed their familiarity with the official army style as well as with Zouave methods. In Philadelphia and Baltimore they continued to dazzle large audiences with drilling, marching, firing and dexterous bayonet play. In Washington, President Buchanan declared that he had never seen such precision. They were "public benefactors"; if other Americans were equally prepared to defend their country, "we may defy a world in arms." The same scenes were enacted in Pittsburgh and in Cincinnati, where an orator assured them, "Our hearts have thrilled with pride . . . as we saw the chivalric Zouaves of Chicago fling down the glove before the corps d'élite of the imperial cities of the Atlantic seaboard and beheld them emerge . . . with no blot or blemish on their bright escutcheon." By way of St. Louis and Springfield they returned to Chicago and a heroes' welcome: fireworks, speeches, a torchlight procession.

Ellsworth had come a long distance from Mechanicville, N.Y. He had given a prodigious stimulus to the volunteer movement. Discarding the "stiff buckram strut of martial tradition," said Hay (perhaps borrowing from O'Brien), "he educated them to move with the loafing *insouciance* of the Indian, or the graceful ease of the panther." Though the style was French, Americans could persuade themselves that it had been theirs all along, especially when introduced to them from what a volunteer speaker from the imperial city of Philadelphia described as "the far West."

Ellsworth's patron was duly elected in November 1860 and he accompanied the President-elect to Washington as bodyguard. Some of his high and probably inordinate hopes were dashed. Denied the chief clerkship of the War Department, and the headship of his dreamed-of militia bureau, he settled for a regular second lieutenant's commission. Then came Fort Sumter, and Ellsworth's third great chance. Resigning his commission for grander vistas, he raised a Zouave regiment among the firemen of New York, bringing 1,100 of them in their brand-new baggy outfits to Washington.

He was soon ordered to advance across the Potomac into Virginia and occupy the town of Alexandria. He and his men enjoyed the assignment, which they carried out without trouble in the early morning of 23 May 1861. It was, so to speak, the early morning of the Civil War itself—a time before Bull Run, before the slaughter and the weariness had set in, a time for bravura.

Young Ellsworth, in his moment of easy triumph, saw a Confederate flag defiantly flying from the roof of a hotel known as the Marshall House. Accompanied by a few men and a delighted newspaper correspondent from the *New York Tribune*, he ran into the building and cut down the flag. As they were descending the stairs with their trophy, exuberance turned to horror. The proprietor of the hotel suddenly confronted them and fired a shotgun point-blank at Ellsworth, who dropped dead with a "heavy . . . headlong weight." His men avenged themselves on the proprietor. Too late: the adored little colonel was dead.

His body was brought to the White House for the funeral service. John Hay sent an eloquent tribute to the *Atlantic Monthly*. It was agreed that the Union's "first martyr" might have developed into a great soldier. For a little while, until more resounding disasters demanded attention, he was remembered and discussed. The public sighed for his bereaved parents and for his presumably heartbroken fiancée, Carrie Spafford of Illinois.

The Civil War Era

14

Kentucky Volunteers
during the Civil War

E. Merton Coulter

Secession led to Southern mobilization, the resignation of many Southern-born officers, the firing on Fort Sumter, and Lincoln's call to arms. Who volunteered, and why? "Patriots," with "patriotic" motives, would be one answer, but it might be one that begged the question. Elmer Ellsworth was a "patriot," but his "patriotism" may have been essentially militaristic, quite different from that of the devout Methodist who volunteered to end "the sin of slavery," or the young editor or mechanic who saw the future of American progress in the national Union. Needless to say, the same question may be asked of Southern volunteers. E. Merton Coulter discusses the phenomenon in Kentucky, a border state that sent thousands north and south in the early stages of the war, and offers an explanation for the interesting and distinctive patterns of volunteering that he found.

THE VIGOROUS SYMPATHIES and sentiments of the times not only cut across family and church, but they also tended to follow a geographical division clearly indicated in voting and volunteering. The fundamental basis for this was the character of the soil itself. The relation of geology to politics is plainly marked here. It was generally true that the hilly country and the thinner soil was the stronghold of Unionism, while the level land and the more fertile soil bred Southern sympathies. This form of sectionalism not

SOURCE: E. Merton Coulter, *The Civil War and Readjustment in Kentucky* (Chapel Hill: University of North Carolina Press, 1926), pp. 121–24, 442–44, 446. Copyright © 1926 The University of North Carolina Press. Reprinted by permission.
EDITOR'S NOTE: Most of the citations to the sources consulted by the author in this essay have been omitted from this volume for brevity and economy. The reader should consult the original source of the essay for the complete scholarly documentation.

only existed in a general way over the state but was reduced to the detailed topography of single counties. Todd County was an excellent exemplification of this fact. Here the hilly parts of the north were boldly arrayed in their strong Unionism against the Southern sympathizers of the rich farming lands of the south; and so intense were their feelings that they refused to let a Southern speaker be heard.[1]

The explanation of this condition is seen in the fact that richer soil meant greater wealth to the possessors with the consequent ownership of slaves, and most likely social ties with the Southern States, and probably economic connections.[2] In 1862, a newspaper correspondent observed, "The disloyal are the wealthy classes, but the Union men are the poor, or 'white trash' as they are called by the slaveholders."[3] The same general observation was made in 1865, after the war was over, that the "poor men mostly—the laboring part of the community—shouldered their guns and by their actions said: We can conquer the South; we can whip the rebellion; we can thrash the life out of this 'Southern chivalry'—this puffed-up slave aristocracy, and we will stand by the Union of our fathers and bear aloft the banner of our country."

A geographical and topographical survey of the state should, therefore, in a general way afford an index into the sympathies of the state as a whole. With the Mississippi alluvial deposits on the west the state gradually assumes a rising altitude until the hills and mountains of the east are reached. Sympathies correspond with this scheme, and the situation was so recognized by Garret Davis, who observed in 1861, "The sympathy for the South and the inclination to secession among our people is much stronger in the southwestern corner of the state than it is in any other part, and as you proceed towards the upper section of the Ohio River and our Virginia line it gradually becomes weaker, until it is almost wholly lost. . . . "

The most pronounced geological formation in Kentucky is the Blue Grass region, ten thousand square miles of the richest land in the state. The wealth and leadership of the state was centered here; and here strong Unionism found its most sterile ground. An eminent Kentucky geologist and historian, Nathaniel S. Shaler, declared that this region "sent the greater part of its men of the richer families into the Confederate army, while the Union troops, though from all parts of the State, came in greatest abundance from those who dwelt on thinner soil." Garret Davis bore out the same conclusion when he said in 1863, "I live in what is called the blue-grass country, and a more wealthy agricultural country does not exist anywhere. I regret to say that the heaviest defection to the Union cause is in the plains, the blue-grass region; and the greatest devotion and fidelity to it is in our mountains and hills.[4]

It should not be inferred that the Blue Grass region was a hot-bed of secession. It was not; but it had no heart for the war against the South and showed it abundantly. One of the surest proofs was its refusal to send its fighters to the Federal armies. The mountain men early in the war looked upon the Blue Grass region as interested only in making money out of the conflict and furnishing the officers. The *Louisville Journal* took occasion early to praise the valiant military exploits of the mountain men, but as for the Blue Grass, "we are sorry to say that the men of this rich and beautiful region of Kentucky have not rallied as they should rally to the defense of the Commonwealth." Many of the Blue Grass counties furnished more soldiers to the South than to the North; notable among them were Bourbon and Scott.[5] By November 1, 1863, the former, the fifth largest slaveholding county in the state, had furnished 700 to the South and 200 to the North; while the latter had furnished only 85 soldiers to the North, a little over one-half of one per cent of the military population. Fayette County, in the very heart of the Blue Grass region, with 1,558 men subject to military duty, had sent only 380 to the Union armies, and over a fourth of them were officers; whereas Pulaski County, lying to the southeast in the mountains, with a military population of 1,560, had sent more than 1,200 men into the Union armies. Twenty of the wealthiest counties, lying in the Blue Grass region and to the west, having 100,000 slaves, being almost half of all the slaves in the state, and valued at $25,500,000, had furnished only 6,000 soldiers to the Union out of a military population of 36,000. This was a little more than sixteen per cent. Forty other counties, with 27,000 slaves, valued at $8,500,000, had sent almost 18,000 soldiers to the Federal ranks out of a military population of 51,000, which amounted to over thirty-five per cent. The lines along which Unionism and Southern sympathies divided, geographically and economically, could be no better exemplified than in the statistics above.

NOTES

1. *Counties of Todd and Christian, Kentucky* (Chicago, 1884), 80, 108, 109. "Phases of life and modes of thought are thus induced which give to different communities and States characters as various as the diverse rocks that underlie them." W. H. Perrin, *History of Bourbon, Scott, Harrison, and Nicholas Counties, Kentucky* (Chicago, 1882), 21, 22.

2. It does not, of course, follow that all slaveholders were Southern sympathizers. There were numerous conspicuous exceptions; but the general statement is undoubtedly true.

3. *Cincinnati Commercial*, March 29, 1862. The non-slaveholders feared for their economic existence if the state should join the South. One small farmer said that if such a happening took place, "every small farmer that is not able to have a negro will be compelled to sell his farm to a slaveholder and be a servant." Otto A. Rothert, *History of Muhlenberg County* (Louisville, 1913), 250.

4. There was long standing enmity between the Blue Grass and the mountains, beginning before the war. See *Cincinnati Gazette*, Feb. 15, 1865.

5. Without compulsion the Blue Grass region would not have furnished nearly as many men to the Federal armies as it did.

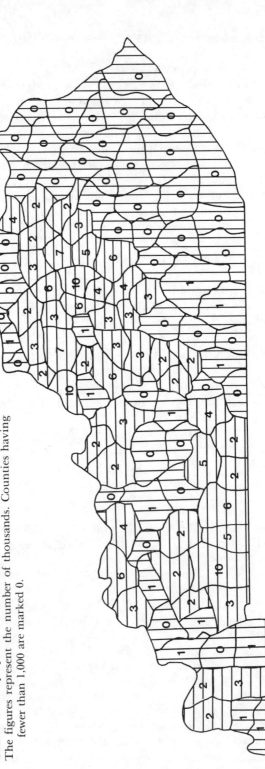

SLAVERY IN KENTUCKY IN 1860

Counties lined horizontally had 2,000 slaves and over.
Counties lined perpendicularly had fewer than 2,000 slaves.
The figures represent the number of thousands. Counties having
fewer than 1,000 are marked 0.

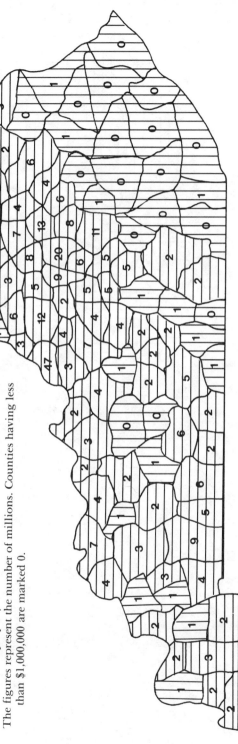

TAXABLE PROPERTY IN KENTUCKY IN 1855

Horizontal lines show counties having property valued at $2,000,000 and over.

Perpendicular lines show the counties having less than $2,000,000 in taxable property.

The figures represent the number of millions. Counties having less than $1,000,000 are marked 0.

KENTUCKY VOLUNTEERS TO THE FEDERAL ARMIES
UP TO NOVEMBER 1, 1863

Horizontal lines indicate counties furnishing 50% and more of men
    subject to military duty.
Perpendicular lines indicate counties furnishing 25% to 50% of men
    subject to military duty.
The other counties furnished less than 25% of men subject to
    military duty.
Information based on statistics in "Annual Report of the Adjutant
    General, January 1, 1964" in *Kentucky Documents*, 1863,
    pp. 15, 16.

15

Mark Twain and His Comrades Kill "an Enemy Soldier"

SAMUEL CLEMENS

The "fear of killing" noted by S. L. A. Marshall and his colleagues during World War II (see Reading #31) was almost certainly not unique to that conflict. This same reluctance to violate a major tenet of the Judao-Christian ethic may be seen in Samuel Clemens's autobiographical "private history of a campaign that failed." Clemens "Mark Twain" was a member of a small company of Confederate volunteers in 1861. He later recalled the first "action" he and his comrades saw after having been warned one evening of the approach of Union troops.

IT WAS LATE, and there was a deep woodsy stillness everywhere. There was a veiled moonlight, which was only just strong enough to enable us to mark the general shape of objects. Presently a muffled sound caught our ears, and we recognized it as the hoof-beats of a horse or horses. And right away a figure appeared in the forest path; it could have been made of smoke, its mass had so little sharpness of outline. It was a man on horseback, and it seemed to me that there were others behind him. I got hold of a gun in the dark, and pushed it through a crack between the logs, hardly knowing what I was doing, I was so dazed with fright. Somebody said "Fire!" I pulled the trigger. I seemed to see a hundred flashes and hear a hundred reports; then I saw the man fall down out of the saddle. My first feeling was of surprised gratification; my first impulse was an apprentice sportsman's impulse to run and pick up his game. Somebody said, hardly audibly, "Good—we've got him!—wait for the rest." But the rest did not come. We waited—listened—still no more came. There was not a

SOURCE: Mark Twain, "The Private History of a Campaign That Failed," in *The American Claimant and Other Stories* (New York, 1899), pp. 276–79.

sound, not the whisper of a leaf; just perfect stillness; an uncanny kind of stillness, which was all the more uncanny on account of the damp, earthy, late-night smells now rising and pervading it. Then, wondering, we crept stealthily out, and approached the man. When we got to him the moon revealed him distinctly. He was lying on his back, with his arms abroad; his mouth was open and his chest heaving with long gasps, and his white shirt-front was all splashed with blood. The thought shot through me that I was a murderer; that I had killed a man—a man who had never done me any harm. That was the coldest sensation that ever went through my marrow. I was down by him in a moment, helplessly stroking his forehead; and I would have given anything then—my own life freely—to make him again what he had been five minutes before. And all the boys seemed to be feeling in the same way; they hung over him, full of pitying interest, and tried all they could to help him, and said all sorts of regretful things. They had forgotten all about the enemy; they thought only of this one forlorn unit of the foe. Once my imagination persuaded me that the dying man gave me a reproachful look out of his shadowy eyes, and it seemed to me that I would rather he had stabbed me than done that. He muttered and mumbled like a dreamer in his sleep about his wife and his child; and I thought with a new despair, "This thing that I have done does not end with him; it falls upon *them* too, and they never did me any harm, any more than he."

In a little while the man was dead. He was killed in war; killed in fair and legitimate war; killed in battle, as you may say; and yet he was as sincerely mourned by the opposing force as if he had been their brother. The boys stood there a half-hour sorrowing over him, and recalling the details of the tragedy, and wondering who he might be, and if he were a spy, and saying that if it were to do over again they would not hurt him unless he attacked them first. It soon came out that mine was not the only shot fired; there were five others—a division of the guilt which was a great relief to me, since it in some degree lightened and diminished the burden I was carrying. There were six shots fired at once; but I was not in my right mind at the time, and my heated imagination had magnified my one shot into a volley.

The man was not in uniform, and was not armed. He was a stranger in the country; that was all we ever found out about him. The thought of him got to preying upon me every night; I could not get rid of it. I could not drive it away, the taking of that unoffending life seemed such a wanton thing. And it seemed an epitome of war; that all war must be just that—the killing of strangers against whom you feel no personal animosity; strangers whom, in other circumstances, you would help if you found them in trouble, and who would help you if you needed it. My campaign was spoiled. It seemed to me that I was not rightly equipped for this awful business; that war was intended for men, and I for a child's nurse. I resolved to retire from this avocation of sham soldiership while I could save some remnant of my self-respect. These morbid thoughts clung to me against reason; for at bottom I did not believe I had touched that man. The law of probabilities decreed me guiltless of his blood; for in all my small experience with guns I had never hit anything I had tried to hit, and I knew I had done my best to hit him. Yet there was no solace in the thought. Against a diseased imagination demonstration goes for nothing.

16

A Study of Morale
in Civil War Soldiers

Peter Maslowski

One of the more elaborate studies of the military that social and behavioral scientists have undertaken dealt with American GIs during World War II (known as the Stouffer study). One of its more intriguing findings concerned the level of commitments to the war effort of those GIs. In this essay Peter Maslowski uses an interesting technique to determine how Civil War soldiers would have answered some of the questions raised by the Stouffer study. What do Maslowski's findings say about differences between the North and South? About change and continuity in American character?

Tolstoy wrote in *War and Peace*: "In warfare the force of armies is the product of the mass multiplied by something else, an unknown x . . . x is the spirit of the army, the greater or less desire to fight and face dangers on the part of all the men composing the army, which is quite apart from the question whether they are fighting under leaders of genius or not, with cudgels or with guns that fire thirty times a minute."

This intangible entity, this x, is the heart of a military machine. Just as a doctor can understand a great deal about a patient by examining his heart, so too can the historian tell a great deal about an army by inves-

Source: Peter Maslowski, "A Study of Morale in Civil War Soldiers," *Military Affairs*, 1970, pp. 122–125. Copyright 1970 by the American Military Institute. Reprinted by permission. No additional copies may be made without the express permission of the author and of the editor of *Military Affairs*.
Editor's note: Most of the citations to the sources consulted by the author in this essay have been omitted from this volume for brevity and economy. The reader should consult the original source of the essay for the complete scholarly documentation.

tigating this quantity. The problem is to establish criteria whereby x may be measured with a high degree of certainty. Samuel A. Stouffer, et al., in the first two volumes of their monumental work, *The American Soldier, Studies in Social Psychology in World War II*, formulated such criteria by demonstrating several ways in which high—or low—morale was manifested in the attitudes of World War II American soldiers.

The authors of *The American Soldier* hinted that their guidelines might be applied profitably to soldiers in other wars. Indeed, this essay was in part inspired by their observation: "If by some miracle a cache should be found of manuscript material telling of the attitudes toward combat of a representative sample of, say, a hundred men in Stonewall Jackson's army, the discovery would be of interest to Civil War historians." Actually, no "miracle" is necessary to provide an abundance of relevant source material since diaries, letters, and memoirs of Civil War soldiers abound in almost every library. Much of this material has been used before. Bell I. Wiley, for example, relied on it almost exclusively when doing his studies of the common soldier. His results were generally "literary" and qualitative; by applying Stouffer's criteria to similar sources the conclusions which emerge should be more quantitative, or, if you will, "scientific."

CLASSIFICATIONS AND METHODOLOGY

Although the criteria which will be used in judging the spirit and morale of Civil War soldiers were suggested by similar topics discussed in *The American Soldier*, there must be an essential difference in methodologies. Stouffer *created* his data by using a questionnaire—almost a public opinion poll—approach, supplemented by interviews and observations. This system is direct and readily adaptable to statistical analysis. On the other hand, the data used in this study already *had been created*, and so the method must be much more indirect and less adaptable to concise statistical analysis. For example, Stouffer asked directly on a questionnaire, "In general, how well do you think the Army is run?" and then followed this with a list of explicit responses such as, "It is run very well; It is run pretty well; It is not run very well; It is run very poorly; Undecided." In the study presented here it was assumed hypothetically that a question like this was asked, and then an answer was sought. Of course, very few such precise remarks as "I think the army is run very well" were found. The conclusions of this paper, accordingly, must be more ambiguous and flexible than those of *The American Soldier*. If Stouffer was prudent in warning his readers to place emphasis on trends and patterns as a whole rather than on specific percentages, the warning seems to be doubly prudent here.

In this treatise several attitude and morale classifications gleaned from the pages of *The American Soldier* were applied to the letters and/or diaries of 50 men who fought in the Civil War. Twenty-five of these men were from the South, and 25 from the North. These will be known henceforth as Group I (Southerners) and Group II (Northerners).[1]

The number of variables involved in a random selection of 50 Civil War soldiers who wrote of their experiences is great. For this study only two variables were held constant. First, each man enlisted as a private and attained no permanent rank higher than Captain, and very few reached this rank. Essentially, then, all 50 could be termed "common soldiers." Secondly, all the men were from rural environments; hence, they probably had some similarities in background and upbringing. No attempt has been made to control such factors as age, marital status, education, whether a man fought in the eastern or western theater, or the length of time spent in the service.

ORIENTATION AND COMMITMENT

One of Stouffer's most interesting attitude classifications dealt with orientation toward and personal commitment to the War. He concluded that World War II soldiers did *not* view the war in terms of ideological principles or causes. Their commitment was a defensive one in that they merely accepted the War as a necessary evil imposed on them by an aggressor nation.

What about Civil War soldiers? Why did they march off to fight and then continue to endure the slaughter? What thoughts sustained them as they slept in the mud, ate hardtack, and marched out periodically to kill and be killed? When Civil War troops stole a few moments to jot down a line or two in their diaries did they discuss the meaning of the war or did they talk about such "base" things as payday and the excitement they encountered on a battlefield?

References to three different criteria, or sub-headings, were regarded as indicative of high ideological commitment. These three, with examples of each, are as follows:

1) Love for one's country: "I love peace but I love my country more." "But always with me the first thing was duty to my country and comfort next."

2) Belief in a better world to come in the future if victory was achieved: " . . . but there is a better time coming, perhaps, for me with others. Perhaps not for me, but for others. Someone will see better times at least."

3) Belief that there were certain basic issues at stake in the War and it was worthwhile fighting for the benefits which would accrue from a favorable settlement of these issues. Among the issues were slavery ("In the heat of battle, the powder and sweat gave us soon the complexion of the black man for whose freedom we were fighting."); the tariff ("The tariff was also a question which divided the sections."); freedom and liberty ("But

I am engaged in the glorious cause of liberty and justice, fighting for the rights of man—fighting for all that we of the South hold dear."); and state rights ("We only fought for our State rights, they for the Union and power. The South fell battling under the banner of State rights, but yet grand and glorious even in death."). The very few references to these supposedly vital issues were startling. Less than one-sixth of the men, for instance, made any comment relating to slavery.

References to four other criteria were assumed to be illustrative of a lack of ideological orientation and commitment. These are:

1) Fighting to gain glory and to "save face" both among fellow soldiers and at home: "Well we have earned our reputation, and although it has cost us something and may cost us some of our best men yet, still I think it will pay to keep it up, cost what it will." "I glory in the honor and pride of a solgers [sic] life."

2) Fighting for adventure and excitement. There were no direct comments to the effect that a man enlisted for the sheer excitement and adventure he expected to encounter in the War. Yet, in reading the diaries and letters one gets the definite impression that some of the soldiers were preoccupied with adventure-seeking, while for others an exciting event at least served to relieve the drudgery of army life and thereby make it more endurable. There is a great deal of indirect evidence bearing on this criterion. When men were enlisting they sometimes commented on the intense excitement which pervaded the atmosphere. Once in the service, raids and battles, foraging, rumors, and other excitement-inducing features of army life were subjects of continual comment. During periods of inactivity there were numerous complaints about the monotony of army life. The quantity of this indirect evidence is so large that this factor has to be accorded considerable weight in any analysis.

Here are several sample statements: "Nothing but positive orders would have induced me to cease firing. I never experienced such excitement and rapture." "During our march, on the previous night, I suggested to young Calmes, a member of the company, that we ride ahead of the advance guard and look for an adventure." "We are delighted to hear for a change and any new adventure will be welcome."

3) Financial and economic considerations: "The great excitement in the army is now about pay. Half of the men in our Regiment are men of families and most of them depend on their wages to support their families." "One important feature in the life of a soldier was the matter of his pay."

4) Fighting just to get the War over with in order to return home to loved ones and "the old way of life:" "Time drags lazily on but each day makes our term of service one less day." "We are already to go to the last; we want to wind the thing up and get home if we live ever to go back."

For each of the 50 men considered, a separate page contained a list of these seven criteria. Each time a statement was found which was applicable to one of these criteria a check was made opposite its listing on the page.

Hence it was a simple matter of addition to determine each soldier's ideological outlook.

Neither the Southerners (Group I) nor the Northerners (Group II) displayed high ideological orientation and commitment. In Group I only 12 per cent of the men made more statements representative of high ideological commitment than low ideological commitment, while 64 per cent had more references indicative of low ideological orientation than they did of high ideological orientation. The remaining 24 percent were even in their comments one way or the other. In Group II the corresponding percentages are 8, 88 and 4. The conclusion is that, like Stouffer's World War II soldiers, the Civil War soldiers studied here were notoriously deficient in ideological orientation. And on each of the specific criteria Northerners and Southerners were very much alike in their orientation. A quick glance at several of the separate sub-headings will illustrate this.

In Group I, 52 per cent of the men made between one and five statements which were illustrative of "love for one's country," four per cent made six or more comments relating to it, and 44 per cent made no mention of anything that could be construed as love for one's country. For Group II the corresponding percentages are 64, 12, and 24. In regard to the meaning and worthwhileness of the War, 64 per cent of the men in Group I made between one and five relevant comments, 8 per cent made six or more, and 28 per cent made no applicable statements. The corresponding percentages for Group II are 52, 4, and 44. Finally, the comments indicative of excitement and adventure as a factor in orientation broke down this way: 52 per cent of the writings in Group I contained between one and five applicable references, 8 per cent six or more, and 40 per cent contained no apt comments. The corresponding percentages for Group II are 48, 16, and 36. Thus, for all three of these criteria the distinct trend for both Groups is this: the majority (in one instance, only 48 per cent) of the writings included between one and five pertinent statements, a large number made no applicable references, and a much smaller number contained six or more germane comments.

The data for the other sub-headings of this classification showed, with but a few minor deviations, the same high degree of similarity between Northerners and Southerners.

The fact that the men of these two Groups were so much like the troops Stouffer studied, and that they were so similar to one another, raised an interesting question in regard to Wiley's conclusion about the orientation of Civil War soldiers. In the concluding chapter of *The Life of Billy Yank*, Wiley states that "Soldiers attitudes as revealed in their letters and diaries leave the impression that Billy Yank was not so deeply concerned with the War as Johnny Reb. Financial considerations seem to have figured more conspicuously in his participation in the conflict, and he appears to have felt less of personal commitment and responsibility." The data found in this study do not support this general statement. As far as orientation and commitment go, *neither* side possessed a high ideological orientation or awareness; and the *patterns and tendencies* in all of the individual subheadings in the orientation classification were identical, with, as mentioned, only minor deviations. Further, if, as Wiley writes, "Billy Yank was fighting to subdue a revolt against national authority and to free the slaves; Johnny Reb was fighting to establish an independent government, but he also was fighting for a peculiar way of life, for the defense of his home, and as it often seemed to him, for life itself," Billy Yank and Johnny Reb did not seem to be particularly cognizant of this themselves. Or, if they were conscious of it, they did not commit their awareness to paper.

COMBAT

A second morale classification to which Stouffer devoted considerable time and energy was attitude toward combat. Under this classification the present study found pertinent information on two criteria. One of these was a man's confidence in his physical and mental stamina, especially during combat. Essentially, this boiled down to how many times a soldier mentioned that he was or was not tired or fatigued by carrying out his military duties. It is assumed that the less a soldier complained the better his morale, and vice versa. Examples were numerous: "In fact we have so much skirmishing and working this week that I am almost broken down." "I have come to the conclusion that I can march as far as most any man in the regiment." "I was on Guard duty, had no rest for four days and nights, am almost exhausted for want of rest."

Only 16 per cent of the Southerners (Group I) had confidence in their stamina, 60 per cent did not, and 24 per cent either made no pertinent statements or else an equal number of positive and negative references on the subject. For the Northerners (Group II) the percentages are 28, 48, and 24. Once again there is very little difference between the soldiers, Reb or Yank: In both Groups most of the soldiers complained of being tired and exhausted more than they commented to the contrary, though Rebs were slightly more prone to carp than their Northern counterparts.

The second sub-heading was whether or not a soldier was willing and eager for combat. Willingness, naturally, would be an indication of high morale; lack of eagerness an indication of lower morale. Most of the relevant statements concerning this matter were direct and to the point one way or the other: "In a few days I was 'spoiling for a fight,' and so were the rest." "I am anxious for the fight to come off." "I hope I will not have to go into another fight as long as I live, for the more I go into the more I dread them."

In Group I, 56 per cent showed a willingness for combat, 20 per cent did not, and 24 per cent either had no apt references or else an equal number of positive and negative responses on the subject. For Group II the corresponding percentages are 44, 20, and 36. In both groups, then, there was a definite willingness to fight, but with a very slight edge in eagerness going to the Rebs.

In a survey applied to 6,280 soldiers, which was designed to determine whether or not a soldier was willing for combat, Stouffer asked two questions. The first was, "Which of the following best tells you the way you feel about getting into an actual combat zone?" This was followed by seven possible gradated responses. 2,970 of the men showed a willingness for combat, 2,624 did not, and 686 had no opinion or answer. The second question was, "Which of the following best describes your own feeling about getting into combat against the Germans?" This was followed by five gradated responses. 4,202 of the men expressed a willingness to fight, 1,763 did not, and 135 had no answer. Thus, in both World War II soldiers and Civil War troops—both Reb and Yank—there was a decided overall willingness for combat.

Wiley may well be overstating the case when he writes that "Moreover, the men who wore the gray fought with more dash, *elan* and enthusiasm . . . Their penchant for recounting the details of combat in home letters suggests that they derived a greater thrill from fighting." True, the data presented here do indicate that Southerners were slightly more willing to "butt heads" with the enemy than Northerners, but the difference is not as dramatic as Wiley's statement suggests.

MILITARY LEADERSHIP

Despite Tolstoy's intimation that x is not necessarily related to leadership, Stouffer found that attitudes toward military leadership were quite significant in the morale of World War II combatants. Three sub-headings in this classification proved fruitful when the writings of Civil War soldiers were applied to them.

The first criterion questioned whether or not a soldier had confidence in his officers. The assumption is that such confidence would be illustrative of high morale. Pertinent statements took two different forms. "Some would be very uneasy about our situation if Gen. [sic] Lee was not in Command." "Suffice it that the army is in good spirits and have confidence in 'Rosy.' " " . . . we are out of Banks' Dep't [sic]. I hope we may never go near it again." Others were far more general in scope: "Had great confidence in our officers." "This state of things has been brought about by the laziness and incompetency of our company officers."

In presenting the data for this sub-heading, repetition cannot be avoided: Southerners and Northerners were remarkably similar. In Group I, 40 per cent of the men thought their officers were competent, 24 per cent did not, and 36 per cent had no comments or an equal number of references one way or the other. For Group II the corresponding percentages are 52, 20, and 28. If anything, there is a slight tendency for Northerners to fare better under this criterion.

The second sub-heading under military leadership dealt with the question of whether or not a soldier's officers "served by example." What this boiled down to in an overwhelming majority of the cases was: Did the officers take their place in the front ranks or were they cowards? It is easy to imagine the depressing effect a cowardly officer could have on the spirit of a common soldier. "When we 'went in' on the above mentioned position old Capt. [sic] Reddish took his place in the ranks and fought like a common soldier." "At this moment, when we had the advantage of position, the cowardice of our advance detachment commander, Lieut. Col. [sic] Park, caused him to order a retreat." "The officers, of course, fared no better than the men—all took the same medicine."

In Group I, 80 per cent and in Group II, 60 per cent of the soldiers studied were satisfied with the personal example displayed by their officers. No one in Group I thought badly of the example set by his officers, and 20 per cent either had no comments or else an equal number of positive and negative responses. In Group II eight per cent were dissatisfied and 32 per cent made no references or else an equal number of pro and con responses. Although both Groups exhibit the same trend in regard to this criterion, it does seem that Group II was not as opinionated about the example set by its officers as was Group I.

The final sub-heading in this classification was designed to discover whether or not a soldier believed that his officers took a personal interest in, and stood up for him. Logically, an officer who took such an interest in his men could be expected to induce higher spirits in them than could a more egocentric officer. This criterion included a whole medley of responses because, basically, any pro or con statement about an officer's behavior which was not applicable to one of the other two sub-headings was included here. "He was not only our beloved Captain, but was comrade, friend, yea, brother and father to us all." "But the officers got busy and went up town and bought, with their own money, something for us to eat." "It seems to us that it is the delight of some officers to see the poor soldier suffer."

The trend that emerged here is identical to that of the previous sub-heading. In Group I, 56 per cent of the men thought their officers took a personal interest in them, only 4 per cent did not, and 40 per cent made no pertinent comments or else an equal number of statements one way or the other. In Group II the corresponding percentages are 36, 24, and 40. Both Groups contained more men who thought their officers took pretty good care of their needs and desires than thought the opposite; yet, again, the men of Group II did not regard their officers as favorably as the men of Group I.

The evidence put forth in these last two sub-headings indicates that Southerners did indeed think more highly of their officers during the War than did Northerners. However, the subheading dealing with the question of general competence of officers presents a real enigma because on this issue Northerners were more favorably disposed toward their officers than were Southerners. Thus, if the emphasis is placed on the absolute percentages in each of these three subheadings there appears to be a contradiction in the evidence. If, however, the emphasis is focused on the general *trends or patterns* in these sub-headings—both individually and collectively—the supposed contradiction disappears and the strong resemblance between the men in the blue and the gray in their awareness of their officers is highlighted.

Not only were Rebs and Yanks similar to each other in regard to leadership, but they also were very much like Stouffer's World War II soldiers on this score. For example, a large majority of Stouffer's soldiers were satisfied with the example set by their officers. In one study which examined attitudes toward officers according to length of time in combat, 60 per cent or more of the men in five different groups of privates, pfcs, and noncoms believed their officers were "willing to go through anything they asked their men to go through." Another survey showed that 70 per cent of the front line troops felt that all or most of their officers were willing to set good examples. In this same study 61 per cent of the front line troops thought all or most of their officers took a personal interest in them. And finally, a study of six companies with pre-determined high morale showed that in all six of them two-thirds or more of the men believed their officers were interested in the men, understood their needs, and were helpful to them.

CONCLUSION

In their attitudes toward leadership and combat and in their orientation and commitment to the War in which they fought, Civil War and World War II soldiers were amazingly similar. A number of other characteristics and attitudes affecting morale were also considered in the original study. These were: 1) discipline; 2) promotions; 3) personal esprit, that is, the soldier's expressed sense of well-being; 4) satisfaction with army job and status; 5) approval or criticism of the army. Like those three classifications reviewed in some detail here, each of these classifications was divided into several criteria or subheadings, all of which were suggested by analogous headings in *The American Soldier*. In all but one instance a high degree of correlation between the soldiers of both Wars was maintained. The contiguity in attitudes of American soldiers separated by a span of 80 years is indeed striking.

The one exception to this contiguity concerned promotions. Stouffer found that World War II troops did not think very highly of the system of promotions—his data showed an unmistakable trend toward an unfavorable view of the promotions policy. On the other hand, the data gathered in this study showed that less than 10 per cent of either Group I or Group II was dissatisfied with the promotions system, while about 50 per cent of each Group was satisfied with the system.[2] This discrepancy is probably related to differences in military organization between 1860 and 1940. Several differences, for example, are readily apparent. One is that in a good many instances (at least early in the War) Civil War soldiers were able to elect their own officers. World War II troops were not given the privilege of participating in the election of their own officers. A second is that Civil War soldiers never had to endure ROTC and Officer Candidate School officers. These officers, who were often regarded as "outsiders," came in for more than their share of scorn and contempt. A third difference is that army organization during World War II not only permitted, but also seemed to encourage a wide official and social gap between commissioned and enlisted personnel. This gap seemed considerably narrower in Civil War armies.

This data on promotions during the Civil War is not in harmony with Bell Wiley's statement, "Still another indication of the Northern soldier's more practical bent was his greater concern about rising in the military hierarchy; certainly his letters and diaries are more replete with comment about promotions." Rebs and Yanks were approximately *equal* in their concern with advancement. If anything, Rebs were slightly more vocal on the subject than Yanks.

Wiley also concluded that "Johnny Rebs seem to have taken more readily to soldiering from their prior mode of life . . . " This conclusion does not seem warranted by the data collected in this study which showed, for instance, that Southerners were consistently in worse mental condition and consistently enjoyed army life less than Northerners.[3] Wiley's assertions that a Rebel's "cheerfulness outweighed his dejection" and that "Adaptability and good nature, in fact, were among his most characteristic qualities" may need substantial revision.

On a number of other issues our data concurred fully with Wiley's findings. In fact, his final verdict that, "In sum, it may be stated that the similarities of Billy Yank and Johnny Reb far outweighed their differences" generally seems to be true; and if Southerners and Northerners by and large resembled each other, it is also true that they closely resembled World War II soldiers on almost all of the attitudes under consideration.

This general conformity, however, should not obscure the fact that this study has raised some interesting and provocative questions in regard to Wiley's conclusions. These center around the issues of personal orientation and commitment, promotions, and mental well-being, but branch out to include such topics as military leadership and willingness for combat where expected differences were not so large and clear-cut as to make them conclusive. Were Civil War soldiers personally aware of the stakes involved in the conflict? Were they at all motivated by high ideological considerations? Were Yanks or Rebs more concerned with promotions? Did Southerners really enjoy fighting more than Yanks? How great was the difference in Southern and Northern attitudes toward their officers? Questions like these still need more definitive answers before we can fully understand the Civil War soldier in the ranks. The method employed here, if projected on a larger and more complex scale, might well provide some of the answers. Certainly the strong correlation between the results set forth here and those obtained by Stouffer suggest this may be the right path to follow.

NOTES

1. In the original study two additional Groups were considered. Group III consisted of twenty-five memoirs or reminiscences written by Southerners; Group IV consisted of twenty-five memoirs or reminiscences written by Northerners. In no instance did the examination of these two Groups result in data contradictory to that derived from Groups I and II. In essence, then, these observations were derived initially from a sample group of 100, not 50, men.

2. The remaining percentage in each Group either had no comments about promotions or else had an equal number of positive and negative references.

3. In Group I, 16 per cent indicated they were in good mental condition, 56 per cent in bad mental condition, and 28 per cent had no relevant comments or an equal number of positive and negative responses. For Group II, on the other hand, these percentages were 32, 40, and 28. Again, in Group I only 40 per cent seemed to enjoy army life, 36 per cent did not, and 24 per cent had no comments or an equal number of pro and con responses. The corresponding percentages in Group II were 88, 8, and 4.

17

Causes of Confederate Desertion

ELLA LONN

It has been said that a Confederate general, riding by a column of men in 1864, spotted a battle-weary sergeant who had served with him earlier in the war. "How are you getting on?" the general asked. "Oh, I'm all right, general, I guess," the sergeant replied. "I'm all right, I guess, but God damn my soul if I ever love another country!" Desertions on both sides were high during the early years of the American Revolution; they were high on both sides during the Civil War. As the war dragged on, the tired, the frightened, and the discouraged on both sides of the lines sometimes walked away from their units. Absenteeism ran from one in every six men (in good times) to one in two (when things were grim). The Union forces lost as great a percentage of their troops as the Confederacy, but Confederate losses tended to count for more, because they (more so than the Union) tended to lose more men as time passed. Entire units were melting away by the winter of 1864–1865. Ella Lonn's study of desertion during the Civil War is the classic work on the subject.* In this excerpt she offers the causes of Confederate desertions.

* See also Richard Bardolph, "Inconstant Rebels: Desertion of North Carolina Troops in the Civil War," *North Carolina Historical Review*, 41 (1964): 163–89.

THE CAUSES OF DESERTION from the Confederate armies are so numerous and complex that to catalogue all in detail would be to tell a considerable part of the story of the Civil War. And yet the enumeration and weighing of these elements of dissatisfaction is the understanding, in no small mea-

SOURCE: Ella Lonn, *Desertion During the Civil War* (New York: Century Co., 1928). pp. 3–7, 10–19.
EDITOR'S NOTE: Most of the citations to the sources consulted by the author in this essay have been omitted from this volume for brevity and economy. The reader should consult the original source of the essay for the complete scholarly documentation.

sure, of the ultimate failure of the effort at disunion. Hence, a brief consideration of the reasons for the manifestation of this great evil is unavoidable.

First, and probably foremost, in the minds of the Confederate leaders as an explanation of dissatisfaction stood the character of many of the privates. Some, untutored and narrow-minded, dragged from the rocky mountains of the Carolinas, Georgia, and Alabama, from the pine hills and lowlands of Louisiana, and from the swamps of Florida and Mississippi, were ignorant of the real issues at stake and were but little identified with the struggle. . . . The illiterate backwoodsman, variously termed "cracker," "mossback," "kasion," "bushwhacker," or "hillbilly," according to the section in which he was located, almost cut off from the mass of his fellow-men, was little interested in the economic aspect of the war, as he could see nothing in it for himself. When dragged from his farm plot into the Southern army, he often proved a passive Union sympathizer, as he was ready to fall back into his neutrality as deserter at the first opportunity. The controlling motive with these men was frequently not love for the Union, but a determination to avoid military service. They cared little for the approbation or condemnation of their fellows, especially distant officials at Richmond. In fact, they showed a conspicuous lack of that quality which we applaud as patriotism, while a few proved, as is true in every army, downright cowards. The usual stories of men maiming themselves to avoid service are to be found.

Still, the fact must be recognized that some of these same ignorant mountaineers were distinctly out of sympathy with the cause of slavery as the foundation stone on which was built the prestige of their proud neighbors of the lowlands, while scattered through the States were a small number, to state the fact conservatively, who cherished a real love for the old Union. The records of conscripts who promptly deserted to the Northern armies are too numerous to be disregarded as evidence. Making all due allowance for insincerity in so explaining their defection, indubitably some spoke the truth when they declared that they did not like the cause in which they were fighting and wished to live once more under the Stars and Stripes. When a deserter raised a company in border territory to enter the service of the Union, his genuineness can scarcely be questioned.

The net of the conscript service, moreover, dragged in men of Northern birth and also foreigners, particularly Germans and Irishmen, who knew little and cared less for the burning American question of State rights. Northern-born men were in most cases holders of considerable property or large traders for their communities. Included in this group were merchants, lumbermen, real estate dealers, bankers, doctors, and even a few planters. Many had gone into the far South recently, after 1850, so that their ties were still mainly with the North and their traditions antislavery. The reports of the Northern officers are full of instances of citizens of Northern States who had settled in the South and who had been impressed into Southern regiments. These reports are sufficiently confirmed by Confederate officers when they tersely remark, "He is a Yankee, gone to his brethren," or when they allude to him openly as a Northern or Union man. Irishmen are encountered frequently who deserted from the rebels and "cheerfully took the oath of allegiance," while the case of a Scotsman was noted who forsook his duties with the commissary department to join the North. . . .

Among the recruits from Kentucky especially were a goodly number bankrupt in fortune and reputation who eagerly embraced the Southern cause, as any change offered hope of possible advantage. Evil propensities brought soldiers into trouble, whereupon, faced with the probability of execution, they fled to the foe. Men, anxious to raise companies or battalions, sought recruits in all quarters and hence sometimes enlisted genuine ruffians. Eggleston tells of some interesting characters who had found release from durance in a Richmond jail by enlistment. One, a pirate and deserter from the British navy, was the most interesting of the group, but helps us to understand the statement that "except as regarded turbulence and utter unmanageability" they proved excellent soldiers. Such men would leave General Morgan's service as readily as they had entered.

Almost from the beginning many of the volunteers were mere boys, fourteen to eighteen years of age, foolish, deluded youths, of whom the Confederates had no right to expect the stamina and courage of mature men. The Conscript Law after April 16, 1862, took in, with some exceptions, every male from eighteen to thirty-five years of age; the second Conscript Act of September 27 following added those between thirty-five and forty-five years; and after February 17, 1864, the draft reached lads just turned seventeen and men up to fifty, while others were liable to service in the home guard up to sixty. Youths of seventeen at military schools were allowed to remain until they had attained the ripe age of eighteen on condition of being regularly drilled and of being subject to be called to the field if necessary. Every one is familiar with the part played by the youths from the Virginia Military Academy at the Battle of New Market, May 15, 1864.

Obviously, men conscripted for service, or hired as substitutes, would be potential material for desertion, as their hearts were not devoted to a cause for which they had failed to volunteer. And conscription became necessary for the Confederacy in the second year of the war. Naturally, a few good soldiers entered the army as conscripts, but for the most part the men whose bodies were dragged in by force had, as Eggleston says, no spirit to bring with them, for they had already learned to brave the contumely of their neighbors for confessed cowardice. But it must not be thought that conscripts had any monopoly of desertion. In northeastern Georgia it was held in 1862 that one half of the men had deserted though the conscript law had not yet been enforced.

Substitutes enjoyed a reputation not much better among the soldiery.

One officer reports that four fifths of his deserters were substitutes, who deserted within twenty-four hours of being received at his headquarters; and in 1863, because of the high average of desertion in this class of recruits, the War Department ordered substitutes accepted only if their moral, physical, and soldierly qualifications clearly equaled those of the soldier excused, and then only on the authority of the commanding general. And in the Confederate Senate it was openly urged in 1863 that it would be no breach of contract to call on those who had furnished substitutes, as the system had excited dissatisfaction among those who had been unable thus to escape service. Such action was taken by the Confederate Congress and warmly defended by Jefferson Davis.

Second in the list of causes came, undoubtedly, lack of the most ordinary necessities for the soldier—food, clothing, pay, and equipment. When men are pinched for food for three months at a stretch, at the same time that they are being subjected to protracted and arduous campaigns and constant exposure; when they have not been paid or furnished with any new clothing in from six to ten months; and when their government is not even able to put arms in their hands, the courage and enthusiasm of the bravest will ebb. The suffering of the Confederate soldier is . . . a prime cause in the tremendous amount of desertion. . . .

The soldiers' pay—the paltry sum of eleven dollars a month in Treasury notes—was almost always delayed, and the depreciation already manifest in the fall of 1862, due to military failures, made it of little value when it did come. The lack of ready funds which kept the men unpaid for from two to eight months in 1861 was still more marked in 1864, when complaints came from all sections that pay was eleven, twelve, and fourteen months behind. Occasionally the difficulty lay in the fact that no one in a given battery, composed of illiterate mountaineers, knew how to make out a proper muster and pay-roll, while that same illiteracy led them to believe that they were being defrauded of their just pay. A private's pay for a month would scarcely buy one meal for his family or a year's pay buy him a pair of boots. This lack of funds operated to make a soldier on leave often unable to defray the cost of reaching his command. The prominence of this factor in desertion is attested by the statement of a group of officers who gave it as their opinion that the recent desertions from the regiment were mainly the result of this discontent, and that the chief causes of this state of feeling were the insufficiency of rations and the failure of the paymaster to pay the men off.

The importance of attention to camp morale, so striking a feature in the recent World War, was not then recognized. The Confederate army, in the opinion of one observer, started wrong the very first winter in its neglect of cleanliness and of exercise. City men, accustomed to stated hours of business and recreation, whose minds were accustomed to the stimulus of thought and recreation, drooped under the monotony of a camp sunk knee-deep in mire, where the only relief from the tedium of long yarns spun around a feeble camp-fire was heavy sleep in a damp bed, curled up in a musty blanket—when there were blankets—in a close tent—when there were tents. And hale, sturdy countrymen, accustomed to the active life of mountain or plantation, found the change to camp life no more agreeable.

And yet only a strong morale could help sustain mortal flesh through the discomforts and hardships inseparable from warfare. Drenching thunder-storms; filth and dirt, which the absence of soap turned into cutaneous diseases; long, jading marches for several days and parts of nights over stony roads, through a country almost entirely without water, were mere incidents of a campaign. "Cooties" were, unfortunately, known before the World War. Cholera, measles, even smallpox, made their appearance in camp, while hospital accommodations were not even decent. . . .

Added to physical want and depression on the part of the soldiers were homesickness and mental anxiety concerning their families, whom they knew to be in need of the necessities of life in the face of ever-soaring prices: flour, fifty dollars a barrel; salt, sixty to seventy cents a pound; bacon, seventy-five cents a pound; and butter, twelve dollars a pound. With the poor mountain whites, the margin of food supplies from a five-acre farm was always necessarily small. The men felt that their services in the army were useless and that their families required their attention, especially when their homes lay hopelessly within the Federal lines. Furthermore, many a man felt himself literally forced to desert in order to defend his family from outlaws. It is small wonder, when soldiers from Arkansas and the western frontier heard of Indians scalping families living on the border, that they left camp at once, with or without leave, to turn their arms to the defense of their homes. Appeals and laments from these same families did not fail to reveal their sufferings. The most familiar tale illustrating the operation of this cause is one which appears in several sources. Such an appeal as the following could not fail to grip a father's heart:

A certain Edward Cooper was being tried by court-martial for desertion. When he was told to produce witnesses, he said his only defense was a letter from his wife, which he handed to the president of the court. It read as follows:

My dear Edward:—I have always been proud of you, and since your connection with the Confederate army, I have been prouder of you than ever before. I would not have you do anything wrong for the world, but before God, Edward, unless you come home, we must die. Last night, I was aroused by little Eddie's crying. I called and said "What is the matter, Eddie?" and he said, "O mamma! I am so hungry." And Lucy, Edward, your darling Lucy; she never complains, but she is growing thinner and thinner every day. And before God, Edward, unless you come home, we must die.

Your Mary

. . . As if it were not enough to be robbed and eaten out by the contending armies, the same sections often became a prey to the arson, murder, and pillage of Tories and deserters. Often three or four families with ten or fifteen children were huddled under one roof with only the charity board between them and starvation. From deserter to Tory was not a difficult step.

The tax-in-kind law, which seized one tenth of the farmers' produce, and the impressment system roused the troops to the point where they were determined to protect their families from injustice and wrong on the part of the government, even to the abandonment of the contest. The law of March 26, 1863, required the impressment of all articles absolutely necessary for the war which could not be purchased. Since the government could regulate the prices for all such articles, and since its agents fixed them far below the market price, no one would sell to the government at one half of the price he could command of his neighbors. The inevitable consequence was that the government never could purchase, but must always impress. These agents operated under no rules—at least, observed none—and were not subject to supervision. Bad and indifferent officers impressed in the way which proved easiest for them, usually on near-by plantations or where the least resistance could be offered. Naturally, wives of absent soldiers were exactly those least able to oppose resistance to impressment, and hence they were often called upon for more than a fair proportion. Soldiers, faced with the choice of serving the State or their families, when famine was stalking through the land, obeyed the stronger of the two obligations. The suspicion was widely entertained that the people employed by quartermasters to buy supplies for the army bought at one price and sold at an advanced figure, sharing the profit with the purchasing officers.

The unredeemed promise of furloughs made at the time that the conscription law was passed was an excuse almost invariably offered by culprits when arrested, at least in North Carolina. And yet by the spring of 1863, if officers had permitted the men to go home, the armies would have been reduced to a corporal's guard, and Governor Vance frankly admitted that he did not see how that promise was to be redeemed. It is interesting to see how General Pemberton "made a virtue of necessity" by proclaiming a thirty days' furlough to his army, "as they had all gone to their homes without leave." The failure to extend to the troops of Georgia, Alabama, and South Carolina, when passing their homes, the same indulgence as had been granted those of Mississippi, gave much dissatisfaction and led numbers to leave the ranks en route.

Another grievance which contributed to desertion was the belief that men were conscripted wrongfully into the service, that this was a "rich man's war but a poor man's fight," since the wealthy seemed to bribe their way to freedom or to comfortable posts as magistrates, overseers, or government officials. Even so important a supporter of the government as

James Phelon, a prominent citizen of Mississippi, wrote President Davis on December 9, 1862: "It seems as if nine-tenths of the youngsters of the land whose relatives are conspicuous in society, wealthy, or influential, obtain some safe perch where they can doze with their heads under their wings." The temporary suspension of the Conscription Bureau in 1863 was interpreted by some citizens as an evidence of the displeasure of the government with it for seizing men. Probably the wretched private had a quite distorted view of the dereliction of the wealthy. Jones, a clerk in the War Department, asserts repeatedly that much defection was due to a deep-seated conviction that the wealthy were enjoying the comforts as usual at home. The absolute necessity of exemption of farmers, manufacturers, and mechanics is perfectly obvious if the country was to be fed, clothed, and armed.

All Southern soldiers had a strong consciousness of themselves as free moral agents; they were wholly unaccustomed to acting on any other than their own motion. They were unused to control of any sort and were not disposed to obey any one except for good and sufficient reason, fully stated. Volunteers held themselves as gentlemen.[1] As free-born American citizens they resented the conscript laws. To illustrate this feeling, a story might be cited of how the death at Manassas of three officers who while serving on a court-martial had sentenced four deserters to be shot, was interpreted by the privates as a divine judgment. Some cherished also a sense of injustice in being subjected to the rigid discipline of Lee's army when bands of partisan rangers, like Mosby's or Forrest's, roamed almost at will. The dashes into enemy country, the brisk adventures, and active movement held a great fascination for all who joined the army as a frolic. So serious did Lee hold the matter that he expressed the hope that all partisan bands except Mosby's would be disbanded in his department.

Conscripts nursed as a grievance the fact that they were not even allowed certain natural rights—to select their own companies with relatives and neighbors. Governor Vance pressed on President Davis the fact that the service lost by attempting to fill up certain regiments first without respect to the wishes of the conscripts. "Large numbers actually threaten to desert before they leave camp," he wrote, "and generally make good their threats." They held firmly to the belief that they were morally free to depart at or near the time of termination of their enlistment. Especially did they insist that they should be allowed to change their service upon renewal of enlistment, as many wanted to be transferred from the infantry to the cavalry. North Carolinians, for instance, used to horseback riding in the mountains, but unaccustomed to walking long distances, felt themselves better fitted for cavalry service.

Men sincerely believed that they had a kind of right to serve in certain localities—usually near their homes, and were averse to being transferred to other points. Numerous desertions followed the transfer of some troops to the Army of Virginia in 1863, and General Jones frankly admitted his doubts whether one half of the Florida troops would honor orders to leave that State. As soon as it was suspected by some Kentucky troops that they were to be led from their own State, they began to desert, while other companies marched cheerfully when they supposed they were going toward Kentucky. An officer had to report bluntly to Richmond, "Our troops here will not go; they will throw down their arms first." A group of Texan troops threatened to take the matter into their own hands unless they were speedily marched back to San Antonio, while other men openly admitted that they had deserted rather than cross the Mississippi.

Closely linked with the right of selecting the company in which the soldier should serve was the right of electing their own officers. Dislike of a commanding officer, dismissal of a favorite officer, absence of a commander, and the false rumor of the resignation of Lee were alleged as causes of desertion. Early in the war even corporals were elected, with, as can be readily surmised, ill results. Until December, 1861, Eggleston declared that he never knew an instance in which a captain dared offend his men by breaking a non-commissioned officer or by supporting one without submitting the matter to a vote of the company. Even in the first instance which occurred after that date the captain had to bolster himself with written authority from headquarters, whereupon followed three weeks of mingled diplomacy and discipline to quell the mutiny which resulted.[2] As late as 1862 a citizen protested to Governor Letcher of Virginia against the elective principle in the army, and especially against inclusion within the rule of the grade of field officers as fraught with the most fatal consequences. . . .

Furthermore, once begun, desertion itself soon became a cause of continued and further desertion; the evil fed upon itself. At first the men feared the Argus eyes of the government agents who should send them back to their regiments and to death. But before long, impunity bred contempt until deserters actually intimidated the poorly armed, inefficient home guards. . . .

From 1863 the element of discouragement and hopelessness of the struggle was added to the natural weariness from the strain of the long, bitterly fought war. Some mail bags captured by the United States officers showed already in 1863 that letters of Southern soldiers breathed but one sentiment—weariness of the war. Soldiers saw, despite desperate and heroic efforts, defeat everywhere, saw their toils and sufferings unproductive against apparently inexhaustible numbers.

A Southern sergeant taken prisoner in April, 1865, voiced to a Union general very accurately the feeling of his comrades: "For six or eight months back, our men have deserted by thousands. Those who remain have been held by a sentiment of honor only. They did not wish to disgrace themselves by deserting their flag. They have done their duty to the best of their ability. As to the Southern Confederacy, although they would have liked to have seen it triumph, they lost all hope of it long since." Grant gauged Southern feeling accurately when in July, 1864, he urged Lincoln to issue a call for 300,000 men as a means to increase desertion from the ranks of the foe. It was notorious that desertion received an impetus from Southern defeats such as Gettysburg and Vicksburg. Lincoln's reelection, with the consequent prospect of the continued prosecution of the war, was assigned by deserters as one ground for despair of success.

Many minor causes contributed locally to promote desertion, such as a threat of invasion of a soldier's home region by the enemy; the excessive number of details to contractors and corporations, whereby so many escaped field service that others in disgust took French leave; the lack of proper discipline in the army, explicable from the manner of its organization and the necessity of bringing it into immediate service, but nevertheless sadly demoralizing; and the promises of immunity to deserters emanating from Washington. Lee states in a letter to Secretary of War Seddon his belief that a circular from Washington authorities, promising immunity to deserters and exemption from military service, had had its due effect.

But more potent than all other causes, except possibly lack of devotion to the Confederacy and personal suffering, was the state of public opinion in the civilian population among the families and neighbors of deserters. Want and suffering undermined the morale, while in some sections, notably in North Carolina, though also elsewhere, the press and some State leaders inflamed the discontent with the government and preached peace at any price, impressing the people with the hopelessness of the cause. General D. H. Hill, who had command in that section, put the situation succinctly in the spring of 1863: "There is a powerful faction in the state poisoning public sentiment and looking to a reconstruction. The soldiers are induced by these traitors to believe that this is an unjust war on the part of the south and that their state soldiers and citizens have been slighted and wronged by the Confederate States Government." Lee also complained of the "evil consequences resulting from crude misstatements of newspaper correspondents." In February, 1865, he charged openly that "the men are influenced by the misrepresentations of their friends at home, who appear to have become very despondent as to our success. They think the cause desperate and write to the soldiers, advising them to take care of themselves, assuring them that if they will return home the bands of deserters so far outnumber the home guards that they will be in no danger of arrest." . . .

NOTES

1. General Lee's statement on this subject, made on his retreat from Gettysburg, is illuminating: "Our people are so little liable to control that it is difficult to get them to follow any course not in accordance with their inclination" (O. W. R., Ser. I, XXVII, pt. III, 1048).

2. The consolidating of odds and ends of paper commands into full regiments often caused disgruntled officers and men to run away (O. W. R., Ser. I, XXXII, pt. I, 346).

From Civil War to World War I

18

Johnson, Stanton, and Grant

A Reconsideration of the Army's Role in the Events Leading to Impeachment

HAROLD M. HYMAN

The surrender of the Confederacy's armies in 1865 ended the formal war, but a decade of guerrilla warfare and terrorism lay before the nation. How was the South to be rebuilt? President Andrew Johnson and the Republican Congress disagreed; for two and a half years Congress fought Johnson, seeking to impose a more thorough remodeling of the recent rebellious states than the president and his supporters were engaging in. The army, the instrument of national policy in the South, found itself drawn inexorably to one side of this controversy. Harold Hyman outlines the development of a crisis that could, in one sense, properly be styled the only coup d'etat in American history. How so? Were not constitutional prerogatives stripped from the President when, in early 1867, Congress refused to accept Johnson's dismissal of Secretary of War Stanton and named Grant the Commander-in-Chief of the armies in the South?

SEVENTY YEARS AGO William A. Dunning saw the involvement of Ulysses Grant and other army officers in the political developments that resulted in Andrew Johnson's impeachment as a " . . . mere accidental feature of

SOURCE: Harold M. Hyman, "Johnson, Stanton, and Grant: A Reconsideration of the Army's Role in the Events Leading to Impeachment," *American Historical Review* 66, 1 (October 1960): 85–96. Reprinted by permission of the author and the American Historical Association.

EDITOR'S NOTE: The citations to the sources consulted by the author in this essay have been omitted from this volume for brevity and economy. The reader should consult the original source of the essay for the complete scholarly documentation.

the general issue . . . throwing over the situation a sort of martial glamour." Accepting this premise without questioning its validity, historians have understated if not altogether ignored the army's role, desires, and needs during the first three years after Appomattox. Studies of the Reconstruction period have stressed political and economic approaches to the impeachment theme, and in the process some writers have created a sentimental and incorrect image of Johnson as a vigorous defender of constitutional rights and presidential prerogatives.

A growing interest in civil-military relations has recently led some investigators into fresh pathways. Lloyd Lewis, for example, while on the trail of Grant's actions during the confused months after Lee surrendered, had by 1947 come to the tentative conclusion that " . . . Grant . . . and the [other] Generals were convinced that Andrew Johnson was going so fast in readmitting 'Rebels' to power, that the nation was endangered." The "modern" view, Lewis continued in a private letter, "that Johnson was merely restoring Lincoln's merciful [Reconstruction] policy and that was all there was to it overlooks a hell of a lot of unreconstructed things the old Bourbons . . . were doing at the time."

Untimely death cut short Lewis' work on Grant in which this judgment might have appeared as a firm conclusion. Lewis was on the right track. The period from early 1865 through 1867 still requires reexamination in order to ascertain what Grant and other generals felt and did about events, and to clarify the ultimately conflicting purposes and policies of President Johnson and his holdover War Secretary, Edwin M. Stanton, the army's civilian overlords. When viewed from the perspective of the professional army officer of this time, these controversial personalities and complex problems gain new illumination.

With the surrender of the last rebel forces, the hurriedly reorganized regulars of the United States Army faced four primary responsibilities. In order to meet them, Stanton and Grant grouped the troops into what in effect were two separate "armies." The first "army" was assigned to relatively traditional duties. It patrolled the Mexican border to impress the French adventurers at the Halls of Montezuma, sought to suppress the Indian tribesmen who had grown bold from wartime incitements, and in smaller detachments garrisoned posts along the unquiet Canadian border and performed training and ceremonial chores in eastern cities. This "army" never became a political issue. Its commanders remained within the traditional pattern of civilian direction from the White House and War Department; Congress was content to let Johnson control it.[1]

In defeated Dixie, however, the war-born military galaxy faced a task unique in American history—the military government of large numbers of their countrymen after hostilities had ceased. Here the second "army" came into being. Its commanders had at hand only the lessons in occupation administration learned since 1861 to guide them. No one in the early months of 1865 knew if these precedents were adequate for peacetime. A new and untried President was in the White House. Marking time until Johnson indicated what he wished the army to do in the South, Stanton and Grant sanctioned the police and welfare activities which local commanders undertook, and devoted their energies to solving demobilization and reorganization problems.

In April 1865 Stanton, Grant, and the senior army officers were prepared to offer Johnson the same cordial support that they had tendered to Lincoln. They assumed that Johnson would give the army the same firm executive backing that Lincoln had done. In the soldiers' terms, this meant that the new President would use the troops in the South to make worthwhile the wartime sacrifices of a hundred thousand Billy Yanks, and that he would employ the powers of his office to protect military personnel who were performing duties to which he had assigned them. Three years later Congress impeached Johnson for attempting to exercise commander in chief powers over the second "army," and in this the legislators had the soldiers' cordial acquiescence. By early 1868 the United States Army units on southern occupation duty were under Congress' command rather than the President's. It had become a separate "army" in law as well as in fact.

Divorce between the White House and the War Department was an improbable eventuality when Johnson announced his Reconstruction and pardon program for the South in May 1865. The President was confident that he was carrying out the spirit of Lincoln's plans, and to be sure, his pronouncements concerning the former rebel states had the ring of his predecessor's. Like Lincoln, Johnson based his Reconstruction proclamation on a broad view of executive power, adequate to employ the army to build new and ostensibly loyal state governments in the South. To this end and for their own protection, the soldiers were to use martial law to expedite the process. True, Johnson ignored the tendency Lincoln had exhibited shortly before the war ended for including some substantial portion of southern Negroes in the electorates of the new states. But the significance of this omission was not immediately apparent.

It soon became obvious, however, to most of the officers on southern duty and to Stanton and Grant who read their reports that fundamental differences existed between the Reconstruction plans of the two Presidents. Lincoln had used the December 1863 proclamation primarily as a war weapon to seduce southern whites away from their allegiance to the Confederacy. Thus conceived and successfully employed by the Union army, Lincoln's plan and his exercise of presidential powers sustained the northern soldier. As Johnson's program developed through 1865, Union officers became convinced that it strengthened only former rebels and returned to positions of official power in the South men who had brought the nation to civil war, but who had since received Johnson's pardons for their rebellious pasts. General Philip Sheridan was later to term Johnson's southern policy "a broad macadamized road for perjury to travel on," by which unrepentant southern whites were encouraged to harass federal soldiers and Unionists, and through vicious legalisms to escape punishment for these transgressions.

Consider one aspect of Reconstruction in 1865 that outraged most soldiers. In southern state courts reborn under Johnson's auspices and through the efforts of the army, former rebels initiated scores of suits against federal military personnel. These claimants asked damages for soldiers' actions made under martial law during and after the war. Army officers on southern duty confessed to the War Department that they were now fearful of exercising their assigned functions, for if these suits succeeded, they would be ruined. In these state courts judges, jurors, and claimants were white men, and almost all were former rebels. What soldier or white or Negro Unionist, officers inquired, could expect fair hearings from such assemblages?

Then, late in 1865, Stanton was sued for damages arising from the wartime arrest of a disloyal northern civilian, Joseph E. Maddox. If Maddox won against the mighty Mars, then similar verdicts would inevitably follow against hundreds of lesser officers.

Maddox's counsel, Caleb Cushing, soon realized that he was involved in something more than a damage claim. Cushing learned that the men who were now the President's chief advisers, the Blair trio (Francis P., Sr., Jr., and Montgomery) and Manton Marble of the New York *World*, had inspired Maddox to sue in order to break Stanton. Marble and the Blairs also wanted to frighten off army officers in the South from enforcing property confiscation and Freedmen's Bureau legislation. Perhaps with Cushing's connivance, Grant and Stanton learned what was afoot. Neither the War Secretary nor the commanding general assumed that the President was privy to the plot. But they were outraged that men close to the White House should involve the army in this combination of personal vendetta and policy struggle. They were bitter that they could not convince Johnson to order the southern state courts to hold off the many damage suits pending against military personnel. The realization sank home at the War Department that the White House was not going to exert itself to protect soldiers from the legal consequences of wartime actions or postwar activities in the South. If something was to be done, army headquarters would have to do it.

Grant arranged a compromise with Cushing so that Maddox dropped the suit against Stanton. Moving to protect army personnel at least so far as suits originating in the South were concerned, Grant and Stanton took advantage of the fact that Johnson's Reconstruction proclamations sanctioned the use of martial law in the former Confederacy. On January 3, 1866, Grant issued General Order 3 to all southern commands. It was designed "To protect loyal persons against improper civil suits and penalties in the late rebellious States." By its terms, soldiers and civilians, including Negroes, who asserted that justice was unobtainable in southern state courts could transfer any suits pending against them to the Freedmen's Bureau paramilitary tribunals or to federal civil courts. In the former, martial law prevailed. In the latter, Congress had prescribed that all federal court personnel, jurors, attorneys, and claimants, had to swear an ironclad oath of past loyalty to the Union.

As a solution to the damage suit problem, General Order 3 was satisfactory if the situation remained static. But a perverse genius for instability seemed to afflict the leading actors and institutions on the political stage. After a nine-year abstention from significant policy pronouncements, the United States Supreme Court introduced a new and unsettling element.

In April 1866 the Court issued a preliminary judgment in the Milligan case. This involved the army's right to employ martial law in noncombat areas. Although the full opinion in this case was not to be issued until the Court's forthcoming December term, it was obvious in April that the jurists did not look kindly upon martial law's being employed anywhere except in the vicinity of battle. Would the Court in December bring forth a decision condemning all martial law usage in the postwar South? As the War Department saw the situation, the White House and the Supreme Court seemed determined to hamstring the army.

Stanton and Grant turned toward Congress in hope that the army might find friends on Capitol Hill. They knew that General Order 3 dealt only with damage suits from the South, but not with those like Maddox's claim, lodged by northern residents over whom the army now claimed no control. The Secretary and the general, therefore, pressured friendly congressmen to amend the 1863 Habeas Corpus Act to provide greater protection for officers who had acted under its provisions anywhere in the nation during the war. Republicans in Congress cooperated. The army was finding its bulwark in Congress, not in the President.

This explains why Stanton and Grant chose to support the Freedmen's Bureau court system in its jurisdictional feud with the provost courts of the army field commands, a carry-over from war organization. Congress had given the Freedmen's Bureau special legislative support lacking in the provost units, which operated only on the wartime executive authority now questioned at the White House and in the Supreme Court as well as in lower federal courts.

But the War Department was still only disturbed, not wrenched away from support of the President. When Congress had convened in December 1865, Stanton and Grant cooperated with Johnson in suppressing the unsavory Smith-Brady Report, which indicated that the state governments set up by Lincoln in the Mississippi Valley were centers of vast corruption rather than of renascent Unionism. Johnson wanted the report suppressed because he believed that he was following Lincoln's policies and did not want his own state creations in the South tarred by the Smith-Brady brush. Grant wanted it hushed up because the report indicated that hundreds of army officers were involved in the sordid peculations discovered in Louisiana, Arkansas, and in parts of Missouri. But it is the fact of the cooperation more than the reasons for it which is significant here.

The Republicans of Congress, like the army officer corps, were not under Radical control in the early months of 1866, but they clearly distrusted Johnson's accomplishments in state making in the South. Congress prevented the "Confederate brigadiers"—the delegates-elect from the former rebel states—from taking seats at the national legislature, and the President and Congress commenced their joust for power. Meanwhile the evidence of southerners' attacks on northern test oath requirements, the inequities of the Black Codes, and the tragic race riot at Memphis gave added weight to Radical arguments that the South was unrepentant and untrustworthy.

As the debate raged, Johnson proved rigid and doctrinaire in his convictions concerning federal-state relations and the power and influence he had at hand to wield. He deceived himself into thinking that he was emulating Lincoln not only in the form of Reconstruction policy, but also in the exercise of executive leadership. He failed to see that Lincoln had never sought perfection, but only realizable goals, had never been willing to battle Congress but instead compromised with or circumvented its leaders, and had never dared lose the support of the Union soldiers.

To be sure, the war was now over, and the last mass armies were replaced by volunteer professionals. But that, to many Republicans legislators and apolitical generals, was the point. It was well enough for Lincoln to have proclaimed emancipation and Reconstruction policies on the basis of war powers, but he had always agreed that these were extraordinary wartime acts, subject to postwar judicial or legislative amendment, and even during the war Congress had protested against Lincoln's assumptions of leadership. Now Johnson insisted that the war was finished, and that no one, therefore, could legitimately limit the revived southern states. Yet he simultaneously claimed a monopoly of pardoning and statemaking power for the executive on which Congress might not infringe. He wanted presidential power and at the same time professed a doctrine of weakness for the entire national government, used the army to get the South on its feet, but refused soldiers the right to shackle the spurred boots of the former rebels so that they might not kick out again. This, at least, was the way many saw the situation.

As if to prove the accuracy of this contention, Johnson on April 2, 1866, almost coincident with the preliminary Milligan decision, proclaimed that the rebellion was ended everywhere and that the southern states were restored to the Union. Army headquarters in Washington soon learned of the intense confusion into which military commanders in the South were cast by this statement and by the Court's pronouncement. Was martial law operating? Did the Freedmen's Bureau, under Congress' authority rather than the President's now lose its power to hold special military tribunals if civil courts failed to provide justice? Did army personnel, insulted and assaulted by jubilant southern whites, now become defenseless?

A week later, on April 9, Grant sent out a confidential circular to military commanders stationed in the former Confederacy. He cautioned them to exercise discreet restraint in dealing with the "reconstructed" state governments and with southern civilians. But he also authorized them to employ martial law whenever they felt it necessary, despite Johnson's clear statement that peace was at hand and in defiance of the Court's inference that martial law was inapplicable in a peacetime situation. In addition, Grant advised his subordinates that the Freedmen's Bureau was exempt from the President's jurisdiction, although it was part of the army, for the general concluded that the Bureau was Congress' creation. Where southern civil authorities failed to provide or obstructed justice to soldiers or to southern Unionists, then the army might still step in.

Clearly Grant was moving toward a sharp break with tradition so far as his view of civil-military relationships was concerned. Events had pushed him and Stanton so far by the spring of 1866 that the two men were willing to use their immense prestige and popularity within the army and with the public to counter what they felt to be error on Johnson's part. They were beginning to align the army with Congress because they felt that the President was leaving the soldiers helplessly adrift.

Neither Grant nor Stanton, however, desired an outright clash with Johnson. Both men still hoped to win him to their views, which at this point approximated those of moderate Republican congressmen. Thus, on May 1, Grant issued through normal army channels General Order 26, specifying compliance with Johnson's April peace proclamation. The general knew that his earlier secret circular had forewarned army commanders to ignore the President's peace policy if necessary. They could be confident that Grant would block any retaliation from the White House.

More evidence accumulated, meanwhile, of outrages in the South directed against soldiers and Negroes. Feeling that they had acted correctly in checking the President's policy, Stanton and Grant were convinced that the army still had work to do in Dixie. They now shared the view of most army commanders assigned to southern stations that former rebels were incapable of true reformation. Grant went a step further to strengthen his subordinates' positions. On July 6 he issued General Order 44, supplementing General Order 3 of the past January. The July order empowered all army commanders in the South down to the post or company level to arrest civilians charged with crimes against federal civil or military personnel, or against "inhabitants of the United States, regardless of color, in cases where the civil authorities have failed, neglected, or are unable to arrest and bring such parties to trial." Those arrested were to stay in confinement "until such time as a proper judicial tribunal may be ready and willing to try them."

This curious document neither imposed martial law nor obeyed the

President's clear statement of April that civil authority must take precedence over military power in the South. In substance, it openly informed Johnson, as many persons including Jonathan Worth of North Carolina complained to him, that Stanton, Grant, and most commanders of the army disagreed with his position and thought the April peace proclamation hasty, ill advised, unfair to military personnel, and an unreal estimate of southern conditions.

Later that month the President prepared to retaliate by reading a proclamation that the rebellion was not only ended, but spelling out that martial law was inoperative everywhere in the country. Thus encouraged, the "reconstructed" governor of Virginia on July 21 informed Stanton that he was reactivating the state militia and requested surplus army weapons for the members, all of whom, Grant learned, were whites, and most of whom were former rebels and holders of the President's pardons. Informed of this by Grant, Johnson refused to cancel the governor's request. To Grant this seemed equivalent to putting arms back in the hands of men still capable of using them against the victors, and the general delayed in complying.

No open rupture yet existed between the White House and the army, but the President's southern policy was forcing individual army officials to make choices concerning their political allegiance. Stanton, Grant, Sheridan, Daniel Sickles, John Pope, M. C. Meigs, and Edward Ord were clearly in sympathy with the Republicans of Congress; William Tecumseh Sherman and Winfield Scott Hancock favored Johnson; E. D. Townsend remained determinedly neutral. But to attach traditional political party labels to these officers seems irrelevant and inaccurate. To be sure, Congress' supporters in the army were becoming "radicals" in the sense that they had come to believe that Negro suffrage must be imposed upon the South as the only means to insure the subordination of the old secessionist class. If Congress was willing to see to it that Negroes voted, then these men were going to favor Congress.

The New Orleans riot seemed to prove the acuity of the "radical" officers' analysis. Soon after that event, General Pope made a speech after first securing Stanton's and Grant's approval for its text. He argued that if the "military power is suspended" in the South, "at once the old political & personal influences will resume their activity," and the Copperheads of the North and the Bourbons of the South would seek again to sunder the Republic. It may be, of course, that Pope was merely spouting Republican propaganda. Yet the man was no politician, and he was risking his professional career by assuming this public position. In openly defying the President's orders, Grant was chancing the political laurels he secretly coveted, and Stanton, who wanted more than all else to get out of politics, was only making it impossible for himself to quit the War Department. These men wanted Pope's words to be clarion calls of warning, to alert a somnolent North to what they feared was a clear and present danger. Aging General Ethan Allen Hitchcock wondered, "Have we run our race as a

Republic? I hope not—but fear it." Grant and Stanton were determined to use military influence to prevent the civilian President from keeping the nation on a disastrous course.

Realizing that so long as Stanton and Grant were working together the army in the South was out of his control, Johnson decided to split the team, replace Grant with a more cooperative commanding general, and then to oust Stanton in turn. He brought the nation's third most popular man, General Sherman, to Washington to be at hand and offered Grant a trumped-up diplomatic assignment to Mexico, intending then to put Sherman in first as commanding general, and once Grant was away to slip either him or Montgomery Blair in as Secretary of War in place of Stanton. But Grant refused to play, Sherman would not take issue with his beloved commander, and the scheme foundered.

Deciding to exploit Grant at home in the 1866 congressional elections if he could not employ him abroad, Johnson swung around the circle with the disgusted general in tow. The results of that "critical" election gave the Republicans a thumping victory and a working majority in Congress adequate to override any veto. Now the question was: Would Johnson acquiesce in the verdict of the ballot boxes? "Things have changed here somewhat since the last election," Grant advised in a confidential note to his protégé, General Phil Sheridan, but he could not predict the nature of the change.

Johnson had no intention of signaling surrender by suggesting that the southern states ratify the pending Fourteenth Amendment. His secretary, Colonel William G. Moore, realized that the President was convinced that the white men of the South would be submerged under a sable sea if the freedmen exercised the ballot. This concern merged with Johnson's views of the nature of the federal system and the purposes of the Civil War, and it combined with his combative personality to help create the critical situation in which the nation found itself. "He seemed never to be happy unless he had some one to strike at or denounce," recalled Hugh McCulloch, Johnson's personal friend, Treasury Secretary, and political supporter. As 1866 closed, Andrew Johnson should have been a very happy man.

Somehow Johnson missed the significance of the 1866 election results, for they were barely counted when he "suggested" to Grant, bypassing Stanton completely, that the army issue ten thousand stands of arms to the revived Virginia state militia. Grant replied properly through Stanton's office that "I would not recommend the issue of arms for the use of the militia of any of the states lately in rebellion in advance of their full restoration and the admission of their representatives by Congress."

The Republicans, now dominating Congress, prepared Reconstruction legislation for the South which included much of what the army had wanted since Appomattox: the continued use of martial law, legal protection for army personnel, and the disfranchisement of most former rebels.

Then in the first weeks of 1867, the Supreme Court threw three bomb-shells into the legislators' works. In the Milligan, Garland, and Cummings decisions, the jurists denounced military trials of civilians and federal and state test oath laws as unconstitutional excesses. This at least was the way excited and indignant Republican spokesmen portrayed the decisions, while Democrats lauded them as noble defenses of civil liberties and individual rights. President Johnson was naturally delighted that his constitutional views now had had judicial support. To the army, however, the Court's pronouncements spelled disaster, and to Radical Republican congressmen, they were reactionary obstructions that must be overcome or ignored.

Now Stanton and Grant leaped fully over the wall into the Radical camp, Stanton openly and Grant still secretly. The two men arranged for Congress to provide for the army's needs. By the military appropriations bill of 1867, Grant was made autonomous of the President so far as the location of his headquarters was concerned and the funnel through which Johnson had to transmit orders to subordinate army commanders. Congress, in brief, determined that Grant, whom the legislators trusted, be the commander in chief as well as the commanding general of the southern section of the army. It would no longer be possible legally for Johnson to replace him, as the President had recently tried to do by sending him to Mexico, or to bypass him and Stanton as Johnson had done with fateful results with General Absalom Baird at New Orleans just before the tragic riot there. And by protecting Stanton in the War Secretary's position through the Tenure of Office Act, the Republican majority in Congress felt that it had effectively blocked the President's power to control the army in the South. To the surprise of many persons, Johnson at last seemed willing to acquiesce in the legislative will, although he did helplessly veto these laws as they emerged from Congress, in what Grant privately described as "the most ridiculous veto message[s] that ever issued from any President."

Buoyed up by the Court's decisions, Johnson now had a new scheme. He intended to water down the effects of the Reconstruction law that Congress passed on March 2, 1867, by having Attorney General Henry Stanbery issue interpretations that would in effect let the President take the teeth from the disfranchising and Negro suffrage provisions. Again the army commanders found themselves at issue with the White House, for most of the senior officers felt that the Reconstruction law was a moderate and necessary enactment.

On March 27, 1867, Sheridan removed from their offices in the Louisiana state government men Johnson had pardoned for rebellion. This was the first test of a military commander's powers under the new law of Congress, and Grant secretly applauded the action. "It is just the thing," Grant confidentially wrote Sheridan, "and merits the approbation of the loyal people at least. I have no doubt but that it will also meet with like approval from the reconstructed." Johnson ordered that no more removals occur until the Attorney General's opinion was available. On April 3 Grant obediently transmitted this order, but also sent Sheridan a private message, warning him that "there is a decided hostility to the whole Congressional plan of reconstruction at the 'White House,' and a disposition to remove you from the command you now have. Both the Secretary of War and myself will oppose any such move, as will the mass of the people." They would oppose it by claiming that in the southern army commands Congress had made officers independent of the President, of the Secretary of War, and of the commanding general. Thus, if the President somehow managed to evade, transfer, or replace Stanton and/or Grant, the Reconstruction acts could still be enforced by local commanders.

Grant assured Sheridan that in the Reconstruction law, Congress "intended to give District Commanders entire control over the civil governments of these [southern] districts." The army commanders in the South " . . . shall be their own judges of the meaning of its provisions." By this analysis, any opinion of the Attorney General, the President's legal representative, would merely be advisory rather than binding on the military officers assigned to Reconstruction duty. The army in the South, Grant inferred, was Congress' army, no longer under the White House or under the War Department except for routine administrative purposes.

To his friend, Congressman Elihu Washburne, Grant wrote " . . . all will be well if Administration and Copperhead influences do not defeat the objects of that reconstruction measure." He advised Sheridan, his favored subordinate: "Go on giving your own interpretation to the law." No wonder that after informing Grant that he intended to remove more of Johnson's state officials, Sheridan boasted to him that "The Attorney General should not hamper me too much; no one can conceive or estimate, at so great a distance, the precautions necessary to be taken . . . here." When General Pope wrote Grant from Georgia that the Milligan decision would have no effect in his command, Grant replied: "My views are the District Commanders are responsible for the faithful execution of the Reconstruction Act of Congress, and that in civil matters I cannot give them an order. I can give them my views, however, . . . and above all, I can advise them of views and opinions here which may serve to put them on their guard." Grant comforted Sheridan with the assurance that "I think your head is safe above your shoulders at least so that it can not be taken off to produce pain." In midsummer the President told Grant that he was thinking of dismissing Sheridan. Warning the younger man, Grant again assured him of his and Stanton's support. "Removal cannot hurt you if it does take place, and I do not believe it will," he wrote. "You have carried out the acts of Congress, and it will be difficult [for Johnson] to get a general officer who will not."

Then the Attorney General issued his opinion. As expected, it watered down the significant aspects of the Reconstruction law and put the military commanders back into almost the same untenable position they had held before Congress enacted this law. Grant and Stanton moved swiftly on two fronts. They had cooperating Congressmen prepare supplements to the Reconstruction law, countering Stanbery's restrictive opinion. And while this was in the works, Grant bolstered sagging army morale by writing to Sheridan and to General Ord in Virginia that "the Attorney General or myself can do no more than give our opinions as to the meaning of the law." Responsibility and autonomy were still where Congress had vested them, in the district commanders, Grant insisted, and he advised them that "Congress may [soon] give an interpretation of their own acts, differing possibly from those given by the Attorney General."

Johnson finally acted, but against Stanton rather than Sheridan. Striking now hard and swiftly, if belatedly, the President in early August suspended Stanton. Giving the slow-thinking Grant little time to ponder, Johnson swept him into the cabinet as combined War Secretary ad interim and commanding general. The President thought he had won the campaign now that Grant was in a frankly Democratic cabinet. Surely the general would benefit from exposure to proper constitutional and political views, and at the same time would become unacceptable as Republican presidential timber in 1868, thereby increasing Johnson's own chances for a Democratic bid, which he greatly desired. But Johnson was to find that Grant, while cooperative enough as Secretary of War in matters of administrative detail, was still acting against the White House when he put on his second hat, the peaked cap of the commanding general of the army.

On the day he took over the War Office, Grant had a trusted friend, General James Forsyth, secretly warn Sheridan of the impending changes, so that "in case the President insists upon your removal, that whoever may be assigned to your command, can be directed by General Grant to carry out the Military Reconstruction Acts as interpreted by you, and foreshadowed by your orders—in fact General Grant wants things in such a condition in Louisiana that your successor (in case you are relieved) will have to carry out the [Reconstruction] Law as you have viewed it; and without the opportunity to change your programme."

Over Grant's vigorous protests in the cabinet, Johnson decided to remove Sheridan from the Louisiana command. Flashing off a secret warning to the younger man, Grant advised him to " . . . go on your course exactly as if this communication had not been sent to you, and without fear of consequences. That so long as you pursue the same line of duty that you have followed thus far in the service you will receive the entire support of these Headquarters." By "these Headquarters" Grant meant himself as commanding general. In this capacity he considered himself autonomous of the President by virtue of Congress' enactments, far more independent than as interim War Secretary. Like Stanton he had learned that the power of this cabinet post was questionable and its tenure uncertain. Grant could not as War Secretary, for example, prevent Johnson from suspending Sheridan, Sickles, Pope, or Ord. As commanding general, however, he saw to it that all the army commanders in the South knew that they had a friend in the cabinet and at army headquarters. Until Congress reassembled in December 1867, when the Senate would judge whether Johnson had acted rightly in suspending Stanton, Grant held the War portfolio in a defensive, caretaker, rear-guard action. Johnson had trapped himself. Thinking that once Stanton was out of the way he could easily overawe Grant, whom he, Gideon Welles, and the Blairs mistook for a simple, malleable soul, the President learned that Grant definitely had a mind of his own.

But he learned it too late. In January 1868 Grant let Stanton return to the war office. When Johnson again sought to oust the sticky War Secretary in favor of General Lorenzo Thomas, Congress impeached the President. During the long weeks from February to May 1868, as Congress tried Johnson for seeking to be commander in chief of the army units stationed in the South, the nation teetered on the brink of renewed violence. Johnson escaped conviction by one vote. Cowed at last, he accepted General John Schofield as a compromise Secretary of War. A total breakdown of the national government was norrowly avoided. For the rest of 1868 Grant remained as commanding general, then he took over the presidency. During that year he saw to it that Johnson kept out of internal army administration. The President, at last brought to caution by the narrowness of the Senate vote on his conviction, accepted what he could not prevent. The Supreme Court sustained Congress' actions in the South, for the jurists had been frightened by the legislators' attacks on them.

Schofield served as a dignified clerk, bearing messages from White House to army headquarters and back, in the manner of prewar Secretaries of War. The military had won. Reconstruction proceeded henceforth in the manner that the soldiers had felt necessary since 1865, and with their own status and safety assured by Congress' laws and sympathy.

Until the complex interaction of the military institution with the civilian political branches of the national government is thoroughly reported, the full story of the background of impeachment will remain partially untold. Thus far the study of this period has suffered from the one-sided nature of the sources most widely utilized. The great *Diary* kept by Gideon Welles, for example, indispensable as it is, in the words of the man who edited it for publication, offers a view of events " . . . too much like sitting at the prize-ring and seeing only one pugilist." The army was another contender, crouched in a posture of self-defense in a ring full of aggressive combatants. It should be invisible no longer.

NOTES

1. Sensing this, William Tecumseh Sherman, who usually tried to stay clear of the political jungle, saw to it that he was assigned to western duties, and except for intervals when he dabbled in the Grant-Stanton-Johnson imbroglio, Sherman escaped serious involvement in the army crisis. See Lloyd Lewis, *Sherman: Fighting Prophet* (New York, 1958), 581–94.

19

The Role of the G.A.R. in the Constitutional Crisis of 1867–1868

MARY R. DEARING

These pages from Mary Dearing's study of the Union Army's political-ideological veteran's organization, the Grand Army of the Republic, provide evidence of a coalescing of the interests of the regular army, on the one hand, and the G.A.R., on the other. They are quite relevant to the preceding selection for two reasons. The G.A.R.'s first national commander, the volunteer General John A. Logan, joined Secretary of War Edwin Stanton in a round-the-clock occupation of the secretary's office at the height of the constitutional crisis in the winter of 1867–1868; and a number of G.A.R. volunteers appear to have gathered in the immediate vicinity of Washington for service in the event that the crisis led to bloodshed and a test of military strength between Johnson and the Congress. Professor Dearing also provides a good account, straight from Monty Python, of the finale to the crisis.

THE PARTICIPATION OF THE GRAND ARMY and other soldiers' organizations in the campaign [of 1866] encouraged wild rumors of violence as the election approached. Each party accused the other of planning to seize the government by force with the soldiers' aid, and excitable individuals on both sides actually proposed such action. Johnson received offers of military aid from a few veterans who despised the Radical cause. Radicals spoke even more seriously of war; the belligerent Butler openly threatened that

SOURCE: Mary R. Dearing, *Veterans in Politics: The Story of the G.A.R.* (Baton Rouge: Louisiana State University Press, 1952), pp. 104–108, 119–121, 134–138. Copyright © 1952. Reprinted by permission.
EDITOR'S NOTE: Most of the citations to the sources consulted by the author in this essay have been omitted from this volume for brevity and economy. The reader should consult the original source of the essay for the complete scholarly documentation.

his party would use veterans to force its will on the President. Threats of force that cropped out vaguely in Radical speeches became more definite in private correspondence. A Wisconsin citizen, imbued with the general spirit of excitement, wrote, "Should Northern Governors not call a convention, at least of themselves, and adopt measures to preserve their own states from a second Civil War, and to protect and defend the Constitution and Union, if again assailed? Arm, arm, arm say we. . . . " Governor Fairchild reported to Senator T. O. Howe that "fears of another civil war" were current, as well as "an undefined fear of general danger. I confess to some little feeling of this kind and to a strong wish to prepare, so far as I am able as the governor of this state, to meet all enemies on their own terms."

Even more alarming were reports regarding military organizations in Missouri, Tennessee, and other states. The most serious threats of violence, however, came from Ohio, Illinois, and Indiana, where G.A.R. leaders apparently were calmly planning military action against the President. Charles O'Beirne, commissioned by Johnson to investigate these rumors, found evidence of the most startling nature and sent excited reports to the President. Journeying through Illinois, Indiana, and Ohio, he forced open Grand Army lodges at night, interviewed army officers who had observed the society's activities, and tried to trace to their source shipments of arms which were being distributed to G.A.R. members.

O'Beirne found a man who claimed to have been present at a meeting in St. Louis where a group of western Radical governors discussed with General Logan the possibility of appointing a dictator. From General James B. Steedman and other officers, O'Beirne learned that Radical politicians planned to have Congress impeach Johnson immediately after it convened. The Grand Army, having completely armed and equipped in the meantime, would then march upon Washington, in readiness to support Congress should the President seek to prevent it from deposing him. While G.A.R. leaders were distributing arms among posts in the West, members were unaware of the purpose for which the society was to be used. O'Beirne informed Johnson, "The G.A.R. are drilled to the sound of the bugle and summoned by the call. This I saw myself." He reported:

> The whole reveals the fact that there is a large body of men in Indiana and Illinois thoroughly organized, partly armed, and drilled to the use of arms. They are sworn to be secret [sic] to obey their commanders. Their intentions are nominally at the start charitable. Beyond this only a small portion of them know what they are politically intended for, and what their leaders propose to do. It is patent that this large organization with kindred branches in some others of the States, will co-operate with and act under the directions of Govr Morton and some four or five other of the Governors of the West. . . .

The investigator concluded:

I think from a full survey of the field that the Radicals mean violence finally and nothing will avert it but a positive determined and fearless attitude of the President backed up by preparations and reliable armed force to execute his constant prerogatives. . . . I regard this as a fit country for military occupation—We had to do it to keep down the Copperheads, and in my mind we ought to do it to keep down the Radicals. . . . Indiana needs reconstruction. . . .

O'Beirne emphasized Steedman's belief that the arms at Springfield should be removed and that "the President should have at least 50,000 stand of arms at Washington."

Evidence exists to substantiate O'Beirne's reports that Radical governors were arming veterans in preparation for an armed attack on the President. Johnson received from General George W. McCook an account of warlike preparations of the Grand Army in Ohio. From Indiana came the report: "Our Governor or some one else has been distributing guns to the 'Army of the Republic' a serete [sic] political organization." General Sol Meredith of Indiana informed Secretary of the Interior Orville H. Browning that Governors Fletcher and Oglesby, as well as other Radicals, planned to seize the government and depose the President if they won the election. Grant, Sherman, and Morton were discussed as possible dictators to be elevated in Johnson's place. Wilson wrote regarding Governor Morton's attitude: "If internecine strife was to follow, he proposed without any dalliance to crush it with the same spirit, and the same men who had crushed the rebellion." Governor Fairchild wrote to Senator Howe:

We . . . will not be induced to swerve from the right path. . . . I feel that we ought to have more arms in our possession, but the state has drawn all its quota. Can we get more? It will certainly do no harm to have them on hand. . . .

If you deem it best will you ask the Secretary of War if he will fill a requisition for 5 or 10 thousand rifles and a batty [sic]—I do not wish to make the request officially until I am sure that it will be granted. . . .

I have been very careful as yet not to show publicly that I have even a shadow of fear for the future.

An Illinois Grand Army leader frankly admitted that Radical politicians would, if necessary, use the society as an armed force to compel Democratic submission to their policies. He wrote to Senator Trumbull: " . . . nominally we are at peace but does it ever occur to you that we may again be driven to arms? The persistent and unyielding course of the Administration in a policy of reconstruction so foreign to the absolute demands of the country . . . will in the absence of the proper checks imposed by a loyal and fearless Congress lead to a rupture that will sink into insignificance the impoverishing war that has just ended. Can you then think in our retaining our Military organization with love to our country and hate to treason any bad results will ensue?"

Newspaper reports supported O'Beirne's statements about mysterious shipments of arms, while later events were to confirm his belief that G.A.R. leaders planned to use the organization for military action.

Alarmed, Johnson took precautions to avoid an uprising. In response to his query, Grant told him that 2,224 troops were within easy reach of the national capital, but that only 1,550 of these were effective. Johnson wrote to Secretary of War Stanton on November 1 that this force was inadequate "in view of the prevalence, in various portions of the country, of a revolutionary and turbulent disposition, which might at any moment assume insurrectionary proportions and lead to serious disorders." He requested Stanton to take immediate steps to ensure the government's safety "and thus discourage any attempt for its possession by insurgent or other illegal combinations." Johnson received various suggestions from anxious Democrats; one urged that the excitement aroused by veterans be directed against England, while another suggested a war with Mexico.

. . . At a meeting to plan Grand Army participation in the 1867 campaign, Pennsylvania's Commander Wagner urged the impeachment of Johnson and cried, "We are ready to quit workshops, factory, desk and farm, to cast aside domestic ties, and arm and fight. . . . "

Members responded willingly with promises to march to the armed defense of Congress. A New Jersey post, for example, asserted its readiness to battle again for "the supremacy of the Constitution and the laws." A Washington post adjutant who had lost a foot in battle wrote to Butler that the time had come to prepare for a struggle, since Johnson's affiliation with traitors meant "fight." He continued:

> We have a Soldiers [sic] organization in this city, known as the Grand Army of the Republic, which can be made of great use to congress situated as we are, if this thing should have to be settled by arms.
>
> We now number about 500, but are organizing colored posts, and think that within a short time, with some encouragement, we will number several thousand. Now it would not take long to organize into Companies and Regiments, and arm ourselves on short notice if an emergency required it. . . . if you think the matter plausable [sic], give us some encouragement. . . . All our workings are entirely secret.

. . . When Sheridan and Sickles returned to the North after Johnson removed them as military governors, the Radicals arranged ovations, which in many cases the G.A.R. managed. At St. Louis, Department Commander Carl Schurz staged a Grand Army torchlight parade, in which more than twenty posts marched to honor Sheridan. When the two generals arrived in Washington, the members of the Grand Army, led by Commander Chipman and accompanied by a blaring band and several regiments of uniformed Negro soldiers, marched to their hotels for enthusiastic demonstrations. As they moved through the East—through Newark, Columbus (Ohio), and Philadelphia—they received similar G.A.R. ovations. Sickles soon dropped out to receive a "handsome reception" from his home posts in New York City and Brooklyn, but Sheridan continued his tour. The Boston posts, under Cushman's leadership, welcomed him with an impressive torchlight procession. "It was the first great stroke in the present year," believed Schurz, "against the Johnson policy."

. . . As the struggle between Johnson and Congress grew increasingly bitter, Logan held the G.A.R. ready to give armed opposition to the President.

In August, 1867, Johnson had finally dismissed Secretary Stanton, whose continued intrigues with Radicals had sabotaged the executive program. But the following January the Senate refused, under the terms of the Tenure of Office Act, to confirm the removal. Grant, the new secretary, immediately turned in his keys; and Stanton triumphantly resumed control. Johnson believed the law unconstitutional; his idea throughout had been to maintain his appointee in control of the department in order to force the act to a court test. In permitting the keys to fall into Stanton's hands, Grant had thwarted this plan. Moreover, the angry President regarded the general's behavior as disloyal and in violation of an express promise. On two occasions Johnson tried to persuade Sherman to accept the post, but the general had no desire to become involved in the imbroglio.

Late in February the Democratic National Committee met in Washington to prepare for its nominating convention. Possibly Johnson believed that by some bold stroke in defiance of Congress he might force himself on the committee's attention as the obvious presidential candidate. Whatever his motive, he suddenly abandoned his dilatory tactics on February 21, and without consulting his advisers appointed General Lorenzo Thomas secretary ad interim.

As adjutant general, Thomas was Stanton's subordinate. The two men had reportedly been on bad terms for years, and the impatient secretary had sent Thomas out on various missions in order to be rid of him. It was with satisfaction, therefore, that the vain old man entered his superior's office to present the President's order. Surprised, Stanton asked if he might have time to remove his personal property. But while Thomas was out of the office, he conferred with Grant; and when the general returned, he announced that he might not obey the instructions. Stanton, stern and nervously irritable, was more than a match for the aspirant; Thomas quickly bowed himself out.

The winner of the first encounter rushed a note to the House; at the same time an announcement from Johnson arrived at the Senate. The effect was electrifying. For two years Radicals had longed to impeach the President; here was their opportunity. In turmoil the senators barred the doors to spectators and went into executive session. Increasingly large crowds huddled about the doors as the news spread, and newspaper reporters gathered like bees. While the Senate voted that the President had no power to dismiss his secretary, rumors developed to terrifying proportions.

Meanwhile crowds thronged the hotels and swarmed about the War Department. A committee of agitated Radical senators hurried to Stanton and begged him to hold his ground. Tears flowed freely, and the secretary vowed that he would never forsake Congress. Urgent letters arrived from other senators, among them a single-word note from Charles Sumner: "Stick." Fearing forcible ejection at any moment, Stanton decided to stay in office quite literally. He ordered his meals sent in, and at night he slept on a sofa in his office. An unsympathetic newspaper remarked that he and his congressional friends were undoubtedly "in no lack of tipple."

General Thomas, enjoying the rapidly mounting excitement, remained downtown most of the evening. He confided to friends that if in the morning his demand for the department was refused, he would apply for troops, and that if he found the door barred, he would break it down. Later, while he nonchalantly attended a masquerade ball, Stanton learned of these conversations.

Despite the armed guard that Stanton had obtained from Grant, the frightened secretary suddenly felt inadequately protected. He swore out a warrant, and before the boastful old Thomas had time to breakfast the next morning, officers appeared to arrest him. Taken before a judge who was a known tool of Stanton, the befuddled general was released on $5,000 bail. Then, after reporting to Johnson, Thomas moved once more upon the War Department. The secretary had spent the night there and now, surrounded by Congressmen, sat like a bewhiskered lord amid his courtiers.

A terse exchange of orders ensued; Thomas insisted upon taking possession, while Stanton sternly demanded that he execute the functions of adjutant general. Finally Thomas crossed the hall to another official's room, and the secretary followed, still issuing orders. Again the general was the first to surrender. The President's appointee remarked sadly to the choice of Congress, "The next time you have me arrested, please do not do it before I get something to eat."

All solicitude, Stanton quickly put his arm around Thomas's shoulders, ran his hand through the general's hair, and turned to an officer.

"Schriver," he called, "you have got a bottle here; bring it out."

Schriver did indeed have a bottle as a "dyspepsia remedy." He produced it, but only a few drops remained. Stanton shared them with his adversary; then he sent out for a full bottle. When it arrived, the two contenders had another drink. "Now," remarked Stanton, "This at least is neutral ground." On that note the general withdrew from the field, vanquished for the moment but a little happier.

As public tension mounted, Democratic and conservative papers urged the President to violence, and again Radicals cried that war was coming. Rumors of Johnson's plans circulated rapidly. Grant, people whispered, had been arrested. Governor Thomas Swann's visit to the White House strengthened the story that he was preparing the Maryland militia, at least ten thousand strong, for a march on Washington. It was reported that the secretary of the navy, "Grandmother" Welles, had offered Johnson the services of four hundred marines stationed in the city. If some Radicals merely made political capital of these rumors, others actually believed the President might seize control of the War Department and maintain his position by force.

On that turbulent Washington's Birthday, excited crowds moved toward the Capitol. "The tramping of thousands of feet," remarked a reporter, "began to sound already like the tread of an army." To frightened Washingtonians, the White House and the Capitol had become castles occupied by opposing forces. Anxious questions flew about; the word "revolution" was whispered everywhere. Inside the Capitol the massive stairways, the corridors—even the dark recesses of the basement—were jammed; and the House galleries had been packed since early morning. Numerous descriptions have been written of the highly theatrical impeachment debate and its most spectacular participant, the feeble, club-footed Radical leader, Thaddeus Stevens.

Real danger of violence hung over the country in these dramatic moments, but it was not to be found in the wild expressions of Old Thad and his confederates, in the nervous tension of the anxious crowds in Washington and other cities, or in the savage threats flung by partisan newspapers. The actual peril lay in the quiet plans of a scowling House member, one of the most venomous of Johnson's opponents, who sat heedless of the debate. General Logan's conviction that the President intended to take the War Department by force seemed confirmed by Thomas' boasts. Logan was determined to block any such contingency, and as head of the G.A.R. he believed he was in a position to do so effectively. While House members declaimed to packed galleries, Logan grasped a pencil and hastily scribbled a note to Chipman, who was still G.A.R. adjutant general as well as commander of District posts.

"It seems that the city is filling up with a Suspicious Class of men," the general wrote.

> That may mean harm Tho no demonstration *has been made*. The House will impeach A. J. and a Row may ensue.
> I hope you will quietly and secretly organize all our boys so that they can assemble at a signal that you may agree upon to report at Hd Qur. &c. ready to protect the Congress of the U.S. in the exercise of their lawful duties. This must be done quietly, and no indiscreet persons must understand or know anything about it, and no demonstration of any kind must be made at all, if no necessity shall occur for us to act at any time then the fact that we are on the alert, must never be known as it would effect many of our boys that hold office &c.
>
> J. A. Logan

All of this must be done by verbal communication as no official orders must be made on the subject at present, or until a necessity might arise to protect The Government against Traitors to it, be discreet, and come and see me tonight. L.

And while attention was centered on the House, where Congressmen spat venom throughout the afternoon and evening, Chipman quietly carried out his instructions. In his own words, he "organized the members of the Grand Army Posts and held them in readiness to rally at a signal in defense of Secretary Stanton or of the Congress." He and Logan formed battalions under former officers and provided countersigns that would bring the men instantly to the War Office. Sentinels stood on duty round the clock at various places in the city, particularly outside the White House and the War Department. Many of these men had no idea why arms and ammunition had been issued to them. Mrs. Logan later remarked, "Through all these trying hours the faithful Grand Army of the Republic were the unknown, silent sentinels that guarded the Capitol and kept vigilant watch. . . . "

Logan, the last speaker that night, proclaimed to the crowded House that Johnson was planning to inaugurate a revolution. Then, crossing the grounds in the pale light from the dome lantern, the general hurried to the War Department to assure Stanton that the G.A.R. was ready for any emergency and that its members were quietly patrolling the city. The secretary was still entrenched in his private office; and on this and succeeding nights, Logan, self-appointed protector, occupied a cot beside him.

Despite Logan's air of secrecy, it soon became public knowledge that he had offered to station 125 Grand Army men at the War Office to "stand by Mr. Stanton at all hazards." And, indeed, excitement became so intense in Washington that for a time it seemed that the G.A.R. guards might actually use their guns. One paper declared: " . . . we are given to understand that blood will flow in our streets in a day or two." Stanton knew that if he left the War Department, General Thomas would immediately take possession. Expecting any moment an attempt at forcible ejection, he remained entrenched there day and night except for a brief daily walk under guard. General Logan was occupied all day as one of the managers of the impeachment trial; but every night, after his conference with the G.A.R. staff in his rooms at Willard's, he hurried to the War Department.

And on that bleak, cold Sabbath, a tumultuous day filled with sensational rumors, messages began pouring in on Logan from the far-flung departments and posts of the Grand Army. For more than a year the *Great Republic* had been shouting for impeachment; when it finally came, members needed no prodding to express themselves in violent language. "Today the mask is stripped from the features of this demon," cried one paper in alarm, "and it boldly offers sword and firebrand to its great patron at Washington. From all parts of the country, say the telegrams, the circles of this military order are tendering their services to Congress."

Logan received many offers of armed assistance. From St. Louis came the wire, "The Grand Army of the Republic of Missouri will give 50,000 men to carry out the action of Congress." The Minnesota G.A.R. declared, "This department will respond promptly to any call in defense of the Government." Commander Palmer, offering military support, stated that Illinois posts were constantly wiring their readiness for immediate action. From New York came the message, "We are ready." From individual posts, too, Logan received numerous offers of aid. As the New York *Herald* observed, the society was "in a great state of excitement"; Republican papers boasted that it was prepared "100,000 strong" to defend Congress by arms.

Many of the war heroes, indeed, were itching for a fight. One inquired of John Covode, "Are the old boys in blue wanted right off? We will come on the click of the telegraph." Another wrote to Butler, "You have got the scoundrel by the throat. Shake him over the jaws of hell and let him drop in. My old regiment is at the service of the government. . . . we could take the field in 12 hours." Wisconsin's Governor Fairchild, high in G.A.R. councils, was overwhelmed with offers. He wrote excitedly to his sister, "Yesterday we were all in commotion on account of receipt of the news. . . . My room was soon crowded with old veterans to offer their services in case trouble and blows come—if it does I'll accept them and hurry troops to W, with all possible speed. If it does come we will stamp all devilish traitors out of existence before peace comes again. . . . I have already full arrangements made for the organization of several regiments. . . . "

He wrote similar letters to Schuyler Colfax and Stanton; and he informed Senator T. O. Howe that veterans from all parts of the state were offering him their services: "Thousands are ready to spring to arms to crush [Johnson] and those who shall attempt to sustain him." To one soldier he wrote, "If Johnson should dare to resist Congress you shall have an opportunity to put on your sword again and battle for the country." Other Radical governors, too, were piling "fuel on the flames of discord" by wiring offers of troops to congressmen. Governor Fletcher telegraphed that Missouri men would rally with bayonets "to crush nullification, headed by Andy Johnson," while the governors of Iowa, Illinois, Pennsylvania, and New York sent similarly threatening messages. General Wallace hurried down to confer with Logan about using the Grand Army in the crisis, but the commander in chief was waiting for some move from Johnson before taking action. The President, however, did nothing. Perhaps he saw little that he could do; dilatory tactics had left him stranded. General Grant, in command of the armies, had gone over to the Radicals, as had also General William H. Emory, commander of the troops around Washington. Before the crisis, Secretary Welles had warned Johnson that the Radicals would arrest and imprison him if they dared, and he asked the President if he could count on any military support in case of a collision. Pacing the room in agitation, Johnson admitted that he could not. He would make Washington a military department, he declared, and order

General Sherman to its command. But the general, who had fled to St. Louis when he saw the political storm brewing, was determined to stay out of the conflict. He refused the appointment. Johnson became painfully aware of his position when he learned that on the evening of Thomas' appointment, all officers under Emory's command had been called back to duty from social functions. Alarmed, he called Emory to ask what orders had been issued and at whose request. But he got no satisfaction from that Radical; Emory promptly spread the tale that the President had sought aid from his troops and that he had coldly replied, "You can't use me."

. . .

While agitated messages were pouring in on congressmen as well as on the President, General Thomas visited the War Department Monday morning to announce for the third time that he would take control. Stanton, his demeanor even fiercer than usual, sternly refused and followed the old man as he bustled from office to office making futile demands for the department's mail. Thomas finally left, reported his failure to Johnson, and then, feeling definitely ill, took a carriage home.

20

Passages from the Writings
of Oliver Wendell Holmes, Jr.

*Some veterans thought of military service essentially as time lost, remembering
mainly the boredom of camp. Many, however, remembered military service as
the most significant and moving experience of their lives. There is good evidence
of this—in diary entries, letters home, and later autobiographies, and speeches.
Oliver Wendell Holmes, Jr., who served in the Army of the Potomac in a Massachusetts regiment, may serve as an example. He was wounded at Ball's Bluff
and left the service in July 1864 with the rank of captain. The following passages
are from his Civil War letters and diary and from speeches delivered a generation
after the war.*

I
DIARY ENTRY

1864, exact date unknown

. . . I WAS QUITE FAINT—and seeing poor Serg^t Merchant lying near—shot
through the head and covered with blood—and then the thinking begun—
(Meanwhile hardly able to speak—at least, coherently)—Shot through the
lungs? Lets see—and I spit—Yes—already the blood was in my mouth. At
once my thoughts jumped to "Children of the New Forest." (by Marryatt)
which I was fond of reading as a little boy, and in which the father of one
of the heroines is shot through the lungs by a robber—I remembered he
died with terrible haemorrhages & great agony—What should I do? Just
then I remembered and felt in my waist coat pocket—Yes there it was—a
little bottle of laudanum which I had brought along—But I won't take it

SOURCE: Diary entry No. 2, as given in *Touched with Fire: The Civil War Letters and Diary
of Oliver Wendell Holmes, Jr.*, edited by Mark DeWolfe Howe (Cambridge, Mass.: Harvard
University Press, 1946), pp. 24–28. Copyright © 1946 by the President and Fellows of
Harvard College; copyright © 1974 by Mary Manning Howe. Reprinted by permission.

yet; no, see a doctor first—It may not be as bad as it looks—At any rate wait till the pain begins—

When I had got to the bottom of the Bluff the ferry boat, (the scow,) had just started with a load—but there was a small boat there—Then, still in this half conscious state, I heard somebody groan—Then I thought "Now wouldn't Sir Philip Sydney have that other feller put into the boat first?" But the question, as the form in which it occurred shows, came from a *mind* still bent on a becoming and consistent carrying out of its ideals of conduct—not from the unhesitating instinct of a still predominant & heroic *will*—I am not sure whether I propounded the question but I let myself be put aboard.

. . , I was taken into the large building which served as a general hospital; and I remember . . . Men lying round on the floor—the spectacle wasn't familiar then—a red blanket with an arm lying on it in a pool of blood—it seems as if instinct told me it was John Putnam's (then Capt. Comdg Co H)—and near the entrance a surgeon calmly grasping a man's finger and cutting it off—both standing—while the victim contemplated the operation with a very grievous mug . . . presently a Doctor of (Baxter's?) Fire Zouaves* coming in with much noise & bluster, and oh, troops were crossing to the Virginia side, and we were going to lick, and Heaven knows what not—I called him and gave him my address and told him (or meant & tried to) if I died to write home & tell 'em I'd done my duty— I was very anxious they should know that— . . .

Much more vivid is my memory of my thoughts and state of mind for though I may have been light-headed my reason was working—even if through a cloud. Of course when I thought I was dying the reflection that the majority vote of the civilized world declared that with my opinions I was *en route* for Hell came up with painful distinctness—Perhaps the first impulse was tremulous—but then I said—by Jove, I die like a soldier anyhow—I was shot in the breast doing my duty up to the hub—afraid? No, I am proud—then I thought I couldn't be guilty of a deathbed recantation—father and I had talked of that and were agreed that it generally meant nothing but a cowardly giving way to fear—Besides, thought I, can I recant if I want to, has the approach of death changed my beliefs much? & to this I answered—No—Then came in my Philosophy—I am to take a leap in the dark—but now as ever I believe that whatever shall happen is best—for it is in accordance with a general law—and *good & universal* (or *general law*) are synonymous terms in the universe—(I can now add that our phrase *good* only means certain general truths seen through the heart & will instead of being merely contemplated intellectually—I doubt if the intellect accepts or recognizes that classification of good and bad). Would the complex forces which made a still more complex unit in *Me* resolve

---

*The 72nd Regiment Pennsylvania Volunteers, under Colonel DeWitt Clinton Baxter, was commonly known as Baxter's Fire Zouaves.

themselves back into simpler forms or would my angel be still winging his way onward when eternities had passed? I could not tell—But all was doubtless well—and so with a "God forgive me if I'm wrong" I slept—

II
HOLMES TO CHARLES ELIOT NORTON
April 17, 1864

Holmes wrote to Norton expressing appreciation of Norton's article in the *North American Review* on St. Louis and Joinville: "I have long wanted to know more of Joinville's Chronicle than I did, but the story seems to come up most opportunely now when we need all the examples of chivalry to help us bind our rebellious desires to steadfastness in the Christian Crusade of the 19th century. If one didn't believe that this war was such a crusade, in the cause of the whole civilized world, it would be hard indeed to keep the hand to the sword; and one who is rather compelled unwillingly to the work by abstract conviction than borne along on the flood of some passionate enthusiasm, must feel his ardor rekindled by stories like this. . . . I am thankful to read of the great dead who have 'stood in the evil day.' No—it will not do to leave Palestine yet."

III
THE SOLDIER'S FAITH
Memorial Day Speech,
Harvard University,
May 30, 1895

. . . Now, at least, and perhaps as long as man dwells upon the globe, his destiny is battle, and he has to take the chances of war. If it is our business to fight, the book for the army is a war-song, not a hospital-sketch. It is not well for soldiers to think much about wounds. Sooner or later we shall fall; but meantime it is for us to fix our eyes upon the point to be stormed, and to get there if we can.

Behind every scheme to make the world over, lies the question, What

SOURCE: Holmes to Norton, April 17, 1864, as given in *Touched with Fire: The Civil War Letters and Diary of Oliver Wendell Holmes, Jr.*, edited by Mark DeWolfe Howe (Cambridge, Mass.: Harvard University Press, 1946), p. 29. Reprinted by permission of the Houghton Library, Harvard University, which holds the original letter.
SOURCE: "The Soldier's Faith," as given in *The Occasional Speeches of Justice Oliver Wendell Holmes*, edited by Mark DeWolfe Howe (Cambridge, Mass.: The Belknap Press of Harvard University Press, 1962), pp. 75–82. Copyright © 1962 by the President and Fellows of Harvard College. Reprinted by permission.

kind of world do you want? The ideals of the past for men have been drawn from war, as those for women have been drawn from motherhood. For all our prophecies, I doubt if we are ready to give up our inheritance. Who is there who would not like to be thought a gentleman? Yet what has that name been built on but the soldier's choice of honor rather than life? To be a soldier or descended from soldiers, in time of peace to be ready to give one's life rather than to suffer disgrace, that is what the world has meant; and if we try to claim it at less cost than a splendid carelessness for life, we are trying to steal the good will without the responsibilities of the place. We will not dispute about tastes. The man of the future may want something different. But who of us could endure a world, although cut up into five-acre lots and having no man upon it who was not well fed and well housed, without the divine folly of honor, without the senseless passion for knowledge out-reaching the flaming bounds of the possible, without ideals the essence of which is that they can never be achieved? I do not know what is true. I do not know the meaning of the universe. But in the midst of doubt, in the collapse of creeds, there is one thing I do not doubt, that no man who lives in the same world with most of us can doubt, and that is that the faith is true and adorable which leads a soldier to throw away his life in obedience to a blindly accepted duty, in a cause which he little understands, in a plan of campaign of which he has no notion, under tactics of which he does not see the use.

Most men who know battle know the cynic force with which the thoughts of common sense will assail them in times of stress; but they know that in their greatest moments faith has trampled those thoughts under foot. If you have been in line, suppose on Tremont Street Mall, ordered simply to wait and to do nothing, and have watched the enemy bring their guns to bear upon you down a gentle slope like that from Beacon Street, have seen the puff of the firing, have felt the burst of the spherical case-shot as it came toward you, have heard and seen the shrieking fragments go tearing through your company, and have known that the next or the next shot carries your fate; if you have advanced in line and have seen ahead of you the spot which you must pass where the rifle bullets are striking; if you have ridden by night at a walk toward the blue line of fire at the dead angle of Spottsylvania, where for twenty-four hours the soldiers were fighting on the two sides of an earthwork, and in the morning the dead and dying lay piled in a row six deep, and as you rode have heard the bullets splashing in the mud and earth about you; if you have been on the picketline at night in a black and unknown wood, have heard the spat of the bullets upon the trees, and as you moved have felt your foot slip upon a dead man's body; if you have had a blind fierce gallop against the enemy, with your blood up and a pace that left no time for fear—if, in short, as some, I hope many, who hear me, have known, you have known the vicissitudes of terror and of triumph in war, you know that there is such a thing as the faith I spoke of. You know your own weakness and are modest; but you know that man has in him that unspeakable somewhat which makes him capable of miracle, able to lift himself by the might of his own soul, unaided, able to face annihilation for a blind belief.

From the beginning, to us, children of the North, life has seemed a place hung about by dark mists, out of which come the pale shine of dragon's scales, and the cry of fighting men, and the sound of swords. Beowulf, Milton, Dürer, Rembrandt, Schopenhauer, Turner, Tennyson, from the first war-song of our race to the stall-fed poetry of modern English drawing-rooms, all have had the same vision, and all have had a glimpse of a light to be followed. "The end of worldly life awaits us all. Let him who may, gain honor ere death. That is best for a warrior when he is dead." So spoke Beowulf a thousand years ago.

> Not of the sunlight,
> Not of the moonlight,
> Not of the starlight!
> O young Mariner,
> Down to the haven,
> Call your companions,
> Launch your vessel,
> And crowd your canvas,
> And, ere it vanishes
> Over the margin,
> After it, follow it,
> Follow The Gleam.

So sang Tennyson in the voice of the dying Merlin.

When I went to war I thought that soldiers were old men. I remembered a picture of the revolutionary soldier which some of you may have seen, representing a white-haired man with his flint-lock slung across his back. I remembered one or two living examples of revolutionary soldiers whom I had met, and I took no account of the lapse of time. It was not until long after, in winter quarters, as I was listening to some of the sentimental songs in vogue, such as—

> Farewell, Mother, you may never
> See your darling boy again,

that it came over me that the army was made up of what I now should call very young men. I dare say that my illusion has been shared by some of those now present, as they have looked at us upon whose heads the white shadows have begun to fall. But the truth is that war is the business of youth and early middle age. You who called this assemblage together, not we, would be the soldiers of another war, if we should have one, and we speak to you as the dying Merlin did in the verse which I just quoted. Would that the blind man's pipe might be transfigured by Merlin's magic, to make you hear the bugles as once we heard them beneath the morning stars! For to you it is that now is sung the Song of the Sword:—

The War-Thing, the Comrade,
Father of honor
And giver of kingship,
The fame-smith, the song master.

. . . .

Priest (saith the Lord)
Of his marriage with victory.

. . . .

Clear singing, clean slicing;
Sweet spoken, soft finishing;
Making death beautiful,
Life but a coin
To be staked in the pastime
Whose playing is more
Than the transfer of being;
Arch-anarch, chief builder,
Prince and evangelist,
I am the Will of God:
I am the Sword.

War, when you are at it, is horrible and dull. It is only when time has passed that you see that its message was divine. I hope it may be long before we are called again to sit at that master's feet. But some teacher of the kind we all need. In this snug, over-safe corner of the world we need it, that we may realize that our comfortable routine is no eternal necessity of things, but merely a little space of calm in the midst of the tempestuous untamed streaming of the world, and in order that we may be ready for danger. We need it in this time of individualist negations, with its literature of French and American humor, revolting at discipline, loving fleshpots, and denying that anything is worthy of reverence,—in order that we may remember all that buffoons forget. We need it everywhere and at all times. For high and dangerous action teaches us to believe as right beyond dispute things for which our doubting minds are slow to find words of proof. Out of heroism grows faith in the worth of heroism. The proof comes later, and even may never come. Therefore I rejoice at every dangerous sport which I see pursued. The students at Heidelberg, with their sword-slashed faces, inspire me with sincere respect. I gaze with delight upon our polo-players. If once in a while in our rough riding a neck is broken, I regard it, not as a waste, but as a price well paid for the breeding of a race fit for headship and command.

We do not save our traditions, in this country. The regiments whose battle-flags were not large enough to hold the names of the battles they had fought, vanished with the surrender of Lee, although their memories inherited would have made heroes for a century. It is the more necessary to learn the lesson afresh from perils newly sought, and perhaps it is not vain for us to tell the new generation what we learned in our day, and what we still believe. That the joy of life is living, is to put out all one's powers as far as they will go; that the measure of power is obstacles over-come; to ride boldly at what is in front of you, be it fence or enemy; to pray, not for comfort, but for combat; to keep the soldier's faith against the doubts of civil life, more besetting and harder to overcome than all the misgivings of the battle-field, and to remember that duty is not to be proved in the evil day, but then to be obeyed unquestioning; to love glory more than the temptations of wallowing ease, but to know that one's final judge and only rival is oneself—with all our failures in act and thought, these things we learned from noble enemies in Virginia or Georgia or on the Mississippi, thirty years ago; these things we believe to be true.

> "Life is not lost," said she, "for which is bought
> Endlesse renown."

We learned also, and we still believe, that love of country is not yet an idle name. . . .

As for us, our days of combat are over. Our swords are rust. Our guns will thunder no more. The vultures that once wheeled over our heads are buried with their prey. Whatever of glory yet remains for us to win must be won in the council or the closet, never again in the field. I do not repine. We have shared the incommunicable experience of war; we have felt, we still feel, the passion of life to its top. . . .

21

The Connecticut National Guard

Many of the volunteer companies of the pre-Civil War years survived to become the core of the National Guard. This national organization of statewide associations of some 100,000 volunteer soldiers was formed in 1879 to lobby for funds in the strike-filled final quarter of the nineteenth century. This photo of early-twentieth-century Connecticut Guardsmen evokes a martial air more suggestive of Wilhelmine Germany than the Nutmeg State.

22

The Wisconsin National Guard in the Milwaukee Riots of 1886

JERRY M. COOPER

Eventually many Guard units acquired a middle-class, "property-rights" char-acter, but others retained their essentially ethnic membership long after that char-acteristic had become quite counterproductive to their new missions. In this regard Jerry Cooper's analysis of the plight of the Kosciusko Guards during a South Milwaukee strike of Polish-American workers in 1886 is instructive.

IN APRIL OF 1886, A. V. H. Carpenter, general manager in Milwaukee for the Chicago, Milwaukee, and St. Paul Railroad, wrote to the Adjutant General of the Wisconsin National Guard, Chandler P. Chapman, on the prevailing labor troubles in the United States. Carpenter expressed par-ticular concern over the current movement within organized labor for the eight hour day and of the workers' apparent willingness to strike to gain this goal. To the Milwaukee railroad man, the entire affair was generated by foreign-born, socialist agitators. The honest, but ignorant, American workingman was unfortunately falling prey to these evil appeals, he thought, and it could only be hoped that Wisconsin railroad workers would ignore the troublemakers. He concluded his letter by expressing the belief that the labor difficulties would pass but that nonetheless, "I am glad the W.N.G. is in good condition—that fact is of itself a great moral power—as well as an inspirator of good order."

SOURCE: Jerry M. Cooper, "The Wisconsin National Guard in the Milwaukee Riots of 1866," *Wisconsin Magazine of History* 55 (Autumn 1971): 31–48. Reprinted by permission of the State Historical Society of Wisconsin.
EDITOR'S NOTE: The citations to the sources consulted by the author in this essay have been omitted from this volume for brevity and economy. The reader should consult the original source of the essay for the complete scholarly documentation.

It was only natural that, as a businessman, Carpenter would express his worries about labor difficulties to the adjutant general of his state, even had the two men not been personally acquainted. A very close correlation between the rise of the modern National Guard in the 1870's and the growing conflicts between capital and labor clearly did exist. It was not until the early 1870's that state governments saw fit to render regular and substantial aid to the volunteer militia and thus give it a basis for a permanent existence. While many men joined the Guard because of a genuine interest in military things and a sincere but vague idea of providing the nation with a military reserve, the states provided money in order to create a force which could deal with domestic disorder engendered by industrial and urban expansion. Inevitably, businessmen came to expect the aid of such a force during strikes and with their access to the loci of power, they more often than not had their expectations gratified. It was in this vein that Carpenter wrote to Chapman.

The development of the Wisconsin National Guard generally paralleled the national trend. The antebellum volunteer militia system, practically destroyed by the war, revived slowly during the late 1860's and early 1870's but always remained ephemeral. The state began providing financial assistance to militia companies in 1873, but the evolution of the modern Wisconsin National Guard, not officially designated as such until 1879, did not reach maturity until the early 1880's. For the most part, the general populace and most state legislators took little interest in the organization. The impact of nationwide labor strife had not yet been felt in Wisconsin and most people saw little need to spend money on the militia. Nonetheless, Guard advocates relied mainly upon the threat of labor disorders as the main justification for financial support of the institution. In 1880, for example, Governor William E. Smith made a strong appeal for a well organized state force, noting that it was always best to be prepared, for "We cannot hope always to escape disorders and tumults similar to those which have arisen in other states and nations." Guard officials serving under Smith, his successor Jeremiah M. Rusk, and other militia advocates all relied upon this argument to gain public and legislative support for the force. A year after Smith made the statement, he sent 300 Guardsmen to Eau Claire to break a strike of lumbermill hands.

By the mid-1880's, this appeal and the diligent work of Rusk's adjutant general, Chandler P. Chapman of Madison, had produced an organized Guard force of about 2,400 officers and men. In 1886, the Guard consisted of thirty-five infantry companies, organized into three regiments and a battalion, with a troop of cavalry and a battery of light artillery, both located in Milwaukee, completing the organization. Serving with Chapman in a variety of posts was Captain Charles King, scion of a prominent Milwaukee family, graduate of West Point and recently retired from active duty with the Fifth United States Cavalry. While both men contributed to the improvement of the service during the early 1880's, many defects remained. The Guard was essentially an amateur outfit, based upon the local company. These companies were as often social-fraternal associations as they were military units, governed by civil rules which determined membership, dues, and the election of officers. They were more often oriented to their own localities than to state matters and were not above using political pressure in attempting to rescind unpopular military decisions made by Chapman and King. Furthermore, the service remained under financial stringencies. Equipped only minimally with material cast off by the Regular Army, Guard units bought their own uniforms and provided from their own resources what little field equipment, such as canteens, tents, overcoats, and field kitchens, that they had.

Following Chapman's assumption of the post of adjutant general, Guard regiments began to hold five-day summer camps on a yearly basis, but these events more often resembled county fairs than genuine military maneuvers, with politicians orating, soldiers drinking, and civilians parading through the camp. What drilling was accomplished at these camps involved intricate battalion and regimental marching on the order of Civil War tactics. The weekly company drills at local armories also concentrated on precision marching with little or no attention to riot drill.

The bulk of the Guard membership throughout the late nineteenth century was located in small cities and towns. The regiments were organized on a geographical basis, ten companies to a regiment. In 1886 the First Regiment, for example, was composed of units from the southeastern section of the state, with companies at such places as Janesville (2), Racine (2), Whitewater, Delavan, Beloit, Monroe, Madison, and Darlington. The other two regiments consisted of companies from towns and cities of similar size in the western and northern portions of the state. In Milwaukee, four infantry companies, the cavalry troop and the light artillery battery made up the local guard forces.

The composition of these units involved varied social and economic classes. Most of the officers came from white-collar groups, though few really wealthy men could be found in the force. Generally, the officers were small businessmen, independent professionals, and professional politicians. The enlisted men came from many occupational groups, although few unskilled workers served. For example, clerks and bookkeepers made up one of the Janesville units but factory workers predominated in the other Janesville company. The Madison unit had many machinists, while the Beloit Guardsmen were primarily paper-mill workers or came from the local shoe shops. In Milwaukee, Company A of the Fourth Battalion counted many iron moulders in its ranks, as did Company B. As a whole, according to Chapman, "The Battalion has a great variety of mechanics and many strong, heavy men." The only units in the Guard which had a definite class cast to them were the cavalry troop and the artillery battery, partly because the troopers and artillerymen had to provide their own horses or

rent them. Adjutant General Chapman observed that the troop was
" . . . composed of young businessmen (mostly in business for themselves)
and is a fair sample of the best blood of Milwaukee," while the battery
contained many men who were " . . . exceptionally bright and intelligent
young men, clerks, students, board of trade officemen and bookkeepers."

The efforts of Adjutant General Chapman and his aide Charles King,
a colonel and chief of inspection by 1885, to give a sense of direction to
the Wisconsin National Guard illustrate the fact that the Guard lacked a
central purpose. The two men could never decide whether to concentrate
on the military or constabulary functions of the service. Chapman and
King attempted to use Regular Army regulations and standards as the
marks with which to measure the Guard. Thus in weekly drills and annual
encampments, Regular Army drills, tactics and maneuvers dominated the
agenda. They applied the Army standards with zeal but in the process
created a great deal of ill-feeling at the local company level, as the officers
objected to King's continual harping on the fine points of officership, while
the enlisted men disliked being subjected to Regular Army discipline. Army
regulations, especially their stress on the gulf between officers and enlisted
men, just did not fit the looser, quasi-fraternal nature of the National
Guard.

At the same time that Chapman and King sought to remake the Guard
in the image of the Army, and thus by implication make it a reserve military force, they also relied upon the argument that the Guard constituted
a state constabulary force as the surest means of gaining financial support
from the legislature and of maintaining a more immediate sense of mission
in the ranks. Chapman continually stressed this function of the Guard in
his annual reports, sometimes referring to the strike duty of National
Guards in such states as Pennsylvania and New York.

Charles King also discussed this aspect of Guard duty. A much more
outspoken man than Chapman, King indicated his pointed views on riot
duty in a stirring lecture to a gathering of Wisconsin Guard officers. Ostensibly King's remarks on riots were to have been merely tactical, but he
talked at length on the political and social aspects of labor strikes, strongly
implying that these were the main sources of riots. The motives of all strikers, regardless of their actions, were questioned by King. He saw most
strikes as " . . . outbreaks in which law, order and property are arranged
on the one hand against a faction or class, driven to temporary insanity,
it may be by fancied wrongs, blind fanaticism, the specious arguments of
designing demagogues or uncontrollable passions. . . . "

His recommendations for dealing with mobs were quite simple. A
Guard unit should make a demonstration of force, and if this did not
dispel the group, "Two volleys by battalion, low, cool, steady, well aimed,
will knock the fight out of any ordinary mob. . . . " King ended his lecture
with speculations on the possibilities of riot duty for the Wisconsin Guard.
He did not foresee any likelihood of riots or labor strife of any consequence

in the state except in Milwaukee, where, King believed, " . . . from whose dregs can be swept up the constituents of a mob [on] whom it might be a municipal blessing to fire. . . . " The city was, in his opinion, woefully unprepared to cope with such an occurrence, as was the Guard. He made several suggestions for preparing both the city and the Guard for such an eventuality, noting that "I speak of this only as illustrative of the apathetic condition of the Milwaukee mind on matters of this character, and while it is to be hoped no rude awakening may come, it is best to be prepared." Two years later, the rude awakening came.

Perhaps the awakening should not have been so rude, for organized labor had made its presence known in Milwaukee throughout the 1880's. In the most important instances, however, business and management had overcome labor's challenges. This was due in large part to the fact that the workers in Milwaukee were divided: divided by their work skills; divided by ethnic antipathies; divided by conflicting ideologies. The nature of Milwaukee's industrial base created the need for both highly skilled laborers and unskilled day workers. The breweries, tanneries, and machine foundries—the core industries of the city's economy—all required men of considerable skill; but each also used many unskilled workers. The skilled workers, of course, received the best pay and job security and because of this, labor leaders found it difficult to unite skilled and unskilled to work for mutual goals. Some of the city's industries were very seasonal, particularly the meat-packing industry. It was always difficult, if not impossible, to organize seasonal workers of limited skill who could be easily replaced by others willing to work.

These differences alone were a challenge to any labor organizer, but they were further complicated by the ethnic makeup of the city. One student of industrialization in Milwaukee has pointed out that a clear ethnic pecking order existed within the city's economic matrix. At the top, among the owners and managers, were native Americans, Scotch and English immigrants, and first- and second-generation Germans. Natives, English, and Germans possessed an almost exclusive hold on skilled jobs, while at the bottom of the industrial order, newcomers made up the vast majority of unskilled laborers, chief among these being the Polish. This ethnic ranking could also be found in local politics, although by the 1880's the Germans, largest and most influential ethnic group in Milwaukee, dominated city and county politics, while native Americans held state and national offices, both relying upon the Republican Party as their vehicle to power. The ethnic divisions within the laboring classes very often prevented the erection of a united labor front. The Germans viewed the Poles with scorn, and in the factories conflicts often developed between the skilled German workers and the unskilled Polish. On the whole, then, the Poles were left out of the best jobs and generally ignored in political affairs except for specific needs in the Polish wards.

It was only logical that this fragmentation within labor and the ethnic groups would affect the approaches various groups would take toward bettering their economic conditions. Native Americans and Germans controlled the craft unions and while the skilled workers were not always content with their lot and used strikes and boycotts on occasion, they were leery of political action and apparently unable or unwilling to act in concert with the unskilled workers. As early as 1880, the craft unions formed a federated trades assembly representing nineteen unions. In 1883, the assembly played a key role in electing Democrat John M. Stowell as mayor but the unions failed to consolidate their victory and the Democrats lost the 1884 city elections. Labor then dropped politics and returned to the policy of strikes and boycotts on a piecemeal basis. There were some radical and militant labor leaders in the city, primarily a small group of German Socialists, but they had only a limited influence with workers.

The two factors which appeared in 1886 to unite these diverse elements of Milwaukee labor into a force to be reckoned with were the Knights of Labor, with their eight-hour movement, and the growth of Paul Grottkau's Central Labor Union. By 1886, the Knights in Milwaukee numbered 16,000 in fifty local assemblies. The Knights of Labor organization crossed skilled and unskilled lines but generally recruited Germans and native Americans. Grottkau, a German-born Socialist, came to Milwaukee in 1883 to edit the Socialist newspaper the *Arbeiter Zeitung*. Early in 1886, he formed the Central Labor Union, the first organization in Milwaukee to recruit actively and to organize unskilled workers on a large scale. As a result, most of Grottkau's following came from the Polish workers. The Milwaukee trades assembly refused to back the eight-hour movement openly, but the appeal of the Knights of Labor and their leader Robert Schilling was strong and many craft unionists joined the cause as individuals. Grottkau and his CLU were much more militant than Schilling's Knights, who were willing to compromise on the eight-hour issue by taking a pay cut for the shorter hours, while Grottkau and his followers wanted eight hours' work for ten hours' pay. In the beginning this difference did not prevent the two leaders and their organizations from enthusiastically declaring a general strike on May 1 if their demands were not met.

Throughout April, organized labor in Milwaukee intensified its campaign for the shorter hours. Local assemblies of the Knights of Labor and the Central Labor Union united to form the Eight Hour League. The League exercised enough influence in the city to gain passage of an ordinance by the Milwaukee Common Council which fixed the legal working day at eight hours. The Council did not establish machinery for the enforcement of the ordinance, however, and few Milwaukee employers took the law seriously. Prior to the May deadline, some firms, notably Milwaukee cigar producers, acceded to the request. Edward P. Allis, owner of the Allis-Reliance Iron Works, also gave in to the demand, but just to an extent, granting only his skilled workers the shorter hours. Some Milwaukee

employers, including the Plankinton and Company packing firm, instituted a lock out before labor could strike, and some workers left their jobs
prior to the deadline.

During the first three days of May the strike developed sporadically
and the course it took indicated that labor was not as united and well
organized as had been implied in the pronouncements of the Eight Hour
League. At two important plants, the Falk Brewery and the Allis-Reliance
Iron Works, skilled workers refused to join the unskilled in the walkout.
On Monday morning, May 3, the situation became tense. Strikers appeared at the Falk and Allis plants and attempted to persuade or force the
workers to quit. The tactic succeeded at the brewery, but at the Iron Works,
Sheriff George Paschen and his deputies barely prevented a riot after Allis
workers turned fire hoses on the strikers. By late afternoon, almost all
factories and shops in the city were closed. Strikers had used coercion to
drive some workers from their jobs and Allis closed his factory on the
advice of Mayor Emil Wallber in order to avoid violence.

At this juncture, many Milwaukee businessmen began to fear the consequences of another day of labor demonstrations. Many doubted either
the ability or the desire of the local civil authorities to control the crowds
of strikers and prevent a work stoppage. Ethnic prejudice dictated this
attitude in part, for Mayor Wallber, Sheriff Paschen, and city Police Chief
Florian Ries were all Germans. The businessmen not only wanted a more
vigorous policy pursued by the city and county police but also wanted the
National Guard called in. Wallber and Paschen were willing to use their
forces to maintain order and prevent violence but apparently were not
willing to attempt to break the strike. Both men knew that to ask for the
National Guard was a politically dangerous move in a city and county
where the labor vote was so important; thus both resisted any pressure in
that direction. The businessmen interpreted this concession to political
reality as sympathy or fear for the strikers, and not a few saw it as mere
collusion between the foreign elements.

This distrust of local officials led some businessmen and Guard officers
in Milwaukee to appeal directly to Governor Rusk for aid. As early as
April 30, Edward P. Allis wrote to Rusk on the troubles and said, "I hope
the emergency may not arise but if it does, trust that the State will act
promptly in my protection." Other leading business leaders, including
Frank Falk and Roswell Miller, of the Chicago, Milwaukee, and St. Paul
Railroad, wrote or phoned Rusk requesting state aid during the strike.
Certain Guard officers, particularly Charles King and Major P. Traeumer
of the Fourth Battalion, also made contact with Madison and recommended that the Guard be alerted for active duty. King maintained daily
contacts with Adjutant General Chapman in Madison during the early
days of the strike and, in order to judge the temper of the strikers, made
daily rides through the residential areas where workingmen lived.

King, a bombastic and nativistic man with an overactive imagination for conspiracy, not only distrusted the many immigrants among the strikers but doubted the loyalties of the overwhelmingly immigrant Fourth Battalion. The Battalion was a peculiar mixture of politics, ethnic brotherhoods, and military comradeship. Each company in the Fourth represented an ethnic bloc—the Sheridan Guards being Irish; the Kosciusko Guards coming from the Polish wards; and the South Side Turner Rifles and Lincoln Guards representing the Germans in the city. Major George Traeumer, Chief of the Board of Public Works and ward politician, ostensibly commanded the Battalion but often found himself at odds with the local company commanders and higher officers in the Guard. The crusty King worked assiduously to have the ethnic companies disbanded and replaced by "American" units, but to no avail. King did not want to rely upon the Fourth in any labor upheaval but instead wanted outside units called in. Despite King's reservations and appeals to Rusk, the onus of restoring order in Milwaukee in 1886 fell to that unit.

Rusk was slow to react to these demands. Some businessmen may even have doubted if the Governor could be relied upon to see their point of view. Early in Rusk's first term, back in 1882, he had refused to use the Guard to dispel a band of angry unemployed railroad hands at Superior. At that time, Rusk had stated, "These men need bread not bullets," and thereafter appeared as a patron of the workingman. This tactic really amounted to the political posturing of a shrewd Republican politician who received his support from Stalwarts within the party, led by the wealthy lumberman Philetus Sawyer. Rusk had no intention of acting precipitately, as would Charles King, but once the Governor saw the direction being taken by the labor disorders in Milwaukee, he acted promptly and decisively.

The tenor of the demonstrations on May 3 brought Governor Rusk, Adjutant General Chapman, and Colonel Samuel Lewis, of the First Regiment, to Milwaukee on the evening train from Madison. The Governor and his party went to the Plankinton House to meet with city and county officials and leading local businessmen. Again, the businessmen accused the local officials of kowtowing to labor and pressed the Governor to mobilize the Guard. The Milwaukee officials, however, " . . . strenuously insisted that the forces at their disposal were then able to maintain order and protect property in the city and county." In light of this, Rusk could do little, for he needed an official request from either Mayor Wallber or Sheriff Paschen before he could order out the Guard. Nonetheless, the local companies were notified to remain on the alert and be prepared to answer the standard signal for riot duty, five double strokes on the fire bells.

On Tuesday, May 4, all the diverse elements involved in the 1886 Milwaukee labor dispute came together. By 7:00 A.M., thousands of eight-hour-day men returned to the streets demanding that those at work lay down their tools and join the general strike. They forced men to quit work at several shops and factories while some 3,000 of them headed for the village of Bay View and the North Chicago Rolling Mills there. Upon their arrival at the mills, the crowd discovered that rumors that skilled workers were on the job at Bay View were true. The strikers, unable to enter the plant, began negotiations with plant officials and sent committees into the factory to urge workers to leave their jobs. The reported tenor and size of the crowd at Bay View and in Milwaukee streets convinced Mayor Wallber and Sheriff Paschen that their forces could not handle the impending disorders and so they made simultaneous requests to Governor Rusk for the National Guard. At 9:00 A.M., riot bells rang in Milwaukee, and members of the Fourth Battalion reported to their armories, dressed for duty, and then left for Bay View. At the same time, Adjutant General Chapman notified units of the First Regiment to prepare for active duty.

At Bay View, company officials continued to negotiate with strike leaders, stalling for time, knowing full well that Guard companies were on the way. Robert Schilling, the Knights' leader, arrived and pleaded with the workers to disperse and avoid violence. Schilling's plea did not take effect immediately, however, and the strikers continued to mill around in front of the plant gate. At this point, the first elements of the Fourth Battalion arrived by train. Most of the troops had reported for duty at the Light Horse Squadron Armory, on Broadway in the downtown area, and then marched to the uptown depot to take trains to Bay View. The train, bearing three companies—the Sheridan Guard, South Side Turner Rifles and the Lincoln Guard—pulled into Bay View at 11:00 A.M. Then, "The crowd yelled at the top of their voices as [the] locomotive and two coaches pulled up at the station and the uniforms of the militiamen became visible."

The presence of any soldiers probably would have offended the strikers but they found the troops of Milwaukee's Fourth Battalion particularly offensive. Aroused by the arrival of local militiamen, the strikers let loose not only with epithets but also with stones and bricks. The Guardsmen knew little about riot tactics and experienced great difficulty in detraining and getting into formation. The crowd pushed in against them, and some soldiers received blows from elbows and fists. Apparently neither Major Traeumer nor his officers had a clear idea of what to do next and took some time in getting the Battalion in formation. Just as they finally massed the unit in front of the plant gate, another train arrived carrying Company B of the Fourth, the Kosciusko Guards. The arrival of the all-Polish Kosciuskos greatly incensed the mob, composed mostly of Polish workingmen. Traeumer ordered the Battalion into the plant grounds, but, according to the *Milwaukee Sentinel*:

> The strikers refused to get out of the path of the soldiers . . . and the latter were compelled to elbow their way through the mob in single file. The Kosciusko guards being the last company to pass through the gate, fared the worst,

as a number of the Poles ran up to the soldiers and struck them from the rear. A shower of stones was also sent after the troops. . . .

Impulsively, five or six of the Kosciuskos turned and fired on the crowd, but their shots were high and hit no one. This unauthorized firing scattered most of the strikers and seemed to temper their bellicosity.

By noon, the threat of a clash between the mob and the Guardsmen seemed to pass. A quick survey of the forces indicated that several of the Kosciuskos had suffered contusions from rocks and bricks, the most seriously injured being Captain Francis Borchardt, the company commander, who had been hit in the head with a brick. With the Guardsmen now inside the plant ground, the crowd outside re-formed and remained there in varying numbers for the rest of the afternoon and evening. Major Traeumer had no orders to disperse the crowd but only to protect the plant and its workers. He posted sentinels around the plant fence to prevent the strikers from entering the grounds but did little else. While the troops took turns at guard duty, the mob outside occasionally booed them and lobbed stones over the fence. Some strikers attempted to scale the fence but none succeeded. The crowd further displayed its distaste for the Guardsmen when it attacked and beat up two late arriving members of the South Side Turner Rifles. The troops maintained a constant vigil until midnight of May 4, but even when they were relieved of duty few could sleep as the night was cold, they had few blankets or overcoats, and most of the men were not yet adjusted to the rigors of domestic warfare.

While the events at Bay View were transpiring, Paul Grottkau addressed a large gathering of workers at the Milwaukee Gardens, urging them to shut down all the business and industry in the city. Inspired by Grottkau's speech, the group marched on the Brand and Company's stove works and forced a work stoppage there. Other strikers continued to march through the city streets chanting slogans. At this point it seemed that labor verged on victory. They had effectively stopped production in Milwaukee shops and factories, and it was only natural that some labor leaders anticipated concessions from management. Indeed, some concessions did come on May 4, as several breweries gave in to the eight-hour demand. Despite the appearance of a near-victory events were already turning against the general strike movement.

Several things began to work against the laborers. First, when it became apparent to Governor Rusk that the Fourth Battalion would be unable to break the strike alone, he had Adjutant General Chapman mobilize the entire First Regiment. This was done at 11:00 A.M. and by 5:30 in the afternoon, the entire unit was in the city. The Madison Governor's Guard arrived first, bringing a Gatling gun, which they set up at the Light Horse Armory. Other companies of the First arrived throughout the rest of the afternoon. Chapman then strategically distributed the units around the city. He sent two companies to reinforce Major Traeumer at Bay View, kept four companies at the Armory as a reserve force, and sent the remaining forces to guard the Allis Iron Works and the West Milwaukee railroad carshops. Colonel King, on Chapman's orders, commanded the cavalry troop and the artillery battery, using these mounted forces to patrol the downtown area and as a mobile force to meet emergencies.

During the night, while the state solidified its position, fatal cracks began to show in labor's united front. Throughout the day there had been little co-operation between the Knights of Labor and the Central Labor Union. A fundamental difference in commitment and tactics existed between the two groups; thus while Robert Schilling had been urging his followers at Bay View to disperse and avoid violence, Paul Grottkau was advocating more militancy in his Milwaukee Gardens speech. The Knights attempted to operate through established channels. They visited Governor Rusk and requested a withdrawal of the National Guard, assuring him that once this was done, the disorder would abate. At the same time, the Knights of Labor issued a broadside urging all Knights to stay off the streets on Tuesday and to refrain from attending any public meetings. The broadside also appealed for the maintenance of law and order and the cessation of union-sponsored demonstrations. When Rusk firmly refused to recall the Guard, the Knights of Labor in effect withdrew from the strike.

By Wednesday morning, May 5, Governor Rusk and his staff appeared to be fully in command of the situation. Adjutant General Chapman had the Second Regiment on stand-by alert for duty in the city and Rusk had issued stern orders to all Guard officers to shoot if crowds refused to obey orders to disperse. Over the telephone, the Governor explicitly ordered Major Traeumer to fire on demonstrators at Bay View if they behaved on Wednesday as they had on the previous night. Very early on Wednesday, a large crowd of laborers, mainly Polish, met at the St. Stanislaus Church and began a march to Bay View. At the mills, Major Traeumer received word of the crowd's progress toward the plant. The Major later stated that he had had it on the best authority that the strikers were " . . . determined to clean out the militia and to set fire to mills." Despite the fact that Traeumer believed this, and despite the orders for stern action, he called Governor Rusk for instructions. The Major was obviously not sure of his authority or of how to best handle the situation. Rusk replied, " . . . that should the rioters again attempt to seek an entrance, 'fight em'."

Traeumer and his command never gave the strikers an opportunity to indicate whether they intended to enter the mill, set fire to it, or merely demonstrate in front of it. As soon as the marchers crossed from the Milwaukee city limits into Bay View, Traeumer, from inside the plant grounds, ordered them to stop and disperse. Apparently the strikers had no single leader and ignored the order. Then, reported the *Milwaukee Sentinel*,

" . . . Maj. Traeumer again warned the crowd to stop, but the mob ignored him and pressed ahead." Without further warning, Traeumer gave the order to fire. The strikers were still about 200 yards from the plant and only two of the six companies, numbering between 35 and 40 men each, fired a full volley. The soldiers remained within the plant grounds and only those standing on high ground could see to fire at the mob. As a result, less than a score of the crowd of 1,500 to 2,000 was hit. Nonetheless, the effect of the firing was immediate and conclusive. Men threw themselves flat on the ground, others dived into ditches and those in the rear ranks literally ran for their lives.

Traeumer quickly marched his men out into the street with fixed bayonets to ensure that the crowd would continue to disperse. The Battalion surgeon, a Catholic priest, county deputies, and some of the braver strikers moved about tending the wounded. In all, the volley killed five people. At least two were not a part of the mob. One of the victims, sixty-eight-year-old Franz Kunkel, was killed by a stray bullet while feeding chickens in his own backyard. The other was a thirteen-year-old boy drawn to the area by adolescent curiosity. The firing ended all demonstrations at the Bay View factory.

The killings at Bay View did not immediately end disorder in Milwaukee, however. Twice during the day, large crowds of strikers gathered at the Milwaukee Gardens for demonstrations and speeches. Both times, hard-pressed Milwaukee police called upon the National Guard reserve at the Light Horse Armory for aid in breaking up these protests. In the morning fray at the Gardens, the Light Horse Squadron rode into the crowd, a tactic which effectively broke up the meeting. Throughout the rest of the day, the Squadron and the other troops at the Armory responded to false alarms of disorder and riot. Each time the National Guardsmen appeared in the street, the crowds jeered and occasionally threw stones, but there was never any need to use force beyond the bayonet, the rifle butt, or the flat of the sword. By the evening of May 5, it was quite evident that Governor Rusk and the National Guard were in control of the city and that the strike was broken.

On Thursday, crowds no longer roamed the streets and city police did not have to call upon Guardsmen at the Armory for aid in maintaining peace. The men of the Fourth Battalion at Bay View were exhausted, according to the *Milwaukee Journal*, having been on duty since Tuesday morning, with little or no sleep. On Friday, May 7, Adjutant General Chapman relieved the Fourth with three companies of the First Regiment and in the afternoon Governor Rusk feted the Battalion, some two hundred men, with a banquet at the Plankinton House. For the Fourth Battalion, the war was over. Units of the Regiment, however, remained in the city until the thirteenth of May, guarding the plant at Bay View, the Allis works and other large factories. When the last companies left Milwaukee, they went with the knowledge that they had broken labor's most serious challenge to management in the city's history.

It is highly unlikely that the individual Guardsman in the ranks thought of himself as a strikebreaker. It is just as unlikely that Governor Rusk, Adjutant General Chapman, or Colonel King saw themselves in this role. To most of these men, the issue had been, from the beginning, a simple one of law and order, although King later rumbled about smashing anarchists and rebellious foreign rabble. Early in the strike, Mayor Wallber and Sheriff Paschen probably sensed that a strict application of law and order would be seen by laborers as strike-breaking. The Mayor and Sheriff, however, evidently frightened by the militancy of the strikers and fearful of losing the support of the solid citizens in the Republican party, acquiesced to pressure and asked for the National Guard. From that point, Rusk took over and applied military force quickly and harshly to bring the disorders to an end. The political and economic *Zeitgeist* dictated such a policy to any regular politician. Later, in a public speech, Rusk stated the assumptions under which he had acted, principles undoubtedly accepted by Chapman, King, Wallber, most Guardsmen, and probably many strikers: " . . . it should be the duty of every citizen that every laborer who desires to work shall be permitted to do so unmolested by those who do not choose to work themselves. And every citizen should be protected in the management of his business against the interference of all comers. This is the only way in which capital and labor can be harmonious. . . . " That these assumptions wholly favored capital over labor and denied the latter the use of such tactics as strikes, boycotts, closed shops, and a union voice in factory matters never occurred to Rusk. In light of this fundamental philosophical fact, Rusk's use of the National Guard is understandable.

It is not completely fair to judge nineteenth-century actions in terms of twentieth-century thought. The historian may find it relatively easy to see the causes of disorder after the fact and to see that the system as a whole worked against organized labor. However, this was not the case for those who lived in the system and strived to better their economic lot under it. The Guard played a central role in breaking the strike, regardless of how that action was justified, and, with good cause, laborers saw the militia as a strikebreaking force. From the very beginning of the Milwaukee general strike, the workers expressed a strong distrust of and distaste for the Guard. The riot bells which called members of the Fourth Battalion to active duty also brought thousands of civilians into the streets. On the first day of mobilization, May 4, a large crowd gathered downtown near the Light Horse Armory and when the troops left for Bay View, according to *The Evening Wisconsin*, " . . . they were greeted with marks of approbation by the immense crowd which had gathered in the street." However, other crowds often greeted troops with jeers, boos and occasional stones.

One reporter observed " . . . that the militia are thoroughly hated by the laborers. . . . " The Bay View Knights of Labor, maintaining that the presence of the Guard was provocative, offered to guard and protect property if the militia were recalled. Their offer fell on deaf ears.

Not surprisingly, the shooting at Bay View on May 5 brought forth the most serious criticism of the National Guard. Robert Schilling wrote in his *Milwaukee Volksblatt*, "The firing was unjustified and cruel, and to say it in plain German, it was cowardly, premeditated murder." The Central Labor Union issued a public statement which accused the police and militia of unnecessary and harsh action throughout the strike and called the killing " . . . over-zealous, unjustifiable and damnable." Indignation and outrage were particularly acute in the Polish wards, again not surprisingly, because except for Franz Kunkel, all those killed or wounded at Bay View had been Polish. Alderman Theodore Rudzinski was caustically critical of the National Guard, charging that it precipitately fired on a peaceful crowd which had a perfect right to demonstrate in front of the Bay View plant.

The Milwaukee Sunday Telegraph, along with most of the English-language papers in the city, deplored the fact that, " . . . demagogues who hope to gain a little political preference will make sneering remarks about the National Guard. . . . " But, the paper pointed out, the shooting at Bay View " . . . had a most wonderfully purifying effect." Praise for the Guard and Governor Rusk's stand during the riots came from these Milwaukee papers, most papers around the state and much of the national press. The Governor received memorials from several business groups in Milwaukee lauding his recent actions, one of which assured him that: " . . . it comes from the hearts of that class which has the best interests of the State and country at heart, and who are interested to so great an extent in the commercial welfare and mercantile interests of the country. . . . "

Such matters did not concern the strikers with their lost cause, however. Unable from the start to gain a hearing for their grievances, the strikers were just as powerless to gain redress for the actions of the Guard. The frustrated workers, particularly the Poles, took out their wrath on the only element of the establishment which they could touch, the Kosciusko Guards. Under the leadership of Alderman Rudzinski, the Polish community imposed a social and economic boycott on the Guards from the afternoon of May 4, after some Kosciuskos had impulsively fired upon the strikers at Bay View. The shooting and killing on May 5 intensified bitter feelings in the Polish wards. Open threats of violence led Adjutant General Chapman to place Guardsmen at the homes of Major Traeumer and Captain Francis Borchardt, commander of the Kosciusko Guards. The boycott sapped the strength of the Polish company. On May 4, fifty officers and men of the company were on duty at Bay View. Two days later, eight enlisted men were absent from duty and on May 7, when the company was relieved, fourteen men were absent. Other companies of the Battalion maintained or added to their strength during the same time.

Since the great majority of the Polish Guardsmen lived in the Polish wards, the boycott became very effective. Most members of the Kosciuskos were small businessmen; grocers, bakers, tavernkeepers, and the like; a few were professionals. By May 10, company members felt the full effect of the ban. Captain Borchardt's law practice disintegrated and the grocers and tavernkeepers in the company lost almost all of their business. The Kosciuskos were ordered out of their armory—the parish school of St. Stanislaus Church—while boys and old women openly insulted the Guardsmen in the streets. Leaders in the larger community soon came to the aid of the Kosciusko Guards. The city's English-language newspapers began a campaign to end the boycott. Governor Rusk summoned Alderman Rudzinski and demanded that he drop leadership of the campaign. Rudzinski persisted, however, and later Rusk revoked his commission as a notary public. A committee of leading Milwaukee manufacturers met and decided that as long as the boycott lasted, they would not hire any Poles who did not have a written recommendation from the Kosciuskos. The committee also promised, according to the *Sentinel*, that " . . . members of the Kosciusko guards will be taken care of in case they do not find employment . . . by giving them positions at the works or shops represented by the committee." Because of this economic support of the company by the local business community, the boycott eventually dissipated.

The reaction of the city's leading newspapers to the boycott accentuated a theme prevalent throughout the disorders. *The Milwaukee Sentinel*, which had been outspokenly anti-Polish during the strike, editorialized: "The Poles of the city are under the greatest obligation to the members of the Kosciusko Guards who alone have prevented the entire race from falling under the public ban."

Most of the city's newspapers and many of the state officials had made much of the ethnicity of the strikers, as though to explain away the troubles by blaming foreigners and outsiders. The *Sentinel*, in particular, continually referred to "Polack" strikers as the real troublemakers. This paper, other segments of the press, and state officials could not resist pointing out that the two leaders of the strike, Robert Schilling and Paul Grottkau, were German-born and Socialists to boot. As noted earlier, many state officials and businessmen believed the troubles arose because Germans dominated local politics and were spineless and untrustworthy. Charles King, almost obsessed with nativism, later condemned all foreigners in the affair, regardless of the role they played. He attacked city and county officials, contemptuously referred to Traeumer as that "German major," criticized the discipline of the Kosciusko Guards, "mainly Polanders, but of a better class," and asserted that the only decent Guard troops in the fray were the cavalry troop and the battery, "all dashing young Americans."

Undoubtedly this antiforeign attitude explains in great part the harsh policy laid down by Governor Rusk and pursued by General Chapman and Colonel King.

Paradoxically, the immigrant companies of the Fourth Battalion carried out the Governor's policy, but the severity of their actions came from poor preparation not antiforeign bias. The Fourth Battalion consistently received the lowest efficiency ratings of all units in the Guard and their performance at Bay View indicates the outfit was poorly trained. The Guard as a whole lacked riot training and the Fourth, often torn by political and social conflicts, frequently performed poorly even at dress parades. Their first day's action at Bay View, when they displayed a total lack of knowledge concerning crowd control, indicated their poor preparation. Furthermore, although Traeumer was under orders to fire if the strikers attempted to enter the plant grounds, he made no effort to determine fully the intentions of the crowd before firing into it. Traeumer displayed indecision throughout the disorders and relied upon ultimate force to cover his indecision. A comment in the *Milwaukee Journal* partially bears out this conclusion, as it noted: "The general opinion of the people of Bay View is that the action of the militia was hasty, and that bloodshed could have been prevented by drawing the militia in line outside the works and menacing the crowd without shooting."

Poor training, lack of discipline, and incompetent leadership, then, were as much a cause of the killing as the resolute stand of the state officials. It is clear that the men of the Fourth were poorly trained for riot duty. Many served throughout the strike in their dress-parade uniforms and went without blankets, overcoats, or hot food for two days when the nights were damp and chilly. On the night following the killing at Bay View the troops remained very jumpy. Twice during the night of May 5–6, nervous sentries awoke other Guardsmen at Bay View by firing at imaginary skulkers in the shadows. Finally, at least some of the Guardsmen, already in an overexcited state, were told by their officers to be ready to kill. Prior to leaving the Armory for Bay View, the captain of the Sheridan Guards gave a short speech to his men, stating in part: "I don't want any of you to show the white feather. . . . Above all things, keep cool. Don't lose your head, but wait for the order to fire before you pull a trigger. And when you do fire, take an aim; pick out your man and kill him." No one in authority bothered to consider these factors, and on May 7 a coroner's jury absolved the militia of any responsibility for the killings at Bay View.
. . . In retelling the story of the Milwaukee riots of 1886, one gains a feeling of *déjà vu*, to say to himself that he too has experienced this upheaval. On the surface, the affair appeared to be a simple one of law and order on the one hand, or a desperate struggle for justice on the other. Beneath the surface, however, one finds complexity, with the National Guard eager to show its mettle yet wholly unprepared to do so; with a sharp division

between state and local officials over methods to control the disorder; with the strikers themselves divided over tactics and goals. The riot was indicative of the difficulty our nation has faced for decades in solving the deep-rooted problems of a pluralistic society. In the one hundred years following the Milwaukee strike, other rude awakenings were to be heralded by five double strokes on the fire bell.

23

Red, White, and the Army Blue

Empathy and Anger in the American West

THOMAS C. LEONARD

Throughout the nineteenth century, regulars served in campaigns against one or another Indian tribe, and some regulars held ambivalent views about their duties and their foes. Ethan Allen Hitchcock's diary entries provide some evidence of this for the pre-Civil War years, as does William Skelton's essay on the subject.* This essay by Thomas Leonard deals with the phenomenon in the late nineteenth century.

*William B. Skelton, "Army Officer Attitudes Toward Indians, 1830–1860," *Pacific Northwest Quarterly* 67 (July 1976): 113–124.

THE POLEMICAL USE of white testimony about the red enemy is the most honored tradition in our histories of the Indian wars. The statements of Indian fighters have seemed eloquent indictments (or, more rarely now, defenses) of the winning of the West. And yet anyone who reads what Army officers said about the final Indian wars must feel that these men have never been listened to closely. As a consequence, I think, a good deal of criticism of American expansion has been blunted in two ways.

SOURCE: Thomas C. Leonard, "Red, White, and the Army Blue: Empathy and Anger in the American West," *American Quarterly* 26 (1974): 176–190. Copyright, 1974, Trustees of the University of Pennsylvania. Reprinted by permission of the author and the publisher, the University of Pennsylvania. *Author's note:* Research for this article now forms part of my *Above the Battle: War-Making in America from Appomattox to Versailles* (New York: Oxford University Press, 1978).
EDITOR'S NOTE: Most of the citations to the sources consulted by the author in this essay have been omitted from this volume for brevity and economy. The reader should consult the original source of the essay for the complete scholarly documentation.

First, it has been easy to forget the limitations of our own empathy and appreciation for native American culture. The officer corps in the last Indian wars provides a useful check on the historian's pride in his cultural relativism and moral compassion. Friends of native Americans can learn humility, I suspect, from some of the red man's old enemies. Second, without paying closer attention to the attitudes of conquerors we cannot identify what distinctive aspects of the dominant culture we wish to criticize. Many 19th century states dispossessed "primitive" natives; it is an open question what special features of American culture affected our conquest of the West. Comparative studies may make this clear (as comparative studies have shown us what was distinctive about American slavery) but we are now a long way from knowing if our Indian fighting was a "peculiar institution." If we listen closely to an articulate group like the officer corps (an institution we find, of course, in most expanding nations) we take the first step toward this comparative approach.

The three decades of border fights after the Civil War climaxed three centuries of cultural conflict in North America. Protestant American culture, however, had never achieved a clear vision of the red man's future. There was broad agreement that Indians must be "redeemed": *from* barbarism and *for* Christian civilization. In practice neither American institutions nor attitudes fit this policy. After the Civil War, the orders and advice that the Army received were most confusing. The rules of war demanded restraint and a fine regard for the enemy's rights, but the author of these orders, Francis Lieber, looked forward to the Indian's "extinction . . . the quicker the better." Military reports and memoirs of this era give an angry picture of civilian obstruction. The government broke treaties and yet expected the Army to keep the peace through trust. Western settlers clamored for protection at the same time their land grabs provoked Indian retaliation. "Friends" of the Indians were a special annoyance. Eastern philanthropic societies damned the Army when blood was shed at the same time that they demanded a forced acculturation: "the Indian as a savage member of a tribal organization cannot survive, ought not to survive the aggressions of civilization." The Army learned that white as well as red society could be enigmatic.

Yet few officers were suited, initially, to play Hamlet. Action seemed the thing to sweep away the complications of the Indian problem. Striking out at the Indian seemed a way to eliminate the source of civilian complaint and punish an incomprehensibly wild enemy. Even Civil War heroes found themselves vilified (and occasionally hung in effigy) if they hesitated to act. In 1870 for example, Philip Sheridan pleaded with General Sherman for authority to react to the upsetting reports that crossed his desk every week: "Since 1862 at least 800 men, women and children have been murdered within the limits of my present command, in the most fiendish manner; the men usually scalped and mutilated, their ——— cut off and placed in their mouth; women ravished sometimes fifty and sixty times in succession, then killed and scalped, sticks stuck in their persons, before and after death." Protests in the East were not going to prevent a righteous revenge in the West. Sheridan came to define the problem as a decision as to who was going to live in his district—red or white—"I have made my choice."

General Sherman appreciated his friend's feelings because he had come to about the same view. The most extravagant threats of "exterminating" the Indian mark much of Sherman's discussion of the West under his command. Both old soldiers proposed that native culture be obliterated; the red man himself, his wife and children, they suggested, were just as expendable. Each was inclined to weigh, in a quite literal way, the destruction of Indian civilization against the material achievements of the frontier—the things that can "be counted, taxed and governed by the laws of nature and civilization." Each often claimed to have made his choice.

This choice, made in passion, looked more complicated when men like Sheridan and Sherman attempted to carry it out. Indian fighters were troubled by various kinds of respect for their enemy. No commander in the West, for example, could conceal his admiration for the red man's fighting skill. Though officially these officers reported a small and very favorable casualty rate, in more candid moments these Civil War veterans complained that Indian fighting was the most dangerous and destructive campaigning ever faced by American soldiers. This high estimate of the enemy's tenacity undermined the Army's pride in its own competence. Sheridan berated the white inefficiency that made campaigns in the West "a series of forlorn-hopes." Sherman explicitly drew the conclusions about Indian resistance that haunted other officers: the red man's military "sagacity and skill surpasses that of the white race." Victory against such valiant opponents was bittersweet; both Sheridan and Sherman confessed a sense of pity and compassion for the native Americans they had set out to destroy.[1]

The tension between civilized and primitive society was felt more intensely by the field officers who served under Sheridan and Sherman. In the West, the Indian often seemed more than a worthy opponent: he cast doubt on the war for civilization itself. Empathizing with the red man while fighting him was an unsettling experience that officers resolved in very different ways. The Army's apologia for its enemy has to be interpreted carefully—but it can tell us much about the military's attitude to the society it was fighting to protect.

Judged by the surviving personal records, few officers escaped a sort of wistful appreciation of primitive society when they learned the folkways of their enemy. A peculiar romantic form of this sentiment stressed the insatiable appetite for war of native Americans and then celebrated this unrestrained aggressiveness. Assimilation and peace were not good enough for Indians. A fight to the death seemed inevitable and strangely exciting to these men:

Oh, what a stirring picture you make as once more I fix my glasses on you! Here, nearly four years after, my pulses bound as I recall the sight. Savage warfare was never more beautiful than in you. On you come, your swift, agile ponies springing down the winding ravine, the rising sun gleaming on your trailing war bonnets, on silver armlets, necklace, gorget; on brillant painted shield and beaded legging; on naked body and beardless face, stained most vivid vermillion.

General Charles King's glorious, doomed Indians seem much like the red men of 20th century popular culture—as indeed they should since King wrote several dozen novels which helped establish the genre.[2]

Similarly, one of Sheridan's favorite generals sought a large audience for his explanation of the temptations of native American culture:

> To me, Indian life, with its attendant ceremonies, mysteries, and forms, is a book of unceasing interest. Grant that some of its pages are frightful, and, if possible, to be avoided, yet the attraction is none the weaker. Study him, fight him, civilize him if you can, he remains still the object of your curiosity, a type of man peculiar and undefined, subjecting himself to no known law of civilization, contending determinedly against all efforts to win him from his chosen mode of life.
>
> If I were an Indian, I often think I would greatly prefer to cast my lot among those of my people [who] adhered to the free open plains, rather than submit to the confined limits of a reservation, there to be the recipient of the blessed benefits of civilization, with its vices thrown in without stint or measure.

General George Custer met the object of his interest at the Little Big Horn two years after his gratuitous advice was published.[3]

Most officers, however, allowed the red man to show his nobility in other ways than in dying at the hands of whites. When officers worked closely with Indians, the white men perceived primitive virtues that made the fight seem tragic. These observers made explicit what their rhapsodic colleagues only implied: civilization was rebuked by the Indians' last stand.

General Nelson A. Miles, one of the officers who tracked the Sioux after Custer's fall, spoke for many in the Army when he praised the Indians' "courage, skill, sagacity, endurance, fortitude, and self-sacrifice of a high order." He was inclined to think that lapses from this standard came as native Americans had "degenerated through contact with the white man." Indeed, even in the midst of campaigns, Miles had serious doubts about the justice of the white objectives. His reflection on the Custer massacre accepted Longfellow's contrite lines on a century of dishonor:

> Whose was the right and the wrong?
> Sing it, O funeral song,
>   With a voice that is full of tears
> And say that our broken faith
> Wrought all this ruin and scathe,
>   In the Year of a Hundred Years.

To many officers, the courage and bearing of native Americans suggested a purer way of life before the coming of the white man. The military frequently searched for Greek and Roman analogies to suggest the virtues of their enemy. And even the Indians' faults might be excused by understanding their lower stage of cultural evolution. General George Crook, perhaps the most skillful Indian fighter in the West, extolled the classical elements in the men he hunted down. Back at West Point for a graduation address, he may have shocked many with the observation that though Indians were cruel, treacherous and unclean, "so were our forefathers." Crook, like Miles, hesitated to condemn even the most ferocious Apache because he respected their spirit and he had come to conclude "we are too culpable as a nation, for the existing condition of affairs."[4]

In a curious way, even the Army's darkest views of native Americans strengthened this expression of compassion and guilt. Colonel Richard I. Dodge, for example, balanced some benign allusions to hostile Indians as Greeks and "natural men" with a harsh critique of their culture. His enemy was bereft of any sense of law or right—"a barbarous, cruel, ignorant, shiftless race." Dodge's criticism was so thorough, however, that the officer was left with deep pity for his enemy. The "wild" Indian, Dodge argued, was not accountable for civilization's concept of "crime." Moral responsibility seemed to rest entirely with whites. Even "the killing of soldiers in battle," Dodge explained, "is not to be regarded as murder or outrage. It is simply the necessary adjunct to our pernicious system of Indian management." Dodge's critique of white responsibility became so vitriolic that he was left with few banners of civilization to carry. American violations of treaties were "more barbarous than anything [the Indians] have done against the whites." The West had become a giant Andersonville for Indian captives—and every American citizen shared the guilt of the crime. In this mood, Dodge refused to see much difference between Indian torture and the evil of his own society: "Barbarism torments the body; civilization torments the soul."

Some officers went further than this. A peculiar cultural relativism is evident in the reflections of many of the men who ostensibly led the fight for civilization. Colonel Henry B. Carrington, for example, was one of the field officers who supplied General Sheridan with the maddening accounts of Indian outrages. Carrington's official report of the fallen soldiers under his command in the Fetterman "massacre" (1866) made grisly reading:

Eyes torn out and laid on the rocks; teeth chopped out; joints of fingers cut off; brains taken out and placed on rocks, with members of the body; entrails taken out and exposed; hands and feet cut off; arms taken out from sockets; eyes, ears, mouth and arms penetrated with spearheads, sticks and arrows; punctures upon every sensitive part of the body, even to the soles of the feet and the palms of the hands.

Carrington's response to this mutilation of his colleagues was reflection, not revenge. A year after this report, Carrington's wife published a study of the land the Army fought to control: *Ab-sa-ra-ka*. The massacre was handled with impressive open-mindedness. Like her husband, Mrs. Carrington never directly condemned this act of war. She noted that "the noblest traits of the soldiers were touchingly developed as they carefully handled the mutilated fragments" from the battlefield. Yet Carrington's wife could not avoid praising the Indian: "In ambush and decoy, *splendid."* Close observers, she wrote, transcended anger to become reconciled and even sympathetic "with the bold warrior in his great struggle."

Colonel Carrington expended on this theme of noble savage resistance as he took charge of enlarged editions of *Ab-sa-ra-ka* in the 1870s. Now he could find no glory in Indian warfare. White barbarities seemed to overshadow the Indian's atrocities. Carrington now appeared to be more bitter about "irresponsible speculative emigration" of whites than the red "massacre." Carrington confessed, like Custer, "if I had been a red man as I was a white man, I should have fought as bitterly, if not as brutally, as the Indian fought."

In 1880 Colonel Carrington stood before the American Association for the Advancement of Science and read again his Official Report of the Fetterman mutilations. Now, however, the atrocities had become artifacts—"startling and impressive." He wanted the scientists to see how the Indian's disposition of enemies was an understandable measure to disable his foe in afterlife. Carrington did not disparage the Indian's set of values, but he closed his address by suggesting some inadequacies of his own culture: "From 1865 until the present time, there has not been a border campaign which did not have its impulse in the aggressions of a white man."

The scalping knife loosened other officers' ties to American culture. General John Gibbon published an account of his discovery of the mutilated men who had fallen with Custer at the Little Big Horn. Gibbon, incredibly, seemed more angry at the "human ghouls" in the Army who had disturbed some Sioux graves than at the warriors who had killed his colleagues. In his assessment, such desecrations "impress one with the conviction that in war barbarism stands upon a level only a little lower than our boasted civilization."

General Gibbon later won a prize from the Military Service Institution for an elaboration of the ways soldiers emulated the savage. The Indian's "blind rage" to mutilate and torture, he explained, "is only another form of the same feeling exhibited every day in a modified way in every so-called *civilized* war." Indeed, Gibbon judged that "civilized nations will at times adopt measures to succeed from which an Indian would turn in horror." The Army, Gibbon suggested, should put itself in the place of its enemy. The record of white treachery and hostility would force any man to fight: "Thus would the *savage* in us come to the surface under the oppression which we know the Indian suffers." Like many officers who addressed the perennial "Indian Question," Gibbon raised more questions about his own culture than he answered about his antagonist's.

Few men in the West raised more unusual questions about both cultures than Captain John Bourke. He entered the campaigns "with the sincere conviction that the only good Indian was a dead Indian, and that the only use to make of him was that of fertilizer." But Bourke found himself haunted by the Indians of the Southwest. His notebooks reveal a man absorbed in the details of his enemy's culture. The master of several Indian languages, Bourke produced an impressive series of monographs on native religious ceremonies. In 1895 he became President of the American Folk-Lore Society. Knowledge proved corrosive to his early cultural pride. At the end of his Army service he was willing to admit that "the American aborigine is not indebted to his pale-faced brother, no matter of what nation or race he may be, for lessons in tenderness and humanity."

Bourke's transformation, like other officers', followed from his disgust with white treaty violations. But his appreciation of native culture was more complex than the respect paid by other Indian fighters. Bourke acknowledged the red man's fighting prowess and noble customs, but he was much more interested in habits that were repulsive to white mores: snake ceremonies and scatological rites. Bourke's interest in the details of these ceremonies was as intense and sustained as his protestations of "horror" during each "filthy" and "disgusting" rite. Such scholarship and prurience could not be confined to the reservation. In *Scatalogic [sic] Rites of All Nations*, Bourke observed these "orgies" throughout the development of Western civilization even surviving in nations of "high enlightenment."[5] Bourke thus went beyond the prevailing sentimental accommodations with native American culture. Noble primitives might teach "humanity" to modern Americans, but even ignoble native customs could encourage compassion by reminding the white race of its own repulsive past. Indian vices as well as virtues could be reasons for peace.

The military's apologia for their enemy finally comes down to a single insight: Indians might be doomed, cruel, repulsive—at least they faced their fate and vices in a spirit of defiant freedom. Primitives had fewer virtues, but also fewer restraints than the civilization these officers defended. Morally, this civilization aimed higher—but were the restraints worth the results?

It is important to realize that all these officers concluded the price of civilization was not too high. Though these men were aware of the ambiguities of their fight for civilization, their sympathies and guilt never swayed them from their duty. I know of no regular Army officer of tender conscience who was provoked to resign his commission. Clearly, cycles of pity and self-censure were consistent with a lifetime of Indian warfare. How could such ambivalence be sustained?

The military's apologia for the red man really met certain professional and psychological needs of the Army in the field. Respect for the Indian's fighting ability, for example, was not altogether disinterested. By defining the Plains Indians as relentless and efficient warriors, the military justified its own ruthless strategy—and setbacks. These officers said little about the ritualistic quality of native American warfare. One learns almost nothing, for example, of the *coup* rituals that turned some combat into a bloodless game of honor. Nor did the military emphasize that their enemy retired from the field during unsuitable weather and ceremonial periods. Most of all, these officers did not see the difficulties Plains Indians faced in turning the white man's cultural offerings into weapons to defend native interests. The horse and rifle, for example, were startling innovations that no tribe had fully integrated. The Plains Indians, themselves sometimes first-generation immigrants from the East, struggled with a culture in some ways as unsettled as that of a white boom town. The Army preferred emphasizing the Indian's strength to showing sympathy for his military weaknesses.

Frontier ethnology was not so innocent either. Men like Crook and Bourke were sensitive to the "inner Indian" and the integrity of his culture—but they had the goal of military containment in mind. And, we must not forget, the officer's praise of Indians was part of the military's effort to convince Eastern critics that the Army deserved the right to take charge of the transformation of Indian culture. For most "friends" of the Indian, in and out of uniform, Indian reform meant a move away from the shelter of the reservation to private farms, the lure of the "cash market" and the responsibilities of the vote. Unlike romantics such as Custer, most officers expected better things for the Indian.

Empathy for the enemy may have made this assignment of "redeeming" the Indian more painful; but there were some emotional satisfactions in the Army's moods of cultural relativism. Empathy was not only compatible with a release of anger; in some cases the appreciation of primitive virtues heightened aggressive impulses. Thus General George Schofield, commander of the Department of the Missouri, could confess that "civilized man . . . never feels so happy as when he throws off a large part of his civilization and reverts to the life of a semi-savage." When Schofield followed this advice on a long hunting trip, he returned invigorated: "I wanted no other occupation in life than to ward off the savage and kill off his food until there should no longer be an Indian frontier in our beautiful country." A similar ominous conclusion from relativistic premises was drawn by one of General Sherman's aides. Sherman's friend praised General Miles' sympathetic account of Indian culture, particularly the nobility of red religion. Further, he granted

There is no doubt the Indians have, at times, been shamefully treated . . . and there is no doubt a man of spirit would rebel. . . . however, it is useless to moralize about the Indians. Their fate is fixed, and we are so near their end, it is easy to see what that fate is to be. That the Indian might be collected, and put out of misery by being shot deliberately, (as it would be done to a disabled animal), would seem shocking, but something could be said in favor of such procedure.

Aggression accompanied by bereavement and guilt will surprise us only if we forget how central anger is to all three reactions. Frustrations of these officers encouraged this most ambivalent response to their job of subduing native cultures. The military commanders in the West found it impossible simply to celebrate or censure white or red aspirations. Indian tactics seemed horrible, yet ingenious. Native culture was repellent, but also alluring because of its integrity. At the same time, a disturbing sense of having been abandoned by an unworthy white civilization is evident in the reports and memoirs of these officers. Army training and experience prevented these men from acting out their anger. Some of the anger of the officer corps against red and white was instead internalized and expressed in the mourning and guilt they confessed so frequently. Appreciation of native Americans for what they had been was combined with determination to punish this society for what it refused to become. Defense of civilized settlement for what it should be was mixed with anger that some virtues, retained by primitives, were slipping away from the white man.

The persistent tension between civilized and primitive virtues was expressed in conflicting strategies to win the West. Like Sherman, many in the Army were willing to concede white inferiority under certain conditions of battle—"man for man." Success, then, required finding some hidden strengths of civilization or, more ingeniously, taking advantage of the savages'. Either choice allowed whites to overcome the inadequacy native Americans had forced these officers to face.

Organization and technology were often perceived as civilization's hidden strengths. Steady, disciplined pursuit would conquer the brilliant but erratic Indian. The most frequent boast of Army officers after the Custer chastisement was that systematic, planned action would eventually restore white pride. Confidence lost on the white man in battle could also be regained by looking at the modern devices held in reserve. Thus General Sherman was willing to make a machine—the railroad—the hero of the winning of the West. "In the great battle of civilization with barbarism," Sherman judged, this machine deserved more credit than the men on the frontier—*it* accounts "fully for the peace and good order that now prevails throughout our country." General Custer, similarly, spoke more warmly of the railroad than of his enlisted men. General Miles credited his victories to the "superior intelligence and modern appliances" that enabled white troops to overcome the considerable Indian military skills. Miles relished his psychological triumph over the Indians who had killed Custer. He allowed two groups of Sioux to talk on the telephone: "Their hands shook visibly, their bodies trembled with emotion, and great drops of perspiration rolled down their bronzed faces." General Miles' own fascination with mechanical achievements was as intense as the Indians'.

The military's celebration of technology and organization was far from unanimous, however. Sherman balanced his awe of the railroad with official warnings that the engineer should not be given greater control in the Army. "Scientific methods" of operation and "modern monsters" of ordnance clearly alarmed the old general. Indeed, some military observers found the Indian's unorthodox warfare an admirable defiance of America's slavery to technology. The red enemy, Bourke explained, "will not brook the restraints which, under our notions of discipline, change men into machines." The Carringtons, similarly, saw the Indian's fight as a warning; his "sense of freedom and independence brings such contrast with the machinery and formalities of much that is called civilized life." Even General Crook officially reported that the war against the Apaches was stalled because the American soldier had become a "machine . . . his individuality is completely lost in his organization." Bourke and Crook followed the logic of this criticism to extremes. They stressed the absolute necessity of Indian scouts and enlistments and further urged that "the civilized soldier must be trained down as clearly as possible to the level of the savage." One Apache chief, at last, seems to have been impressed by Crook's re-education: "He's more of an Indian than I am.' "

Native Americans, then, were caught between some officers who sought to harness the Indians' strengths and others who struggled to master science. Compassion and guilt were hardly enough to restrain white men who could identify with such compelling features of both a traditional and a modern society. But these were troubled alliances—each aimed at destroying a culture that was respected. If we appreciate the military's doubts as well as commitments, the tragedy in the West does not go away; it deepens. Was there an escape from the emotional trap the Army fell into between red and white?

Refusing to win the West required the renunciation of faith in American progress and civilization. Sentimental cultural relativism had to yield to a serious commitment to primitivism as the way to truth. Technology and organization had to seem more horrible prospects than any of these officers imagined. Anger with America had to come out in the open. Such a conversion is hard to imagine without an immense shock outside the military life.

The cultural odyssey of one lieutenant in the Nez Percé war illustrates, however, that this transformation was possible. Charles E. S. Wood served on General O. O. Howard's staff and translated the very moving speeches of the defeated Chief Joseph. Wood's reflections on these campaigns in the early 1880s set the conventional balance between regret and pride. He surveyed the shameful record of white treaty violations and warned his Army colleagues that retribution might follow. Yet necessity seemed to excuse bad faith: forces were "silently at work, beyond all human control."

Indian culture and tribal organization now seemed expendable in Wood's view. He was ready to bring the "martial spirit" to save the Indian—enlistment in the Army offered the red man "the advantages of contact with whites, drill and discipline."

Wood eventually participated in the somewhat crowded celebration by Army officers of the culture they had worked to destroy. He emphasized the color and nobility of the Indians, qualities that seemed poignant by their passing. In the 1870s Wood rejected the program of assimilation: the Indian "receives from civilization little or nothing which benefits him." But, significantly, Wood refused to condemn directly the civilization that had corrupted and supplanted native Americans. Wood's fashionable relativism did not sound much different from General Custer's.

But Wood was to change. He pursued his literary and legal interests outside the Army. Not satisfied with the standard literary culture and pessimistic about legal reform, Wood became an ally of the IWW and searched for a literary form to express his growing anarchistic perspective. The fruit of this veteran's rehabilitation was a long experimental poem: *The Poet in the Desert* (1915 and 1918). Wood's effort is an effective personal renunciation of "civilization" and a call for the revolt of the masses against privilege. The "silent forces" that Wood had bowed to earlier now seemed the roar of machine-like civilization that drove men to war. Seeing this, Wood was able to use his radical perspective to re-evaluate his part in the Indian campaigns and express his guilt clearly for the first time:[6]

> I have lain out with the brown men
> And know they are favored.
> Nature whispered to them her secrets,
> But passed me by.
>
> I sprawled flat in the bunch-grass, a target
> For the just bullets of my brown brothers betrayed.
> I was a soldier, and, at command,
> Had gone out to kill and be killed.
>
> We swept like fire over the smoke-browned tee-pees;
> Their conical tops peering above the willows.
> We frightened the air with crackle of rifles,
> Women's shrieks, children's screams,
> Shrill yells of savages;
> Curses of Christians.
> The rifles chuckled continually.
> A poor people who asked nothing but freedom,
> Butchered in the dark.

Wood's polemic is more straightforward, I believe, than many made today on behalf of native Americans. He learned that respect and compassion for another culture were very unsure checks on violence. And it is important to keep in mind that peace in the West required more than the abundant good will of our polemical histories of the Indian wars.

Wood and his troubled colleagues also can clarify the historian's work as they provide a model of civilizing agents to be compared with other armies on other 19th century frontiers (in Burma, the steppes of Europe and in Argentina, for example). Certainly, indictments of American culture cannot be precise until such studies have been made. It will be deeply ironic if American sympathy for the enemy turns out to be a "peculiar institution" that we wish to condemn.

NOTES

1. Sherman, *Report of the Secretary of War*, I (1876), 36. Robert G. Athearn, *William Tecumseh Sherman and the Settlement of the West* (Norman: Univ. of Oklahoma Press, 1956), gives the most balanced picture of Sherman's anger (pp. 99–101, 223, 301) set against his moments of pity for the enemy he had to fight (pp. 64, 67, 82–83, 321). General Sheridan's compassion for the defeated Indian is very clear in his *Report of the Secretary of War*, I (1878), 38. See also Henry E. Fritz, *The Movement for Indian Assimilation* (Philadelphia: Univ. of Pennsylvania Press, 1963), pp. 127–28. Sheridan's private papers show the same attitude, e.g., draft of letter to General Townsent (?) Dec. 1878 in Sheridan Papers, Library of Congress, Box 92. It is also significant that Sheridan approved of the viewpoint of his regiment's war correspondent, De Benneville Randolph Keim, *Sheridan's Troopers on the Borders* (New York: D. McKay, 1885). An endorsement from the General served as an introduction to these reports. Keim wrote that whites were generally at fault in the Indian conflicts and that contemporary civilization was "selfish and aggressive." Neither judgment, however, took much away from his joy in these campaigns, pp. 294, 283. Sheridan's ambivalence is also clear in his *Personal Memoirs* (New York: C. L. Webster, 1888), I, 88–89, 111.

2. *Campaigning with Crook*, 2nd ed. (1890; rpt. Norman: Univ. of Oklahoma Press, 1964), p. 33. King, the great-grandson of Rufus King, can be compared with another connoisseur of Indian lore, General Hugh Lenox Scott—the grandson of Charles Hodge. General Scott paused in his campaigns to rejoice in becoming a part of "primitive America," studied Indian culture closely, and feared for native Americans faced with the "blighting power" of civilization. *Some Memoirs of a Soldier* (New York: Century, 1928), pp. 30–32, 156–57. It is perhaps appropriate that the descendants of these two antebellum conservatives should appreciate some alternative to the culture of modern America—at the same time they fought to defend the nation.

3. Custer also confessed he enjoyed the heroic escape of Indians he pursued and he predicted that as the Indian yielded to civilization, he would grow weak and die, pp. 201, 21. Custer's admiration of the Indian seems to have been partly reciprocated. His body was not mutilated on the battlefield—an honor in Sioux warfare.

4. Officers very often sought to understand and even excuse Indian "outrages"

by pointing to white provocations. General John Pope stressed this point in his official reports, *Report of the Secretary of War*, I (1874), 30; ibid, I (1875), 76. See also, Colonel James B. Fry, *Army Sacrifices* (New York: Van Nostrand, 1879), p. 4.

5. Bourke's attitude is particularly evident in *The Snake-Dance of the Moquis of Arizona* (New York: Scribner's, 1884), p. 162; *Scatalogic (sic) Rites of All Nations* (Washington, D.C.: W. H. Loudermilk, 1891), pp. iv, 467. Bourke was not alone in combining serious anthropological work with the military life. Washington Matthews' major research on the Sioux and Navaho was done as he served as a doctor with the Army in the West. What is most significant, however, is the respectful attention ordinary officers paid to the culture of their enemy. A further example of this is the manuscript "Notes on Indians" ca. 1876 in Walter Scribner Schuyler Papers, section B, Henry E. Huntington Library.

6. Wood, *The Poet in the Desert* (Portland, Ore.: F. W. Baltes, 1915) develops the case against technology especially pp. 77 and 107. In the 1918 revision, a detailed recollection of the Indian campaigns is given (pp. 90–95), quoted 90 and 92. The longer 1915 version of the poem used the last line of this passage (p. 103) but avoids the detailed references to Indians that Wood put in the briefer 1918 revision. It seems that Wood's memory and guilt sharpened as his disillusionment with World War I deepened.

24

Armed Progressives

The Military Reorganizes for the American Century

PETER KARSTEN

For many reasons the late nineteenth century represented watershed years for the regular army and navy—years in which these services developed the outlooks and strategies familiar to us today. This essay explores the impulses within each service that facilitated their rationalization and modernization.

THE U.S. MILITARY underwent a virtual revolution in the late 19th and early 20th centuries—a revolution involving new missions, managerial and technological streamlining, professionalization, and sheer growth. Professional military men, mostly graduates of West Point and Annapolis, looked with admiration on the vast military machines of late 19th-century European powers, and with chagrin on Congressional foes who could see no value to their constituents in a big navy, a large standing army, or a system of national conscription. These officers and their allies in and out of government came to believe that a modern, nationally managed military system was a necessity for America in the dog-eat-dog world of international commerce, imperial rivalries, conscription armies, and Dreadnaught navies.

In the process the military was compelled to reorganize its own houses. Junior officers, "armed progressives," were depressed with military condi-

SOURCE: Peter Karsten, "Armed Progressives: The Military Reorganizes for the American Century," in *Building the Organizational Society*, ed. Jerry Israel (New York: Free Press, 1972), pp. 196–232.
EDITOR'S NOTE: Most of the citations to the sources consulted by the author in this essay have been omitted from this volume for brevity and economy. The reader should consult the original source of the essay for the complete scholarly documentation.

tions and more anxious about their own careers than were many of their superiors. They and their more senior allies, often acting in such organizations as the Naval Officers Association, the Marine Corps Association, and the Infantry Association, were the prime organizers of the military revolution.

The services could never have reorganized themselves without the sustained support of civilian allies in the Army or Navy Leagues, the Congress and the Executive, the worlds of agriculture, commerce, banking, and war-related industries. The impressive social credentials of virtually every Secretary of War or Navy from the 1880s to the present demonstrates the concern that the national elite have for the military establishment. But men like William Whitney, Benjamin Franklin Tracy, Redfield Proctor, Theodore Roosevelt, Elihu Root, Hilary Herbert, Henry Stimson, and Franklin D. Roosevelt, appreciative as they were of the need for change, could never have accomplished such a thorough reorganization of America's Indian-fighting Army and sail-and-spar Navy without the efforts of the "armed progressives."

THE NAVY

The Civil War U.S. Navy was modern and impressive. But it aged, and was left behind in the technological race. By 1880 the Navy was a third-rate assemblage of wooden, or thin-skinned iron-plated sailing ships with the capacity, but without the inclination, to burn coal. The Civil War blockade had demonstrated the merit of steam power, but steam-powered vessels burned too much coal to suit economy-minded administrators. In "showing the flag" on foreign stations, sail power was more efficient and strategically feasible than the somewhat unpredictable, coal-dependent steamer with its small cruising radius.

The ships themselves were a motley lot, in various states of disrepair. Training cycles were infrequent or nonexistent, and the gunnery, even by contemporary European standards, was erratic. Officers ordered to cruise on foreign stations in "old tubs" felt "wounds" to their "sense of professional pride." More than one officer, mortified by the sneers of their counterparts in foreign services, sensed that the U.S. Navy had become "the laughing stock of the Naval World."

Younger officers, many experiencing their first naval cruises, were hardest hit. Older men had witnessed the slow decline over a long period of years and many had at least learned to live with it. But the striking differences between the American, and the French, British, Italian, or Chilean navies made the idealistic officer fresh from the Acadamy "feel sort of insignificant and ashamed."

Many spoke of the need for a "new navy," to be sure, and in 1873 a group of progressive naval officers founded the Naval Institute, a semi-official organization "having for its object the advancement of professional and scientific knowledge in the Navy." But in the 1870s the federal government offered little support for naval revitalization. Most American statesmen saw little need for expensive warships that would be obsolete in a matter of months. Three thousand miles of bounding main separated them from the evolving European arms race. The nation was expanding, but it was still primarily expanding over land, not sea. Railroads and local matters drew more attention than foreign affairs or the Navy.

Decaying ships and antique equipment were not the Navy's only woes; there were personnel problems as well. The service had an excess of officers. Consequently promotions were few and far between. The careers of many younger officers lay becalmed. The Civil War had been a glorious period for junior officers. But with the termination of hostilities in 1865 came a termination in career growth. Even after the departure of civilian volunteers and enlisted wartime appointees the ranks of the naval officer corps remained swollen out of proportion to their obligations. Between 1861 and 1865 some 858 midshipmen had been admitted to the Academy. The graduates of the classes of 1864, 1865, 1866, 1867, and 1868 filled and blocked the lower echelons of the naval officer hierarchy. The 12 top graduates of the Class of 1868 remained lieutenants for 21 years. In 1866 there were many lieutenant commanders with less than eight years of post-Annapolis service; in 1896 there were many ensigns with over 15 years of service in that grade. Each year the time one was required to remain in the same grade increased. Promotion was strictly linear; there was no way, in peacetime, that one might advance any more rapidly than the sum of the deaths or retirements of senior officers. Every officer who had received a note of thanks from Congress during the Civil War (and there had been quite a few) could be retired only with his permission unless he had committed a felony or had compiled no less than 55 years of naval service. The rest of the Civil War "Hump" were free to stay for 40 years, or until age 62. "What is this but a life thrown away," one lieutenant bemoaned, and his anxiety was echoed by many others. The weary waiting for automatic advancement dulled many an officer's ambition. Navy lieutenants grew grey, "broken by the heart-sickening prospect of always being compelled to perform the same duty they did in their youth." And to such junior officers the sense of futility was compounded whenever contact was made with a British warship, whose captain was often younger than the senior American lieutenant on board, and all of whose junior officers were significantly younger than their American counterparts.

Consequently, many junior officers resigned. No less a figure than the senior U.S. naval officer himself, Admiral David D. Porter, told one of his former subordinates: "I think you are wise in leaving the Navy as there is little inducement for remaining in it." More than one junior officer, in submitting his resignation, gave as his reasons "the slowness of promotion, the overcrowded conditions of the lower grades of the Service, and the low rate of pay for which I would have to serve for a number of years." But many were reluctant to give up what little they had achieved. "There is nothing else for me but the Navy," Cadet-Midshipman Frank Bunts (U.S.N.A. '81) told his brother in July, 1882. "I have spent nearly six of the best years of my life endeavoring to perfect myself in this profession and I feel totally unable to enter into any other profession with that zest, interest, and spirit necessary to insure success." A few made efforts to find attractive civilian employment, but failing to meet success, they returned to the Navy. Many never bothered to try. "I expect that after all the Navy is the most comfortable place for me," Lieutenant Albert Caldwell (U.S.N.A. '65) wrote his aunt.

By 1882 there was one naval officer for every four enlisted men, and the growing criticism of "this swarm" of officers moved Congressmen and naval authorities alike to demand "radical change." The officer complement had to be decreased in numbers. Several options were available: "deadwood" could be pruned out of the upper ranks; provision could be made for more rapid rates of advance for meritorious officers; or the size of the graduating classes of the Academy could be reduced.

The second of these—promotion on merit—had some defenders, but many critics. Officers and politicians alike were too conscious of the power of "political, social and personal influences" in such a method to press for its acceptance. In any event, few could see how such a provision could effect much change in the officer complement. "Selection-up-or-out" was not to come for several decades.

The first option—that of pruning and retiring officers of the senior ranks—was vigorously opposed by Admiral David D. Porter and most of the senior officers, who inveighed against such *total disregard & ignoring of Seniority.* "Stand by me and see that this injustice is not done me," Admiral Porter, fearing involuntary retirement himself, wrote to Representative William E. Robinson of the House Naval Affairs Committee. "Pruning," or "plucking," had an ample store of powerful, if hoary, foes.

That left only the proposal to reduce the number of Academy graduates. This plan advanced by Rear Admiral C. K. Stribling and Commander A. T. Mahan as early as 1876, and pressed again in 1881 by Academy Superintendent C. R. P. Rodgers, drew attention to the fact that Academy graduates were without hope of advancement for years, and called for a reduction in the sizes of Academy classes and an immediate cut-back in the number of graduates commissioned. It was this scheme that was adopted by Congress and made law on August 5, 1882.

The Act of August 5, 1882, specified the exact number of officers intended for each rank, but the actual complement of 1882 revealed a surplus of at least 115 officers in the upper ranks. Under such conditions, the Act required the creation of two vacancies in each higher rank before anyone from a lower rank might be advanced—this in order to arrive eventually at the stipulated allowances for each grade. Thus officers began to speak of "this curious legislative freak" as "the system of promotion which required the death or retirement of 64 Commodores or 128 Rear Admirals to promote one Ensign." One result was that for several years only a handful of Academy graduates—the top 25 per cent of each class—were given commissions. Another was that the tenure of cadet midshipmen in "interim," precommissioned status was extended from four to six years. "After six years of study and service at the school, in competition with several hundred," one observer noted in 1891, "the [midshipman] frequently is disappointed by finding no vacancy in the navy, and has to go off with an honorable discharge, and a year's pay, bitterly chagrined." When he completed his six years of apprenticeship, Cadet-Midshipman Robert Coontz (U.S.N.A. '83) was compelled to race about Washington for days to convince Navy Department officials that enough officers had died or retired to allow for his commissioning. Only 7 per cent of those who entered the Academy in 1881 received commissions in 1887.

The reaction of junior officers to this new, palpable impediment to their careers should have been predictable. The Academy erupted into its most violent period of fighting, hazing, and chaotic abuses of discipline. In the winter of 1882–1883, Superintendent Francis Ramsay (U.S.N.A. '56) faced a "virtual mutiny." All junior officers were upset. Ensign C. C. Marsh (U.S.N.A. '75) wrote to a classmate:

> You know, of course, long before this of the infernal bill that our sage lawmakers passed concerning the Navy. Prospects before dark are now blacker than damnation. What to do? is a question that flies through my brain every time I get my pipe and seat myself. . . . What is to come?

Midshipman Frank Bunts considered the act "enough to dishearten and paralyze a young officer." "What am I to do?" he asked his mother, and himself. One anonymous officer, whose pamphlet *National Defense* appeared shortly after the passage of the August 5 act, drew an analogy between the despondent junior naval officers and the junior members of another profession:

> What would the gentlemen of the legal profession say and feel if an arbitrary law was in existence, to wit, that none shall be permitted to rise in their profession above that of an attorney, until regularly promoted through a vacancy, created by the death of a judge or counsellor, and that only by seniority.

The legal profession would be outraged, of course, as were the junior officers of the naval profession. The August 5 act was a blow to their ambitions. The young Annapolite had read his Benjamin Franklin, but neither virtuous behavior nor hard work had as yet caused success to smile on him:

> What has a Lieutenant to show for his thirty years of service? Nothing, absolutely nothing . . . while his contemporaries in civil life have accumulated wealth or high position. *They have reached the goal they started for.*

Act of August 5 or no, most junior officers still found it difficult to give up their plans of a naval career. The service was not an avenue of golden opportunity to the junior officer in the 1880s, but after years of preparation for its mysteries, it was still a desirable career to many. "A man's tastes," a petition of the Class of 1883 observed, could not be "so easily transferred from one mode of living to another." With the "aptitude and liking for one profession comes the unfitness for any other."

The junior officers, their professional careers threatened, drew analogies between their own condition and what they deemed to be the precarious state of the Navy itself. By 1883 the U.S. had no modern warships to speak of, and from the junior officer's perspective it was unclear as to when it would. Many were persuaded that the threat was not simply to their own careers, but to the entire Navy. In any event, a decline in naval strength meant even fewer billets for junior officers and more attrition. The expression "Don't give up the ship" had taken on new meaning and urgency. Officers noted with alarm the arguments of the pacifists, arbitrationists, and foes of a "big navy" policy, and feared their strength. Such deadly foes of the service, who were heard "to clamor for its extinction," had to be countered. But even if their foes only managed to preserve the *status quo*, without actually abolishing the service, such a standing-still, in reality, amounted to the gradual dismemberment of what remained of the great Navy of Hull, Decatur, and Farragut. "Not to progress was to die," one officer observed. "We had reached a point when the very life of the Navy seemed at stake," Casper Goodrich later wrote of the 1880s.

The junior officers responded to the Act of August 5, 1882, and to what they conceived to be the threat of the Navy *per se* in three ways. First, they organized to fight for the repeal of the obnoxious promotion provisions of the 1882 law. Second, they made themselves as useful to the Navy as possible and became instrumental in the creation of the "new navy." And third, they and many of their more senior colleagues aggressively strove to change the attitude of Congress and the public regarding the role the Navy played in the national life. The stakes were high. Each increase in naval expenditures meant more ships, more billets, and thus greater career security to these "Young Turks." In a host of ways the Navy's "armed progressives" sought to demonstrate the desirability of a "new navy."

The first response—that of organized opposition to the 1882 promotion system—was reflexive and immediate. Various Academy classes, among them 1881, 1882, and 1883, hired Washington attorneys and lobbied for repeal or exemption. The effort to gain reinstatement for 145 midshipmen who had been released upon graduation in the first three years after the passage of the "obnoxious" clause of the Act of August 5, 1882, failed to receive a favorable Senate committee report in 1886, and was lost. The Class of 1881 published its own annual reports, and many a member voiced his hope to meet his exiled classmates "again on the quarter-deck, or the forecastle—Doesn't matter much which, just so we are wearing the 'blue and gold'." But the exiled classmates remained beyond the pale.

Those who survived the purge, however, had learned a lesson; they had discovered that much of their opposition wore "blue and gold" too. Many senior officers regarded the "selection-up-or-out" promotion reform measures introduced by the "Young Turks" to be the products of "a clique of ambitious officers who want to get on top by whatever means they can bring to bear." "A large majority of the older line officers openly and actively opposed us," one ensign-lobbyist wrote in late 1886. This opposition appeared to have guaranteed their defeat. The junior officers reacted by arguing for the forced retirement of their elder adversaries. "*Old men and old material must be got rid of at all hazards.*" A "new life, a young life," must be given to the service "to prepare for the work so soon expected of it." Admiral Porter had used the same argument in early 1862 when he tried to persuade the Navy department to recall and retire his rival, Flag Officer David Farragut. Porter was 75 in 1882.

The intra-service division was largely junior versus senior, but not all senior officers were unsympathetic. Morris Janowitz has postulated that "the lower the rank, the greater . . . the officer's sense of professional and service frustration." This certainly describes the situation with regard to the 1882 promotion law. But many grey-haired lieutenants, lieutenant commanders, and commanders, for whom the future was bleak, also fought for promotion and materiel reform even if they, personally, could "derive no profit" from their labors. In spite of age and individual career interest, many a senior officer's lifelong perspective led him to sympathize with the "youngblood" striving to assert itself and to reinvest life in the Navy. Complaints of a weakening of the "feeling of comradeship and brotherhood among the officers," and of officers "watching one another to detect trivial errors," led to the creation of the Naval Academy Graduate Association in 1886. This organization sponsored regional and annual get-togethers to boost sagging morale during the "doldrum" years, and was "a powerful means of keeping alive the feeling of devotion to the service" when many suffered from "slow promotion" and "a feeling of lack of appreciation." In 1888 Academy Superintendent Captain William Sampson argued before a Senate committee for an increase in the number of billets for Academy graduates reacting to an appeal from the Class of 1887 who had found only 12 openings available for their class. "I wouldn't be too sure that promotion will be very slow [from now on]," Ensign John Bernadou wrote to Lieutenant (j.g.) George Foulk in the late '80s "[T]he head of the Senior Lieutenants lists [sic] is being squeezed from both ends, and the cry of the selectionists is growing louder." Many young line and staff officers even rejected much of the logic of the perennial line-staff controversy, and argued that the two branches should "combine for the general good." In 1890 three line ensigns and three assistant engineers actually collaborated to draft a bill that would guarantee both ranks promotion to lieutenant (j.g.) and its engineer equivalent upon the completion of ten years of service. "We cannot all be Nelson" one crusader remarked, "but we can and must be a band of brothers."

The second response of junior officers to the 1882 promotion law and their perception of the state of the service in the 1880s consisted of efforts to make their professional careers as functional and meaningful as possible. There was no inconsistency here; dissatisfaction with the promotion system and zealous attention to naval affairs were two sides of the same coin— a coin intended to buy naval reform and career security. With or without immediate promotion incentive, these sons of Horatio Alger and Horatio Nelson, filled with 19th-century American self-reliance and Annapolis-bred enthusiasm for the Navy, were possessed with what David McClelland calls a high "need for achievement." They sensed the significance to their careers of a "long peace." As one advised another, the nation was not going to go to war for quite some time, "and the only chance for fellows like you and I, to get along, is to have a specialty and work hard at it." Alfred Mahan often maintained that "the only stimulus in peace to exertion beyond the simple line of duty" was one's interest in "matters professional for their own sake." This "sense of duty" or "professional enthusiasm" created initiative and sustained energy, "thus becoming a productive force for personal improvement, as well as for naval progress."

In the 1880s, with the decommissioning of a number of old wooden vessels many junior officers were forced ashore for periods of from three to five years. There they "naturally" became interested in "the absorbing question of rebuilding the Navy." Ensign Bernadou wrote Lieutenant (j.g.) Foulk in early 1887 of the "whole fields open" in a stateside shore billet. There was "a chance for a man" to "make a name." Foulk was advised to go in for some professional specialty. Senior officers who had damned the "Young Turks" for "launching out in a ruthless process of reconstructing [the naval] personnel [laws]," actively encouraged them to reconstruct the naval operating forces and support services.

The contributions of junior officers to the creation of the "new navy" in the 1880s were impressive. Assistant Naval Constructors brought ideas home from the Royal Navy people at Glasgow and Greenwich and were assigned to shipyards all over the U.S. "Young Turk" ordnance inventors of the 1880s studied British and European techniques vital to the armor process developed at Pittsburgh. Other "young Turks" pioneered in electrical and hydroelectrical inventions and in important steam turbine modifications in these years. Lieutenant Bradley Fiske (U.S.N.A. '74), whose *Electricity in Theory and Practice* appeared in 1883 while he was attached to the Bureau of Ordnance, patented no less than 17 key inventions— among them the battle-order telegraph, the hydroelectric turret train, the stadimeter, the telescope sight, the first electric gun director system, and the first electric interior communications system. Those assigned to billets at industrial sites, especially those who worked under Frederick W. Taylor himself, later brought these managerial techniques to bear on naval problems such as those involving the installation on the U.S.S. *Minnesota* in 1905 of the Sims-Scott continuous-aim fire control system. Consequently, the views of two civilian efficiency experts who inspected the *Minnesota* were predictable:

> The synchronization of gun operations, fire control, and engine room was a model exhibition of scientific management—stopwatch work, no waste effort, no lost motion, but every movement standardized and unified to the shortest possible time.

"The subject of naval reorganization seems now to be in the air and to occupy naval thought," one officer observed. Whether the subject was Navy yards, supply systems, enlisted personnel, war planning, or fleet maneuvers, every aspect of the naval establishment was subjected to the test of efficiency. Pork-barrel yard politics might be essential to the vitality of local political machines, but they clashed with the more functional objectives of the builders of the "new Navy" and were condemned. The shortcomings of the fragmented bureau system demonstrated the need for the "introduction of business methods into our system of naval administration." Managers trained to "think for the railroad" by correlating the various facets of the company and noting the activity of rival lines and local legislators could "watch the future and prepare their systems to draw all possible advantage from events. . . . " Such skills, long "employed by the great commercial companies," could be utilized by a trained Navy general staff as well. Vital military resources, such as oil and steel, should be developed with "method and system" and an eye for the future. Discipline should be re-designed to breed coordination rather than the less efficient *sub*ordination. Efficiency ("E") awards should be granted to vessels with low rates of fuel consumption or high rates of target destruction. Sailors should receive national citizenship training to improve their "productive capacity," and enable them to "produce better children, govern their families better, and [prove] more stable in conduct." Venereal disease should be eliminated as it constituted "a crime both against ourselves and the State." In short, every aspect of naval life was to be rationalized and made harmonious with the mission of the "new Navy" in the coming century, when America would assume far-reaching world "responsibilities."

Invention and managerial reorganization were but two of the talents young officers exercised. Others included the writing of naval history, the drafting of fresh surveys of inlets, harbors, and seas, the publication of exploring and navigation treatises, and the analyses of foreign cultures, economies, and naval establishments. The publications of U.S. naval officers gradually increased in numbers throughout the late 19th century, reaching a peak during the Spanish-American War, but the 1880s appear as a kind of "take-off" period, a decade in which all naval publications of junior officers nearly tripled.

Among the more active "Young Turks" were those attached to the Office of Naval Intelligence. Inspired by British and German views on naval intelligence, a group of lieutenants, headed by Theodorus Mason (U.S.N.A. '68), persuaded Commodore John G. Walker (U.S.N.A. '56) Chief of the Bureau of Navigation, to create the office in 1882. Thereafter, young naval attachés were dispatched as overt spies to London, Berlin, Paris, Vienna, St. Petersburg, Rome and other capitals, and by 1914 the United States had more attachés abroad than any other nation. The O.N.I.'s many publications served as media through which activist naval strategy found expression. Thus in 1889 one pace-setting O.N.I. volume, entitled *Naval Mobilization and Improvement in Materiel*, contained a piece by Lieutenant Sidney A. Staunton (U.S.N.A. '71) which called for formal war planning and a naval general staff, and an essay by Lieutenant John Forsythe Meigs (U.S.N.A. '67), calling for a "gun control" system and more gunfire exercises.

By 1880 a Torpedo School was in operation at Newport, training future destroyer captains, and in 1893 a Naval Architecture program at M.I.T. began to train designers of the Navy of the American Century. Elsewhere activists at the Naval Academy were helping to provide "practical and progressive" courses in electricity, construction, photography, steam engineering, and modern gunnery. Others argued for the creation of a naval postgraduate school to provide advanced training in math, mechanics, physics, chemistry, astronomy, metallurgy, torpedoes and ordnance, ship-handling, naval architecture, steam engineering, international law, naval history, strategy, and tactics.

The plan of Commodore Stephen Luce (U.S.N.A. '48) for a naval war college that would focus on the last four subjects did not satisfy the more progressive of the younger officers, but when it became clear that the department and its senior naval advisors would approve of no more extensive a program of postgraduate training than Luce's scheme encompassed, the progressives accepted the Luce War College—and made the best of it. After all, as Army Colonel Emory Upton had told Luce in 1878, a war college could "keep the officers occupied as one means of preventing reduction of the Navy." War College Presidents A. T. Mahan (U.S.N.A. '59) and Henry Clay Taylor (U.S.N.A. '63) appeared to many "young Turks" to "point backward instead of forward." They presented strategy as something "independent of mechanism" and thus of limited value in an era of rapid technological change. Somewhat hostile to the innovations of modern naval technology, they were ideologically wedded to the 18th-century romantic world of topside seamanship, of sails and spars. But if Mahan's "Department of Ancient Naval History" was virtually useless to the task of preparing for the American Century, the "more practical and progressive" courses—War Gaming and "Problem Solving," taught by Lieutenant William McCarty Little (U.S.N.A. '75), Staff and Intelligence, taught by Lieutenant C. C. Rogers (U.S.N.A. '76), and International Law, taught by young Academy Professor James Russell Soley—were more to the point.

As every young officer knew, an increase in the number and size of commissioned warships meant an increase in the number of officers required to man them with a consequent increase in the rate of promotion. Thus it was natural to expect that the Navy's "Young Turks" of the 1880s would make every effort to increase the number of vessels on the lists, or, at the very least, to retain the same number of vessels in commission. "Any reduction would stop promotion, already very slow, and would cause dissatisfaction and want of zeal," as Lieutenant R. M. G. Brown (U.S.N.A. '68) put it.

The "Young Turks" therefore, constituted a body of amateur, but aggressive Navy public relations men. In or out of the service, every naval progressive was expected to "lose no opportunity" to sell the Navy to any prominent relation, friend, or to any member of Congress he might "happen to know." "The Nazareth of public opinion" was not overtly responsible to "service needs" in the 1880s as Lieutenant J. D. Jerrold Kelley (U.S.N.A. '68) put it:

> And so it went from bad to worse, until in sheer desperation the remedy had, at last, to come from within the service. A number of officers . . . began a campaign of education.

The first, and perhaps most amenable, targets of this campaign were the special industries affected by naval construction—shipbuilders, steel firms, and weapons manufacturers. These interest groups, Rear Admiral Thornton Jenkins told a Naval Institute audience in 1885, should be led to "recognize their opportunity, and find that their interests lie in supporting our efforts." From the Office of Naval Intelligence and other Bureau of Navigation retreats of "Young Turks" and their sympathizers came a steady stream of "Naval Profession Papers," distributed throughout the 1880s "to manufacturers who might be interested in their contents."

The second target of this "campaign of education" was that group of businessmen and lobbyists affiliated with the U.S. Merchant Marine. The interests of the two services, in the words of Lieutenant R. M. G. Brown, were "so closely bound together," that "when speaking of the rebuilding of one we must necessarily provide for the other." Ensign William David (U.S.N.A. '77) won the Institute's essay prize in 1882 with a paper on the state of the U.S. Merchant Marine, but he made the order of his loyalties quite clear. "It does not follow," he told his fellow officers, "that a strong navy will produce a merchant marine; but the reverse does follow." Every blow dealt for the "revival" of the Merchant Marine was a blow dealt for the "new Navy." Commander N. H. Farquhar (U.S.N.A. '64) who chaired the meeting at which David's paper was read, told the assemblage that, "as naval officers, we should keep the subject of the revival of the merchant marine before the public, for its revival will benefit the Navy." A year later Captain A. P. Cooke told a similar group of officers that closer relations between merchant mariners and the Navy "would very materially increase the sphere of usefulness of navy officers." And in 1890 Ensign J. B. Bernadou (U.S.N.A. '80) repeated to a Naval Institute audience that the best way to "obtain a powerful navy" was to "build up a merchant service." Naval officers consistently argued for federal legislation that might aid the U.S. Merchant Marine, but fundamentally they had the interests of their own service in mind.

A third target of the "campaign of education" was the American public, the most important and the most difficult of the three. "The navy is not popular with the people at large," one officer confided to a colleague, "and our existence depends on our keeping up a high standard of usefulness." In 1884 Lieutenant J. D. J. Kelley obtained orders to duty at James Gordon Bennett's New York *Herald*, where he could bring his "new Navy" salesmanship directly to bear on the public's pulse. Others settled for less convenient, but only slightly less effective arrangements with other publishers.

At the heart of each argument lay one principle with which every one of the "band of brothers" was familiar—warships were invaluable aids to U.S. businessmen abroad. In the 19th century the foreign offices of many U.S.-owned commercial firms left "spare seats at the dinner table every day," which naval officers were expected to fill without formal invitation whenever they were ashore. These merchants knew the many uses of the Navy. It was the great mass of American businessmen with local concerns, far from these African, Asiatic, and Latin American marts of trade, who were generally less conscious of the Navy's importance to their livelihoods, and consequently less enthusiastic about new ships. "Our businessmen practically control our national expenditures," one "Young Turk" observed. Those immersed in domestic pursuits simply had to be made aware of the Navy's role in facilitating the movement of cattle, grains, cotton goods, manufactured goods, and other raw and finished commodities to and from the "Great Middle Kingdom" and her foreign markets and sources of supply. The "history of trade" told one clear story: There was "no diplomatic sentence so short as '*justice or shells*'."

Navy progressives outdid one another throughout the 1880s in their published efforts to persuade the public of the historical value of the Navy to commerce. They frequently underscored the importance of the "command of the sea," of fleet tactics, heavy guns and armor, concentrated forces, and available coaling stations. They cited the isthmian regions of Central America as strategic objectives of the highest value. They maintained that history, day-to-day observation, and common sense all established that the nation's health and growth required trade expansion and commercial security abroad, and that a strong Navy, capable of taking the offensive, was a prerequisite for such development.

The officers of "the rising generation" were in the van of the movement to demonstrate the importance of naval power to the public in the 1880s, but on this score they met with very little opposition in the service. "Young Turks" and "Old Salts" were both "looking outward." Captain A. T. Mahan (U.S.N.A. '59), President of the War College and thus official custodian of the philosophy of sea power, was the most renowned of the Navy's publicists and exponents of the American century, though he was, relatively, a latecomer.

But all the arguments of the Navy's armed progressives would have been without effect if it were not for the fact that there were many civilian groups "looking outward" in the 1880s, too. Exporters, shipbuilders, manufacturers, and agricultural leaders had learned new managerial skills in the late 19th-century national marketplace, and their lobbies sought to conquer Uncle Sam's share of the fabled markets abroad. The Navy's publicists spoke their language, and their allies in Congress and the Executive department were earnest navalists themselves. Anti-navalists, like Jerry Simpson of Kansas and Oscar Callaway of Texas, fought virtually every new naval appropriations bill tooth and nail, but their foes, led by such cosmopolitan figures as John T. Morgan of Alabama, Washington Whitthorne of Tennessee, William V. Allen of Nebraska, Henry Cabot Lodge of Massachusetts, Benjamin F. Tracy of New York, and William E. Chandler of New Hampshire, slowly overcame the localists by persuading more and more of their colleagues to support a navy second to none.

By the 1890s, all naval officers, young and old, were becoming adept at the art of lobbying. Whether the issue was the future of the Naval War College, promotion reform, or, as was more frequent, greater naval appropriations, it was now certain that officers would seize every opportunity to tell their countrymen of the importance of the Navy to their own interest. By 1900, this propagandizing, crowned as it was by Manila and Santiago, had achieved a measure of success. "Our Navy has never been intrenched more firmly in the popular heart than at this very hour," Assistant Navy Secretary Frank Hackett rightly told a group of Annapolites in that year.[1]

But Mahan's messmates didn't rest on their laurels. As one officer put it in 1902: "we naval officers as a class can each do a little toward advancing the good of the service by judicious missionary work at times when some effect is likely to be produced."

In 1909 ex-Annapolites John Sanford Barnes and John Forsythe Meigs and Rear Admirals Luce, Chadwick, and Davis created a Naval History Society designed to affect public opinion and public interest in the Navy. Barnes sought to found a Society repository for naval memorabilia. This willingness to "sell the Navy" reflected the Annapolite's rejection of the strictly apolitical habit. Retired Rear Admiral Mahan assured his active brethren that politics were the proper concern of naval progressives and sought "by sustained apprehension, communicated to the nation, to maintain a pressure which shall constantly ensure . . . a navy. . . . " The Navy League, surely the most effective pressure group the Navy was to enjoy in the 20th century, was born in the same year that Mahan's words were set in print.

The Navy League was not Mahan's idea, but it was fundamentally the invention of naval officers.[2] Numerous Annapolites had for some time sought to create such a lobby. One, Lieutenant Commander J. H. Gibbons (U.S.N.A. '79), regarded a Navy League as central to the "important missionary work of spreading the naval propaganda among the people at large." He favored conferences with superintendents of public schools "and other educators" to spur courses of instruction in naval history and customs, "beginning with toys of the kindergarten, fashioned after naval models, and working up through the stages of sea stories and nautical adventures to that of comparative history and the influence of sea power." He also sought a series of lectures and pamphlets, prepared in collaboration with "chambers of commerce, shipbuilding interest, marine underwriters and other organizations. . . . " As Captain Marbury Johnston put it, "the Navy is a fierce business proposition, and to get results we must use business methods." Gibbons, Johnston, and many of their colleagues had become highly skilled in public relations and Congressional lobbying.

The naval publicists' efforts on behalf of the Merchant Marine may have facilitated the passage of the Ocean Mail Act of 1891 and a similar Act of May 10, 1892, designed to encourage the construction of U.S.-owned and operated merchantmen. But neither act stemmed the flow of trade to foreign-registered bottoms. Naval officers could not have been *too* upset. After all, merchant marine expansion had been fundamentally a means of securing naval expansion to them. And if merchant marine growth was slow, *naval* tonnage grew at a better pace. Four ships were authorized in 1883, and four more in 1885. Between 1885 and 1889, 30 more vessels were allowed. Between 1890 and 1894 four battleships were authorized, and in April, 1895, in the same week that one of the battleships, *Iowa*, and several torpedo-boat destroyers were completed, two more battleships were authorized. As one junior officer told his mother, it had been "a *grand* week for the naval service."

As Congressional appropriations flowed more easily and foreign navies burgeoned, naval officers constantly revised their estimates of a minimal rate of naval construction. Commander French Chadwick first set his sights on "nothing less than 150 ships." Three months later the figure had risen to "nothing less than 200 ships as a minimum." By 1903 the Navy General Board wanted first 40, and then 48, battlewagons—one for every state or territory. The number 48 had less strategical significance than it had political potential. As ex-Navy Secretary John Long recalled,

Every state, of course, desired to have its name given to a man-of-war. No state was content with anything less than the biggest battleship. One senator came to me in great distress fearing that he would lose his re-election because a ship of not quite that size had been named for his state.

With the Anglo-German naval arms race and World War I, naval officers revised their goals again. Rear Admiral Bradley Fiske now spoke of the need for "superadequateness." By 1919 the Navy had its "navy second to none."

As naval appropriations grew in the 1890s, so did pressures for resolution of internal tensions. In 1890 Navy Secretary Benjamin F. Tracy advised the Senate Naval Affairs Committee of several "organizations among naval officers not authorized by the Navy Department" that were "designed to advance the interests" of certain types of officers by "influencing Congressional legislation." These were the Line Officers Association, a similar association of naval engineers, an association of medical and disbursing officers, and an ensigns association. By 1900, only one remained.

As early as 1868, Navy Secretary Gideon Welles had realized that the line-engineer controversy could be "prevented in only one way." "The officers must themselves become engineers as well as sailors." Welles failed to persuade either branch of the merits of merging. Thirty years later Captains Bowman McCalla and Robley Evans proposed, and Assistant Navy Secretary Theodore Roosevelt approved, the same "amalgamation" principle that Welles and his Chief of Engineers, Benjamin Isherwood, had advanced in 1867. The situation was different. "The engineering profession throughout the country had become a party to the issue," Navy Secretary John Long recalled, "and was demanding that its representatives in the navy should receive that measure of official recognition (absolute rank) which the higher character of the calling requires." The 1899 Naval Personnel Act amalgamated the two corps. Younger line and engineering officers who had joined forces to lobby for promotion reform in 1890 were delighted; older ones were less enthusiastic.

The most urgent professional tension, the promotion bottleneck, was also relieved in these years, but this was not as simple a business as the resolution of the line-engineer controversy. The Naval Personnel Act of 1899, which provided for the amalgamation of the two feuding officer corps, also provided for a radically different system of promotion.

By 1891, the dissatisfaction among junior officers with the Act of August 5, 1882, had reached such proportions that the Navy Department convened a special board, chaired by Academy Superintendent Captain R. L. Phythian (U.S.N.A. '56), to report upon stagnation of officers in the Navy. This board argued for the restoration of 29 senior billets that had been cycled out of existence in accordance with the provisions of the 1882 Act. The "new Navy" had created a need for more of these senior billets, and the Phythian board saw their resurrection as a means of temporarily accelerating promotion. The board also recommended a voluntary retirement plan for captains, and in a radical gesture, suggested a system of forced retirement, "plucking," for captains who had not demonstrated sufficient ability to be awarded flag rank. The impetus for this final recommendation may have come from the board's "progressive" members, one of whom wrote to Lieutenant Nathan Sargent (U.S.N.A. '70) in the month the report was submitted of his pleasure with its form. Promotion law revision was "inevitable," he told Sargent, "and must come in spite of the open or secret resistance of those who are in a position to profit by the present preposterous state of affairs."

Initially nothing came of the report's ambitious "plucking" recommendation, but the naval progressives persisted. In 1894, a joint Congressional Naval Committee heard testimony on naval promotion problems. Senior officers suggested a merit system by which a few exceptional junior officers might experience an accelerated promotion rate; junior officers countered with an appeal for sufficient "plucking" of senior officers to guarantee enough vacancies to provide for a proper promotion flow. Lieutenant Commander William Cowles (U.S.N.A. '67) wrote from his post as Naval Attaché, London, to Assistant Secretary McAdoo, urging promotion law reform that would "avoid the necessity of having gray-haired men in the Ward Room." British journalists were not being very "polite" in their treatment of U.S naval promotion laws," Cowles advised McAdoo, but their criticism "certainly could not have been more true."

The result of Congress's investigation of naval officer promotion problems was the drafting of the so-called Meyer Bill which proposed "to pluck" officers from "the Hump"—that is, from those classes that entered the Academy between 1861 and 1865. The Line Officers Association, controlled by "conservative" senior officers, fought this bill tooth and nail. Younger "radicals," in turn, sought support for the Meyer Bill. "We cannot stand this stagnation in promotion any longer," Ensign Roger Welles (U.S.N.A. '84) dramatically confided to his father, in October, 1895:

> . . . and we (the junior officers particularly) are doing all we can to relieve it. The Junior Officers are a large majority of the whole Navy and I think will accomplish something; but it will only be done by our work and by the work of those interested in us, principally the latter. . . . Unless something is done this Congress your son will spend the best days of his life in subordinate grades.

A month after Welles wrote this letter, he and his fellow junior officers overthrew the leadership of the Line Officers Association. On November 23, 1895, an unusually large number of junior officers attended the scheduled annual business meeting of the Association. Some 65 officers in all were present, the majority being lieutenants, lieutenants (junior grade), and ensigns. Lieutenant W. H. Schuetze, a Phythian board veteran, and "one or two others" held the proxies of 297 junior officers. After defeating a senior officer motion to elect new officers by rank, Lieutenant David

Peacock (U.S.N.A. '74) nominated an entire slate of junior officers, and with the support of a few senior officers such as Captain William Sampson and Commander French Chadwick, the junior officer majority elected their own kind to take the helm of their profession's primary lobbying organization.

Within a week, senior line officers were hard at work organizing a group of their own, "The Naval Association." Mrs. Captain George Remey reported to her son on November 29 that her husband had gone to a meeting of senior officers the previous evening "in regard to matters of the Navy which are to be brought before the Congress this session." There were "many younger officers working against the older ones." "I think there is danger of injustice to many of your father's grade and higher."

The Naval Association proposed to fight "the essential features of the Meyer Bill," and to "substitute one of its own, drafted upon conservative lines." All officers with the rank of lieutenant or above were invited to join. Membership was to be confined, a Naval Association circular explained, "to Line Officers of experience." Among its first members were Commodore Edmund O. Matthews (U.S.N.A. '55), the ousted head of the Line Officers Association, Captain George Remey (U.S.N.A. '59), Commander Charles Sigsbee (U.S.N.A. '64), Commander Benjamin Lamberton (U.S.N.A. '65), and Lieutenant Dennis Hart Mahan, Jr. (U.S.N.A. '69), Captain Mahan's younger brother. The Naval Association conceived of its parent, the Line Officers Association, now in the hands of junior line officers, as an instrument for promoting class legislation, injurious to the Navy. Naval Association leadership sought to persuade Congressmen, and senior members of the officer corps who had not yet thrown in their lot with either group, that the Line Officers Association was no longer representative of the line, and that the Navy ought to "repress" its publications and directives.

The Naval Association gambit was bold, but it failed to crush the revolt. Two days before the senior group's circular was dispatched, the new officers of the Line Officers Association were already in communication with uncommitted personnel. They were fully aware of the "bitter feeling" among "many senior officers," and they advised the profession of the resignation of 10 disaffected senior men, all known opponents of the Meyer Bill. The new leaders of the Line Officers Association accurately advised uncommitted officers that a number of senior officers sided with them and favored the Meyer Bill as a means of relieving stagnation. "In unity of action alone, can success of any kind be secured," Ensign Thomas Magruder (U.S.N.A. '89), the new Secretary of the Line Officers Association, wrote to one key Captain, Caspar Goodrich (U.S.N.A. '65). Magruder asked for Goodrich's support.

Goodrich was not altogether satisfied with the Meyer Bill. He preferred a "more conservative" measure. But he was willing to accept the "Young Turk" coup as a *fait accompli* and to lobby for the Meyer Bill until something more reasonable was offered. "Our condition is such that any change is better than nothing," he told Commander "Ben" Lamberton of the Naval Association faction on December 8.

It took three-and-a-half more years for the "Young Turks" to persuade Congress and the Navy Department (represented in 1897–98 by Lieutenant Commander Cowles' brother-in-law, Assistant Navy Secretary Theodore Roosevelt) to cut the deadwood out from among the senior officers and thus spur promotion, but the 1899 Naval Personnel Act did the job.

The passage of this act, with its provision for the "plucking" of unsatisfactory captains, capped a string of victories for the "Young Turks." A "new Navy" had been built, the Service had covered itself with glory during the war with Spain, a more efficient recruitment and training policy had been initiated in order to attract more "native Americans" into the enlisted ranks, the line-engineer controversy had been resolved, and now the promotion bottleneck had been eliminated. The officer corps had dwindled from 1,866 officers in 1881 to 1,399 officers in 1897, and career anxiety had been high. But by 1899, the Annapolites had won their "struggle, against bigotry and caprice, for a mere continued existence." In 1903 Congress increased the pay and allowed complement of each level of the line officer corps, and doubled the number of Academy appointments allowed each Congressman. By 1904, there were 2,014 active duty naval officers, and by 1925, the figure had burgeoned to 8,916—over six times the 1897 complement. In the 1880s and '90s the Academy graduated an average of 31 Annapolites per year. By 1905 the figure had risen to 114, and it continued to grow thereafter.

The "Young Turks" of the 1880s had risen to the top by the first decade of the 20th century (albeit by attrition and by-the-numbers promotion). But the rise of a new generation of naval leaders was not the panacea some may have imagined it would be. Coordination of the Office of Naval Intelligence, the War College, the General Board, the Bureau of Navigation, and the Board of Inspection produced a reasonably effective jury-rig of a naval general staff by 1902, but it would be another two decades before the decentralized bureau system would give way to a more centralized organization under a Chief of Naval Operations. The creation of the office of C.N.O. represented a victory for the "progressive" proponents of managerial reorganization, but World War II clearly demonstrated that the bureau system was virtually as vital as its *fin de siècle* defenders had claimed. And when aviation attracted a number of young officers during and after World War I, they met with opposition from battleship-oriented veterans of the appropriations battles of the late 19th century. It was not until the late 1940s that carrier-oriented commanders were able to wrest the strategy-planning initiative from battleship-oriented admirals. Apparently the progressive junior officers only remained "progressive" as long as they were junior officers. With seniority and rank came a decline in career anxieties—and, generally speaking, a concurrent decline in innovative propensities.

Ironically, the new promotion rules were neither immediately useful to nor terribly popular with much of the "progressive" generation of Annapolites. The men who had suffered from "the Hump" and the Act of August 5, 1882, obtained little relief from the 1899 Naval Personnel Act; on the contrary, a good many of them suffered from it. Some officers had foreseen this situation, of course. As early as 1895, Captain Caspar Goodrich saw that the "selection out" or "plucking" system "puts selection at the wrong end"—that is, Goodrich favored a selection process that weeded out the unfit while they were still junior officers. Rear Admiral McCalla argued for promotion for merit. Lieutenant Commander Lyman A. Cotten favored promotion by competitive process. Others favored the creation of selection or "screening" boards for each rank, and this plan, which provided for "plucking" at all levels, became law in the Act of August 29, 1916, and is essentially the system which is still in operation today.

The Navy's progressives succeeded in securing amalgamation and promotion reform, but the concurrent growth of the new navy took them by surprise on their flank, and created a new "enemy" that slowly infiltrated their ranks and weakened the Annapolite's control of the service and its codes.

As more and more new steel vessels were added to the Navy in the 1880s and '90s, Congress and the Navy Department began to give consideration to the need for naval militia or reserve forces to back up the fleet. If sea power *was* essential, and numerous warships of all sorts *were* necessary, then there might come a day when Annapolis would not by itself be able to supply enough fresh officers to the fleet.

State naval militia units were utilized in 1898, as they had been in the Civil War, but these units proved to be little more than a training ground for wartime replacements for the fleet. Naval militia units were rarely deployed intact. Moreover, they were state troops, under the control of state governors. In 1898 too many local interests had asked that a warship be detached from the battle fleet to protect their section of the waterfront. Militia units were not deemed to be the most effective of naval forces from the point of view of those professional regulars planning the naval war machine for the American century.

Some officers recommended the creation of additional naval academies, but this was rejected as too expensive by Congress. A national naval reserve was the final choice of the Navy and the lawmakers.

The first naval reserve legislation in 1900 showed the stamp of the Annapolites. Reserve officers were clearly subordinated to Academy graduates. Reserve officers found promotion and tenure difficult to obtain. World War I legislation, designed to flesh out the burgeoning battle fleet with reserves, contained a built-in safeguard for Annapolites which prevented reserve officers from rising above the rank of lieutenant commander in peace-time. The Act of June 4, 1920, permitted the 1,200 best reserve officers to become coopted into the regular officer corps, but reserve promotions were brought to a standstill. No less than 25,000 reserve officers were dropped from the reserve rolls by September, 1921. Reserve officer corps morale sank, and career anxieties rose among naval reservists. In 1922 a group of naval reserve officers formed the Naval Reserve Officers Association (NROA), and began lobbying for reserve officer permanence and prerogatives. By late 1924, these reservist "Young Turks" had secured their first breakthrough—448 reserve officers were finally given long-over-due promotions. In 1925 the NROA and their allies persuaded Congress to create the first peacetime Naval Reserve Officer Training Corps. As many as 1,200 students at selected colleges would take approved courses and receive a reserve commission upon graduation. Status-conscious children of an upwardly mobile middle class were sorely needed to manage the growing, increasingly technical Navy. By 1928, the reserve officer corps had been integrated with the Annapolites on a reasonably equitable basis, with one reserve commodore and eight reserve captains; reserve morale was good.

The depression destabilized everything. Appropriations for the Navy declined in the early thirties, halting promotions, and reducing pay by 15 per cent. When it became clear that Annapolites, who still held all the top posts in the naval establishment, were cutting reserve budgets to the bone, the NROA went into action once again, infuriating many of the "band of brothers." Admiral William Standley (U.S.N.A. '95), Chief of Naval Operations, rebuked the NROA in don't-rock-the-boat language reminiscent of the senior-junior promotion struggle of the 1880s and '90s. The NROA's lobbying, Standley charged, would only harm the Navy and cause uncertainty and confusion in the minds of the Naval Affairs Committee. But reservists countered by charging that the "band of brothers" continually refused to consult them on appropriation or policy matters. They demanded an end to Annapolite opposition to the reserve officer aviation program. They demanded an end to the ban on flag rank for reservists. They demanded the "running mate" system of reserve promotion. And by 1938 they had won on all three counts.

The naval reserve officers corps continued to grow during and after World War II. The non-Annapolite is now the backbone of the service, vastly outnumbering his Annapolis counterparts. Annapolis graduates continue to hold disproportionate numbers of key posts in the naval establishment, but this propensity is clearly passing, and the coopted reservists seem virtually as orthodox in their navalism as their Annapolis counterparts.[3]

THE ARMY

The officers of the post-Civil War Army faced problems similar to those of their naval counterparts. While European armies grew throughout the late 19th century, sporting new weapons and reorganized command structures, the Regular Army, to its chagrin, declined steadily. By 1895 the Army numbered but 27,500 officers and men.

As the Indian wars came to an end, Army posts scattered throughout the West settled into a stultifying state of inactivity. "Commanding officers are puzzled to know how to employ their subordinates," 2nd Lieutenant Frank Eastman (U.S.M.A. '79) wrote from one such post in 1890,

> . . . and the people are beginning to wonder what the Regular Army is good for and to believe they can just as well get along without it. . . . It would be well for officers to . . . take the lead in introducing radical changes—called innovation by some—in the organization . . . and uses to be made of the Regular Army. If they don't we may wake up some day from the Rip Van Winkle sleep to find our occupation gone.

Moreover, regular officers commissioned during the Civil War, "the '61 to '64 men," had created a "choke" in the Army's seniority-only promotion system similar to that in the Navy's. "Every officer . . . of five year's service has a right to aspire to the command of a regiment in war," wrote 1st Lieutenant S. M. Foote (U.S.M.A. '84), who had 13 years of service at the time. But aspiring to command was not the same as commanding. One first lieutenant begged his senior comrades-in-arms in 1883 to "make a fight" on behalf of "the youngest officers" to rectify the inequities in "the system of promotion":

> . . . as I figure it . . . unless there should be a war, I could not possibly be promoted to a Captaincy under 15 to 20 years from now . . . in other words, after a period of 30 years, at least, as a Lieutenant.

Promotion reform may have been urged by some senior commanders; the reports of the Secretary of War in the late 1880s contain several recommendations to Congress for new promotion legislation. But it was not the kind of reform that junior army officers sought. As had been the case with the 1882 naval legislation, the army promotion reforms of 1890 had little effect on "the '61 to '64" hump of army officers. Efficiency reports were now due of all officers, but for years these were but perfunctory things, and examination for promotion was ordered only for those junior ranks below field grade (first lieutenant and captain). Since 1882 senior officers had been compelled to retire at age 64 (compared to the Navy's 62), but this had provided but slight relief. Most Civil War veterans had another 10 or 15 years active service left in them in 1890, and few appeared anxious to give it up. The average first lieutenant in 1891 was 45 years old, and the youngest captain of artillery was older than the oldest captain of artillery in the British Army. In 1896 the ranking officers of the Military Service Institute of the U.S. (the counterpart of the U.S. Naval Institute) called once for promotion reform to clear the way for "youthful ambition," and then fell silent. Junior army officers were "not without *aim* or energy or *ambition* in life," as one aspiring officer candidate put it in 1888, but the cards were not exactly stacked in their favor.

In the 1880s many Regular Army officers came to sense a new threat to their service. Shortly after the bloody summer of 1877, when railroad strikers clashed with state and federal troops, a group of leaders of state volunteer units met to form an "organized militia." By 1879 the National Guard Association (N.G.A.) was on its feet, and throughout the 1880s and '90s it secured the revision of the militia codes in every state to facilitate the arming of urban businessmen and their allies against the "communistic" and "anarchistic" strikers of the era. By 1896 nearly $3 million were being appropriated each year by the states for an organized militia of over 100,000 officers and men, a force four times as large as that of the Regular Army.

This was bad enough, but when in 1887 the N.G.A. secured a doubling of annual federal support, a jump from $200,000 to $400,000, and urged its members to maintain "a steady pressure upon Congress and public opinion," the Regular Army became alarmed. Some feared that the Guard, already comprising "the regular army of the states," might in time displace "the regular army [of] the nation" as well. After all, N.G.A. officials consistently argued that the Guard constituted a "a popular West Point," and that is was "the only thing" that could "unite against the army" if the Regulars should ever move to usurp the government. The Regular Army, "separated in interest and aspirations from the great body of the people," was less desirable, according to Representative James Slayden of Texas, than the guardsman "who stays at home and does a citizen's work while he keeps alive his sympathies with his fellow citizens."

Incensed, regulars attacked Congressional support of the Guard. Since it was deemed "unconstitutional," as well as impossible, to oblige guardsmen to fight abroad, 1st Lieutenant S. M. Foote (U.S.M.A. '84) and Arthur Wagner (U.S.M.A. '75), Captains William Carter (U.S.M.A. '73) and A. P. Schenck (U.S.M.A. '67), and many others, insisted that "the Army should be given a Reserve of its own," fully federalized and quite independent of the Guard and the local political "bosses," to fight the expanding nation's future wars of empire. The nation's "commercial intercourse must be enlarged," wrote Captain Arthur Williams (U.S.M.A. '61). America must claim her "rightful share of the trade of the world." The process was fraught with hazards. "We cannot meddle in other people's affairs without getting involved," Williams explained, and were Americans to get involved, as was likely, "we should be prepared to do so successfully. . . . " Captain Lewis Green observed that the United States was "being continually brought into closer contact with other nations," and that she would "ultimately be called into the deliberations of the world." The nation was "not isolated," in any sense of that word. John Schofield (U.S.M.A. '53), maintained that the Army was prepared to govern "any national outposts or other possessions which the interests of the country may require it to hold" in the Pacific or Caribbean. In fact, he was of the opinion in 1897 that "the best and most satisfactory government any island of the West Indies can have in the next hundred years will be a military government under an officer of the U.S. Army." For such a defense of America's overseas empire an Army Reserve was vital, but it would have to be a Reserve "entirely independent of the National Guard." Reversing the traditional civilian fear of the regulars, regulars warned that the National Guard constituted "a system of standing armies for the States." At the same time they were but "a broken reed upon which to lean for our [national] security." The Guard was simply not an efficient instrument for the conduct of national military policy.

If the Guard was to remain, its ranks should be nationalized by rigorous application of Regular Army standards of training, weaponry, and uniforms, and frequent Regular inspections. Joint maneuvers and encampments with the Guard might "in due time bring the orderly and well-disposed part thereof to regard the [regular] army with an increasing interest," to see things the Regular Army way, and to abandon any ambitions to usurp the Regular's status as the national defender. The Regular Army, after all, had often been called in to put down strikers that the Guard had proven unable to handle. Regulars had the advantage of being strangers to the community and its problems. Guardsmen, recruited locally, their officers often elected, "might hesitate," as one local official put it, but "them Reg'lars are the fellers that shoot!" The regulars would be better prepared to deal with strikers if the Army were augmented and a number of Western posts were to be relocated in the vicinity of key industrial centers. Army progressives like Lieutenants Wagner and Guy Huse (U.S.M.A. '79) regularly urged such relocation,[4] and the number of Army posts was steadily reduced, from 120 in 1888, to 77 by 1896, and 40 by 1912. But guardsmen insisted that the states were "fully competent" to handle local "lawlessness" with their own "military establishments." The N.G.A. seemed a thorn in the side of the Regular Army and its eager young Academy graduates.

The same year that the N.G.A. persuaded Congress to double its federal subsidy saw the posthumous publication of Senator (and Volunteer Major General) John A. Logan's *The Volunteer Soldier of America*. Logan, a friend of the National Guard until his death in 1886, was highly critical of the West Point "aristocracy" and full of praise for the state militia system. Unlike his Regular Army counterpart, Colonel Emory Upton (U.S.M.A. '61), Logan placed his faith in a decentralized system of national defense wherein the military academies would be abolished and all officer training would be conducted at state colleges.

Colonel Upton's unpublished manuscript on "The Military Policy of the United States" was passed about in the Regular Army after his death in 1881, and his views were summarized by West Point Professor Peter S. Michie (the counterpart to Annapolis Professor James R. Soley) in an 1885 edition of *The Life and Letters of General Emory Upton*. Upton was scornful of the combat record of militia and volunteers, and urged reliance upon an "expansible" Regular Army, in which a force of national reserves would be trained by regulars for incorporation into the ranks of regular regiments under regular leadership. Increasingly, the Regular Army's "young Turks" became "disciples" of Upton's elitist policies, for here were both critique of, and solution to, the threat of Logan and the Guard.

Simultaneously, a number of nationally prominent elites—cosmopolitan Congressmen, business leaders, editors—were evincing an interest in the future of the national Army, which they saw as a force for national integration. Void of the traditional fear of standing armies, these elite sought an increase in military appropriations, the application of sound management practices, and the introduction of a system of promotion by merit. "Shall we compell the Army to die from slothfulness and want of vigor?" asked Representative George Steele in 1882. But Upton's disciples and their civilian allies notwithstanding, the Guard continued to grow; the Army, to mark time.

In 1890, four years after his graduation from West Point, John J. Pershing was still a long way from 1st lieutenant. "Think of a man of his ability only a second lieutenant!" a civilian friend wrote of Pershing, "Why does he remain in the Army?" Why indeed? Many officers did resign their commission; Pershing seriously considered resigning his. But he remained in the service, and so did most of his comrades-in-arms.

As had been the case with the young Annapolites in the 1880s, most West Point graduates had become so enamored of the national service that they found it impossible to throw in the sponge. So they fought for promotion reform, jockeyed for position with the National Guard, and looked about for ways to make their mark in the Army. Captain E. L. Zalinski studied artillery trajectories and developed the pneumatic dynamite gun. 1st Lieutenants Sidney Stuart (U.S.M.A. '78) and Frank Hobbs (U.S.M.A. '78) joined naval progressives supervising ordnance construction at Midvale and Bethlehem between 1888 and 1892. 1st Lieutenant Enoch Crowder (U.S.M.A. '81) studied law and transferred to the judge advocate general's department at an opportune time in 1891; he was immediately advanced to Captain. 1st Lieutenant Tasker Bliss (U.S.M.A. '75) transferred to the Commissary Department, served at the Naval War College, and then carded and tabulated officer efficiency records in the War Department. 2nd Lieutenant John Pershing tried to transfer to the Quartermaster Corps, where promotions were faster; he was eventually selected for a staff billet and fast promotion several years later. 1st Lieutenant Arthur Wagner urged his Regular colleagues to become masters of the "Science of War," and Wagner, John Bigelow (U.S.M.A. '77), Matthew Hanna (U.S.M.A. '97), and Matthew Steele (U.S.M.A. '83) went on to write a number of first-rate military works. Wagner was instrumental in making the Fort Leavenworth Infantry and Cavalry School into an effective staff college. Major W. R. Livermore (U.S.M.A. '65) and 2nd Lieutenant C. A. L. Totton (U.S.M.A. '73) devised an "American Game of War,"

Strategos. And many others contributed articles on European military developments, weapon technology, and the implications of these innovations for tactics and strategy to the *Journal of the Military Service Institution of the U.S.* (founded in 1880), the *Cavalry Journal* (founded in 1885), the *Journal of the U.S. Artillery Corps* (founded in 1892), or the Infantry Association's Journal (founded in 1904, ten years after the Association itself was organized).

Agencies designed to bring the Army up to date, sponsored by Army "Young Turks" and their older allies, began to materialize. The Military Information Division, created in 1889, grew under the guidance of Captain Daniel Taylor (U.S.M.A. '69), Major William Volkmar (U.S.M.A. '68), and Colonels Arthur Wagner and William Simpson (U.S.M.A. '75). Echoing the Office of Naval Intelligence, in 1893 the Military Information Division began to publish policy papers, including ones on the colonial occupation armies of European powers and the subordination of the National Guard in a scheme of national mobilization. In 1887 a Cavalry and Light Artillery School at Fort Monroe was modernized. By 1903 the Army's postgraduate system had grown further to include a school of theory—the Army War College—and two schools of application—the School of the Line, which grew out of the Fort Leavenworth Infantry and Cavalry School, and the Army Staff College, headed by Brigadier General Wagner and staffed by Colonel Eben Swift (U.S.M.A. '76) and Major John Morrison (U.S.M.A. '81), who introduced map war games. By 1904 a Signal Corps School was operating at Fort Leavenworth, and in 1907 and 1911 infantry and field artillery schools were added at Presidio, California, and Fort Sill, Oklahoma. First Lieutenant Elmer Hubbard (U.S.M.A. '85) and a host of other young West Pointers sought to update their alma mater. A U.S. Military Academy Graduate Association was created in 1897. Advocates of weapons reform insured the standardizing of modern rifles and artillery pieces by 1903. Others argued for Army imitation of the managerial techniques of large business organizations. In language strikingly similar to that used by the Navy's Rear Admiral Henry Clay Taylor only two years before, Lieutenant Colonel William H. Carter suggested that Army leaders were akin to railroad directors: "groups of men whose principal work was to observe rival lines, to consider state and local laws, and to prepare their systems to derive all possible advantage from future growth. . . ."

In order to insure for the proper mobilizing and managing of modern forces, the Army's progressives sought a General Staff, an organization that might, in the words of General Schofield, emulate the "Kaiser-Moltke relationship." The General Staff would serve the same coordinating, supervising, and planning roles as those of the boards of directors of great corporations. War Secretary Elihu Root, fresh from Wall Street director meetings and styled "the personification of capitalistic efficiency" by one student of his administration, was a natural ally of the Army progressives.

Root ran into stiff resistance from some of the bureau chiefs, whose perspective was often that of the 19th-century Indian-fighting Army, but he persevered, and saw the creation in 1903 of a small, but potentially effective, General Staff. The older army traditionalists, men like non-Academy General Nelson A. Miles, tended to sympathize with their Civil War volunteer colleagues in the N.G.A. and disapproved of several of the "progressive" innovations. Arthur Wagner felt compelled to seek relief from "superannuated individuals who have not kept pace with the march of events."

The line-staff struggle between the progressives and more traditional bureau chiefs simmered until 1911. In that year the minority report to the War Department Board on Business Methods, written by Captains Matthew Hanna (U.S.M.A. '97) and James Moss (U.S.M.A. '94), recommended the streamlining of muster rolls, payrolls, and other inventories. Major General Fred C. Ainsworth, the non-Academy champion of the Army's bureau system, took offense, struck out at the "Young Turks" and their supporters, Chief of Staff Leonard Wood and War Secretary Henry Stimson (another veteran of Wall Street board of directors meetings). Within a year Ainsworth had been maneuvered into resigning. The bureaus, long supreme in their bailiwicks, were steadily being forced to yield to the supervision of a breed of systems managers whose ability to coordinate and plan made them appear invaluable to their civilian elite counterparts in the age of organizations. In the process of making their mark and defending their Service, the Army's progressives were becoming truly professional.

They were also becoming deft public relations men and lobbyists. According to Colonel James Fry, one of the reasons for the founding of the Military Service Institution of the U.S. had been "to bring about a unanimity of sentiment" among those officers planning to testify at Congressional appropriations hearings. "The interests of the people in military matters must be aroused," Lieutenant Wagner maintained, "and must become a perpetual spur to the action of the national legislators. . . . " In Wagner's view one of the more effective ways to arouse public interest was "to encourage a martial spirit in [the] younger generation, to disseminate military knowledge among the young men, and to institute systematic tactical training among the people." Wagner, Frank Eastman, and many Regular colleagues urged high schools and colleges to compensate for the "loss of manliness" in unmilitary America by providing for a "steady growth of military virtue" in military courses that would "popularize the Army" among the roughly 5,000 college students receiving such training each year. Eventually, these college-bred Cincinnati would demand "a more liberal spirit in military legislation." As a measure of the Army's commitment to such a policy, no less than 40 young Regulars were stationed on the campuses of American state colleges by 1890.

Some guardsmen tended to sympathize with the regulars. Some foresaw the role that the Army of the 20th century might be called upon to play in defense of the Open Door. Regulars were invited to inspect Guard summer encampments in a dozen states by 1885, a fact that must have resulted in just the sort of sympathetic "interest" in the Army that regulars had hoped for. Brigadier General Albert Ordway of the District of Columbia National Guard went so far as to seek to persuade Congress that the Guard could and would serve as a ready reserve force for the Regular Army.

A number of regulars were pleased and gratified, but others remained distrustful of these potential allies. One, revealing an intense loyalty to both his nation and his service, complained that "the subordinate principality of New York" provided for an armed force larger than all the Regular Army. Major General G. W. Wingate of the New York Guard, the President of the N.G.A. in the 1880s, and one more sympathetic to the regular point of view than most of his associates, was none the less highly critical of Uptonian "military theorists" among the regulars, "who want the French, Prussian, or Austrian system, or more commonly some little system of their own, and who object to any scheme but their own. . . . " The army leadership it appears, had "turned a cold shoulder" on Wingate's plans to have Regulars assigned in peacetime as adjutants and chiefs of staff of National Guard regiments, brigades, and divisions.

But Wingate also noted that the regular distrust of the Guard was reciprocal. Many guardsmen regarded his plan to incorporate regulars into their staffs "with suspicion." Cooperation between the Army and the Guard was seen to be as much a victim of the "local jealousy" of guardsmen as it was the national jealousy of regulars. "Localism" was the very essence of the Guard, whose officers and men lived and worked in the same community where their armory was to be found. Guardsmen were, after all, little more than part-time state militia, and that was what most guardsmen felt they should remain. Thus in the mid-nineties the N.G.A. was captured from the more cosmopolitan Wingate and his colleagues by a group of guardsmen who were more committed to the principle of local control. These localist guard leaders tended to regard their institution less as a pool of reserves for a national army with overseas missions (Wingate's "great training school for any future war") than as a confederation of state-controlled minutemen, pledged to riot-control and the defense of the homeland. Connecticut guardsmen, their adjutant general explained, would "defend the country in Connecticut or any other State in the Union, but have no desire for foreign service." The New York Guard, according to Major General John F. O'Ryan (N.G., N.Y.) existed for "purely defensive purposes," and was unavailable for any "war of conquest." In 1897 localists actually renamed their organization the "Interstate National Guard Association." The Regular-Guard rivalry grew more polarized and more intense.

The rivalry turned into open warfare on the eve of war in March, 1898. Regulars had persuaded John Hull, Chairman of the House Military Affairs Committee, to offer Congress legislation designed to triple the size of the Regular Army (speeding promotion) and to identify each regular regiment with an individual state or Congressional district which would then serve as that regiment's recruiting ground. This would have given the Army the same local roots that had made the Guard so powerful. Interstate N.G.A. leaders properly perceived this to be an effort to vitiate the Guard, and they rallied their Congressional allies and were instrumental in the Hull Bill's defeat. The Guard then secured the guarantee that its units would be called in the impending war and that they would be committed intact, with state designations. The regular desire for state identification with regular regiments (linked battalions) lingered on, of course. Thus one regular told a meeting of the Minnesota N.G.A. in late 1906 of the merits of "localizing" army regiments in order to create "a thoroughly national body, with home and state pride aiding to keep them with the colors," and to "furnish a solid basis for the establishment of a Regular Army reserve." His audience was understandably unreceptive.

Neither military organization was fully prepared to fight the Spanish-American War nor to conduct the ensuing Philippine campaign, but the regulars were more prepared than the decentralized Guard, and they had sufficient vested authority as the nation's official military professionals to enable them to subordinate the Guard throughout the combat period. Consequently, the regulars were most displeased with the *manner* by which Congress tripled the Regular Army between 1899 and 1902.

In 1878 West Pointers had secured from Congress a slight advantage over their non-Academy counterparts in the Regular Army when West Point graduates were assured priority in the commissioning process. Over the next 20 years this had resulted in a considerable increase in the percentage of West Pointers (the most cosmopolitan of all the regulars) in the lower and middle ranks of the service, until by 1898 over 80 per cent of the junior officers were Point graduates. The army increases were for the next several years too much for the Point to handle, and, as had been the case with the Navy, the Army was forced to turn elsewhere for officer material. Over 1,000 new officer billets were created between 1899 and 1902, and many of these billets went to graduates of military colleges, graduates of state colleges with military training programs, and to interested volunteer and National Guard officers, many of whom had seen service in the Philippines. West Pointers came disproportionately from cosmopolitan, urban, Eastern backgrounds. Over 95 per cent of candidates representing the District of Columbia, New Jersey, New York, Massachusetts, Connecticut, and Rhode Island were able to pass Academy entrance examinations in the late 19th century, while less than 30 per cent of those from Idaho, Colorado, Nevada, and West Virginia were admitted in the same period. Moreover, the Point, like Annapolis, tended to shear away local identities and to inculcate broad, national values and interests. But only 22 per cent of the 1899–1902 breed of lieutenants were West Pointers. Known to young Point graduates as "the crime of '99," this influx of unannointed civilians (many from the enemy's own Guard encampments) was most unsettling.

Then in 1903 the same Congress that had created the General Staff also recognized the National Guard as first-line defenders of the nation. In spite of their local identifications and loyalties, the leaders of the Interstate N.G.A. had been drifting toward such a national role for several years. Guardsmen had always vaguely *assumed* that they were the nation's first-line defense in wartime. Only the more cosmopolitan guardsmen had been willing to see the organized militia used as a manpower pool to flesh out Regular-controlled volunteer units. But this appeared to be what the future had in store for the Interstate N.G.A., unless the Association could firmly establish itself as the nation's first-line reserve force for international warfare. Guardsmen had heard the arguments of regulars for a new model army to meet the challenges of world leadership and world order in the 20th century—challenges such as those summarized by Major Edwin Glenn (U.S.M.A. '77):

> The holding of colonies at great distances from home, the immense development of trade relations in all foreign countries, and particularly in the Orient and tropical countries, the development and settlement of labor questions both at home and abroad, and the opening up and controlling of important international highways.

Guardsmen had participated in overseas campaigns in Puerto Rico and the Philippines. They knew that hostile regulars felt that the Guard was "never intended as a military power of a great nation, to give weight to its international policies and interests in its relations with foreign states." They sensed that the national leadership was thinking less of the policing of internal disorders and more of the preparation for external order.

As the commitment of guardsmen to their role as a first-line national force grew, their commitment to internal police duties declined. They insisted to labor leaders that the Guard was without prejudice or class loyalty. They aided in the creation of separate state police forces to relieve them of many of their police duties. They sought entry into Regular Army professional postgraduate schools. They fought the Army's policy of awarding medals for overseas duty only to regulars. They began to espouse the cosmopolitan view that international trade was as vital to America as "the circulation of blood is to the individual." And they sought to make the Guard "one hundred per cent efficient" to defend "our trans-oceanic possessions" as well as "our enormous coast line." In short, the Guard had come to accept the Regular argument for a national reserve force, locally based. But unlike the regulars, the Interstate N.G.A. believed that the Guard should do the job—that an effective reserve force could "only come through the increase of voluntary organizations having already a local habitation and a name to build on." A separate Army Reserve system would be wasteful duplication.

In 1908 Congressional friends of the Guard acted to remove a formidable barrier to the Guard's case by authorizing the mobilization of Guardsmen for overseas campaigns. This action, of dubious constitutionality, was designed to undermine the Uptonian argument that such militia as the Guard would be unavailable for the wars of the American century, wars for which a Regularly-managed Reserve force would be required. By 1909 the Guard was receiving from the national treasury some $4 million annually, 10 times the sum granted in 1887. Minimum standards were imposed on the Guard; the Division of Militia Affairs, established in the 1890s, was expanded; Regulars were provided as inspectors and instructors. But to some West Pointers it may not have seemed clear as to whether the Regulars were supervising the Guard, or whether the Guard was in fact infiltrating and enveloping the Regular Army.

It is at this point that the Army's progressives began to speak openly of the need for conscription, to praise the Swiss system of universal military training. The Swiss were surrounded by no less than four major powers, all of whom had conscription programs, while 3,000 miles of bounding main and the "new Navy" offered Americans real security and rendered somewhat superfluous such a departure from the tradition of Logan's state-controlled "volunteer soldiers." But the Regulars persevered, for conscription would mean an Army-controlled Reserve that would undermine the need for a National Guard, and the Guard *had* to be dislodged from its role as the first-line reserve, which (Regulars believed) it was neither large enough nor national enough to fulfill.

Recalling the arguments of the 1880s, the regular establishment insisted that the 1908 Guard legislation was unconstitutional—that state militia troops could not be ordered by the federal government to serve overseas. In 1912 the U.S. Attorney General obligingly agreed. The Guard was off-guard.

Army Chief of Staff Leonard Wood (non-Academy, but a staunch Regular) then proceeded to launch a vigorous "preparedness" campaign, stressing the need of some form of conscription. General Wood spoke of the hidden values to America of a vast Army Reserve system, and offered arguments with much appeal to many policymakers and industrial planners. Conscription would return to civil life "a more valuable industrial factor [sic] because of his better physique, his improved mental and physical discipline and [his] greater respect for the flag, law and order, and his superiors," all with "the minimum of time taken from his industrial career." Conscription would unite the country by transcending class, section, and ethnic difference. It would reduce crime. It would provide for "the moral organization of the people: an organization which creates in the heart of every citizen a sense of his obligation for service to the nation in time of war or other difficulty."

Full mobilization of the nation's manpower would also require an organizing of "the industrial resources of the country" to insure proper logistical support for a war machine capable of throwing a million men overseas. In 1915 a number of Army Ordnance Corps officers were given indefinite leave to assume supervisory positions in munitions plants.

The Mexican Revolution gave regulars an opportunity to accelerate the process of modernization. The effort to mobilize 20,000 troops on the Mexican border took too long to satisfy Army progressives. The Army had been closing outdated Western posts and consolidating its forces for many years, but always in the teeth of porkbarrel politicos whose false-front hamlets thrived on the Army's trade. Throughout 1912 the concentration of forces proceeded at a somewhat more rapid pace, and when a second mobilization was ordered in early 1913, the Army was ready.

"Progressive" civilian leaders were impressed. While Guardsmen were objecting to service on the Mexican border during the Mexican Revolution, Pershing and the Regulars were in hot pursuit of Pancho Villa. Guardsmen returned home more sympathetic to the notion of conscription; in addition to the personal inconvenience they had experienced, they had, in many cases, suffered financial loss. The call-up had made a shambles of some firms as clerks and executives alike were shuttled off to Texas. The New York Mayor's Committee on National Defense noted that businessmen preferred "a system to which business could fairly adjust itself." A draft would reach all elements of the population; and it could be raised selectively, so as to permit "vital" sectors of the economy to continue to function. Grenville Clark, a Wall Street lawyer who had "thought the matter out," advised Senator John Weeks of Massachusetts that "the thinking part of the community" was ready for conscription.

Regulars scored other gains. Friends of the Army formed the Army League (counterpart to the Navy League) in 1912, and launched a sustained effort on behalf of conscription and a comprehensive reserve system. In 1913 students from some 50 colleges voluntarily attended five-week summer camps at Gettysburg, Pennsylvania, and Monterey, California, where they received "a true knowledge of what our military policy . . . should be. . . . " These camps were later reproduced at Plattsburg, New York, at the behest of the very upper class "Committee of 100" (headed by Grenville Clark), and were the models for the camps that trained officers in 1917 and 1918. In late 1914 a group that the *New York Times* styled "sober-minded . . . merchants, financiers, professional men of all shades of political opinion," organized the National Security League. Joined by the National Civic Federation and the vast majority of college presidents, they urged military training programs under Regular control. By 1916 the Progressive Party's National Committee was espousing conscription, and was attacking the "state-dominated militia with its menace of shiftless incompetence, spoils politics, and organized snobbery. . . . " And in early 1917 a coalition of Regulars, Army Leaguers, Plattsburgers, National Security Leaguers, and Progressives created the National Committee of Patriotic Societies, with a central bureau in Washington and a card index of community leaders throughout the country who favored conscription. The cosmopolitans were in high gear.

The N.G.A. fought back, to be sure. It fought Regular efforts in 1913 to discontinue Guard staff positions. It fought Regular efforts to provide for further nationalizing of the Guard. It fought Regular efforts to establish a reserve bureau in the War Department. It dropped the "interstate" label from its name. And, of course, it fought both the reserve system (the "Continental Army" scheme) and all talk of peacetime conscription.

The issues were most clearly joined at the 1913 convention of the Interstate N.G.A. where Brigadier General Albert Mills (U.S.M.A. '79), head of the Army's Division of Militia Affairs, defended the Regular plans to standardize Guard units and discontinue many Guard adjutant generalcies. Mills politely advised the guardsmen that they looked at things "too much from a State point of view and too little from the Federal point. Local and State pride is a large factor in securing efficiency," he admitted, "but beyond this there is a national vista. . . . " A minority of guardsmen representing populous industrial Eastern and mid-Western states, agreed. "New York stands ready," Guard General H. D. Hamilton of New York announced,

> . . . to listen to the War Department and to the [professional Regular] officers.
> . . . We may have our [local] notions, but when the War Department speaks
> we listen. . . . We take no narrow-minded view in New York [nor any] eastern
> or coastwise view. I look at this thing as I wish the militia all over the country
> [would].

But the majority of Guardsmen agreed with Adjutant General John Chase of the Colorado Guard, who noted that the interests and needs of New York, as a commercial, cosmopolitan center, differed from those of less advanced communities. New York was concerned with national and international issues, but it was "difficult in Colorado." There Guardsmen were still performing police duties: "I judge we have 15,000 strikers and some of them are pretty good shots . . . —and I tell you that I will need every man I have got. . . . "

On the one hand, guardsmen resisted what they deemed "the federalization of the Organized Militia." But on the other hand, they insisted that Congress provide drill pay for the Guard, since the federal government "gets the most benefit" from the Guard's newly-adopted first-line "war availability." Regulars had long considered the strings that could be attached to "National aid" to the Guard as the best means of binding the Guard to "National as well as State defense." The Guard and its allies won battles on many fronts, but in the end they were forced to yield to additional nationalizing in exchange for Congressional authorization for drill pay.

The Guard-Army rivalry continued throughout the war and postwar years. Guardsmen engaged in secret maneuvers to beat army and marine regulars to France in the summer of 1917. Guard-Regular friction was constant in the AEF. Regulars discharged all Guard personnel at major depots in 1919, ignoring their Guard obligations and causing many of them to trickle back to their states individually. This disrupted Guard administration and made it difficult for guardsmen to conduct loyal victory parades or other group ceremonies in their communities. Many Guard officers were coopted into the Army's Reserve Officer Corps by offers of promotion in exchange for quitting the Guard. General Peyton C. March (U.S.M.A. '88), Chief of Staff from 1918 to 1921, and members of the newly organized Universal Military Training League urged Congress to continue the draft in peacetime.[5] Colonels P. S. Bond (U.S.M.A. '00) and C. F. Martin (U.S.M.A. '00) drove the conscription argument home in a 1920 publication entitled *Your Boy and the Other in Universal Training*, where they maintained that it was "the destiny of America to be the greatest, the wealthiest, and most powerful nation the world has ever seen," and insisted that it was "vitally necessary that the rising generation" be given military training, first in youth camps, and then in Army Reserve programs, in order to insure that "proper habits of thought and action be inculcated in our young men." Conscription "alone" would "meet the urgent needs." It would be "the most powerful instrument in history for the development on a gigantic scale of a race of . . . supermen" who alone could create and maintain America's "greater civilization."

March and his allies were countered by Colonel Bennett Clark of the Missouri Guard, President of the N.G.A., who vowed before the 1919 N.G.A. convention to "smash the Regular Army." They were also countered by one of their own, Lieutenant Colonel John McAuley Palmer (U.S.M.A. '92), of General Pershing's staff.

Palmer's grandfather had been a "volunteer soldier" in the Civil War and, as a member of the Senate Military Affairs Committee in the 1890s, old General Palmer had explained to his grandson the unpopularity of Upton's giant Army Reserve scheme. The proposal Colonel Palmer recommended to Congress in 1920 involved conscription, but it retained a prominent role for the National Guard. Guard training centers would be established with federal funds and with War Department cooperation. Assurances were given that the Militia Bureau at the War Department would in the future be headed by Guardsmen. The Guard had proven its effectiveness in the war, and the Congress was unwilling to maintain peacetime conscription. Pershing, with several years of teaching experience at the University of Nebraska, was no Uptonian. Volunteers and Guardsmen would suffice—so long as they were trained and controlled by Regulars. Cooption of the Guard was all that the Regulars like Pershing, Palmer, and Colonel George Marshall felt they could hope for in 1920. And they were right. As one Guardsman advised Congress in 1919, conscription was favored only by the Regular, "the employer, and the man who appears prominently before the public"—in effect, by cosmopolitan elites. "The majority," composed of "workers and farmers," were opposed to conscription, making UMT politically unfeasible in 1920. Palmer's plan, more palatable to Americans, was chosen over March's.

But the Army-Guard rapprochement was brief. The appropriation fights of the 1920s and '30s resulted in the renewal of hostilities. Congressional retrenchment resulted in Regular retrenchment and further professionalization. Guard training camps were disbanded as funds began to cut into new Regular programs, such as the Army Industrial College (1924) and a variety of Infantry, Quartermaster, Ordnance, and Engineering Corps activities.

Like the naval reservists, Guardsmen fought to insure their survival. In 1933 they secured legislation stipulating that the Guard was to be an official Reserve for the U.S. Army and that Guard units would be committed to action intact, under Guard command. In 1940 they fought conscription again, this time in the form of the Selective Service System. Guard Major General Milton A. Reckord warned a 1940 N.G.A. convention in Washington, D.C. that "you have got to keep men here who see this thing as we see it and who will carry the fight, if necessary, to Congress to see that the necessary legislation is provided to protect the National Guard as an institution." They insured themselves a piece of the aviation action with the creation of the Air National Guard. They were unable to prevent the passage of peacetime conscription in the Selective Service Act of 1948, but they managed to insure their own role in its execution. They fought Brigadier General Palmer's efforts to reduce the Guard to a minor home defense role in World War II, though they continued to serve a local function, offering disaster relief and riot-control.

In the process of vying for power with a larger, more professional Army, the Guard has lost a good deal of its 19th-century independence. The price of Guard survival has been the progressive silencing of its defense-of-the-homeland localism and its growing acceptance of the Regular's vision of military reality. The Guard, with its Washington headquarters facing the Capitol, is truly National today. But it is the modern, professional Regular Army and its Reserve that constitute the primary military authority of the nation, and in that sense the Regular Army's "progressives" have carried the day.

FINAL OBSERVATIONS

Perceiving threats to their services and their careers in the *fin de siècle*, Annapolites and West Pointers fought successful campaigns against those who continued to define military policy in local, home-defense terms. Envisioning vast, well-trained conscript armies and mighty, efficient fleets, they offered military policies attractive to the statesmen planning America's international role in the 20th century. In the process of reorganizing the military, both services streamlined their recruitment, training, promotion, procurement, and administrative faculties, produced aggressive, anti-radical intelligence services, and steadily developed closer and closer relations with American business and industry.[6]

The roots of naval progressivism and modern navalism may be traced to the career anxieties of junior officers in the 1880s. The process was intraservice; naval militia units played no role. Naval reservists fell out with the Annapolites briefly in the 1920s and '30s, but eventually they were effectively integrated into the Navy of the *Pax Americana*.

Army progressives faced many of the same intraservice problems as their naval compeers (though "generation gap" was less significant in the Army), but they faced an external problem as well. Local militia infantry units, sorely needed to deal with the unrest of the *fin de siècle*, emerged in the National Guard as a viable competitor to the Regular Army, whose traditional Indian-fighting role was dwindling rapidly. But as America's interest in international trade and investment intensified, first the Regulars, and then the Guard moved to adopt the philosophy of national organization for international warfare. And thereafter the two military organizations simply struggled for appropriations, power, survival. Guardsmen espoused federalism, but practiced nationalism. Regulars criticized locally based military organizations, and then created a locally based reserve of their own and called for "little groups of neighbors" to administer conscription. Consistency was for those who could afford it.

Quite naturally, neither the Army nor the Guard, nor for that matter the Navy, acted without first giving considerable attention to their own institutional interests, which goes a long way toward explaining the fact that none of these services has ever recommended a significant decrease in their own appropriations or missions. The military of the American Century has come a long way—both ideologically and financially—from the home-defense concepts of the 19th century, and there is no evidence that it has any desire to return—or that it could find its way back if it wanted to.

NOTES

1. For more on anti-navalist "locals" see Thomas Coode, "Southern Congressmen and the American Naval Revolution, 1880–1898," *Alabama Historical Review* (1968), 89–110; John M. Cooper, "Progressivism and American Foreign Policy," *Mid-America* LI (1969), 265; *Literary Digest* (23 Jan. 1915), 137. Coode notes (109) that the personal papers of anti-navalist Congressmen are filled with correspondence from constituents concerning entirely local matters, while my own examination of the correspondence of Congressmen favorable to the Navy revealed a substantial constituent interest in international and naval affairs. See also Walter LaFeber, *The New Empire* (Ithaca, 1963), 235.

2. Armin Rappaport feels that the munitions men and shipping magnates associated with the Navy League "might have been motivated by economic interest," but that it is "just as likely" that their motive was "patriotism" (p. 22). He quotes approvingly Navy League denials that the steel, nickel, shipping, and munitions interests of such League founders as J. P. Morgan, H. L. Satterlee, Henry Clay Frick, J. H. Schiff, C. H. Dodge, J. P. Grace, H. C. DuPont, John Jacob Astor, R. W. Thompson, H. P. Whitney, and Charles Schwab were of any significance (p. 54). Perhaps men whose profession it is to make ships or weapons can *persuade* themselves that what is good for industry is good for the country. Consider, for example, the remarks of Clement Griscom, president of a forerunner of the Navy League, the Society of Naval Architects and Marine Engineers: "A technical society of this kind has no *raison d'etre* if there are no ships to build; and if its labors . . . result in reawakening general interest in the development of our great marine resources, there will be little doubt that the inception and growth of [this] society . . . is a national blessing (Prolonged applause)." *Transactions of the Society of N. A. and M. E.,* I (1893), xxii. See also *Transactions,* III (1895), xxvi-xxvii.

3. See Peter Karsten, "Two Breeds or One? A Note on ROTC- and Academy-Trained Officers," *IUS Newsletter,* September 1979, pp. 4–7. However, there are indications that non-Annapolis *junior* officers, from NROTC and OCS programs, are less absolutistic, less authoritarian, and less belligerent than their Academy counterparts. See E. Berger, L. Flatley, J. Frisch, M. Gottleib, J. Haisley, P. Karsten, L. Pexton, and W. Worrest, "ROTC, Mylai, and the Volunteer Army," *Foreign Policy,* I (Feb. 1971).

4. Similarly, marine officers hoped that their participation in riot control and strike-breaking would be recalled when appropriation-time came. See Captain Louis Fagan, U. S. M. C., to Captain H. C. Cochrane, Sept. 11, 1877, Cochrane Papers, M. C. Museum, Quantico.

5. The Universal Military Training League's founders included 6 manufacturers, 5 investment bankers, 5 prominent religious figures (including Russell Conwell), 4 newspaper publishers, 4 presidents of communication and transportation companies, 3 educators, 2 prominent merchants, 2 bonanza farmers, 1 engineer, 1 rancher, 1 Knights of Columbus official, the Rotary Secretary, the President of the U.S. Chamber of Commerce, the Vice-president of the American Federation of Labor, and the ubiquitous Henry Stimson. Mauritz Hallgren, *The Tragic Fallacy* (N.Y., 1937), 11n–12n.

6. In World War I, the Army developed close liaison, in the persons of Brigadier General Hugh Johnson (U. S. M. A. '03) and Brigadier General Frank R. McCoy (U. S. M. A. '97), with the civilian War Industries Board. The post of Assistant War Secretary for Economic Mobilization was created in 1920, and four years later the Army Industrial College began to train future managers of war. See Paul Koistinen, "The Industrial-Military Complex in Historical Perspective: World War I," *Business History Review,* XLI (1967), 378–403; and "The Industrial Military Complex in Historical Perspective: The Interwar Years," *Journal of American History,* LVI (1970), 819–39. Navy-industrial liaison developed along similar lines some 30 years earlier. See Karsten, *Naval Aristocracy,* end of Chapter 4.

25

The Spanish–American War and the Small-Town Community

GERALD LINDERMAN

The contrast between the more localistic National Guard and the cosmopolitan and professional Regular Army, noted in the previous reading, is evident also in these passages from "The War and the Small-Town Community," a chapter in Gerald Linderman's study of the Spanish–American War, The Mirror of War. *Ask yourself whether the comradeship of the Galesburg or Clyde Guardsmen may not have made up for what they lacked in discipline and training.*

WILLIAM MCKINLEY knew that the regular Army, a lean professional force of fewer than thirty thousand men, was inadequate to defeat an enemy that deployed six times its numbers in Cuba alone. He recognized too that whatever the Army's capacities, the popular clamor for participation would compel a broad expansion of American land forces; the war would be a people's war in its execution as in its origins. In a situation offering little room for maneuver, the president attempted to compromise political and military requirements. By inviting the mobilization of the citizen-soldiers of the National Guard he moved to accommodate popular pressure while upholding the necessity for some minimal military proficiency among thousands of insistent volunteers.

Regular Army units, themselves doubled in size and barely able to maintain cohesion, won the battles, but the hometown National Guard

SOURCE: Gerald Linderman, *The Mirror of War: American Society and the Spanish-American War* (Ann Arbor: University of Michigan Press, 1974), ch. 3.
EDITOR'S NOTE: Most of the citations to the sources consulted by the author in this essay have been omitted from this volume for brevity and economy. The reader should consult the original source of the essay for the complete scholarly documentation.

company became the prism through which many Americans viewed and interpreted the Spanish–American War. In peace the company played an important role in the life of its town. In war soldiers and townsmen alike saw the company, wherever located, as an extension of their community. This perception supported greater social informality and wider spheres of individual action than professional soldiers thought consistent with the demands of a national military effort. Throughout the war the Army attempted to stamp volunteers with a greater respect for hierarchy and discipline. This effort, impeded by the regular Army's own structural weakness and political vulnerability, was vigorously opposed by guardsmen who unhesitatingly invoked hometown ties to resist the imposition of bureaucratic order. . . .

Whatever their military capabilities in 1898, the National Guards offered to a harried president existing organizations staffed with men who thought themselves soldiers. Their expansion and deployment would channel volunteer fervor, leave regular Army units to cope with no more than a two-fold expansion, and assuage powerful state political organizations gratified to see militias recognized and strengthened, though no less determined to control their use. In the end there was no choice but to call on the guardsmen.

The method of their mobilization caused some hesitation. The president himself had doubts about the constitutionality of ordering Guard units beyond America's borders, so the War Department devised an artifice to bring state units intact into the national Army. Governors would mobilize their Guards *en bloc*. At assembly camps throughout the country regular officers would then call on each guardsman individually to enlist for the duration of the war. Once pledged to federal service, the guardsman would immediately rejoin his fellows in reelecting his former officers, thus reconstituting the old state unit within the national Army.

The Spanish-American War "was as hard to get into as later world wars were hard to keep out of." It was, a postbellum Army War College study would conclude, "the most popular foreign war in which the United States has ever been engaged. . . . " Thousands of young men were, like the light-hearted Tennessean and later secretary of state, Cordell Hull, "wildly eager to leave at once." The regular Army might reject 77,000 of 102,000 applicants—75 percent—and the volunteer forces refuse 25 percent in pre-muster physicals and an equal proportion after induction, but the commanding general would still complain that the Army had admitted 100,000 more than were needed or could be equipped. This popular enthusiasm had forced McKinley to a war from which he shrank; it continued to distract the administration insofar as military units had to be chosen from and within the various states with the same delicacy that the most succulent political plums were apportioned. As Governor John R. Tanner of Illinois set out the problem: "If no one wanted to go, and the government had to draught, any one Congressional district would object to allowing more than its proportionate share. On the other hand, where everybody wants to go . . . the equities suggest that each . . . district have its proportionate share in the glory."[1] Perplexing as were these problems, volunteer enthusiasm did spare Washington at least one of Abraham Lincoln's difficulties. It enabled the government to exact terms of enlistment more stringent than those of 1861. There would be no three-month or hundred-day men among the 233,000 guardsmen who moved by this circuitous route into the national army.

Though regular Army units were to be decisive in the land victories of the Cuban campaign, the small-town National Guard company was in the view of many Americans the essential and preeminent unit of the Spanish–American War. Americans thought it appropriate, indeed necessary, that a foreign war should be fought by the hometown military unit acting as an extension of their community.

If it is true, as the Kansas editor William Allen White wrote, that "Johnny of the American Army, the Johnny who responded to the President's call for troops is a country boy—a boy of the country town,"[2] it is also true that in 1898 the place held by the small town in the consciousness and daily life of its citizens was diminishing. American small towns were losing their self-sufficient and self-contained qualities. The older sense of belonging in totality within the local community was rapidly slipping away as 1900 approached. The railroads, regional and national advertising, standardized products and the mail order houses had already established in men's minds many points of reference and identification beyond the town limits. Large-scale movements toward corporate concentration which small towns were powerless to influence—but also their own desires for superior services and more and cheaper goods—prodded townspeople into a larger world and made them increasingly dependent on decisions made there.

Though weakening, the power of locale remained in 1898 a measurable force in American life. Most Americans continued to believe that there were important distinctions between the values, virtues, and styles of life prevailing in their own and other corners of the United States. Locale still served them as a primary focus of emotional attachment and allegiance. An Ohioan serving in the Fifth Mississippi Volunteer Infantry in 1898 wrote the father of a dead soldier, "I know it is some comfort to you to know that an Ohio boy was with your son when he died. After he learned I was from Ohio he called me 'brother'." Brigadier General William C. Oates, a former Confederate soldier, spent much of his time and all of his influence in 1898–99 attempting to obtain Alabama staff officers and Alabama regiments for his command. He wanted Alabamans for what he deemed their unique qualities, and he was angry when Alger ignored all of his petitions.

To the more cosmopolitan, this identification with locale was a residual provincialism, an American failing. They rejoiced at evidence of new national standards and congruencies. Augustus Peabody Gardner, the son-in-law of Senator Henry Cabot Lodge of Massachusetts, was pleased and proud "to see [in the Army] thousands on thousands of lads with clean-cut faces and clean habits all looking exactly alike whether from North, South, East or West." . . . Both defender and detractor testified that localism retained some force.

The National Guard company was a local institution with a prominent niche in the social and political life of its community. For the old, the hometown unit was a source of pride and security and commemoration; for the young, it signified excitement and adventure and social aspiration.[3] Carl Sandburg, twenty years old in 1898 and a member of Company C, Sixth Illinois National Guard Regiment, called his unit a "living part" of the town of Galesburg. His company, like others throughout the country, paraded on holidays, mustered for important vistors, sponsored an "annual ball and reception," and conducted in its own armory a weekly drill that had all the marks of a public entertainment. With companies from surrounding towns it traveled to a summer encampment. There each guardsman might fire five or ten cartridges in target practice, provided that the legislature had not eliminated the ammunition appropriation as a matter of economy and that the men had not eliminated weapons firing as a matter of preference. There were few hours given to serious training, almost none to long marches. Civilian caterers provided the food; regimental armorers looked after the rifles. The same hometown relations and friends who gathered for drill nights often came along to summer camp, sometimes in chartered excursion trains. The five-day schedule of these "regimental maneuvers" ordinarily included a little close-order drill, a sham fight, and the governor's review. Summer camp was truly a "jolly lark."

The only company activity that moved beyond the ceremonial, social, or political was the riot duty to which a state administration would occasionally summon a hometown unit. The governor of Illinois called out Galesburg's Company C against striking laborers in East St. Louis in 1886 and against striking miners in Pekin and Spring Valley in 1894. Sherwood Anderson's hometown unit—Company I, Sixteenth Ohio National Guard Regiment, of Clyde, Ohio—moved into Tiffin on riot patrol in November 1895 and later helped to control disorders in Cincinnati and a strike near Wheeling. Though obviously less than a "jolly lark," such duty was seldom onerous. The appearance of Guard units was usually sufficient to restore order. Violent confrontations were rare.

With so little necessity for rigorous military performance, the company mirrored with minimal distortion the social patterns of its community. Although upholding in principle democratic and cooperative ideals, the town seldom realized them in its social setting. There existed instead an influential scale of deference, though one whose increments were so subtle that the modern eye would perhaps miss them and whose gradations remained inseparable even to that exemplar of small-town life, William Allen White.

Based on shifting combinations of wealth, occupation, education, and term of residence, it operated principally to diminish the expectations of those at the bottom: neither Carl Sandburg nor Sherwood Anderson thought himself entitled to earn as much money as the town's banker or to become the captain of the town's company. Though this system did impart to townspeople an almost intuitive sense of social superiors and inferiors, few seem to have thought it oppressive. It seldom jeopardized the town's ambience of intimacy. (Wrote Carl Sandburg of his company, "I knew most of the privates. [I] had worked for Corporal Cully Rose at the Auditorium and had gone to school with the Q[uincy railroad] boiler-maker, Con Byloff, who was first lieutenant.") It was, moreover, deemed "the town's way," and thus a mark of the community's independence from external control. Most important, individuals generally found the resultant social patterns sufficiently limber to permit a latitude of action they thought satisfactory.

Thus, all anticipated that those respectables who had lobbied legislative authority at the state capital and had done the preliminary work of organizing the town's military unit would be those whom the enlisted men would select as their officers in the required company elections—a fair return, it was understood, for the positions they occupied and the uses to which they had put the attached status. Retention of command, however, by a major or captain who had assumed his rank by virtue of a station accorded deference depended on the maintenance of social relationships consonant with the fluidity of community patterns, often as interpreted by the company's privates. They *spoke* of the shoulderstrap not as the emblem of their deference but as the sign of a neighbor's greater interest in military affairs or his willingness to work a bit harder or even his endowment with a certain leadership ability. They remained suspicious that the wearer, if unwatched, would develop dangerous tastes for the prerogatives of office. They required that he give frequent signs that he thought himself not much better than those he ranked. They expected that officers and men would address one another by first name.

Action the men considered unduly arbitrary might produce a move for new elections or a flurry of resignations. With the strength of the local company a mark of the town's standing in competition with its neighbors, such disaffection could be a serious matter. Town officials thus tended to support the men's assumption that authority inhered principally not in community status nor in the rank of officer but, democratically, in commonly recognized qualities of the incumbent. With the men retaining the right to reconsider their choice of officers on social grounds and with the community sometimes standing in their support, the officer's sphere of command was a narrow one. The call to war did not alter these essential relationships within National Guard companies.

The pattern of interaction between regular and volunteer soldiers during the Spanish–American War was one of muted conflict; the regulars attempted to impose hierarchical controls on hometown units; the volunteers, determined to uphold the informal relationships of the Galesburgs and Clydes, resisted. In the end, organizational weakness within the regular Army, the brevity of the war, and the multiplicity and resilience of the National Guard company's links with home enabled the volunteers to forestall major change.

Professional soldiers equated discipline and technical proficiency in a way alien to volunteer thought. Guardsmen were confident of their ability to do everything that a war would require of them, and they saw no necessary connection between what they did and how they did it. Regular Army leaders, insisting that control and performance were inseparable, recognized from the first that the chain of command would lack the power to constrain volunteers until informal social relationships between officers and men were suppressed. It was apparent with the first attempts, however, that the Army leadership would be unable to force observance of military manual relationships. In part, the Army's own structural weaknesses were responsible. . . .

[T]he regular Army was able to enforce few standards of organization, procedure, or performance. It could decree but it could not enforce in the new national Army the discipline of the constabulary. Moreover, unlike the Civil War, the Spanish–American War did not go badly enough or last long enough to compel organizational unity and discipline as matters of military necessity.

Even without problems of its own, the regular Army would have found it difficult to assimilate National Guard units because of the diversity and vitality of the latters' links with their communities. Each Galesburg, each Clyde assumed that the hometown company was *its* military unit, an extension first of itself rather than the nation. The community thereby accepted the largest measure of responsibility for the unit's welfare, and that meant hard work to establish and maintain ties to its soldiers.

Communication was the foremost problem. How were people at home to remain in contact with a company that had marched away? The difficulty of obtaining information increased of course with the distance between town and unit, but the community was seldom without detailed news of the condition of its soldiers. While the company remained in an assembly camp within the United States, streams of curious and voluble visitors shuttled back and forth on excursion trains. Sick soldiers convalesced at home and could be counted on for the latest news. More reliable than either of these links, however, was the correspondent.

Large-city newspapers assigned a correspondent to accompany each of the state's regiments wherever it might go. In a common pattern the Chicago *Daily News* had reporters with each of Illinois' three regiments, and their dispatches were distributed to small-town newspapers within the regiment's home territory. Smaller papers strained their resources to send a regular correspondent with the local company, a practice that delighted the townspeople but disgusted professional war correspondents. Richard

Harding Davis publicly prophesied the demise of quality reportage as the result of the small-town amateur's invasion of his fraternity.

When there was insufficient money to send a reporter, the local newspaper ordinarily commissioned a soldier to send back regular letters for its columns. Though Carl Sandburg apparently aspired to the job, Private George Martin, a miner's son and the former captain for the Knox College football team, served as the correspondent of the Galesburg *Evening Mail.* In five months he sent home for publication more than thirty letters filled with innumerable details of daily routine; of the poor food served and promised rations undelivered; of activities in and out of camp; of sickness and morale. Such reports were personal and candid. Galesburg read in another of its newspapers, the *Republican-Register,* the letters of the company commander reporting the progressive deterioration into insanity of a Company C private identified by name. That was a collective concern just as much as the accounts of adventure and mischief or the daily denunciations of those held responsible for the troops' misfortunes.

Such dispatches continued to appear regularly in most newspapers after the secretary of war formally prohibited military personnel from writing for publication. Many units simply ignored Alger's order. Where it did receive notice, it was circumvented. Correspondents addressed their letters to hometown friends who in turn offered them to the newspapers as of "possible interest" to the community. Privates, noncommissioned officers, chaplains, occasionally lieutenants and captains—and, according to the journalist Ray Stannard Baker, naval officers acting as correspondents aboard war vessels—constituted an informal communications network more extensive than has been appreciated.

Regular sources of information, often revealing the troops' immediate needs, guided those at home who were committed to the support of the company. The first steps of organization actually preceded the boys' departure: the farewell reception, the speeches, the parade to the railroad station, the presentation of company colors. The town ladies soon discovered that some of the soldiers had left needy families behind and that the trains that carried away their sons would soon pass through again with other hungry and thirsty boys. These concerns required new organizations. A Women's Auxiliary War League, a Citizens' War Committee, or an Army–Navy League appeared in every town. As news reached them from their companies, these groups expanded their activities. Many established commissary operations. They made or bought articles company members said were needed. A popular, though probably unsolicited, effort at the beginning of the war was the knitting of red or white bellybands, abdominal protectors of stitched flannel believed to ward off tropical fevers. The boys threw them away; the food, pieces of clothing, pocket cases of pins, needles, buttons, and thread they kept.

The arrival of news was often the prelude to other varieties of community action, for on very few counts did the community conceive its role as a passive one. The town dispatched special delegations to check reports of soldier sickness or suffering. It occasionally sent local doctors and even hospital trains to camps in the southeastern United States. Hometown leaders were equally dedicated to another kind of guardianship: they watched for news of promotions and were quick to bombard their congressmen with indignant delegations and complaining letters if an officer vacancy was filled by someone from another company or regiment.

Clearly, hometown companies affected the way small-town citizens thought about the war. Though the quantum leaps in communications were still in the future and all Americans except those on the eastern shoreline must have realized that there was virtually no chance that they would experience war directly, people had less difficulty than one might imagine in engendering a feeling of the immediacy of war. The existence of Company C testified that it was Galesburg, Illinois, and only secondarily the federal government, that was waging war. Galesburg and other small towns assumed—without justification, as it turned out—that theirs would be a decisive influence on the war's outcome. Confident of their power to affect what happened to their companies, they had little sense of consigning their young men to the care of the federal government, and thus assumed that Washington would interpose only infrequently and unimportantly between them and their military companies.

Those at home seldom pressed the War Department to release news of their sons, for the simple reason that they did not view the United States government as an important source of information. Controlling their own lines, townspeople felt with justification that they had fuller information about their boys than had the secretary of war. And for news of the broader movements of the war they could rely on the wire services feeding the local newspaper. Local people celebrated of course the great victories of Manila and Santiago, but they did so without impinging on the centrality of the relationship between town and company. Many of the manifestations of that relationship seem today merely quaint. At the same time that the nationally minded Theodore Roosevelt was soliciting Rough Rider testimonials in a forlorn attempt to win the Congressional medal of honor for his actions on Kettle Hill, the women of the Clyde Ladies Society began to collect funds to provide each of the members of Company I a medal (cost: fifty cents) struck on behalf of the town. To the ladies, the gesture did not lack substance. Service to the community should be rewarded by the community.

In 1917–18 and 1941–45 Americans would again follow the large movements of war in their newspapers and would trace in personal letters the exploits of their sons. In twentieth-century wars, however, the federal government would control newspaper content, and letters like those of 1898 conveying full details of daily routine, diet, illness, and adventure, would be censored as damaging to morale and security. Tied in such ways to their soldiers, many of America's small towns experienced the Spanish-

American War more intimately than would be possible for civilians in subsequent wars.

No doubt many young men welcomed war as an escape from monotonous jobs—or as an invitation to adventure of a sort rarely available to them. Happy to enlist, they nonetheless conceived their escape as strictly temporary. Anticipating nothing more exceptional than a return home at the war's end, officers and men were content to accept their role as representatives of their communities. On the occasion of his unit's departure for the Caribbean, Carl Sandburg's company commander acknowledged Galesburg's mandate by addressing a farewell letter to the entire town.[4] Letters home bear similar evidence that the soldiers recognized themselves as guardians of the town's honor. They too would work to retain links between town and unit and to resist any intrusive element threatening to make the company less representative of its community.

When shortly after the passage of the war resolutions the House of Representatives debated an Army bill that endangered the election of company officers by increasing the governors' appointive powers, the Galesburg *Republican-Register* reported that the "boys [of the National Guard company] were worked up and vowed they would not go into service with other than their own officers."[5] In this instance the House bill became law, but so strong was small-town opposition that politically sensitive governors invited local "recommendations" for officer positions, thereby preserving the substance of the elections system.

In cases where there were no such concessions to community control, the men sometimes acted on their threats to stay at home. The members of Galesburg's Artillery Battery B remained civilians rather than merge with another town's battery, a condition stipulated by the War Department for Battery B's activation. "In this [amalgamation]," explained the *Evening Mail*, "they would lose their organization, identification and officers, and they did not choose to accept the offer."

Those who did accept did not cease to concern themselves with the composition of the unit. When, following the departure from home of most National Guard organizations, the War Department directed that companies be increased from sixty-eight to one hundred and eight, sergeants returned to home towns to recruit the additional men. Such soldiers, to whom the manpower depots of World War I would have seemed alien inventions, assumed that replacements should come from home. "The boys are hoping," wrote Sergeant A. I. Robinson, the correspondent in Sherwood Anderson's company, "that the . . . new men will all be from Clyde."

The soldiers were less exercised than their townsmen over the promotion of outsiders, but it remained a point of dissatisfaction. Robinson wrote home in mid-May of 1898 that "members of the company were very much chagrined" at the appointment of a "Toledo man" as captain of

Company I, "but like good soldiers they made the best of it." Later he was less resigned. The men suspected "political chicanery" when a Clyde man was passed over in favor of a candidate from rival Fremont; that constituted "an outrage." Unit sentiment as reflected in his letters throughout the war strongly supported promotion from the company ranks. There is in his criticisms of the Toledo men who would "hog" promotions something beyond small-group solidarity and normal desire for personal preferment. His opposition, and the protests of those at home, signal the deeper conviction that other officers were less capable and trustworthy *because* they were not from Clyde.

Men from home made easier the maintenance of informal social relationships, perhaps the soldiers' principal concern beyond their safe return to civilian life. Out of this concern grew their resistance to the pretensions of their own officers and the incursions of regular officers intent on establishing professional discipline and impersonality. A complicating factor in this struggle was a measure of ambivalence in volunteer attitudes toward the regulars. Hometown soldiers admired the capabilities of the professionals. "As good as the regulars" was an encomium that volunteer units would happily accept, so long as professional leadership was not imposed on their own ranks. Volunteers could not entirely ignore the returns of professionalism, even when they calculated its price too high to pay. In one of his letters to the Galesburg *Evening Mail*, Private Martin assured townspeople that the order and discipline in Company C would be "much the same" as in the regulars, but, he added with no sense of contradiction, "of course, the officers will hardly be as strict." Carl Sandburg wrote with less ambiguity of the same volunteers: "They elected their own officers and you could hear fellows [say], 'No West Pointers in *this* regiment.'" The Seventh New York, perhaps the best National Guard regiment in the country, refused induction into federal service because its members feared they would be compelled to serve under West Point graduates.

The source of such widespread aversion to the regular officer was the volunteer's conviction that professional discipline would cheat him of the critical personal experience that the war was expected to supply. Close ties of company and town and their united resistance to external authority in no sense implied a high degree of subordination of the volunteer to his hometown unit. The "boy of the country town" still thought of warmaking as personal expression and scarcely at all as concerted group action. Face to face with the enemy, the individual was the integer of meaning. It was he testing himself. It was his battle performance—and only peripherally his unit's—that counted. Many volunteers considered their membership in a company a matter of administrative convenience, the result of their need for a vehicle that would carry them to war. Once there, each would be judged, by himself and others, as an individual combatant.

It was this individual expression in warfare that the volunteers believed regular officers determined to prevent: West Point martinets would compel the volunteer to subordinate himself to an organization. So believing, volunteers throughout the war resisted those attempts at discipline and regimentation that threatened their image as personal combatants. It was thus not only the familiarity and security of the hometown unit, the presence of childhood friends, that brought volunteers to the company's defense against the threat of outside control. In equal measure it was the freedom offered in such units to fight in a style that volunteers thought would supply the personal meaning of war.

Volunteers further resisted the imposition of impersonal authority because they saw no basis for a careful distinction between officer and enlisted man. They were unpersuaded that anything inherent in the category "officer" established superior soldiership. Relevant military experience earned the volunteers' respect, but almost all their officers were as innocent of it as they were. Neither regular nor volunteer had faced a European enemy or fought over a tropical terrain. Moreover, the implements of land warfare, unlike those huge, complex and risky machines employed since the 1880s in the United States Navy, required no specialized training. Volunteers were confident that their proficiency with the weapons available to fight Spaniards in Cuba equaled—many thought surpassed—that of the regulars. In the eyes of the men, their officers had no claim to authority or even respect—neither superior experience, expertise, nor anything else by which they had *earned* the right to issue peremptory orders and enjoy privileges denied the men.

The writings of Sherwood Anderson make clear the volunteer's assumption that hometown social patterns should prevail and his determination to resist their suspension. "I was a soldier," he wrote a quarter century later, "and had picked the right war. We of the local military companies were taken into the national service just as we were. Our local companies had been built up on a democratic basis. I had got what I wanted. . . . " To keep what he wanted required some effort. The professionals, fearing that intimacy would translate into partiality in combat, insisted on the social separation of officers and men. But Anderson had grown up with his lieutenants, had lived side by side with them on terms of intimacy and informality and expected to resume such a life in Clyde as soon as the war was over. At first the situation in each company must have resembled that described by a citizen of neighboring Fremont who visited his town's company at Camp Bushnell in Columbus. "There are no regular Army officers in camp . . . and officers and men of the Guard mingle on a plane of beautiful equality. Privates invade the tents of their officers at will, and yell at them half the length of the street. The recruits talk and smoke cigars in ranks, and officers frequently associate in the pastimes of the men." The Army's adjutant-general would later cite as one of the most serious defects in the American military effort the "utter disregard for the most elementary principles of military life in large camps."

In mid-May 1898 volunteer companies received orders prohibiting officers and men messing together. Anderson was at first bemused. "Ed and Dug [company officers] are all right. They have to live off by themselves and act as though they were something special, kind of grand and wise and gaudy. It's kind of a bluff, I guess, that has to be kept up. . . . " He took delight in his inability to separate the company commander from the janitor he had known at home. In his mind the first lieutenant would remain a celery-raiser and the second lieutenant a knife-sharpener. Throughout the war Anderson doubted the Army's ability to invest those men with additional powers that he would be inclined to recognize.

Some intrusions of formality were simply laughed away. Returning from an evening in town without benefit of pass, Anderson mocked the challenging sentry. "Ah, cut it Will, you big boob. Don't make such a racket." With that, he proceeded into camp.

The limitations of jeering became obvious, however, as volunteers found restrictions imposed by the regular Army increasingly onerous. The men then made clear to their own officers that they would appeal questions of personal relationships, not to higher military authority but to the home town. In one form the process involved threats of a vigilante justice that volunteers expected the community to condone. Wrote Anderson: "An officer might conceivably 'get away' with some sort of injustice for the moment—but a year from now, when we were all at home again[?] . . . Did the fool want to take the chance of four or five huskies giving him a beating some night in the alleyway?"

More overt and genteel appeals to community values were equally effective. Newspapers did not hesitate to print letters, from their own correspondents or unnamed persons, denouncing the "airs" put on by an always-named officer. One potent petition to the people at home was that of Wiz Brown, a private in Sandburg's unit. The company commander, Captain Thomas Leslie McGirr (whom Sandburg described as "a second-rank Galesburg lawyer") believed that Brown had threatened him and resolved to retaliate by giving the private a dishonorable discharge. When he learned of the matter, Brown apparently gave no consideration to an appeal through the chain of command. Even if the idea had occurred to him, a reversal of McGirr's decision would not have accomplished his purpose, for Brown was much less disturbed by the nature of his discharge than by the effrontery of McGirr's conduct. Instead he instigated an article that appeared in the Galesburg *Evening Mail* on the day before the company's return. It reported that all except three of the unit's members had signed a petition, requesting that McGirr be denied the honors of homecoming, leading the parade, and making the principal speech. Specifically, the signers charged the captain with improprieties in the maintenance of the company accounts and with treating some of the men with favoritism, others with undue severity. The newspaper seems to have accepted Brown's letter as prima facie evidence of McGirr's guilt; it summoned no more in his defense than the observation of one of the captain's friends that "he is not well." Nothing more was heard of the charges against McGirr. He did speak, very briefly, at the banquet given the returned heroes by the Army and Navy League at the Universalist Church. Whatever the justice of the matter, Captain McGirr, and all those other volunteer officers so precariously balanced between town, company, and Army, must have been acutely aware of the narrow range of the command prerogative.

Those in command positions could not miss the fact that the men judged them on their willingness to maintain pliant social relationships. In an angry diary Private Charles Johnson Post reserved a special rage for the chaplain who pressed charges against shipboard food thieves and later ousted enlisted men from a Y.M.C.A. tent reserved for officers. To acknowledge the official division between officers and men was mischievous, to enforce it intolerable. Conversely, a Captain Rafferty won Post's praise when he joined the men each night at the fire for reminiscence and discussion of religion and politics. Enlisted men whose letters filled hometown newspapers could find no higher compliment for an officer than the assertion that military life had in no way altered his demeanor. Colonel D. Jack Foster of Sandburg's regiment was one who retained popularity because he continued to act like a civilian. There was about him "no assumed military dignity nor overbearing manners."

To volunteers the handshake was the litmus of the egalitarian ideal. A Rough Rider cowboy introduced himself to Leonard Wood, his regimental commander: "Say, Colonel, I want to shake hands with you and tell you that I like you a damn sight better than I expected to. . . . " Another began his harangue of the Rough Riders' second in command, Theodore Roosevelt, with "Well, Colonel, I want to shake hands and say we're with you. . . . " There was tentative flattery and further testing in these remarks. An officer willing to shake hands was an officer whose men assured one another that they could expect "man-to-man" treatment. On the other hand, volunteers despised the salute[6] and castigated as a tyrant the officer who insisted upon it. So caustic were the men on this count that even regular officers ceased to require military courtesy. A career officer of the Tenth United States Cavalry, Captain John Bigelow, Jr., wrote with self-mocking resignation at the end of the war, "Few of the enlisted men whom I pass on the streets of Huntsville [Alabama] salute: I do not know why, unless it is that they are not in the habit of saluting their officers."

If Bigelow typifies regular officers frustrated by their inability to enforce the professional ideal, William Jennings Bryan might stand for that minority of volunteer officers who escaped the tension between egalitarian and professional ideals by remaining unconscious of the latter's existence. A colonel in a Nebraska regiment accurately described as a "neighborhood organization."[7] The Great Commoner perceived no distinctions between officers and men. Not the drillfield but the campfire—and the opportunities it offered to discuss with the men "how to live and how to die"[8]—fixed the pivot on which his Army life turned. Nothing professionals said of military efficiency or discipline chipped his vision of the Army as co-operative movement. For Bryan and others who thought as he did there was no interior conflict. Larger numbers of volunteer officers, however, found themselves jostled between personal desires to make their units "as good as the regulars" and the volunteers' disapproval of officer "airs." Again the experience of the unhappy McGirr is instructive. On a hot march from Guanica to Ponce during the Puerto Rican campaign the tired, dust-covered boys of Galesburg's Company C saw a chance to spare their backs by transferring blanket rolls to a hired ox cart. McGirr hesitated; he "did not think it a military thing to do." Confused, a bit embarrassed, a bit angry at his inability to feel in full control of the situation, he finally gave his consent. His was the dilemma of the hometown company officer.

The efforts of Theodore Roosevelt and Leonard Wood to reshape an older friendship to meet the requirements of a new hierarchical relationship reflected all the tensions inherent in a dual approach to war. Eager for a commission, Roosevelt cited as one of his qualifications for a lieutenant colonelcy his very perfunctory service in a New York National Guard unit. Wood, Roosevelt's fellow outdoorsman and nominal superior, had by contrast more than a decade's experience in the old Army as regimental surgeon and Indian fighter. In the year prior to the war Roosevelt, while serving as assistant secretary of the Navy, had built friendships with Wood and a group of young naval officers. Influenced by such associations, Roosevelt became a convert to the standards of the regulars. When war came, he announced his determination to be "professional" in all aspects of soldiering. To his surprise he could not shed the preconceptions planted in his National Guard days. Pleased when a contingent of Rough Riders properly executed a difficult drill, he showed his appreciation by buying each man a schooner of beer. Wood, with other officers present, rebuked his friend for unprofessional conduct. Stung at first but soon repentant, Roosevelt returned to tell Wood, "I wish to say, sir, that I agree with what you said. I consider myself the damndest ass within ten miles of this camp."

Contrition did not insulate the future president from his basic ambivalence on the proper manner of producing American soldiers. He said of his Rough Riders that "what was necessary was to teach them to act together, and to obey orders." To this professional formula Roosevelt the guardsman added: "The men were singularly quick to respond to any appeal to their intelligence and patriotism."

Biographer Hermann Hagedorn saw here the essential difference between professional and volunteer. Wood, he said, came to the Rough Riders expecting to command and be obeyed; Roosevelt felt it essential "to win over the minds" of his men. It must be added that if Roosevelt's problem was the inability to reconcile his persuasion-inspiration tactic with a power theoretically self-sufficient, Wood's was the frustration of dedication to an ideal beyond realization. Passing sprawling soldiers, he heard his corporal rebuke one of the lounging volunteers: "Didn't yo' hear me shout

ATTENTION?" Came the reply: "Sure, I did. I thought yo' jest wanted me to look alive to somethin' interestin'."

Friedrich Wilhelm von Steuben had observed of American soldiers one hundred and twenty years earlier that "one must first explain—and then give the order." His remark was no less applicable to the volunteers of 1898, although professional soldiers were by then less likely than von Steuben to regard the trait as a part of the genius of the American people. Unable to enforce orders, the Leonard Woods of the Army were loath to explain them. Like his friend Theodore, he pondered whether the officer's duty was to instill in his men automatic response to command, or to offer a personal example of intelligence and patriotism inspiring others to follow where he led.

The Spanish–American War proved partially correct the regulars' contention that social informality would produce volunteer indiscipline and officer indecision. While still near their communities, volunteers so comported themselves that Alger advised his commanders to transport troops from their home states as soon as possible, an obvious effort to escape what an investigating commission chaired by Grenville M. Dodge would later term "the disturbing influences of home locality." Distance, however, proved no panacea. In training camps the men simply disregarded elementary sanitary precautions; repeated orders and daily inspections were unavailing. Fist fights between individual officers and men were frequent. In the war zone, ranks often crumbled when there was the prospect of a view or a show, whether bombardment or dance troupe. Tired marchers regularly ignored orders and pitched into the jungle scarce supplies of ammunition. Officers hesitated to invoke military justice. Shafter reported that in the Fifth Corps "not an officer was brought to trial by court-martial, and, as far as I know, no enlisted man." In extreme cases where discipline fell below the minimal standard necessary to maintain the semblance of a military unit, the Army could at best request the resignations of officers it held accountable.

Ultimately, however, despite such evidence, the professionals' indictment proved unpersuasive, for in the crucial moments the volunteers' battle discipline—resting not on officer authority but on a particular personal motivation—was adequate to the test of combat.[9] To most Americans, that alone was the performance that counted.

Better than any other writer, Stephen Crane captured the tension that played between volunteer and professional concepts of war. In Crane's short story, *Virtue in War*, Private Lige approaches the tent of Major Gates, a former regular commanding a volunteer unit:

"Well, Maje," said the newcomer, genially, "how goes it?"

The major's head flashed up, but he spoke without heat. "Come to attention and salute."

The private looked at him in resentful amazement, and then inquired: "Ye ain't mad, are ye? Ain't nothin' to get huffy about, is there?"

"I—Come to attention and salute."

"Well," drawled the private, as he stared, "seein' as ye are so darn particular, I don't care if I do—if it'll make yer meals set on yer stummick any better."

Drawing a long breath and grinning ironically, he lazily pulled his heels together and saluted with a flourish.

"There," he said, with a return to his earlier genial manner. "How's that suit ye, Maje?"

There was a silence which to an impartial observer would have seemed pregnant with dynamite and bloody death. Then the major cleared his throat and coldly said: "And now, what is your business?"

"Who—me?" asked the private. "Oh, I just sorter dropped in." With a deeper meaning he added: "Sorter dropped in in a friendly way, thinkin' ye was mebbe a different kind of feller from what ye be."

The inference was clearly marked.

It was now Gates's turn to stare, and stare he unfeignedly did. "Go back to your quarters," he said at length.

The volunteer became very angry.

"Oh, ye needn't be so up-in-th'-air, need ye? Don't know's I'm dead anxious to inflict my company on yer since I've had a good look at ye. There may be men in this here battalion what's had just as much edjewcation as you have, and I'm damned if they ain't got better *manners*. Good mornin'," he said, with dignity; and passing out of the tent, he flung the flap back in place with an air of slamming it as if it had been a door. He made his way back to his company street. . . . He was furious.

Lige complains to his friends that Gates "won't have no truck with jest common—*men*, like you be." He and the major are both wounded in an attack on a Spanish blockhouse. Again, Lige attempts to persuade Gates to acknowledge his individuality. As if his pardon were important to Gates, Lige tells the major he is no longer angry. Again Gates responds from the manual, ordering Lige to "Go to the rear!" Lige refuses, though the major rather desperately threatens him with drawn revolver. The volunteer stays, but he can do nothing, neither win Gates' recognition of his personal worth nor save the major's life. In the end Lige perceives a "certain hopeless gulf" separating him from the other man.

In contemplating the quandary of 1898's professional officers, whether Leonard Wood or Crane's Major Gates, one must take care not to rely on too strict a dichotomy between the desire for automatic response and the necessity of inspirational leadership rooted in character. In fact, the issue was not so sharply etched in 1898. Not even the most dedicated professionals yet conceived of the Army as a machine, or soldiers as cogwheels that could be made to rotate independently of individual will. Men continued to believe in varying degrees that the success of an army flowed from the personal qualities of its members: professionals insisted that obedience to command was the most important, not the sole, quality required. No one, least of all those generals like Oates who insisted in surrounding themselves with men from home, thought of a national army of inter-changeable parts. No one, least of all those who in 1898 believed that directing others in peacetime pursuits constituted grounds for refusing direction in war, foresaw that another war would dissolve those large areas of continuity between civilian and military life, leaving all equally vulnerable to a power of command enhanced psychologically and institutionally.

Change thus came with no rush to the American Army of 1900–1917. With many officers still professing to value a certain latitude in individual behavior, with an American public persistent in its belief that the experience of 1898 had validated the nation's reliance on a volunteer system, and with the exemplar of individualized warfare sitting in the White House, the interwar debate on military reform quite understandably focused on inefficiency rather than on discipline. (Although professionals asserted to one another that the volunteers would have fared poorly in combat without the heavy stiffening of the regulars, incompetence, especially in the care of the sick, had in truth cost far more lives than had lack of discipline in battle.) The objective of Army reformers was thus a "more intimate relation" between the general government and National Guard units, one assuming that the militiaman taught *how* to act professionally would thereby *wish* to act professionally. Sufficient exposure to the values of the regulars would of itself purge informality, without resort to coercion. As the Dodge Commission concluded, "Until the individual soldier appreciates the necessity of complying fully with the regulations and confines himself to the regular food—and this the soldier never does until *experience* teaches him the necessity—he will drink polluted water, eat noxious food . . . and will not take care of himself, and *no discipline or watching will prevent it.*"

Varieties of proposals were offered to shape the experience of guardsmen toward professional standards. Secretary of War Elihu Root opened to members of the National Guard the Army's new specialized schools. The Dick Act of 1903 provided that the Guard was to be organized, equipped, and trained in uniformity with the regular Army. The latter, moreover, received authority to detail to the states professional instructors and to establish minimum standards for weekly drill and summer camp. From other sources came suggestions for combined maneuvers, joint encampments, and experimental mobilizations. If ideas were profuse, however, movement was rare. Old exhortations could not do work for which new mechanisms were required. In 1908 the election of officers continued in the Guard units of several states. In 1916 the mobilization of the National Guard during the Mexican border crisis revealed so few organizational advances beyond 1898 that Leonard Wood's claim of the previous year that the volunteer system had proven a failure seemed borne out.

To be sure, the pace of change was already accelerating with the approach of war in Europe. Americans, granted almost three years to contemplate from afar the horrors of trench warfare, were untouched in 1917 by the massive enthusiasm of 1898. Guard rosters were as a rule under-subscribed; even the introduction of conscripts sometimes failed to fore-stall the consolidation of units. Guardsmen for the first time took a double oath, to the national as well as the state government. Within a year of America's entry into war, most divisions thoroughly blended regulars, guardsmen, and draftees.

In 1917–18 the homogeneous hometown unit—and with it any inter-mediate level of loyalty and identification between soldier and the national Army—was rapidly disappearing. A stronger military institutional struc-ture, a growing national-mindedness and the exigencies of a war of im-mensely greater scope and severity were combining to produce units of greater geographical mix and officers whose professional qualifications rather than community affiliations would become the requisites of military leadership.

In the spring of 1898 Sherwood Anderson had quit his job in a Chicago cold-storage warehouse and had returned to Clyde to rejoin Company I, a gesture for which even the hoboes on the train on which he stole a ride had paid him honor. In 1917 fewer Americans felt so strongly a direct relationship between war and hometown. No longer did many feel it im-portant to approach a national conflict through one's local community.

The same Sherwood Anderson who ridiculed the command preten-sions of "Ed and Dug" did seem to enter a strikingly different conceptual cosmos when in 1917 he wrote a book presenting man as "ineffectual until, absorbed into a faceless mass led by a charismatic leader, he contributed his will and body to an invincible social entity." Though rich in hyperbole when applied to the American soldier of 1917–18, such a statement does help to mark the diminution of individualized expression in war. It gives shape to a tendency advanced by the introduction during World War I of psychological placement and standardized testing. And it finds rough counterparts in the professionals' reconceptualization of war. Reflecting on the experience of 1917–18, General Henry Jervey told brother officers in 1920:

> A man could not be considered as merely a man. He was something more. He was part of [a] machine made up of many different parts, each a man it is true, but having to play a highly specialized part. Consequently it became necessary to economize the specialized abilities of these various spare parts and assign them where their specialized abilities would do the most good. In other words, round pegs had to be selected to fill round holes. This required a careful classification of the men before assignment . . .

Invincible social entity. A machine of many parts. Pegs and holes. No longer would men discuss war in the imagery of character, citizenship, energy, and physical prowess.

If by 1920 no issue survived, twenty-two years earlier two conceptions of warmaking still remained in an unstable suspension.

The Spanish–American War did not bridge the gulf between volunteer and professional. The enemy was too weak and the war too short to force efficiency; the weapons were not so destructive as to force discipline. The nation for the last time thought appropriate, and could afford, volunteer informality.

NOTES

1. Tanner to Corbin, May 19, 1898, in "Muster In War With Spain," The Office of the Adjutant General, National Archives, Washington, D.C. (Hereafter cited as AGO Records.) Close political calculus is evident in Shelby Cullom's telegram to Adjutant General Corbin; the senator asked "whether it is possible for me to prevail upon the Gov't to accept a battery from Galesburg . . . Gov't has accepted a battery from Danville on east side of state. This one is on the west and are [sic] exceedingly anxious to be accepted." Cullom to Corbin, May 3, 1898, ibid. In his reply of May 4, Corbin refused Cullom's request.

2. William Allen White, "When Johnny Went Marching Out," *McClure's Magazine*, XI (June 1898), 199. See also Hill, *Minute Man*, p. 126: "He [the National Guardsman] and his comrades were small people from farms, villages and main street stores."

3. Sherwood Anderson's enlistment in the local National Guard company, one of his biographers reports, was recognized as "a boost socially." William Alfred Sutton, "Sherwood Anderson's Formative Years (1876-1913)" (Ph.D. dissertation, Ohio State University, 1943), p. 84.

4. *Evening Mail*, July 11, 1898. George Martin wrote in a letter published in the July 12 edition, "Company C boys hope to behave with honor to themselves and to their beloved city."

5. *Republican-Register*, Apr. 23, 1898. Millis, *Martial Spirit*, pp. 156-57, quotes Congressman Oscar Underwood of Alabama addressing his colleagues: "There is hardly a man on this floor who has not received letters from his constituents stating that they would be glad to volunteer, glad to fight for their country, if they can be officered by their home men. They want to know their officers and be officered by men who have been raised [,] and who have lived [,] among them."

6. At Tampa Wood dispatched a trooper to locate ammunition for the regiment's Colt machine guns. Meeting General Adna R. Chaffee, the volunteer blurted out, "Say, Colonel Wood wants the cartridges for the Colt guns a heap pronto. We are a-going aboard the ship." Shot back Chaffee, "Don't you know enough to be a soldier? You should dismount, salute, and stand at attention until I notice you." Saying little but speaking volumes, the soldier replied, "I ain't no soldier. I'm a Rough Rider." Virgil Carrington Jones, *Roosevelt's Rough Riders* (Garden City, New York, 1971), p. 62.

7. Willis J. Abbot, *Watching the World Go By* (Boston, 1933), pp. 228-29. Bryan's regiment was "largely a neighborhood organization, recruited in Nebraska, and its men to a surprising number were known to their colonel."

8. Anna Maus, "Reminiscences," USAMHRC. Nurse Maus was puzzled by the

determination of an ill soldier to leave her recuperation hospital, one the men called "the best place on earth," and to return to Bryan's unit. He "said that nothing could take the place of his Colonel. 'We sit around him every evening and he tells us how to live and how to die.'"

9. It is no surprise that those commended for heriosm often seemed to combine courage in the face of the enemy with resistance to the orders of their officers. Two of three Rough Riders whom Roosevelt recommended for Congressional medals of honor fell in this category. (Theodore Roosevelt to William H. Carter, Mar. 20, 1899, Roosevelt Papers.) Disobedience appeared to give a fillip to heroism.

The Era
of World War I

26

Conscripting for Colossus

The Progressive Era and the Origin of the Modern Military Draft in the United States in World War I

JOHN WHITECLAY CHAMBERS II

The friends of conscription in 1916 tended to be cosmopolitans; the foes, localists. The alliance between "progressives" ("cosmopolitans"? "modernizers"?) and the regular army and navy mentioned in the preceding essay is also in evidence in the following one, an original essay on the origins of the draft in 1917 by John Chambers.

The volunteer system, like the stage coach, served its purpose in primitive times, but like that stagecoach, it proved unequal to the expanding needs of modern time. . . . [The people] know that the volunteer system has been a failure wherever tried, and seeking efficiency they prefer the selective draft system, just as seeking speed they would prefer a locomotive to an oxcart.

—Henry Watterson, 1917

THE ADOPTION OF THE DRAFT in World War I heralded a radical departure from the traditional method of raising armies in America's wars. For generations, the country had relied upon militia or local units of the U.S. Volunteers to provide most of its wartime troops. These volunteer citizen-soldiers—from the Minute Men to the Rough Riders—had occupied a hal-

SOURCE: John Whiteclay Chambers II, "Conscripting for Colossus," adapted from a paper presented at the annual meeting of the Organization of American Historians, April 18, 1972, Washington, D.C. Full scholarly citations may be found in John Chambers, *To Arm a Nation: The Draft Comes to America* (New York: Free Press, forthcoming, 1987).

lowed place in the nation's history. Americans had inherited English antimilitarism and distrust of large professional armies, and that tradition fit both the needs and values of their new society. In a country of widely scattered settlements, men elected their own officers or enlisted behind popular local leaders to preserve their community's honor and safety. Even when the first national draft was adopted midway through the Civil War, it sought primarily to prod local volunteering. In the face of massive resistance, less than 2.5 percent of the Union Army was drafted. After Appomattox, Union and Confederate veterans paid homage to the volunteer tradition both North and South.

Yet, in World War I, the tradition of local voluntarism was summarily ended and replaced by a centrally directed system of compulsory military service. For the first time, the government adopted national conscription at the beginning of a war as the primary means of raising an army, and for the first time it sent conscripts overseas. Rather than stimulating enlistment, the government, through the draft, sought to help allocate the nation's human resources more efficiently in a program of total national mobilization. Before the war ended, authorities prohibited any voluntary enlistment as wasteful. The Selective Service System became the central dispenser of manpower for the armed forces and to a lesser degree, through the manipulation of deferments, for the civilian economy as well. In eighteen months, 72 percent of the doughboys entered the army as conscripts in what the draft administrator labeled as a "revolutionary" change in military policy.

The changing social values of a newly industrialized nation as well as more immediate actions triggered by the World War, precipitated this revolution. Although historians have generally concentrated on the proximate causes rather than on the underlying reasons, neither can be fully understood without the other. The new military policy was a sign of a new America.

U.S. entry into the war and President Wilson's decision to demand adoption of the draft provided the immediate causes of the radical change in military policy. In 1916, the president had opposed peacetime conscription. Even after the break in diplomatic relations with Germany in February 1917, he seems to have thought that in wartime conscription should be adopted only after volunteering had failed. However, within a few days after his decision of March 20, 1917 to enter the war, Wilson reversed his position and decided to rely primarily upon a selective draft, from the outset, to build a national army.

Wilson apparently based his decision on both political and ideological considerations. Circumstantial evidence suggests that Wilson decided to abandon his initial plan for first calling out the volunteers because of a challenge from his former rival, Theodore Roosevelt. Faced with the Rough Rider's demand that, as an excommander in chief, he be allowed to raise and lead a volunteer division for service in France, Wilson decided to prohibit local volunteer units and to keep the army under the central control of the professional military and the administration.

The draft also appealed to Wilson's increasing desire for efficient national solutions to the country's problems, and he explained his decision on that basis. He saw it as the fairest and most effective method of allocating manpower in a war that required industrial and agricultural as well as military mobilization. Several weeks after his decision, he explained:

> The idea of the draft is not only the drawing of men into the military service of the Government, but the virtual assigning of men to the necessary labor of the country. Its central idea was to disturb the industrial and social structure of the country just as little as possible.

In recommending the draft, the general staff had praised both its reliability for producing as many soldiers as were wanted and its ability to keep skilled workers at home to maintain production of ships, munitions, and supplies. The English experience had shown that such industrially valuable men often rushed to the colors only to die in the trenches. But under conscription the government rather than the individual could determine where each man would serve his country. "It is not an army that we must shape and train for war," the president declared as he signed the draft law, "it is a nation. . . . The whole nation must be a team in which each man shall play the part for which he is best fitted."

Draftees with serialized identification tags replaced the individualistic Rough Riders, and the rather colorless professional John J. Pershing instead of the flamboyant amateur Teddy Roosevelt took the troops to France. In this rationally planned conscription system, the secretary of war admitted, the government did not expect enthusiasm; obedience would suffice.

Military institutions reflect the societies that employ them. The underlying causes of the adoption of the draft in the United States in World War I were attitudinal changes among key elite groups in a rapidly modernizing nation. By the early twentieth century, the United States had emerged from a decentralized, rural, agrarian land to a more centralized, urban, industrial nation. Industrialization and massive immigration put great strains on the social order, widening the sense of distance between rich and poor, native and immigrant. But it also enhanced the power of a nation that was bursting into world markets and international politics and imperial rivalries. The new cosmopolitan elite—corporation managers, financiers, Wall Street lawyers, heads of the new professional associations, and others—sought to rationalize the social order. To the new decision makers in modern America, efficiency, predictability, and order superseded older values of localism, individualism, and voluntarism. National conscription corresponded to a number of the values important to the leadership of a society in flux. A variation of the long-despised European conscript system came to the United States during World War I because an urban elite saw it as the most efficient means of mobilizing an industrial nation for total war.

Led by a coterie of Eastern patricians and supported by some of the wealthiest men in America, a conscription crusade emerged as an elite social movement to revitalize and protect America through the inculcation of military values. Between 1915 and 1917, an intensive propaganda campaign for compulsory military training and service under federal control helped to mold sentiment in favor of national conscription and to ensure its adoption when the United States finally entered the war. Many of the leaders of this campaign had been early advocates of American participation on the side of the Allies. In their public statements and even their private discussions, however, they did not urge universal military training (UMT) in preparation for aiding the Allies. Rather, they advocated such increased military measures to protect the United States and its expanding markets, especially in Latin America and the Far East, from the invasion or trade war that they feared would follow the war in Europe. They gave equal weight—indeed some gave greater importance—to the domestic reasons for UMT. The conscriptionists believed that military training would help restore harmony, order, and vitality to a society that they believed was being fragmented and debilitated by individual selfishness, class and ethnic divisions, and local and regional parochialism. The cosmopolitan elite was determined to modernize American institutions. The conscriptionist members of that elite sought to create a truly national American citizen-army.

Collective biographical analysis shows a remarkable similarity among the conscriptionist leaders who included politicians such as Theodore Roosevelt; soldiers such as Generals Leonard Wood and Hugh Scott, the army chief of staff; Wall Street lawyers such as Joseph Choate, Grenville Clark, Elihu Root, and Henry Stimson (the last two both former secretaries of war); college presidents such as Charles Eliot of Harvard, John Hibben of Princeton, Arthur Hadley of Yale, and Henry Drinker of Lehigh; and New York financiers including George Perkins, Robert Bacon, and Willard Straight of J. P. Morgan and Company and Guy Emerson of the National Bank of Commerce. A sample of forty-two leaders of the National Security League, the Plattsburg training camp movement, and other conscriptionist groups as well as individual advocates of UMT showed that the majority belonged to families of long residence and comfortable means, were educated at Ivy League colleges or West Point, grew up as Episcopalians and Republicans, and worked in finance or corporate law in the Northeast or with the general staff in Washington.[1]

This elite group feared that America was threatened by great internal and external dangers. The lack of assimilation of millions of immigrants from southern and eastern Europe and the burgeoning ghettoes in the cities appalled them. They were shocked by increasing crime and disease, class consciousness and labor violence, and the growth of radical organizations such as the Anarchists, the Socialist Party, and the Industrial Workers of the World. To the conscriptionist leaders, the old agencies of socialization and social control—the family, the church, the school—seemed to have become ineffective, and grubby self-interest, materialism, and pacifism appeared to sap the vitality of the nation and its ability to resist the peril. The patricians feared the physical and moral deterioration of what they liked to call "the race" at a time when they feared it was confronted with its greatest challenge.

The challenge came not only from within but from without. The conscriptionists thought that America had to be made strong to play the world role dictated by its destiny and its great industrial power. As the country joined the international race for colonies and foreign markets, these men believed that only armed force could limit the greed of other nations; adequate preparation was the only antidote for war. Many of them thought that America should help the Allies militarily and protect the Western Hemisphere from German economic penetration and colonization. All feared that after the European war, Germany, England, or Japan would seek to recapture the wealth and markets that America had gained during the conflict.

Universal military training would provide the panacea for these problems. Every able-bodied young man in the country when he reached nineteen would be required to spend six months to a year or more in military camp, trained by professional soldiers in obedience, sanitation, citizenship, and combat. UMT would establish a large and relatively inexpensive army—wages, pensions, and wartime enlistment bounties would be eliminated. This army would be based primarily on millions of army-trained civilians in ready reserves. Universal military training was the only way to maintain peace, one of the country's railroad tycoons warned, "in face of the envy, hatred and malice towards us which will be in the hearts of all Europe and Japan when the present war is over and our country alone will be rich and prosperous."

Besides providing a shield against outside attack, universal military training would also strengthen America internally according to the conscriptionists. It would implant the military values of duty, discipline, respect, and national loyalty and would restore order and unity to the country. The experience at training camp would teach the immigrants American values and customs, reduce class consciousness and violence, and teach rich and poor to understand each other and work together for mutual benefit. It would build better men, physically as well as morally, and would fashion superior workers who were mature, obedient, and productive.

"Obviously the problems ahead are problems of labor and capital and in some degree of race," one young Wall Street lawyer warned the president. "They appear to arise in very great part through misunderstandings created by rumors, newspapers and lack of personal contact." UMT, where boys from Groton and from the Bowery mingled together, tended to

THE ERA OF WORLD WAR I

"obliterate the so-called class distinctions. I really believe," he wrote, "that nothing else will so surely aid in making us a united and understanding people." Theodore Roosevelt, with characteristic exuberance, claimed that "the military tent, where all sleep side-by-side, will rank next to the public school among the great agents of democratization."

The word "democracy" has many definitions. To the conscriptionists, UMT was democratic because it distributed military obligations among all citizens. They advised that those who shared the privileges of citizenship also had to share its burdens. They equated universal military service with universal male suffrage, and they argued that military service like taxation had to be compulsory to be effective. But critics pointed out that, although all might train together, the burden of the loss of the trainee's civilian wages upon affluent families and upon impoverished families, which needed every penny of income, would hardly be the same. And, because not all would serve in the trenches in time of war, there really could never be an equitable sharing of the supreme risk faced by the front-line soldier.

If democracy means popular government as well as equity, many conscriptionists could be considered antidemocratic, for they sought to remove the military establishment from popular control. These men had lost faith in the National Guard and the U.S. Volunteers, which they thought were influenced by state politics and popular whim. Furthermore, many were contemptuous of Congress, which they believed concerned itself with parochial interests rather than national defense. To achieve predictability, efficiency, and cost saving, the conscriptionists sought to remove the national military policy from the politicians of Capitol Hill and the state houses and to place it in the hands of a nonpartisan board of experts composed of men such as themselves. The Council of National Defense that they proposed aimed at the same kind of depoliticization as the city-manager form of government and the U.S. Tariff Commission. Many of the same persons and groups supported each of these plans.

Even equity had its limits among most conscriptionists. Critics such as the socialist editor of *The Masses* charged that, although members of the elite spoke of sharing pup tents with the poor, they had little intention of sharing their wealth with their less fortunate tentmates. Many of the conscriptionists had ardently opposed the income tax, and, when war came, many of them contested proposals for high income and corporate taxes. Significantly, the plan for wartime conscription of wealth came primarily from reformers who had fought unsuccessfully against the conscription of men.

The support of corporate leaders for the conscription movement led to charges that they were attempting to suppress democracy through militarization. "The Wall Street interests that are behind the campaign for compulsory service," the lawyer-reformer Amos Pinchot asserted, "wanted . . . a meek and disciplined labor group that will make no trouble at home, and will fight obediently to defend the American dollar abroad." Such accusations found acceptance among many workers and farmers who already feared the expanding power of big business.

The financial records of the conscriptionist organizations confirm that the bulk of their funds came from wealthy New Yorkers and that the major contributors were linked to some of the largest corporations in America. Among them were such industrialists as Arthur C. James, vice president of Phelps Dodge Mining and a director of several railroads, who had inherited $26 million; T. Coleman DuPont, who had sold his holdings for $14 million after building the DuPont Powder Trust; John T. Pratt, son of one of the organizers of the Standard Oil Trust and a major stockholder in the company; Oliver Payne, a former trustee and treasurer of Standard Oil and American Tobacco; Henry Clay Frick, the steel magnate; Henry Walters, president of two of the three major railroads in the South; members of the Guggenheim mining family; Wall Street financiers such as J. P. Morgan and several of his partners, Henry Davidson, George Perkins, and Robert Bacon; plus Bernard Baruch and Mortimer and Jacob Schiff of Kuhn, Loeb and Company. After the declaration of war, when the conscriptionists sought to replace selective service with a permanent policy of UMT, these contributors were joined by John D. Rockefeller, Jr., and the Carnegie Corporation, with Elihu Root, of the National Security League, on its board of directors. These sixteen men contributed at least $144,000, in addition to the $100,000 supplied by the Carnegie Corporation.

It is difficult to verify fully the reasons behind human behavior, but the motivation of the conscriptionist leaders may be suggested from an analysis of their careers as well as their ideologies. Born into old American families with fathers who were businessmen or professionals, most of them grew up during the rapid industrialization of the late nineteenth century. Adapting to this economic change, they succeeded in occupations that were linked to the industrialization of the country and its expansion as a world power. These cosmopolitan leaders—industrialists, financiers, corporation lawyers, and soldiers—believed in the new large-scale corporate enterprise and in international expansion. But they found the country threatened by retaliation from foreign competitors and dissatisfaction among lower-income groups at home. The president of the National City Bank of New York spoke for many other conscriptionists when he told the American Bankers Association:

> It is the duty of everyone of us to do what we can to induce wage-earners to examine their relations to the industrial system as a whole and to be loyal to the industrial system as a whole rather than to any narrow and mistaken opinion of class interest. The whole idea of separate class interests is an illusion and, if cherished, fatal to the welfare of all classes.

These men, Hobbesian in their distrust of people as motivated chiefly by self-interest and greed, frightened by the rise of urban ghettoes and labor violence and concerned about foreign trade wars and invasions, placed their faith in the military model for protection and social control. As Lt. Gen. Samuel Young (U.S.A., Ret.), president of the Association of National Service, confided in 1916, "The urgent need for a system of National Military Training for America is not military at all, but economic." It was needed to form the "habits of personal hygiene, discipline and respect for authority and, through service to the State, a love of and devotion to the fundamental ideals of Democracy." General Leonard Wood was even more direct. "I am for the universal service," the former chief of staff told a congressional committee, "even if I knew we were never to have a war, for its moral and physical training and building up of the citizenship-responsibility idea, which is so largely lacking in this country." To those who seek stability, order, and unity, nothing appears so comforting as long, neat rows of soldiers marching behind the flag, all so uniform, so orderly, and so reliable.

During 1915 and 1916, the conscriptionists worked through newspapers and magazines, through speeches, lobbying, preparedness parades, and Plattsburg encampments to ally military, business, and professional groups behind the movement for universal military training. Aided by the mass media, they sought to discredit the National Guard and the U.S. Volunteers as historically unreliable and politically dominated and to enhance the image of the regular army that for years had been pictured as a refuge for criminals, sluggards, and industrial failures. The conscriptionists interpreted the lessons of America's past wars, of England's current wartime experience, and of the 1916 mobilization of the National Guard on the Mexican border against Francisco "Pancho" Villa. History showed (the admirers of UMT said) that the volunteer method failed to supply enough troops, took essential workers and managers, created undue hardship for the patriotic, their families, and their employers, disrupted the economy, and was unnecessarily expensive.

By the winter of 1916–1917, their propaganda campaign seems to have convinced significant numbers of public opinion leaders throughout the country. Polls showed compulsory military training and service supported by 270 major newspapers, more than two hundred mayors representing cities with nearly eighteen million residents, and by local chambers of commerce in every state but one. Some conscriptionists believed that universal military training might be adopted by Congress during 1917.

Yet the United States probably would never have adopted conscription without the country's entry into World War I. Among the masses of citizens and the majority of lawmakers, antimilitarism and reliance upon America's traditional safeguards—the navy, the National Guard, and the U.S. Volunteers—remained too strong and the necessity for conscription too vague. Only a minority of Americans really believed the conscriptionists' warnings that the country was in danger of invasion, and most denied that the volunteer system had failed. The country responded to danger in the traditional manner, by reinforcing existing institutions and forming temporary voluntary associations. Those who thought there was a need for increased national defense often joined organizations for military drill or target practice like the Plattsburg training camps, the National Guard, and the hundreds of military units being established by schools, clubs, and businesses. By the end of 1916, 1.5 million persons had engaged in formal rifle shooting, and several hundred thousand had taken military drill. Although many of these voluntary trainees, like the "Plattsburgers" urged compulsory military training, the majority of Americans continued to reject compulsion. Even after the diplomatic break with Germany, the Senate quietly tabled a UMT bill that had been recommended by the military affairs committee, and the House blocked an attempt to rush the bill through as a rider.

Opposition to the conscription crusade came especially from the South and the trans-Mississippi West with their strong traditions of dedication to local institutions and hostility to the wealthy financiers and industrialists of New York and Chicago. Many farmers, workers, and some merchants in this rural heartland became increasingly suspicious of the movement for conscription because it was dominated by wealthy urban interests, the metropolitan press and professional army officers.

These rural anticonscriptionists believed in the traditional Jeffersonian values of individual liberty, equality, majority rule, and local self-government. Freedom concerned them more than duty. They distrusted the experts of the newly created general staff, and they considered the military inimical to democracy and reform and they suspected that Wall Street and the military had joined in what William Jennings Bryan called the "Munitions-Militarist Conspiracy." Furthermore, these agrarians generally opposed American involvement in the commercial and dynastic struggles of Europe, saw little danger to the United States for years to come, and condemned the conscriptionist schemes as requiring an unnecessary drain on farm labor and an unjustified tax increase.

With over half the population of the country living in rural areas, opposition to conscription from the Grange, the Farmers Union, and other agrarian groups carried considerable influence in Congress. Midwestern progressive Republicans, such as Senators La Follette of Wisconsin, Norris of Nebraska, and Gronna of North Dakota, and many Southern Bryanite Democrats led by House Majority Leader Claude Kitchin of North Carolina thundered against compulsory military service or an exclusively national army in 1916 and early 1917.

After the declaration of war, they attacked conscription as a device to force the poor to fight without adequate wages in a foreign war three thousand miles away. They argued instead for the volunteer system so that the war would be fought by those who wanted to fight it. They wanted men to serve together in local units under officers they knew and trusted.

Included among these anticonscriptionist politicians were many Southerners who feared that compulsory national military training would endanger local white supremacy and perhaps lead to armed rebellion by the blacks in the South. Blatant racists like Vardaman of Mississippi, Watson of Georgia, Blease of South Carolina, and Catts of Florida vigorously opposed conscription, which, as Vardaman explained, would put "arrogant strutting representatives of the black soldiery in every community." Some sought to prevent black men from being accepted in the regular army or even from being drafted once the country joined the war. The Southerners tried to maintain the National Guard and the U.S. Volunteers that would allow communities to respond to the call for troops without disturbing local institutions and race relations.

Some black leaders such as James Weldon Johnson, the New York columnist and author, urged the adoption of universal military training as a major step toward recognition of equal rights as well as duties for black Americans. Johnson blamed Southern racists for blocking UMT. Later, he sharply criticized what he called the "Jim Crow Wilson Administration" for advocating a selective draft to select only whites, at least for combat service. If blacks were drafted at all, Johnson predicted in 1917, it would be for menial tasks that would not help their claim for equal citizenship.

Although Secretary of War Newton Baker refused to exempt blacks from the draft, he did assure the Southern-dominated House Military Affairs Committee that black soldiers would be segregated and that the administration would not threaten the social structure of the South. At the same time, the draft administrator suggested to the congressmen a plan to keep blacks working in the cotton fields during the war. Many Southern representatives appear to have been assuaged by this, for many of them eventually voted in favor of wartime conscription that in effect nationalized the military establishment and directly involved the War Department in race relations in the South.[2]

Not all opposition came from rural areas; labor organizations formed a second major element in the voluntarist forces. The United Mine Workers and many union locals and city labor councils bitterly attacked a movement that they feared was aimed at breaking unions and strikes. So did more radical workingmen's organizations such as the Industrial Workers of the World, with its strength among the miners and lumberjacks of the West. Anarchists and Socialists scattered in New York, Chicago, San Francisco, Milwaukee, and a host of smaller cities as well as in the sharecropping regions of Oklahoma and Texas assailed compulsory military service. Worker opposition was weakened, however, by the policy of Samuel Gompers and most of the leadership of the American Federation of Labor. The A.F. of L. opposed universal military training in peacetime, but it endorsed Wilson's expansion of the army in 1916 and 1917 and offered only perfunctory opposition to the selective draft bill.

Many immigrants who had fled their native lands partly to avoid European conscription or who sympathized with the Central powers against the Allies belonged in the anticonscriptionist camp. Millions of German-

Americans, Irish–Americans who hated the British, and Russian Jewish–Americans who bitterly recalled the Czarist pogroms, felt little desire to be drafted or have their sons drafted into service on the side of England and Russia. However, many of the immigrant leaders supported the administration, and, after the declaration of war, pledged their loyalty to their adopted country. Although antiwar and antidraft sentiment remained strong among these ethnic groups during the first year of American belligerency, no major antidraft movement emanated from the ethnic areas.

The rather amorphous anticonscriptionist sentiment among farmers, workers, immigrants, and others lacked central leadership, but a handful of urban liberal pacifists sought to supply it. The American Union against Militarism (AUAM) was formed by such social workers as Lillian Wald, Jane Addams, and Paul Kellog; journalists such as Oswald Garrison Villard of the *Nation* and the *New York Post* and Max Eastman of the *Masses*; labor lawyers including Crystal Eastman, Amos Pinchot, and Hollingsworth Wood, the Quaker chairman of the Urban League; and ministers such as Unitarian John Haynes Holmes and Presbyterian Norman Thomas.

As with the conscriptionists, the leaders of the American Union against Militarism came from old established or professional families in New England or the Middle Atlantic states, attended prestigious Eastern colleges, and then took up residence in New York City. However, the pacifists included women as well as men, and their careers and attitudes differed sharply from the conscriptionists' pattern of corporate or military success. Instead these antimilitarists had responded to the needs of groups that found themselves exploited and suppressed in urban-industrial America. Active reformers, generally progresssive Republicans but including a few Socialists, they campaigned for legislation to guarantee equal rights and opportunities for women, blacks, and recent European immigrants.

Having put their faith in education and public regulation and improvement—a few of them even encouraged union organization—these pacifistic progressives feared war and militarism as totally destructive to their promotion of peaceful achievement of liberty and democracy. They held an optimistic belief in humankind and in the ability to enhance life through the improvement of the urban and international environment. Consequently, they shuddered at the idea of mass military training that they thought would destroy individual responsibility and initiative and cripple the people's ability to govern themselves. Fearing unrestricted power, even in the hands of the government, they warned that military and industrial interests sought to create a subservience to the state just as heinous as the slavery of the Old South.

Raising its limited funds primarily from Philadelphia Quakers, wealthy New York women, and the members of its own executive committee, the American Union against Militarism staged a propaganda campaign to counter the conscriptionists' arguments and to work for peaceful international mediation. Beginning in the spring of 1916, the AUAM attacked compulsory military training and service as an expensive departure from American tradition that would suppress reform at home and encourage jingoism abroad. Even after the United States declared war, AUAM leaders warned that the people would not stand for such a violation of American principles and that enforcement of the draft would trigger rioting and bloodshed in the streets.

Although some of the pacifists put their faith exclusively in international mediation and the barrier of the vast oceans to keep America secure, most anticonscriptionists relied on the navy and the traditional military system. Some advocated drastic changes in the regular army including shorter terms of service and longer periods in the civilian reserve, higher pay (even snow-shovellers earned more than a private's wages of $15 a month). Some proposed vocational training, more attractive surroundings and daily routine, and democratization of the army through elimination of the caste system that separated officers and enlisted men. A number of anticonscriptionists had argued successfully in 1916 for a program to expand the National Guard. Others continued to urge reliance on local volunteer units in wartime under the new Volunteer Act of 1914.

But the volunteer system never received a fair trial in 1917. The general staff and the administration committed themselves to a National Draft Army and held only a mild recruiting campaign for the regulars and the National Guardsmen. Even the War Department itself later admitted that recruiting had not been intensive during the war. Offers from Theodore Roosevelt, Polish–American leaders, and others to raise several volunteer divisions for service overseas were rejected by President Wilson. The government summarily abandoned the volunteer system in World War I despite evidence that it could have provided adequate home defense and even a reasonable expeditionary force.

War proved the catalyst that ended established traditions. The president as commander in chief obtains, in wartime, enormous legal and latent powers to unite the nation behind his policies. When the president decided for war and a selective draft, he received vital backing from the press and the conscriptionist organizations. Together they undermined the remaining support for the local volunteer tradition. The president cajoled, then threatened, recalcitrant congressmen who wanted to call for volunteers first. The conscriptionists and the metropolitan press worked to arouse grass roots support for the draft by urging local editors and businessmen to exert pressure on the congressmen whom they accused of "blocking the President in his fight against Germany" and giving "aid and comfort to the enemy."

An avalanche of mail cascaded upon Capitol Hill, and the letters showed that, although many Americans still opposed the draft, "the most substantial citizens" in communities throughout the country endorsed the administration's plan for temporary and selective conscription. This plan would exempt skilled industrial workers and managers and critical farm labor. Businessmen, professionals, and many farm leaders believed that the draft would keep necessary workers at home and send the unskilled, the unessential, and the "slackers"—idlers, delinquents, and the unassimilated immigrants—into the army. Although most politicians spoke of compelling the sons of the rich to fight alongside the poor, the English experience had shown that those of comfortable means were the first to volunteer and that conscription was used to force the alienated and the lower-income groups into military services. "I implore you [to] vote for conscription," one Chicago executive wrote to various members of Congress, "and let the loafers and unsympathetic naturalized foreigners do their part." Many others also demonstrated this loss of faith in the ability of voluntarism to produce an equitable response, across class and ethnic lines, by the entire community.

Bowing to enormous pressure, the House of Representatives staged one of the most complete reversals in its history and in three weeks swung from opposition to endorsement of the draft. Tempers flared and party lines snapped as traditionalists sought to halt the stampede, but in the end Congress gave the president essentially what he wanted. In the key vote, the lawmakers accepted conscription by three to one in the House and four to one in the Senate. Representatives from the urban Northeast provided the most united backing for the draft. The voluntarists clustered in the delegations from the rural southern and western states. The Senate, which has been more fully examined by historians, clearly divided along ideological as well as sectional lines. The majority of reformers there attacked the draft bill that had the support of virtually every conservative in the upper chamber. Acceding to the inevitable, Senator Hiram Johnson, a California progressive, cautioned his colleagues that Americans unlike other peoples had little knowledge of drastic restrictive measures and had enjoyed more liberty than most other men. "The draft," he prophesied, "will be a rude awakening."

The revolutionary change in American military policy encompassed in the adoption of the wartime draft in the spring of 1917 resulted from both circumstance and design. America was emerging as an urban, industrial, and highly heterogeneous nation; and a group of Eastern patricians and businessmen sought to create a military establishment that they believed would be commensurate with the needs of this new colossus. Even with major newspaper support, their conscription crusade failed to achieve permanent universal military training, but it did create the climate of opinion that resulted after the American declaration of war in the abandonment of the volunteer tradition and adoption of a wartime selective draft based on universal male military liability to service.

U.S. entry into the war and the president's decision to demand the draft were as essential as the conscriptionist campaign and the support of the press to the adoption of compulsory military service, but so too was the changing attitude of American elites. Community leaders had lost their faith in the ability of traditional institutions such as local volunteering to function equitably and effectively in raising troops during wartime. They believed that the best men would go and the worst stay behind, and as a result they supported the selective draft in which the government rather than the individual would decide where each man would serve his country. This, as the president's confidential secretary later remarked, was the argument that won for wartime conscription.

This attitude reflected a sense of the loss of community homogeneity and mirrored new beliefs in rational planning and order, and compulsion as a necessary concomitant. As the *New York Tribune* commented after the crucial vote on the draft:

> It has been an up-hill fight to overcome the tradition of voluntaryism. The idea that one may serve the State or not, as he pleases, had taken deep root in our easygoing American individualism. It fitted in with the loose structure of our national organization and with our frontiersman habits of thought. In young and sparsely settled countries volunteering is in harmony with popular temper. . . . But in a country which has attained, or is attaining, its growth, where economic and industrial conditions are complex, volunteering handicaps efficiency. It hampers national effort, because it prevents unification and scientific selection. It is a policy of muddling and waste.

Yet the draft was no more inevitable than the scale on which the United States eventually participated in the war. Alternatives had been available more in keeping with the traditional American values of localism, voluntarism, and distrust of the professional officer corps. Indeed, a volunteer army of 500,000 to 1,000,000 men would have been more suited to the kind of economic and naval warfare that many in April 1917 saw as America's major role in the war. It might have limited the country's military response to a more traditional pattern. Only the draft permitted the eventual raising of an army of four million men to fight in the trenches of Europe. Significantly, not until the day he signed the Draft Act did President Wilson announce that he was sending an American Expeditionary Force to France.

The adoption of the draft in World War I represented a victory for the values of a cosmopolitan urban-industrial elite over localistic rural-agrarian traditions, but the victory was not complete. Local elites had supported conscription only as a temporary wartime measure, and after the armistice, even though the president, his secretary of war, the general staff, and many of the old conscriptionists argued for permanent peacetime universal military training, Congress refused to adopt it. With the war over, the necessity for such an expensive and radical policy disappeared, and the revival of civilian contempt and neglect of the military pared the Army practically to its prewar status—a small, isolated appendage to society.

Nevertheless, there had been a revolutionary change in military policy. The country might not be ready to accept peacetime conscription, but it had agreed to primary reliance upon a national wartime draft for the first time in its history and sent its first conscripts overseas. The military and its civilian allies successfully relied upon such public acceptance of a draft in time of war or national emergency in their preparations for fighting the country's battles for at least the next fifty years, until the war in Vietnam caused a major reexamination of the necessity and compatibility of conscription in American society.

NOTES

1. Analysis showed that the avearge age in 1916 was fifty-seven; 29 percent were born in mid-Atlantic states; 73 percent claimed descent from pre-Revolutionary War families; 52 percent were children of professionals or businessmen; 76 percent were college graduates (43 percent Ivy League graduates); 83 percent of those whose religion could be determined were Episcopalian or Presbyterian; 72 percent of those whose party affiliation could be ascertained were Republican; and 35 percent had previous service with the military or with the War Department. Biographical data were obtained from the *Dictionary of American Biography, National Cyclopedia of American Biography, Who's Who in America,* and obituaries in the *New York Times.*
2. The Southerners apparently wanted assurance that the blacks would be exempted for work in the cotton fields but that southern whites would not be required to make up the remainder of the quota. U.S. Congress, House Committee on Military Affairs, *Increase of the Military Establishment: Hearings,* pp. 28, 259; General Crowder suggested that blacks could be exempted if the president ruled cotton an essential industry because of its relation to explosives. Informal memorandum from E. H. Crowder to Sen. McKellar of Tennessee, April 17, 1917, Crowder MSS, Box 2.

27

Uncle Sam's Little War in the Arkansas Ozarks

"I didn't raise my boy to be a soldier," began a popular song of 1916. Opposition to conscription was considerable; some 300,000 failed to respond to the call altogether, and tens of thousands deserted within thirty days, never to be seen again.* In 1919, the Literary Digest *reprinted this account of the response of one localistic rural community in Arkansas to the draft.*

*Secretary of War Newton D. Baker to President Woodrow Wilson, 13 May 1920, Box 13, N. D. Baker Papers, Manuscripts Division, Library of Congress. (I am indebted to Professor Edward Coffman for making me aware of this letter.)

WHEN THE UNITED STATES entered the war with Germany, Cecil Cove did not. This little valley in the remote fastnesses of the North Arkansas Ozarks practically seceded from the Union for the duration of the war. The older men cooperated with the eligibles to resist the draft. They defied Uncle Sam, being well stocked with arms and prepared to hold out indefinitely in their hiding-places. When they finally gave up it was by no means an unconditional surrender, for the authorities accepted all the terms of the slacker gang, after a number of attempts to round them up had proved unsuccessful. A writer in the Kansas City *Star* attributes the incident to "a combination of plain ignorance, Jeff Davis politics, *The Appeal to Reason*, and mountain religion." He adds that another fact may throw some light on the happenings in Cecil Cove, namely, that "it was a notorious hiding-place for men who were neither Federals nor Confederates in the Civil War," and who "found a refuge in the caves and fastnesses of the Cove exactly as did the slacker gang of 1917–1918."

Cecil Cove—some twelve miles long and eight miles wide—lies high up

SOURCE: "Uncle Sam's Little War in the Arkansas Ozarks," *Literary Digest*, 8 March 1919, pp. 107 ff.

in Newton County, which has not been penetrated by the railroad. The people there form an isolated mountain community, suspicious yet hospitable, reticent, "trained and accustomed to arms," and also trained and accustomed, boys and girls, men and women alike, to using tobacco, as snuffers, smokers, and chewers. If we are to believe *The Star*, they are "unerring spitters," and "the youngest of the family is considered deserving of a reprimand if he can not hit the fireplace at ten paces."

When the news of the draft came the Cove prepared for war, but not with Germany. To quote *The Star*:

> The country roundabout was scoured for high-power rifles. Stocks of the Harrison and Jasper stores were pretty well depleted. Repeating rifles of 30–30 caliber and great range and precision began to reach the Cove from mail-order houses. Quantities of ammunition were bought—report has it that "Uncle Lige" Harp bought nearly $60 worth at one time in Harrison.

A number of young men were drafted, but refused to report for duty. The sheriff sent word he was coming after them, but seems to have thought better of it when he received the answer: "Come on, but look out for yourself!" Four United States marshals or deputies, several special investigators, and an army colonel all visited Newton County in turn, did some questioning and searching, and alike returned empty handed. We read in *The Star* that the people in the Cove were all related through intermarriage, and practically all of them were in sympathy with the slackers. They agreed to stick together, and it has been reported that some sort of covenant was signed. The Cove, we are told, "is a region of multifarious hiding places, studded with boulders and pocketed with caves; a searcher might pass within six feet of a dozen hidden men and see none of them." It is reached and penetrated only by steep mountain-trails, which are easily threaded by the "sure-footed mountain horses and mules and their equally sure-footed owners," but which are almost impassable to strangers. Moreover, continues the writer in *The Star*:

> So perfect were means of observation and communication a stranger could not enter the Cove at any point without that fact being known to all its inhabitants before the intruder had got along half a mile.
>
> Nearly all the families in the Cove have telephones. It is a remarkable fact that these mountaineers will do without the meanest comforts of life, but they insist upon having telephones. This and the other varied methods of intercourse, peculiar to the mountains, gave the Cecil Cove slackers an almost unbeatable combination. They always knew where the searchers were and what they were doing, but the searchers never were able to find anything except a blind trail.
>
> The telephone-lines might have been cut, but that would have served little purpose. News travels by strange and devious processes in the mountains. The smoke of a brush-fire high up on a peak may have little significance to the uninitiated, but it may mean considerable to an Ozark mountaineer. The weird, long-drawn-out Ozark yell, "Hia-a-ahoo-o-o" may sound the same always to

a man from the city, but there are variations of it that contain hidden significances. And the mountaineer afoot travels with amazing speed, even along those broken trails. Bent forward, walking with a characteristic shuffle, he can scurry over boulder and fallen log like an Indian.

A deputy marshal "with a reputation as a killer" spent a month in Newton County, but made no arrests, telling some one that it would be "nothing short of suicide" for an officer to try to capture the slacker gang. The officer second in command at Camp Pike, Little Rock, took a hand in the affair and told the county officials that some of his men who were "sore at being unable to go across to France" would be very glad to "come up and clear out these slackers." But about this time the War Department offered something like amnesty to the Cove gang and apparently promised that a charge of desertion would not be pressed if the men were to give themselves up. Word was passed around, whether or not from official sources, that the boys would be "gone only from sixty to ninety days, that they would all get a suit of clothes and a dollar a day." At the same time a new sheriff, Frank Carlton, came into office. He knew the neighborhood and its people. He got in touch with some of the leaders of the hiding men and finally had an interview with two of them. They agreed to give themselves up if certain concessions were made and finally told the sheriff to meet them alone and unarmed and thus accompany them to Little Rock. As we read:

> The next day the gang met the sheriff at the lonely spot agreed upon. They caught a mail-coach and rode to Harrison and then were taken to Camp Pike.
> The morning after their arrival Joel Arnold asked the sheriff:
> "Do they feed like this all the time?"
> The sheriff replied that they had received the ordinary soldier fare.
> "We've been a passel of fools," Arnold replied.

The slackers are still held in custody at Camp Pike, and, according to the writer in *The Star*, authorities there will make no statement as to the procedure contemplated in the case. In showing how such different influences as religion, socialism, and sheer ignorance operated, the writer lets certain of the Cove leaders speak for themselves. Uncle Lige Harp backed up the slackers strongly with all of his great influence in the community. "Uncle Lige" is now an old man, but in his younger days had the reputation of being a "bad man." He tells with glee of a man who once said he would "just as soon meet a grizzly bear on the trail as meet Lige Harp." In his heyday Uncle Lige "was accounted a dead shot—one who could put out a turkey's left eye at one hundred yards every shot." Here are Uncle Lige's views:

> "We-all don't take no truck with strangers and we didn't want our boys takin' no truck with furriners. We didn't have no right to send folks over to Europe to fight; 'tain't a free country when that's done. Wait till them Germans come over here and then fight 'em is what I said when I heard 'bout the war. If

anybody was to try to invade this country ever' man in these hills would git his rifle and pick 'em off."

"Aunt Sary" Harp, between puffs at her clay pipe, nodded her approval of "Uncle Lige's" position.

France Sturdgil and Jim Blackwell say they are Socialists. They have read scattering copies of *The Appeal to Reason*. To be fair, it should be added that this Socialist paper, now *The New Appeal*, has taken an attitude in support of the Government's war-policy. Said Sturdgil:

"It's war for the benefit of them silk-hatted fellers up in New York. We don't want our boys fightin' them rich fellers' battles and gittin' killed just to make a lot of money for a bunch of millionaires. Why, they own most of the country now."

To the writer of the *Star* article this sounds very much like the sort of argument which Jeff Davis used for many years in persuading the "hill billies" of Arkansas to elect him regularly to the United States Senate. George Slape, the Cove's religious leader, is "a prayin' man."

"The good book says, 'Thou shalt not kill.' We didn't want our boys takin' nobody's life. It ain't right 'cause it's contrary to the Bible and the good Lord's teachin's," declared Slape.

Asked to explain the difference between fighting Germans and preparing to resist the draft authorities, both likely to result in death, Slape said:

"The boys wasn't goin' to kill nobody unless they had to. It's different killing a man who tries to make you do wrong and killin' somebody in war."

None of these leaders ever admitted they knew anything about where the boys were hiding. It was a common report that the slackers "lived at home except on those occasions when an officer was discovered to be prowling about." It is the Ozark way: "nobody ever has seen a hunted man, tho a rustling of the leaves, the crackling of a dead twig, might betray the fact that the fugitive was there only a moment before."

Cecil Cove had its loyal men. At least one young man defied home opinion and threats of violence by reporting for duty when he was drafted. He was sent to France and became an excellent soldier. Loyal citizens living on the fringe of the Cove were shot at and threatened on a number of occasions, and several were ordered to keep away from the community. "Uncle Jimmy" Richardson, a Confederate veteran, loyal and fearless, was not afraid to go straight to some of the parents of the slackers and tell them what he thought of them.

"You're a gang of yellow bellies," he said. "If you've got any manhood in you, them boys will be made to go and serve their country."

"Uncle Jimmy" got his answer one day when he ventured a little way into the Cove. A shot rang out and a bullet whistled past his ear.

"The cowardly hounds wouldn't fight fair," he said. "In the old days of the Civil War them kind was swung up to the nearest tree. I'm past seventy-three now, but I'd have got down my rifle and gone in with anybody that would have went after them. I don't like to live near folks who ain't Americans."

"Uncle Jimmy" does not speak to the slacker folks in the Cove now. He says he never will again. If he did, he says, he would feel ashamed of the more than a dozen wounds that he received in the Civil War.

Loyalists in the Cove were forced by fear into what amounted to a state of neutrality. "We couldn't risk having our homes burned down or our stock killed, let alone anything worse," said one of them, who added "I'm not afraid of any man face to face, but it is a different proposition when you're one against thirty-six, and them with all the advantage and willin' to go anything." . . .

28

The American Military
and the Melting Pot in World War I

BRUCE WHITE

The military had for many years drawn heavily upon the foreign-born population for its recruits and had long maintained separate black and Indian units. But World War I saw the entry into military service of such persons in numbers several orders of magnitude greater than at any time since the Civil War. Bruce White describes the military's designs regarding this population during the world war in this essay.

AMERICAN MILITARY HISTORY has in the past seemed barren ground to students of social history. They have left the field to historians primarily interested in strategy, technology, or political relationships, to sociologists such as Morris Janowitz, and to Civil War buffs and others who write "bugles in the afternoon" histories of warfare. There are probably two reasons for this. First, the American military during most of the history of the United States has seemed weak and isolated from the mainstream of American life. Second, since army officers are admitted social conservatives who do not consider the army a proper agency to initiate social reforms, it has appeared that any study of military social thought would be dull reading indeed, and perhaps the shortest book ever written.

Nonetheless, the army's experiences with ethnic and racial minorities

SOURCE: Bruce White, "The American Military and the Melting Pot in World War I," in *War and Society in North America*, eds. J. L. Granatstein and R. D. Cuff (Toronto: Thomas Nelson & Sons, 1971), pp. 37–51. Reprinted by permission of the author and the publisher.
EDITOR'S NOTE: Most of the citations to the sources consulted by the author in this essay have been omitted from this volume for brevity and economy. The reader should consult the original source of the essay for the complete scholarly documentation.

constitute an important and neglected aspect of American social history. Immigrants, blacks, and Indians who served in the army during peacetime were affected in various ways,[1] and during major wars the attention of the nation has been focused on military activities and thus on ethnic and racial minorities in the army. The opportunity thus existed for creating a more favourable public image of minorities and for stimulating a sense of identity among members of minority groups themselves.

The Civil War is a good example of a conflict which benefited the immigrant. As Maldwyn Jones has shown, nativism declined because of "the realization that, in the new situation brought about by the war, immigrants were not a menace to the existing order but one of its stoutests props." Moreover, military service in national units stimulated a sense of identity among immigrant nationalities. "The many thousands who fought for the Union," Jones concludes, "did so upon terms of equality with the native population, and thus lost the sense of inferiority which had dogged them since their coming to America." The potential for social change was even greater during the First World War, although the handicaps to be overcome were also more considerable. The immigrant was on the defensive because of the adverse reaction to the "new immigration" from Southern and Eastern Europe, because of the fact that certain nationalities could be identified as the enemy or possibly in sympathy with him, and because of the growing fear of "bolshevism." In such a situation ethnic groups needed, even more than during the Civil War, the opportunity to display their commitment to America by forming national units.

In this situation military policy was to prove on the whole detrimental to immigrant needs. Since the 1890s the army had been hostile to the enlistment of immigrants, but military attitudes began to change as the European situation deteriorated. Army officers began to campaign for their panacea of preparedness through universal military training. This coincided with the increasingly popular Americanization movement in the United States, and the army was quick to see the possibilities this movement offered in furthering the cause of universal training; the army could provide the needed alembic for the Americanization of the immigrant. Unleashing their verbal armouries against the traditional educational institutions of the home, family, church, and school, military men charged that these agencies had left the immigrants concentrated in urban ghettos, speaking only their native tongues and clinging to their former customs. Obviously, concluded General Leonard Wood, the high priest of preparedness, some institution should remove them from this physical and mental environment and force them to make outside contacts so that they might "speak American and think American." It took very little imagination to guess which institution Wood believed could best do the job.

Ironically, what had been a rationale for universal military training turned into unpleasant reality after the declaration of war on April 6th, 1917 and the subsequent Selective Service Act, which provided for the registration for military service of all men between the ages of 21 and 30, inclusive. The problems created by the massive influx into the army of non-English-speaking aliens and illiterate native Americans were all too real. The widely publicized statistic that 24.9 per cent of those drafted were unable to read and understand a newspaper or write letters home was too high, but it revealed the extent of the problem. Convinced that in the army everyone must be treated alike, many officers and NCO's were highly frustrated when it became apparent that those who could not understand simple military commands in English would have to be treated differently. An officer at Camp Meade may have been exaggerating when he claimed that the first time he called roll not a single man recognized his own name, but that when he sneezed ten men stepped forward; his point was made, though, about the lack of communication. The potential for misunderstandings was great, and often an alien's lack of compliance was misinterpreted as stupidity or surliness. At one camp a recruit reportedly had his jaw broken and some teeth knocked out by a sergeant who became enraged when the private could not spell his own name. In another instance a Polish recruit was court-martialled for answering a question in Polish, and a Russian spent six weeks in the guardhouse for evading the draft before it was learned he had been arrested before receiving his draft notice. Not being able to speak English, he could not communicate this fact.

Naturally, those who could not understand commands in English could not be sent into battle, at least in integrated units. Such men, as well as those considered security risks, the physically handicapped, and others who were simply not wanted for one reason or another, usually ended up in depot brigades in the South, where they were put to work at menial tasks such as kitchen and police duty. The army's ultimate response to this potentially dangerous situation was the establishment in May 1918 of development battalions, which were to be set up in each National Army, National Guard, and Regular Army divisional camp. The battalions were to be filled with those considered unfit for general service, and the officers of these battalions were to decide which of them were capable of being trained for some duty, to train these, and to discharge all others. The order specifically stated that all soldiers with an insufficient knowledge of English were to be transferred to these units.

As a result of preliminary experiments with instruction in English in the battalions, the War Department issued a circular in July 1918 directing the establishment of schools to teach English. Classes were to be normally for four months, with instruction from two to three hours daily, preferably in small groups and segregated according to progress. A designated officer was to be in charge of each school, attendance was to be compulsory, and the Y.M.C.A. was to furnish instructors, books and other supplies. The Y.M.C.A. system of instruction for foreign-born adults, developed by Peter Roberts and featuring oral instructions and carefully structured lessons dealing with everyday experiences, was adapted for military use. The curriculum was subsequently broadened to include French, American history and government, citizenship, and geography.

Most instruction in the schools continued to be given by army officers and enlisted men, although the educational secretaries of the Y.M.C.A. supervised the work, conducted normal school courses for instructors, and did some of the teaching themselves. Volunteers from nearby communities also were recruited as instructors. As early as February 1918, almost 25,000 illiterates and non-English-speaking soldiers were receiving instruction, and by the end of the war, despite a variety of problems including personnel and unit transfers and a chronic shortage of textbooks, equipment and supplies, 107 development battalions were in operation.

The development battalions might well have been a vehicle for creating a favourable public image of ethnic groups and might even have been a force toward cultural pluralism had they resulted in the creation of large ethnic units. It must have occurred to military men that a thorough knowledge of English was not so vital for the rank and file had this been done. The War Department did, in fact, draw up a memorandum recommending that the battalions be subdivided into companies by nationality and that the officers and non-commissioned officers of each company be of the same nationality as their men, or at least familiar with that ethnic group. In one of the two earliest experiments with development battalions, at Camp Gordon, Georgia, Major Bernard Lentz of the Operations Division of the General Staff divided the battalion into two companies, a Slavic one under Polish and Russian-speaking officers, and an Italian one under officers of that nationality. He not only initiated intensive instruction in English, but also instituted a broad indoctrination and training program and special activities and religious services. More sensitive than most army officers to ethnic needs and problems, he even instructed the cooks to prepare racially and religiously acceptable food.

The Camp Gordon plan was highly successful, and ethnic segregation, as well as the other aspects of Lentz's program, was begun at other camps. The potential inherent in this concept was not realized, however. This was partly due to the exigencies of the situation and partly because of the opposition of high-ranking officers who argued that aliens could better learn English when integrated into units of English-speaking soldiers. In addition, they concluded, the time and expense involved in transportation to the new units and the training of them could be saved. Undoubtedly, many officers also worried about the potential for enemy propaganda.

The major reason, however, for the lack of more enthusiasm for the creation of national units from the development battalions was that the focus throughout the war was on the enlistment of "foreign legions." The War Department announced in March 1918 that it opposed such organizations. "It is not the policy of the United States Army," wrote Brigadier General Henry Jervey to Isaac Kushner, "to encourage or permit the formation of distinctive brigades, regiments, battalions or other organizations composed exclusively or primarily of the members of any race, creed or political or social group. This policy will be adhered to whether the proposed recruit unit is intended for service within the American Army, or with the armies of our Allies."

If the War Department was really serious about Americanization, then this alone might explain its stand. But the circumstances surrounding the announcement suggest there were other motivations. First, the War Department had been resisting without much success the recruitment of aliens in the United States not subject to the American draft for service in Allied armies. Second, Isaac Kushner was one of three civilians who had sent a telegram to President Wilson advocating recruitment of American Socialists into a "Red Guard" to fight in Russia against the Germans. The War Department viewed this proposal with less than unbounded enthusiasm. Third, the army had been urged by H. A. Garfield, United States Fuel Administrator, and by representatives of the coal industry, to resist attempts by Polish workmen to organize an army because they were needed in the mining districts.

During the following two months the controversy over "foreign legions" continued to centre on the question of Polish volunteers, and although other armies now had the authority for enlistment of Poles in the United States, their enlistment as a national unit in the American army was still opposed by the War Department. This was partly because of the resolute opposition of General Pershing to ethnic units and the expressed opinion of the War Plans Division that if this request were granted "a precedent would be set which, if followed in other cases, would tend toward inefficiency by greatly complicating the military machine."

A dramatic reversal, however, was about to take place. President Wilson and Marshal Foch were favourable to the formation of such units; the advantages of utilizing the services of many Poles, Yugoslavs, Czechoslovaks, and Ruthenians who were eager to fight in the American army but could not because they were technically enemy aliens were obvious. The potential dangers in ignoring them were also clear. The moral effect "of large, powerful, nationalistic units," wrote Brigadier General Lytle Brown, Director of the War Plans Division, "fighting for the freedom of their compatriots will be of inestimable value." The lack of commitment of the army to Americanization was revealed when a staff report concluded that "It may rightly be claimed that such segregation of races into regiments, etc., does not make American citizens and possibly this is true, but we are not in this war to make more American citizens, we are in to win the war. . . ."

As a result of the War Department's change of attitude, a Slavic Legion was authorized by Congress in July 1918. Arrangements were made for local draft boards to act as recruiting agencies for the Legion, but the war ended before the plan could be carried out. Nonetheless, the immigrant was to loom large in army plans for the future, for the success of the development battalions set military minds to thinking. By the beginning of 1919 a movement was under way to continue the concept in the peacetime army as part of a broader program of educational and vocational training, the so-called "university in khaki" concept. The objective was, as usual, universal military training, and once again army officers argued that since civilian Americanization agencies had failed to do their job the army must step in.

Taking advantage of wartime emergency powers, recruiting officers began the enlistment of illiterates and non-English-speaking aliens and citizens for a period of three years. Recruiting was actively pursued by means of posters in foreign-speaking localities, advertisements in the foreign language press and other means, but confined to members of the white race. Aliens were required to declare their intention of becoming citizens before they could enlist. Immediately following induction, illiterates and non-English-speaking recruits were sent to the Recruit Educational Center at Camp Upton, New York, where they were taught English and instructed in the duties of a good soldier and citizen. At the end of their three-year term of service aliens would receive their final naturalization papers and be sent forth into the world to spread the army's version of what it meant to be a good citizen.

The army was successful in obtaining authorization in June 1920 for the peacetime enlistment of non-English-speaking citizens and aliens and five additional Recruit Educational Centers were established to supplement the original center. A course entitled *Army Lessons in English* had already been prepared, designed not only to teach English but also to inculcate citizenship and to influence the civilian community as well. The first project was a letter home by the end of the first two weeks, to be followed by others. Suggestions were made as to content and, of course, these were more than suggestions since they were almost the only English words the recruit knew. The results must have been disturbing to some civilians. In the first lesson, for example, one of the assigned sentences was "We want to learn to use a gun, a book and a pencil." Suggestions for letters included encouragement for others to enlist, for improved sanitation methods, and warnings of the dangers of bolshevism. The more advanced English lessons concentrated on stories of immigrants who had been successful, on native American and foreign heroes, and on vignettes of military life with a moral. One of the stories, entitled "The American Way," included the following:

'You did!' shouted José, madly. 'Don't tell me I did,' yelled Rudolf. And as José seized a knife from the mess table, Rudolf picked up a chair and swung it at the wrathful José's head.

With a leap, Sergeant Hart sprang between the two men. 'Stop that!' he ordered. 'Drop that knife and put down that chair. We will not stand for any European methods of settling arguments around here.'[2]

In a visit to Camp Upton, Willis Fletcher Johnson also found that recruits were being taught the army version of economics:

> He was, I believe, an Italian. He listened with rapt attention to a discussion of the high cost of living and strikes, and what not else, dawning appreciation kindling in his face till at last it blazed forth in words:
> 'I see! I see! I get two dollar a day. Not enough. So I strike, get four dollars; twice as well off as before. Pretty soon fellow in shop across the street, he strikes, too. He get four dollars. Some other fellows strike; all get more wages. So many strikes, so little work done, things get scarce, prices go up. Pretty soon when I go to buy things, my four dollars not buy as much as two did. Strike no good!'

To promote enlistment, a detachment from Camp Upton representing fourteen nationalities toured fifteen major cities east of the Mississippi River. The group demonstrated the "cadence system" of drill, in which an officer gave orders and the soldiers being drilled repeated them in unison and executed the movement on their own commands. The system was developed by Bernard Lentz, who believed it would synchronize "oral, verbal, and motor impressions." The detachment was especially well received by industrial firms; Henry Ford was so impressed he made movies of the occasion and distributed them to theatres across the country. In the following summer Lentz formed five smaller units which joined the Radcliffe Chautauqua circuit, thus spreading the army's message to dozens of smaller cities and towns. Their repertoire included drills, sitting-up exercises, singing, and dramatic entertainment, and they now called themselves the "Americans-All Detachments," after a war-time poster showing a list of names representing various nationalities.

Despite all this publicity, and in spite of the authorization of peacetime enlistment of non-English-speaking aliens, the experiment was short-lived. The familiar problem was Congress, whose niggardly appropriation forced the army to suspend recruiting in 1921 and to close all Recruit Education Centers. The experiment, which had looked so promising in the rosy sunset of victory, died in the cold financial dawn of peace.

As in the case of the immigrant, military prejudices against the black man increased during the 1890s, and by the first decade of the twentieth century equal justice for the Negro in the army was no longer possible. The black infantry and cavalry regiments continued to exist, but in 1907 a committee of the General Staff concluded that Negroes lacked the requisite intelligence to become artillerymen, and several years later the Judge Advocate General ruled that their enlistment in the Coast Artillery was not legal because Congress had only designated that infantry and cavalry regiments could be formed. The implication was that they could not serve in any other branches. General Leonard Wood was successful in excluding Negroes from the Plattsburg training camp, commenting that he didn't even want anyone in the country "with whom our descendants cannot intermarry without producing a breed of mongrels; they must at least be white."

Thus by the declaration of war in 1917 military policy toward blacks was one of discrimination and segregation. Before 1917 the latter policy was acquiesced in by blacks in the United States. The National Association for the Advancement of Colored People, for example, petitioned Congress in 1916 to create four more black regiments. After the United States entered the war, however, there was less unanimity about accepting segregated black units. W.E.B. DuBois of the N.A.A.C.P. was severely criticized for his call to "close ranks" and put aside domestic grievances until the end of the war, and Joel E. Spingarn, also of the N.A.A.C.P., was equally attacked, especially by the Negro press, for his advocacy of a segregated military training camp for black officers and his circular letter urging Negroes to sign up for it.

Spingarn's critics argued that such a camp would be a tacit approval of racial segregation. Spingarn, however, had by far the sounder argument, pointing out that the black man needed, above all, the opportunity to demonstrate his potential for leadership. He was right, at least so far as the military was concerned; since the Civil War the greatest barrier of prejudice Negroes had had to surmount had been the difficulty of entering the ranks of commissioned officers. The black man had had few opportunities to demonstrate his competence to lead other men, and few stereotypes about him were more firmly entrenched than the belief that he was innately incapable of doing so. Spingarn also correctly pointed out that the army had displayed great reluctance to train Negro officers at all, arguing that all fourteen of its camps were too full to accommodate a single black officer candidate. Under increasing pressure, the War Department did allow some blacks to enter officer training, but not as many as Spingarn was able to have admitted at the Negro training camp at Des Moines, Iowa. Furthermore, although Spingarn did not give much credence to this argument, it was certainly true that black officers and officer candidates integrated into white units would not get a fair chance. It would be a relatively easy matter to pass them over for promotions, to give them the most menial of assignments, and to discriminate against them in a hundred other ways.

Some of Spingarn's critics argued that there were enough NCO's in the already existing black regiments who could be commissioned, but he replied that most of them lacked the literary skills to function in the higher officer grades, or even in many cases as lieutenants. This was subsequently borne out at Fort Des Moines; many of the candidates from the Negro regiments (250 out of 1,250) were reportedly "scarcely literate." There were many shortcomings in the carrying out of the plan, to be sure. The instruction at Fort Des Moines was generally poor, with instructors in some cases reading from army manuals without comment. Des Moines graduates were somewhat prepared for infantry assignments, but were woefully un-prepared for assignments in other branches, and subsequent officer train-ing was haphazard and marked by race prejudice at every step. These were failures of operation, however, not of concept, and the failures in subse-quent officer training merely underscored Spingarn's objections to inte-grated training.

The demand for black officers in other branches than infantry was occasioned by the decision to form a Negro division. There was never any question about the use of black soldiers in the war, but there was a justified fear that most blacks would be used only in labour organizations. Spingarn and Robert Russa Moton, Booker T. Washington's successor at Tuskegee Institute, began agitating for the creation of a black combat division, and the War Department was increasingly receptive to the idea when it became apparent how many Negroes would be enlisted and how many combat divisions would be needed.

The crucial question for the army was not whether such a division or divisions would be created, but who would be the officers. It was now inevitable that blacks would serve as company grade officers, but army officers were generally repulsed at the thought of having a black man as a superior officer. The immediate problem was Charles Young, a black West Point graduate, the popular choice of Negroes to command the di-vision because of his almost unique position as a black officer. The army got rid of him, to the chagrin and anger of Negroes, by declaring him medically unfit. In January 1918, it also made clear that blacks were to be confined, so far as possible, to the company grades. Negroes, explained the Assistant Chief of Staff, were not entitled to any proportion of officers as a matter of right; it was a matter of efficiency only. "The best officers," he concluded, "are to be found among candidates possessing the greatest mentality, natural intelligence, initiative and qualities of leadership. These qualities exist among white candidates to a greater extent than elsewhere." This was to be official War Department policy for the remainder of the war and, more than any other War Department action, it crippled the Negro's chances to prove his leadership potential. A great many of the white officers in the resulting 92nd Division and the black regiments which were supposed to constitute the 93rd Division were openly antagonistic toward both the black officers and enlisted men in these units. Many of them seized every opportunity to discredit black officers and to have them replaced, often successfully, and openly criticized the performance of the enlisted men. The Chief of Staff of the 92nd Division, Colonel Allen J. Greer, ridiculed the fighting abilities of the men of his own division and tried to have the division's black officers reassigned. Even the division commander, Major General Charles C. Ballou, was convinced that the Negro lacked initiative and the capacity for leadership.

Friction between black and white officers was primarily responsible for the incident in which two battalions of the 368th Infantry Regiment of the 92nd Division crumbled and were routed in France, and this incident did more than anything else to perpetuate the stereotype that the black man was an adequate soldier only under white leadership. Again, the concept of segregation was not to blame; it was the most effective road toward overcoming race prejudice and convincing the American public that the Negro had undeveloped potential. It was the way in which the policy was carried out that was at fault. If the 92nd Division had been entirely officered by well-trained Negroes, and had it been well-equipped, the rout of a portion of the 368th Infantry would never have occurred. Since the record of the division was otherwise good, and that of the other regiments brigaded with the French ranged from good to excellent, it would have been considerably harder for officers and civilians, black as well as white, to perpetuate the time-honoured stereotypes.

Not surprisingly, army officers were overwhelmingly critical of the performance of black officers during the war and determined that they be eliminated from the post-war army.[3] The wartime experience had, however, benefited the black man by releasing a powerful force not planned or desired by whites. The First World War, as the editor of the *Southwestern Christian Advocate* commented, had "lifted the Negro problem out of the provincialism of America into the cosmopolitanism of the civilized world." Returning black veterans would no longer acquiesce in the pre-war patterns. Thousands of blacks who had moved north during the war, lured by wartime employment opportunities, would ultimately no longer be willing to accept a subordinate position in American society. They would force America to awake to the fact that discrimination was a national, rather than a regional, problem.

The army's experiences with ethnic and racial minorities during World War I reveal that the military was unable to make good on its often stated promise of equal treatment. Military men have had little tolerance for differing backgrounds and customs; their relationships with minority groups have been marked by constant attempts to apply the time-honoured army rules and regulations, to fit all comers into a common mould. It is essentially an Anglo-Saxon mould, which is not surprising in view of the upper-middle class, Anglo-Saxon, Protestant background of most army officers. But the army does implicitly promise that prejudice has no place within its ranks, and it does not always fulfill this promise. In its relationships with the immigrant during World War I and in other periods, nativism has been an undercurrent which occasionally rises to the surface. Army policy toward the black soldier has to a greater degree been determined by racial prejudice.

When the common mould does operate as intended, minorities are not necessarily aided. During World War I strict segregation, rather than integration, and unequal, rather than equal, treatment would have most benefited immigrants and blacks. The military was not, of course, taking the needs of minorities into account in determining its policies, but the decisions it made affected minority groups, especially during wartime. The relationship can best be described as tangential. The army has been concerned with problems of professionalism and functionalism; ethnic and racial minorities have been concerned with identity, mobility, acculturation, and integration. During the nineteenth century this tangent aided minority groups; during World War I it hindered them.

NOTES

1. The army, for example, had a recruitment problem during most of the nineteenth century; this spelled opportunity for thousands of immigrants who were unable to find employment. In the army they learned American customs and the English language, or at least the army versions of both. For many of them the army meant mobility, for the immigrants were recruited in eastern seaboard cities and transported to the frontier, where many of them settled. The recruitment problem also led to the formation of four black regiments following the Civil War, which meant economic, if not physical security, for a number of Negroes. Both immigrants and blacks benefited from the army post educational system established after the Civil War.

   The army's relationships with the American Indian were, of course, less peaceful ones. Since the War Department controlled Indian affairs, until the creation of the Department of the Interior in 1849, and almost regained control during the 1870s, army officers exercised control over Indian reservations and prisoners for considerable periods of time, and frequently served as Indian agents on the reservations. Their collective record showed the army was not the proper agency to effect the acculturation of the Indian, but it was a considerably better one than civilian agents compiled during the same time. In addition, a number of Indian scouts served with the army, and during the 1890s the army experimented with Indian units.

2. The "American Way" turned out to be with boxing gloves.

3. A good example was the comment of Major Fred R. Brown, who had served in the 92nd Division during the war. "History has repeatedly proven," he wrote to the Assistant Commandant of the General Staff College in April, 1920, "that normally the negro, as a race, is and has always been lacking in bravery, grit, and leadership, as well as some other qualities which are necessary in an officer." No amount of training could overcome this. During the war, he charged, all Negro officers had displayed "inertia, lack of dependability, and lack of appreciation of the responsibility resting upon officers. . . . " They were completely devoid of courage or initiative. Fred R. Brown to Assistant Commandant, General Staff College, April 5, 1920, Office of the Chief of Military History, Records of the Historical Section Army War College, file 3272.

   In comparison, no such hostility existed toward the American Indian. After the army experiment with Indian regiments failed during the 1890s, mainly because of the army's inflexibility, the War Department was convinced that the Indian should be integrated as completely as possible into white units. Thus during the World War I period there were few Indian units. It was a mistake from the Indian's standpoint, for whites needed to be constantly reminded that the Indian was a part of society, with potentiality and personality, and the Indian needed to develop his own leadership and a sense of racial pride in order to stimulate the confidence of others. His basic problem was the continuing apathy of whites.

29

Reenlistment and Desertion in the Navy, 1900–1940

FREDERICK HARROD

Economic distress has always helped military recruiters fill their quotas, and the Great Depression of the 1930s was no exception. Frederick Harrod has compiled reenlistment and desertion rates for the navy in the years from 1900 to 1940, and correlates the former with national unemployment rates in these tables.

Reenlistments and Extensions of Enlistment, 1905–1939

Fiscal Year	Rate of Reenlistment and Extension	Rate of Unemployment for Calendar Year	Fiscal Year	Rate of Reenlistment and Extension	Rate of Unemployment for Calendar Year
1905	54	3.1	1923	49	3.2
1906	43.1	.8	1924	76.7	5.5
1907	32.2	1.8	1925	72	4.0
1908	57	8.5	1926	75	1.9
1909	65	5.2	1927	61.7	4.1
1910	61	5.9	1928	68.5	4.4
1911	57	6.2	1929	72.8	3.2
1912	54	5.2	1930	71.9	8.7
1913	57	4.4	1931	78.5	15.9
1914	65	8.0	1932	90.07	23.6
1915	72	9.7	1933	93.25	24.9
1916	72	4.8	1934	76.10	21.7
1917	78.6	4.8	1935	80.86	20.1
1918	83.4	1.4	1936	83.67	16.9
1919	35.9	2.3	1937	81.75	14.3
1920	35.6	4.0	1938	72.21	19.0
1921	78.6	11.9	1939	80.81	17.2
1922	72.2	7.6			

SOURCE: Reenlistment rates: Annual Report of the Chief of the Bureau of Navigation for the years 1905–39. Unemployment rates: U.S. Department of Commerce, Bureau of the Census, Historical Statistics of the United States, Colonial Times to 1957 (Washington: GPO, 1960), p. 73. Reprinted from page 185 of Manning the New Navy: The Development of a Modern Naval Enlisted Force, 1899–1940 by Frederick S. Harrod and used by permission of the publisher, Greenwood Press, Inc., Westport, Connecticut.

Desertion, 1900–1940

Fiscal Year	Enlisted Force June 30	Number of Desertions	Desertions as Percentage of Enlisted Force
1900	16,832	2,452	14.5
1901	18,825	3,158	16.8
1902	21,433	3,037	14.1
1903	27,245	4,136	15.1
1904	29,321	4,488	15.3
1905	30,804	4,427	14.4
1906	32,163	4,867	15.1
1907	33,027	5,105	15.5
1908	39,048	6,054	15.5
1909	42,861	3,836	8.8
1910	45,076	3,549	7.9
1911	47,612	3,284	6.9
1912	47,515	3,055	6.4
1913	48,068	3,237	6.7
1914	52,667	2,728	5.2
1915	52,561	2,320	4.4
1916	54,234	2,064	3.8
1917	100,539	2,826	2.8
1918	435,406	3,133	.7
1919	250,833	6,138	2.5
1920	108,950	10,036	9.5
1921	119,205	10,261	8.6
1922	85,580	not available	
1923	82,355	5,820	7.1
1924	87,327	7,787	8.9
1925	84,289	4,657	4.9
1926	82,161	2,675	3.2
1927	83,566	3,123	3.8
1928	84,355	2,906	3.5
1929	85,321	2,055	2.4
1930	84,938	1,884	2.2
1931	80,910	1,123	1.4
1932	81,120	757	.9
1933	79,243	604	.8
1934	80,359	580	.7
1935	82,839	332	.4
1936	93,077	318	.3
1937	100,178	467	.5
1938	104,888	473	.5
1939	110,196	338	.3
1940	139,554	442	.3

SOURCE: *Annual Report of the Chief of the Bureau of Navigation* for the years 1900–1940. Reprinted from page 198 of *Manning the New Navy: The Development of a Modern Naval Enlisted Force, 1899–1940* by Frederick S. Harrod and used by permission of the publisher, Greenwood Press, Inc., Westport, Connecticut.

The Era
of World War II

30

Who Volunteered for Service in World War II?

The Selective Service Act of 1940, revised in 1941, governed the flow of most of those who served in World War II, but a substantial fraction of those who served enlisted (most of them prior to 1943). Where did those who chose to join come from?

THE ACCOMPANYING TABLE, correlating enlistment rates with an index of industrial development for each county in one state (South Carolina), indicates that the typical enlistee was from an industrialized, urbanized place, not from the countryside.

If industrial workers were to have been especially favored with exemptions by the Selective Service system, then these figures of enlistments as a percentage of all inductees might be extremely misleading. In fact, however, *agricultural* occupations were favored with exemptions from Selective Service.[1] Hence these percentages would *understate* the greater propensity of persons from industrial regions to enlist. And that is exactly what they do. If we divide the numbers enlisting from each county into the total population of each county, we find that the least industrial counties (Lowest Quarter) saw only 1 enlistment for every 66 persons, whereas in the most industrial counties (Highest Quarter) 1 in every 24 persons enlisted, a ratio of 2.75, which figure is greater than the ratio (2.0) of our averages shown in the table.

However, it might still be the case that persons from industrial areas were enlisting precisely in order to avoid being drafted into less desirable, combat roles. Surely this would explain some of these enlistments. However, when we compare enlistments by county in an obviously high-risk combat service (the Marine Corps) with those in an obviously low-risk

Percent of Enlistments of All Those Entering the Military from South Carolina, 1940–46, by County's Index of Industrial Development[a]

LOW LEVEL OF INDUSTRIAL DEVELOPMENT						HIGH LEVEL OF INDUSTRIAL DEVELOPMENT	
Lowest Quarter (Index of 0–20)		Second Quarter (Index of 21–40)		Third Quarter (Index of 41–100)		Highest Quarter (Index of Over 100)	
County	*Enlisted (%)*	*County*	*Enlisted (%)*	*County*	*Enlisted (%)*	*County*	*Enlisted (%)*
Allendale	6.2	Bamberg	7.8	Barnwell	6.6	Anderson	14.4
Calhoun	7.0	Berkeley	5.9	Charleston	15.2	Cherokee	11.4
Clarendon	4.7	Chesterfield	9.8	Jasper	8.5	Chester	13.1
Colleton	8.8	Dillon	10.9	Lexington	12.0	Darlington	11.4
Edgefield	8.4	Dorchester	8.5	Marion	10.0	Greenville	15.6
Horry	8.9	Florence	11.4	Ocone	12.8	Greenwood	14.8
Lee	5.8	Hampton	8.1	Pickens	13.8	Lancaster	11.6
Saluda	6.8	Kershaw	12.6	Richland	16.5	Laurens	11.9
Williamsburg	5.6	Marlboro	9.1	Sumter	9.1	Newberry	12.8
		Orangeburg	8.6	Union	15.8	Spartanburg	14.5
						York	14.8
Average	7.3	Average	9.3	Average	12.0	Average	14.6

[a]Index of Industrial Development = Value added by manufacture per capita in county.

SOURCES: Compiled from the 16th Census of U.S., *1940, Manufactures, 1939, Vol. III,* pp. 942–43, and Holmes Springs, *Selective Service in South Carolina, 1940–1947* (Columbia, S.C., 1948), 70–71.

combat service (the Coast Guard), we find that the ratio of Marine Corps to Coast Guard recruitment in highly industrial areas (Highest Quarter) is 9.0, whereas it is only 2.5 in the least industrial areas (Lowest Quarter). It would seem that industrial areas in World War II yielded more persons per capita "willing to fight" than did agricultural areas, a phenomenon that other data would appear to confirm for World War I.

What accounts for this propensity? I suspect that it is largely due to the fact that persons in industrial areas tend to be more cosmopolitan than their localistic agrarian counterparts. Persons whose informational diet is purely localistic, who are rarely told of the link between distant events and their own lives, rights, values, jobs, standard of living, and so on, are simply less likely to see the need for military action than those who are routinely so informed.[2]

We do know that blacks were disproportionately located in nonindustrial areas and that until recently they were much less willing to enlist than whites.[3] For several reasons blacks were very "localistic" when it came to World War II. This explains part of the industrial–nonindustrial differential, not all of it. If we manipulate county census materials and selective service records in order to isolate the white population, we find that eligible whites in heavily industrial areas enlisted at a rate 33 percent greater than that of eligible whites in the least industrial areas.

NOTES

1. Holmes Springs, *Selective Service in South Carolina, 1940–1947* (Columbia, S.C., 1948), p. 85.
2. For more on the significance of the local–cosmopolitan rift see Samuel P. Hays, "Political Parties and the Community-Society Continuum," in W. N. Chambers and W. D. Burnham, eds., *The American Party Systems* (New York, 1967), pp. 152–81.
3. See, for example, Springs, *Selective Service in South Carolina*, pp. 63, 65; Arthur Barbeau and F. Henri, *The Unknown Soldiers: Black Soldiers in World War I* (Philadelphia: Temple University Press, 1974); and S. Stouffer, *et al.*, *Studies in Social Psychology in World War II*, 4 vols. (Princeton, N.J.: Princeton University Press, 1949–50), I: 334 and II: 524.

31

Combat Behavior
of Infantry Companies

S. L. A. MARSHALL

Much was learned of the GI and his world by the social and behavioral scientists participating in the Stouffer study.* An equally important study, conducted by similar personnel of the Human Resources Research Office, concerned the combat behavior of several hundred infantry companies in the European and Pacific theaters. Brigadier General S. L. A. Marshall, who was in charge of the study, describes its surprising major finding in these selections from the 1961 edition of his book Men Against Fire. *Why wouldn't over 75 percent of the men fire their weapons?*

*Samuel Stouffer et al., Studies in Social Psychology in World War II, 4 vols. (Princeton, N.J., 1949–50).

AT FORT BENNING, GA., the citadel of the infantry spirit in modern America, there is today a superior system for bringing infantry weapons under command control so that in the crisis of battle their response will be decisive. It is called *Train Fire.*

As a system, scientifically applied over the known distance ranges, so that riflemen and integral support weapons groups will acquire fire habits which will fortify them and keep unity of action steadfast when they face the enemy, Train Fire owes its origins formally to the Human Resources Research Office of the Army and to the imaginative tacticians who advise that body of scientists. . . .

SOURCE: S. L. A. Marshall, *Men Against Fire* (New York: Apollo Editions, 1961), pp. 5, 5–10, 50–51, 53–60, 70–72, 74–80. Originally published by Harper & Row in 1947. Reprinted by permission of Mrs. S. L. A. Marshall and Peter Smith, Publishers.

I had anticipated that, provided [this] book had something important to say, the American people might gradually be won to its truths, and over 10 years or so, their good opinion would superinduce change in the Army toward needed reform. It was a naive expectation. There was practically no public response to the book. Civilian periodicals ignored it almost unanimously. But within less than six months, the United States Army, and other military systems abroad, had taken it up seriously, and such fortune as it has had, they made.

True, in the beginning, the most noteworthy reaction was that some of the older generals (especially those who had been division commanders) read it but to damn it. They felt compelled to believe that whatever it said about troops performing somewhat less than perfectly under fire, might hold true of some other commander's people, but never of their own. Of such loyalty as this great legends are made, but it is hardly conducive to the smoothing of operations and the correcting of error. The grumbling hurt no one and after the grumblers had heard from some of their battalion and company commanders, who being released from service, were ready to sound off immoderately about these same problems, they quickly lapsed into silence, as did certain of the service schools which initially objected that the criticisms were too radical.

The Army institutionally immediately welcomed the book and put the main ideas to use within the training system. With especial gratitude, I recall the support given it by General J. Lawton Collins, Chief of Staff, General Jacob Devers, chief of field forces, and Lieutenant General Raymond S. McLain, then Army chief of information. The department publication, "Officers' Call," gave it a first ringing endorsement.

Out of the text, what was said about fire ratios—that less than 25 per cent of our infantry line employed hand weapons effectively when under fire—drew main attention and stirred initial controversy. The data so said and the Army didn't contest it. Instead, at centers like Fort Benning, Knox and Riley, during the years 1948-49, to overcome weapons inertia, imaginative trainers instituted wholly new methods, some of which were suggested in the book.

Their pioneering paid off splendidly in Korea from 1950 till the end. When on returning from my first tour there, in April, 1951, I reported to Secretary of the Army Frank Pace, Jr., and General Charles L. Bolte, vice chief of staff, I was able to say that active weapons participation in our infantry line had risen beyond 55 percent both in night defense and daytime attack—more than doubling the World War II output.

General Bolte then raised the question: "Is this not because the perimeters are isolated and the men know they must shoot to survive?" To that I perforce answered: "No, knowledge of the conditions would but increase the impact of fear, which freezes the trigger finger. The improvement has to be the product of an improved training system." What was most noticeable in Korea was that every infantry company was aware of the problem. Their fire volume was a point of pride with them. In World War II, junior leaders, without exception, disregarded the factor. . . .

Now I do not think I have seen it stated in the military manuals of this age, or in any of the writings meant for the instruction of those who lead troops, that a commander of infantry will be well advised to believe that when he engages the enemy not more than one quarter of his men will ever strike a real blow unless they are compelled by almost overpowering circumstances or unless all junior leaders constantly "ride herd" on troops with the specific mission of increasing their fire.

The 25 per cent estimate stands even for well-trained and campaign-seasoned troops. I mean that 75 per cent will not fire or will not persist in firing against the enemy and his works. These men may face the danger but they will not fight.

But as I said in the beginning, it is an aspect of infantry combat which goes unheeded. So far as the records show, the question has never been raised by anyone: "During engagement, what ratio of fire can be expected from a normal body of well-trained infantry under average conditions of combat?"

This is a very curious oversight, inasmuch as the problem of how much fire can be brought to bear is the basic problem in all tactics. In fact, it *is* tactics in a nutshell, and the other elements of tactics are simply shaped around it. . . .

Why the subject of fire ratios under combat conditions has not been long and searchingly explored, I don't know, but I doubt that it is because of any professional taboo, and I suspect that it is because in earlier wars there had never existed the opportunity for systematic collection of the data.

It is the human nature of the commander to believe that the majority of his troops are willing, for unless he so believes, he is aware of his personal failure. But it is not less true that to his mind willingness and loyalty are virtually synonymous with initiative and voluntary risk at the point of danger. During battle it is physically impossible for him to make a check of the action of all of his men without neglecting other and more decisive responsibilities. Nor can his immediate subordinates do this for him without taking undue risks. After battle the question is of less moment and the commander becomes occupied with the duties of his next employment. It does not occur to him that the rate of effective fire in the command is the core of his whole problem and that the means for taking a reasonably accurate measure of it is his for the asking. The average soldier will tell the absolute truth when asked if he has used his weapon.

In the course of holding post-combat mass interviews with approximately four hundred infantry companies in the Central Pacific and European Theaters, I did not find one battalion, company, or platoon commander who had made the slightest effort to determine how many of his men had actually engaged the enemy with a weapon. But there were many who, on being asked the preliminary question, made the automatic reply: "I believe that every man used a weapon at one time or another." Some added that wherever they had moved and viewed, it had seemed that all hands were taking an active part in the fighting.

Later when the companies were interviewed at a full assembly and the men spoke as witnesses in the presence of the commander and their junior leaders, we found that on an average not more than 15 per cent of the men had actually fired at the enemy positions or personnel with rifles, carbines, grenades, bazookas, BARs, or machine guns during the course of an entire engagement. Even allowing for the dead and wounded, and assuming that in their numbers there would be the same proportion of active firers as among the living, the figure did not rise above 20 to 25 per cent of the total for any action. The best showing that could be made by the most spirited and aggressive companies was that one man in four had made at least some use of his fire power.

Naturally, the commanders were astonished at these findings, though at the conclusion of the critiques, there was no case of a commander remaining unconvinced that the men had made a true report.

Most of the actions had taken place under conditions of ground and maneuver where it would have been possible for at least 80 per cent of the men to fire, and where nearly all hands, at one time or another, were operating within satisfactory firing distance of enemy works. Scarcely one of the actions had been a casual affair. The greater number had been decisive local actions in which the operations of a company had had critical effect upon the fortunes of some larger body and in which the company itself had been hard-pressed. In most cases the company had achieved a substantial success. In some cases, it had been driven back and locally defeated by enemy fire.

The critiques covered all that took place from the opening to the end of action. The spot checks were made by a showing of hands and questioning as to the number of rounds used, targets fired upon, etc., usually after all witnesses had been heard and the company had received a well-rounded impression of the action as a whole. There is no reason to doubt that the men were reporting honestly and objectively; they quickly realized that it was something to their credit if they could establish that they had participated in the fire fight.

There was an occasional exception to the almost uniform pattern of the results but there was no exception to my earlier statement that the commanders had not been trained to interest themselves in this problem.

To return to the beginning, in the Makin Island fight, which was a part of the Gilbert Islands invasion in November, 1943, one battalion of the 165th Infantry Regiment was stoutly engaged all along the front of its defensive perimeter throughout the third night. The enemy, crazed with sake, began a series of banzai charges at dusk, and the pressure thereafter was almost unremitting until dawn came. The frontal gun positions were all directly assaulted with sword and bayonet. Most of the killing took place at less than a ten-yard interval. Half of the American guns were knocked out and approximately half of the occupants of the forward foxholes were either killed or wounded. Every position was ringed with enemy dead.

When morning brought the assurance that the defensive position had weathered the storm and the enemy had been beaten back by superior fire, it seemed certain to those of us who were close enough to it to appraise the action that all concerned must have acted with utmost boldness. For it was clear that the whole battalion was alive to the danger and that despite its greatly superior numbers, it had succeeded by none too wide a margin. We began the investigation to determine how many of our men had fought with their weapons. It was an exhaustive search, man by man and gun crew by gun crew, each man being asked exactly what he had done.

Yet making allowances for the dead, we could identify only 36 men as having fired at the enemy with all weapons. The majority were heavy weapons men. The really active firers were usually in small groups working together. There were some men in the positions directly under attack who did not fire at all or attempt to use a weapon even when the position was being overrun. The majority of the active firers used several weapons; if the machine gun went out, they picked up a rifle; when they ran out of rifle ammunition, they used grenades. But there were other witnesses who testified that they had seen clear targets and still did not fire.

It is true that these were green troops who were having their first taste of combat. Likewise, it is to be observed that the nature of perimeter defense, as it was then used in the Pacific, limited the freedom of fire of troops inside the perimeter.

But thereafter the trail of this same question was followed through many companies with varying degrees of battle experience, in the Pacific and in Europe. The proportions varied little from situation to situation. In an average experienced infantry company in an average stern day's action, the number engaging with any and all weapons was approximately 15 per cent of total strength. In the most aggressive infantry companies, under the most intense local pressure, the figure rarely rose above 25 per cent of total strength from the opening to the close of action.

Now maybe I should clarify the matter still further. I do not mean to say that throughout an engagement, the average company maintained fire with an average of 15 per cent of its weapons. If that were it, there would be no problem, for such a rate of fire would necessarily mean great volume during the height of an assault.

The thing is simply this, that out of an average one hundred men along the line of fire during the period of an encounter, only fifteen men on the average would take any part with the weapons. This was true whether the action was spread over a day, or two days, or three. The prolonging of the engagement did not add appreciably to the numbers.

Moreover, the man did not have to maintain fire to be counted among the active firers. If he had so much as fired a rifle once or twice, though not aiming it at anything in particular, or lobbed a grenade roughly in the direction of the enemy, he was scored on the positive side. Usually the men with heavier weapons, such as the BAR, flamethrower or bazooka, gave a pretty good account of themselves, which of course is just another way of saying that the majority of men who were present and armed but would not fight were riflemen.

Terrain, the tactical situation, and even the nature of the enemy and the accuracy of his fire appeared to have almost no bearing on the ratio of active firers to non-firers. Nor did the element of battle experience through three or four campaigns produce any such radical change as might be expected. The results appeared to indicate that the ceiling was fixed by some constant which was inherent in the nature of troops or perhaps in our failure to understand that nature sufficiently to apply the proper correctives.

One of the principal effects of battle seasoning is apparently to make junior leaders cognizant of some of the proportions of the problem so that when the company engages, a larger percentage of NCOs will use direct methods to increase the fire power of the immediate group. But the best of NCOs cannot for long move up and down a fire line booting his men until they use their weapons. Not only is that an invitation to sudden death but it diverts him from supporting and encouraging the relatively few willing spirits who are sustaining the action. Also, regardless of what the book says to the contrary, that is not his real role on the battlefield. When the heat is on, he is more likely to be working hard with his own weapon, trying to beat back the enemy with his own hands and strength of purpose.

It seems to me, therefore, that there is every reason why the fire ratio factor should be treated primarily as a most vital training problem and secondarily as a subject for critical inquiry and treatment in the early stages of combat.

During the Kwajalein battle, in working with the companies of the 7th Infantry Division, we first found that the percentage of men who engaged with all weapons was about constant in all companies, despite extreme variations in the local tactical situations. Then attention was drawn to one other significant fact. Though there were a few minor shifts, with new men coming forward and others leaving the fight because of death or wounds, in the main the same men were carrying the fire fight for each company day after day. The willing riflemen, grenadiers, and bazooka men who had led the attack and worked the detail of destruction upon the enemy on a Monday would carry the attack when the fight was renewed in a different part of the island on Wednesday. The hand that pulled the trigger was the same hand that was most likely to be found tossing a grenade, setting a satchel charge, or leading a sortie in the next round.

Of course there were many other active files doing yeoman service in supply, communications, and other missions. Men do not progress in battle by fire alone, and without the work of the others the efforts of the firers would have been unavailing. But the point is that among those present for duty with the weapons, the same names continued to reappear as having taken the initiative and relatively few fresh names were added to the list on any day.

You could pick out your man who would probably keep going until he was dead. Or for that matter, after a few trial rounds, you could spot the man who would probably never get going though his chances of dying were relatively good.

For it must be said in favor of some who did not use their weapons that they did not shirk the final risk of battle. They were not malingerers. They did not hold back from the danger point. They were there to be killed if the enemy fire searched and found them. For certain tasks they were good soldiers. Nor can it be doubted that as riflemen many of them were of sound potential. The point is that they would not fire though they were in situations where firing was their prime responsibility and where nothing else could be as helpful to the company.

It was also conspicuous that the men who used their weapons were the same men who took the lead in outflanking an enemy fire trench or in blowing an enemy shelter. It should be obvious that these things go hand-in-hand, since the act of willingly firing upon the enemy is of itself an instance of high initiative on the battlefield, though commanders have long considered it as simply a natural derivative of sound training. On that subject I will have more to say later.

How much then does training have to do with it? Probably this—that it enables the willing soldier, the man who will fight when he gets the chance, to recognize the breadth of each opportunity and to know when and where to use his fire to full advantage and with regard for his own need of protection. It may also stimulate and inform the man who is already fixed with a high sense of duty so that in him the initiative becomes simply a form of obedience.

But more than that it is not likely to do under present methods and until the principles by which we attempt to establish fire discipline are squared with human nature. We are on infirm ground when we hold to the belief that the routine of marksmanship training and of giving the soldier an easy familiarity with his weapon will automatically prompt the desire to use the weapon when he comes under fire.

There is no feature of training known to any company commander I have met which enabled him to determine, prior to combat, which of his men would carry the fight for him and which would simply go along for the ride. Discipline is not the key. Perfection in drill is not the key. The most perfectly drilled and disciplined soldier I saw in World War I was a sergeant who tried to crawl into the bushes his first time over the top. Some of the most gallant single-handed fighters I encountered in World War II had spent most of their time in the guardhouse. It is all very well for such an authority as Major General J. F. C. Fuller to assure us that the yardsticks of loyalty and obedience are the means of measuring beforehand the probable response of the soldier in battle. Many others have said it before Fuller. But I deny that it is true. It may have applied to the ranks in the days of closed formations but it does not apply to our present soldiery. . . .

Since the average man likes to fire a weapon and takes unreluctantly to instruction on the range, it cannot be doubted that a majority would participate freely with their weapons under conditions approximating a field exercise.

But combat cannot ever approximate the conditions of field maneuvers. Fears of varying sort afflict the soldier in battle. The unit commander soon comes to realize that one of his difficulties is to get men to leave cover because of enemy bullets and the fear they instill. In training, there being no real bullet danger even on the courses which employ live ammunition, every advance under a supposed enemy fire is unrealistic. Too, in training, the soldier does not have a man as his target. He is not shooting with the idea of killing. There is a third vast difference in the two conditions: The rifleman in training is usually under close observation and the chief pressure upon him is to give satisfaction to his superior, whereas the rifleman engaging the enemy is of necessity pretty much on his own, and the chief pressure on him is to remain alive, if possible.

When the infantryman's mind is gripped by fear, his body is captured by inertia, which is fear's Siamese twin. "In an attack half of the men on a firing line are in terror and the other half are unnerved." So wrote Major General J. F. C. Fuller when a young captain. The failure of the average soldier to fire is not in the main due to conscious recognition of the fact that the act of firing may entail increased exposure. It is a result of a paralysis which comes of varying fears. The man afraid wants to do nothing; indeed, he does not care even to think of taking action.

Getting him on his way to the doing of one positive act—the digging of a foxhole or the administering of first-aid to a comrade—persuading him to make any constructive use of his muscle power, and especially putting him at a job which he can share with other men, may become the first step toward getting him to make appropriate use of his weapons under combat conditions. Action is the great steadying force. It helps clear the brain. The man who finds that he can still control his muscles will shortly begin to use them. But if he is to make a rapid and complete recovery, he requires help from others. . . .

The diagnosis of the disease must precede the remedy; the object of search must be known before there can be intelligent seeking.

Once oriented toward the problem, the commander would work more carefully with his junior leaders in training. They would be told that in combat it would become one of their tasks to mark well the men who take the initiative with the rifle or other hand weapons. When these men are identified, it then becomes incumbent on the junior leader to devote more of his effort to personal work among the nonstarters, encouraging them to work up to favorable fire positions and giving them direct orders to begin fire with the weapon.

This will not produce a cure-all but it is at least a start. The survey of the company and an organized knowledge of how its individuals respond under actual fire conditions should precede all else; correction of this study should continue thereafter.

When the tendency of all members of the unit has been thus appraised, the commander may find that for maximum combat effectiveness it is necessary to make a number of personnel adjustments. Men previously overlooked will be marked for promotion. The man who is always a self-starter under fire is not *ipso facto* qualified for junior leadership; there must be other substantial elements in his character. But on the other hand, the NCO who cannot exercise fire initiative will lose the respect of his men as quickly as his weakness is observed by them in battle. Even the soldier who cannot overcome a similar weakness in himself will look with contempt on a superior who appears to shirk his duty because of danger.

The men who show no disposition to use the small weapons, even when properly urged and directed, can be switched to the gun crews. There, the group will keep them going. Men working in groups or in teams do not have the same tendency to default of fire as do single riflemen. This is such a well-fixed principle in human nature that one very rarely sees a gun go out of action simply because the opposing fire is too close.

As another experiment, unwilling riflemen may be switched to heavier and more decisive one-man weapons. This sounds like a paradox—to expect greater response to come from increased responsibility. But it works. I have seen many cases where men who had funked it badly with a rifle responded heroicially when given a flame-thrower or BAR. Self-pride and the ego are the touchstone of most of these remarkable conversions. A man may fail with the rifle because he feels anonymous and believes that nothing important is being asked of him. (Though that is a false feeling and the rifle must remain the prime weapon of the infantryman, I remind the reader that we are considering human nature in its relation to weapon efficiency.) The switch to a heavier weapon is a challenging form of recognition. It is a chance for the man to show others that he has been held in too lowly esteem.

Whether there is any sure cure with the rifle itself I am not at all certain—whether it would be possible by special techniques to break down a rifleman's resistance against employing his weapon upon human targets. To think that the job can be done simply by giving the man confidence in his weapon or working him up to the point where he enjoys firing it is a gross miscalculation. These things are a valuable part of the conditioning process but they will not remove the final mental block.

To my knowledge, no sustained experiments have ever been made during combat to see whether and how a group of non-firers can be converted to willing use of the rifle. Moreover, I doubt that a test under non-combat conditions would have value. The only thing that counts is how the man responds when he is given opportunity to fire at an object for the direct purpose of taking another man's life. Let me cite an example:

> In the 184th Infantry Regiment's sector during the Kwajalein battle, we saw two objects floating by, 200 yards out in the lagoon. They looked like the heads of swimming men. From forward of us, there was a spattering of fire which kicked up the water around the objects. The riflemen close around me— there were about ten of them—held their fire. I then turned my field glasses over to them, saying: "Take a look and you will see that those men are wasting their ammunition on blocks of wood." They did so, and within a few seconds they were all firing like mad at the objects. They had found a release in the very information which I had supposed would cause them to hold their fire.

There were numerous incidents in this battle and in others wherein enemy soldiers walked deliberately into the open in full daylight, exposing themselves long enough for a score or more men to get a sustained view of the target, without one shot being fired.

As to the main problem, I suspect, and my psychologist friends assure me that it is so, that if any treatment is likely to work it would be to dispose the rifleman where he has a clear sight of an enemy target, then handle him as one would a recruit on the range, making certain that he continues the fire for an extended period. By that, I do not mean necessarily a live target. They are not that convenient. The instructor who has his pupil hold fire until he sees a man to fire on will usually have a very long wait indeed. But it is necessary that the fire be aimed against a position where the enemy is presumed to be located.

It seems reasonable to believe that there is a definite advantage to getting the soldier into the habit of free firing in combat while the situation is still such that his target is a position rather than a man moving clear. It becomes easier for the supervisor to regulate his own work and it is the logical and most promising approach to the problem, if only for the reason that the average firer will have less resistance to firing on a house or a tree than upon a human being. To clear up this point, it is necessary to take a somewhat closer look at the average, normal man who is fitted into the uniform of an American ground soldier.

He is what his home, his religion, his schooling, and the moral code and ideals of his society have made him. The Army cannot unmake him. It must reckon with the fact that he comes from a civilization in which aggression, connected with the taking of life, is prohibited and unacceptable. The teaching and the ideals of that civilization are against killing, against taking advantage. The fear of aggression has been expressed to him so strongly and absorbed by him so deeply and pervadingly—practically with his mother's milk—that it is part of the normal man's emotional make-up. This is his great handicap when he enters combat. It stays his trigger finger even though he is hardly conscious that it is a restraint upon him. Because it is an emotional and not an intellectual handicap, it is not removable by intellectual reasoning, such as: "Kill or be killed."

Line commanders pay little attention to the true nature of this mental block. They take it more or less for granted that if the man is put on such easy terms with his weapon in training that he "loves to fire," this is the main step toward surmounting the general difficulty. But it isn't as easy as that. A revealing light is thrown on this subject through the studies by Medical Corps psychiatrists of the combat fatigue cases in the European Theater. They found that fear of killing, rather than fear of being killed, was the most common cause of battle failure in the individual, and that fear of failure ran a strong second.

It is therefore reasonable to believe that the average and normally healthy individual—the man who can endure the mental and physical stresses of combat—still has such an inner and usually unrealized resistance toward killing a fellow man that he will not of his own volition take life if it is possible to turn away from that responsibility. Though it is improbable that he may ever analyze his own feelings so searchingly as to know what is stopping his own hand, his hand is nonetheless stopped. At the vital point, he becomes a conscientious objector, unknowing. That is something to the American credit. But it is likewise something which needs to be analyzed and understood if we are to prevail against it in the interests of battle efficiency. I well recall that in World War I the great sense of relief that came to troops when they were passed to a quiet sector such as the old Toul front was due not so much to the realization that things were safer there as to the blessed knowledge that for a time they were not under the compulsion to take life. "Let 'em go; we'll get 'em some other time," was the remark frequently made when the enemy grew careless and offered himself as a target.

To get back to my main point, however, it would likewise seem reasonable to believe that if resistance to the idea of firing can be overcome for a period, it can be defeated permanently. Once the plunge is made, the water seems less forbidding. As with every other duty in life, it is made easier by virtue of the fact that a man may say to himself: "I have done it once. I can do it again."

As for those other men, the self-starting men who somehow have managed to overcome their inhibitions and have proved their initiative under fire beyond all doubt, the good commander will cherish and protect them as if his own life depends on it, for surely his professional reputation does. However, it is self-evident that for the good of the company such men should not be wasted on rear area or communications duty unless the signs of cracking from battle strain become evident. When that happens, arranging some special assignment which will afford the good soldier temporary relief is the commander's obligation. On patrol, outpost, or other hazardous duty, the commander would be ill-advised to concentrate these moral leaders of the company, though they should be present in the minimum numbers which will provide a safe binder for the other files so assigned. Too, he will take care that they are never driven by his other subordinates; they do not require driving and there can be no surer way to destroy their mettle.

Finally, when the rewards of battle are handed out, he will make certain that these are the men who are honored first. In my judgment the soldier who consistently addresses the enemy with fire is full worthy of decoration. But what honors are commonly given such men under our present awards system? None whatever! It is the almost universal practice of boards sitting in judgment somewhere safely in the rear areas (I do not speak from inexperience, having sat on four such boards) to dismiss all such cases with the comment: "He was only doing his duty." Until it is formally recognized that there could be no higher tribute than this to the combat soldier, our system of distributing awards will tend toward the discouragement of the fighting line rather than otherwise. . . .

32

American Military Ethics in World War II: The Bombing of German Civilians

RONALD SCHAFFER

In October 1918, Colonel William Mitchell asked Secretary of War Newton D. Baker to direct the air service to conduct the sort of strategic bombing raids that General Trenchard of the R.A.F. favored. Baker replied that the United States would not participate in an offensive "that has as its objective the promiscuous bombing upon industry, commerce, or population in enemy countries." In 1940 Secretary of State Cordell Hull condemned the Japanese for their "bombing and machine-gunning of civilians from the air at places near which there was no military establishments or organizations." He called incendiary weapons "ruthless" and attacks on civilians "terrorism." The United States would have none of it. But within four years the United States was doing precisely what it had openly condemned others for doing. Ronald Schaffer has made use of oral history collections and the Freedom of Information Act to reveal the private views and moral attitudes of U.S. Army Air Force leaders as they planned and carried out the strategic bombing of Europe.

SOURCE: Ronald Schaffer, "American Bombing Ethics in World War II: The Bombing of German Civilians," *Journal of American History*, LXVII (September 1980): 318–334. For his most complete analysis see Schaffer, *Wings of Judgement: American Bombing in World War II* (Oxford University Press, 1985).

EDITOR'S NOTE: Most of the citations to the sources consulted by the author in this essay have been omitted from this volume for brevity and economy. The reader should consult the original source of the essay for the complete scholarly documentation.

DURING WORLD WAR II the United States Army Air Forces (AAF) enunciated a policy of avoiding indiscriminate attacks against German civilians. According to this policy, American airmen were to make selective strikes against precise military and industrial targets, avoiding direct attacks on the populace. Although some noncombatants would inevitably be killed or wounded, these casualties would be the result of accidents of war, not of intention. The AAF policy appears as a noteworthy phenomenon in a savage, atrocity-filled war. It seems to distinguish the United States from such nations as Japan, Germany, and Great Britain, which intentionally attacked civilian-populated areas. It also seems to tell something about the ethical codes of American air force leaders, for official historians of the United States armed forces strongly suggest that those men agreed with the policy for moral reasons. According to the official AAF history, General Carl Spaatz, commander of the United States Strategic Air Forces in Europe, consistently opposed recommendations "frankly aimed at breaking the morale of the German people." Spaatz repeatedly "raised the moral issue" involved in bombing enemy civilians and was strongly supported, when he did so, by AAF headquarters in Washington. Another AAF commander, General Ira C. Eaker, stated that "we should never allow the history of this war to convict us of throwing the strategic bomber at the man in the street." Citing the official AAF history, army historian Kent R. Greenfield contended that "the Americans not only believed [selective bombing] to be more effective: they were opposed to the mass bombing of civilians." The views of AAF leaders in World War II appear to provide a standard against which to measure the ethics of military professionals.

Yet when the evidence is examined closely, it is clear that the ethical codes of these men did little to discourage air attacks on German civilians. Prewar American air plans and doctrine and the development of operations during the war reveal that official policy against indiscriminate bombing was so broadly interpreted and so frequently breached as to become almost meaningless. Statements of air commanders that supposedly indicate abhorrence of terror bombing, when analyzed in context, mean something very different. In the end, both the policy and the apparent ethical support for it among AAF leaders turn out to be myths; while they contain elements of truth, they are substantially fictitious or misleading. How did these particular myths arise? What were the actual views of AAF leaders on the morality of bombing civilians? How does a more accurate reconstruction of moral attitudes in the war against Germany affect understanding of the history of American military ethics?

Prewar doctrine of the American Army Air Corps had developed under the influence of a group of air power theorists, particularly the Italian Giulio Douhet. Douhet prophesied that offensive aircraft would decide the war of the future. Instead of sending waves of soldiers to slaughter each other, as on the Western Front in World War I, belligerents would use aircraft to destroy vital centers behind the lines: naval bases, transportation junctions, military depots, factories, and centers of population. Civilians would panic at the mere sight of approaching warplanes. Repeated bombings would lead to the utter collapse of the enemy's society.

The authors of official United States air warfare manuals were ambivalent about the strategy of attacking civilians. A 1935 Air Corps Tactical School manual declared, in a paraphrase of Douhet's words, that the morale of an enemy's populace was even more important than the spirit of its troops because military morale could be revived after it was damaged, while a breakdown in civilian morale might decide the war. A 1938 Air Corps training text declared that among the methods used to break the enemy's will to fight were denial of necessities of life to civilians and direct intimidation of the populace. Nevertheless, prewar doctrine recommended against striking directly at civilians, chiefly on the ground that it was inefficient to do so.

Efficiency was crucial to American air planners during the years before the attack on Pearl Harbor, for they understood that, at the start of the coming war, the number of American planes would be severely limited while the number of possible enemy targets was extremely large. Most of these targets were connected by the web of functions that linked together a modern industrial society. Accordingly, the primary purpose of American air power would be to disintegrate the enemy society by striking the most vital points in the web, such as oil refineries and power stations. American bombers would also attack more immediate sources of military power, such as tank factories, aircraft engine plants, and warships.

Direct attacks on civilians employed air power resources inefficiently, reducing the ability of the air force to strike at more vital targets. In 1941 AAF commander Henry H. Arnold and Eaker stated that, except in special situations, human beings were not "priority targets." Bombers in far greater numbers than were then available, they observed, would be required to "wipe out" enough people to break the will of a whole nation. The AAF's 1941 war plan, AWPD/1, also gave civilian targets less than top priority at the start of a future war. Its authors proposed that in a conflict with Germany, the AAF might begin morale attacks only after German industry had begun to crumble, after the structure of the state was breaking apart, and after the populace was despondent.

Neither the Arnold–Eaker study nor the AAF war plan promised permanent safeguards for enemy civilians. The first implied that when bombers became available in far greater numbers than existed in 1941 they could be used against civilians. The second suggested that after Germany's industrial fabric began to come apart and her people were becoming demoralized, the AAF might bomb German cities to destroy morale completely. It would appear, then, that the men who developed the prewar strategy of the AAF had no objections in principle to the use of air power against noncombatants.

Prewar plans and the airpower doctrine that emerged before Pearl Harbor are obviously not sufficient as tests of the ethics of AAF leaders. What has to be analyzed is the way those leaders acted as the air war evolved.

At first glance the record of early AAF actions in Europe seems to uphold the view that American air force commanders wished to avoid bombing enemy civilians. It shows that they dispatched their planes in daylight to hit precise military and industrial targets and that when the British asked them to join in night raids on urban residential areas they refused. The Royal Air Force (RAF) was committed to urban area bombing. It had tried precision raids but found that its own losses far outweighed the damage inflicted on the enemy. Unable to bomb German factories effectively, the British decided to attack residential districts, hoping to "dehouse" and otherwise incapacitate factory workers, striking at the German economy through its labor force and demoralizing the enemy population. Prime Minister Winston Churchill and British military leaders thought the U.S. Eighth Air Force should send some of its planes on night saturation raids, but at the Casablanca Conference of January 1943 the AAF persuaded the Allied leaders to let its precision daylight raids continue. "We had won a major victory," Arnold wrote about this agreement, "for we would bomb in accordance with American principles, using methods for which our planes were designed."

These principles did not include moral objections to bombing the residents of German cities, a fact that emerges from the arguments that Eaker, then commander of the Eighth Air Force, used to persuade Churchill to agree to continued American day attacks. American heavy bombers, Eaker observed, were designed for daylight operations and were equipped with precision bombsights that worked correctly only when the target could be seen. American crews, who were trained for precision bombing, could hit small but important installations. When they flew in daylight they would draw out and destroy enemy day fighters. Attacking by day, while the British bombed at night, they would, in Eaker's words, "give the devils no rest."

Every one of Eaker's arguments was pragmatic. None implied any solicitude for the welfare of German civilians. Indeed, Eaker told an Air Force historian after the war that his colleagues in the AAF never objected on moral grounds to bombing the people of Germany. "I never felt there was any moral sentiment among leaders of the AAF," he explained. "A military man has to be trained and inured to do the job. . . . The business of sentiment never enters into it at all."

After the Casablanca Conference, Arnold made it clear that he did not intend to exempt German civilians from American air attacks. In April 1943 he told a logistics officer that the Eighth Air Force was going to use incendiary bombs to burn densely built-up sections of towns and cities in daylight raids. Shortly afterward, he had an aide inform members of the Air Staff in Washington that "this is a brutal war and . . . the way to stop the killing of civilians is to cause so much damage and destruction and death that the civilians will demand that their government cease fighting. This doesn't mean that we are making civilians or civilian institutions a war objective, but we cannot 'pull our punches' because some of them may get killed."

The meaning of Arnold's last point was brought home to German civilians when American planes bombed outside the target area—something that happened frequently when weather was poor or enemy opposition was strong and that occasionally occurred when there was no opposition at all. Sometimes the killing of civilians was not entirely accidental. On October 10, 1943, 236 Eighth Air Force planes bombed Münster in clear weather, using the center of the town as their aiming point. At a conference eleven days later, some of the officers involved explained that houses as well as factories were good aiming points because they enabled airmen to "put down enough bombs to destroy the town." This made it unnecessary to go back and hit the target again.[1]

As a direct attack on a civilian area in good weather, the Münster raid was an exception to AAF practice at this stage of the war. But shortly after it took place, the Americans began a series of bombings through cloud cover that were tantamount to urban area attacks. European weather was unusually foul in the fall of 1943, and AAF planners felt they would have to abandon the strategic bombing offensive if their planes could only attack in clear skies. They chose instead to guide the bombers toward their objectives with radar. Since radar could not distinguish targets precisely at that time, the result was the killing and wounding of large numbers of noncombatants.

This lack of precision looked like a virtue to some American officers who wanted to find a way to launch massive direct attacks on civilians. Colonel Henry A. Berliner, an intelligence officer on Arnold's staff, thought that radar-assisted attacks on German cities would disperse Luftwaffe fighter defenses, weaken enemy morale, and by driving civilians from their homes in wintertime, force the Nazi government to use up resources caring for the victims of bombardment. He believed that, without diminishing the precision bombing offensive, the AAF could stage at least one raid a month like the Hamburg operation—a series of joint British-American attacks in the summer of 1943 that had killed at least 60,000 Germans and incinerated a large part of the city. Eaker also thought radar bombing should be used to erode enemy morale when weather prevented raids on higher priority precision objectives. "We learn from enemy reaction from secret sources," he told another officer, "and from his squealing and press and propaganda, that he abhors these attacks on his cities. They cause great gloom in Germany." On November 1, 1943, Arnold directed that when daytime precision raids were impossible, heavy bombardment units should attack area targets in Germany using radar.

A few weeks after Arnold issued this order, AAF planners began to consider a further step: making civilian morale an explicit target system.

Officers appointed to study bombing programs for the next phase in the war examined this possibility but concluded that morale would not be a suitable objective. They believed that bombing might actually strengthen civilian determination to fight. But even if it were possible to destroy civilian morale, they thought that the feelings of the populace could not bring an early end to the war since no group or combination of groups in Germany was strong enough to overcome Nazi control. One member of the committee, told that morale was bad in Berlin, remarked that the "only morale worth considering now is the morale of the people in high places— the people in power, the High Command."

While none of these officers raised anything but pragmatic objections to morale bombing, other persons, outside the armed forces, had begun to criticize area attacks as immoral, and their complaints had an important effect on the AAF. In March 1944 twenty-eight noted clergymen and antiwar activists signed an introduction to an article in *Fellowship*, the journal of the pacifist organization Fellowship of Reconciliation, stating, among other things, that "Christian people should be moved to examine themselves concerning their participation in this carnival of death." The *New York Times* printed a front page story about the incident and a flurry of controversy followed in religious and secular media.

This show of dissent alarmed officials in the War Department and the AAF. Undersecretary of War Robert P. Patterson publicly denounced the protestors, claiming that they were encouraging the enemy. Robert A. Lovett, the Assistant Secretary of War for Air, visited AAF leaders in Europe and briefed them on the problem of adverse publicity at home. Shortly after D-Day, he informed Spaatz at the headquarters of the United States Strategic Air Forces in Europe (USSTAF)[2] that there was genuine feeling in the country and in Congress about the inhumanity of indiscriminate bombing and advised utmost caution in pursuing such a program. Lovett predicted serious trouble if indiscriminate attacks became the announced policy of the AAF.

Lovett touched on an issue of the highest importance to air commanders—the public image of the AAF. During the years between the wars, officers like Spaatz, Eaker, and William L. ("Billy") Mitchell had worked diligently to develop a favorable image, testifying at congressional hearings, staging exhibitions of flight endurance and bombing demonstrations, and cultivating journalists who could help them make the American people feel positively about the air corps and the doctrine of strategic air power. After Pearl Harbor, public relations was just as important to the air commanders, for not only did they want to contribute as much as possible to the winning of the war, but they hoped that by making a massive display of effective strategic bombing, they would insure their preeminence in the postwar military establishment as an independent air force. As Arnold told Eaker in June 1943, "We want the people to understand and have faith in *our way of making war.*"

Eaker was so concerned about public perceptions of the AAF that he sought to control the way its history would be written. He warned an officer in Arnold's headquarters that no criticism of the conduct of the war in any theater of operations should appear in official correspondence without clearance from the "war chiefs." To General Clayton L. Bissell, the assistant chief of air staff for intelligence, Eaker wrote: "We have got a mass of historians at both ends watching all this correspondence and these things cannot but creep into the official documents unless we are all on guard."

Even before Lovett's warning, AAF leaders had begun to fear that area bombing might jeopardize the reputation of their service at home. Large numbers of Americans did not appear to hate the German people, even after the Nazi government declared war. There were, of course, millions of German-Americans in the United States and many citizens, regardless of ancestry, felt their country should not have become involved in war with Germany in the first place. AAF generals knew about these attitudes, felt that making war against civilians conflicted with national ideals, and worried about the way Americans might react to stories of American attacks on German women and children.

It was this concern for the image of the AAF, together with reluctance to divert resources from the precision bombing offensive, that led Spaatz, in summer 1944, to turn down proposals for morale bombing. Some of these originated with the British, while others were developed in Spaatz's own headquarters where the deputy director of intelligence, Colonel Lowell P. Weicker, promoted a psychological warfare bombing plan. Weicker wanted to broadcast warnings that particular German towns and cities were about to be destroyed, then issue black propaganda, purporting to originate with the Nazi government, that would tell the inhabitants that the Americans could not harm them. Finally, American planes would bomb the designated places, showing the German people that their government could no longer defend them.

The chief British proposal was for a massive Allied air attack on Berlin, operation THUNDERCLAP, that would supposedly bring down the German government through the collapse of civilian morale. "I have been subjected to some pressure on the part of the Air Ministry," Spaatz told Arnold, "to join hands with them in morale bombing. I discussed this matter . . . with Lovett when he was here and have maintained a firm position that our bombing will continue to be precision bombing against military objective[s]. . . . There is no doubt in my mind that the RAF want very much to have the U.S. Air Forces tarred with the morale bombing aftermath which we feel will be terrific."

If, as the official historians say, Spaatz raised the moral issue in opposing frankly stated recommendations to break German morale by bombing, he did so with practical intentions. "It wasn't for religious or moral reasons," he explained after the war, "that I didn't go along with urban area bombing." Although the official history claims that AAF headquarters backed up Spaatz when he raised the moral issue, the record shows that this was not because the chief of the AAF rejected terror bombing. When the British offered proposals for attacking morale, Arnold did not turn them down. Rather, he asked his staff to study them. Arnold had what an aide called an "open mind" on the subject.

For a while Spaatz's viewpoint prevailed. Dwight D. Eisenhower, the supreme allied commander who then held control over the activities of USSTAF, at first supported Spaatz's wish to avoid open war against civilians. But at the end of August, with Allied armies stalled on the Western Front, he changed his mind. "While I have always insisted," Eisenhower told Spaatz on August 28, "that U.S. Strategic Air Forces be directed against precision targets, I am always prepared to take part in anything that gives real promise to ending the war quickly." Less than two weeks later, he notified Spaatz to have the Eighth Air Force ready to bomb Berlin at a moment's notice. Spaatz then instructed the Eighth Air Force commander "that we would no longer plan to hit definite military objectives but be ready to drop bombs indiscriminately" on the Nazi capital when Eisenhower gave the order.

Preparations for THUNDERCLAP continued at different levels. At the September 14 meeting of the Combined Chiefs of Staff, Arnold brought up a British proposal to have the chiefs endorse morale bombing, which would have given the sanction of the highest Anglo-American military body to raids like the one proposed for Berlin. President Franklin D. Roosevelt's chief military advisor, Admiral William Leahy, told the chiefs it would be a mistake to "record" such a decision. (He did not, as the AAF history states, express opposition to morale bombing.) At USSTAF headquarters, Spaatz's deputy commander for operations, General Frederick C. Anderson, Jr., told the planners to incorporate into THUNDERCLAP Weicker's proposal for breaking morale with preannounced raids and black propaganda. Execution of THUNDERCLAP was delayed, however, until 1945, not for ethical reasons or because of the AAF policy against indiscriminate bombing, but because of problems in assembling the required forces.

The AAF had started working, meanwhile, on other programs which offer additional proof that the official policy did not conform to practice. One of these was the War Weary Bomber project, designed to take hundreds of worn-out bombers, fill them with explosives, and aim them at enemy targets. After the crews bailed out over friendly territory, automatic devices would direct the winged bombs toward their objectives. This project was America's response to the German V-1 and V-2 missiles, which were falling indiscriminately on the English. The robot planes were intended to blow up industrial targets and military installations, such as the V-1 launching sites. AAF leaders also hoped they would disrupt the German economy, force the enemy to mobilize large numbers of people for defense, and reduce the German will to resist. They could serve, in addition, as prototypes for guided missiles to be used against Japan.

It was obvious to air force commanders that the employment of robot bombers was really indiscriminate air warfare, and it is equally evident that the generals had no moral objection to using them. "I can see very little difference," Arnold wrote Spaatz in November 1944, "between the British night area bombing and our taking a war weary airplane, launching it, at say, 50 or 60 miles away from Cologne and letting it fall somewhere in the city limits." Arnold then suggested turning the robot planes loose all over Germany so the Germans would be as afraid of them, not knowing where they would hit, as the English were of V-1s and V-2s. "I think that the psychological effect on the morale of the German people would be much greater this way." Spaatz replied that war-weary aircraft would have the greatest chance of success if directed against reasonably large, undefended towns. While he did not think they would affect the outcome of the war significantly, he saw no reason for not attacking those towns with robot planes if they had military or industrial targets "associated with them."

Early models of war-weary bombers were so inaccurate that Leahy described their use as an "inhumane and barbarous type of warfare with which the United States should not be associated." Even after the AAF equipped the experimental robot planes with radar guidance late in the war with Germany, they were estimated likely to hit somewhere within a mile and a half of their targets, leading the War Department to wonder if they did not violate the official policy against indiscriminate bombing. Arnold's staff was able to allay this concern by redefining indiscriminate bombing. It notified the War Department that robot aircraft were more accurate than radar bombing (which the AAF had employed on a large scale since the fall of 1943), and since robot bombers were bound to affect enemy production when they exploded within large industrial targets, they would not be indiscriminate. Reassured that the weapon was accurate enough to use in Germany, the War Department approved its employment.

Only a few of the robot planes ever flew, for the British government feared that the Germans would retaliate against London with robot bombers of their own and induced the military chiefs to delay the project until the last few days of the war. But another program, even more deadly to civilians, did go into effect: operation CLARION, which sent American fighters and bombers all over Germany to attack targets in small towns and villages. Its purpose was to persuade the German people that they were defenseless against air attacks and that additional resistance was futile—in other words, to break civilian morale.

Air planners set to work on this project in earnest during the late summer of 1944. In September, Colonel Charles G. Williamson, a USSTAF planning officer, told General Laurence Kuter, chief of plans at AAF headquarters, about the kind of attacks Williamson's group had in mind. The targets should be in "relatively virgin areas" and should include transportation facilities in small towns, small machine shops, and other targets, no matter how small, "resembling known industrial establishments." A few days later, at a meeting with Kuter and Williamson, Arnold proposed that planning begin for attacks lasting six or seven days against widespread German targets. Arnold felt that if these raids were carried out at the right time they might decide the war. He stated that they were not to be obliteration attacks aimed at the people of Germany. Rather, groups of roving fighters and bombers should hit numerous types of military objectives throughout Germany "to give every citizen an opportunity to see positive proof of Allied air power."

Given the probable accuracy of the attacking planes, this distinction meant virtually nothing, for there was no way that the attackers could avoid obliterating villages or parts of larger communities if they struck at small machine shops or at railroad stations and other transportation targets. Spaatz and others had made exactly this point before the D-Day invasion, arguing against proposals to hit transportation facilities in French and Belgian towns because too many civilians would be killed and wounded. Furthermore, AAF planners had long regarded transportation bombing as a form of antimorale warfare because of its effects on nearby civilians.

Nevertheless, in response to Arnold's wishes, USSTAF developed the CLARION plan, gving it the euphemistic subtitle: GENERAL PLAN FOR MAXIMUM EFFORT ATTACK AGAINST TRANSPORTATION OBJECTIVES. AAF commanders had no difficulty understanding what was really being prepared, and several of them protested. General James H. Doolittle, who then commanded the Eighth Air Force, warned Spaatz that widespread strafing of German civilians behind the battle lines might so enrage the enemy populace that they would retaliate against Allied prisoners of war. German propagandists would use CLARION to justify Nazi brutality, and if the operation led to substantial Allied losses, the American people might begin to ask why the AAF had changed its strategy. The commander of the Fifteenth Air Force, General Nathan F. Twining, added his own cautions, warning of potential heavy losses for the attackers and urging Spaatz to consider how the enemy and the American people would react to the inevitable civilian casualties.

Eaker offered the most vehement objections. In a letter for Spaatz's eyes only, he predicted that CLARION would absolutely convince the Germans "that we are the barbarians they say we are, for it would be perfectly obvious to them that this is primarily a large scale attack on civilians, as, in fact, it of course will be." Eaker reminded Spaatz that CLARION was completely contrary to what Lovett had said about sticking to military targets and added that it entailed an inefficient and excessively risky employment of strategic bombers. Eaker wrote:

If the time ever comes when we want to attack the civilian populace with a view to breaking civil morale, such a plan . . . is probably the way to do it. I personally, however, have become completely convinced that you and Bob Lovett are right and we should never allow the history of this war to convict us of throwing the strategic bomber at the man in the street. I think there is a better way we can do our share toward the defeat of the enemy, but if we are to attack the civilian population I am certain we should wait until its morale is much nearer [the] breaking point and until the weather favors the operation more than it will at any time in the winter or early spring.

It should be noted that each of these arguments was pragmatic. Eaker worried about German propaganda and excessive risks and losses. He expressed, not moral objections to bombing civilians, but concern over the shifting of resources from more efficient modes of warfare, over the timing of the operation, and over the way CLARION would make the AAF appear in the history of the war. In fact, Eaker explicitly denied, several years later, that he had meant to indicate in this letter that he opposed bombing that endangered enemy civilians. The civilian who supported national leaders in war, he contended, was just as responsible as the military man.

While Spaatz seemed hesitant about carrying out CLARION, there was considerable enthusiasm at higher levels for sending United States planes against large and small German targets in a series of widespread sweeps. Secretary of War Henry L. Stimson and Assistant Secretary John McCloy found the idea, in Stimson's words, "intriguing." Chief of Staff George C. Marshall declared that he wanted to see attacks all over Germany. And on January 9, 1945, Lovett himself urged Arnold to begin the operation. "If the power of the German people to resist is to be further reduced," Lovett explained, "it seems likely that we must spread the destruction of industry into the smaller cities and towns now being used for production under the German system of dispersal."

Eisenhower's headquarters finally ordered CLARION to proceed. On February 22 and in the early morning hours of February 23, thousands of bombers and fighters of the Eighth, Ninth, and Fifteenth Air Forces, joined by RAF units, ranged over Germany, bombing and strafing transportation objectives and targets of opportunity.

CLARION was only one of a series of operations in 1945 officially described as attacks on transportation but really aimed largely at reducing civilian morale. General Haywood S. Hansell, one of the designers of the pre-Pearl Harbor plan AWPD/1, observed that during the last weeks of the war, the strategic air forces dropped great quantities of bombs on German marshaling yards and stations, some of them in cities, although the German rail system was already wrecked. In reality, Hansell observed, the marshaling yards were area bombing targets. By this time the conditions for area bombing that Arnold, Eaker, and Hansell had predicated before the war had been met. Since bombers were available in greater numbers than were required to eliminate the remaining important precision targets, they could be used against civilians with no loss of efficiency. The German industrial system was so devastated that the AAF could devote a substantial part of its resources to breaking civilian morale.

The most publicized instances of the now fully formed program of American area bombing were the raids, early in 1945, on Berlin, Dresden, and other east German cities. Substantial impetus for these raids came from a Russian offensive into Germany that began the second week of January. Added to the hope of ending the war by breaking enemy morale and destroying Nazi administrative centers was a belief that AAF and RAF bombers could assist the Soviet advance. By battering the remnants of German transportation and by dislocating the German rear, American and British aircraft could make it harder for the Germans to bring up supplies and reinforcements to resist the Red Army.

In addition, some staff officers thought the attacks would be useful in shaping Soviet attitudes toward the Western Allies. A week before the Yalta Conference, General David M. Schlatter, the deputy chief of air staff at Supreme Headquarters, Allied Expeditionary Force (SHAEF), noted in his diary: "I feel that our air forces are the blue chips with which we will approach the post-war treaty table, and that this operation [a massive bombardment of Berlin] will add immeasurably to their strength, or rather to the Russian knowledge of their strength." The British Joint Intelligence Committee likewise believed that raids in east German cities would be politically advantageous as a show of Anglo-American support for the Russians.

First of these huge attacks would be THUNDERCLAP, the operation against the German capital that had been suspended months before. Doolittle, whose Eighth Air Force would have to bomb the administrative center of the city, did not like THUNDERCLAP at all. He pointed out to Spaatz that American planes would have to fly within range of hundreds of heavy antiaircraft guns to reach an area where there were no important strictly military targets. Even as a terror operation the raid would not be successful, because German civilians would have ample warning to take shelter. Besides, terror was induced by fear of the unknown, not by intensifying what the people of Berlin had experienced for years. And as perhaps the last and best-remembered air force operation of the war, THUNDERCLAP would "violate the basic American principle of precision bombing of targets of strictly military significance for which our tactics were developed and our crews trained and indoctrinated." Doolittle recommended that the RAF be assigned to area bomb Berlin while the Americans hit precise military targets.

Spaatz was also worried about the effects of the raid on the way people thought about the AAF. This is evident from his suggestion to Doolittle that news summaries of the operation stress the effort to create administrative confusion and disrupt reinforcements. He said nothing about breaking morale, though he knew that this was one of the chief objectives for those who advocated THUNDERCLAP. The British felt that way and so, as Spaatz had recently learned, did Chief of Staff Marshall. Not only did Marshall want to hit Berlin, but when its inhabitants were evacuated to places like Munich, he wanted to attack Munich too, showing the eva-cuees there was no hope.

After some hesitation Spaatz proceeded with the bombing of Berlin, arranging for it to occur as a radar-guided, blind-bombing operation. He also had his staff prepare for the attack on Munich that Marshall had requested. Following Spaatz's instructions, nearly a thousand B-17s blasted targets in Berlin on February 3, 1945. Although American bombardiers were able to do visual bombing through holes in the clouds and hit several military targets, perhaps 25,000 civilians were killed.

Other raids on east German cities followed, climaxing February 13 and 14 in an attack on Dresden, where British planes created a vast firestorm that swept across the city. Then more than three hundred American bombers roared high over the still flaming ruins, aiming through dense clouds at the marshaling yards, while American fighters strafed moving targets down below.

The east German raids, particularly the attack on Dresden, produced just the kind of publicity that Spaatz and Doolittle wished to avoid. At Eisenhower's headquarters, RAF Air Commodore C. M. Grierson told a press briefing that one object of these raids was to disrupt the German economy by forcing the German government to move supplies around to care for bombed-out civilians, by attacking towns from which relief was being sent, and by destroying places to which refugees were evacuated. An Associated Press story based on Grierson's interview was passed by a SHAEF censor, and soon people in the United States were reading that "Allied air commanders have made the long-awaited decision to adopt deliberate terror bombing of the great German population centers as a ruthless expedient to hasten Hitler's doom."

The briefing and news story, both essentially correct, caused consid-erable alarm at AAF headquarters. "What do we say?" Arnold's chief of information asked Spaatz. "This is certain to have a nation-wide serious effect on the Air Forces as we have steadfastly preached the gospel of pre-cision bombing against military and industrial targets." Anderson, Spaatz's deputy commander for operations, replied that, after discussing the matter with Eisenhower, it had been decided that USSTAF would issue no official explanation and that all questions on the subject would be answered by saying:

A. That there has been no change in bombing policy;
B. The United States Strategic Air Forces have always directed their attacks against military objectives and will continue to do so;
C. The story was erroneously passed by censor.

Anderson informed Washington, on Spaatz's behalf, that while the bombing of Berlin had not been expected to be precise, it was justified by the city's military significance and that the same was true of Dresden and the other cities in eastern Germany. "It has always been my policy," he told Arnold (in Spaatz's name), "that civilian populations are not suitable military objectives." Anderson did not say what Spaatz's practice had been—which was to permit indiscriminate bombing of German civilians when his superiors required him to.

We are now in a position to explain how the myth arose of an AAF policy against indiscriminate bombing. There was a policy—on paper. Sometimes it was adhered to; often it was not, or it was so broadly reinterpreted as to become meaningless. High-ranking officers sent official messages to one another which caused the record to suggest that AAF practice fitted with the official policy. Yet these officers knew this was not the case. Thus, in the aftermath of the raids into eastern Germany, Anderson cabled Arnold that the commander of USSTAF did not regard civilians as appropriate targets even though Anderson himself, three months earlier, had requested USSTAF planners to include a terror bombing proposal in their preparations for THUNDERCLAP. Anderson and his colleagues were protecting the image of the AAF from historians and other investigators.

The official historians of the AAF noted some of the deviations from stated policy. They remarked that bombing directives were sometimes issued for the record and that bombardiers and air force commanders sometimes ignored them. But they did not pursue systematically the question of how meaningful the policy was to AAF leaders. Had they done so, they presumably would have concluded that, regardless of what the leaders said for the record, the official policy placed insignificant restraints on the bombing of German civilians.[3]

Whatever restraints there were did not arise out of the consciences of the men who ran the AAF, for the record provides no indication that they objected on moral grounds to radar bombing, inaccurate robot plane attacks, sweeps against small towns and villages, or the devastation of cities calculated to break morale. While these men did prefer precision bombing to area attacks, at least until the last weeks of the war, it was not for reasons of conscience. Rather, it was because they considered selective bombing more efficient militarily, better suited to the image they wished to project, more likely to verify their theory of strategic air power and, for all these reasons, a more effective way of establishing the preeminence of their service after the war. When Spaatz and his colleagues "raised the moral issue," they were expressing not personal repugnance to the bombing of noncombatants, but apprehension over the way others would regard the actions of the AAF. Their approach to the business of war was essentially pragmatic.

This does not mean that they never thought about the ethical implications of air warfare. Certainly Arnold did. In June 1943 he sent a memorandum to his combat commanders in which he warned that bombing was bound to add to the horrors of war and likely to intensify feelings of hatred in the "victim populations" that could poison international relations after the war ended. As a "spur to conscience," he reminded the commanders that increased accuracy of bombing meant lives saved (though whether he meant enemy or American lives is not clear). The bomber, he observed, "when used with the proper degree of understanding . . . becomes, in effect, the most humane of all weapons" and, depending on how it was employed, could be either "the savior or the scourge of humanity."

These sentiments appear to conflict with Arnold's willingness to burn down enemy cities, his desire to see robot bombers fall indiscriminately among the German people, and his acceptance of morale attacks. Yet they are more than lip service or words for the historical record. They represent a moral attitude inherent in air power theory, a position that goes back to World War I—the idea that bombing is a way of preserving lives by ending wars quickly and by providing a substitute for the kind of ground warfare that had killed so many soldiers a quarter century earlier. Anderson reflected this view when he wrote, in July 1943, that his Eighth Bomber Command would so devastate the German economy that there would be no necessity of an invasion of the continent "with the consequent loss of thousands and possibly millions of lives." Eventually, American airmen were sent to attack German civilians and the German economy as a way of rapidly ending the war (and saving the lives of those who would otherwise be killed).

Despite his claim that AAF leaders never evinced moral sentiments, Eaker himself defended area bombing with a moral argument—that civilians could legitimately be killed in air attacks because they supported the enemy's war effort. As Eaker put it, the man who builds a weapon is as responsible for its use as the man who carries it into battle. Eaker also contended that the avoidance of a greater evil justified endangering civilians, for he regarded the entire conflict with Nazi Germany as a war against evil in which it was necessary to attack bad people in order to save the good, the righteous, and the just. While Eaker offered these arguments long after the end of the war, there is no reason to doubt that something like the same sentiments occurred to him while it was going on. If so, then he, like other AAF leaders held moral attitudes about the bombing of civilians, attitudes that did not forbid such bombing but rather made it permissible.

This reinterpretation of World War II bombing policy and moral attitudes has several consequences for the history of American military ethics. It makes it somewhat harder to distinguish the ethical conduct of the United States in World War II from its conduct in Vietnam and in other wars and from the morality of other nations that practiced terror bombing. It raises the question whether feelings for the welfare of enemy civilians can ever be compatible with military success. And it invites us to scan the history of American warfare to see what other myths affect our perception of the role of moral constraints.

NOTES

1. Wesley Frank Craven and James Lea Cate describe the raid as directed against railroads and waterways. Craven and Cate, eds., *Army Air Forces in World War II*, 7 vols. (Chicago, 1948–58), II, 850. To understand why these officers wanted to avoid returning to a target, one should note that on August 17 their planes had taken tremendous losses in attacks on Schweinfurt and Regensburg. Yet on October 14, four days after the Münster raid, they had to go back to Schweinfurt again.
2. United States Strategic Air Forces, formed in January 1944, coordinated strategic bombing by the U.S. Eighth and Fifteenth Air Forces. In April it passed from formal control by the Combined Chiefs of Staff to control by the supreme Allied commander. In September it reverted back to the Combined Chiefs of Staff. Even after that date, however, Dwight D. Eisenhower continued to influence its activities through understandings with Carl Spaatz.
3. Craven and Cate, eds., *Army Air Forces*, III, 721, 726. A secret Air University study prepared in 1969 makes the point more bluntly: "Americans were not much concerned about civilian casualties resulting from attacks on objectives in the Reich." [Charles A. Ravenstein and Maurer Maurer], "Constraints on AAF Operations" (Maxwell Air Force Base, Ala., 1969), 4. A copy is available at Simpson Historical Research Center.

33

Fifteen-Item Neuropsychiatric Screening Adjunct Scores of Flying Personnel with and Without Combat Flying Experience

Yossarian, Joseph Heller's terrified bombardier, antihero of Catch-22, was not utterly imaginary. He lives in the report of psychiatrists Roy Grinker and John Spiegel on bomber crews in the Mediterranean–North African theater* and the multivolume Studies in Social Psychology in World War II, *from which this table is drawn. Flak, enemy fighters, long hours, and the sight of a B-17 disintegrating beside them took their toll on the nerves of bomber crews.*

*See Roy Grinker and John Spiegel, *Men Under Stress* (Philadelphia: Blakinston, 1945).

SOURCE: S. Stouffer et al., *Studies in Social Psychology in World War II*, 4 vols. (Princeton, N.J.: Princeton University Press, 1949–50), II: 376.

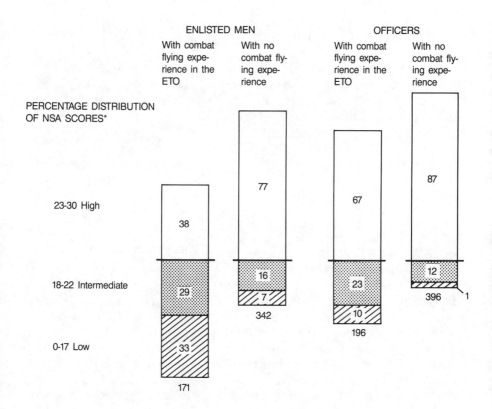

ENLISTED MEN

With combat flying experience in the ETO | With no combat flying experience

OFFICERS

With combat flying experience in the ETO | With no combat flying experience

PERCENTAGE DISTRIBUTION OF NSA SCORES*

23-30 High

18-22 Intermediate

0-17 Low

*A low score indicates marked psychoneurotic tendencies.

(Based on a survey of officer and enlisted air crew members in one very heavy bombardment, B-29, wing in training in the United States, May 1945)(numbers at the bottom of the bars = numbers of cases on which percentages are based.)

34

A World War II Tailgunner Feels Guilt for Killing Germans

The fear of being killed was the more powerful fear, but the fear of killing, or reluctance to take human life, caused some G.I.s anguish. A psychiatrist offered this "case history" of a former Army Air Force bomber crew member whose disorder appeared to stem from his sense of guilt.

BORN TO A VERY RELIGIOUS Midwestern family, P.P.T. started attending church at an early age. As well as being the religious center of his community, the church was also a major factor in much of its social life. As he grew up, graduating from high school and taking his first job, he came to accept the religious precepts as basic to his way of life. He attended services twice a week and participated actively in church affairs. Religion was his guide as well as his solace. To flout its doctrines was to flout not only his God and his family, but the whole community of which he was a part. After leaving school P.P.T. worked for four years as a truck driver and construction laborer before entering the Army at age of twenty-two.

During the first nine months of his service career he was shifted rapidly from one air field to another—Florida, Utah, Colorado, Washington, Oregon, Nebraska. By the time this training was completed he was qualified to work as a gunner on the large bombers and had attained the rank of sergeant. Although this was not the type of duty he would have chosen he accepted it. Next he was sent to England and joined a bomber squadron that had already amassed an impressive record in raids over France and Germany. His first mission was an easy one, but after that it was very difficult. The flak was almost always heavy and enemy fighters were everywhere. His pilot was killed on one raid, his bombardier on another. Once

SOURCE: Eli Ginzberg *et al.*, eds., *The Ineffective Soldier: Vol II: Breakdown and Recovery,* (New York: Columbia University Press, 1959). Excerpt is from pp. 113–15.

they just barely made it back to England after losing three engines and putting out a fire in the cockpit.

P.P.T. was frightened, but even more, he felt terribly guilty. Every time his plane went up its only purpose was to drop bombs on defenseless people. His job as a gunner was to kill enemy fliers and he did his job. But it seemed all wrong to him. This was contrary to his religion and everything that he had learned prior to entering the Army. He felt that he was guilty of participating in a never ending series of heinous crimes for which his family, his community, and his God must always condemn him. He became jittery, could not sleep, and vomited frequently. Yet he kept going and completed his twenty-five missions in a commendable manner. Seven months after leaving the United States he was on his way home again.

After a furlough, he returned to duty still completely obsessed with guilt. If anything, his state was worse than when he had been in combat. He didn't want to do anything, could not eat or sleep and had the sensation that ants were crawling all over his body. Hospitalized, he poured forth his preoccupations to the doctor: "There was the raid the day before Christmas. We had to go. I didn't want to kill those poor people. . . . I shot down a man, a German. I feel guilty about it. We shouldn't kill people. Here they hang people for that. . . . I guess that is what bothers me most. I killed somebody. . . . I think about that German I shot down. I know it was him or me, but I just can't forget that I saw him blow up. Up to then it was just an airplane. Then I realized that there was a man in the plane. . . . I keep trying to think that it is all behind me, but I can't. I just think about it and get upset. I can't read or go to classes without thinking about it. You have fighters coming at you in bed and you can't do anything about it. I keep dreaming about it. I just can't help it." The doctor tried to convince him that he had only been doing his duty, but to no avail, and he was finally discharged virtually unimproved by his hospital stay.

Within two months of leaving the Army P.P.T. started work in a steel plant. At first he found it difficult to work; he was plagued with frequent thoughts and dreams of combat. He did not go to church or associate with his old friends. Gradually, however, he began to participate in community activities and finally started going to church again. By 1948, although still rather restless and suffering from insomnia, he had almost fitted himself back into his old pattern of life. He enjoyed his job, went hunting and fishing for recreation, and was thinking of getting married. He felt far less guilty than he had when he returned from Europe. Later he married and had two children. He feels very much a part of his community again and has, as he sees it, returned to a religious way of life.

35

Bill Mauldin Captures the Civilian's View of Combat Vets in 1946

Many Vietnam veterans resent the assumption held by some Americans that military service had transformed them into psychotic, dangerous men. But the feeling is not unique to Vietnam veterans, as this cartoon of Bill Mauldin's shows. Mauldin's World War II veteran comrades were just as annoyed by the "violent man" assumption.

SOURCE: Bill Mauldin, *Back Home* (New York, 1947), p. 54. Drawings copyrighted 1944, renewed 1972, Bill Mauldin; reproduced by courtesy of Bill Mauldin and Wil-Jo Associates, Inc.

"There's a small item on page 17 about a triple ax murder.
No veterans involved."

The Cold War Years

36

Troops in Segregated and in Integrated Units Answer a Question About Race Relations, 1951

Black troops were, with only a handful of exceptions, assigned to segregated units throughout U.S. military history until President Harry S. Truman ordered the integration of the armed services during the Korean War. Truman was responding to appeals from Civil Rights leaders, to political advisers, and to arguments advanced by army social and behavioral scientists that black troops would be more effective in integrated units and that white soldiers would accept the assignment of blacks in their units largely without deterioration of morale or unit standards.* These behavioral scientists then surveyed opinion as integration took place and found their theories verified by responses such as this one.

*See Richard Dalfiume, *The Integration of the U.S. Armed Forces: Fighting on Two Fronts, 1939–1953* (Columbia: University of Missouri Press, 1969); and Leo Bogart, ed., *Social Research and the Desegregation of the U.S. Army* (Chicago: University of Chicago Press, 1969).

How Quartermaster Corps Personnel in 1951 Answered the Question: "As Time Goes on, Do You Think That White and Colored People in the United States Will Get Along Better Together Than They Do Today, Not as Well as They Do Now, or About the Same as Now?"

	QUARTERMASTER			
	Whites in All-White Units	Whites in Integrated Units	Negroes in Integrated Units	Negroes in All-Negro Units
Answers:				
They will get along better together	13%	68%	85%	82%
They will get along about the same as now	65	23	13	15
They will not get along as well as now	22	7	1	2
No answer	0	2	1	1
N(100%) =	(68)	(99)	(73)	(144)

SOURCE: Leo Bogart, ed., *Social Research and the Desegregation of the U.S. Army* (Chicago, 1969), pp. 176, 353, 355.

37

The Selective Service System

Channeling Manpower

The Selective Service System (the "draft") was designed to serve several ends in the era of the Cold War: (1) to provide for basic military manpower needs yet (2) to exempt those with skills "vital to the national interest" and, in the words of President Truman, to (3) "raise the physical standard of the nation's manpower, [4] lower the illiteracy rate, [5] develop citizenship responsibilities, and [6] foster the moral and spiritual welfare of our young people." This memo, prepared for the information of new draft board members, was produced by the office of General Lewis Hershey, head of the Selective Service System, in 1965. What are some of the consequences that "channeling" may have had on America in the 1960s?

ONE OF THE MAJOR PRODUCTS of the Selective Service classification process is the channeling of manpower into many endeavors and occupations; activities that are in the national interest. This function is a counterpart and amplification of the System's responsibility to deliver manpower to the armed forces in such a manner as to reduce to a minimum any adverse effect upon the national health, safety, interest, and progress. By identifying and applying this process intelligently, the System is able not only to minimize any adverse effect, but to exert an effect beneficial to the national health, safety and interest.

The line dividing the primary function of armed forces manpower procurement from the process of channeling manpower into civilian support is often finely drawn. The process of channeling by not taking men from certain activities who are otherwise liable for service, or by giving deferments to qualified men in certain occupations, is actual procurement by

SOURCE: *The Selective Service: Its Concepts, History, and Operation* (Washington, D.C.: Government Printing Office, September 1967).

inducement of manpower of civilian activities which are manifestly in the national interest.

While the best known purpose of Selective Service is to procure manpower for the armed forces, a variety of related processes takes place outside delivery of manpower to the active armed forces. Many of these may be put under the heading of "channeling manpower." Many young men would have not pursued a higher education if there had not been a program of student deferments. Many young scientists, engineers, tool and die makers, and other possessors of scarce skills would not remain in their jobs in the defense effort if it were not for a program of occupational deferment. Even though the salary of a teacher has historically been meager, many young men remain in that job seeking the reward of deferment. The process of channeling manpower by deferment is entitled to much credit for the large amount of graduate students in technical fields and for the fact that there is not a greater shortage of teachers, engineers, and other scientists working in activities which are essential to the national interest.

The opportunity to enhance the national well-being by inducing more registrants to participate in fields which relate directly to the national interest came about as a consequence, soon after the close of the Korean episode, of the knowledge within the System that there was enough registrant personnel to allow stringent deferment practices employed during war time to be relaxed or tightened as the situation might require. Circumstances had become favorable to induce registrants, by the attraction of deferment, to matriculate in schools and pursue subjects in which there was beginning to be a national shortage of personnel. These were particularly in the engineering, scientific, and teaching professions.

In the Selective Service System, the term "deferment" has been used millions of times to describe the method and means used to attract to the kind of service considered to be the most important, the individuals who were not compelled to do it. The club of induction has been used to drive out of areas considered to be less important to the areas of greater importance in which deferments were given, the individuals who did not or could not participate in activities which were considered essential to the Nation. The Selective Service System anticipates evolution in this area. It is promoting the process by the granting of deferments in liberal numbers where the national need clearly would benefit.

Soon after Sputnik I was launched it became popular to reappraise critically our educational, scientific, and technological inventory. Many deplored our shortage of scientific and technical personnel, inadequacies of our schools, and shortage of teachers. Since any analysis having any connection with manpower and its relation to the Nation's survival vitally involves the Selective Service System, it is well to point out that for quite some time the System had been following a policy of deferring instructors who were engaged in the teaching of mathematics and physical and biological sciences. It is appropriate also to recall the System's previously invoked practice of deferring students to prepare themselves for work in some essential activity and the established program of deferring engineers, scientists, and other critically skilled persons who were working in essential fields.

The Congress, in enacting the Universal Military Training and Service legislation declared that adequate provisions for national security required maximum effort in the fields of scientific research and development, and the fullest possible utilization of the Nation's technological, scientific, and other critical manpower resources. To give effect to this philosophy, the classifying boards of the Selective Service System defer registrants determined by them to be necessary in the national health, safety, or interest. This is accomplished on the basis of evidence of record in each individual case. No group deferments are permitted. Deferments are granted, however, in a realistic atmosphere so that the fullest effect of channeling will be felt, rather than be terminated by military service at too early a time.

Registrants and their employers are encouraged and required to make available to the classifying authorities detailed evidence as to the occupations and activities in which registrants are engaged. It is not necessary for any registrant to specifically request deferment, but his selective service file must contain sufficient current evidence on which can be based a proper determination as to whether he should remain where he is or be made available for service. Since occupational deferments are granted for no more than a year at a time, a process of periodically receiving current information and repeated review assures that every deferred registrant continues to contribute to the overall national good. This reminds him of the basis of his deferment. The skills as well as the activities are periodically reevaluated. A critical skill that is not employed in an essential activity does not qualify for deferment.

It is in this atmosphere that the young man registers at age 18 and pressure begins to force his choice. He does not have the inhibitions that a philosophy of universal service in uniform would engender. The door is open for him as a student to qualify if capable in a skill needed by his nation. He has many choices and he is prodded to make a decision.

The psychological effect of this circumstantial climate depends upon the individual, his sense of good citizenship, his love of country and its way of life. He can obtain a sense of well being and satisfaction that he is doing as a civilian what will help his country most. This process encourages him to put forth his best effort and removes to some degree the stigma that has been attached to being out of uniform.

In the less patriotic and more selfish individual it engenders a sense of fear, uncertainty, and dissatisfaction which motivates him, nevertheless, in the same direction. He complains of the uncertainty which he must endure; he would like to be able to do as he pleases; he would appreciate a certain future with no prospect of military service or civilian contribution, but he complies with the needs of the national health, safety, or interest—or he is denied deferment.

Throughout his career as a student, the pressure—the threat of loss of deferment—continues. It continues with equal intensity after graduation. His local board requires periodic reports to find out what he is up to. He is impelled to pursue his skill rather than embark upon some less important enterprise and is encouraged to apply high skill in an essential activity in the national interest. The loss of deferred status is the consequence for the individual who has acquired the skill and either does not use it, or uses it in a nonessential activity.

The psychology of granting wide choice under pressure to take action is the American or indirect way of achieving what is done by direction in foreign countries where choice is not allowed. Here, choice is limited but not denied, and it is fundamental that an individual generally applies himself better to something he has decided to do rather than something he has been told to do.

The effects of channeling are manifested among student physicians. They are deferred to complete their education through school and internship. This permits them to serve in the armed forces in their skills rather than as unskilled enlisted men.

The device of pressurized guidance, or channeling, is employed on Standby Reservists of which more than 2½ million have been referred by all services for availability determinations. The appeal to the Reservist who knows he is subject to recall to active duty unless he is determined to be unavailable is virtually identical to that extended to other registrants.

The psychological impact of being rejected for service in uniform is severe. The earlier this occurs in a young man's life, the sooner the beneficial effects of pressured motivation by the Selective Service System are lost. He is labeled unwanted. His patriotism is not desired. Once the label of "rejectee" is upon him all efforts at guidance by persuasion are futile. If he attempts to enlist at 17 or 18 and is rejected, then he receives virtually none of the impulsion the System is capable of giving him. If he makes no effort to enlist and as a result is not rejected until delivered for examination by the Selective Service System at about age 23, he has felt some of the pressure but thereafter is a free agent.

This contributed to establishment of a new classification of I-Y (registrant qualified for military service only in time of war or national emergency). The classification reminds the registrant of his ultimate qualification to serve and preserves some of the benefit of what we call channeling. Without it or any other similar method of categorizing men in degrees of acceptability, men rejected for military service would be left with the understanding that they are unfit to defend their country, even in war time.

From the individual's viewpoint, he is standing in a room which has been made uncomfortably warm. Several doors are open, but they all lead to various forms of recognized, patriotic service to the Nation. Some accept the alternatives gladly—some with reluctance. The consequence is approximately the same.

The so-called Doctor Draft was set up during the Korean episode to insure sufficient physicians, dentists, and veterinarians in the armed forces as officers. The objective of that law was to exert sufficient pressure to furnish an incentive for application for commission. However, the indirect effect was to induce many physicians, dentists, and veterinarians to specialize in areas of medical personnel shortage and to seek outlets for their skills in areas of greatest demand and national need rather than of greatest financial return.

Selective Service processes do not compel people by edict as in foreign systems to enter pursuits having to do with essentiality and progress. They go because they know that by going they will be deferred.

Delivery of manpower for induction, the process of providing a few thousand men with transportation to a reception center, is not much of an administrative or financial challenge. It is in dealing with the other millions of registrants that the system is heavily occupied, developing more effective human beings in the national interest. . . .

38

Why We Fight

A Study of Indoctrination Activities in the Armed Forces

Thomas A. Palmer

The Korean War POW brouhaha clearly stimulated the creation of such "troop information" programs as the "Code of Conduct" and Admiral Radford's "Militant Liberty" campaign, but "troop information" and political indoctrination of troops had roots in World War I, as Bruce White's essay demonstrates, and were in full bloom by 1944, as Thomas Palmer indicates in this essay, written in the 1970s. Moreover, the "troop information" program of the Cold War years had more staying power than its predecessors, and many of the films and programs described by Palmer as having been created in the 1950s or early 1960s are still being utilized both within the armed services and without, by other, anti-communist and conservative groups in America. What distinguishes "troop information" from "political indoctrination"? Which is more likely to be effective in the U.S. military? Is the officer corps generation gap described by Palmer in the 1970s still extant?

IT IS COMMONLY AGREED that political societies must instill a loyalty of country and its institutions without which there can be no effective cooperation. And, since no political structure can last without a certain degree of effective cooperation from most of its members, this process of political socialization has been the concern of all governments.

In the contemporary international milieu, nations, reflecting this concern, consider it of special importance to provide some measure of political indoctrination for their Armed Forces. The methods, scope, and intensity

EDITOR'S NOTE: The author's citations of sources are omitted to save space and expense. Readers interested in the sources can consult the first edition or the author, Department of Political Science, College of Charleston, Charleston, SC 29424.

of this indoctrination vary significantly from state to state, but the objectives are not completely dissimilar. Most military indoctrination programs seek to improve individual morale, achieve unity, stress national or ideological objectives, and develop a hatred of or, at least, a distrust toward an actual or potential enemy.

Political indoctrination efforts within the military are not endemic to totalitarian states. Democratic societies have not been reluctant to undertake such activities in times of crisis or when considered to be in their best national interest. The United States is no exception. Formal and regularly scheduled indoctrination efforts have taken place in America's armed forces since 1941. They have alternately been called the Troop Information Program, Non-Military Instruction, or Information and Education Activities. "Troop Information," the most commonly accepted generic term for these activities designates what is today a required training program in the armed forces embracing such nonmilitary subjects as citizenship, democracy vs. communism, forces for freedom, and world affairs. The program is directed by a civilian-led Pentagon agency, the Office of Information for the Armed Forces (IAF), which, administratively, is part of the Office of the Secretary of Defense.

Exposure to Troop Information materials comes on a routine, perhaps daily, basis for Americans in uniform. Orientation posters are prominently displayed throughout military installations, Troop Information material is provided for reproduction in some 1,500 service newspapers, pamphlets and other printed matter are circulated to all units, multiple copies of over one hundred films produced by Troop Information are maintained for indoctrination purposes throughout the armed forces, and Troop Information lectures and discussion periods are regularly scheduled for service personnel as an integral part of their military training. Added to these media is a massive communications complex of 300 radio and 60 television stations which dispenses indoctrination material along with music, news, and entertainment to armed forces personnel serving abroad.

Troop Information was originally instituted to counter the sagging morale of poorly motivated pre-World War II conscripts. The program grew rapidly, if somewhat haphazardly, during the war years while attempting to fulfill the adage that the American soldier was to be "not just the best trained soldier in the world, not just the best equipped soldier in the world, but the best informed soldier in the world."

After the end of World War II military leaders considered that retention of the Troop Information program would offer certain advantages in shaping the postwar armed forces. The program was restructured to deal with internal communications problems resulting from the continuing flow of short-term enlistees and conscripts required for a military structure that could not return to its limited prewar strength. Equally important it was recognized that the armed forces were unable to revert to their isolated position in American society, and Troop Information resources were adapted to a public relation role designed to "make understandable the Army, its purposes, its requirements, and its ideas."

Nineteen forty-nine proved to be a transitional year for Troop Information. The trend toward centralized control of the military structure set in motion by the National Security Act Amendments of 1949 led to a basic reorganization of indoctrination activities. In July 1949, administrative control of Troop Information, which up to this time had been an army function, was transferred to the Department of Defense. Henceforth, all major policy and planning decisions affecting the program would be made at that level. Concurrently, the hardening lines of the Cold War focused increased attention on the importance of the "war of ideas" in the worldwide confrontation with communism.

It was, however, the aftermath of the Korean conflict that induced the greatest pressures for the ideological "toughening" of Americans in uniform. Acceptance of the need for stronger measures to enhance political awareness within the armed forces was based on the allegations of widespread collaboration of United States personnel captured in Korea and the refusal of twenty-one prisoners to accept repatriation. These events gave Americans a national sense of uneasiness. There was widespread debate and discussion on the erosion of traditional values. In turn, the prisoner-of-war issue served as a catalyst that led to increased political involvement and public scrutiny of the Troop Information program.

On September 16, 1953, President Eisenhower mirrored the nation's concern. The occasion was a presidential press conference in which Mae Craig, Washington correspondent for several Maine newspapers, invoked Eisenhower's view as a general, president, father, and grandfather on the behavior of the youthful POWs. The question drew an embarrassed titter from other members of the press corps which quickly died when the president earnestly plunged into the subject. He stated that "commanders responsible for employing our youth in war had been appalled by the lack of knowledge on what America is—the fundamental values of America and why they were fighting." Eisenhower stressed his interest in Troop Information while in uniform and said that he was surprised that more American POWs had not succumbed to communist indoctrination in view of their lack of knowledge about their heritage as free Americans.

Dr. James H. Hannah, a prominent educator who left his post as president of Michigan State primarily to revitalize the Troop Information program, supported the president by asserting that "unless a majority of our service personnel have firmly-held convictions of what this nation means there is no assurance that our country will come out right in the end. . . . Teaching such fundamentals should be done at home and in school but it is not being done and the services provide the *last chance* for society to do the job" (italics added).

But if there was agreement on the need for a stronger indoctrination program there was less consensus on the content of this program.

Previous indoctrination materials and methods had allegedly been inadequate in alerting the armed forces to the dangers of communism. What should be used to replace them? There were officials who felt that one of the great advantages of the communists in the Cold War was the possession of a clearly enunciated ideology. One of the major reasons for Soviet and Red Chinese "victories," so this reasoning went, was that the communists had ready, even though spurious, ideological answers for every question while members of democratic societies were often unable to explain "what they stood for." This thesis was supported by the assertions of an official investigating group which stressed that Americans captured in Korea could have resisted more effectively had they only possessed a more thorough grounding in the principles of democracy.

The growing demand for an easily understood explanation of competing political systems within the framework of the Cold War indicated clearly that both the domestic political environment and the international milieu were presenting new complications for Troop Information activities in the armed forces. The definition of indoctrination functions within the military establishment, never characterized by a precise doctrinal foundation, was becoming ever more complex as Troop Information was increasingly called upon to undertake political functions.

Symptomatic of this problem was the development of an indoctrination program known as "Militant Liberty," which was designed for communication to the troops in "Battle for Liberty" kits. "Militant Liberty" originated in the office of Admiral Arthur Radford, chairman of the Joint Chiefs of Staff, and was injected into the Troop Information program with the enthusiastic approval of Secretary of Defense Charles Wilson.

This unusual indoctrination concept described the conflict between the Western and Soviet blocs in terms of competing ideologies. The communists had been able to make substantial gains during the past decade, it was explained, because of the dynamism of their ideology. They could be defeated then only by a more dynamic ideology. The purpose of Militant Liberty was to provide this ideology to give articulation and shape to the philosophy of freedom "in terms which are meaningful to all people, regardless of geographic area, culture, and social, or economic conditions. . . . " This formidable task was to be undertaken by a unique system of contrasting our own and the communist worlds. The basis of the "Free World ideology" was described as the "sensitive individual conscience" which stood diametrically opposed to the "annihilated individual conscience" of the communists. The degree to which a nation either nurtured or annihilated the conscience of the individual reflected the degree of freedom that existed within its borders.

Once this postulate was grasped the next step was the construction of a yardstick of freedom whereby any nation could be measured on a scale ranging from minus one hundred to plus one hundred in the annihilation of the individual conscience. This assessment further involved breaking a nation down into six categories (discipline, religion, civics, education, social order, and economic order) and placing an assigned value opposite each category. The total of the combined values would indicate the nation's position on the "freedom scale."

The alleged utility of all this was to provide an understanding and guidance for Americans "to work with the nations of the free world toward a position of plus one hundred as opposed to the communist position which stood at minus one hundred." Militant Liberty stressed that the closer all nations move toward the "free world's position of strength (plus one hundred) the stronger the free world will be" and this will mean that "it is the free people who will provide the wave of the future."

For some Militant Liberty was a test case of whether the United States could come up with something to match the wares of the graduates of the Lenin Academy or whether the construction of a "dynamic ideology" would be inimicable to the workings of a pluralistic society. One scholar who shared the latter view characterized Militant Liberty as a "warning symptom of the derangement of American civil-military relationships." In the end the services led by the navy and the marine corps resisted the incorporation of Militant Liberty into their Troop Information programs and the concept quickly faded into obscurity.

But if distribution of an "in-house" ideology was rejected by the armed forces, what have been some of the images and perceptions offered to several tens of millions of Americans in uniform over the past three decades?

At the outset two factors must be recognized:

1. A great deal of Troop Information material has little political content. There are scores of pamphlets, films, and broadcasts which are concerned with personal affairs, materials to "introduce" the serviceman to a country to which he has been assigned, and instructions on the Code of Conduct, which governs behavior in the event of capture. A lion's share of the planning effort does, however, go into the production of politically oriented material.

2. Troop Information encounters a number of significant problems in the production of indoctrination material. Research has demonstrated, for example, that Americans in uniform are not particularly receptive to indoctrination training. Further, there are powerful congressmen, high-ranking military, bureaucratic elites, and elements of the public sector who cannot be offended by specific indoctrination material. Then too, there is the problem of changes in national policy which reduce the credibility of indoctrination materials. Consider, for example, the effect of the president's détente policy with the People's Republic of China on the various anti-communist Chinese indoctrination items being circulated in the armed forces.

In spite of these problems much Troop Information material produced over the years has been balanced and well presented. Certainly one can never underestimate the difficult environment in which the propagandist must operate. Still, there often seems to be a curious overdrawn, uneven quality inherent in Troop Information fare offered to American service personnel. In the words of one defense official, "Troop Information materials are perpetually out of phase. They seem to start too late and continue too long."

During World War II indoctrination themes were direct and uncomplicated. Americans in uniform were exposed to

1. motivational material that stressed the need to work or to fight harder ("Now is the crucial time," "What's ahead is worth fighting for," etc.),
2. material aimed at creating abhorrence of the enemy (this issue was often presented in general terms of defining the evils of fascism rather than stressing specific acts or atrocities performed by the Axis powers),
3. measures taken to reassure soldiers concerning things of personal concern ("The home folks know what you are doing," "Your top commanders know their jobs," "The greatest production machine in history is behind you," etc.).

Of some interest, in view of the Cold War years that followed, was the Troop Information treatment of Russia. During the war years there was anxiety within the Troop Information staff that distrust of Russia among American soldiers would have a negative effect on prosecution of the war. Troop Information films did their best to create a sympathetic understanding, not only of Russia's valor, as at Leningrad and Stalingrad, but also of Russia's foreign policy and domestic accomplishments. Orientation lectures, training aids, and discussion sessions were also frequently directed toward the reduction of anti-Soviet prejudice.

These activities, it was stressed, were not designed to endorse communism, but often the material provided a surprisingly simplistic point of view concerning Russia's actions and objectives. The provisions of the 1936 Soviet Constitution were liberally quoted to show that Russia was a leader in granting individual rights to its citizens. In one passage a Troop Information pamphlet asserted "that Fascism treats women as mere breeders whereas the Soviet Union has granted political and economic equality to women to an unprecedented degree." In an effort to defend prewar Soviet policies it was blandly asserted that the USSR's attack on Finland was valuable because it ultimately strengthened the Allied cause.

Instructions used to provide guidance for Troop Information officers paralleled prevailing Soviet propaganda objectives designed to portray Russian wartime victories as communist, not national, accomplishments. Troop Information lecturers were admonished to "speak only of the Red Army, never of the Russian Army," to use "battle of the USSR, not battle of Russia," and to "speak only of Red soldiers, Russian Soldier is incorrect."

On balance, during World War II, the mission of Troop Information was defined as "assisting commanders in maintaining a high state of morale."

An official memorandum of June 1944 probably came closest to identifying the themes and objectives that Troop Information found itself undertaking by the end of the war. This memorandum stated in part:

> The general purpose of orientation is to make soldiers fight better, work harder, and return as better citizens. . . . To accomplish these new objectives it is necessary that soldiers know their enemies and their allies, know and take pride in their outfit, know the news and its significance, have confidence in their leadership, in the Army, in the home front and in the future; and that the soldier have a sense of importance in his job.

By 1951, the international system had been shaped along quite different lines than that anticipated by World War II indoctrination materials. The Cold War, especially the Korean Conflict, shifted the primary emphasis of indoctrination toward the theme of anti-communism. Much of this material was more strident and emotionally oriented than that directed at Germany and Japan in the war years. Programming over Armed Forces Radio could be particularly harsh. Some of the episodes in one anti-communism series went something like this:

The Bishop of Springfield—Story of what would happen to a man of God if communism took over America.

The Traitor—Story of what might happen to an individual citizen if communism took over America.

No Escape—Story of what might happen to any girl if communists took over America.

No Other Way—A communist regime interferes with all normal living, even love and marriage.

Sapphire Anniversary—Story of what would happen to an American farmer if communism took over America.

The Pledge—Story of what would happen to a Boy Scout if communism took over America.

Handicap—Story of a racetrack under communist control.

The Toss-Up—A communist-controlled basketball tournament.

It was with this series and a film of the same period that the technique of portraying "hometown" USA after it was taken over by the communists was initiated. The 1951 film entitled *Face to Face with Communism* was described as "a realistic presentation of what life in this country would be like if Communists were in control. Life becomes a nightmare for Sergeant

Conway of the Air Force, in town on furlough, until he learns that the seizure of the town was staged by the citizenry to show what could happen."

In 1963 a "major emphasis" Troop Information film was produced, entitled *Freedom and You*. In this motion picture an "American citizen suddenly finds his town taken over by the communists and is jolted into a full realization of the importance of his civic responsibilities (which in this case consisted mainly of attending PTA and scout meetings). Again in 1965 the film *Red Nightmare* was produced. This film "deals with the nightmare situation of an American citizen who finds himself in a communist village and is rudely awakened to his civic responsibilities."

Another recurring theme is based on the thesis that the armed forces are a special target for communist subversion and hence need counterindoctrination in a period of protracted Cold War. Toward this end, a number of films, publications, and posters are in being which warn against communist efforts to compromise Americans in uniform. There are, for example, the Troop Information materials:

Enemy Agent and You—Alerts servicemen to the dangers of enemy espionage activities.

Espionage Target You—Explains how to avoid becoming ensnared by communist espionage agents.

Confidentially Yours—Alerts servicemen to some of the techniques used by the enemy and strengthens their determination and ability to safeguard classified information.

One such warning film entitled *The Con Men* shows how "three notorious confidence men—Hitler, Mussolini, and Tojo—deceived their people and warns against the false promises and appeals of Communism today." In this 1964 film, a series of Hollywood actors appear in the garish carnival dress of "con men." As each goes into his "pitch," the scene fades into a newsreel clip of a totalitarian leader making a speech. After this brief opening the remainder of the film is devoted to the warning not to let the false promises of Communism "con you."

Troop Information materials in dealing with competing political systems have thus often tended toward the presentation of a stark, bipolar view of international relations in which neutrality is discouraged and anticommunist movements encouraged.

In order to give maximum coverage to "major themes" various devices have been used to coordinate indoctrination images throughout all Troop Information media by means of a THEMAT (themes and materials plan). A directive to Troop Information staff and field activities urged implementation "to the fullest" of the THEMAT "democracy vs. communism." It went as follows:

Support Plan I. *Threat to Freedom Objective:* to increase awareness of the methods used by Sino-Soviet Bloc and the threat that these methods pose to the Free World. *Film and Publication materials to be used*

"Challenge of Ideas"	"Korean Armistice"
"The Struggle for Liberty"	"Red China"
"Communist Europe"	"A Study of the USSR"
"Communist Target Youth"	

Instructions to Radio and Television Division
Conduct TV chalk talk on spread of Communism in Europe, 1945 to present.

Reissue TV network feature which highlights growing Communist threat, "Face of Red China" and "Nightmare in Red."

In addition procure and circulate recent films "The Spy Next Door," "The Red Sell," "Revolt in Hungary," "Riot in East Berlin," and "Poland on a Tightrope."

Program series of short documentaries on each of Russia's satellite countries showing how they fell under the Communist yoke and what they have done, if anything, to regain their freedom.

Spot announcements, programs, features and fillers will be prepared on a continuing basis in support of this project.

All this was to be buttressed by three additional radio series, "Who Will Win the World," "Yardstick for Freedom," and "The Great Challenge."

A 1970 analysis of the thirteen major Troop Information films on Communism shows that eight were produced 8–12 years ago, four were produced 5–7 years ago, and the most recent of the thirteen was released in 1967. The major films on democracy are only slightly more recent. Of the ten major films in this area, one is over 17 years old, two are 14 years old, one is ten years old, and the others were produced between 1963–1967.

The aging quality of the material is recognized and to a degree is accepted within the program. In the 1968 budget hearings a Troop Information official could say " . . . when we put out a film on some aspect of Communism, for instance, it was not really necessary to have saturation quickly. It may take months or even several years for the troops to see a particular film." The result of these distribution limitations can be the presentation of conceptions of the world which may have little currency. If the Troop Information instruction, for example, is on Eastern Europe, a 1961 film, *Communist Europe*, is the major motion picture available. This film portrays an international situation that is unrecognizable in terms of changes in Europe in the past decade.

The major Troop Information film dealing with guerrilla warfare was produced in 1963. In 1970, while only 7 years old, it is completely out of date in terms of the events that have transpired in Vietnam. Certainly, the troops have reservations about the continued distribution of a film showing the anti-guerrilla capabilities of American forces with the strong inference that this nation has the capability to deal with such conflicts quickly and decisively wherever they may arise.

But if various factors seem to contribute to a one-dimensional view of world affairs in Troop Information materials, they, in turn, pose a series of questions as well. What should Troop Information disseminate? Are there continuing and valid themes? How should the presentation of change in these themes be handled?

In dealing with these considerations Troop Information is on surer ground in the presentation of its materials on citizenship. This area heavily emphasizes traditional views of American history, privileges and responsibilities of the American citizen, and exhortations to participate in "civic" programs, including absentee voting, the purchase of savings bonds, and patriotic letter-writing contests. For over twenty years there was almost a timeless quality about this material. What was produced in 1945 could have been used in 1965 with little concern over the appropriateness and suitability of the views presented.

Rapid social change in this country, particularly since 1965 has, however, demanded that images and roles be re-examined in this area of indoctrination. Young officers and enlisted personnel are bringing new perceptions of American institutions and international affairs into the services. Newly commissioned officers as compared to their seniors are generally more liberally oriented. They tend to be more concerned with domestic issues than international issues, more worried about issues of social justice, less worried about issues of national security, more often are mildly isolationist and on any given circumstance, less often favor the use of military force.

Young enlisted personnel, mirroring contemporary civilian attitudes, are often vocal in their criticism of service traditions and administrative procedures. In one European-based American army unit, the Information NCO edits an official newspaper called the "Joint Concern." Much of the prepared Troop Information material is dispensed with and the army is pictured as "indifferent, incompetent and inconsistent." This is far from an isolated situation and Troop Information faces increasing pressures to introduce material which Americans in uniform consider more relevant.

Indicative of the Troop Information response to these challenges is the widespread attention currently devoted to merchandising the "Human Goals" program. This Department of Defense concept, aimed at dispelling the image of the "green machine," is designed to "show respect for the serviceman as a person, recognizing his needs, aspirations and capabilities" (as well as increasing the attractiveness of a career in defense).

Notwithstanding the new content of Troop Information, the significance in the field of political socialization of the fact that our government presents political viewpoints to American troops still poses a wide range of complexities. Can a pluralistic society successfully undertake this sort of activity without, to a degree, engaging in the same sort of techniques and aspects which are more characteristic of a totalitarian state?

Again, where does one draw the boundaries between interference between the individual and his political beliefs, on one hand, and the official policies of the government, on the other?

There is also the problem of the ill-defined relationship between peacetime and wartime. Certain undertakings are considered excusable under the duress of total mobilization as in World War II. But the semi-war of Korea or Vietnam poses a different set of conditions which result in less clearly defined distinctions between political involvement by the military. This problem highlighted by the widely publicized excesses of a handful of officers in undertaking "Cold War Education" measures and formal congressional scrutiny of indoctrination activities in the early 1960s has been a central issue for the Troop Information program.

Of equal concern are the internal strains imposed by the indoctrination experience of the American military. The creation of political awareness is a complex process, one which has led the officer corps into unfamiliar instructional roles. Not the least of these problems has been the possibility of negative-type reactions on the part of the indoctrinatees and the danger of inviting outside attacks (as has been the case of Senator Fulbright's criticism of indoctrination activities which has spanned a full decade).

In the 1970s these and other equally nagging issues have placed difficult strains on the Troop Information program. The diminution of the Cold War and the Nixon administration's overtures to Red China have eroded many of the standard indoctrination themes of the past two decades. Compensatory actions on the part of the Office of Information for the Armed Forces to shift the emphasis of its "education" measures to domestic conflict and internal problems have not been wholly successful.

In the eyes of defense officials, no contemporary issue facing the armed forces is more serious than that of racial dissent. Civil rights, however, is not a problem that Troop Information has traditionally found appropriate to publicize. The stance toward this issue was set in 1943. Instructions to Troop Information officers at that time directed them, when producing indoctrination material, to avoid, "popular stereotypes of minorities no matter how kindly in intent, such as grinning, singing, dancing, happy-go-lucky, crapshooting negroes," "but," the instructions cautioned, "problems of race are a proper concern of the Army only insofar as they effect the efficiency of the Army—no more, no less. The Army is given no authority for the initiation of social reform." As late as 1963, a film designed to "depict the depth of America's struggle to safeguard freedom," discusses the historic problem of minority rights in America in terms of an unsuccessful attempt to deny a Chinese laundryman his license.

Perhaps in part because of previous Troop Information inattention in this area, responsibility for indoctrination procedures and material on civil rights and racial harmony within the armed forces has been placed with the newly created Defense Race Relations Institute (DRRI).

Similarly, responsibility for indoctrination of service personnel on the problem of drug abuse is being shifted from Troop Information to yet another Pentagon agency. Between 1967 to mid-1970 Troop Information was able to construct what some observers called "the largest drug information program in the world." Responsibility for this massive program on the dangers of the illegal and improper use of drugs (and alcohol) is now to be transferred to the Pentagon's assistant Secretary of Defense for Health and Environment.

The most damaging blow to the Troop Information Structure could well be the recent service trend toward decentralization of training. Under this concept there will be less Defense-wide training guidance. Commanders operating under a broad general mandate will make a greater determination as to the instruction their personnel will receive. In spite of the widely publicized case of Major General Edwin A. Walker, there is little historic evidence to suggest that unit commanders will be eager to use scarce training time for indoctrination activities. Indeed, quite the opposite may well be the case.

As Troop Information casts about for a redefinition of its mission within the American military it seems paradoxical in the extreme to consider that the greatest impact of our military indoctrination activities is perhaps achieved among foreign nationals.

In the process of distributing orientation materials to American service personnel abroad, Troop Information has acquired an unofficial, little publicized, but extremely important mission as an indoctrination channel for furthering American policies among foreign populations and presenting a favorable image of the United States throughout the world.

This role is carried out at times by the printed word. Each year large quantities of Troop Information publications, camp newspapers, and the like "find their way into the hands" of foreign nationals. But by far the most important Troop Information communications medium is Armed Forces Radio and Television Service (AFRTS).

Although AFRTS programs are designed specifically to provide entertainment, news, and indoctrination messages for American servicemen and their dependents stationed overseas, they have attracted an "eavesdropping audience" which in some areas of the world is estimated to be many times that of the Voice of America's broadcasts in English.

Twenty years ago when there were no Armed Forces Television facilities and considerably fewer radio outlets, the foreign audience was estimated at 90 million. Today with over twice as many stations beaming programs to a wider global area the number of foreign nationals reached by AFRTS broadcasting may well be as high as 300 million.

Armed forces broadcasting is popular for two basic reasons: (1) foreign nationals tune in with the firmly held conviction that the United States has no desire to propagandize its own citizens, and (2) Troop Information broadcasting is designed for a predominantly youthful American service audience. The programming, as it is structured, tends to attract foreign youths as well. The Armed Forces Network in Europe was some years ago called "the most popular station with young people in half of Europe" by a magazine of the German radio and television industry. The informal, breezy style affected by many youthful "G.I." announcers and "disc jockeys" creates a rapport with indigenous youth that would be extremely difficult to match by an official propaganda organ.

Armed Forces Radio and Television facilities in Washington, D.C. beam "timely and accurate seat-of-government news and information, military and general news and sports and special events programming" on a 24-hour-a-day basis to AFRTS outlets abroad. Shortwave, direct program circuits, and teletype are all used to transmit this flow of material. Each hour of transmission from Washington consists of a news program for the first 15 minutes followed by 5–15 minutes of sports. A 5-minute news summary follows on the half-hour and the remaining 25 minutes of each hour are filled with "feature programming." These programs include, among others, selected episodes of the following: "Meet the Press," "Face the Nation," "Hometown USA," "Vietnam Update," "Voices in the Headlines," "Washington Week in Review," "Issues and Answers," "CBS Dimension," "NBC Emphasis-Monitor," "Armed Forces Digest," "Firing Line," "Capital Cloakroom," "Paul Harvey," "Washington Window," "Georgetown University Forum," "Pace College," and "Opinion."

Once received by AFRTS outlets, these programs are "patched in" with popular music, interviews, and other items of local interest to form the typical AFRTS broadcast day. The result is a rather impressive amount of material that is collectively designed to present a favorable view of the United States. The official rationale for the existence of all this is to provide Department of Defense personnel with information they need in order that they may

1. comprehend the values of our government and our American heritage;
2. be fully aware of the threat to free nations;
3. understand ideologies inimical to the free institutions upon which the United States is founded; and
4. realize the responsibilities and objectives of the individual military citizen.

If, at the same time, these perceptions are imparted to millions of foreign nationals then a significant dimension is added to the United States' inventory of psychological instruments of national power. Throughout all this, Troop Information officials are careful to disassociate their efforts with any propaganda function. But, as one analyst phrased it, "Propaganda by any other name is just as sweet," and "the conviction of the propagandist that he is not a propagandist can be a real asset."

Troop Information then, in addition to the mission of "informing the

Troop" has, quite by accident, acquired an overseas propaganda function of some magnitude. This adds yet another dimension to the complexities that surround this facet of American military training.

In spite of scepticism in some quarters as to the overall value of Troop Information, it seems probable that the program will continue to function if for no other reason than the rather broad support it enjoys from sources outside of the military establishment. The rationale for this support is sometimes reminiscent of the reaction of some soldiers in World War II who remembered virtually nothing about the Troop Information materials they were exposed to, but nonetheless "felt better about the Army" if they believed it was trying to keep them informed. Similarly, influential backers of Troop Information in Congress, the executive, and elements of the private sector seem to "feel better about the Armed Forces" if efforts are made to transmit indoctrination material to service personnel, even though little formal proof is forthcoming that those efforts are effective in instilling patriotic values or providing more than a marginal understanding of communism.

Troop Information, after 30 years of existence, has been shaped in a number of ways that would surprise the original proponents of the program. One can view with some irony the fact that indoctrination efforts have had, on the whole, perhaps more impact on foreign audiences than among Americans in uniform.

Still, the contemporary environment may provide more positive challenges. As many American youths undergo the process of political socialization through unconventional sources it may prove important to insure that other institutions including the services provide a more traditional view of our national heritage and democratic experiences. Certainly, by introducing a high degree of quality and credibility into its materials Troop Information can help overcome some of the internal strains within the American military establishment.

Nonetheless it has become increasingly difficult to explain to Americans in uniform "why we fight." Future indoctrination efforts must be undertaken with care, intelligence, and sophistication if Troop Information is to play a constructive or even an accepted role in the armed forces of the 1970s.

The Vietnam Era
and Beyond

39

American Military Performance in Vietnam

Background and Analysis

KURT LANG

The debate continues over the wisdom, morality, and effectiveness of various American military policies in Vietnam, but some aspects of American involvement can be put into perspective. Kurt Lang compares the American military experience in Vietnam to studies of other military systems undergoing the stress of combat, and offers an explanation of the observed decline in cohesion and unit effectiveness as the war wore on.

A RUSSIAN ARCHDUKE is reported to have said that he hated war because "it spoiled armies." His observation fits, most uncomfortably, the American experience in Vietnam. There signs of partial dissolution of the armed forces coincided with increasingly strident opposition at home to further involvement in the conflict. Increases in the various indicators of military ineffectiveness pretty much paralleled the rising curve of anti-war sentiment, as measured by polls.[1]

That the military faced a problem in Vietnam is clear, though its exact nature and extent remain in dispute. Military self-examinations have sometimes ignored the escalation of peace protests. Other analysts have blamed unsoldierly conduct or the permissiveness of American society[2] or argued

SOURCE: Kurt Lang, "American Military Performance in Vietnam: Background and Analysis," *Journal of Political and Military Sociology*, VIII (1980): 269–286.
EDITOR'S NOTE: Most of the citations to the sources consulted by the author in this essay have been omitted from this volume for brevity and economy. The reader should consult the original source of the essay for the complete scholarly documentation.

that the brutalizing nature of the warfare moved soldiers to recognize the immorality and illegitimacy of the U.S. intervention in Southeast Asia but said little about the countervailing role of organizational and home-front support for the war.

This paper seeks to review what happened in Vietnam within the context of other twentieth-century wars. It focuses on five propositions each of which is supported by a considerable body of evidence and/or is useful as a postulate to help explain the progressive demoralization of armies:

1. The effects of combat stress are cumulative and tend to depress performance below officially prescribed levels.
2. Organizational disintegration results from the failure of groups in which soldiers function to transmit and/or enforce appropriate norms of conduct.
3. The extent of dissolution is affected more by concrete tactical and organizational realities that directly affect soldiers than by the more abstract moral and political principles to which national leaders tend to appeal.
4. Political dissent typically spreads from civilians to troops rather than the other way around.
5. Rising antiwar sentiment on the home front affects dissolution in two ways: directly, by tacitly condoning or explicitly encouraging some forms of deviance, and indirectly, by limiting the sacrifices authorities can legitimately demand and the range of options available for countering deviant tendencies.

The basic question is this: do these propositions hold for Vietnam? If war "spoiled" the American army, does the explanation these propositions provide suffice? Or must we view Vietnam as a unique historical experience?

Support for these propositions comes from studies of past wars. In two cases—the South African War (1899–1902) between the British and the Boer Republic and the French effort to pacify Algeria (1954–1961)—there are similarities to the Vietnam experience: a disparity of strength between opponents with a major power employing its arsenal of modern weapons against an essentially guerilla force. In strictly numerical terms, this disparity was even greater in the Boer and Algerian confrontations than in Vietnam. Yet the British expedition proved unexpectedly costly, especially in lives lost, while the French effort ended in what can only be called a defeat, with the Algerian nationalists gaining full independence. In both wars atrocities were charged. A resettlement program through which the British sought to separate the Boers from their supply base anticipated one element of American Vietnam policy. Nor was the measurement of progress against an invisible enemy by body counts, strict inventories of weapons and ammunition captured, and the mapping of "pacified" areas new to Vietnam. Used by the French in Algeria, these indicators were criticized, as they would be in Vietnam, as having only a tenuous relation to reality. These "little wars," it should also be noted, were launched with considerable popular support, with opposition being muted at first but becoming more vocal as the war bogged down. In terms of demands placed on individuals in the name of the national interest, there is a more meaningful comparison to be made between the Vietnam experience and the world conflicts of 1914–18 and 1939–45.

The troops (as opposed to the officers) who ultimately brought victory in South Africa were essentially a mercenary force, mostly recruited among the poor and therefore considered expendable. In Algeria, the elite paratroopers did most of the fighting; the draftees did little more than serve as garrison troops in the towns.

Within this comparative framework, we shall now take up each of the propositions, examining in turn (1) the effect of stress, (2) the value of group cohesion, (3) tactics and strategy, (4) political influences and (5) the process of politicization in understanding the performance of U.S. troops in Vietnam.

1. THE STRESS FACTOR

It is difficult for anyone not directly involved to realize how disorienting and debilitating combat can be, and until fairly recently, military historians have not provided much information on the battle experience of soldiers at the tactical level. S. L. A. Marshall pioneered by documenting the large number of combat soldiers in World War II who failed to direct fire against the enemy even when clearly in a position to do so. The battle outcome, obviously, rested on relatively few men. Further disquieting news was found in reports of the behavior of American POWs held in North Korean and Chinese camps. Though only a score refused repatriation, many more, including officers, falsely confessed to germ warfare or otherwise "collaborated" with their captors. In the American soul-searching that followed, the universal aspect of such responses (for example, among Communist soldiers in Korea . . .) was often overlooked.

The Korean war was not the first occasion on which the not-so-total commitment of citizen soldiers to self-sacrifice became a political issue. In World War I psychological casualties gave rise to controversy: should a soldier without debilitating physical injury but unable or unwilling to go on be granted casualty privileges? Did a diagnosis of "shell-shock"—repeated close hits affecting a man's nervous system causing him to lose control—imply a legitimate injury? As the war dragged on, the notion of psychiatric breakdown due to stress gained some acceptance; but the British army, continuing to emphasize its disciplinary aspects, executed an unusually large number of men for desertion.

American experience in Vietnam reenforced observations in World War

II: a disproportionate number of evacuations for neuropsychiatric reasons occurred during initial exposure to combat when anxiety was at its peak and the "new guy" had not yet been integrated into the informal soldier group. Psychiatric facilities close to the battle zone were designed to speed and maximize the return to active duty of those men with less serious symptoms.

The logistic revolution brought on by the military exploitation of the railroad, of motor transport, and of aircraft has underlined the cumulative effects of stress. While increased mobility has favored the quick knock-out blow, as in Hitler's *Blitzkrieg* campaigns, it also has speeded the flow of replacements so that armies now carry on where heavy losses would once have meant an end to hostilities. Until World War I there were always more deaths from disease than battle deaths, but protracted combat with increasingly lethal weapons has reversed the balance. Meanwhile military planners have become aware that after a certain time spent in combat, even the most effective soldier becomes indifferent and may end on the neuropsychiatric casualty list.

Certain measures can, however, extend the period of combat effectiveness indefinitely. One is giving troops frequent brief breaks. However, Ahrenfeldt while noting the positive effect of the American belief that every man has a "breaking point," found that more frequent rest periods sometimes contributed to ineffectiveness. A strictly delimited tour of duty probably had similar effects. For instance, when the Americans increased the number of missions required for rotation, delaying the potential date for going home, the onset of anxiety symptoms among air crews was correspondingly delayed. Thus treating anxiety as a medical rather than a disciplinary problem has side effects. Still, by using the medical channel to rid themselves of misfits, unit commanders could avoid time-consuming steps that might ultimately reflect on their own competence.[3]

In Vietnam the kind and amount of stress on troops was affected by the specific nature of the warfare being waged. Intermittent but brief contact with the enemy; fairly large permanent base camps that, while not so secure as rear echelons in previous wars, provided time for rest, clean up and equipment care between periodic forays; precisely delimited tour of overseas duty; and screening procedures designed to weed out the unfit all helped reduce American neuropsychiatric casualty rates far below those of the Second World War and Korea. Until late 1968, neuropsychiatric casualty rates among American soldiers whether stationed in Vietnam, Europe, or the United States were quite similar, and there was general satisfaction with the morale and good health of troops in the combat zone.[4] Yet one familiar problem resurfaced—the "short-termer's syndrome"—with a marked decline in effectiveness among fliers as the date of expected return approached. With so many reluctant to be killed just before going home, some "veterans," I have been told, were allowed to mark time in anticipation of their near-departure.[5] This reduction of pressure may help explain the finding, in at least one study, that the lowest incidence of neuropsychiatric casualties occurred within the last two months of a Vietnam tour.

However, in the second half of 1968, the neuropsychiatric rate in Vietnam began a perceptible rise, becoming over twice that in other military theaters by summer 1970. The Vietnam pattern was unique: where battlefield and psychiatric casualties had always been strongly correlated, now the neuropsychiatric rate rose as the war was winding down. Furthermore, the increase was in behavioral and character disorders, not in psychotic or neurotic disorders which are more often associated with a prior psychiatric history. Thus the rise could not be readily attributed to some slack in induction screening procedures. On the contrary, the psychiatric record of draftees who began to reach Vietnam in 1967, though not up to that of the Special Forces, was somewhat better than that of "regulars."

Two caveats are in order. First, though the risk of injury may have lessened, it did persist. By 1970 injuries from exploding mines and booby traps accounted for 80 percent of all battle wounds. Concern about triggering such devices may have been more debilitating than fear of encountering the enemy in combat.

Second, some reports suggest that soldiers in Vietnam occasionally behaved so as to provoke an early return from overseas on psychiatric grounds, while others not yet in Vietnam sought undesirable, even punitive discharges hoping the type of discharge could later be changed. It was during this period that increases in the number of attacks on officers ("fraggings") and collective refusals to obey an order were noted and that drugs were identified as a serious problem[6] either as a cause or a symptom of disintegration.

A review of the literature suggests that, in Vietnam, as in other wars, there was a gap between performance expected and actual performance. Yet where such performance gaps have generally reflected the cumulative effects of combat stress, the gap in Vietnam widened towards the end of the sixties when stress seemed to be subsiding. Nor can organizational practices which do affect the modes of escape from stress account for changing behavior in Vietnam since policy scarcely changed throughout the war.

2. GROUP COHESION

Nineteenth-century writers like Ardant du Picq and commentators on the First World War like Kurt Hesse insisted that bonds of comradeship (now called peer cohesion) were a precondition for effective leadership at the tactical level. Intuitively they sensed the importance of the informal group in providing motivational support for soldiers in combat. But it took the more systematic evaluation of psychological warfare and morale studies during World War II to raise what had been a folk theorem to a sociological principle. Summarizing the Psychological Warfare Board experience with German prisoners of war, Shils and Janowitz found the strength of national socialist convictions contributing little to the *Wehrmacht's* ability to resist disintegration. The key to sustained morale was the primary group built around an experienced cadre of non-commissioned officers.

The World War II experience provides other evidence on the importance of group support. For example, the replacement joining his unit in combat as an individual was likely to be less effective than one arriving as part of a group. The same was true of soldiers temporarily separated from their unit during an operation. Groups of stragglers often continued to function, while individuals picked up by "strange units" tended to be useless militarily. "Straggling" could, of course, be a deliberate effort to avoid danger, with such soldiers being less well integrated into their own groups than others. Evidence from the Korean war confirms the fundamental import of these findings.

These findings have raised two issues: what conditions facilitate cohesion on the level of the informal group, and to what extent do the group's norms sustain and support organizational objectives?

Interpersonal ties develop largely but not solely as a spontaneous response to the common experience of separation from the family and from familiar civilian surroundings. Factors promoting the formation of cohesive ties include leadership behavior, practices that encourage participation, weapons whose operation requires teamwork, general norms of comradeliness, shared pride and feelings of eliteness related to one's unit or branch of service or just being a soldier, and common background and allegiance to secondary symbols. Turnover, on the other hand, is the main cause of group disruption. Absorption of new members always causes some strain, but where the turnover is necessitated by casualties, both increased anxiety among the survivors and the mourning of lost "buddies" present an increased burden. The ability to form new relationships has limits.

Much turnover in Vietnam was mandated by the rotation policy, but the effect of rotation on the cohesion of those left behind has probably been exaggerated. To begin with, such policies had long governed military assignment to isolated posts and to hazardous duty without destroying group bonds. Second, in combat yearly casualties of military units often exceeded 100 per cent of average troop strength. By comparison, any disruption attributable to rotation seems rather benign. Moskos confirms that, rotation notwithstanding, military units in Vietnam were indeed held together by a network of primary ties based largely on mutual self-interest and characterized by a degree of detachment. Third, it is highly probable that the concept of overseas service as an individual contract between each man and the military made it easier to remain detached. There was less reason to identify with one's unit or to perceive a link between one's own fate and victory. Fourth, the direct effects of rotation on leadership were probably more significant than its effects on the troops. The average tenure of officer commands was less than six months.[7] This constant change hardly allowed time for the establishment of trust and close working relationships between leaders and subordinates who were themselves being rotated. This generated a feeling of impermanence in everyone, further loosening any links between individuals and the larger organization.

The front-line environment mandates a degree of solidarity that can eliminate the divisive influence of traditional social position, like class, race, and religion, but does not assure organizational effectiveness. For one thing the informal group "up front" functions within a framework of military directives, and the effort to control their own environment can produce conflict with higher authority. In fact, tension between the work group—civilian or military—and official authority has been a major focus of organizational research. In the military, it has a special relevance because of two cleavages: risk and rank. Risks cannot be equally shared but fall heavily on a relatively small minority, while officers, regardless of their echelon of risk, enjoy a disproportionate share of the privileges. There is, however, a highly visible contrast between privilege distribution in rear areas and in combat zones. In combat, rank *per se* counts for less, with certain deviations from regulations being widely tolerated, even condoned.

The most pervasive form of "indiscipline" is not open mutiny but subterfuge by which an informal group quietly disregards a directive or surreptitiously circumvents an order contrary to its own norms of conduct. Examples include unofficial "truces" during World War I with occupants of opposing trenches withholding fire to allow the rescue of the wounded in "no man's land" or simply to exchange Christmas greetings; the use of intoxicants (and drugs); the occasionally harsh treatment meted out to prisoners; and traffic with civilians, such as the wholesale violation of General Eisenhower's order against fraternizing with German women, soon rescinded as impossible to enforce.

Such deviations from official directives have always occurred, with most having only a marginal bearing on organizational effectiveness. But some informally sanctioned "indiscipline" can and does occasionally interfere with the attainment of military objectives, for example, the determination of American infantrymen in World War II to see to the care of wounded comrades. There is also the casual expenditure of property in combat. Neither behavior has official sanction, but higher authority does little to try to change it. Furthermore, most combat offers multitudinous ways of subtly sabotaging the superior who, through ineptness or over-eagerness to please those higher up, creates excess risks. Men fail to warn him of personal danger, or he may meet with an unexpected "accident." Enlisted lore is full of such stories, many being exaggerations or just plain lies. That they circulate in every army, however, surely attests to some substance in fact.

By the same token, the collective refusal to obey reflects not a weakening of group cohesion but the endemic conflict between those who issue orders and those expected to run grave risks in complying.

In August 1969, the men of A Company in the 196th Light Brigade refused to mount an attack in the area north of Da Nang. But while this unit had just experienced unusually high casualties, high casualty rates alone cannot account for the growing disjunction between informal norms and official directives that came to characterize the war in Vietnam. Military operations there have been described as a "commander's war." Radio communication enabled a division commander to maintain direct contact right down to the level of platoon, thereby making unit leadership in the traditional sense somewhat superfluous. When troops out on a mission made enemy contact, the immediate response was to call the division command for concentrated fire. Massive amounts of ammunition would be expended on objectives whose importance later on turned out to be trivial but still had to be justified. The familiar conflict between echelons centered on the measurements of success, which the military as a whole was geared to produce. When, as in Vietnam, troops learn how easily counts can be faked and how readily they are accepted, the inflation of figures (of enemy casualties, weapons captured, areas pacified, etc.) becomes part of the informal code of self-protection. Superiors have nothing to gain from questioning such counts; to do so might only depress their own performance rating. The overall effect of the widely practiced circumventions was to discredit organizational authority.

In addition to the customary cleavages related to the two echelons of rank and risk, troop behavior in Vietnam was complicated by three others: by the coexistence of two mutually hostile subcultures, by attitudes toward drug use, and by race.

The friction between "lifers" and "grunts" and the way these two social types sorted themselves out is too well known to merit much comment. The cleavage, partly generational, interfered with the induction of younger recruits into military ways by those who had made the army their way of life. For various reasons, old-timers in Vietnam were unable to assume the role played by the senior NCO in the *Wehrmacht*, that of the leader, respected though feared, who could insist and see to it that every order was punctiliously carried out. Enjoying only limited respect, the NCO had his own reasons for tolerating deviant practices that did not jeopardize his position vis-à-vis his own superiors.

The extent of drug use by troops in Vietnam touched off something close to a national scandal. One need not take sides in the argument over physiological effects to recognize the consequence of a policy that made alcoholic beverages available through official supply channels but proscribed the use of drugs. To assure their supply, drug users were forced to participate in the illicit network. Conflict with organizational authority over the use of drugs usually generalized to other issues as users developed their own code of behavior.

Race had little effect on relations in combat, but outside combat there were clear signs of cleavage along racial lines. Conflicts over orders or discipline, where one party was black and the other white, could readily develop racial overtones. Race undoubtedly played a role in some "fraggings," but in the majority of cases both perpetrator and victim evidently belonged to the same race.

3. TACTICAL AND STRATEGIC FACTORS

The amount of control the military group exercises in combat is highly contingent on its ability to provide unit members minimal comfort and the best possible chance of survival. As the military situation changes, not only neuropsychiatric but other casualty rates change.

Typically, the neuropsychiatric casualty rate is higher when the military situation has stabilized than during a retreat when, evacuation facilities being scarce, those unable to stick it out are likely to fall into the hands of the enemy. During a rapid advance with small units operating more autonomously, troops more typically get "lost" temporarily, then rejoin their unit. Desertion in Vietnam was unviable mainly because civilian life there held little attraction for most Americans while escape home or to a more Westernized country was hampered by dependence on military transport, distance, and language barriers. With the strategic situation hardly desperate, the preferred solution was to limit one's risk by routine performance and thus ultimately return to the "land of the great PX."

The tactical and strategic situation also influences available stratagems for minimizing risk—whether by feigned illness, self-mutilization, claims of family emergency, behavior that forces evacuation, just going over the hill, or military insubordination. In Vietnam there was no military disaster comparable to those suffered by some belligerents in the two world wars. There was no strategic collapse, and the Tet offensive (1968) was, in strictly military terms, an American victory. But, given prior claims, it was a serious setback—a calamity akin to General Nivelle's promise, early in 1917, that his frontal assault on the German lines would be the first step to victory. For ordinary troops, the disconfirmation of expectation inevitably calls into question the credibility of the high command. Criticism, especially as it is increasingly shared by higher officers, gets communicated down the line. It was after Tet that certain deviance rates began to climb, and desertions increased, not in Vietnam, but among soldiers determined to avoid being sent there. It was also at this point that a variety of political factors came into play, not the least of which was President Johnson's announcement, made less than two months after Tet, that the USA stood ready to enter negotiations. The effect of these developments on the strategic perspectives of troops is not to be discounted in the light of previous history.

4. POLITICAL INFLUENCES

The thrust of the argument so far has been based on an image of combat as a world apart, as a passage out of the normal world to which the individual soldier ultimately returns. Leed (1979) has highlighted the "liminal" aspects of this experience. Although the change in perspective due to the disruption of ties is very real, troops are not totally removed from civilian influence nor from the currents of public opinion. Political opposition to war typically spreads from the front to the rear.

The apparent threat to the nation when war is declared gives new meaning to patriotic appeals. Criticism is muted and potentially divisive issues shelved in the name of national unity. But solidarity is temporary; it does not always survive the duration of the war. Civilian politicians are forever sensitive to the strategic picture and not averse to capitalizing politically on any military setback. Further, as the costs of war mount, old conflicts are reactivated. Appeals for greater sacrifice begin to ring hollow since the burden is never distributed equally.

The growth in dissension during World War I is indexed by a rising curve of strikes in every major European country involved as a belligerent. Nothing comparable occurred in World War II, which did not to the same degree become a conflict of attrition with neither side harboring much hope of achieving a clear victory.[8] Generally, the longer a war drags out, the greater the war-weariness. So it was that American opinion exhibited much the same downward trend in three wars. Initially high support for American participation in the second world war and for military involvement in Korea gradually eroded as victory proved elusive, just as it did in Vietnam.

Homefront opinion will inevitably make its way to the front through the pre-service socialization of recruits, through the mail and other communications with home, through observations relayed from soldiers on home leave, and through whatever mass media are available. To the extent that soldiers are self-selected, their positive (or, at least, not negative) attitude towards the task at hand will affect their reactions to political developments, including news of war-weariness. But even where troops are young, apolitical and highly patriotic, they cannot be expected to remain intractably hostile to every expression of the desire for peace.

To what extent, then, are political factors determining for the behavior of troops? First, their influence is manifest in the characteristics of manpower attracted to military service. If a war has enthusiastic support, appeals to flag and country (or some political ideology), attract large numbers of volunteers of higher quality—physically, mentally, and "morally"—than manpower usually attracted to military service. The extent of public support has little effect on those in the military who regard war as release from the more prosaic existence of bourgeois society. For a majority, however, the passage into a new military role requires justification or at least a tacit acceptance of the declared objectives for which a war is being fought. Both the importance and the manner in which ideology is expressed varies. Thus veterans of the anti-Franco Abraham Lincoln Brigade, recruited on ideological grounds in the Spanish Civil War, ranked horror of the world the enemy intended to create as a more effective antidote against fear than traditional military palliatives, such as leadership, training, and unit pride. Yet in World War II, which from the Allied side was a war against the same Fascist enemy, men fought bravely even without the strong convictions of the Lincoln Brigade volunteers.

Patriotism and allegiance to the symbol of democracy were nevertheless the basis for American consensus about entry into World War II. And, after that entry, public opposition was always minimal. Military groups functioned and orders were issued within a context of fundamental legitimacy: the war was a "just" war, forced on America by its enemies. Studies that emphasize group ties as the key to military morale nevertheless acknowledge the importance of this moral consensus. Within the *Wehrmacht*, faith in Hitler was identified as a secondary symbol remarkably resilient to strategic reverses. In addition, there was the sizable hard core of fanatical Nazis ready on ideological grounds to repress any defeatist statements as traitorous activity harmful to the nation. Recognizing the morale-sustaining value of ideology, some armies have institutionalized the political commissar who monitors all indicators of dissension from behavior to expressions of opinion.

The manner in which America drifted into the Vietnam War, without any declaration or sense of national emergency, goes a long way toward explaining the limited commitment of both troops and civilians. Enthusiasm for the military endeavor was limited and there was more than the usual reluctance to serve, especially as anti-war protests gained strength. The ease with which deferments could be obtained—not only by students but also on a variety of occupational, medical, religious, and other grounds—resulted in a military force disproportionately poor and working class. Most sought to discharge their military obligation with a minimum of inconvenience and risk. Yet even the "unlucky" minority of the age-eligible cohort sent to Vietnam, mostly against their will, exhibited an abiding faith in America. The core elements of this "latent ideology," as Moskos (1970) calls it, are a high valuation of the American way of life and its familiar comforts, which leave an unassailable residue of feelings that underlie other more pragmatic beliefs. This sufficed to prevent open disloyalty but provided little immunity to the general disaffection.

Statistics on Vietnam, so far as I have been able to examine them, give no indication of a compositional effect at work. To be sure, the Special Forces, very much in evidence during the early phase of American involvement, progressively disappeared from the scene as ever larger numbers of Marine Corps and Army moved in. No adverse effects have been attributed to the influx of young draftees,[9] whose overall performance was more than equal to the regular army personnel they replaced. Increasingly, however, they were affected by the American youth culture, including its acceptance of non-conventional drug use. Moreover, it is highly probable that, as peace protests gained in momentum and public opinion began to turn against the war, each new cohort of arrivals resented more deeply the injustice of a system that afforded some the freedom to protest but pushed others into the military and into the least desirable assignments.

The military–civilian contact most disruptive to morale in World War I was home leave. This removed a soldier, however temporarily, not only from combat but also from military discipline. All kinds of contact with family, friends, associates, and even strangers left him open to political influence from civilians, and the most frequent form of desertion was to overstay one's home leave.

In Vietnam home leave was foreclosed until a tour of duty ended. It is difficult to overestimate how dependent the morale of soldiers was on mail and other forms of communication from home. But contrary to the Nazis who, aware that not all news is good news, had pressured letter writers to omit less cheerful items about shortages and bomb damage, Americans did not monitor the mail in this fashion. Rather, the main effort was to facilitate communication with home, making it easy for soldiers to telephone overseas.

Although a tract, song, or poem of the peace movement would occasionally be sent by a civilian friend to a like-minded soldier for circulation, most limited correspondence to personal concerns. Since civilians were not suffering deprivations comparable to those in other conflicts, most letters probably reinforced the desire to get home but did not otherwise undermine morale.

The mass media serve as another channel of civil–military contact, one with more political message content, and a greater potential for disseminating news the military would prefer soldiers not be exposed to. The direct impact of mass media messages is usually limited. For instance, German soldiers paid little attention to appeals contained in Allied propaganda leaflets dropped on them during World War II.[10] On the other hand, DeGaulle's radio appeal, urging French troops in Algeria not to support their officers' attempt to block peace negotiations, met with instantaneous approval. Partly this was because DeGaulle, though under challenge, addressed them as the legitimate head of state, partly because negotiations held out the best promise for a quick return home.

The mass media, by creating an awareness of political issues, can have more indirect effects on morale. In World War I, publicity given the various calls for a negotiated end to military stalemate, such as that issued in Stockholm by the 1917 congress of socialist parties, undoubtedly had some resonance among the troops of the several belligerents. Similarly, the sailors at Kiel had become aware of changes in the German government and pending peace initiatives. Their action to foil their officers' plan for a final naval sortie against the British can only be understood within that political context. While officers plotting the 20th of July attempt to assassinate Hitler justified this as a prelude to a negotiated peace, their action was thereafter effectively discredited as a betrayal of German soldiers shedding their blood for the fatherland. No call for peace came from anyone with real moral authority.

The true feelings of combat troops about manifestations of anti-war sentiment are usually ambivalent and therefore hard to gauge. Vietnam was too remote to allow for political links to be formed or even for an effective dialogue. Troops could fully comprehend neither the motivation of protesters nor Johnson's decision to shift course and seek a negotiated settlement. But the peace goals of both were consistent with the characteristic nostalgia of troops for home. In this way, the elements of "latent ideology" can work against the goals of military organization. One need only recall the demobilization riots, mild as they were, of impatient American soldiers in Europe at the end of World War II. Neither their disaffection nor that experienced by many in Vietnam reflected ideological opposition to U.S. policy or moral revulsion against the conduct of the war. Some without previous political interest did end up in the anti-war movement, but their change of heart usually took place only after their return to the states, and exposure to the changed civilian attitudes. The few "conversions" during the Vietnam tour seem to have come about under the tutelage of a local person, usually a woman with whom the soldier had formed a stable relationship.

5. THE PROCESS OF POLITICIZATION

One proposition has almost achieved the status of a truism: the cohesion of an army in the field depends only to a very limited degree on the soldiers' allegiance to secondary symbols. Organizational factors, like informal group solidarity, the quality of leadership, and the adequacy of command and supply channels, have a more direct effect than ideology. Still, the impact of ideology should not be ignored. While clearly it provides an insufficient defense against disintegrative tendencies, it remains the necessary foundation on which the edifice of a citizen army is built. That is, controversy over a war and open expressions of defeatism are of some consequence—mostly, it will be argued, by politicizing deviance whatever its cause and by influencing the ways the organization deals with it.

To be sure, few infractions or refusals to fight have an overtly political content, however much is later read into them. This applies even to Vietnam, which in its later phases became a rather unpopular war. Notwithstanding all the publicity, the typical deserter there was no different from the deserters in other wars. Rarely did they abandon their unit in combat. Most were individuals plagued by multiple personal problems having nothing to do with their beliefs about American involvement in the Vietnam conflict. Some of these later adopted the rhetoric of the anti-war protest.

One must be cautious in generalizing from individual characteristics to social processes reflected in changing rates. Increases in psychiatric malaise, indiscipline, and other indicators of disaffection are the inevitable result of attrition. And as rates rise, individual characteristics become less predictive of susceptibility. Thus the profile of the mutineer conforms more closely to that of the typical soldier than does that of the deserter. While chronic troublemakers are to be found among the disaffected, most have excellent prior records, even decorations. What mainly differentiates the mutineer from other troops is exposure to unusually heavy stress.

The question then becomes: how does the loss of popular support contribute to the dissolution of an army?

Open criticism of the war is more concentrated among the educated. This same characteristic makes them less prone to commit a disciplinary offense. Nevertheless, their presence in large numbers can serve as a catalyst for the delinquency of others, who depend on firm authority to keep their own dispositions in check. Some such phenomenon was observed with the influx during the Korean war of a large number of draftees. Not only were these men better educated but they were also more negative toward the military than were regular army personnel. Units with large numbers of draftees had higher delinquency rates than units where the number was small, yet it was the regulars and not the draftees who committed most of the offenses. The inference is that derogatory attitudes toward the army, openly expressed by many, changed the atmosphere sufficiently to trigger delinquency by others who were previously well-behaved.

Civilian society may simply refuse to back the kind of sanctions by which the military seeks to enforce discipline. This can take the form of legislative hearings, such as the inquiry into the *Kitty Hawk* incident (involving racial tension to the point of near mutiny during the Vietnam War) or of open criticism, such as widespread concern in and out of Congress about protecting the right of free expression against incursions by overly zealous commanders. But there are other, more subtle encouragements of deviance. In a study of AWOLs from the German *Bundeswehr*, many claimed that they almost never had to justify their behavior to civilians. Many were able to find employment even without required papers, and in only 14 per cent of the cases did the parents urge their son to return to his unit voluntarily. Refusal to cooperate out of sympathy is still short of active subversion.

Where pacifist and revolutionary slogans have surfaced among troops, this has more frequently occurred near centers of anti-war activity than among units most exposed to the danger and brutality of war. Nevertheless when disaffection is rife, whatever its actual causes, soldiers are prepared to embrace the rhetoric that justifies their behavior, be it the rhetoric of class, of race, or simply of anti-militarism.

Because combat perspectives are too parochial, too pragmatic, and too obsessed with personal survival to generate more than sporadic protest, the politicization of deviance requires a link-up with civilian political organizations which contest the claims of hierarchical command authority by putting forth their own claims to legitimacy. What happened in World War I on a fairly large scale was inhibited in Vietnam by the sheer physical distance of the theater of war. But there can be no question that troops on returning home were severely shocked to encounter so little understanding of an ordeal that was outside the normal categories of civilian experience. The shock was intensified by the change of mood in the country, many veterans returning to find themselves not heroes but pariahs.

The American government was able to absorb the anti-war protest with but a minimal loss of legitimacy, largely because the anti-war movement failed to capitalize sufficiently on the sentiment for peace, both inside and outside the military, to mobilize a more general social movement directed at broader and equally pressing domestic problems the American government was not prepared to face up to. The effect on the military was less benign. Concern over legitimacy encourages policies with side effects that, from a strictly military viewpoint, may be undesirable. We have mentioned two such policies. One was the handling of milder forms of indiscipline through medical channels by issuing administrative discharges. This afforded some an easy escape but was preferable to strict enforcement of discipline that could have courted rebellion. The same trade-off characterized rotation policy. It had serious adverse effects, yet by individualizing the war for every individual, the contracted tour of duty not only distributed the burden of sacrifice but lessened the possibility that any discontent might coalesce.

An alternative policy for the military, faced with loss of popular support, is to insulate itself from the political cross-currents of civilian society. The volunteer force, implemented at the end of Vietnam operations, was a deliberate step in this direction. Its mere existence has raised new issues about the adequacy of manpower obtained through the volunteer mechanism and about the political and moral desirability of a force that over-represents the poor and blacks. Given modern means of communication it seems most unlikely that the military can fully insulate itself from the intrusions of public opinion whether in peace or war, especially when, as in Vietnam, public disaffection becomes epidemic. All this suggests that there are serious limits to the use of military force, except for small ventures, without significant popular support.

CONCLUDING REMARKS

Illuminating what became in the end the American Fiasco in Vietnam through other historical instances points to the utility of the propositions outlined at the beginning of the paper in understanding this phenomenon.

A further lesson to be drawn from these comparisons relates to the inadequacy of single-factor explanations for something as multi-faceted as the overall American performance in Southeast Asia. In every one of the instances drawn on for comparison, the decomposition was the joint effect of narrowly military, of organizational, and of human inadequacies and defects. Not only do these typically interact, but they exert their influence within a context of beliefs that are political, not necessarily in the most conventional meaning of the term but in the deeper and more profound sense of relating to the legitimacy of the demands being made on soldiers. It is in this sense also that the American failure in Vietnam was political, even though nothing there resembled even remotely a general revulsion against American policies by troops or fraternization between them and the "enemy" in order to put a speedy end to war.

To emphasize the political is not to deny the existence of organizational, strategic, and even logistic deficiencies in the military effort which, if remedied, might have made a difference. Evaluations from a strategic or managerial viewpoint are beyond this analyst's competence, even though he is convinced that a *post hoc* analysis would reveal many errors and failings, as they have with regard to every military venture and especially the ones that ended in stalemate or defeat. The political factor in the broader sense, we insist, sets limits to the effective use of military force, not only because the amount deployed needs to be measured against the foreign policy objective sought but also because lack of popular support means fewer soldiers motivated to fight and less leeway for the military leadership to pursue what might be considered most efficient on strictly military grounds. Even when the friction between lack of commitment to the war effort and military exigency fails to push soldiers to open mutiny and in the absence of red flags of protest, it still has important direct effects. The case material sketched out here is intended to underline this pervasive influence of the political factor.

NOTES

1. The main shift against the war seems to have taken place in the second half of 1967 and the first half of 1968. See Gallup Opinion Index, Nos. 30, 52, and 93.

2. These are reminiscent of reaction to allegations of "collaboration" by large numbers of American prisoners of war held captive in North Korean and Chinese prison camps. See A. D. Biderman, *March to Calumny* (New York: Macmillan, 1963).

3. See A. J. Glass "Conclusion and summary," in W. S. Mullins, ed., *Overseas Theaters*, Vol. II of *Neuropsychiatry in World War II*. (Washington: GPO, 1973), p. 1013. "The relatively small incidence of NP disorders can readily be hidden or absorbed in the much higher disease and injury rates, as well as such de-

viant behavior categories regarded as disciplinary problems, as AWOL, desertion or even drug addiction." See also A. J. Glass, "Observations upon the epidemiology of mental illness in troops during warfare," in *Symposium on Preventive and Social Psychiatry* (Washington, D.C.: Walter Reed Army Institute of Research, 1957), pp. 185–197. Also R. L. Pettera, *et al.*, "Psychiatric management of combat reactions with emphasis on Vietnam," *Military Medicine*, 134 (1969): 673–679.

4. E. M. Colbach and M. D. Parrish, "Army mental health activities in Vietnam: 1965–1970," *Bulletin of the Menninger Clinic*, 34 (1970): 33–342. See also William S. Allerton (1969), "Army psychiatry in Vietnam," in P. G. Bourne, *The Psychology and Physiology of Stress* (New York: Academic Press, 1969), pp. 1–18. "Vietnam incidence rates were one-tenth of the highest rate ever reported in World War II and less than one-third of rates reported during stressful periods in the Korean conflict" (p. 14). Psychiatric casualties were reported during stressful periods in the Korean conflict" (p. 14). Psychiatric casualties were also a remarkably low percentage of all medical evacuations represented by NPs.

5. This "lying low" is not very different from what has been reported about French conscript troops in Algeria.

6. Statistics on "fragging" are bound to be unreliable. The generally accepted official DoD figure is "about 800" between 1969 and 1972, with a steady increase for each year through 1971, by which time troop strength had declined dramatically. This figure compares with 370 cases of "violence against superiors" brought to courts martial during the eighteen months of World War I, which involved over 4.7 million troops. No statistics on "refusal to fight" have come to this author's attention. Drug abuse was first officially recognized as a problem when the Army established its first amnesty program in October 1969. The problem was not unique to Vietnam, although the incidence there of heroin use was no doubt higher than in other theatres. See L. N. Robins, *The Vietnam Drug User Returns: Special Action Office Monograph*, Series A, No. 2 (Washington: GPO, 1973), ch. 6.

7. This is the thrust of the Savage and Gabriel argument in *Crisis of Command*, 1978. A. E. Ashworth, "The Sociology of Trench Warfare," *British Journal of Sociology*, 19 (1968): 407–423.

8. According to U.S. Army Surgeon General's Office, combat deaths per 100 of average yearly troop strength was 51.9 in World War II, 43.2 in Korea, and 18.0 in Vietnam.

9. For example, T. F. Hartnagel, "Absent without leave—a study of the military offender," *Journal of Military and Political Sociology*, 2 (1974): 205–220, notes more "volunteers" were AWOL than draftees. According to Robins, 65 per cent of the drug users but only 44 per cent of the non-users were "regular army."

10. H. Speier, *Vietnam Drug User*, "Psychological Warfare Reconsidered," in D. Lerner and H. D. Lasswell (eds.), *The Policy Sciences* (Stanford: Stanford University Press, 1951). This was the case except for the "Safe Conduct" pass to be used after troops were no longer under disciplinary control.

40

Who Served in Vietnam?

The recruits entering the U.S. armed services in the 1960s were composed of "true" volunteers, "draft-motivated" volunteers (seeking a service or military specialty of their choice on the eve of being drafted), and draftees. The draftees (about 37 percent of the whole) tended to be slightly overrepresented in the combat arms (28 percent of draftees, 23 percent of "regular army" volunteers).* One's level of education or socio-economic status were not linear predictors of the likelihood of one's serving, as Michael Useem and this national survey in the fall of 1968 demonstrated†—that is, both the rich and well-educated and the poor and undereducated were underrepresented in the armed services of the Vietnam era. (Many of the latter could not pass mental or physical exams.) But, those who actually served in Vietnam were disproportionately poor and undereducated (see table). Consequently, as had been the case in Korea, the poor were overrepresented among the casualties.‡

*Charles Moskos, *The American Enlisted Man* (New York, 1970), p. 203.
†M. Useem, "The Educational and Military Experiences of Young Men During the Vietnam Era: Non-linear Effects of Parental Social Class," JPMS, VIII (1980): 15–29.
‡*U.S. News and World Report*, February 20, 1953, p. 18; Gilbert Badillo and G. David Curry, "Social Incidence of Vietnam Casualties," *Armed Forces and Society*, II (1976): 403; Thomas McIntyre, "One Body at a Time: The Political Economy of Vietnam Combat Death," unpublished Ph.D. dissertation, University of Pittsburgh, 1986.

"Have you or any of immediate relatives been in the armed services and stationed in Vietnam over the previous five or six years?"

	Vietnam (%)	Armed Services (%)	Ratio	N
	PROPORTION WITH SELF OR RELATIVE IN			
Education				
10th grade or less	14.0	24.7	0.57	(393)
11th grade	12.9	25.8	0.50	(248)
12th grade	12.1	30.9	0.39	(528)
At least some		27.1	0.27	(439)
college	7.3			
Family income				
$4,000 or less	13.5	27.5	0.49	(415)
$4,000 to $7,000	12.9	26.7	0.48	(363)
$7,000 to $12,000	10.9	31.7	0.34	(524)
$12,000 and over	8.8	26.3	0.33	(319)

SOURCE: M. Useem, *Conscription, Protest, and Social Conflict* (New York: John Wiley & Sons, Inc., 1973) p. 141.

41

"Dopin' Dan" Comments on Racism, "Heads," and the Primary Group

Good cartoonists can sometimes capture the essence of war and military life. Bill Mauldin is certainly an example. Some of the strips from the Vietnam-era comic-book "Dopin' Dan" have those qualities as well. This particular sequence suggests three phenomena social scientists point to with regard to Vietnam:* the decline in racism on the battlefield, the tendency of many GIs to take drugs (typically marijuana) in the field, and the importance of primary group relationships ("your buddies").

*See John Helmer, *Bringing the War Home* (New York: Free Press, 1973); and Charles Moskos, *The American Enlisted Man* (New York: Russell Sage, 1970).

42

Did Vietnam Turn GIs into Dope Addicts?

Some have claimed that the opportunity to acquire drugs in Southeast Asia, and the tensions of the war, transformed many "straight" GIs into regular drug users. What does this table indicate about the risks of addiction or chemical dependence for those using pot or pills? Those using opium derivatives?

Taking pot or pills in Southeast Asia during the war did not necessarily mean that a GI would become an addict, as this table indicates. Only those who used opium derivatives ran heavy risks of addiction.*

*See also Spencer Rich, "Fears of Narcotics Wave Among Vets Exaggerated," *Washington Post*, February 25, 1980, p. A3.

Incidence and Frequency of Drug Use Among Vietnam Enlisted Returnees, Oakland Overseas Processing Center—1–13 March 1971 (1,010 Vietnam Enlisted Separatees—E-1-6, Age 26 or Below)

	BEFORE VIETNAM		DURING VIETNAM		CURRENT (LAST 30 DAYS)	
Marihuana: total users	45.80%	(461)	58.50%	(592)	37.10%	(374)
Amphetamines: total users	14.00	(141)	16.40	(165)	5.76	(58)
Barbiturates: total users	11.32	(114)	15.46	(156)	7.04	(71)
Acid (LSD, peyote, and the like): total users	12.67	(127)	9.54	(96)	4.16	(42)
Heroin or morphine: total users	6.17	(62)	22.68	(228)	16.15	(163)
Opium: total users	7.75	(78)	19.59	(196)	9.14	(92)

SOURCE: K. E. Nelson and J. Panzarella, "Prevalence of Drug Use, Enlisted Vietnam Returnees Processing for ETS Separation, Oakland Overseas Processing Center," unpublished ms., 1971, cited in John Helmer, *Bringing the War Home* (New York: Free Press, 1974), p. 78.

43

American Response to the Trial of Lt. William L. Calley

Herbert C. Kelman and Lee H. Lawrence

Many combatants in Vietnam more or less scrupulously observed the laws of warfare, but a number, on both sides, did not. The massacre by American GIs of several hundred unarmed Vietnamese civilians at My Lai was the most notorious of these violations.* Lieutenant William Calley was tried by General Court-Martial and convicted of these murders on good and ample evidence, but many suspected, incorrectly, that he was as much a victim as an executioner, that he was essentially a scapegoat for the Vietnam policy. Herbert C. Kelman and Lee H. Lawrence analyze an elaborate poll of the public's views on the Calley case in this perceptive and provocative essay. What are the characteristics of those who disapproved of Calley's being tried? Of those who approved?

*See Peter Karsten, *Soldiers, Law and Combat* (Westport, Conn., 1978); Gunther Lewy, *America and Vietnam* (New York, 1978); and Seymour Hersh, *My Lai 4* (New York, 1970).

In 1945 the United States Government put Japanese General Tomoyuki Yamashita on trial because men under his command had committed war crimes. His defense was that he had not ordered his soldiers to commit the crimes. The Americans decided that Yamashita was nevertheless responsible for his men's actions, and duly convicted and executed him.

In 1946 an International Tribunal found 19 Nazis guilty of war crimes. Their defense was that they were following orders handed down by their superiors. The Tribunal decided that there is a point, even in war, at which

Source: Herbert C. Kelman and Lee H. Lawrence, "American Response to the Trial of Lt. William L. Calley," *Psychology Today*, June 1972, pp. 41–45, 78–81. Copyright © 1972 Ziff-Davis Publishing Company. Reprinted by permission.

obedience must defer to morality. Accordingly it convicted the Nazis and sentenced them to death or imprisonment.

The American people, flushed with victory and horrified at the reports of wartime atrocities, supported these trials and considered the verdicts just and wise. Even 15 years later, when Israel captured, tried and hanged Adolf Eichmann for "crimes against humanity," some pitied Eichmann and some despised him, but few said he should go free.

In 1971 the United States Government brought Lt. William L. Calley to trial for the massacre of unarmed Vietnamese civilians at My Lai. While everyone acknowledged the horror of what happened there, only a minority of Americans held Calley responsible. His conviction invoked outrage and protest.

Social scientists were at a loss to explain the widespread disapproval of Calley's trial. Rarely do 70 percent of a national sample agree on anything, especially current political issues; yet here were all sorts of strange bedfellows: hawks and doves, liberals and conservatives, whites and blacks, young and old, rich and poor, veterans and nonveterans. The standard dichotomies did little to predict which groups supported Calley and which did not. Nor could one predict a person's attitude by knowing whether he supported the war and the military.

At the time of Calley's conviction we were exploring the dynamics of obedience to authority. How does someone behave when a legitimate authority tells him to act against a third person? Stanley Milgram's famous experiments suggest one answer: he obeys. The majority of Milgram's subjects, following the experimenter's instruction, administered electrical shocks of increasing intensity to their victims.

To us, one key to understanding a person's response in such a situation—be it a controlled experiment or the realities of My Lai—is his perception of the locus of responsibility. That is, he may engage in actions that he would normally regard as immoral if he feels that, although he personally caused these actions, the responsibility for them lies elsewhere. Similarly, in assessing the actions of others—such as Calley's actions in My Lai—people may absolve the actor of guilt if they feel that he was not personally responsible for actions he caused.

Social scientists and laymen alike have generally assumed that causation and responsibility are linked: the person who intentionally causes an event is responsible for its consequences. (Intention is critical: we generally do not hold a person accountable for effects he did not intend.) In such terms most Americans should have held Calley responsible for what happened at My Lai: he caused a great many deaths, and clearly intended to do so. He did not plead insanity or accident. What was different about this situation, however, was that—in the eyes of many Americans—Calley was acting under the orders of legitimate authorities.

Calley rested his defense on the assumption that actions ordered by legitimate authorities *must* be carried out. This assumption breaks the link between causation and responsibility; it says that though a man's actions may be personal and intentional, responsibility for them can be deferred elsewhere.

Once this link is broken, a person may be able to perform acts that violate his own moral standards simply because his standards are no longer the issue; he suspends personal judgment. Milgram notes that once an individual has acknowledged an authority as legitimate, his moral concern shifts. Instead of trying to meet his own moral demands, he worries about how well or poorly he is meeting the expectations of the authorities.

The prosecution in the Calley case did not challenge the principle that legitimate orders may erase an individual's culpability. Rather, they challenged Calley's claim that he acted under legitimate orders. Their argument was two-fold: either (1) Calley acted without orders, in which case he must be held personally responsible for violating the rules; or (2) he acted under orders that clearly were illegal—and Calley, as an officer, should have realized this and refused to obey.

Both prosecution and defense, then, acknowledged that personal responsibility may be waived in a situation of authority. The question at hand was whether that authority was legitimate.

When Calley was convicted, we undertook a national survey of reactions to the trial. We wanted to understand better the widespread outcry against his sentence, and to examine this reaction in the light of attitudes about authority and responsibility. Further, we wanted to get some sense of how ready Americans are to be "good Germans"—to commit whatever violence the authorities say is necessary.

The interviews (conducted for us by the Roper Organization) took place in May and early June 1971, about two months after the trial had ended. The sample consisted of 989 respondents representative of the American population over the age of 18. The interview focused on attitudes toward the trial, the war, and Calley's actions at My Lai; and it included some questions about related incidents—real and hypothetical—so that we could generalize beyond My Lai. We also probed for reasons behind the respondents' opinions, giving them many opportunities to expand on their answers.

About 58 percent of our sample disapproved of the trial against Calley; only one third approved (34 percent) and eight percent had no opinion. (Some surveys conducted immediately following the trial found an even higher proportion of Americans opposed to the trial—close to 70 percent. Presumably by the time we began our interviews, the intensity of feelings had abated somewhat and attitudes had stabilized.)

The true complexity of feelings about the trial, however, emerged when we asked respondents to indicate *why* they approved or disapproved. We gave each person a list of five statements that might explain his attitude, and asked him to choose as many as he endorsed. We then asked the respondent to select the one *most important* reason of the five. (We offered each an opportunity to add his own motives, but very few did so; apparently our choices covered the ground adequately.)

Among respondents who approved of the trial, the most frequently chosen reason was that *even a soldier in combat has no right to kill defenseless civilians*—a belief that affirms the responsibility of the individual soldier. Another item captured this belief in more abstract form: *the trial conveys the idea that every man must bear responsibility for his own actions.* Almost half (45 percent) of those who approved of the trial chose one of these two statements as the most important reason for their approval. An additional one fifth explained their attitude by their opposition to the war (*the trial shows the immorality and cruelty of the Vietnam War . . .*); smaller proportions said that they were primarily concerned with the integrity of the military or with equity in the army's treatment of soldiers.

We offered parallel items for those who said they were opposed to the trial. Forty-five percent of them explained that they consider it *unfair to send a man to fight and then put him on trial for doing his duty*—a belief that affirms the responsibility of the authorities. An additional 15 percent chose another version of this idea, that *the trial used Calley as a scapegoat; Calley shouldn't be blamed for the failures of his superiors.* A relatively small number opposed the trial because they opposed the war and the way it was being fought (nine percent); or because the trial might weaken army morale (11 percent); or because it was unfair to single out Calley when other soldiers have done what he did (15 percent).

In order to penetrate the complexity of public reactions of approval and disapproval, we decided to contrast our respondents on the basis of the primary *reasons* for their reaction to the trial. So we divided supporters into three groups, and critics into three groups, according to the most important reason they gave:

1. Those who based their attitude on how responsibility should be allocated—to the individual or to the authorities;
2. Those who based their attitude on their opposition to the war;
3. Those who based their attitude on their concern with the integrity or morale of the army.

While we compared all of the resulting six groups, we will discuss only the two largest groups here—those who supported or opposed the trial on the issue of responsibility. These two groups anchor the extreme positions; the other four tend to fall between them on most issues. In addition, the responsibility groups give us the clearest basis for understanding why the trial provoked such ambivalence and anger.

Thus the respondents we will contrast are:

1. Those who approved of the trial on grounds of personal responsibility (PR approvers): respondents who supported the trial because they believe that each soldier is responsible for his actions. To these respondents, Calley was therefore accountable for the deaths at My Lai.

2. Those who disapproved of the trial on grounds of Government responsibility (GR disapprovers): respondents who opposed the trial because they believe that a good soldier follows orders, and that the authorities are therefore responsible for what happens. To these respondents, Calley was doing his duty and was therefore not liable for the deaths at My Lai. (Of course we will not be dealing with everyone who opposed the trial, or everyone who favored it.)

We then contrasted these groups on three major topics: their attitudes toward the trial itself and toward the larger question of war crimes; toward Calley's action—whether he was justified, and why; and toward the Vietnam war and the Government's military strategy.

The two groups differed significantly in their ideas about who should be tried for war crimes, in their assessment of Calley's sentence, and in their attitudes toward some of the protest actions that took place after the trial.

Who should be tried for the events at My Lai? Very few respondents said that *only* Calley was responsible; even among the PR approvers, no more than six percent chose this option. They regarded Calley as personally responsible, to be sure, but 80 percent of them also agreed that the higher authorities must share the blame. The GR disapprovers, on the other hand, were more likely to say that neither Calley nor his superiors should have been tried (43 percent compared to three percent of the PR approvers).

For the vast majority of the whole sample, bringing Calley to trial and sentencing him to life imprisonment are two distinct issues: three fourths of the respondents thought that the sentence was too harsh. This proportion increases to virtually all of the GR disapprovers (93 percent). However, even among the PR approvers, 42 percent thought that the sentence was too harsh—possibly because, as we saw, they felt that Calley's superiors shared the blame and should share the punishment. Similarly, only four percent of the GR disapprovers considered the sentence fair, compared to 41 percent of the PR approvers.

After Calley's conviction, a few draft boards engaged in a form of civil disobedience: in protest against the sentence, they refused to draft young men. Slightly more than half of the GR disapprovers thought that these draft boards were doing the right thing, but only 15 percent of the PR approvers did. This finding was noteworthy since the GR disapprovers are otherwise oriented toward law-and-order values and are unwilling to defy legitimate authority. The fact that so many of them condoned an act of civil disobedience indicates the strength of their feelings about the case.

> I don't think Calley should have been prosecuted alone and the draft boards are taking that means to show how unfair his treatment is. They don't want to subject any others to it.   —A respondent

Only a small number of PR approvers supported the draft-board protest (15 percent); but of these, half did so because they thought such action would lead to a reevaluation of national policies or because they opposed the draft. The motives of the GR disapprovers were different: 73 percent of those who condoned such protest did so because (1) they believed that Calley's conviction was wrong and that he was entitled to public support; or, more commonly, (2) they felt that draft boards should not draft men who eventually will be punished simply for following orders.

> If they are going to train people to be good professional cool killers and send them out to war and tell them they're back of them and put them in an area where they HAVE to fight and then let the men down—it's wrong to draft them.   —A respondent

GR disapprovers felt that the trial has placed soldiers in a double bind: "You're damned if you do and damned if you don't," many of them said. You are court-martialed if you don't obey orders—and now it appears that you are convicted if you do obey them. This was a clear indication of the deep sense of betrayal that these respondents felt: the Calley trial violated the understanding, the tacit contract, under which men have been drafted.

> They should not draft a man, then send him to prison for doing what he is sent out to do.   —A respondent

A majority of all respondents approved of President Nixon's intervention in the case (by ordering Calley's release from the stockade and by announcing that he would personally review the conviction). But the GR disapprovers were considerably more likely to support Nixon's action than PR approvers, 81 percent to 51 percent. Again, the reasons were different for each group. GR disapprovers most frequently expressed a concern for Calley: many agreed with Nixon's action because they thought he might help Calley; because they felt the conviction was unjust; or because they felt Calley had been treated unfairly. PR approvers, however, cited reasons that were independent of Calley: many agreed because they thought the case was complicated and needed a higher review; because Nixon, as Commander-in-Chief, had a right to be the final reviewer in the case; or because they felt the President had to respond somehow to the strong public outcry.

We asked respondents what they thought about the World War II precedents for My Lai—specifically, the Yamashita and Nuremberg trials—and what they thought should happen to American generals and officers in similar cases.

(We must view their answers with some caution: we brought up the international comparisons *after* asking about the Calley trial, so presumably many respondents realized that they were being tested for consistency. Some may have said that the Yamashita and Nuremberg convictions were wrong because they had just criticized the Calley trial; and the fairly substantial number who chose the "don't know" alternatives may have done so to avoid acknowledging their inconsistency.)

Even with these caveats, we found that Americans are more willing to convict a Japanese Yamashita than an American one, and to sentence German officers than American ones. Thus while 45 percent of the total sample thought Yamashita should *not* have been convicted, fully 62 percent thought American generals should not be convicted for war crimes they do not order. About the same number (44 percent) said that Germans at Nuremberg should not have been convicted for following orders; but the percentage jumps to 57 percent who thought that American officers—like Calley—should not be convicted on the same grounds.

PR approvers were consistent on these questions, holding Americans as culpable for war crimes as Japanese or Germans. But the GR disapprovers were inconsistent: while they were the least inclined of any group to convict anyone for war crimes, they approved more of trials for Japanese and Germans than they did for Americans. For example, while only 23 percent of the GR disapprovers thought that the Nuremberg trials were right, fewer than half that many—10 percent—thought that American officers should be convicted for following orders.

Close to the beginning of the interview, before we asked anything about the Calley trial itself, we gave respondents a hypothetical situation: soldiers in Vietnam are ordered to shoot all inhabitants of a village suspected of aiding the enemy—including old men, women and children. We asked: what do you think *most* people would do in this situation—obey orders and shoot, or refuse to shoot? Then we asked respondents what they thought they would do in that situation.

Two thirds of the total sample believed that "most people" would follow orders and shoot; a smaller proportion, but still a majority, said that they themselves would shoot in such circumstances. The fact that a majority of our respondents "admit" that they would shoot is surprising only if we assume that "refuse to shoot" is the socially desirable answer to this question. But it is not: for many respondents, the desirable response is to follow orders. The 51 percent who say they would "follow orders and shoot" are not necessarily admitting to moral weakness—rather, they may be expressing the view that such action represents their moral obligation.

I'm a great disciplinarian. In this type of situation, if I had been told to do it and trained to do it, I would follow orders.   —A respondent

I would shoot, because there are no civilians in Vietnam. They're either for you or against you. They all have killing in their minds.   —A respondent

Attitudes toward trial of Lt. Calley

REASONS		AGREE WITH THIS REASON	MOST IMPORTANT REASON
Among respondents approving of trial:			
1. Even a soldier in a combat situation has no right to kill defenseless civilians and anyone who violates this rule must be brought to trial:	PR approvers	53%	27%
2. The trial helps to put across the important idea that every man must bear responsibility for his own actions:		48%	18%
3. The trial helps to make clear the immorality and cruelty of the Vietnam war and of the way we are fighting it:		45%	20%
4. To preserve its honor, the Army has to bring to trial anyone accused of breaking its rules of warfare:		45%	14%
5. Many other U.S. soldiers have been tried for crimes in Vietnam; it would be unfair to let Lt. Calley off without a trial:		40%	8%
6. None of these or don't know:		14%	14%
Among respondents disapproving of trial:			
1. It is unfair to send a man to fight in Vietnam and then put him on trial for doing his duty:	GR disapprovers	83%	45%
2. The trial used Lt. Calley as a scapegoat; one young lieutenant shouldn't be blamed for the failures of his superiors:		67%	15%
3. The trial keeps us from facing the real issue; what's wrong is the war and the way it is being fought, not just the actions of an individual soldier:		43%	9%
4. The trial is an insult to our fighting men and weakens the morale of the U.S. army:		64%	11%
5. Many other U.S. soldiers have done the same kinds of things as Lt. Calley; it is unfair to single out one man and put him on trial:		69%	15%
6. None of these or don't know:		3%	5%

ATTITUDES TOWARD TRIAL: Respondents gave a variety of reasons for their approval or disapproval of Calley's trial. These fell into three categories: (1) attitudes based on the issue of responsibility (reasons one and two in each group); (2) attitudes based on opposition to the war; (3) attitudes based on concerns with the integrity or morale of the army (reasons four and five). [The reasons are not in the order in which respondents saw them.]

It follows that respondents who disapproved of the trial because Calley was only doing his duty—GR disapprovers—would be the most likely group to say that they would do the same thing in Calley's shoes. More than eight in 10 of them (82 percent) thought that most persons would shoot, and 68 percent believed that they themselves would obey such orders. Among the PR approvers, by contrast, only 37 percent say that most people would do what Calley did—and only 19 percent believed that they themselves would.

GR disapprovers, in short, regarded the shooting of civilians as a necessary evil of war. Given legitimate orders, obedience is normal behavior: for "most people," for Calley, for themselves.

> It's either shoot or be shot and one must take orders from the commanding officers. I don't approve of women and children being killed, but unfortunately in war these things happen.
> —A respondent

PR approvers were consistent in the opposite direction. For them, refusing to shoot is the morally correct course; correspondingly, they maintained that most people would agree with them and refuse to obey orders that were immoral. Hence their condemnation of Calley: 43 percent of them felt that his action was a violation of "principles of morality."

> I would tell superior officers to go to hell because it is immoral—the whole war is wrong.
> —A respondent

> [I wouldn't shoot] because I can't imagine old women, men and children could be part of the war.
> —A respondent

Of the few PR approvers who said they might shoot civilians if they were ordered to do so, some acknowledged that they would be contradicting their moral standards. "I don't believe in shooting animals, let alone a human being," said one, but he added, "being in the Army you would have to follow orders or be court-martialed." Another thought he would shoot "because Vietnam has your mind messed up and so therefore you don't think."

The two groups, then, seem to have entirely different definitions of the situation in which Calley found himself. Of the two verbs in the response *follow orders* and *shoot*, GR disapprovers focus on the first, PR approvers on the second.

Dehumanization of the victim or enemy has been a central concept in many theories of mass murder and war. How many respondents, we wondered, justified Calley's actions by perceiving his victims as less than human—either because of Communist ideology or because of race?

Over one third of the total sample (37 percent) thought that Calley was justified if the persons he shot were Communists—whatever their sex or age. We must be cautious here, however: to many respondents the word *Communist* may automatically evoke an image of an armed and dangerous guerrilla. Still, more than half of the GR disapprovers agreed with this statement, compared to only 11 percent of the PR approvers.

A larger proportion of the total sample, 47 percent, justified Calley on the grounds that *it is better to kill some South Vietnamese civilians than to risk the lives of any American soldiers.* To test the hypothesis, however crudely, that many Americans consider Orientals to be more dispensable than Caucasians, and their lives less valuable, we asked a parallel question about German civilians in World War II. If anything, the results countered the expectation of racism: a slightly *larger* number of respondents, 53 percent, would justify killing German civilians to protect American lives.

PR approvers were less inclined than GR disapprovers to dehumanize the enemy. Only 17 percent of them condoned Calley because it is better to lose South Vietnamese lives than to risk American lives; but two thirds of the GR disapprovers agreed with that statement.

We next asked respondents to compare Calley's actions—"in terms of rights and wrongs"—with American bombing raids that also kill Vietnamese civilians. About half of the PR approvers (51 percent) regarded these two actions as quite different, compared to only one fourth of the GR disapprovers. When we asked them why the events were different, 72 percent of the PR approvers who chose this answer explained that the killing of civilians in bombing raids is unintentional, while Calley's action involved intentional and deliberate murder. Again they based their attitude on the issue of personal causation and responsibility. To the GR disapprovers, though, Calley and the bombardier both operate under the constraints of legitimate authority.

PR approvers of the trial were as likely as GR disapprovers to oppose the Vietnam war. For example, 66 percent of the total sample favored the McGovern–Hatfield amendment to bring all the troops home by the end of 1971; 23 percent opposed the plan. As many GR disapprovers supported this proposal as PR approvers.

There was disagreement between the groups, however, on other attitudes about the war. We prepared 12 statements: five highly correlated with each other, that represented "hawk" beliefs; two more neutral statements; and five, also highly intercorrelated, that represented the "dove" position. GR disapprovers agreed more often than PR approvers with the "hawk" items and less often with the "dove" items, but the differences are small and inconsistent.

Although there is no clear-cut dove–hawk distinction between the two groups in their attitudes toward the war, the PR approvers were much more likely to label themselves doves: 44 percent to 28 percent of the GR disapprovers. (GR disapprovers may regard the dove label less as a description of their position on Vietnam than as an ideological act of opposition to the Government. This may explain why they are reluctant to identify with, and call themselves, doves.)

Demographic factors, usually good predictors of public attitudes, had a minor role in distinguishing approvers from disapprovers. PR approvers were somewhat more likely than GR disapprovers to live in the East or West, rather than in the Midwest or South; to live in metropolitan rather than in rural areas; and to be female. They were less likely to fall in the over-50 age bracket or to be Protestant. Race differences were negligible.

Considerably stronger demographic differences appeared in socioeconomic status. (Interviewers rated each respondent's home and personal possessions on a 10-point scale, which we in turn collapsed into five standard social-class categories.) Approvers tend to fall in the upper three categories, disapprovers in the lower two. Similarly for education level: 42 percent of the PR approvers, compared to only 25 percent of the GR disapprovers, had some college or more.

In earlier research, Kelman identified several routes by which individuals become integrated into the national system. A citizen learns the norms, values and behaviors that his country expects at one of three levels:

1. The normative level, through adherence to system rules. Such an individual regards compliance as highly proper; he accepts the system's right to define and enforce standards of behavior for its members. He is committed to the state as a sacred object or to the belief that law and order are the guarantors of fairness. He will obey system demands to the extent that he perceives them as the wishes of the leadership or the requirements of law. Like Julian B. Rotter's externally controlled individual, he feels that he has little say in shaping Government policies; he sees himself more as a pawn of the system than an active agent.

2. The role-participant level, through identification with system roles. Such an individual is bound to the system by the roles he plays, roles that are important determinants of his self-concept. He will meet system demands to the extent that situational factors have made his roles salient.

3. The ideological level, through internalization of system values. Such an individual is bound to the system by the values and beliefs that transcend role and rule. He will meet the demands of the system so long as he perceives them as consistent with the values to which he is committed.

These distinctions, together with the data from the survey, may give us a deeper understanding of public reactions to Calley's trial.

The largest group of opponents to the trial were those who felt that Calley was unjustly accused for doing his duty. For these respondents, perhaps, the trial and conviction may have threatened the basis of their *normative* integration into the social order: the principles that laws are just, that authorities are legitimate and to be obeyed.

According to our hypothesis, normatively integrated individuals (and we suggest that many of the GR disapprovers belong to this category) relate to the system in terms of an implicit understanding. They will give up control over matters of national policy, but, in return, the authorities must accept responsibility for the consequences of such policies. The individual loses some freedom of choice, but gains some freedom from guilt.

But the Calley trial betrayed this bargain, creating for a large segment of the population a deep sense of confusion, anxiety and anger.

This reaction was further exacerbated by the depth of public identification with Calley himself. Calley, like most of the GR disapprovers, is relatively low in socioeconomic status and education. His public image was less that of an officer than of a simple soldier and little man—and the fact that he is little reinforced his role as victim. Further, Calley's views of authority are the same as those of the GR disapprovers. For all of these reasons, the disapprovers saw Calley as one of their own.

The fact that most GR disapprovers are disenchanted with the war only adds to their sense of dismay. They do not think that the war reflects their own wishes and inclinations, and this makes them even less inclined to accept personal responsibility for it. They would not turn their personal misgivings into active disobedience; but they regard it as unfair to be held responsible for the consequences of a war about which they have such doubts.

We may draw an analogy here to Milgram's study. An individual in a laboratory experiment sees the situation as one that the experimenter defines and controls. Only the experimenter knows the dimensions and requirements of the procedure: the subject knows that he must do as he is told. By the same token, the experimenter is responsible for the subject's actions. In the Calley trial, it was as if one of Milgram's subjects were sentenced for administering shocks to another person—and the chief of the laboratory came to testify against him.

The very premise of the situation—I'll do what you ask, but you must know what you're doing—has been violated.

Milgram's experiments provoked worried speculation about the potential of Americans for following orders even when such obedience contradicts their moral standards. Certainly the disclosure of the events at My Lai provoked far more soul-searching, among many more people, about the potential for crimes committed in the name of obedience. The question remains: to what extent can Americans be mobilized, by appeals to authority, to commit large-scale violence?

Clearly, not everyone finds the demands of apparently legitimate authorities equally compelling. Not all of Milgram's subjects shocked their victims with the highest voltage. Nor did every soldier under Calley's command follow his orders to kill unarmed civilians. Those who resist in such circumstances have apparently managed to retain the framework of personal causation and responsibility that we ordinarily use in daily life.

Yet our data suggest that many Americans feel they have no right to resist authoritative demands. They regard Calley's actions at My Lai as normal, even desirable, because (they think) he performed them in obedience to legitimate authority. One might then infer that this large group

Trial-related Attitudes

	TOTAL SAMPLE	PR APPROVERS	GR DISAPPROVERS
A Who should have been tried for My Lai events?			
Calley and higher officers:	46%	80%	26%
Only Calley:	2%	6%	0%
Only higher officers:	11%	2%	16%
Neither:	28%	3%	43%
B Should Yamashita have been convicted for war crimes he did not order?			
Yes:	26%	35%	21%
No:	45%	39%	48%
Don't know:	30%	26%	31%
C Should American generals be convicted for war crimes they did not order?			
Yes:	22%	35%	16%
No:	62%	49%	68%
Don't know:	16%	17%	16%
D Should German officers at Nuremberg have been convicted for war crimes ordered by superiors?			
Yes:	39%	67%	23%
No:	44%	20%	57%
Don't know:	17%	14%	20%
E Should American officers be convicted for war crimes ordered by superiors?			
Yes:	29%	68%	10%
No:	57%	20%	75%
Don't know:	14%	11%	15%
F Was Calley's sentence:			
Fair?	16%	41%	4%
Too harsh?	75%	42%	93%
Too light?	1%	3%	0%
G Reaction to draft boards that would stop drafting men until Calley's sentence is reversed:			
Approve:	38%	15%	52%
Disapprove:	45%	67%	34%
H Reaction to Nixon's intervention in Calley case:			
Approve:	70%	51%	81%
Disapprove:	22%	41%	13%

would be susceptible to violence in similar conditions; indeed many ac-knowledged that they would take actions similar to those Calley took, if they were ordered to do so.

We are not prepared to make this inference from respondents' answers

Attitudes Toward Calley's Actions

	TOTAL SAMPLE	PR APPROVERS	GR DISAPPROVERS
A What would most people do if ordered to shoot all inhabitants of a Vietnamese village?			
Follow orders and shoot:	67%	37%	82%
Refuse to shoot:	19%	42%	9%
B What would you do in this situation?			
Follow orders and shoot:	51%	19%	68%
Refuse to shoot:	33%	65%	17%
C Overall opinion of Calley's action:			
Right—what any good soldier would do under the circumstances:	29%	3%	49%
Wrong—but hard for him to know right or wrong in this situation:	39%	33%	34%
Wrong—clear violation of military code:	6%	15%	3%
Wrong—violation of morality regardless of military code:	17%	43%	5%
D Calley's actions justified if people he shot were Communists?			
Agree:	37%	11%	53%
Disagree:	51%	85%	34%
E Calley's actions justified because better to kill some S. Vietnamese civilians than risk lives of American soldiers:			
Agree:	47%	17%	67%
Disagree:	39%	70%	21%
F In World War II it would have been better to kill some German civilians than risk lives of American soldiers:			
Agree:	53%	29%	68%
Disagree:	29%	57%	15%
G In terms of rights and wrongs, how do Calley's actions compare with bombing raids that also kill Vietnamese civilians?			
Similar:	56%	38%	63%
Different:	32%	51%	24%

to hypothetical questions. Their reactions in a real My Lai would depend on the precise structure of the situation and their perception of the rules that governed it. Their behavior would be contingent on (1) specific orders and (2) the conviction that the orders were legitimate. Most respondents apparently felt that both criteria were met in Calley's case, but this is not entirely clear. (We incline to the view that Lt. Calley's actions, even if they were not directly ordered, were well within the range of actions that were encouraged or at least condoned in Vietnam.)

Attitudes Toward Vietnam

Percent who agree with each of the following views:		TOTAL SAMPLE	PR APPROVERS	GR DISAPPROVERS
1 If S. Vietnam goes Communist, so will other Asian countries:	HAWK	46%	40%	55%
2 Important to keep non-Communist government in power there:		41%	39%	46%
3 "Blood bath" if American troops leave too fast:		31%	30%	35%
4 Must show world we keep commitments:		32%	34%	32%
5 Should fight to preserve democracy when it is threatened:		45%	39%	48%
6 Normal military tactics cannot win guerrilla war:		43%	45%	40%
7 War undermining morale of U.S. armed forces:		51%	51%	53%
8 War destroying national unity and pride:	DOVE	58%	60%	54%
9 War hurting American economy:		48%	44%	51%
10 War diverting attention from serious domestic problems:		51%	58%	48%
11 An immoral and destructive war:		45%	49%	44%
12 Too many American lives have been lost:		77%	73%	77%
Percent who agree with following reasons for Vietnamization:				
1 Anything that brings troops home is a good move:		50%	55%	49%
2 No right to keep interfering in S. Vietnam's affairs:		24%	27%	20%
3 It's their war—let S. Vietnamese take the casualties:		37%	33%	38%
4 Can maintain military control from the air with less loss of lives:		20%	16%	22%
Self-description on issue of Vietnam war:				
Strong hawk:		8%	3%	11%
Moderate hawk:		14%	13%	17%
Middle of the road:		29%	26%	29%
Moderate dove:		17%	25%	15%
Strong dove:		14%	19%	13%

GENERAL ATTITUDES TOWARD WAR CRIMES, CALLEY'S ACTIONS, VIETNAM WAR. PR approvers differed from GR disapprovers in many of their attitudes toward war crimes in general and toward Calley's trial in particular. Their views on Vietnam did not diverge so strongly, though GR disapprovers tended to endorse more hawkish opinions than PR approvers did, and to consider themselves hawks as well. [Both the wording and order of the above items differ from their presentation in the actual interview.]

Behavior in the actual situation also depends on the balance between binding and opposing forces on an individual. *Binding forces* are those features of a situation that make it difficult for a person to extricate himself. In the Milgram study, for example, the experimenter's presence in the room was a binding force on the subject; when the experimenter left the room, this factor was reduced. *Opposing forces* refer to the strength of a person's inhibitions against performing the act.

The military situation is typically marked by strong binding forces that lock the soldier into obedience.

> My husband has been in Vietnam and he said, "You either follow the order of your superior officer or you will be put in the brig," that when you are arrested for not following orders you can be put in prison for five to 10 years. Besides, you are there fighting a war and you shoot or be killed.
>
> —A respondent

In an event like My Lai, however, there are also strong inhibitions against killing unarmed civilians, especially women and children. To the extent that one can dehumanize the victims, one may overcome such inhibitions; but we think that most persons would find it difficult to do so.

> [I couldn't shoot them because of] a commitment to a higher moral law . . . I don't believe all these people are really my enemy. Somewhere along the line I would have to draw a line between a three-year-old child and someone who is out to take my life.   —A respondent

> I'd rather disobey and face the consequences than live with my conscience if I shot them.   —A respondent

We assume that Lt. Calley's actions at My Lai resulted not only from powerful situational pressures, but also from personal motives which our GR disapprovers do not necessarily share. (For example, Seymour Hersh's account of the events before and during My Lai suggests that Calley was strongly motivated to prove himself as an officer and hero.) Many of our respondents, lacking Calley's special motives, would probably have found the authority structure at My Lai less compelling than they imagined it was for Calley. Also, they might well have felt more inhibited by opposing forces than they realize. On balance, therefore, we believe (perhaps we want to believe it) that many GR disapprovers would not have done *what Calley did*, had they actually found themselves in a similar situation. On the other hand, it is far more likely that they would have done *what the enlisted men under Calley did*—and that is obey Calley's explicit orders to kill civilians.

Clearly, we can only speculate about what our respondents would or would not *do* if they actually found themselves in a My Lai. Our data do suggest quite strongly, however, that there is a *readiness* for violent actions of the type committed by Calley and his men in large segments of the American population. Readiness for such acts is linked to commonly held attitudes toward authority. These attitudes can help us understand how people allocated responsibility for the events at My Lai and why so many felt a deep sense of betrayal at the conviction of Lt. Calley. The public reactions to the Calley trial make it clear that My Lai must be viewed not as a mere aberration, but—at least in part—as the product of a political ideology that exempts authoritative orders from the demands of individual conscience.

44

Letter of Resignation from an Air Force Officer

If few deserters were essentially motivated by matters of conscience, some were. Resignation was another option available, although it was not easy to accomplish unless the individual's term of service was expiring. Captain Dale Noyd, USAF, was one who sought to resign early, for conscientious reasons. Portions of his letter of resignation, dated 8 December 1966, are reprinted here. Does Captain Noyd have counterparts in America's past?

1. I, Dale Edwin Noyd, Captain, FR28084, under paragraph 16m, AFR 36–12, hereby voluntarily tender my resignation from all appointments in the USAF. . . .

2b. I am opposed to the war that this country is waging in Vietnam; and for the past year—since it has become increasingly clear that I will not be able to serve out my obligation and resign from the Air Force—I have considered various stratagems that would obviate my participation in, and contribution to, that war. Among other alternatives, I have considered grounding myself or seeking an assignment other than in Southeast Asia. But these choices were not an honest confrontation of the issues and they do not do justice to my beliefs. The hypocrisy of my silence and acquiescence must end—I feel strongly that it is time for me to demand more consistency between my convictions and my behavior. Several months ago I came to a decision that would reflect this consistency and sought counsel in what alternatives I might have. This letter is a result of that decision.
. . .

2c. Increasingly I find myself in the position of being highly involved and *caring* about many moral, political, and social issues—of which the war in Vietnam is the most important—and yet I cannot protest and work

SOURCE: U.S. District Court, Denver, Colorado, *Noyd v. McNamara, Secretary of Defense, et al.,* 1967. Records and briefs.

to effect some change. Not only may my convictions remain unexpressed and the concomitant responsibilities unfulfilled, but I am possibly confronted with fighting in a war that I believe to be unjust, immoral, and which makes a mockery of both our constitution and the charter of the United Nations—and the human values which they represent. Apart from the moral and ethical issues, and speaking only from the point of view of the super-patriot, it is a stupid war and pernicious to the self-interest of the United States. I am somewhat reluctant to attempt an analysis of the role of this country in the affairs of Southeast Asia for two reasons: First, I have nothing to say that has not been eloquently stated by men such as Senators Fulbright and Morse, U Thant, Fall, Sheehan, Morgenthau, Goodwin, Scheer, Terrill, Raskin, Lacouture, and, of course, the spokesmen for most of the nations of the free world; and secondly, any brief statement almost of necessity will hazard the same defects that have been characteristic of our foreign policy and its public debate—simplistic and obfuscated by cliches and slogans. Nevertheless, because of the gravity of my circumstances and the unusual nature of my resignation, I shall state some of the observations and premises from which I have made my judgments. First of all, in a nation that pretends to an open and free society, hypocrisy and subterfuge have pervaded our conduct and policy in Southeast Asia at least since 1954. This is not only in relations with the Vietnamese and in our pronouncements to the other nations of the world, but also with the American people. One need look no further than our public statements in order to detect this. I insist on knowing what my government is doing and it is clear that this right has been usurped. Although I am cognizant that an open society may have its disadvantages in an ideological war with a totalitarian system, I do not believe that the best defense of our freedoms is an emulation of that system. . . .

2g. It is an immoral war for several sets of reasons. It is not only because our presence is unjustified and for what we are doing to the Vietnamese—as I have discussed above—but also because of our "sins" of omission. This country is capable of achieving for its people, and encouraging in other nations, enormous social advancement, but we are now throwing our riches—both of material and of purpose—into the utter waste of the maelstrom of increasing military involvement. If we as a nation really care about people, then we had best make concepts like freedom and equality *real* to all our citizens—and not just political sham—before we play policeman to the world. Our righteousness is often misplaced. Our behavior in Vietnam is immoral for another set of reasons which concern our conduct of that war. As many newsmen have witnessed, time and again we have bombed, shelled, or attacked a "VC village" or "VC structures" and when we later appraise the results, we label dead adult males as "VC" and add them to the tally—and fail to count the women and children. Our frequent indiscriminate destruction is killing the innocent as well as the "guilty." In addition, our left-handed morality in the treatment of prisoners is odious—

we turn them over to the ARVN for possible torture or execution with the excuse that we are not in command but are only supporting the South Vietnam government. Again, this hypocrisy needs no explication. Also frighteningly new in American morality is the pragmatic justification that we must retaliate against the terrorist tactics of the VC. Perhaps most devastatingly immoral about the war in Vietnam are the risks we are assuming for the rest of the world. Each new step and escalation appears unplanned and is an attempt to rectify previous blunders by more military action. The consequences of our course appear too predictable, and although we as a people may elect "better dead than red," do we have the right to make this choice for the rest of mankind?

2h. I am not a pacifist; I believe that there are times when it is right and necessary that a nation or community of nations employ force to deter or repel totalitarian aggression. My three-year assignment in an operational fighter squadron—with the attendant capacity for inflicting terrible killing and destruction—was based on the personal premise that I was serving a useful deterrent purpose and that I would never be used as an instrument of aggression. This, of course, raises the important and pervasive question for me: What is my duty when I am faced with a conflict between my conscience and the commands of my government? What is my responsibility when there is an irreparable division between my beliefs in the ideals of this nation and the conduct of my political and military leaders? The problem of ultimate loyalty is not one for which there is an easy solution. And, unfortunately, the issues are most often obscured by those who would undermine the very freedoms they are ostensibly defending— by invoking "loyalty" and "patriotism" to enforce conformity, silence dissent, and protect themselves from criticism. May a government or nation be in error? Who is to judge? As Thoreau asked, "Must the citizen ever for a moment, or in the least degree, resign his conscience, to the legislator? Why has every man a conscience, then? I think that we should be men first, and subjects afterwards. It is not desirable to cultivate a respect for the law, so much as for the right. The only obligation which I have a right to assume, is to do at any time what I think right. . . . Law never made men a whit more just; and, by means of their respect for it, even the well-disposed are daily made the agents of injustice." The individual *must* judge. We as a nation expect and demand this—we have prosecuted and condemned those who forfeited their personal sense of justice to an immoral authoritarian system. We have despised those who have pleaded that they were only doing their job. If we are to survive as individuals in this age of acquiescence, and as nations in this time of international anarchy, we must resist total enculturation so that we may stand aside to question and evaluate—not as an Air Force officer or as an American, but as a member of the human species. This resistance and autonomy is difficult to acquire and precarious to maintain, which perhaps explains its rarity. Camus puts it succinctly: "We get into the habit of living before acquiring the habit of thinking." We must not confuse dissent with disloyalty and we must recognize that consensus is no substitute for conscience. As Senator Fulbright has stated, "Criticism is more than a right; it is an act of patriotism—a higher form of patriotism, I believe, than the familiar ritual of national adulation. All of us have the responsibility to act upon this higher patriotism which is to love our country less for what it is than for what we would like it to be." . . .

2j. I have attempted to sincerely state the values and beliefs that are both most meaningful in my life and relevant to my present dilemma. It would appear that I am no longer a loyal Air Force officer if this loyalty requires unquestioning obedience to the policies of this nation in Vietnam. I cannot honestly wear the uniform of this country and support unjust and puerile military involvement. Although it may be inconsistent, I have been able to justify (or rationalize) my position here at the Academy by my belief that my contribution in the classroom has had more effect in encouraging rationalism, a sense of humanism, and the development of social consciousness than it has had in the inculcation of militarism. My system of ethics is humanistic—simply a respect and love for man and confidence in his capability to improve his condition. This is my ultimate loyalty. And, as a man trying to be free, my first obligation is to my own integrity and conscience, and this is of course not mitigated by my government's permission or command to engage in immoral acts. I am many things before I am a citizen of this country or an Air Force officer; and included among these things is simply that I am a man with a set of human values which I will not abrogate. I must stand on what I am and what I believe. The war in Vietnam is unjust and immoral, and if ordered to do so, I shall refuse to fight in that war. I should prefer, and respectfully request, that this resignation be accepted. . . .

45

Vietnam and the Vets

JACK LADINSKY

The effects and aftermath of Vietnam service have provoked heated arguments and much hyperbole. This first half of a review essay by Jack Ladinsky is the best analytical survey of the literature and of the issues.

AT THE END OF EVERY WAR a nation pauses and anxiously reflects on the manifold difficulties involved in demobilization and the reintegration of millions of returning veterans. For social institutions and for the individual veterans, even under the best of conditions back home, adjustments are vexing and strained. The end of the Vietnam conflict was no different; indeed it was destined to be more troublesome in many respects than prior demobilizations, despite the fact that 12-month rotations from Vietnam mitigated some of the pressures of reintegrating large numbers of returnees over a short period of time. There was no victory to celebrate, and it was an unpopular war beset by violent protests. It was scarred by gross inequities in who fought the war, by widespread media publicity of heavy drug abuse in Vietnam, and by the shocking events surrounding the My Lai affair. Moreover, largely because of the costs of the war, the American economy, to which veterans returned in search of jobs, was unable to absorb them very swiftly. Fed by the instant and stereotyped imagery of our visual and printed media, a public ambivalence appeared toward the returning veteran. By 1971 there was a mood strikingly different from the ceremonialism and merriment after World War II or the more subdued

SOURCE: Jack Ladinsky, "Vietnam, the Vets, and the VA," *Armed Forces and Society* 2 (Spring 1976): 435–467. Copyright 1976 Inter-University Seminar on Armed Forces and Society. Reprinted by permission.
EDITOR'S NOTE: Most of the citations to the sources consulted by the author in this essay have been omitted from this volume for brevity and economy. The reader should consult the original source of the essay for the complete scholarly documentation.

elation and relief after Korea. Norma Wikler, in her study of the political consciousness of Vietnam returnees, makes the point that public uneasiness about the veterans began to appear when there were signs that they might return and cause trouble.

Once large numbers of Vietnam veterans were home, troubles did begin. Complaints began to mount about various problems they were encountering: unemployment, inadequate educational and training benefits, poor medical care, ineffective drug treatment facilities. Some veterans were saying that public neglect was leading to the loss of a whole generation of men.

At the same time, the military posture toward manpower procurement was undergoing a substantial change. Partly because of the manpower instabilities experienced in the protracted conflict in Southeast Asia, and partly because of larger changes in the technology of modern defense preparedness, the military was calling for an all-volunteer enlisted force with substantially upgraded pay scales and fringe benefits. The Congress complied, and the all-volunteer concept became official policy in 1973.

In 1969 when more than one million veterans already had returned from Vietnam, a few books and articles began to appear. By 1972 thousands of pages of congressional testimony had piled up on the veterans and the assistance, or lack of it, offered to them by the Veterans Administration. 1973 and 1974 witnessed a flurry of volumes and all sorts of articles in scholarly and popular publications. (Penthouse Magazine is still running a series on the Vietnam veteran—"America's Prisoners of Peace"— that began in March, 1974.) . . .

I
POPULAR IMAGES OF THE VIETNAM VETERAN

Beginning in 1969, as troop involvement wound down and men began to return home in substantial numbers, one could discern in newspapers and magazines the emergence of a variety of images of what the Vietnam returnees were like. Wikler has a very perceptive chapter reviewing these images, which she divides into the "radical" and the "normal," along political lines. Drawing upon the works under review, I have arranged these images somewhat differently, but the picture is similar.

Scattered throughout the *Source Material* volume are representative newspaper and magazine articles whose captions portray the components of the images:

"The Invisible Veterans"
"The Vietnam Veteran: Silent, Perplexed, Unnoticed"
"The Veterans—Aliens in Their Land"
"Postwar Shock Besets Veterans of Vietnam"

"Vietnam Vets: An Unpopular War Rubs Off"
"Coming Home With a Habit"

One of the most vivid captions I have seen appeared above a two-part article on Vietnam veterans ("a different breed") in a Madison, Wisconsin, newspaper: "Alienation Follows the Horrors of Asia." It is not reprinted (fortunately) in *Source Material*.

The most powerful and controversial image is illustrated by the Levy book, *Spoils of War*. It is a series of vignettes that purvey the view of Vietnam veterans; they are so brutalized by their war experiences as to have become "human time bombs" in the words of the *Philadelphia Enquirer*—men with an uncontrollable capacity for violence. Starr (p. 36) credits Levy with being the principal source for this view, and extensive exploration of the literature suggests Starr is correct. Allusion to the violent veterans, when it appears, invariably refers to Levy's work.

Levy did his three-year study out of the Laboratory of Community Psychiatry at Harvard Medical School. He studied 60 Marine veterans and later 60 Army veterans in the same Boston working-class neighborhood. His respondents were not a random sample of veterans. They were gathered from community contacts and referrals. In late 1970, over two years into the study period, and apparently before he interviewed the Army veterans, Levy and his colleague Dr. Gerald Caplan, Director of the Laboratory, testified before Senator Cranston's Subcommittee on Veterans' Affairs of the Committee on Labor and Public Welfare, which was looking into unemployment and other readjustment problems of Vietnam veterans. They painted a vivid picture of estrangement, brutalization, and dehumanization, which at least some of the subcommittee members found hard to swallow. At one point Senator Randolph asked Caplan:

> these veterans who return. I have rather felt that you placed them all under one umbrella and say they all return in the same mental attitude. . . . What is the percentage of young people in the United States, let's say young men, that are not in Vietnam but are in the United States, who crack up?
>
> Dr. CAPLAN. Well, first, I don't have the figures, and I wouldn't like to give an estimate on something as important as that. I would be suspicious of any figures you get because I am not familiar with any really adequate way of answering that question from a scientific point of view.
>
> But, Senator. I did not say all veterans were in the same boat with regard to these unpleasant and painful reactions. I said that there are a significant proportion of them who have difficulties. I don't know what that proportion is, because we still haven't been able to conduct the research to answer that question. But enough of them suffer from these reactions to make it not at all difficult to find them as research subjects in an ordinary population in the city. So all I would say is that there is a significant number who have problems, certainly not all.

It is curious that Caplan hesitated to generalize about "something as important as" the number of young men in the United States who "crack up," because it is hard to get scientific information, but was quite willing to talk about a "significant proportion" of Vietnam veterans who are *prone* to violence in the absence of scientific information beyond 60 Boston working-class Marine veterans. Levy showed the same lack of inhibition. Later Senator Saxbe quizzed him:

> Now, what kind of control group did you establish on this study?
>
> Dr. LEVY. The control group was in effect each succeeding veteran that I spoke to. In other words, I was continually trying to find out whether I was talking to a peculiar instance or whether there was a pattern.

And further along Saxbe asked:

> Do you want to generalize from your study of 60 veterans that the characteristics that you have shown are representative of approximately 4 million that have served in this Vietnam era?
>
> Dr. LEVY. I would be cautious about that, naturally. But I think at the same time it is not entirely improbable that one can make such an extension if one is to rely on their testimony, for instance, they describe what seem to be patterns in Vietnam that would indicate that this sort of thing was not uncommon.

The Senators were not alone in their wariness about generalizing. During his testimony later in the hearings, Professor Charles C. Moskos, Jr. of Northwestern University and author of *American Enlisted Men*, stated:

> I would like to make a passing remark about the so-called killer instinct that veterans are alleged to bring back after serving in combat. There is not one shred of data or evidence that support that proposition that veterans come back with a higher rate of this killer instinct. Then you should not forget that even in Vietnam only 15 percent of all soldiers are actually frontline combat soldiers and this proportion is even dropping in recent times. If one prorates in 1970 the total number of men under fire with the total number of men in uniforms, less than 3 percent of all people in uniform in 1970 are actually in combat, and even among that 3 percent, there is no evidence of a killer instinct.

So much for the brutalization hypothesis. One does not hear much about it anymore. Levy claims to have had requests for assistance from veterans, their families, and their lawyers, from "every type of background in all parts of the country" (p. viii) after he gave his Senate testimony. However, the nation, at least so far, does not appear to have been terrorized by exploding veterans. Nor did anyone take seriously Levy's suggestion that returning Vietnam troops be put through a special "boot camp in reverse" to unlearn their violence proneness.

A related image of the Vietnam veteran is illustrated in Lifton's book, *Home From the War*. Lifton says that the Vietnam veteran is confused, guilt-ridden, and depressed by his immoral behavior in the cause of a corrupt and depraved war. Lifton is a prominent psychiatrist at Yale University who has written numerous volumes among which is an award winning book, *Death in Life: Survivors of Hiroshima*. Lifton writes from extensive experience with antiwar veteran rap groups and studies of the My Lai episode, which included intensive interviews with participants. But antiwar and My Lai veterans do not a universe make. His neo-Freudian conclusions suffer from the same lack of inhibitions to generalize that we saw in connection with the brutalization image. Lifton feels *all* Vietnam veterans suffer these problems, as does the society at large. The theme runs throughout the book. At the 1972 Annual Convention of the American Psychiatric Association, during the discussion period of the panel in which he delivered a paper on rap groups. Lifton was asked what distinguishes a prowar veteran from an antiwar veteran. His answer (which he labeled a "guess") was that both groups have similar issues of guilt and rage to resolve over the dirty business with which they cooperated, but that the former group, the prowar veterans, buries it whereas the latter group, the antiwar veterans, confronts death and guilt. Failing to confront guilt, of course, means maladjustment and the prospect of future acting out of the disturbance. In this regard Lifton comes close to the brutalization image. However, he is more guarded in his predictions. In fact, he could hardly be wrong because he covers himself on all sides:

> we can expect various kinds of psychological disturbances to appear in Vietnam veterans, ranging from mild withdrawal to periodic depression to severe psychosomatic disorder to disabling psychosis. Some are likely to seek continuing outlets for a pattern of violence to which they have become habituated. . . . Similarly, many will hold onto a related habituation to racism and the need to victimize others. Any of these patterns may appear very quickly in some, but in others lie dormant for a period of months or even years and then emerge in response to various internal and external pressures.

Just about the only way Lifton could err is if Vietnam veterans manifested absolutely no deviant behavior ever. In that unlikely event they would be "deviant" by any reasonable standards of comparison to the male civilian population of the same age.

Of course, as stated, this is not a readily testable proposition. But by any reasonable behavioral test one can point to contradictory findings. In a study of 577 Vietnam Army returnees contrasted with 172 non-Vietnam Army men on the same garrison post, Jonathan Borus found no significant differences between the two groups in incidence of maladjustment. Robins, in her study of a random sample of returnees (n = 470) found they showed no more treatable psychiatric problems than other soldiers, and they showed no sign of more disciplinary problems than other veterans (*The Vietnam Drug User Returns*, p. 46).

Lifton's writings and lectures, like Levy's, have captured little continuing attention into the present. Neither have been very prominent because, I suspect, their dire predictions about visible and spectacular behavioral problems among the three million Vietnam returnees now living in American society have not come true.

A third image of the Vietnam veteran is the returnee alienated from people and from society. On a simpler level this image is reflected in one variation or another of the popular news article where the "gung ho" youth goes off to fight what turns out to be a wretched and unpopular war and returns to find the country has changed, there is no work to be found, and he is watched guardedly by his fellow Americans. He is "disillusioned and cynical." At a deeper level the veteran is seen as becoming alienated in the Marxist sense of subjective disaffection, rejection of government, and ultimately politicization into radical, even revolutionary, activity. [John Helmer's *Bringing the War Home*] reflects the latter view. Unlike the other works under review, Helmer's book is a lengthy and complex, indeed, in places a tangled, sociological treatise. I found the book exasperating, but, at the same time, the most provocative of the materials under review. Helmer is cavalier with data, loose with concepts, and bold with unsubstantiated assertions, but his basic argument is sociologically intriguing. Helmer begins with three "samples" of 30 veterans from whom he obtained extensive survey interviews. Group I, the "straights," were all members of Veterans of Foreign Wars in Boston and other parts of the Northeast. They were selected from lists of names supplied by "friendly" post officials and from "random" sampling of members taken at varying times when they happened to be at the post. Group II, the "addicts," were selected as they "randomly became available" by appearing at a Boston methadone center, or by admission to a Boston area VA program or clinic, or through veteran addicts who volunteered to do interviews with other addicts who they knew were not in a program. Group III, the "radicals," were members of Vietnam Veterans Against the War in Boston, and were chosen so as to include only active members.

Helmer presents data on these 90 respondents in well over 150 simple, descriptive, number and percent tables which allow comparisons of the three groups. No tests of significance are shown. No other analytic techniques are applied. In conjunction with these cross-tabulations, Helmer presents an intricate explanation of the evolution of alienation among these men. It is not presented in any one place; I have tried to piece it together from 300 pages of text.

Prior to service these 90 men were quite similar. All came from conventional working-class families. None held strong political beliefs about the war or service. None were radicals or drug addicts. They were drafted or joined to avoid the draft. During training there were no differences, and once assigned to Vietnam there were no major differences in the conditions they faced. All three groups had similar exposures to combat. Differences began to emerge after first combat experiences. Addicts and radicals came to have more respect for the enemy and for civilians, and more often to feel that the war was unwinnable and unjustifiable than did the straights. What caused these attitudinal differences to emerge? To answer this Helmer draws upon the primary group, that social concept so often applied in military sociology since the *American Soldier* studies during World War II. Very quickly after arrival in Vietnam, Helmer says, the men became identified with one of two mutually exclusive groups—the "juicers" or the "heads." The former were characterized by drinking and the latter by drug use. "Straights were juicers and no juicer was a head. Addicts and radicals were heads, and heads could not also be juicers" (p. 187). There was no selectivity of men into one or the other group. The sorting took place by happenstance, a product of the random assignment of men to units and to barracks replacing men who rotated back home or were permanent losses as casualties of the war. "The process by which the men sorted themselves into primary groups seems almost pure spontaneity" (p. 188). Helmer likens the process to Rosa Luxemburg's spontaneous mobilization of revolutionaries from a mass base of workers, rather than through the Leninist idea of recruitment by a vanguard elite. The men themselves were "silent" about why they became juicers or heads (p. 190), presumably because it was done unconsciously.

The juicers and the heads became primary group identities and provided ideologies that affect the way men perceived what happened to them day-by-day, and the way they evaluated the purpose of American military presence in Vietnam. The real deprivations and frustrations of Vietnam were the same for all, but the two groups provided different contexts for subjectively experiencing these deprivations. Drugs symbolized heads' solidarity against booze, rednecks, straights, and lifers. Beer symbolized the juicers' solidarity around the enlisted men's club, whorehouse raids, gang rapes, arson, shooting civilians, and fights with blacks. This identity was the first stage of a development in which the men were ideologically and behaviorally transformed into compliers with military rules and discipline and noncompliers:

> Our data cannot be indicative of the full power of the primary group variable in the process of ideological mobilization. . . . without it . . . the working class soldier in Vietnam would not have reached the point of noncompliance that he did, and noncompliance in itself, where it occurred, would not have been followed by considerable ideological change, formal opposition to continuation of the fighting, and within the limits of the circumstances, active revolt against the military. [p. 199]

By active revolt Helmer means fragging, a behavior presumably carried out almost entirely by heads.

Head and juicer groups were broken for the men when they departed from Vietnam for other assignments or for separation. During the period of reassignment, the heads group was reestablished for most radicals and some addicts at bases in Japan, Europe, or continental United States through affiliation with the radical antiwar activists who set up units around military installations. This was especially true for the radicals who disproportionately reenlisted. Inclined toward antiwar sentiment, radicals sought such affiliations, and their radical perspectives were sharpened. Straights by and large did not get reassigned, but were separated after Vietnam, and, hence, missed this further socialization to radicalism. Most addicts also were separated soon after Vietnam. How can their behavior be explained? Helmer admits he cannot explain why these men became addicts, some during and some after service:

> There can be no satisfactory sociological explanation of why the men of Group II became addicts—that is, men who spend more of their waking hours under the influence of a narcotic than they did anything else. I can specify the social factors associated with the onset of addiction and also its social consequences insofar as these are commonly shared. But these do not make theories of motivation, and in a study of this kind the psychological and physiological elements of the situation are simply beyond reach. [pp. 237–238]

The social fact associated with onset of drug use, says Helmer, was the marijuana crackdown by the military command in Vietnam in 1969–1970. Group II men came to Vietnam right after that, when heroin was substituted for marijuana. Helmer also suggests that addiction, like head and juicer recruitment, was "spontaneous," by men ready for mobilization.

Upon separation from service, juicers and heads had different experiences that further influenced their behavior. Radicals found that they now had little in common with their working-class families, especially over feelings about the war. Tensions developed, and the men moved out of the house. In time they found their ideological home, Vietnam Veterans Against the War (VVAW). Straights, on the other hand, returned to families with whom they had no trouble. However, they found that the friends they had left were more "headlike" now—voicing antiwar sentiments and using drugs. Straights sought new friends closer to their conservative views, and they found them at the Veterans of Foreign Wars (VFW).

In order for radical activism to emerge, says Helmer, two conditions had to exist. First, local ties to family and friends had to be destroyed. Second, there had to be a civilian counterpart of the heads primary groups: "Radicals came to satisfy both of these conditions; the addicts only the first" (p. 219). Addicts were too preoccupied feeding a habit to participate in organized militant activism, although they agreed with it in principle.

Thus, VFW served to integrate the straights into civilian life, recreating the juicers' primary group and supporting their ideological position on the war. For the radicals, VVAW was a continuation of the heads group they left in service. In the last chapter Helmer comments on the fate of alienation and radicalism. In their activism the radicals came to reject violence as a political response at home. They did not, in principle, embrace nonviolence, but in VVAW opted for reform, not revolution. Given the reformist stance of VVAW, Helmer predicts that true radicals ultimately would take to underground activism.

This, put briefly, but I believe accurately, is Helmer's thesis. The problem is that his data are incapable of supporting this formidable edifice. It takes countless heroic leaps of faith to get from the data to the post hoc interpretations. Rarely can a table be seen as a direct support of an assertion. His 90 veterans are not subsamples of the universes to which he wishes to generalize. Retrospective answers are open to doubt, and by respondents as firm in their convictions as are these men—given the way they were selected—hindsight feelings are very suspect. Moreover, close to half of the straights are Marines who joined up, trained, and shipped out together, many on the buddy system. Helmer either ignores or dismisses these technical problems as he dauntlessly pursues his theory. In the end he has glossed over serious gaps in his explanation, and he succumbs to myths about the war that are untenable. I can only comment here on the more egregious among them.

First, Helmer does not explain the dynamics of primary group processes. The two primary groups are black boxes. We are not told what is in them. Where did juicer and head groups come from? What characterized them aside from alcohol and drugs? Why did one elicit honorable and the other abject behavior? I do not question that there were juicers and heads in Vietnam. The terms are not Helmer's; similar aggregates of men existed during the Korean conflict, in more recent years among troops stationed in Europe, and perhaps elsewhere. One properly can question whether the universe of Vietnam troops were divided between the two, and it taxes the sociological imagination to believe that there was no selectivity into them. It is obscurantism to assert that propinquity led to spontaneous identity. Rosa Luxemburg was not concerned to explain alternative choices by the depressed working class. In reaction to Leninist centralism, she maintained that revolutionary action and creative leadership would emerge among the masses through continued political education, but without the organizational assistance of advanced sectors of the party. Vietnam did not create such conditions. Helmer has posed a theory that requires explanation of the dynamics of group identification, and the way in which group experiences led to ideological commitments and attitudes. An intriguing sociological explanation remains critically incomplete. He cannot provide the explanation from the data he has accumulated. More important, he cannot provide it, I suggest, because the distinctiveness he implies is not there to begin with. Head and juicer identities, real as they were for some men, were partial or nonexistent for most. They were not intense or inclusive primary groups, and, therefore, they could not guide world views as thoroughly as Helmer would have us believe. The juicer-head distinction is useful, and could yield insights into behavior in Vietnam, but elevated to such prominence, it is an exaggeration of reality.

Second, Helmer makes assertions about the role of drugs in Vietnam that are unwarranted. He claims that psychiatric casualties were significantly lower than during World War II because of drugs "that transformed individually experienced stress into collective grievance" (p. 199, n. 53). It is true that the incidence of psychiatric problems in combat were substantially lower in Vietnam than during either World War II or the Korean conflict. It is a fact, as Bourne has emphasized, that many drugs can provide physiological relaxation from stress, and this is reflected in the variety of reasons men gave for using drugs.[1] Alcohol has the same effect, and undoubtedly for many in Vietnam drugs replaced alcohol. But there is no evidence I have seen that drug use was a primary factor in ameliorating psychiatric distress. There is common agreement that the 12-month rotation period was the most important reason. In addition, combat in Vietnam was less intense and less sustained than in prior wars. Soldiers did not spend long periods in trenches or foxholes, and they were rarely under continuous bombardment by artillery or airplanes. Moreover, they had more of the small luxuries of life in Vietnam, and the time to enjoy them insofar as that was possible back in camp, in Saigon, or during rest and recuperation leave. Vietnam combat was no picnic, but neither was it the hell of World War II or even Korea. Drug use was very high in Vietnam, a fact that is explored further below. But it is inaccurate to assert that drugs were the primary agent in holding down psychiatric casualties.

Helmer also suggests, as noted above, that the marijuana crackdown in Vietnam drove men to use harder drugs, especially heroin. He is not the only writer to make this argument. Indeed, it is an obvious, almost reflective, response by social scientists who are inclined to look for replacements in social behavior under conditions of legal control. But the argument also assumes that the military (using dogs to detect the smell of marijuana, burning fields, imposing stiff penalties for use, and so on) has been more effective than civilian authorities in curbing the traffic in drugs. The available evidence does not bear this out. Robins' data show that 70% of a sample of men in Vietnam right after the crackdown said marijuana was always available, and 22% more said it was usually available. Only 8% said it was scarce (pp. 25–26). The Harris survey reported similar high figures from a sample of veterans in Vietnam about the same time. Three-fourths judged that marijuana was very accessible. Another 12% judged that it was somewhat accessible. Only 2% said "not at all." These bits of evidence are not an ideal test, but they do cast doubt on the replacement thesis.

Third, Helmer implies, in various places through the book, that the Vietnam war was fought by a "poor man's army" (p. 3), heavily black and largely "New Standards" men. Helmer's own respondents were hardly poor. They were, by and large, from solid working-class families.[2]

There is evidence that during the Vietnam era, liberalized acceptance standards and draft deferment policies operated to reduce upper-middle-class participation, and to increase the proportion from lower strata. There is also evidence that casualty rates were higher for blacks, and they were probably higher for lower-class whites. But these facts do not justify the conclusion that a lumpenproletariat was shipped to Vietnam.

Acceptance standards were relaxed between 1963 and 1965, and again in 1968. Despite this, overall entrances to the Army were at, or only a percentage point above, black representation in the population. The differences begin to show when entrances are separated into inductions and enlistments by race. Black inductions are greater than black population representation in most years between 1961 and 1968 by from one to six percentage points, whereas black enlistments are usually at or below black population representation during the same period. In short, blacks were drafted beyond their presence in the population during much of the Vietnam war. Relaxed standards played the major role but they had to be coupled with student and occupational deferments to get the effect. But even with this obvious bias, military acceptance standards still excluded 31% of all youths, and 72% of black youths. These exclusions at the bottom precluded the creation of a poor man's army. The exclusions at the top guaranteed that it would look more like a working-class army.

It was also impossible for New Standards men to comprise very much of the fighting force in Vietnam. There simply were not enough of them. New Standards men were military entrances who would have been disqualified under regular mental and physical standards. They came in with "Project 100,000," which was launched in 1966 by then Secretary of Defense Robert McNamara, to rehabilitate some of America's disadvantaged youths. The program was the military's contribution to the war on poverty. It was always controversial, and, ultimately, not terribly successful. It was terminated by Congress in 1971. However, the quotas of New Standards entrants already had begun to fall substantially during the prior two years in all the services as they prepared for the advent of the all-volunteer military.

Between 1966 and 1971, about 350,000 New Standards men entered the services. Attrition ran about 10%, leaving 315,000 to serve out their tours of duty. If all these men had gone to Vietnam, an unlikely event, they would have represented 13% of the active force. If all of them had seen combat, also unlikely, they would have represented 21% of the combat troops. More realistic, but liberal, estimates would be something closer to 7% or 8% of all Vietnam troops, and perhaps 11% or 12% of combat troops. These are high estimates, pulled from very rough calculations. There are no published data to draw from. I have calculated on the high side because the evidence is clear that New Standards men were heavily black (40%) and ended up disproportionately in combat MOSs (37%). Although we do not have data on what proportion saw duty in Vietnam, it is reasonable to assume that it was higher than for any regular entering cohort.

If these estimates are even close to correct, they may be grounds for grave concern about the fate of New Standards men. They undoubtedly were casualties disproportionate to their representation in the military. But surely the figures do not suggest that these men were a major component of the Vietnam force.

Fourth, Helmer implies that many heads, presumably a substantial number of the Vietnam returnees after the addicts were separated out, were politicized into radical antiwar activity. The weakness of sustained opposition by an antiwar faction does not fit with this view. Organized militant action was sporadic and short-lived. Antiwar militancy has been diffused further since the last troops left Southeast Asia; the takeovers of South Vietnam and Cambodia by Communist regimes have all but killed the opposition. Veterans appear to be more concerned with G.I. benefits than with antigovernment actions. There is one study that suggests a conclusion the reverse of Helmer's. In 1970–1971, Wikler studied political consciousness among 140 veterans who returned from Vietnam to the San Francisco Bay Area. She concluded that the majority of the men remained pre-political thinkers. Once home the commonest response was dissipation of political consciousness, not radicalization. A second study also casts doubt on the politicization theme. Jennings and Markus studied 328 veterans who were part of a panel interviewed prior to service (1965) and after separation (1973). They reported that while military service overall had little impact on political orientation, men with Vietnam service more often adopted a "non-active citizenship norm."[3]

An inevitable conclusion is that Helmer's work suffers from the same malady that overcame Levy's and Lifton's: exaggeration in the service of a sense of outrage about American military action in Vietnam.

A fourth image of the returning Vietnam veteran is as a drug-hooked G.I., wasted by a habit that he innocently picked up using potent narcotics, a habit he developed while searching for relief from the pains of Vietnam. Some of the journalistic accounts are reprinted in *Source Material* (pp. 237–245, 257–262). They provide vignettes about discontented men in treatment centers, and they describe the uneasiness among authorities about the growing but unknown extent of the problem. There were others that painted more somber pictures of men, some in medical units, some not, all unfit for regular employment and viewed suspiciously by their friends and families.

A drug abuse literature has accumulated on the Vietnam soldier. It is not a large body of literature, but it is diffuse and often contradictory; but no more so than the drug abuse literature on the United States generally. Much of the writing on drugs and youth in the United States is devoted to favored explanations of the cause of addiction, followed by cures consistent with the theories. For every theory of cause and cure there are critiques that purport to show them wrong or inadequate. Starr briefly reviews the history of drug abuse in the United States, and he endorses the theory, simply put, that America created the contemporary drug problem by labeling it and driving it underground, whereas England took the more sensible step of treating drug abusers in low-cost clinics, and thereby avoided widespread addiction and the secondary deviance that has followed from the American approach. My limited familiarity with the literature suggests that this view is not universally accepted. However, it is not my intention to enter this arena of debate. My concern is primarily with understanding, insofar as it is possible, the extent of drug abuse in Vietnam, and the consequences of it for the returning veterans. For this purpose, *The Vietnam Drug User Returns*, by Lee Robins, is the most insightful research available. Starr, who is usually more careful, wrongly dismissed this study as unreliable because it was based on interviews with veterans (p. 151), who, presumably, would not be honest out of fear of losing benefits or for other reasons. He apparently saw only a Department of Defense release about the study, which announced that most heroin users in Vietnam gave it up after returning home, and that the readdiction rate was so small as to not add substantially to the drug problem in the United States. (A *New York Times* article on the Defense Department release is reprinted in *Source Material*, pp. 257–258.) The release was, as Starr charges, self-serving, but it was a reasonably accurate statement of the findings from Robins's interim report. (The interim report is reprinted in *Source Material*, pp. 262–289. The final report differs from the interim report primarily in detail.)

The Robins study was not a Defense Department project. It was undertaken by the Special Action Office for Drug Abuse Prevention, with joint funding by the Departments of Defense and Labor, the National Institute of Mental Health, and the Veterans Administration. Interviewing and preliminary data processing were carried out by the National Opinion Research Center. Respondents were Vietnam enlisted returnees in September, 1971. They served in Vietnam during the period of heaviest heroin use. Two samples were studied. The first, a general sample consisted of 470 men randomly selected from the close to 14,000 returning that month. The second, a drug-positive sample of 495 men was randomly drawn from approximately 1,000 men found to be drug positive in the urine screening when departing from Vietnam. In 1972, eight to 12 months after their return, the men were interviewed and asked for urine samples. At the same time, their military records were abstracted and their names sought among VA claims files. Cooperation was remarkably high. Ninety-six percent of those interviewed "readily agreed" to be interviewed; interviews were completed for 95%; urine samples were granted by 92%. Many questions about discreditable events were answered accurately. For example, 97% of those with records of heroin use in Vietnam admitted to it on the interview (pp. 13–16). Concordance was not always so high, but there was no evidence of patterned concealment or evasion. There is no reason to seriously question overall validity. Moreover, the rate of urine positives for narcotics was very close to the respondents' own reports. Three percent expected to have positive urines, and 2% did (p. 15). There were problems, of course, but generally the results appear to be as reliable and valid as any comparable survey research on sensitive topics.

The data reveal that illicit narcotics use was extremely high in Vietnam. Forty-three percent of the general sample used narcotics at least once (p. vii). Sixty-two percent of narcotics users were regulars (p. 31). Only 11% of the sample had been exposed to these drugs before Vietnam service (p. 21). Thirty-three percent of the sample began use of narcotics in Vietnam for the first time, and 19% began regular use. Let us assume that these proportions held across some three million men who served in Vietnam. That would suggest that 800,000 men were regular narcotics users in Vietnam, or 27% of those who went over. About 570,000 became regular users in Vietnam. Further assume that one-fourth of these new regular users would have been "at risk" anyway, and would have become regular users had they not served in Vietnam. This probably is a liberal estimate, since most men by age 20 who would have used drugs very likely had done so before assignment to Vietnam. That would still leave over 427,000 introduced to regular narcotics use in Vietnam, or 14% of the men who served there. Even if we reduce this figure by half to adjust for the fact that hard drug use was less prior to 1970, it is a very high proportion.

What about drug use just before departure from Vietnam and after return to the United States? Robins estimates that 10.5% of the general sample was drug positive at the time of departure from Vietnam (p. ix). This figure is based on urine screening at time of departure and adjusted for possible errors. Again assume that this figure held over the three million men who served in Vietnam. That means 315,000 men could have returned to the United States with a positive rating for illicit drugs. Of course, many of these would have been caught in the screening, once it began, and detoxified. However, Robins reports later in the volume that detoxification did not prove very effective for this group (p. 61). They were no less likely to use narcotics and use them heavily after Vietnam than a comparable group of users who had not been detected and detoxified. Moreover, there was no evidence that placement in an Army treatment center after returning to the states made a difference in later narcotics use (p. 67). She further notes that 10% reported using a narcotic since returning, but only 2% of the general sample continued use of drugs up to time of interview (p. 57). Again generalizing, that would come to 60,000 continuing users. This estimate might well be too conservative because it excludes those who did not admit use in the interview. This would appear to be a small bias. However, the figure is also inflated because drug use was less in the earlier years. On balance the estimate is probably not out of line.

The above figures speak only to drug use, not addiction. Robins estimates that since returning from Vietnam about 1% had been readdicted (p. viii). Twenty percent reported symptoms of addiction in Vietnam (p.

viii), a figure that is double the pickup rate on the departure urine screening. Of those who began narcotics use in Vietnam, 93% stopped altogether after service (p. 81). Two-thirds, however, did use some other drugs, especially marijuana (p. 82). Among men introduced only to marijuana in Vietnam, 86% never used it on return (p. 82).

Clearly drug use in Vietnam was very widespread, and addiction was by no means trivial. Vietnam service introduced thousands to hard drugs who likely would not have been exposed. Given these facts, the extent of remission after leaving Vietnam is striking. It should not be interpreted to mean drug abuse in Vietnam has left no problems. Robins found that men who used narcotics in Vietnam and continued after return had significantly more arrests, psychiatric treatment, unemployment, and divorce than did nonusers (p. 73). And even allowing for high preservice exposure to drugs among these men, they carried a heavy burden of social adjustment due to their Vietnam experience. But the high remission rate does suggest that the problems are not overwhelming. There are not masses of drug-crazed veterans loose menacing the nation. Of course, it remains to be seen whether the remissions hold up over time. Robins has now completed a second follow-up, which reveals that the low rate of narcotic dependency does continue after three years.

The abatement of hard drug use once stateside suggests, as Starr and others have noted, that most users in Vietnam were able to reequilibrate once out of that milieu. In Vietnam, drug use was accepted and sociable, and drugs like heroin were cheap, pure (which allowed smoking rather than injection), and easy to procure. Allowing for the fact that many shifted to softer drugs once home, the important point is still that most men did not define themselves as part of the stateside drug scene and were not willing to pay the economic and social costs imposed on drug users in American society.

These findings suggest that there is something to the juicer-head distinction as a limited description of collective behavior in Vietnam. Other evidence in Robins's report reinforces this conclusion. Prior to Vietnam, drug and alcohol intake were highly correlated for the men. In Vietnam the correlation reversed. After Vietnam the correlation became positive again. Another supporting fact is that first narcotics use occurred very early in Vietnam. Sixty percent of users began within the first two months, and usually before first combat experiences. Both facts suggest that drug use was a reaction to being in Vietnam and being in contact with a certain cluster of other men. It apparently was not a reaction to the trauma of combat.

Robins's data on best preservice predictors of drug use in Vietnam do not support Helmer's argument about lack of selectivity into the primary groups. Preservice use of marijuana was the strongest predictor of use of drugs in Vietnam. Also important was being a first-term enlistee (as opposed to draftee) and having a preservice history of narcotic or amphetamine use. When being under 21 years of age, having an arrest history preservice, a truancy history preservice, and unemployment at time of induction are added to the equation, 36% of the variance in drug use is explained (p. 41). However, these variables did not predict heavy drug use in Vietnam. The same seven variables explained only 9% of the variance (p. 42), which suggests that, once in Vietnam, background attributes were predisposing, but immediate social and environmental conditions took over as determinants of extent of involvement with drugs. Primary group interaction surely played some part in encouraging or retarding drug use, but it is not immediately obvious how, or what social processes operated.

One final finding from the Robins study is worth reporting. Overall, the majority of the men showed remarkably little apprehension about their drug problem, in contrast to the alarm manifested in the Congress, the press, and ostensibly in the public at large. Few felt their drug use was deleterious. Only 10% of users felt drugs had hurt them; even in the drug-positive sample only 31% felt it was a harmful experience (p. 43). Moreover, few drug users expressed interest in treatment—1% of the general sample and 5% of the drug-positive sample (p. viii). This did not appear to result, as Starr suggests, from being "turned off" by how the military handled drug abuse, or by the VA "hassle." Those treated were generally satisfied with the treatment (pp. 43, 67). Ninety percent favored urine checks, and 78% even favored surprise urine checks (p. 88). They did not feel drug use was a reason for punishment or denial of benefits, nor did they feel it was a reason for special services. Eighty-one percent favored honorable discharges for drug users who performed well; 53% favored medical discharges for those who performed poorly; 82% felt no special VA benefits should exist for drug users (pp. 88–89). These findings suggest that most men did not see drugs as a serious problem. If men functioned well, drugs were "OK." If men did not function, they had problems comparable perhaps to alcoholics, and treatment was in line. This nonchalance or matter-of-fact perspective appears in part to be age linked. Only the older, career NCOs depart from the above opinions, but the separation is not great. It would be difficult to pin a very clear juicer-head dichotomy on these findings. There remains a gap in our understanding of an important social process.

In the above discussion of images of Vietnam veterans, my remarks have been highly critical. They should not be interpreted as insensitivity to the wrongfulness and the anguish of the Vietnam war. Vietnam was American vainglorious intemperance. Political opposition precluded the launching of an aggressive, offensive war, and national pride, in the face of a tenacious and indefatigable jungle enemy, prompted us to lash out with all the technical military superiority we could muster short of nuclear holocaust. At that reluctant point of withdrawal into Vietnamization we were already hip deep in miscalculation and blind indulgence. The consequences have been appalling at home and abroad. As a nation we have suffered dearly in social and economic terms. Although quite unheralded, Vietnam also added a good measure of damage to the reputation and the stability of the military.

Nor do I mean to dismiss the frustration and hardship inflicted on American soldiers in Vietnam, and the difficulty of their adjustment once home. They faced the trying conditions of limited combat offensive composed mainly of search and destroy operations, of green junior officers and senior NCOs, and of at least lingering doubts and some skepticism about the purpose of the war. They faced a perplexing situation where allies were viewed with contempt and distrust, and where it often was impossible to separate foe from friend. Some men yielded to cruelty and inhumane behavior, some to fragging. All of these conditions made the Vietnam war different from other wars this nation has fought. Ultimately and fundamentally, however, it was the same in one way. Like all wars, men had to face the fear of death and disfigurement. All these facts notwithstanding, some of the works under review—Levy's, Lifton's, Helmer's—are too often mere caricatures. The passions of indignation against an unjust and immoral war elicited overreactions that do justice neither to the veterans they characterize nor to responsible scholarship. . . .

[In the second half of this review essay, Professor Ladinsky reviews five works dealing with the Veterans Administration and veteran's benefits—Ed.]

NOTES

1. See Robins, p. 32, and the Louis Harris Survey, *A Study of the Problems Facing Vietnam Era Veterans on Their Readjustment to Civilian Life*, Committee on Veterans Affairs, United States Senate, Ninety-Second Congress, Second Session, Senate Committee Print No. 7 (Washington, D.C.: U.S. Government Printing Office, January 31, 1972), pp. 169–171.

   It should be noted, however, that the responses men give are not uniformly high for relief of stress as the primary reason for drug use. In the Harris survey "boredom" outranked "pressures," "escape," or other more direct tension-producing causes. The Robins study shows "boredom" in third place after "more tolerant of Army rules and regulations," and "less homesick and lonely." This was in response to an open-ended question. When asked directly, "less bored" ranked first. Thus, it is not at all clear that drug use was a direct response to the pressures of service in Vietnam such as combat. Indeed, most drug users began before their first combat experiences, as Robins notes. However, one might argue that this merely shows drug use during the buildup of tensions in anticipation of combat. There is no way to resolve this dilemma from the data available. For what it is worth the Harris Survey shows that 40% of men serving in Vietnam agreed that drugs made it easier for men to tolerate abuse from officers, but only 15% agreed that the only way to face the killing and violence of combat was to use drugs. Twenty-five percent agreed that without drugs military life would have been unbearable (p. 171).

2. Helmer argues from family income figures that one in three came from a "severely deprived environment" (p. 58). Neither the income breakdown nor other background characteristics support this claim. Moreover, levels of education and rates of utilization of G.I. Bill benefits, especially in Groups I and III, do not suggest that these are highly disadvantaged youths (pp. 58, 225). Indeed, middle class would seem to be a better title for many, despite their subjective identifications.

3. M. Kent Jennings and Gregory B. Markus, "Political Participation and Vietnam-Era War Veterans: A Longitudinal Study," University of Michigan, unpublished paper, n.d., p. 14. The authors also reported on participation in public protests by period of service, but were not able to separate respondents by tour in Vietnam due to small numbers. Protest activity was highest among those who served during the later periods (1969–1970 and 1971–1973). Many of them had engaged in antiwar protest in an earlier, civilian period (p. 25).

46

The Public Rates
American Institutions

As America withdrew from Vietnam in the early 1970s, some officers began to speak bitterly of the public's "blaming" the military for Vietnam and to worry openly of future support for the armed services. But as this national opinion poll (conducted by social scientists at the University of Michigan) shows, the public gave the military high marks in the year after the last troops withdrew.

	Rating
U.S. Military	5.50
Colleges and Universities	5.48
Churches and Religious Organizations	5.26
Small Businesses	5.21
Public Schools	4.95
News Media	4.89
U.S. Supreme Court	4.82
Large Corporations	4.72
U.S. Congress	4.59
State Governments	4.47
All Courts, Judicial System	4.35
Local Governments	4.33
Labor Unions	4.26
Federal Government	3.86
President & Administration	3.30

Scale: 0 (Very Poor) ← 2.0 2.5 3.0 3.5 4.0 4.5 5.0 5.5 → (Very Good) 8

The Public's Rating of American Institutions: How Well They Are Serving the Country

Scale shows overall rating from 0 to 8 (from very poor job to very good job)

SOURCE: Institute for Social Research, *Newsletter* (Winter 1974), p. 8. (The survey was conducted in 1973.)

47

The American Enlisted Man in the All-Volunteer Army

Alarmed by reports of increased use of drugs among GIs, the Army commissioned a study of four representative companies at "Fort Marshall," an Army post in the Eastern United States, in 1973–74. A team of professionals from the Walter Reed Army Institute of Research moved into the barracks and began to monitor the daily life of the privates and NCOs. Their findings were remarkable: The increased pay available to members of the All-Volunteer Force had made it possible for married GIs to live in separate housing, generally off the base. The remaining privates lived essentially by themselves, with very little monitoring by officers or NCOs. Except for the handful on guard duty, "their time was their own" from 4:30 P.M. until 7:00 A.M. Most used alcohol (chiefly beer), which was not new to the 1970s, and about half regularly used illicit drugs—chiefly marijuana—which use was relatively new to the Army, for "recreation, group affirmation, and ceremony."* These uses provided small groups of men with social bonds. The availability of cash, the relatively unsurpervised, partly segmented barracks design, and the easy access to drugs and alcohol, coupled with the social role such use played in the life of soldier groups, largely explained the increased use of these substances. The research team also assessed the NCOs and officers who commanded these companies.

---

*By 1983 the Army estimated that the percentage of users had declined to less than 30 percent of first-term enlistment soldiers.

SOURCE: Larry H. Ingraham, *The Boys in the Barracks: Observations on American Military Life* (Philadelphia: Institute for The Study of Human Issues, 1984), pp. xviii–xxi, 57–58, 64–66, 69–70, 91–93, 100–101, 119, 122–124, 133, 165, 177, 178, 180, 181, 184, 187, 188, 201. See also Sar Levitan and K. C. Alderman, *Warriors at Work: The Volunteer Armed Force* (Beverly Hills, Calif.: Sage, 1977), 186.

ULTIMATELY, drugs and alcohol as used by the boys in the barracks contribute to the formation of these "emotional bonds of group integration."
This is not to say that other social behaviors do not also serve this purpose.
Nor is it to deny that there may also be negative consequences attached
to the use of drugs and alcohol by barracks dwellers. It is simply to assert
that the use of drugs and alcohol facilitates the bonding between isolated
individuals who find themselves living together largely by chance rather
than choice and who are held in place by a number of specific environmental structures, both physical and social.

Emphasizing the bonding effect of drugs and alcohol does not wash
away the differences between smoking and drinking with regard to their
legal status. Nor does it explain the psychological and physiological "high"
that comes from a six-pack or a joint. The bonding yield referred to comes
from the clustering of prior and present commonalities which soldiers can
identify and construct while they are using; semidurable meanings and
memories are ascribed to these commonalities and a semblance of social
stability emerges from the mutual participation.

It may well be that drug use in an Army unit is positively correlated
with unit cohesion and morale, rather than negatively correlated, as is
generally supposed. The present data strongly suggest that the patterns of
drug and alcohol use are largely determined by the patterns of social interaction in the barracks after duty hours which in turn are bounded by
the patterns of interaction permitted within the formal structure during
the duty day. The soldiers we studied tended to spend their leisure time
with those they knew best, and those they knew best were usually those
with whom they spent the most time during working hours. Therefore,
insofar as the mission, structure and operations of a military unit encourage soldiers to know one another better, these factors also generate those
conditions of interpersonal knowledge and trust that enable efficient drug
distribution and discreet use. It should follow, all else being equal, that
military units at highest risk for drug use are those that are most cohesive.
However, those with the least cohesion will appear to be highest in drug
use because they have insufficient group solidarity to prevent or mask public exposure of drug involvement.

For whatever reason and for whatever purpose, the fact is that drug
use among common soldiers in the United States Army is now endemic,
just as alcohol use has always been in the American military. It becomes
essential to understand what is involved in this phenomenon. The findings
and interpretations presented here demonstrate the need to understand
the soldiers' lives in general before meaningful comment is possible on any
single aspect of them, whether it be drug and alcohol use, venereal disease,
absenteeism, performance effectiveness or whatever. There has been
enough whispering and denial. It is time to define the nature of the existent
social order so that the behaviors which occur within it will be predictable
and manageable rather than unexpected and alarming.

As a rejoinder someone is certain to ask, but just who are these boys in the barracks? Whom do they represent? Dare we allow them to speak for the entire Army? Are they not merely a tiny minority of common soldiers—support troops at that—stationed at a "backwater" post with every reason to be dispirited and uninspired, and in constant search of manufacturing their own excitement? Had one of the elite combat units been the focus of observation, would the findings have been quite different?

The question of generalizability is a matter for future research. Unknown are the limits under which drug and alcohol use facilitates group bonding. Unknown, for example, are the consequences on group cohesiveness of drug use by soldiers deployed to a combat zone. Unknown as well is the extent to which gains in social solidarity are offset by immediate physiological costs. Mythology would have it that soldiers traditionally drink hard during pauses in battle, but we do not know in any kind of systematic fashion how such diversions affect group functioning or individual performance in the heat of the conflict.

However, to ask *who* our boys are is the wrong question when it comes to shedding light on the generalizability issue. The domain of generalization is defined by the barracks, not by the boys. Given common social structures, common behavioral patterns result. These patterns can take the form of horseplay, verbal banter, roughhousing, sex talk, whoring, smoking and drinking, clique formations and affiliations, among many others. The personalities and demographics of the individuals housed by the social structures are essentially irrelevant to the generalization question. Social structures determine the patterns of social behavior; individual differences determine who specifically fills what role (the script for which is already written), or who in particular is assigned which label (the content of which is already fixed). It matters little if the soldiers are black or white, rich or poor, tall or short, high school dropouts or college graduates, and, most probably, male or female. The important question is: How similar are the social structures?

Readers of drafts of this book have reacted with shock, dismay, and even disgust at some of the descriptions of barracks living. The tone of barracks life is often thought to be bleak and depressing, if not thoroughly repulsive and obscene. But it is well to remember that the boys in the barracks are not deviants or delinquents. They are American soldiers who do their jobs as they have been trained—and constrained—to do them. They are the next generation of Army sergeants. They will fight America's next war.

In the final analysis we are not talking about titillating tales and bawdy humor. We are concerned with the fate of our country, with the ability of our army to maintain itself on the field of battle. Obviously the picture that emerges here does not conform to the highest American middle-class values, aspirations and ideals regarding either the Army or American youth, but that is all beside the point. The lives of the soldiers in the barracks—bleak as these barracks may seem—depend on each other's, and ours on theirs.

. . . There are two kinds of barracks: those characterized by open bays (traditional) and those divided into individual rooms (modern). With the advent of the volunteer Army, traditional barracks were renovated by partitioning the bay into rooms to increase privacy; modern barracks were built at some posts. Some of the observations at Fort Marshall were made in the traditional barracks, in which only the sergeants are accorded private rooms while the privates share a single large bay.

The bays at each end of the building measured 30 by 60 feet. Each bay accommodated a platoon of up to 50 soldiers when bunk beds were carefully arranged. The rooms opening on to the connecting corridor were reserved for sergeants with the exception of one room occupied by the cooks who kept irregular hours.

The ambience of an open bay was more like that of an institution than a home or residence. There were no curtains at the windows that began five feet off the floor and ran the length of the bay, and the globe lamps, before fluorescent lighting, hung on their chains from the exposed steel beams that supported the concrete ceiling. The room was furnished with iron bunk beds, metal wardrobes (wall lockers), three or four desks, and a few straight-back iron chairs. The monotony of the brown tiled floor, murky green painted walls, and battleship gray furniture was relieved only by an occasional area rug or art poster taped to a wall or wall locker.

The placement of the wall lockers and beds divided the large room into smaller two-, three-, and four-man living areas. To discourage theft, all personal possessions were kept in the wall lockers equipped with hasps and heavy padlocks.

The increasing number of married soldiers served to reduce the need for barracks space. The trend, therefore, was to remodel existing barracks and partition them into individual rooms affording single soldiers greater privacy. Each room was approximately 12 feet square, and the ambience was more like a college dormitory. Fluorescent fixtures hung in suspended ceilings, and the light reflected pleasantly from the pastel painted walls. Each room contained a bed, desk, chair, and wall locker, and many rooms had carpets on the floor. The furniture was still iron, painted gray, but the curtains at the windows and the art posters, fish netting, trophies, pictures, and personal possessions on display provided some diversion. The soldiers were allowed to arrange and decorate as they chose within rather broad limits. Because the barracks often were included in tours given to visiting dignitaries, the display of Confederate flags, swastikas, and certain pictures of nude women ("tits and ass are OK, but no hair") was actively discouraged. Remodeled barracks frequently had recreation and laundry rooms for the convenience of the residents. . . .

The Army is racially integrated in every area of military life governed by the rules and statutes of the formal organization and the directives of those in legitimate authority. Formal rules and legitimate authority do not apply when soldiers are on their own time. Army regulations, for example, require that all soldiers, regardless of race, be admitted to the dining hall, but no regulation requires soldiers of different races to eat at the same table. When soldiers are on their own time, the Army is quite rigidly segregated.

In the dining hall individuals have considerable freedom to define relationships to other people by where they choose to sit. In the barracks, however, there was almost no choice, for bunks were assigned on a first-come, first-placed basis as space became available. Hence a diagram of the barracks would show greater racial integration than the mess halls, but behaviorally the barracks were every bit as segregated. Under no conditions was a white ever incorporated into an informal group of blacks. Only under very special conditions was a black incorporated in an informal group of whites in the barracks.

Life in the barracks after duty hours was controlled by the majority group, and blacks were not in the majority. While blacks maintained formal, day-to-day business relations with their white barracks-mates, they typically changed clothes immediately after duty and left the barracks to associate with other blacks. To meet other blacks they had to cross intra- and intercompany boundaries; hence race provided a notable exception to the impermeability of these boundaries. A similar exception to this rule involved Spanish-speaking soldiers, who commonly segregated themselves from both the blacks and the whites, and had to cross organizational boundaries to do so. The means of scaling work-group barriers was provided in the dining halls and the ethnic bars on or near the post; the motive was the tension between the majority and minority groups.

The reasons for interracial tension are woven into the fabric of American society, and the same threads simply assume different configurations in that section of the tapestry that is the Army.

The following excerpts come from two different group interviews, one with all white members and the other with all black. The excerpts are juxtaposed to demonstrate that the two groups hold essentially the same views toward each other with respect to the three central issues of Army life: work, discipline, and food.

WHITE: "You're damned right there's discrimination against us. The blacks are always coming up with some phony excuse and getting over on the sergeants; 'course we all do that [laughter], but the blacks definitely sham [loaf on the job] more than the whites, which means we have to do all the work."

BLACK: "I wouldn't call it discrimination, but there's sure as hell a lot of prejudice. Who does all the shamming? Right, the whites. Whenever there's a dirty, stinky job to do, you don't see no whites around. No, let the nigger do it."

WHITE: "The thing that really burns my ass is the two standards of discipline in the Army. Whenever an NCO or officer jumps on a brother, they scream 'prejudice' all the way to the colonel. Us whites just get slapped with fines, extra duty, and restrictions."

BLACK: "There's definitely two standards of discipline in the Army. Sir, you just check the company records. Blacks always get more Article 15's [punishments], and whitey just gets off with a warning. The blacks get heavier punishments, too. Check it out."

WHITE: "They think the world owes them something special all the time. Y'know what we had in the mess hall last week? Pig guts and tomato sauce. Yeah, man, no kidding. Soul food, special for them; I'm Italian and I don't see no cooks making ravioli for me."

BLACK: "Sometimes I just get so hungry for chitlins, beans, and rice, and a side of greens. What do we get in the mess hall? Spaghetti at least three times a week. The man just won't even let us eat right."

What are the facts? Fact: Greens and black-eyed peas were served as frequently as brussels sprouts and stewed tomatoes. They may not have been prepared like mother's, but a variety of ethnic food was available in the mess halls. Fact: An examination of disciplinary records over a 12-month period revealed no significant relationship between race and either the frequency or severity of punishment in the four companies studied. Fact: In work assignment, sergeants were scrupulous to the point of obsession in avoiding any hint of discrimination.

The tensions between blacks and whites, then, had little to do with the Army as an institution *per se*. The Army simply provided yet another setting for the definition and testing of majority–minority power differentials rooted in the larger society. In the barracks the power edge was maintained and honed through repeated interpersonal assaults that made it practically impossible for the barracks dweller to cross racial lines to select leisure time associates.

. . . Part of the soldier's sense of social isolation stems from an unwillingness to make extensive personal commitments to other soldiers. In the effort to recruit and maintain an all-volunteer force, the Army attempted to assign personnel as close to their homes as possible. The recruits typically had every expectation of returning to hometown, family, and friends, when they completed a three-year tour; hence they went home as often as possible to maintain their place in the social network. For the barracks dweller, the Army post was not a community, but a place to work; their community was the hometown to which they had to return each weekend. The barracks was viewed simply as a dormitory.

Personal relationships in the Army were not made with the expectation that they would extend beyond the time the parties were stationed together. Army companies experienced continual personnel turnover as soldiers were recruited, discharged, and reassigned to other posts. All personal relationships were bounded by the brief time that the individuals were together—typically no more than 12 months, and often less.

The fundamental social unit in the barracks was the dyad—two soldiers who consider themselves buddies or partners. Their relationship generally was established and maintained more by circumstance than choice, and typically emerged from proximal bunk assignments in the barracks and being forced to work together during the duty day. The dyad is the most intimate of all barracks relationships, but is commonly acknowledged as only temporary. The Army buddy who remains a lifetime personal friend may emerge from shared combat experience, but this is highly unlikely in the garrison Army. The silliest question to ask a soldier is to name friends in the unit, because the answer is always, "I have no friends in the Army."

. . . The annual "organization day" is designed to foster unity and cohesion within the companies and pride within the battalion. This ceremonial event descends from the old regimental field days when the enlisted men in the companies competed with each other before the admiring eyes of the colonel and his officers and guests. Competition included military skills like marching and marksmanship as well as boxing, baseball, and track and field events. The guests included girlfriends, wives, and families as well as townspeople who joined in with food, drink, music, and dancing at the end of the day. In an age without radio, television, or rapid transportation, and in an organization in which enlisted soldiers may have served with each other under the same officers for five years or more, the field day was one of the highlights of the year and was well attended and eagerly anticipated. Times and organizations have changed, however, and the observer noted little enthusiasm for the present-day battalion picnic:

> I mentioned to Corwin that I was going to the battalion picnic tomorrow. He said I was wasting my time, since no one would be there but the lifers. He then yelled out, "There's nobody here going to the lifer picnic, is there?" He then snapped out the names of the men in turn. "Conner, you're not going, are you? Johnson? Eggers?" No one said that he was going.

The enlisted men viewed attendance at the picnic as positive sentiment toward the Army, thus in a battalion of over 900 men, less than 200 went to the "organization day." The observer noted:

> Most of the people congregated around the beer truck. They seemed to segregate themselves by companies, and the overwhelming majority were sergeants and officers. Someone tried to initiate a tug-of-war between my company and another unit, but there weren't enough interested to form a team.

The result was scarcely different with required attendance. In one battalion the men assembled in formation in the morning, marched to the athletic field, were addressed by the colonel, and were encouraged to join in the tent pitching, pie eating, and greased pole climbing contests.

> Most of the men sit in groups of two or three clustered by platoons within companies and by companies. They drink their beer and grumble about the day being a waste of time, evidence little enthusiasm for the competition, and

grudgingly "volunteer" to participate when the lieutenant encourages them. As the sergeants and officers become more drunk and more involved, the men quietly slip away to their cars or to the barracks to sleep.

Company parties and picnics were also scheduled. Voluntary attendance was greater than for battalion functions, and participation in the activities was a bit more spirited, although anti-Army sentiments continued to run high.

. . . The authorities at Fort Marshall did not sanction the use of alcohol when on duty, the drinking of wine or hard liquor in the barracks, or any drinking that resulted in property destruction or vandalism. Enlisted soldiers routinely ignored all of these prohibitions, but were cautious in overstepping the limits.

Standing guard at night was the most eligible occasion for drinking on duty. Guard duty consisted of walking around the perimeter of a motor pool or patroling parts of the battalion area. Soldiers served on guard patrol for two hours and then had four hours off before returning to their posts. No one ever did much talking while on guard duty, so between shifts the guards returned to the barracks and their buddies. . . .

Walking guards worked from 4:00 in the afternoon until 6:00 the following morning during the work week, and pulled a 24-hour shift on weekends and holidays. Tower guards in the stockade worked 8-hour shifts without breaks and sometimes used alcohol in the towers. . . .

A final instance of drinking on duty was observed during field training. Most soldiers did not look forward to going to the field because of the work involved in loading the trucks, pitching the tents, digging foxholes, and running through exercises with limited blank ammunition. In the field there were long stretches of inactivity, punctuated with drinking.

On the first night after the base camp was set up and the evening maneuvers were cancelled, the men sat around in small groups, talking and drinking sodas they had brought with them. Wilson had filled his canteen with daiquiris; Jones had a fifth of bourbon; and Lemsen had a pint of vodka. Several men had brought six-packs of beer along, and the motor pool crew managed to stash three cases in among their gear. The sergeants stayed to themselves, and didn't bother us the entire evening.

. . . Ceremonial drinking at Fort Marshall involved more than a single clique, and going-away parties provided a prime occasion. Each soldier has an ETS date—that is, the day he is scheduled to leave the service. Soldiers at the post began describing themselves as "short" about a month from their departure, and marked off the days, hours, and minutes remaining on "short-timer" calendars. Not everyone merited an ETS party. Companies organized into a few large work groups, like platoons, tended not to have ETS parties for departing members. If any note was taken of a departure at all, it was among intimates in the manner of a birthday celebration. Companies that were organized into multiple, small work groups tended to have ETS parties involving many people from the company. Such occasions provided one of the few opportunities to affirm social bonds beyond the usually fragmented cliques. Whether an individual merited an ETS party depended upon his status in the barracks and the availability of sufficient people from his original cohort to organize the celebration.

ETS parties provided an opportunity to observe both the coalition of all of the work-group cliques into a momentary unity and the allocation of status within the entire barracks social structure. . . .

[D]rinking rituals were neither inevitable nor invariable at ETS parties; rather they were invented at the moment and performed as if they had long-standing traditional significance:

> Murphy then proposed a "beer-for-Cressey" ceremony. He opened a bottle of beer and proceeded to each person, urging him to have a drink of Cressey's beer. He carried the beer bottle in both hands at his stomach, and lifted it to each of us in turn with great formality and solemnity.

A considerable number of soldiers had recently arrived in the barracks. The old order was clearly passing, but some way was needed to communicate to everyone how the barracks was organized and who determined the policies. It was also necessary to initiate the newcomers into the ways of the village:

> After everyone in the circle has taken a sip, Murphy decides that everyone on the bay should wake up and participate. The new black accepts with no argument. The new guy in my area accepts, and gets up to join us. The three new guys next to Murphy and Barker accept. Next is Simpson, and I expect some trouble. Simpson awakes, is told to sip from Cressey's beer, looks at the crowd, and takes the beer. He also gets up. The new guy in Peterson's area takes a sip and gets up. The last man on the bay is a new man on the far end. He refuses to drink and is booed roundly. Murphy persists in pushing and poking the guy and telling him to drink. He refuses and rolls to face the wall. We leave the area and return to the other end of the bay; whereupon Murphy decides he isn't finished yet. We return to the new man, and after much pushing and yelling he finally sips the beer, pleading that he didn't understand what Murphy wanted to do at first.

The barracks residents were now united, and the new men were ready to learn why "this is the most fucked-up company in the whole Army." A new out-group had to be defined.

> Murphy, Roberts, and Frisco troop to the other end of the building, determined that the other platoon share the ceremonial beer. They return shortly, bragging that only one man refused, but they would get him yet. The ceremony is then forgotten. No one presents the empty bottle to Cressey; it is thrown out the window with all the other bottles.

Having had the outsiders defined for them, the new men were now ready to learn the rites of the in-group.

Cressey, "the torch," then made his final showing. He got out his lighter fluid and sprayed it on his wall locker. Frisco set it on fire as he continued spraying circles and zig-zags on the floor. We all cheered as he put away his fluid for the last time, but there was no formal passing of the torch to the new generation.

The next "lesson" involved dealing with the low-status people. One target was the individual whose highly polished floor was burned some weeks earlier.

> Murphy instructs Simpson to shoot a beer. We all crowd around him and he is successful at shooting, but not at making friends. Roberts then decides to throw Simpson's television set out the window. It is an old cabinet model that will not fit through the window, and the pane breaks as Roberts tries. Simpson just stands back, looks relieved, and mutters that it didn't work that well anyway. The television is left leaning between the window and the desk. Next Rembolt is told to shoot a beer. He swallowed about half way through, and Gross jerked the can from his hand, finished it, and threw it disdainfully on the floor. Rembolt smiled in embarrassment and left the party.

From the day they arrived, the newcomers heard stories of the kind of barracks they joined. The oral history reached back little more than a year and recounted exploits of the "real crazies" who weren't afraid of anything or anybody. The newcomers had been told that the barracks had settled down a lot since the "crazies" left, but that some of the tradition was carried on by those who knew them. Now the drunken revelers re-enacted some of those scenes from yesteryear.

> For some unknown reason Cressey pours a beer over Frisco's bed-pillow, sheets, blankets, and mattress. Frisco laughs, walks to the hallway, and returns with a fire extinguisher which he empties on Cressey's bed. Gross comes in with a 24 oz. glass of urine, and tries to get people to try his "beer." Everyone recognizes it for what it is, and Roberts takes it toward the latrine. Instead of dumping it there, he proceeds to the other platoon area, and returns, bragging that he poured it "in that fucking faggot Benzoni's bed and somebody else." Ten minutes later Gross comes screaming down the hall. "Roberts, your mother sucks cunt. You cocksucker, you poured piss all over my bed." Roberts denies it, and the incident is quickly forgotten.

As if on cue, a staff sergeant who lived in one of the private rooms was awakened by the melee, came to the bay, and demanded quiet. The observer noted:

> Very bald Sergeant Blumer came into the bay, and in a disgusted tone demanded that we hold down the noise so others could sleep. Frisco yelled out, "Fuck you, shine. If you can't take it, move out with the rest of the goddamned lifers." Blumer left in angry, disgusted resignation only to return in a few minutes and demand that the party stop at once and the mess be cleaned up. Preston said, "Cool it, Sergeant Blumer, we'll clean it up like we always do, and it would be just so much easier if you would just go back to your room

and don't hassle us." Blumer stalked out again, shaking his head in disgust. Murphy and Barker then began beating on the metal wall lockers, and Cressey disassembled his bunk.

At 1:00 they sent out for more beer, but the party was over. . . . Most of the interviewees at Fort Marshall were in junior and senior high school during the nationwide proliferation of drug use that peaked in the late 1960s. Virtually every one of them had either been exposed to or had used drugs before coming into the Army.

Every Army company had an extensive reservoir made up of the pre-induction drug experiences of its members. The most common experiences were with marijuana, chemical hallucinogens, amphetamines, and barbiturates. Moreover, every company was likely to have at least one member who had used cocaine and heroin and who knew how to use a hypodermic syringe. A soldier who had not used a particular substance had no difficulty in finding an experienced teacher among his comrades.

It is now widely believed that drug use declines sharply when individuals enter the Army and undergo the isolation and stress of basic training. Use often increases during Advanced Individual Training, which is less stressful and provides more leisure time. After assignment to a permanent duty station, use typically returns to or exceeds pre-Army levels. . . .

What do drugs do for the maintenance of barracks social structure that alcohol doesn't? There are essentially two fundamental problems of social organization faced by barracks soldiers. The first is how to keep social relationships vital and alive in circumstances in which there is neither an expectation of future interaction nor a storehouse of past affiliation. The second is how to create and maintain group identification and group boundaries under unstable conditions: how to create a sense of "we" and define a contrastive "they," given the constant personnel turnover in an Army unit.

Alcohol use contributes in a major way to the solution of the first problem, while drug use contributes heavily to the solution of the second. Alcohol and illicit drugs each make a *unique* contribution to the social structuring of barracks living; as a result their use cannot be taken as interchangeable.

Alcohol is particularly helpful in generating distinctive, memorable episodes involving brawls, "broads," and bad news so that the participants can recall and recount evidence for the meaningfulness of their relationship and what they have been through together. Drug use is far less effective in this respect; it is personal and private. . . .

The life of a first-line supervisor in the Army is not an easy one; it is filled with interpersonal unpleasantries that require considerable training and experience in personnel management. Attempting to intervene can be embarrassing, as in the episode in the barracks when the sergeant attempted to break up a raucous party and was hooted from the area. . . .

Coupled with the belief that the NCO corps was inexperienced was the belief that the best way to train NCOs was formal schooling in classroom settings. The Army runs a virtual university of courses in leadership principles, human relations, equipment maintenance, and office organization. Promotion points are weighted in favor of such training, and the ambitious sergeant acquires all the formal instruction he can. One problem with this scheme is that the sergeants felt it favored the least competent. Whenever there was an opening in one of the schools, the officers were thought most likely to appoint the sergeant they could best do without; hence the most competent sergeants stayed behind and managed the company while the least competent were sent to school and promoted. There seemed no system of reward for looking after the troops. . . .

[Another] problem in equating classroom instruction with training was the chasm between what is written in notebooks and what is enacted in the unit. A first sergeant, unmindful of the irony as he watched his sergeant rush to the automobiles after work, commented, "The job of the NCO begins at when duty ends." Sergeants "knew" that the best rewards for enlisted men were praise and time off, yet it became too embarrassing to ask for the most recent use of these rewards. The more dedicated sergeants could easily recite the 11 principles of military leadership; they noted the second principle, "know your men," by carefully compiling personnel data cards on each of their charges, yet they could not say why they collected the information or what they might use it for. . . .

It is not so much that the senior officers and NCOs did not know how to deal with their men; they could all recount leadership strategies that worked in the past, and while they faulted the younger officers and men for inexperience, they also recognized that the Army had changed. The organization seemed to have become even more impersonal with the advent of computers and centralized services. Everyone, from the private to the general, felt estranged and helpless in view of the social constraints against individual action. . . .

Nothing rankled the leaders more than the changes in the legal system. For any violation of the Uniform Code of Military Justice, soldiers are advised of their right to counsel and a hearing before a military judge. Cases would be thrown out of court or delayed for months when the paperwork was not in proper form, down to the last comma. The authority to confine a soldier to the stockade has been sharply curtailed, and all instances must be approved by an officer in the Judge Advocate General Corps. Pretrial confinement was carefully monitored, and harsh prison conditions have disappeared. Restrictions on confinement authority, in the words of one captain, "took the sword away from the company commander." . . .

A collage of confusion, alienation, and perceived helplessness in a world of eroding values and social restraints marked the beliefs and attitudes of leaders at Fort Marshall. They were fundamentally unconcerned about alcohol misuse, or drug use, or even the men in the barracks. Their basic concerns were promotions, maintaining authority, and avoiding the suspicion of incompetence. For each officer and NCO these issues posed significant psychological questions: Where do I fit in this organization called the Army? Am I really important? If I am, what is the evidence that tells me so? The plaintive cry of the men in the barracks expressed in one group interview—"Nobody gives a shit about us"—was echoed by the leaders as they struggled to maintain a stable place in the amorphous social order . . .

How have the leaders changed? [One NCO remarked:]

"They don't care anymore. We're not putting the Army first anymore; there's too much moonlighting, and the Army comes second. There's no sense of community like when all the sergeants got to know each other and spend time together. We've got to get back to professionalism at every level. You can't run an Army where the first four ranks are all recruits. We need professional privates who can drive any rig in the lot and handle any weapon in the arms room. They could teach the younger guys more than the sergeants. But the Army doesn't see it that way; it's either up in rank or out of service. They think that every NCO should be bucking for sergeant major of the Army; hell, there's but one of them. Everybody is evaluated on education and test scores that can be read by the computer. Qualitative management they call it; brought to you by the same goddamned dummies who got us into Vietnam."

48

The All-Volunteer Force
Versus the Draft

*The shift to an all-volunteer force in 1974 was highly controversial. It was equitable, economical, and the "American Way," one school argued. It was inequitable, uneconomical, and dangerous to the "American Way," another school insisted. It would weaken/strengthen the military. It was fair/unfair to blacks. These figures may answer some of the questions about the all-volunteer force.**

*See U.S. Congress, Senate Armed Services Committee, *Status of the All-Volunteer Force* (Washington, 20 June 1978), and R. V. L. Cooper, *Military Manpower and the All-Volunteer Force* (Rand Corp. R-1450-ARPA, September 1977), for conflicting views. See also Morris Janowitz and Charles Moskos, "Five Years of the All-Volunteer Force, 1973–1978," *Armed Forces and Society* 5 (Winter 1979): 171–218.

Lottery Draft-All-Volunteer Forces (AVF)
UCMJ Comparisons (per 1,000)

	COURTS-MARTIAL	VIOLENT CRIMES
1st Quarter '73 (Lottery Draft)	7.01	2.02
1st Quarter '76 (All Volunteer)	3.18	1.65

SOURCE: Department of the Army, *Information Paper*, March 1977.

• 471 •

Absenteeism and Desertion in the Active Enlisted Force

(Rate per 1000)
Fiscal Year

Category/Service*	1964/65	1968/69	1973/74	1974/75	1975/76	1976/77	1977/78	1978/79	1979/80	1980/81	1982/83	1983/84	1985/86
Absenteeism													
Army	53.7	89.7	159.2	129.9	95.4	70.3	47.0	40.4	38.0	41.6	29.0	19.6	12.5
Navy	**	14.4	21.7	53.8	73.0	77.5	76.9	78.3	83.4	82.0			
Marine corps	**	87.6	243.3	287.3	300.9	201.8	103.5	97.5	86.7	83.6			
Airforce	**	3.6	16.1	17.3	13.0	7.8	3.8	4.6	5.9	6.7			
Desertion													
Army	13.4	29.1	52.1	41.1	26.0	17.7	16.7	15.4	18.1	19.6	12.0	7.1	6.1
Navy	6.2	8.5	13.6	21.2	22.4	24.8	31.6	30.4	29.6	27.0			
Marine corps	17.8	30.7	63.2	89.2	105.0	69.2	47.0	39.9	37.9	34.2			
Airforce	0.6	0.4	2.2	2.4	1.9	1.2	0.6	0.7	1.1	2.2			

*The varying experiences of the four services over time, and the great disparities among them at any given year, preclude the computation of meaningful aggregate DOD averages.

**Missing data for these years.

It should also be noted that reporting procedures for the several services changes at somewhat different points between 1975/76 and 1978/79, and abrupt changes from one year to the next within that period should be read with caution.

SOURCES: Department of Defense, *Annual Report FY1979*, p. 338; US Senate, Armed Services Committee, *Hearings on FY1979 Defense Authorization*, 95th Cong., 2nd sess., Pt. 4, pp. 2760–1; and data from the Office of the Assistant Secretary of Defense (Manpower, Reserve Affairs, and Logistics) (Manpower Policy Plans), March 1978, February 1979, February 1980, and February 1981; U.S. Army Military Police Operations Agency, Washington, D.C., 22041; Department of the Army, *The Posture of the U.S. Army for Fiscal Year 1987* (Washington, D.C., GPO, 1986), 63.

Active Duty Nonprior Service Male and Female Enlistees by Parents' Earnings—May 1975

PARENTS' EARNINGS	ARMY %	NAVY %	MARINES %	AIR FORCE %	DoD %	U.S. FAMILY %
0–10,990	53	38	47	40	44	40
11,000–19,999	34	41	40	44	39	37
20,000 or more	14	21	14	16	16	22

SOURCE: OASD (MRA&L) December 31, 1978.

Distribution of Enlisted Male 1972 High School Graduates

MILITARY SERVICE BY 1976	SOCIOECONOMIC STATUS			
	LOWER QUARTILE %	MIDDLE HALF %	UPPER QUARTILE %	N
Navy	28.5	55.6	15.8	165
Army	44.1	40.2	15.6	179
Marines	36.7	50.0	13.3	60
Air Force	30.8	52.8	16.4	195
DoD[a]	35.9	46.5	17.6	1041
Did not serve	24.3	48.1	27.7	8671

SOURCE: National Longitudinal Survey. [This table and the one preceding are reprinted from John Faris, "The AVF: Recruitment from Military Families," *Armed Forces and Society*, VII (1981): 547.—Ed.]

[a]Discrepancies of percentages and sample size reflect the inclusion of cases where branch of service data are missing.

Percentage Distribution of Army Male Entrants (nonprior-service) by Mental Group Level: Selected Years

YEAR	I	II	III	IV	TOTAL
1960	8.2	24.1	50.7	17.0	100.0
1964	5.7	28.0	46.4	19.9	100.0
1969	6.1	28.3	38.1	27.5	100.0
1973	3.4	27.5	51.8	17.3	100.0
1975	4.5	30.3	55.1	10.0	100.0
1977	2.3	17.9	36.4	43.4	100.0
1979	1.7	14.4	35.1	48.7	100.0
1981	2.2	21.4	44.5	30.9	100.0
1983	3.5	33.0	51.5	12.0	100.0
1985				8.5	

SOURCE: Charles Moskos, "The American Enlisted Man in the All-Volunteer Army," in David R. Segal and H. W. Sinaiko, eds., *Life in the Rank and File* (Pergamon Press, 1986). Department of the Army, *The Posture of the U.S. Army for Fiscal Year 1987* (Washington, D.C., GPO, 1986), 23.

Percentage of Black Participation in the Army by Pay Grade: Selected Years

	1964	1972	1979	1981	1983	1984
Officers:						
O-7 and above (general)	—	1.8	5.2		6.3	
O-6 (colonel)	.2	1.5	4.3		4.8	
O-5 (lieutenant colonel)	1.1	5.3	5.3		4.9	
O-4 (major)	3.5	5.0	4.5		4.8	
O-3 (captain)	5.1	3.9	6.9		10.0	
O-2 (1st lieutenant)	3.6	3.4	9.7		14.7	
O-1 (2nd lieutenant)	2.6	2.2	9.4		11.9	
Warrant	2.8	4.5	5.9		6.2	
Total Officers	3.3	3.9	6.8		8.8	9.5
Enlisted:						
E-9 (sergeant major)	3.3	8.6	19.0		24.7	
E-8 (master sergeant)	5.8	14.4	23.9		28.6	
E-7 (sergeant first class)	7.9	19.9	25.2		23.9	
E-6 (staff sergeant)	12.2	23.9	22.8		29.1	
E-5 (sergeant)	14.8	16.9	28.6		38.8	
E-4 (specialist 4)	12.5	14.1	33.7		38.1	
E-3 (private first class)	11.9	16.7	37.8		29.3	
E-2 (private)	11.6	18.5	37.9		26.4	
E-1 (private)	6.4	18.4	37.3		24.4	
Total Enlisted	11.8	17.4	32.2	36.9	32.2	30.7

SOURCE: Charles Moskos, "The American Enlisted Man in the All-Volunteer Army," in David R. Segal and H.W. Sinaiko, eds., Life in the Rank and File (Pergamon Press, forthcoming), and David Petraeus, "The Antagonists: A Review Essay," Military Affairs, XLIX (January 1985): 17–18.

First-Term Attrition in the Active Force (Percentage Not Completing Minimum Three-Year Obligation)

SERVICE	FISCAL YEAR ENTERING SERVICE									
	1971/72	1972/73	1973/74	1974/75	1975/76	1976/77	1977/78	1978/79	1979/80	1980/81
Army	26%	28%	31%	38%	37%	37%	34%	31%	32%	34%
Navy	28%	32%	34%	38%	35%	31%	29%	26%	27%	27%
Marine Corps	31%	24%	32%	37%	38%	35%	29%	30%	29%	28%
Airforce	21%	26%	30%	31%	29%	26%	26%	29%	27%	27%
DOD total:	26%	28%	32%	37%	35%	34%	31%	29%	29%	30%

Note: FYS 1971–7 are actual data; 1978/79 are estimated data; 1980 is projected.

SOURCES: Data from Office of the Assistant Secretary of Defense (MRA and L) (MPP) 31 October 1980 and February 1981; and R.W. Hunter and G. Nelson, "The All-Volunteer Force: Has It Worked? Will It Work?" Paper presented to the Hoover Institution Conference on Military Manpower and the All-Volunteer Force (Stanford, CA, December 1979) p. 37.